Lecture Notes in Computer Science 3338

Commenced Publication in 1973
Founding and Former Series Editors:
Gerhard Goos, Juris Hartmanis, and Jan van Leeuwen

Stan Z. Li Jianhuang Lai
Tieniu Tan Guocan Feng
Yunhong Wang (Eds.)

Advances in
Biometric
Person Authentication

5th Chinese Conference on
Biometric Recognition, SINOBIOMETRICS 2004
Guangzhou, China, December 13-14, 2004
Proceedings

 Springer

Volume Editors

Stan Z. Li
Tieniu Tan
Yunhong Wang
Chinese Academy of Sciences
Institute of Automation, P.O. Box 2728, Beijing, 100080, China
E-mail: {szli,tnt,wangyh}@nlpr.ia.ac.cn

Jianhuang Lai
Guocan Feng
Sun Yat-sen University
Center of Computer Vision, Guangzhou, 510275, China
E-mail: {stsljh,mcsfgc}@zsu.edu.cn

Library of Congress Control Number: 2004116259

CR Subject Classification (1998): I.5, I.4, I.3, H.5, C.3, K.6.5

ISSN 0302-9743
ISBN 3-540-24029-2 Springer Berlin Heidelberg New York

Springer is a part of Springer Science+Business Media

springeronline.com

© Springer-Verlag Berlin Heidelberg 2004
Printed in Germany

Typesetting: Camera-ready by author, data conversion by Scientific Publishing Services, Chennai, India
Printed on acid-free paper   SPIN: 11364870   06/3142   5 4 3 2 1 0

Preface

Following the previous four annual conferences, the 5th Chinese Conference on Biometrics Recognition (Sinobiometrics 2004) was held in Guangzhou, China in December 2004. The conference this year was aimed at promoting the international exchange of ideas and providing an opportunity for keeping abreast of the latest developments in biometric algorithms, systems, and applications. The 1st Biometrics Verification Competition (BVC) on face, iris, and fingerprint recognition was also conducted in conjunction with the conference.

This book is composed of 74 papers presented at Sinobiometrics 2004, contributed by researchers and industrial practitioners from Korea, Japan, Singapore, Hong Kong, France, UK, US, as well as China. Of these, 60 papers were selected from 140 submissions and 14 were invited. The papers not only presented recent technical advances, but also addressed issues in biometric system design, standardization, and applications.

Included among the invited were four feature papers on the ideas and algorithms of the best-performing biometric engines, which were either competition winners at the Face Authentication Test (FAT) 2004 or the Fingerprint Verification Competition (FVC) 2004, or they were the best-performing iris and palmprint recognition algorithms.

The papers were complemented by five keynote lectures on biometrics, and face, fingerprint, and iris authentication and multimodal fusion by Arun Ross (West Virginia University) and Anil K. Jain (Michigan State University), Josef Kittler (University of Surrey), John Daugman (University of Cambridge), Raffaele Cappelli (University of Bologna), and Stan Z. Li (Chinese Academy of Sciences).

We wish to express our gratitude to all those who helped organize Sinobiometrics 2004 and who contributed to the conference. We would like to thank the Program Committee who selected the best papers from a large number of submissions. Special thanks are due to the organizing team at Sun Yat-sen University and the Institute of Automation for their effort to make the conference a success.

December 2004

Stan Z. Li
Jianhuang Lai
Tieniu Tan
Guocan Feng
Yunhong Wang

Organization

Advisory Committee

Anil K. Jain, Michigan State University, USA
Zhaoqi Bian, Tsinghua University, China

General Chairs

Daren Huang, Sun Yat-sen University, China
Tieniu Tan, Institute of Automation, Chinese Academy of Sciences

Program Chairs

Stan Z. Li, Institute of Automation, Chinese Academy of Sciences
Yunhong Wang, Institute of Automation, Chinese Academy of Sciences
Daoqing Dai, Sun Yat-sen University, China

Program Committee

Xilin Chen, Harbin Institute of Technology, China
Guocan Feng, Sun Yat-sen University, China
Dewen Hu, National University of Defense Technology, China
Jianmin Jiang, University of Bradford, UK
Jianhuang Lai, Sun Yat-sen University, China
Mingquan Quan, Northwest University, China
Arun Abraham Ross, West Virginia University, USA
Shiguang Shang, Chinese Academy of Sciences, China
Zheng Tan, Xi'an Jiaotong University, China
Xiaoou Tang, Chinese University of Hong Kong, Hong Kong, China
Yuanyan Tang, Hong Kong Baptist University, Hong Kong, China
Yangsheng Wang, Institute of Automation, Chinese Academy of Sciences
Chaohui Wu, Zhejiang University, China
Xihong Wu, Beijing University, China
Hong Yan, City University of Hong Kong, Hong Kong, China
Jingyu Yang, Nanjing University of Science and Technology, China
Lihua Yang, Sun Yat-sen University, China
Pong C. Yuen, Hong Kong Baptist University, Hong Kong, China
Changshui Zhang, Tsinghua University, China
David Zhang, Hong Kong Polytechnic University, Hong Kong, China

Organized by

Sun Yat-Sun University, China
Institute of Automation, Chinese Academy of Sciences, China
Guangdong Society of Image and Graphics, China

Organizing Committee Chair

Jianhuang Lai, Sun Yat-sen University, China

Organizing Committee Members

Guocan Feng, Sun Yat-sen University, China
Miao Hong, Institute of Automation, Chinese Academy of Sciences
Xing Li, Sun Yat-sen University, China
Yuan Wang, Institute of Automation, Chinese Academy of Sciences
Lihua Yang, Sun Yat-sen University, China
Pong C. Yuen, Hong Kong Baptist University, Hong Kong, China
Weishi Zheng, Sun Yat-sen University, China

Web Publishing

Miao Hong, Institute of Automation, Chinese Academy of Sciences

Steering Committee

Tieniu Tan, Institute of Automation, Chinese Academy of Sciences
Anni Cai, Bejing University of Posts and Telecommunications, China
Wen Gao, Chinese Academy of Sciences, China
Stan Z. Li, Institute of Automation, Chinese Academy of Sciences
Pengfei Shi, Shanghai Jiao Tong University, China
Jie Tian, Institute of Automation, Chinese Academy of Sciences
Guangyou Xu, Tsinghua University, China

Sponsors

Institute of Automation
Chinese Academy of Sciences

Sun Yat-sen University

Omron Corporation

National Natural Science Foundation of
China (NSFC)

China Society of Image and Graphics

Chinese Association of Automation

Table of Contents

Part III Face Recognition

Face Localization

Pose Estimation

Face Recognition

3D-Based Methods

Subspace and Discriminant Analysis

Systems and Applications

Part IV Fingerprint Recognition

Fingerprint Preprocessing and Minutiae Extraction

Part VI Speaker Recognition

Part VII Other Biometrics

Biometrics: When Identity Matters

Arun Ross[1] and Anil K. Jain[2]

[1] West Virginia University, Morgantown, WV 26506 USA
[2] Michigan State University, East Lansing, MI 48824 USA
ross@csee.wvu.edu, jain@msu.edu

Establishing the identity of a person is becoming critical in our vastly inter-connected society. Questions like "Is she really who she claims to be?", "Is this person authorized to use this facility?" or "Is he in the watchlist posted by the government?" are routinely being posed in a variety of scenarios ranging from issuing a driver's licence to gaining entry into a country. The need for reliable user authentication techniques has increased in the wake of heightened concerns about security and rapid advancements in networking, communication and mobility. Biometrics, described as the science of recognizing an individual based on her physiological or behavioral traits, is beginning to gain acceptance as a legitimate method for determining an individual's identity. Biometric systems have now been deployed in various commercial, civilian and forensic applications as a means of establishing identity. These systems rely on the evidence of fingerprints, hand geometry, iris, retina, face, hand vein, facial thermogram, signature, voice, etc. to either validate or determine an identity.

Biometrics offers several advantages over traditional authentication schemes, including: (a) enhanced convenience, since the user does not have to recall complex passwords or possess surrogate tokens of identity such as ID cards; and (b) enhanced security, as biometrics can deter or detect impostors more easily and is an effective measure to address repudiation claims. Therefore, biometrics is an enabling technology that can make our society safer while imparting convenience to the users of the system. For example, the problem of identity fraud can be effectively addressed by adopting a biometric-based authentication scheme.

A biometric system provides three broad functionalities: (a) user verification ("Is this person who he claims to be?"); (b) large-scale identification ("Who is this person?"); and (c) screening ("Is this person on a wanted list?"). Note that traditional authentication schemes cannot reliably provide functionalities (b) and (c). Thus, biometrics is especially advantageous in scenarios which require large throughput with minimum or no human supervision.

There are several issues that render biometric recognition as a challenging problem. (a) Noise in sensed data: A fingerprint image with a scar, or a voice sample altered by cold are examples of noisy data. (b) Intra-class variations: These variations are typically caused by a user who is incorrectly interacting with the sensor (e.g., incorrect facial pose), or when the characteristics of a sensor are modified during authentication (e.g., optical versus solid-state fingerprint sensors). (c) Inter-class similarities: In a biometric system comprising of a large number of users, there may be inter-class similarities (overlap) in the feature space of multiple users. (d) Non-universality: The biometric system may not be

S.Z. Li et al. (Eds.): Sinobiometrics 2004, LNCS 3338, pp. 1–2, 2004.
© Springer-Verlag Berlin Heidelberg 2004

able to acquire meaningful biometric data from a subset of users. A fingerprint biometric system, for example, may extract incorrect minutiae features from the fingerprints of certain individuals, due to the poor quality of the ridges. (e) Spoof attacks: This type of attack is especially relevant when behavioral traits such as signature or voice are used. However, physical traits such as fingerprints are also susceptible to spoof attacks.

Some of the challenges listed above can be addressed by adopting a multi-modal biometric system. A multimodal system (unlike a unimodal one) utilizes the evidence presented by multiple biometric cues in order to establish identity. By consolidating multiple sources of biometric information (e.g., multiple fingers of a user, or multiple matchers operating on the same biometric, or multiple traits such as fingerprint and iris), these systems improve matching performance, increase population coverage, deter spoofing, and facilitate indexing. Since no single biometric trait can efficiently meet all the requirements imposed by a large-scale application (involving a large number of enrolled users), it is commonly agreed that multimodal systems will play an important role in the identity management systems of the future.

In order to deflect (as well as prevent) attacks directed at a biometric system, it is important to deal with issues pertaining to fake biometrics, replay/insertion attacks, channel eavesdropping and template integrity. The introduction of cancelable biometrics and template watermarking can address some of the concerns related to safeguarding templates. Similarly, a combination of liveness detection algorithms and challenge-response mechanisms can be used to ensure that a fake biometric is not being presented. However, substantially more research is needed in order to identity and resolve the vulnerabilities in a biometric system. Furthermore, there are several privacy concerns associated with the use of biometrics: (a) Will the government use biometric data to track people secretly? (b) Will an insurance company use the biometric data of an individual to elicit his medical history (c) Will an organization employ the biometric data of its members for the intended purpose only or will there be functionality creep? A legal framework may be necessary to ensure that these concerns are satisfactorily handled.

Biometrics is an exciting pattern recognition application but is not yet a 'solved' problem. Specifically, issues such as the following have to be addressed. (a) Representation: How can the biometric of a person be effectively modeled using the limited number of samples obtained during enrolment? (b) Scaling: How does one reliably predict the performance (accuracy, speed, vulnerability) of a large-scale biometric system that has several million identities enrolled in it? (c) Security: How can one ensure the security and integrity of the templates stored in a database? (d) Privacy: What type of legal and technical procedures are necessary to ensure the privacy of individuals enrolled in a biometric database?

Considering the recent mandates of several governments for the nationwide use of biometrics in delivering crucial societal functions, it is evident that biometrics would profoundly impact the way identity is established in the 21st century.

Face Recognition: Technical Challenges and Research Directions

Stan Z. Li [1,2]

[1] Center for Biometrics Research and Testing
[2] National Laboratory of Pattern Recognition,
Institute of Automation, Chinese Academy of Sciences,
Beijing 10008, China
szli@nlpr.ia.ac.cn

Abstract. Face recognition performance has improved significantly since the first automatic face recognition system developed by Kanade. Face detection, facial feature extraction, and recognition can now be performed in "realtime" for images captured under favorable, constrained situations. Although progress in face recognition has been encouraging, the task has also turned out to be a difficult endeavor, especially for unconstrained tasks where viewpoint, illumination, expression, occlusion, accessories, and so on vary considerably. In this talk, I will analyze challenges from the viewpoint of face manifolds and points out possible research directions towards highly accurate face recognition. I will show that the challenges come from high nonconvexity of face manifolds, in the image space, under variations in lighting, pose and so on; unfortunately, there have been no good methods from theories of pattern recognition for solving such difficult problems, especially when the size of training data is small. However, there are two directions to look at towards possible solutions: One is to construct a ``good" feature space in which the face manifolds become less complex i.e., less nonlinear and nonconvex than those in other spaces. This includes two levels of processing: (1) normalize face images geometrically and photometrically, such as using morphing and histogram equalization; and (2) extract features in the normalized images which are stable with respect to the said variations, such as based on Gabor wavelets. The second strategy is to construct classification engines able to solve less, although still, nonlinear problems in the feature space, and to generalize better. A successful algorithm usually combines both strategies. Still another direction is on system design, including sensor hardware, to make the pattern recognition problems thereafter less challenging.

S.Z. Li et al. (Eds.): Sinobiometrics 2004, LNCS 3338, p. 3, 2004.
© Springer-Verlag Berlin Heidelberg 2004

Fingerprints: Recognition, Performance Evaluation and Synthetic Generation

Raffaele Cappelli

Biometric Systems Lab – DEIS,
University of Bologna
Via Sacchi 3, 47023 Cesena (FC), Italy
cappelli@csr.unibo.it

Abstract. Fingerprints are the most widely used characteristics in systems that recognize a person's identity, for their proven uniqueness and stability over time. Although automatic fingerprint recognition was one of the first pattern recognition application, it is not a solved problem. In this talk, the main automatic fingerprint recognition approaches will be reviewed, concentrating on feature extraction and matching techniques (minutiae-based, correlation-based texture-based), and discussing some of the most important challenges in this field. Furthermore, the fingerprint evaluation campaigns organized in the recent years will be described, focusing on the three editions of the Fingerprint Verification Competition (FVC). Independent and reliable evaluation of the advances in fingerprint recognition is extremely important for several reasons: 1) to give governments, organizations and to every potential user a clear panorama of the potentiality and current limits of this technology; 2) to compare and rank different solutions (academic and commercial); 3) to provide unambiguous benchmarks/protocols to researchers to track their advances. Finally, a method for generating synthetic fingerprints with the aim of creating large test databases at zero cost will be introduced. The synthetic images are randomly generated according to few given parameters; the method captures the variability which characterizes the acquisition of fingerprints through on-line sensors and uses a sequence of steps to derive a series of "impressions" of the same "artificial finger".

S.Z. Li et al. (Eds.): Sinobiometrics 2004, LNCS 3338, p. 4, 2004.
© Springer-Verlag Berlin Heidelberg 2004

Recognising Persons by Their Iris Patterns

John Daugman

The Computer Laboratory, University of Cambridge, CB3 0FD, UK
john.daugman@CL.cam.ac.uk
http://www.CL.cam.ac.uk/users/jgd1000/

Abstract. Algorithms developed by the author for recognizing persons by their iris patterns have now been tested in many field deployments, producing no false matches in millions of iris comparisons. The recognition principle is the failure of a test of statistical independence on iris phase structure, as encoded by multi-scale quadrature 2D Gabor wavelets. The combinatorial complexity of this phase information across different persons spans about 249 degrees of freedom and generates a discrimination entropy of about 3.2 bits/mm^2 over the iris, enabling real-time decisions about personal identity with extremely high confidence. These high confidence levels are important because they allow very large databases on even a national scale to be searched exhaustively (one-to-many "identification mode"), without making false matches, despite so many chances. Biometrics that lack this property can only survive one-to-one ("verification") or few comparisons. This paper explains the iris recognition algorithms, and presents results of 9.1 million comparisons among eye images from trials in Britain, the USA, Japan, and Korea.

1 Introduction

Reliable automatic recognition of persons has long been an attractive goal. As in all pattern recognition problems, the key issue is the relation between inter-class and intra-class variability: objects can be reliably classified only if the variation among different instances of a given class is less than the variation between different classes. For example in face recognition, difficulties arise from the fact that the face is a changeable social organ displaying a variety of expressions, as well as being an active 3D object whose image varies with viewing angle, pose, illumination, accoutrements, and age [1], [2]. It has been shown that for "mug shot" images taken at least one year apart, even the best current algorithms can have error rates of 43% to 50% [14], [15], [16]. Against this intra-class (same face) variation, inter-class variation is limited because different faces possess the same basic set of features, in the same canonical geometry.

Following the fundamental principle that inter-class variation should be larger than intra-class variation, iris patterns offer a powerful alternative approach to reliable visual recognition of persons when imaging can be done at distances of less than a meter, and especially when there is a need to search very large databases without incurring any false matches despite a huge number of possibilities. Although small (11 mm) and sometimes problematic to image, the iris has

S.Z. Li et al. (Eds.): Sinobiometrics 2004, LNCS 3338, pp. 5–25, 2004.

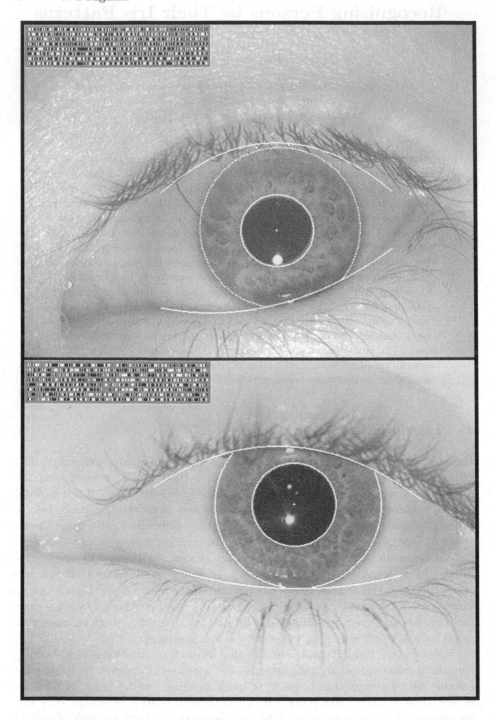

Fig. 1. Examples of human iris patterns, imaged monochromatically at a distance of about 35 cm. The outline overlays show the results of the iris and pupil localization and eyelid detection steps. The bit streams pictured result from demodulation with complex-valued 2D Gabor wavelets to encode the phase sequence of each iris pattern

the great mathematical advantage that its pattern variability among different persons is enormous. In addition, as an internal (yet externally visible) organ of the eye, the iris is well protected from the environment, and stable over time. As a planar object its image is relatively insensitive to angle of illumination, and changes in viewing angle cause only affine transformations; even the non-affine pattern distortion caused by pupillary dilation is readily reversible in the image coding stage. Finally, the ease of localizing eyes in faces, and the distinctive annular shape of the iris, facilitate reliable and precise isolation of this feature and the creation of a size-invariant representation.

The iris begins to form in the third month of gestation [13] and the structures creating its pattern are largely complete by the eighth month, although pigment accretion can continue into the first postnatal years. Its complex pattern can contain many distinctive features such as arching ligaments, furrows, ridges, crypts, rings, corona, freckles, and a zigzag collarette, some of which are seen in Fig. 1. Iris colour is determined mainly by the density of melanin pigment [4] in its anterior layer and stroma, with blue irises resulting from an absence of pigment: long wavelength light penetrates while shorter wavelengths are scattered by the stroma. The striated trabecular meshwork of elastic pectinate ligament creates the predominant texture under visible light, whereas in the near infrared (NIR) wavelengths used for unobtrusive imaging at distances of up to 1 meter, deeper and somewhat more slowly modulated stromal features dominate the iris pattern. In NIR wavelengths, even darkly pigmented irises reveal rich and complex features.

The author's algorithms [8], [9], [10] for encoding and recognizing iris patterns have been the executable software used in all iris recognition systems so far deployed commercially or in tests, including those by British Telecom, NIST, TSA, Sandia Labs, UK National Physical Lab, Panasonic, LG, Oki, EyeTicket, IrisGuard, Sensar, Sarnoff, IBM, SchipholGroup, Siemens, Byometric, Sagem, IriScan, and Iridian. All testing organizations have reported a false match rate of 0 in their tests, some of which involved millions of iris pairings. This paper explains how the algorithms work, and presents new data on the statistical properties and singularity of iris patterns based on 9.1 million comparisons.

2 Finding an Iris in an Image

To capture the rich details of iris patterns, an imaging system should resolve a minimum of 70 pixels in iris radius. In most deployments of these algorithms to date, the resolved iris radius has typically been 80 to 130 pixels. Monochrome CCD cameras (480 x 640) have been used because NIR illumination in the 700nm - 900nm band was required for imaging to be unintrusive to humans. Some imaging platforms deployed a wide-angle camera for coarse localization of eyes in faces, to steer the optics of a narrow-angle pan/tilt camera that acquired higher resolution images of eyes. There exist many alternative methods for finding and tracking facial features such as the eyes, and this well-researched topic will not be discussed further here. Most images in the present database were acquired without active pan/tilt camera optics, instead exploiting visual feedback via a mirror or video image to enable cooperating Subjects to position their own eyes within the field of view of a single narrow-angle camera.

Image focus assessment is performed in real-time (faster than video frame rate) by measuring spectral power in middle and upper frequency bands of the 2D Fourier spectrum of each image frame and seeking to maximize this quantity either by moving an active lens or by providing audio feedback to Subjects to adjust their range appropriately. The video rate execution speed of focus assessment (i.e. within 15 msec) is achieved by using a bandpass 2D filter kernel requiring only summation and differencing of pixels, and no multiplications, within the 2D convolution necessary to estimate power in the selected 2D spectral bands.

Images passing a minimum focus criterion are then analyzed to find the iris, with precise localization of its boundaries using a coarse-to-fine strategy terminating in single-pixel precision estimates of the center coordinates and radius of both the iris and the pupil. Although the results of the iris search greatly constrain the pupil search, concentricity of these boundaries cannot be assumed. Very often the pupil center is nasal, and inferior, to the iris center. Its radius can range from 0.1 to 0.8 of the iris radius. Thus, all three parameters defining the pupillary circle must be estimated separately from those of the iris. A very effective integrodifferential operator for determining these parameters is:

$$\max_{(r,x_0,y_0)} \left| G_\sigma(r) * \frac{\partial}{\partial r} \oint_{r,x_0,y_0} \frac{I(x,y)}{2\pi r} ds \right| \tag{1}$$

where $I(x,y)$ is an image such as Fig. 1 containing an eye. The operator searches over the image domain (x,y) for the maximum in the blurred partial derivative with respect to increasing radius r, of the normalized contour integral of $I(x,y)$ along a circular arc ds of radius r and center coordinates (x_0,y_0). The symbol * denotes convolution and $G_\sigma(r)$ is a smoothing function such as a Gaussian of scale σ. The complete operator behaves as a circular edge detector, blurred at a scale set by σ, searching iteratively for the maximal contour integral derivative at successively finer scales of analysis through the three parameter space of center coordinates and radius (x_0,y_0,r) defining a path of contour integration.

The operator in (1) serves to find both the pupillary boundary and the outer (limbus) boundary of the iris, although the initial search for the limbus also incorporates evidence of an interior pupil to improve its robustness since the limbic boundary itself usually has extremely soft contrast when long wavelength NIR illumination is used. Once the coarse-to-fine iterative searches for both these boundaries have reached single pixel precision, then a similar approach to detecting curvilinear edges is used to localize both the upper and lower eyelid boundaries. The path of contour integration in (1) is changed from circular to arcuate, with spline parameters fitted by statistical estimation methods to model each eyelid boundary. Images with less than 50% of the iris visible between the fitted eyelid splines are deemed inadequate, e.g. in blink. The result of all these localization operations is the isolation of iris tissue from other image regions, as illustrated in Fig. 1 by the graphical overlays on the eyes.

Because pupils are generally not exactly round, the inner boundary of the iris coordinate system should not be forced to be a circle. Instead, once the approximate circular boundary has been determined, an active contour ("snake") is allowed to deform into the true pupillary boundary by seeking equilibrium between internal (smoothness) and external (edge data) "energy" terms. A general principle in model-based computer vision is that where the data is strong, weak constraints should be employed, whereas strong constraints should be employed where the data is weak. For irises imaged in infrared illumination as illustrated in Fig. 1, the outer boundary of the iris with the sclera (the limbus) is often a very weak signal, sometimes having only about 1% contrast. Such weak edge data should be localized under the strong constraint that this contour will be a circle. But the pupillary boundary offers such strong edge data of high contrast that it can be determined reliably with weak constraints, and so an active snake with only weak smoothness constraints is allowed to fit its true contour for setting the inner boundary of the pseudo-polar coordinate system.

3   Iris Feature Encoding by 2D Wavelet Demodulation

Each isolated iris pattern is then demodulated to extract its phase information using quadrature 2D Gabor wavelets [6], [7], [11]. This encoding process is illustrated in Fig. 2. It amounts to a patch-wise phase quantization of the iris pattern, by identifying in which quadrant of the complex plane each resultant phasor lies when a given area of the iris is projected onto complex-valued 2D Gabor wavelets:

$$h_{\{Re,Im\}} = \mathrm{sgn}_{\{Re,Im\}} \int_{\rho} \int_{\phi} I(\rho,\phi) e^{-i\omega(\theta_0-\phi)}$$
$$\cdot e^{-(r_0-\rho)^2/\alpha^2} e^{-(\theta_0-\phi)^2/\beta^2} \rho d\rho d\phi \tag{2}$$

where $h_{\{Re,Im\}}$ can be regarded as a complex-valued bit whose real and imaginary parts are either 1 or 0 (sgn) depending on the sign of the 2D integral; $I(\rho,\phi)$ is the raw iris image in a dimensionless polar coordinate system that is size- and translation-invariant, and which also corrects for pupil dilation as explained in a later section; α and β are the multi-scale 2D wavelet size parameters, spanning an 8-fold range from 0.15mm to 1.2mm on the iris; ω is wavelet frequency, spanning 3 octaves in inverse proportion to β; and (r_0, θ_0) represent the polar coordinates of each region of iris for which the phasor coordinates $h_{\{Re,Im\}}$ are computed. Such phase quadrant coding sequences are illustrated for two irises by the bit streams shown graphically in Fig. 1. A desirable feature of the phase code definition given in Fig. 2 is that it is a cyclic, or Gray code: in rotating between any adjacent phase quadrants, only a single bit changes, unlike a binary code in which two bits may change, making some errors arbitrarily more costly than others. Altogether 2,048 such phase bits (256 bytes) are computed for each iris, but in a major improvement over the author's earlier [8] algorithms, now an equal number of masking bits are also computed to signify whether any iris region is obscured by eyelids, contains any eyelash occlusions, specular reflections,

Phase-Quadrant Demodulation Code

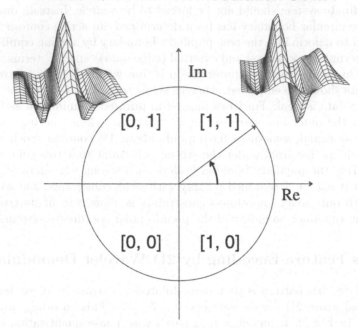

Fig. 2. The phase demodulation process used to encode iris patterns. Local regions of an iris are projected (2) onto quadrature 2D Gabor wavelets, generating complex-valued coefficients whose real and imaginary parts specify the coordinates of a phasor in the complex plane. The angle of each phasor is quantized to one of the four quadrants, setting two bits of phase information. This process is repeated all across the iris with many wavelet sizes, frequencies, and orientations, to extract 2,048 bits

boundary artifacts of hard contact lenses, or poor signal-to-noise ratio and thus should be ignored in the demodulation code as artifact.

The 2D Gabor wavelets were chosen for the extraction of iris information because of the nice optimality properties of these wavelets. Following the Heisenberg Uncertainty Principle as it applies generally to mathematical functions, filters that are well-localized in frequency are poorly localized in space (or time), and *vice versa*. The 2D Gabor wavelets have the maximal joint resolution in the two domains simultaneously [6], [7], which means that both "what" and "where" information about iris features is extracted with optimal simultaneous resolution. A further nice property of 2D Gabor wavelets is that because they are complex-valued, they allow the definition and assignment of phase variables to any point in the image.

Only phase information is used for recognizing irises because amplitude information is not very discriminating, and it depends upon extraneous factors such as imaging contrast, illumination, and camera gain. The phase bit settings which code the sequence of projection quadrants as shown in Fig. 2 capture the

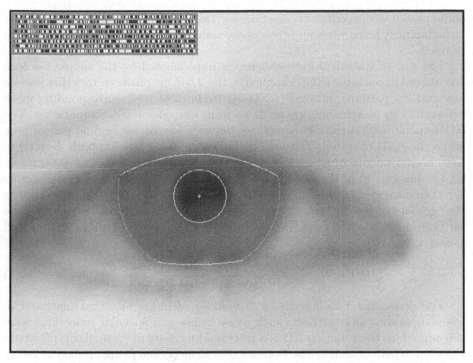

Fig. 3. Illustration that even for poorly focused eye images, the bits of a demodulation phase sequence are still set, randomly by noise. This prevents poorly focused eye images from falsely matching each other, as they may do in amplitude-based representations

information of wavelet zero-crossings, as seen in the sign operator in (2). The extraction of phase has the further advantage that phase angles remain defined regardless of how poor the image contrast may be, as illustrated by the extremely out-of-focus image in Fig. 3. Its phase bit stream has statistical properties such as run lengths similar to those of the codes for the properly focused eye images in Fig. 1. (Fig. 3 also illustrates the robustness of the iris- and pupil-finding operators, and the eyelid detection operators, despite poor focus.) The benefit which arises from the fact that phase bits are set also for a poorly focused image as shown here, even if based only on random CCD thermal noise, is that different poorly focused irises never become confused with each other when their phase codes are compared. By contrast, images of different faces look increasingly alike when poorly resolved, and can be confused with each other by appearance-based face recognition algorithms.

4   The Test of Statistical Independence: Combinatorics of Phase Sequences

The key to iris recognition is the failure of a test of statistical independence, which involves so many degrees-of-freedom that this test is virtually guaranteed to be passed whenever the phase codes for two different eyes are compared, but to be uniquely failed when any eye's phase code is compared with another version of itself.

The test of statistical independence is implemented by the simple Boolean Exclusive-OR operator (XOR) applied to the 2,048 bit phase vectors that encode any two iris patterns, masked (AND'ed) by both of their corresponding mask bit vectors to prevent non-iris artifacts from influencing iris comparisons. The XOR operator $\otimes$ detects disagreement between any corresponding pair of bits, while the AND operator $\cap$ ensures that the compared bits are both deemed to have been uncorrupted by eyelashes, eyelids, specular reflections, or other noise. The norms ($\|\quad\|$) of the resultant bit vector and of the AND'ed mask vectors are then measured in order to compute a fractional Hamming Distance (HD) as the measure of the dissimilarity between any two irises, whose two phase code bit vectors are denoted {codeA, codeB} and whose mask bit vectors are denoted {maskA, maskB}:

$$HD = \frac{\|(codeA \otimes codeB) \cap maskA \cap maskB\|}{\|maskA \cap maskB\|} \tag{3}$$

The denominator tallies the total number of phase bits that mattered in iris comparisons after artifacts such as eyelashes and specular reflections were discounted, so the resulting HD is a fractional measure of dissimilarity; 0 would represent a perfect match. The Boolean operators $\otimes$ and $\cap$ are applied in vector form to binary strings of length up to the word length of the CPU, as a single machine instruction. Thus for example on an ordinary 32-bit machine, any two integers between 0 and 4 billion can be XOR'ed in a single machine instruction to generate a third such integer, each of whose bits in a binary expansion is the XOR of the corresponding pair of bits of the original two integers. This implementation of (3) in parallel 32-bit chunks enables extremely rapid comparisons of iris codes when searching through a large database to find a match. On a 300 MHz CPU, such exhaustive searches are performed at a rate of about 100,000 irises per second; on a 3 GHz server, about a million iris comparisons can be performed per second.

Because any given bit in the phase code for an iris is equally likely to be 1 or 0, and different irises are uncorrelated, the expected proportion of agreeing bits between the codes for two different irises is HD = 0.500. The histogram in Fig. 4 shows the distribution of HDs obtained from 9.1 million comparisons between different pairings of iris images acquired by licensees of these algorithms in the UK, the USA, Japan, and Korea. There were 4,258 different iris images, including 10 each of one subset of 70 eyes. Excluding those duplicates of (700 x 9) same-eye comparisons, and not double-counting pairs, and not comparing any image with itself, the total number of unique pairings between different eye images whose HDs could be computed was ((4,258 x 4,257 - 700 x 9) / 2) = 9,060,003. Their observed mean HD was $p = 0.499$ with standard deviation $\sigma = 0.0317$; their full distribution in Fig. 4 corresponds to a binomial having $N = p(1-p)/\sigma^2 = 249$ degrees-of-freedom, as shown by the solid curve. The extremely close fit of the theoretical binomial to the observed distribution is

Binomial Distribution of IrisCode Hamming Distances

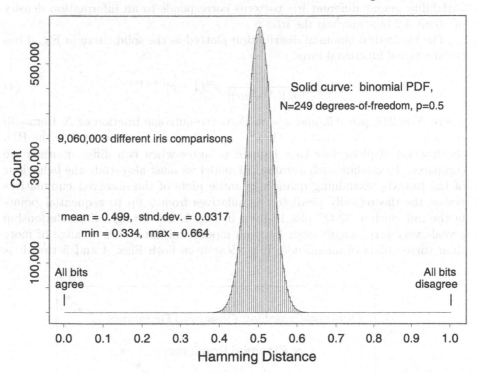

Fig. 4. Distribution of Hamming Distances from all 9.1 million possible comparisons between different pairs of irises in the database. The histogram forms a perfect binomial distribution with $p = 0.5$ and $N = 249$ degrees-of-freedom, as shown by the solid curve (4). The data implies that it is extremely improbable for two different irises to disagree in less than about a third of their phase information

a consequence of the fact that each comparison between two phase code bits from two different irises is essentially a Bernoulli trial, albeit with correlations between successive "coin tosses."

In the phase code for any given iris, only small subsets of bits are mutually independent due to the internal correlations, especially radial, within an iris. (If all $N = 2,048$ phase bits were independent, then the distribution in Fig. 4 would be very much sharper, with an expected standard deviation of only $\sqrt{p(1-p)/N} = 0.011$ and so the HD interval between 0.49 and 0.51 would contain most of the distribution.) Bernoulli trials that are correlated [18] remain binomially distributed but with a reduction in N, the effective number of tosses, and hence an increase in the σ of the normalized HD distribution. The form and width of the HD distribution in Fig. 4 tell us that the amount of difference between the phase codes for different irises is distributed equivalently to runs of 249 tosses of a fair coin (Bernoulli trials with $p = 0.5, N = 249$). Expressing this variation as a discrimination entropy [5] and using typical iris and pupil diameters of 11mm and 5mm respectively, the observed amount of statistical variability among different iris patterns corresponds to an information density of about 3.2 bits/mm² on the iris.

The theoretical binomial distribution plotted as the solid curve in Fig. 4 has the fractional functional form

$$f(x) = \frac{N!}{m!(N-m)!} \, p^m (1-p)^{(N-m)} \tag{4}$$

where $N = 249$, $p = 0.5$, and $x = m/N$ is the outcome fraction of N Bernoulli trials (e.g. coin tosses that are "heads" in each run). In our case, x is the HD, the fraction of phase bits that happen to agree when two different irises are compared. To validate such a statistical model we must also study the behaviour of the tails, by examining quantile-quantile plots of the observed cumulatives versus the theoretically predicted cumulatives from 0 up to sequential points in the tail. Such a "Q-Q" plot is given in Fig. 5. The straight line relationship reveals very precise agreement between model and data, over a range of more than three orders of magnitude. It is clear from both Figs. 4 and 5 that it is

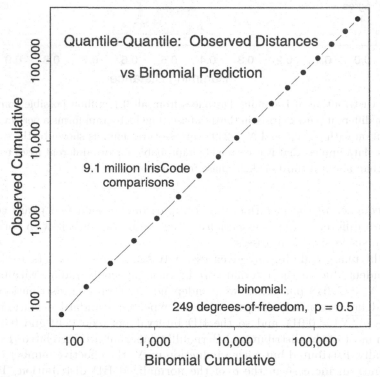

Fig. 5. Quantile-quantile plot of the observed cumulatives under the left tail of the histogram in Fig. 4 versus the predicted binomial cumulatives. The close agreement over several orders of magnitude strongly confirms the binomial model for phase bit comparisons between different irises

extremely improbable that two different irises might disagree by chance in fewer than at least a third of their bits. (Of the 9.1 million iris comparisons plotted in the histogram of Fig. 4, the smallest Hamming Distance observed was 0.334.) Computing the cumulative of $f(x)$ from 0 to 0.333 indicates that the probability of such an event is about 1 in 16 million. The cumulative from 0 to just 0.300 is 1 in 10 billion. Thus, even the observation of a relatively poor degree of match between the phase codes for two different iris images (say, 70% agreement or HD = 0.300) would still provide extraordinarily compelling evidence of identity, because the test of statistical independence is still failed so convincingly.

I also compared genetically identical eyes in the same manner, in order to discover the degree to which their textural patterns were correlated and hence genetically determined. A convenient source of genetically identical irises are the right and left pair from any given person; such pairs have the same genetic relationship as the four irises of monozygotic twins, or indeed the prospective $2N$

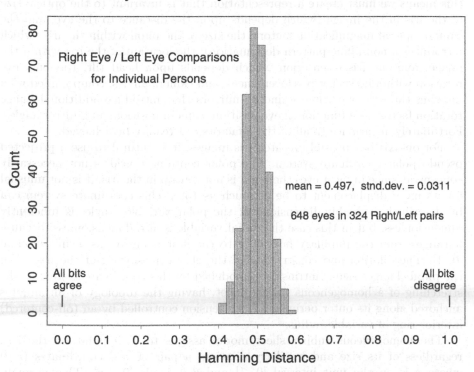

Fig. 6. Distribution of Hamming Distances between genetically identical irises, in 648 paired eyes from 324 persons. The data are statistically indistinguishable from that shown in Fig. 4 comparing unrelated irises. Unlike eye colour, the phase structure of iris patterns therefore appears to be epigenetic, arising from random events and circumstances in the morphogenesis of this tissue

irises of N clones. Although eye colour is of course strongly determined geneti-cally, as is overall iris appearance, the detailed patterns of genetically identical irises appear to be as uncorrelated as they are among unrelated eyes. Using the same methods as described above, 648 right/left iris pairs from 324 persons were compared pairwise. Their mean HD was 0.497 with standard deviation 0.031, and their distribution (Fig. 6) was statistically indistinguishable from the dis-tribution for unrelated eyes (Fig. 4). A set of 6 pairwise comparisons among the eyes of actual monozygotic twins also yielded a result (mean HD = 0.507) expected for unrelated eyes. It appears that the phenotypic random patterns visible in the human iris are almost entirely epigenetic [12].

5 Recognizing Irises Regardless of Size, Position, and Orientation

Robust representations for pattern recognition must be invariant to changes in the size, position, and orientation of the patterns. In the case of iris recognition, this means we must create a representation that is invariant to the optical size of the iris in the image (which depends upon the distance to the eye, and the camera optical magnification factor); the size of the pupil within the iris (which introduces a non-affine pattern deformation); the location of the iris within the image; and the iris orientation, which depends upon head tilt, torsional eye rotation within its socket (cyclovergence), and camera angles, compounded with imaging through pan/tilt eye-finding mirrors that introduce additional image rotation factors as a function of eye position, camera position, and mirror angles. Fortunately, invariance to all of these factors can readily be achieved.

For on-axis but possibly rotated iris images, it is natural to use a projected pseudo polar coordinate system. The polar coordinate grid is not necessarily concentric, since in most eyes the pupil is not central in the iris; it is not unusual for its nasal displacement to be as much as 15%. This coordinate system can be described as doubly-dimensionless: the polar variable, angle, is inherently dimensionless, but in this case the radial variable is also dimensionless, because it ranges from the pupillary boundary to the limbus always as a unit interval [0, 1]. The dilation and constriction of the elastic meshwork of the iris when the pupil changes size is intrinsically modelled by this coordinate system as the stretching of a homogeneous rubber sheet, having the topology of an annulus anchored along its outer perimeter, with tension controlled by an (off-centered) interior ring of variable radius.

The homogeneous rubber sheet model assigns to each point on the iris, regardless of its size and pupillary dilation, a pair of real coordinates (r, θ) where r is on the unit interval [0, 1] and θ is angle [0, 2π]. This normali-sation, or remapping of the iris image $I(x, y)$ from raw cartesian coordinates (x, y) to the dimensionless non-concentric polar coordinate system (r, θ) can be represented:

$$I(x(r, \theta), y(r, \theta)) \to I(r, \theta) \tag{5}$$

where $x(r, \theta)$ and $y(r, \theta)$ are defined as linear combinations of both the set of pupillary boundary points $(x_p(\theta), y_p(\theta))$ and the set of limbus boundary points along the outer perimeter of the iris $(x_s(\theta), y_s(\theta))$ bordering the sclera, both of which are detected by finding the maximum of the operator (1).

$$x(r, \theta) = (1 - r)x_p(\theta) + rx_s(\theta) \tag{6}$$

$$y(r, \theta) = (1 - r)y_p(\theta) + ry_s(\theta) \tag{7}$$

Since the radial coordinate ranges from the iris inner boundary to its outer boundary as a unit interval, it inherently corrects for the elastic pattern deformation in the iris when the pupil changes in size.

The localization of the iris and the coordinate system described above achieve invariance to the 2D position and size of the iris, and to the dilation of the pupil within the iris. However, it would not be invariant to the orientation of the iris within the image plane. The most efficient way to achieve iris recognition with orientation invariance is not to rotate the image itself using the Euler matrix, but rather to compute the iris phase code in a single canonical orientation and then to compare this very compact representation at many discrete orientations by cyclic scrolling of its angular variable. The statistical consequences of seeking the best match after numerous relative rotations of two iris codes are straightforward. Let $f_0(x)$ be the raw density distribution obtained for the HDs between different irises after comparing them only in a single relative orientation; for example, $f_0(x)$ might be the binomial defined in (4). Then $F_0(x)$, the cumulative of $f_0(x)$ from 0 to x, becomes the probability of getting a false match in such a test when using HD acceptance criterion x:

$$F_0(x) = \int_0^x f_0(x)dx \tag{8}$$

or, equivalently,

$$f_0(x) = \frac{d}{dx}F_0(x) \tag{9}$$

Clearly, then, the probability of not making a false match when using criterion x is $1 - F_0(x)$ after a single test, and it is $[1 - F_0(x)]^n$ after carrying out n such tests independently at n different relative orientations. It follows that the probability of a false match after a "best of n" test of agreement, when using HD criterion x, regardless of the actual form of the raw unrotated distribution $f_0(x)$, is:

$$F_n(x) = 1 - [1 - F_0(x)]^n \tag{10}$$

and the expected density $f_n(x)$ associated with this cumulative is

$$f_n(x) = \frac{d}{dx}F_n(x)$$
$$= nf_0(x)[1 - F_0(x)]^{n-1} \tag{11}$$

Each of the 9.1 million pairings of different iris images whose HD distribution was shown in Fig. 4, was submitted to further comparisons in each of 7 relative

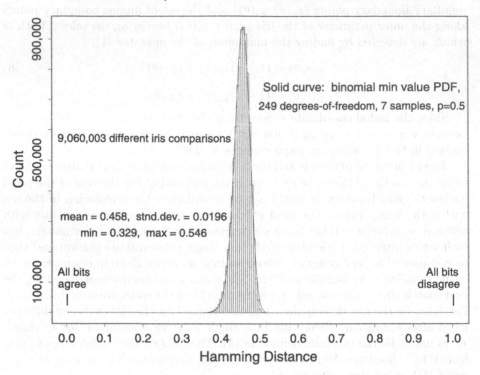

IrisCode Comparisons after Rotations: Best Matches

Fig. 7. Distribution of Hamming Distances for the same set of 9.1 million comparisons shown in Fig. 4, but allowing for 7 relative rotations and preserving only the best match found for each pair. This "best of n" test skews the distribution to the left and reduces its mean from about 0.5 to 0.458. The solid curve is the theoretical prediction for such "extreme-value" sampling, as described by (4) and (8) - (11)

orientations. This generated 63 million HD outcomes, but in each group of 7 associated with any one pair of irises, only the best match (smallest HD) was retained. The histogram of these new 9.1 million best HDs is shown in Fig. 7. Since only the smallest value in each group of 7 samples was retained, the new distribution is skewed and biased to a lower mean value (HD = 0.458), as expected from the theory of extreme value sampling. The solid curve in Fig. 7 is a plot of (11), incorporating (4) and (8) as its terms, and it shows an excellent fit between theory (binomial extreme value sampling) and data. The fact that the minimum HD observed in all of these millions of rotated comparisons was about 0.33 illustrates the extreme improbability that the phase sequences for two different irises might disagree in fewer than a third of their bits. This suggests that in order to identify people by their iris patterns with high confidence, we need to demand only a very forgiving degree of match (say, HD $\leq$ 0.32).

6 Uniqueness of Failing the Test of Statistical Independence

The statistical data and theory presented above show that we can perform iris recognition successfully just by a test of statistical independence. Any two different irises are statistically "guaranteed" to pass this test of independence; and any two images that fail this test must be images of the same iris. Thus, it is the unique failure of the test of independence, that is the basis for iris recognition.

It is informative to calculate the significance of any observed HD matching score, in terms of the likelihood that it could have arisen by chance from two different irises. These probabilities give a confidence level associated with any recognition decision. Fig. 8 shows the false match probabilities marked off in cumulatives along the tail of the distribution presented in Fig. 7 (same theoretical curve (11) as plotted in Fig. 7 and with the justification presented in Fig. 4

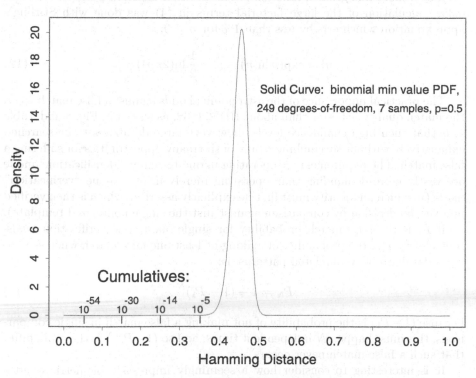

Fig. 8. Calculated cumulatives under the left tail of the distribution seen in Fig. 7, up to sequential points, using the functional analysis described by (4) and (8) - (11). The extremely rapid attenuation of these cumulatives reflects the binomial combinatorics that dominate (4). This accounts for the astronomical confidence levels against a false match, when executing this test of statistical independence

Table 1. Cumulatives under (11) giving single false match probabilities for various Hamming Distance (HD) decision criteria

HD Criterion	Odds of False Match
0.26	1 in 10^{13}
0.27	1 in 10^{12}
0.28	1 in 10^{11}
0.29	1 in 13 billion
0.30	1 in 1.5 billion
0.31	1 in 185 million
0.32	1 in 26 million
0.33	1 in 4 million
0.34	1 in 690,000
0.35	1 in 133,000

and Fig. 5). Table 1 enumerates false match probabilities, the cumulatives of (11), as a more fine-grained function of HD decision criterion between 0.26 and 0.35. Calculation of the large factorial terms in (4) was done with Stirling's approximation which errs by less than 1% for $n \geq 9$:

$$n! \approx \exp(n \ln(n) - n + \frac{1}{2} \ln(2\pi n)) \tag{12}$$

The practical importance of the astronomical odds against a false match when the match quality is better than about HD ≤ 0.32, as shown in Fig. 8 and Table 1, is that such high confidence levels allow very large databases to be searched exhaustively without succumbing to any of the many opportunities for suffering a false match. The requirements of operating in one-to-many "identification" mode are vastly more demanding than operating merely in one-to-one "verification" mode (in which an identity must first be explicitly asserted, which is then verified in a yes/no decision by comparison against just the single nominated template).

If P_1 is the false match probability for single one-to-one verification trials, then clearly P_N, the probability of making at least one false match when searching a database of N unrelated patterns, is:

$$P_N = 1 - (1 - P_1)^N \tag{13}$$

because $(1 - P_1)$ is the probability of not making a false match in single comparisons; this must happen N independent times; and so $(1 - P_1)^N$ is the probability that such a false match never occurs.

It is interesting to consider how a seemingly impressive biometric one-to-one "verifier" would perform in exhaustive search mode once databases become larger than about 100, in view of (13). For example, a face recognition algorithm that truly achieved 99.9% correct rejection when tested on non-identical faces, hence making only 0.1% false matches, would seem to be performing at a very impressive level because it must confuse no more than 10% of all identical twin pairs (since about 1% of all persons in the general population have an identical twin). But even with its $P_1 = 0.001$, how good would it be on large databases?

Using (13) we see that when the search database size has reached merely $N = 200$ unrelated faces, the probability of at least one false match among them is already 18%. When the search database is just $N = 2000$ unrelated faces, the probability of at least one false match has reached 86%. Clearly, identification is vastly more demanding than one-to-one verification, and even for moderate database sizes, merely "good" verifiers are of no use as identifiers. Observing the approximation that $P_N \approx NP_1$ for small $P_1 << \frac{1}{N} << 1$, when searching a database of size N an identifier needs to be roughly N times better than a verifier to achieve comparable odds against making false matches.

The algorithms for iris recognition exploit the extremely rapid attenuation of the HD distribution tail created by binomial combinatorics, to accommodate very large database searches without suffering false matches. The HD threshold is adaptive, to maintain $P_N < 10^{-6}$ regardless of how large the search database size N is. As Table 1 illustrates, this means that if the search database contains 1 million different iris patterns, it is only necessary for the HD match criterion to adjust downwards from 0.33 to 0.27 in order to maintain still a net false match probability of 10^{-6} for the entire database.

7   Decision Environment for Iris Recognition

The overall "decidability" of the task of recognizing persons by their iris patterns is revealed by comparing the Hamming Distance distributions for same versus for different irises. The left distribution in Fig. 9 shows the HDs computed between 7,070 different pairs of same-eye images at different times, under different conditions, and usually with different cameras; and the right distribution gives the same 9.1 million comparisons among different eyes shown earlier. To the degree that one can confidently decide whether an observed sample belongs to the left or the right distribution in Fig. 9, iris recognition can be successfully performed. Such a representation of the decision problem may be called the "decision environment," because it reveals the extent to which the two cases (same versus different) are separable and thus how reliably decisions can be made, since the overlap between the two distributions determines the error rates.

Whereas Fig. 9 shows the decision environment under less favourable conditions (images acquired by different camera platforms), Fig. 10 shows the decision environment under ideal (almost artificial) conditions. Subjects' eyes were imaged in a laboratory setting using always the same camera with fixed zoom factor and at fixed distance, and with fixed illumination. Not surprisingly, more than half of such image comparisons achieved an HD of 0.00, and the average HD was a mere 0.019. It is clear from comparing Fig. 9 and Fig. 10 that the "authentics" distribution for iris recognition (the similarity between different images of the same eye, as shown in the left-side distributions), depends very strongly upon the image acquisition conditions. However, the measured similarity for "imposters" (the right-side distribution) is almost completely independent of imaging fac-

Decision Environment for Iris Recognition: Non-Ideal Imaging

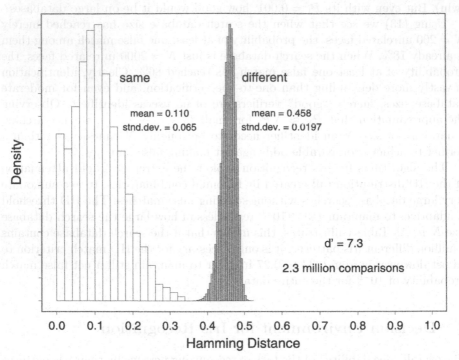

Fig. 9. The Decision Environment for iris recognition under relatively unfavourable conditions, using images acquired at different distances, and by different cameras

tors. Instead, it just reflects the combinatorics of Bernoulli trials, as bits from independent binary sources (the phase codes for different irises) are compared.

For two-choice decision tasks (e.g. same versus different), such as biometric decision making, the "decidability" index d' is one measure of how well separated the two distributions are, since recognition errors would be caused by their overlap. If their two means are μ_1 and μ_2, and their two standard deviations are σ_1 and σ_2, then d' is defined as

$$d' = \frac{|\mu_1 - \mu_2|}{\sqrt{(\sigma_1^2 + \sigma_2^2)/2}} \tag{14}$$

This measure of decidability is independent of how liberal or conservative is the acceptance threshold used. Rather, by measuring separation, it reflects the degree to which any improvement in (say) the false match error rate must be paid for by a worsening of the failure-to-match error rate. The performance of any biometric technology can be calibrated by its d' score, among other metrics. The measured decidability for iris recognition is $d' = 7.3$ for the non-ideal (crossed platform) conditions presented in Fig. 9, and it is $d' = 14.1$ for the ideal imaging conditions presented in Fig. 10.

Decision Environment for Iris Recognition: Ideal Imaging

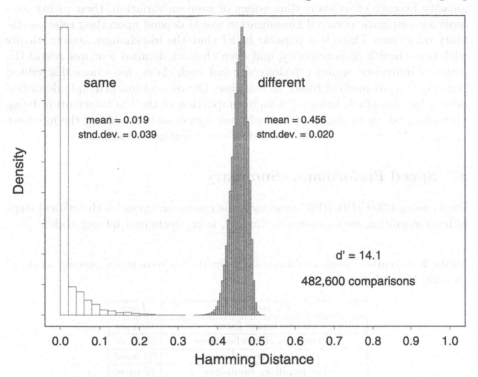

Fig. 10. The Decision Environment for iris recognition under very favourable conditions, using always the same camera, distance, and lighting

Based on the left-side distributions in Figs. 9 and 10, one could calculate a table of probabilities of failure to match, as a function of HD match criterion, just as we did earlier in Table 1 for false match probabilities based on the right-side distribution. However, such estimates may not be stable because the "authentics" distributions depend strongly on the quality of imaging (e.g. motion blur, focus, noise, etc.) and would be different for different optical platforms. As illustrated earlier by the badly defocused image of Fig. 3, phase bits are still set randomly with binomial statistics in poor imaging, and so the right distribution is the stable asymptotic form both in the case of well imaged irises (Fig. 10) and poorly imaged irises (Fig. 9). Imaging quality determines how much the same-iris distribution evolves and migrates leftward, away from the asymptotic different-iris distribution on the right. In any case, we note that for the 7,070 same-iris comparisons shown in Fig. 9, their highest HD was 0.327 which is below the smallest HD of 0.329 for the 9.1 million comparisons between different irises. Thus a decision criterion slightly below 0.33 for the empirical data sets shown can perfectly separate the dual distributions. At this criterion, using the cumulatives of (11) in Table 1, the theoretical false match probability is 1 in 4 million.

Notwithstanding this diversity among iris patterns and their apparent singularity because of so many dimensions of random variation, their utility as a basis for automatic personal identification would depend upon their relative stability over time. There is a popular belief that the iris changes systematically with one's health or personality, and even that its detailed features reveal the states of individual organs ("iridology"); but such claims have been discredited (e.g. [3], [17]) as medical fraud. In any case, the recognition principle described here is intrinsically tolerant of a large proportion of the iris information being corrupted, say up to about a third, without significantly impairing the inference of personal identity by the simple test of statistical independence.

8   Speed Performance Summary

On a low-cost 300 MHz RISC processor, the execution times for the critical steps in iris recognition are as shown in Table 2, using optimized integer code:

Table 2. Execution speeds of various stages in the iris recognition process, as timed on a 300 MHz RISC processor

Operation	Time
Assess image focus	15 msec
Scrub specular reflections	56 msec
Localize eye and iris	90 msec
Fit pupillary boundary	12 msec
Detect and fit both eyelids	93 msec
Remove lashes and contact lens edges	78 msec
Demodulation and IrisCode creation	102 msec
XOR comparison of two IrisCodes	10 μs

The search engine can perform about 100,000 full comparisons between different irises per second on each such a CPU, or 1 million in about a second on a 3 GHz server, because of the efficient implementation of the matching process in terms of elementary Boolean operators $\otimes$ and $\cap$ acting in parallel on the computed phase bit sequences. If a database contained many millions of enrolled persons, then the inherent parallelism of the search process should be exploited for the sake of speed by dividing up the full database into smaller chunks to be searched in parallel. The confidence levels shown in Table 1 indicate how the decision threshold should be adapted for each of these parallel search engines, in order to ensure that no false matches were made despite several large-scale searches being conducted independently. The mathematics of the iris recognition algorithms, particularly the binomial-class distributions (4) (11) that they generate when comparing different irises, make it clear that databases the size of an entire country's population could be searched in parallel to make confident and rapid identification decisions using parallel banks of inexpensive CPUs, if such iris code databases existed.

References

1. Adini, Y., Moses, Y., Ullman, S.: Face recognition: the problem of compensating for changes in illumination direction. *IEEE Trans. Pattern Analysis and Machine Intelligence* **19** (1997) 721-732
2. Belhumeur, P.N., Hespanha, J.P., Kriegman, D.J.: Eigenfaces vs. Fisherfaces: Recognition using class-specific linear projection. *IEEE Trans. Pattern Analysis and Machine Intelligence* **19** (1997) 711-720
3. Berggren, L.: Iridology: A critical review. *Acta Ophthalmologica* **63** (1985) 1-8
4. Chedekel, M.R.: Photophysics and photochemistry of melanin. In *Melanin: Its Role in Human Photoprotection*. Valdenmar (1995), 11-23
5. Cover, T., Thomas, J.: *Elements of Information Theory.* Wiley: New York (1991)
6. Daugman, J.: Uncertainty relation for resolution in space, spatial frequency, and orientation optimized by two-dimensional visual cortical filters. *J. Opt. Soc. Amer. A* **2** (1985) 1160-1169
7. Daugman, J.: Complete discrete 2D Gabor transforms by neural networks for image analysis and compression. *IEEE Trans. Acoust., Speech, Signal Processing* **36** (1988) 1169-1179
8. Daugman, J.: High confidence visual recognition of persons by a test of statistical independence. *IEEE Trans. Pattern Analysis and Machine Intelligence* **15** (1993) 1148-1161
9. Daugman, J.: U.S. Patent No. 5,291,560: *Biometric Personal Identification System Based on Iris Analysis.* (1994) US Government Printing Office, Washington DC
10. Daugman, J.: Statistical richness of visual phase information: Update on recognizing persons by their iris patterns. *Int'l J. Computer Vision* **45** (2001) 25-38
11. Daugman, J., Downing, J.: Demodulation, predictive coding, and spatial vision. *J. Opt. Soc. Amer. A* **12** (1995) 641-660
12. Daugman, J., Downing, C.: Epigenetic randomness, complexity, and singularity of human iris patterns. *Proceedings of the Royal Society: Biological Sciences* **268** (2001) 1737-1740
13. Kronfeld, P.: Gross anatomy and embryology of the eye. In: *The Eye.* (H. Davson, ed.) Academic Press: London (1962)
14. Pentland, A., Choudhury, T.: Face recognition for smart environments. *Computer* **33** (2000) 50-55
15. Phillips, P.J., Martin, A., Wilson, C.L., Przybocki, M.: An introduction to evaluating biometric systems. *Computer* **33** (2000) 56-63
16. Phillips, P.J., Moon, H., Rizvi, S.A., Rauss, P.J.: The FERET evaluation methodology for face-recognition algorithms. *IEEE Trans. Pattern Analysis and Machine Intelligence* **22** (2000) 1090-1104
17. Simon, A., Worthen, D.M., Mitas, J.A.: An evaluation of iridology. *J. Amer. Med. Assoc.* **242** (1979) 1385-1387
18. Viveros, R., Balasubramanian, K., Balakrishnan, N.: Binomial and negative binomial analogues under correlated Bernoulli trials. *The American Statistician* **48** (1984) 243-247

Multiple Classifier Fusion for Biometric Authentication

Josef Kittler

Centre for Vision, Speech and Signal Processing,
University of Surrey,
Guildford, Surrey GU2 7XH, UK
j.kittler@eim.surrey.ac.uk

Abstract. Individual biometric modalities are continuously developed to improve their performance by sensor, system and algorithmic improvements. However, a very attractive alternative is to gain enhanced performance and robustness of biometric systems by combining multiple biometric experts. Recent research has demonstrated that both, the fusion of intra-modal experts as well as multi-modal biometrics impact beneficially on the system performance. In the former case the benefits derive from pooling the opinions of individual intra-modal experts. In the latter, complementary biometric information is brought to bear on the personal identity authentication problem. The issues involved in multiple biometric expert fusion and its potential will be discussed and illustrated on the problem of combining face and voice based identification.

Performance Evaluation in 1 : 1 Biometric Engines

Ruud M. Bolle, Nalini K. Ratha, and Sharath Pankanti

IBM Thomas J Watson Research Center, Yorktown Heights, NY 10598

Abstract. Performance of a biometric system is characterized by its speed, accuracy, and cost. This paper presents fundamentals of 1 : 1 biometric match engine accuracy performance metrics and its evaluation. Here, we explain the basic terminology, performance metrics and related system issues. We also discuss practical methods used for evaluating 1 : 1 biometric match engine accuracy performance and provide a summary of the state-of-art of biometric identifier accuracies.

1   Introduction

The specifications for a biometric authentication system will usually include requirements like maximum allowable error rates. There are a number of biometric error types, expressed as error rates or error percentages, that need to be understood before a solution is designed and before a particular biometric is selected. Some of these errors are inherent with biometric authentication being just a kind of pattern recognition application; other errors are more specifically related to biometric authentication systems. What is clear is that any biometric authentication system will make mistakes, and that the *true* value of the various error rates for a matcher cannot be computed or theoretically established; it is only possible to obtain statistical estimates of the errors using test databases of biometric samples.

In this paper, we present an intuitive and theoretical meanings of the various error types that are found in the biometrics literature, concentrating mainly on the errors made in a 1 : 1 biometric match engine. A similar exposition for 1 : N biometric match engine is not dealt with here because of space limitation and the reader is referred to elsewhere [1] for analysis of 1 : N biometric match engine.

This paper is organized as follows. Section 2 presents the fundamental concepts related to matcher, matcher scores, score distributions, and underlying match engine error rates. Accuracy of biometric systems is limited by the fraction of the population who can and are able to use such system; these peculiarities of biometric system are narrated in Section 3. Section 4 is devoted to the Receiver Operating Characteristics, its variations, and other accuracy performance metrics. Section 5 introduces the concept of computing confidence intervals for the error estimates. In Section 6 we briefly overview the system performance tradeoffs in the context of positive authentication and relate them to the underlying biometric match engine accuracies. In Section 7, we introduce the different

S.Z. Li et al. (Eds.): Sinobiometrics 2004, LNCS 3338, pp. 27–46, 2004.
© Springer-Verlag Berlin Heidelberg 2004

type of testing methodologies. Section 8 provides a quick summary of the state of the art of various 1 : 1 biometric identifiers. Finally, in Section 9, we present conclusions and directions for future research.

2   Matchers, Scores, Error Rates

A matcher is a system that takes two samples of biometric data and returns a score s that indicates their similarity. Let us assume that the higher the score, the more similar the samples.

The reliability of the score in comparing two biometric samples is influenced by many factors. There is variability in the live real-world biometric input signal, there is variation from sensor to sensor, and there is much variability in the sampling process, i.e., the process of acquiring signal from a biometric identifier. The latter is mainly due to variability in the way a subject presents the real-world biometric for sampling. This variability is much higher from one sampling to the next as compared to (say) the variability for authentication methods like password entry, where the error is generally only due to input (typing) error. Rather, when we have two samples from an identical biometric (e.g., two impressions of left index finger of John Doe), the similarity score rarely reflects a perfect match score. Similarly, when we have two biometrics from two different individuals (e.g., an impression of left index of John Doe and an impression of left index finger of Jane Doe) the similarity score rarely reflects the lowest possible score. What we can say is that when samples originate from a single biometric identifier, the match score is usually high, while when samples originate from different identifiers, the score is usually low. This is shown in Figure 1, where the probability density $p_n(s)$ of the non-match scores (left) and the $p_m(s)$ of the match scores (right) are depicted. The non-match or *imposter scores* resulting from matching samples from different biometric identifier tend to be low and the match or *genuine scores*, representing samples from same biometric identifier tend to be high.

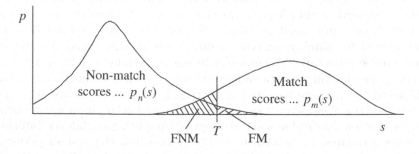

Fig. 1. The non-match scores are on average lower than the match scores; in this case, the threshold T is set high to minimize false matches

Given two biometric samples and a score threshold T, the matcher engine has to decide between two outcomes:

$$\begin{aligned} &\text{The } \textit{null} \text{ hypothesis}: \qquad H_o \Rightarrow \text{the two samples match;} \\ &\text{The } \textit{alternate} \text{ hypothesis}: H_a \Rightarrow \text{the two samples do } \textit{not} \text{ match.} \end{aligned} \qquad (1)$$

We define the error rates of a biometric matcher according to its correctness in deciding between these *two* outcomes. Consequently, a matcher can make two types of errors ([2]). (i) False match (FM) error occurs when score $s > T$ and matcher engine erroneously decides H_o when indeed H_a is true (also known as Type I error; and (ii) False non-match (FNM) error occurs when score $s \leq T$ and matcher engine decides H_a when indeed H_o is true (also known as Type II error). The *False Match Rate* (FMR) and the *False Non-Match Rate* (FNMR) are then the frequencies at which FM and FNM occur, respectively.

The FMR is the area of the hatched region on the right under the non-match (mismatch) score density curve $p_n(s)$, the proportion of the time $s > T$ when H_a is indeed true:

$$\text{FMR}(T) = 1 - \int_{s=T}^{\infty} p_n(s) \, ds. \qquad (2)$$

Similarly,

$$\text{FNMR}(T) = \int_{s=-\infty}^{T} p_m(s|H_a) \, ds. \qquad (3)$$

Unfortunately, for biometric applications, the non-match score distribution $p_n(s)$ and the match score distribution $p_m(s)$ in Figure 1 always overlap, so it is not possible to choose a threshold for which both $FMR = 0$ and $FNMR = 0$. Therefore the threshold T in decision rule needs to be selected in such a way that the biometric system operates in an "optimal" fashion. Choosing the threshold involves assessing the consequences of the two types of errors. In a first approximation, a biometric matcher needs to be "tuned" to operate at acceptable False Match and False Non-Match rates for a given population of subjects. This threshold can only be determined through a process of training and testing where some more-or-less representative sample of the user population is available. In Figure 1, an operating point T is selected so that the FM rate is less than the FNM rate.

The threshold T controls the tradeoff between FMR(T) and FNMR(T) as expressed by the Receiver Operating Characteristic (ROC) curve (see, e.g., [3]) discussed in Section 4. A matcher operating at a high threshold T has a low FMR but high FNMR; a low threshold, conversely, means high FMR and low FNMR.

The cumulative probability distributions $G(y)$ and $F(x)$ of the non-match scores and match scores respectively are defined as follows:

$$\begin{aligned} G(y) &= \int_{-\infty}^{y} p(s|H_a) \, ds = 1 - \text{FNMR}(y) \\ F(x) &= \int_{-\infty}^{x} p(s|H_o) \, ds = \text{FMR}(x). \end{aligned} \qquad (4)$$

These can be used interchangeably with FMR and FNMR because there is 1-1 correspondence as shown in Figure 2.

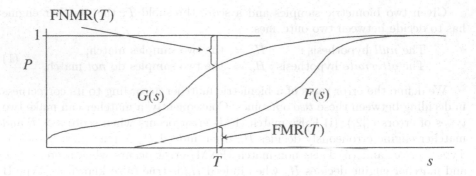

Fig. 2. Cumulative probability distributions of non-match and match scores, $G(s)$ and $F(s)$; the FNMR(T) and FMR(T) at threshold T are indicated

2.1   Definitions of FAR and FRR, Positive Authentication

Positive verification ("*I am who I claim I am*") systems can make two kinds of errors, a *False Accept* or a *False Reject*:

I.   *False Accept* (FA): Deciding that a (claimed) identity is a legitimate one while in reality it is an imposter; deciding H_o when H_a is true. The frequency at which false accept errors are made is called the *False Accept Rate* (FAR).
II. *False Reject* (FR): Deciding that a (claimed) identity is *not* legitimate when in reality the person is genuine; deciding H_a when H_o is true. The frequency at which false rejects occur is called the *False Reject Rate* (FRR).

When biometrics are used for securing a logical or physical site the errors have certain consequences. A FA results in security breaches, with an unauthorized person being admitted. A FR results in convenience problems, since genuinely enrolled identities are denied access to the application, or at least will have to undergo some further check to be admitted.

2.2   Estimating Errors from Data

Given a set of M match (genuine, suspect) scores $\mathbf{X}$ and a set $\mathbf{Y}$ of N non-match (imposter, legitimate) scores. We further need estimates of the true underlying match score distribution $F(s)$ and non-match score distribution $G(s)$. Estimates of the match distribution $F(x)$ is given by

$$\hat{F}(s) = \frac{1}{M} \sum_{i=1}^{M} \mathbf{1}\,(X_i \leq s) = \frac{1}{M}(\# \, X_i \leq s), \qquad (5)$$

computed from the match scores $\mathbf{X} = \{X_1, ..., X_M\}$. The mismatch scores $\mathbf{Y} =, \{Y_1, ..., Y_N\}$ on the other hand, give an estimate $\hat{G}(s)$ of the non-match score distribution

$$\hat{G}(s) = \frac{1}{N} \sum_{j=1}^{N} \mathbf{1}\,(Y_j \leq s) = \frac{1}{N}(\# \, Y_j \leq s). \qquad (6)$$

Again, these probability distribution estimates are called *empirical distribu-*
tions[1].

3   Error Conditions "Specific" to Biometrics

In addition to the fundamental type I and type II misclassification errors, and
their multiple aliases, there are other error rates that are more specific to biometrics.

1. The *Failure to Acquire* (FTA) rate is the percentage of the target population
   which do not deliver a usable biometric sample, either because of lack of such
   biometric or because of sensor unable to acquire sufficiently good signal.
2. The *Failure to Enroll* (FTE) rate is the proportion of the population that
   somehow cannot be enrolled because of limitations of the technology or procedural problems [4].Both FTA and FTE are partially due to intrinsic biometric properties and limitations in state of the art of the biometrics.
3. In addition to FTA and FTE, mainly for voluntary applications, the "failure
   to use" FTU rate can be defined as FTE rate plus the proportion of the
   population that for some reason does not enroll, or enrolls and fails to continue using the biometrics system. For voluntary biometric authentication
   applications, the difference between the FTU and FTE rates will be due to
   convenience (usability) problems with the voluntary applications.

The design parameter FTE can be artificially increased for a given installation, which will improve the overall quality of the enrolled population samples at
the expense of increased exception handling and inconvenience. The system variable FTE enables a tradeoff between *manual* versus *automated* authentication,
which in turn is related to maintenance cost *versus* upfront cost.

4   The Receiver Operating Characteristic (ROC)

The error rates FMR(T) and FNMR(T) can be plotted against each other as a
two dimensional curve ROC(T) = (FMR(T), FNMR(T)), referred to as Receiver
Operating Characteristic (ROC) curve [5,3]. An example of a ROC curve is
shown in Figure 3. Any point on the ROC defines an *operating point* of the
matcher and it can be specified by choosing any one of T, FMR or FNMR,
with the other two then being implicitly defined. For a given matcher, operating
points are often given by specifying the threshold since this is something that
can be chosen in the matcher, and FMR and FNMR can only be estimated given
a threshold. On the other hand, when specifying a biometric application or a
performance target, or when comparing two matchers, the operating point is

---

[1] The is empirical cumulative distributions $\hat{G}(y)$ and $\hat{F}(x)$ are sometimes used interchangeably with 'FMR' and 'FNMR', which are also used to refer to $G(y)$ and $F(x)$,
respectively.

specified by choosing FMR or FNMR since the threshold is a number that is
only meaningful for a particular implementation of a particular matcher.

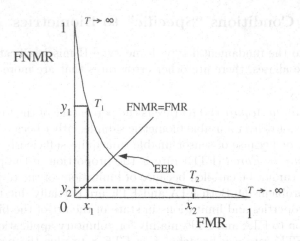

Fig. 3. The ROC curve expresses the tradeoff between FMR and FNMR

There are a number of variations of ROCs that are used for expressing the
same information. Naturally, the FAR and FRR can equally well be plotted in
ROCs, as can the FNR and FPR we will see in Section **??**, or the axes can be
inverted by plotting correct rates instead of error rates. In addition, quite often
one or both of the probabilities (FMR and FNMR) in the ROC is plotted on a
logarithmic scale. More commonly, a log-log plot of ROC is used as it magnifies
the typical region of interest (operating area). Sometimes researchers plot the
Correct Match Rate (i.e., $1 - $ FNMR) *vs.* the FMR. This form of curve comes
from detection theory, and is called the *Detection Error Tradeoff* (DET) curve.
Along the y axis, we have $(1 - $ FNMR$)$ which is the correct detection rate, or
simply the detection rate; along the x-axis, we still have the FMR, here more
usually termed the False Accept Rate or the False Alarm Rate.

What the ROC curve of an operational biometric installation is, and at what
point the system is operating, will depend entirely on the enrolled population and
the desired security—which should be defined with respect to the real enemies
of the system. For positive identification systems, false accepts may never be
detected; for negative identification systems may never be detected.

4.1   Other Metrics of Performance

When comparing the performance of two or more matchers, a single number
representing the quality of a matcher independent of operating point is often
desired. This requirement has led to various expressions which attempt to reduce the information in the ROC to a single number. Here we present some

performance summary figures that attempt this: the equal error rate, d-prime, expected overall error and expected cost. These measures have severe limitations [1] but in some circumstances but can be useful for summarizing matcher performance and comparing matchers when the ROCs do not cross.

The Equal Error Rate. The Equal Error (EE) operating point, as shown in Figure 3, leads us to the Equal Error Rate (EER) which is an obvious, simple choice to judge the quality of a matcher. The Equal Error point of a biometric matcher is the operating point at the intersection of the line FMR = FNMR with the ROC of the matcher. The equal error rate is the value of the error rates at this point EER = FMR_{EE} = FNMR_{EE}.

The EER (subject to statistical significance [1]) can certainly tell us that one matcher is better than another, but only does so for a narrow range of operating points in the neighborhood of the EER operating point. Very often matchers operate with highly unequal FMR & FNMR making the EER an unreliable summary of system accuracy.

d-Prime. Another way of judging the quality of a matcher is to measure how well the non-match score probability density $p_n(s)$ and the match score probability density $p_m(s)$ are separated, (see Figure 1). A measure of this separation for a matcher is d-prime:

$$d' = \frac{\mu_m - \mu_n}{\sqrt{(\sigma_m^2 + \sigma_n^2)}}, \tag{7}$$

as suggested by Daugman [6]. Here μ_m and σ_m are the mean and variance of the match scores of genuine users; μ_n and σ_n are the mean and variance of the (non-)match scores of mismatching finger prints (or estimates thereof). Figure 4 shows how two different matches with identical d' can have significantly different performance at different operating points.

Expected Overall Error. The equal error rate and d-prime implicitly treat the false match and a false non-match errors as equally likely and of equal importance or cost. A measure which takes into account the likelihood is the expected overall error rate, $E(T)$ which can be calculated from the ROC for any threshold T, based upon the prior probability $P_\mathcal{I}$ of a random user being an imposter and the prior probability $P_\mathcal{G}$ of a user being genuine:

$$E(T) = \text{FMR}(T) \times P_\mathcal{I} + \text{FNMR}(T) \times P_\mathcal{G}, \tag{8}$$

with $P_\mathcal{I} + P_\mathcal{G} = 1$. This is the expected probability that a random trial will result in an error. The minimum overall error of a matcher is defined as

$$E_{\text{min}} = \min_T E(T) \tag{9}$$

This is visualized (Figure 9) as the point where the ROC intersects a diagonal line (marked L_d in Figure 5) from the family $\text{FMR} \times P_\mathcal{I} + \text{FNMR} \times P_\mathcal{G} = k$, with

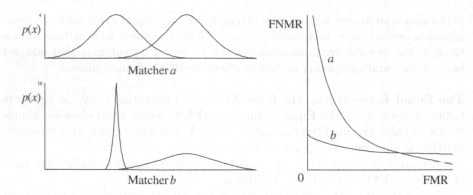

Fig. 4. Different ROCs for two hypothetical matchers a and b with identical d'. Here Gaussian score distributions with identical means and different variances lead to the same d' but different ROCs

k the lowest value for which such an intersection takes place. Changing the prior weights changes the gradient of the lines for which we seek an intersection. Given the priors, this is another matcher-independent way of specifying an operating point, as well as giving a performance measure for comparing matchers.

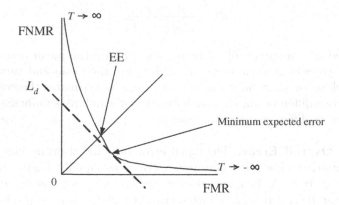

Fig. 5. The minimum expected error will not generally be found at the same operating point as the equal error rate

For simplicity, and in the absence of knowledge about the values of $P_\mathcal{I}$ and $P_\mathcal{G}$ a single (but not necessarily meaningful) measure of accuracy can be derived by setting $P_\mathcal{I} = P_\mathcal{G} = 0.5$. This gives a measure akin to, but (as shown in Figure 5) not in general the same as, the equal error rate discussed above.

Cost Functions. A refinement of the overall expected error is to associate a cost with each of the errors and to calculate the expected cost of each match decision:

$$Cost = C_{\mathrm{FNM}} \times \mathrm{FNMR} \times P_{\mathcal{G}} + C_{\mathrm{FA}} \times \mathrm{FM} \times (1 - P_{\mathcal{G}}).$$

The minimum cost operating point can be visualized in the same way as the minimum expected error point, with the relative costs affecting the gradient of the family of straight lines. If $C_{FM} = C_{FNM}$ the minimum cost operating point will be the same as the minimum expected overall error point, but by putting real costs into the equation (e.g. dollar amounts at risk) the cost function becomes a meaningful number: the expected cost per use of the system. Cost functions are used in the NIST Speaker Identification evaluations [7].

5   Confidence Intervals

A ROC in itself does not mean much. We need to report the data set size of biometric samples that is used to compute these statistics. In addition, some indication should be given about the quality of biometrics samples, e.g., the conditions under which the samples were collected and a description of the subjects used for acquiring the database. Of course, if the subjects used in the test are not representative of the target population, it is dubious whether the accuracy estimates are useful at all. But given that the database samples are representative, the accuracy of the estimates depends only on the database size, the larger the size, the more accurate the estimates. Accuracy of the estimates (significance) can be addressed by computing error margins.

To evaluate a biometric authentication system, a set of mated pairs $\mathbf{M} = \{a_1, ..., a_M\}$ and a set of non mated pairs $\mathbf{N} = \{b_1, ..., b_N\}$ need to be acquired. Here $M < N$ because collecting prints from subjects always results in more non matching than matching pairs. (From this it immediately follows that the FAR can be estimated more accurately than the FRR.) Matching these sets of pairs results in M scores X_i of matching fingers and N scores Y_j of non matching fingers. We denote these sets of scores by $\mathbf{X} = \{X_1, ..., X_M\}$ and $\mathbf{Y} = \{Y_1, ..., Y_N\}$, respectively. For the set $\mathbf{X}$, assume that this is a sample of M numbers drawn from a population with distribution F. That is, $F(x) = Prob(X \leq x)$. Let $\mathbf{Y}$ be a sample of N numbers drawn from a population with distribution $G(y) = Prob(Y \leq y)$. Here $x \geq 0$ and $y \geq 0$, because the random variables X and Y are similarity measures (scores). Let us first concentrate on the distribution F. The function F is the probability distribution or cumulative distribution function of match scores X of matching pairs. We can study this sample $\mathbf{X}$ in order to estimate $F(x_o)$, the value of the distribution F at some fixed $x = x_o$. Just as the distribution function F of match scores, the distribution of $F(x_o)$ is of unknown form. An unbiased statistic, $\Gamma(\mathbf{X}) = \hat{F}(x_o)$ may be used to estimate $F(x_o)$ from the data $\mathbf{X}$. We have estimates $\hat{F}(x_o)$ and $\hat{G}(y_o)$, i.e., estimates of the match and mismatch score distributions at specific score values x_o and y_o. These estimates themselves are random variable, e.g., $\Gamma(\mathbf{X}) = \hat{F}(x_o)$

is a random variable, for which intervals of confidence can be established. We concentrate on cumulative distributions $F(x)$ and $G(y)$, however, it is easily seen that $\text{FRR}(T) = F(T)$ and $\text{FAR}(T) = 1 - G(T)$.

To compute the confidence intervals, we have a choice between using parametric or non parametric methods. For both methods there are inherent assumptions, which should be expressed explicitly.

5.1   Parametric Confidence Intervals

Parametric evaluation methods impose assumptions about the shape of the distribution of the available data. Under such assumptions, determining confidence regions reduces to estimating a few parameters of a known distribution. These methods further assume that multiple matching pairs (and non matching pairs) of a given fingerprint provide i.i.d. match scores – irrespective whether these match scores are from the same individual or not.

An estimate of $F(x_o)$ is given by

$$\Gamma(\mathbf{X}) = \hat{F}(x_o) = \frac{1}{M} \sum_{i=1}^{M} \mathbf{1}\,(X_i \leq x_o) = \frac{1}{M}(\# \, X_i \leq x_o), \tag{10}$$

obtained by simply counting the $X_i \in \mathbf{X}$ that are smaller than x_o and dividing by M. Expression 10 is a discrete function approximating the true F and is called *the empirical distribution*. For the moment, let us keep $x = x_o$ fixed and let us determine the confidence region for $\hat{F}(x_o)$. First define Z as a binomial random variable, the number of successes in M trials with probability of success $F(x_o) = Prob\,(X \leq x_o)$ (i.e., success $\equiv (X \leq x_o)$). This random variable Z has mass distribution

$$P(Z = z) = \binom{M}{z} F(x_o)^z (1 - F(x_o))^{M-z},$$

$z = 0, \dots, M$.

The expectation of Z, $\text{E}(Z) = MF(x_o)$ and the variance of Z, $\sigma(Z) = MF(x_o)(1 - F(x_o))$. From this it follows that the random variable Z/M has expectation $\text{E}(Z/M) = F(x_o)$ and variance $\sigma(x_o) = F(x_o)(1 - F(x_o))/M$. Then when M is large enough, using the law of large numbers, Z/M is distributed according to a normal distribution, i.e., $Z/M \sim \mathcal{N}(F(x), \sigma(x))$. Now, it can be seen that $Z/M = \hat{F}(x_o)$ of (10) where M is the number of samples that is used. Hence, for large M, $\hat{F}(x)$ is normally distributed, with an estimate of the variance given by

$$\hat{\sigma}(x) = \sqrt{\frac{\hat{F}(x)(1 - \hat{F}(x))}{M}}. \tag{11}$$

So, confidence intervals can be determined with percentiles of the normal distribution, e.g., a 90% interval of confidence is

$$-1.645\,\hat{\sigma}(x) < \hat{F}(x) < 1.645\,\hat{\sigma}(x) \tag{12}$$

5.2   Bootstrap Confidence Intervals

We have the set of match scores $\mathbf{X}$ and we want to have some idea as to how much importance should be given to $\Gamma(\mathbf{X}) = \hat{F}(x_o)$. That is, we are interested in a $(1 - \alpha)100\%$ confidence region for $\hat{F}(x_o)$ in the form of $[q^*(\alpha/2), q^*(1 - \alpha/2)]$. The $q^*(\alpha/2)$ and $q^*(1 - \alpha/2)$ are the $\alpha/2$ and $1 - \alpha/2$ quantiles of $H(z) = Prob\,(\hat{F}(x_o) = \Gamma(\mathbf{X}) \leq z)$. Here, $H(z)$ (which is a function of the data $\mathbf{X}$), is the probability distribution of the estimate, $\hat{F}(x_o)$.

The sample population $\mathbf{X}$ has distribution $\hat{F}(x)$, called empirical distribution, defined as

$$\hat{F}(x) = \frac{1}{M} \sum_{i=1}^{M} \mathbf{1}\,(X_i \leq x) = \frac{1}{M}(\# \, X_i \leq x) \tag{13}$$

which puts equal mass $1/M$ at each observation X_i. It should be noted that the samples in set $\mathbf{X}$ are the only data we have and the distribution (13) is the only distribution we have. The bootstrap proceeds, therefore, by assuming that the empirical distribution $\hat{F}$ is a good enough approximation of the true distribution F. Now, to draw samples that are distributed as $\hat{F}$ one can sample the set $\mathbf{X}$ *with replacement*, that is, placing back the sample into set $\mathbf{X}$. Hence, any statistic, including $\Gamma(\mathbf{X}) = \hat{F}(x_o)$, for fixed x_o, can be re-estimated by simply resampling.

The bootstrap principle prescribes sampling, with replacement, the set $\mathbf{X}$ a large number (B) of times, resulting in the bootstrap sets $\mathbf{X}_i^*$, $i = 1, ..., B$. Using these sets, one can calculate the estimates $\hat{F}_i^*(x_o) = T_i^*(\mathbf{X}_i^*)$, $i = 1, ..., B$. Determining confidence intervals now essentially amounts to counting exercises. One can compute (say) a 90% confidence interval by counting the bottom 5% and top 5% of the estimates $\hat{F}_i^*(x_o)$ and subtracting these estimates from the total set of the estimates $\hat{F}_i^*(x_o)$. The leftover set determines the interval of confidence. We are able, however, to determine a bootstrap confidence interval of $\hat{F}(x_o)$ by sampling with replacement from $\mathbf{X}$ as follows.

1. Calculate the estimate $\hat{F}(x_o)$ from the sample $\mathbf{X}$. This is the empirical distribution of $\mathbf{X}$.
2. *Resampling.* Create a bootstrap sample $\mathbf{X}^* = \{X_1^*, ..., X_M^*\}$ by sampling $\mathbf{X}$ with replacement.
3. *Bootstrap estimate.* Calculate $\hat{F}^*(x_o)$ from $\mathbf{X}^*$.
4. *Repetition.* Repeat steps 2-3 B times (B large), resulting in $\hat{F}_1^*(x_o)$, $\hat{F}_2^*(x_o)$ ... $\hat{F}_B^*(x_o)$. The distribution $\hat{H}^*$ of $\hat{F}(x_o)$ is given by

$$\hat{H}^*\left(\hat{F}(x_o)\right) = \hat{H}^*(z) = \frac{1}{B} \sum_{i=1}^{B} \mathbf{1}\,(\hat{F}_i^*(x_o) \leq z)$$

$$= \frac{1}{B}(\# \, \hat{F}^*(x_o) \leq z)$$

To obtain a confidence interval for $\hat{F}(x_o)$, we sort the bootstrap estimates in increasing order to obtain $\hat{F}_{(1)}^*(x_o) \leq \hat{F}_{(2)}^*(x_o) \leq ... \leq \hat{F}_{(B)}^*(x_o)$. A $(1 - \alpha)100\%$ bootstrap confidence interval is $(\hat{F}_{(q_1)}^*(x_o), \hat{F}_{(q_2)}^*(x_o))$, where $q_1 = \lfloor B\alpha/2 \rfloor$ is the integer part of $B\alpha/2$ and $q_2 = B - q_1 + 1$. In Fig. 6, we show the confidence interval computation for FRR using simple bootstrap as well as other variations described in [1].

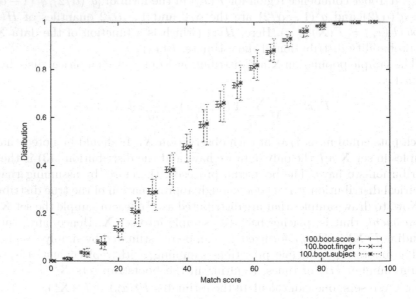

Fig. 6. Confidence intervals for FRR

6   Tradeoffs

The tradeoff between the FMR and FNMR rates largely expresses itself as a security versus convenience tradeoff. The tradeoff between security and cost of the biometric authentication system is related to the tradeoff between errors. Obviously, by setting FRR = 0 and FAR = 1, we have a very cheap but totally insecure system. By setting FAR = 0 and FRR = 1, the biometric system is not accepting anybody and one has to rely on costly human and manual labor. Hence the FRR can be used as some measure of cost of an authentication system; the higher the FRR, the more expensive an application is because more subjects are incorrectly *identified* and therefore subject to denial of service or the exception handling process. The FAR is a measure of security since a lower FAR implies smaller FMR and hence smaller likelihood of an intruder matching erroneously matching to a falsely claimed identity (under zero-effort attack model assumption).

For screening (or negative authentication) systems

$$Security = (1 - \text{FNR}),$$

i.e., the lower the chances of missing undesirable subjects d_n, the higher the security. The convenience of such a negative authentication system is related as

$$Cost = FPR,$$

where falsely matched innocent subjects d are inconvenienced because they will
be subject to further interrogation. We summarize various errors and their implications in Table 1.

Table 1. Quantitative error rate pairs for biometric match engines and applications

FM	Falsely matching two biometrics.
FNM	Falsely *not* matching two mated biometrics.
FA	False accept of an intruder causing security problems.
FR	False reject of an authorized user in **M** causing inconvenience.
FN	Erroneously missing a match in **N** causing security problems.
FP	Detecting a false match in a screening database **N** causing inconvenience; this is also called a *false alarm*.

Table 2 lists the two authentication scenarios with the associated errors and
the consequences of these errors to the application. For positive authentication, a
FA (caused by FM) is a security problem and a FR (caused by FNM) is a convenience problem. For negative authentication, on the other hand, a FN (caused by
FNM) is a security problem and a FP (caused by FM) is a convenience problem.
When a subject d is denied access, either through a false reject, or by erroneously
matching undesirable subject d_n, this certainly amounts to inconvenience, both
to the subjects and to the staff operating the biometric system.

Table 2. Error parameters of our two biometric applications

Positive authentication	Negative authentication
FA = FM $\Rightarrow$ *security problem*	FN = FNM $\Rightarrow$ *security problem*
FR = FNM $\Rightarrow$ *convenience problem*	FP = FM $\Rightarrow$ *convenience problem*

Note that the causes of a FA and a FP are the same, i.e., the occurrence of
a False Match. The consequences of such a false match are quite different. It is
a security problem in case of a FA and a convenience problem in the case of a
FP. Similarly, the cause for a FN and a FR are the same, a False Non-Match,
but here a FN is a security problem and a FR is a convenience problem. The
definitions of the errors depend on the application and hence on the definition
of the hypotheses H_o and H_a.

7   Measuring Performance

There are three prominent testing methodologies for biometric matcher evaluation, *technology evaluations*, *scenario evaluations* and *operational evaluations*

[8]. Evaluations are often organized in the form of a competition between vendors and developers of biometric matchers that compute the similarity $s(B',B)$ between samples or templates B and B'. Because biometrics is such a relatively young research area, the contestants in these evaluations are often both commercial vendors and academic institutions. Furthermore, biometric system testing is focussed on the $1:1$ verification systems. The fundamental error rates FAR (FMR) and FRR (FNMR) derived from an ROC using correctly labeled databases of biometric samples. Such tests are also called *bench marks* in that various biometric matchers can be compared on "*frozen*" biometric databases.

7.1   Technology Evaluations

In technology evaluations, the match capabilities of core $1:1$ matchers are estimated and compared and not the FAR/FRR or FPR/FNR of some biometric application. In this type of evaluation the contestants have a certain period of time to train their biometric match algorithms on some "training data" which are made available by the contest organizers. In the next step of the evaluation, the matching algorithms are tested on newly made available, labeled sequestered "test" data and the performance statistics that are to be measured are defined and it is defined how these parameters are estimated from test data.

Good biometric data is important, both for system testing and system training. Errors in labelling result in data that are not "clean"; this can have rather dramatic effects on the estimated error rates when such databases are used for testing. Similarly, if poorly labelled databases are used to train the matcher this will result in a faulty match engine. Moreover, all databases evolve over time as individuals are added into and deleted from the database. It is important to be careful about the integrity of the database over its entire lifetime, else a good database may go bad.

The face biometric has a long history of testing face matching algorithms in this way [9–11]; such testing has been started more recently in the fingerprint area [12, 13]. Influenced by the rigorous testing procedures of speech recognition algorithm, the area of speaker recognition also has a good history of competitive algorithm testing (see [14, 15]).

Two common and easy ways to make mistakes in biometric system design are:

1. *"Testing on the training set"* – the test score databases $\mathbf{X}$ of and $\mathbf{Y}$ are somehow used to train a biometric match engine.
2. *Overtraining* – The training databases $\mathbf{X}$ and $\mathbf{Y}$ are used too extensively to optimize the associated FAR/FRR ROC curve. A sign that a system may be overtrained is exceptionally good performance on just *one* particular data set.

Classical books like [16] warn for these pitfalls.

All these database are from samples obtained from a finite number of volunteer subjects. As long as all this data is considered to be acquired from the user population of the biometric application, this data is a *closed* database of samples. When these databases are also used to generate false match error conditions, the associated error estimates like the FAR and FNR are so-called "zero-effort" error estimates, as introduced by the signature research community [1]. It is unclear, in general, how these zero-effort estimates differ from the true (false accept and false negative) error rates. Since biometric data is often not available from the true enemies of an application, it is hard to generate true false accepts and false negatives. Estimates of these unmeasurable error rates, of course, are impossible to compute without somehow modelling this population. The error conditions that are easy to detect are a false reject and a false positive, and therefore the FRR and FPR estimates are more meaningful estimates of the true false reject rate and true false positive rate.

When examining ROC tradeoff error curves, one should always be suspicious about how the false accepts and false negatives are determined (from the available samples or otherwise).

7.2   Scenario Evaluations

This type of evaluation takes place in a testing facility, e.g., as shown in Figure 7. The biometric authentication devices (1:1 matchers) are installed in an "office environment" as in the figure (loosely the test facility layout used in [17]) and the biometric devices are tested.

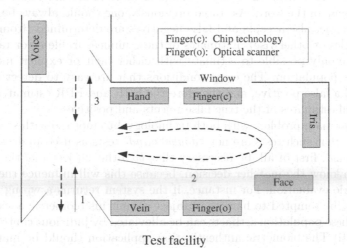

Test facility

Fig. 7. Scenario evaluation where volunteers are drafted to use several biometric systems on a regular basis. Adapted from [17]

A group of volunteer subjects is drafted, and this group uses the system periodically over some duration (ideally months or even years to capture the temporal variability of the biometrics) while statistics are collected. Many such evaluations will try to compare different biometrics or different vendors' technologies at the same time, so the test facility will contain all the systems being tested, and each volunteer will generally use all of them in sequence. This of course creates a database of biometric samples that can subsequently be used for technology evaluations. Any estimate of a FAR should be scrutinized carefully because the false accept error condition may be somehow artificially inferred.

7.3   Comparison: Technology and Scenario Evaluations

Both evaluation methods are used by the biometric industry but it seems that academia tends to use (often public) databases, i.e., technology evaluations. Of course, during scenario evaluation, databases of biometric samples are processed (and may be collected) and the estimation of error rates becomes a matter of computing estimates based on sample data.

A scenario evaluation using "end-to-end" biometric authentication systems is very different from a technology evaluation. In technology evaluations, biometric matchers are tested on databases with no control of the acquisition procedure (possibly collected from volunteers); in scenario evaluations of the entire end-to-end biometric systems, including acquisition, are tested on volunteers. It is unclear how the test results obtained with such disparate testing procedures are to be compared.

A first problem with most scenario evaluations is that the user population is a closed set and during the test the biometric devices are not really attacked in the true sense of the word. As stated previously, one should always be suspicious about how the false accepts and false negatives are determined (from the available samples or otherwise). Estimates of these unmeasurable error rates are, of course, are only possible to estimate with either tacit or explicit modelling of the enemy population. The error conditions that are easy to detect are a false reject and a false positive, and therefore the FRR and FPR estimates are more meaningful estimates of the true false rejects and positives.

Another main problem with both technology, but more so with scenario evaluations, is that such tests are not "*double blind*" tests as used in drug discovery [18]. It would, first of all, be necessary that *both* the subject *and* the testers do not get to know the matcher decision, because this will influence the results of the scenario evaluation. For instance, if the system returns a wrong result, the tester may be tempted to have the subject submit his biometric a second time. Some of these population artifacts can be alleviated by judicious control over test subjects: (i) The biometric authentication application should be mandatory to the whole user population or rules for the selection of a subset of the volunteers need to be developed, as hinted at in [8]; (ii) A related requirement is that the user population should be fairly represented in the test; and (iii)The subjects themselves should probably be unaware of the matching decision.

7.4   Operational Ealuation

Clearly, to measure accuracy fairly and in an unbiased fashion one may find other requirements but it seems that, because of the fact that people are involved, biometric matcher evaluation is a wide open area of research. However, at a minimum, the evaluation should be performed under the most realistic circumstances and maybe the only place to perform biometric testing is at the actual installation, this type of testing is called an *operational evaluation*.

In the mean time, when reporting realistic error rates for the various biometrics, we have to deal with what we have. The biometrics face, finger, and voice are ahead in terms of technology evaluations. Public databases are collected and maintained by universities (e.g., the University of Bologna) or by government agencies such as NIST and DoD and comparative evaluation reports are available as already mentioned. On the other hand, for estimating error rates of commercial and academic authentication systems that use iris or hand, no public databases are available and no open competitions are being held. This could be attributed to the lack of competing systems using these biometrics. Therefore, for these biometrics, we have to resort to public reports on biometric technology commissioned by government agencies or other institutions that are mainly scenario evaluations. The signature biometric is a class in itself because much of the signature verification testing is done with technology evaluations but not in a very systematic way.

Incidentally, while an operational evaluation of a biometric system is clearly desired, one cannot measure the *true* false accept rate for positive authentication systems and the *true* false negative rate for negative or screening biometric authentication systems. Ironically, an operational evaluation cannot measure how well the biometric system can detect the very event that a biometric system is trying to prevent. The error condition could be granting unauthorized access or granting access to undesirable subjects. If it happens, nobody except the actual subject will ever know. Statistics that an operational evaluation can measure is the false reject rate as function of a threshold for positive authentication, the false positive rate as function of a threshold for negative identification systems; or rank order statistics that are related to the expected length of candidate lists.

Any attempt at measuring these "hidden" system parameters (i.e., true false accept rate for positive authentication) will be by actively trying to defeat a biometric system. These are forgeries, impersonations, disguises etc. and it is not clear what error rates would actually be measured. Are we measuring the skills of the intruders, or the system error rates? The use of rank probability mass (RPM) [1] statistics to evaluate this type of *operational data* is, perhaps, one neutral way of estimating underlying error rates.

Although the operational evaluation results realistically measure the system error performance, it may be infeasible because of excessive cost of evaluation both in terms of resources and time. Secondly, by its very nature, the operational evaluations results cannot be easily extrapolated to other applications and scenarios.

8   Biometric Verification Accuracies

Due to space limitations we will not be able to present details of the state of the art of the biometric verification accuracies. We will instead present an overview. Table 3 summarizes *the best error rates* that we found in the literature and as they are discussed else where [1]. The last column give the type of testing, done for the particular biometric, T is technology and S is scenario evaluation. It cannot be emphasized enough that face, finger and speech are tested with technology evaluations; iris and hand are mainly tested with scenario evaluations; and signature is tested with both technology and scenario evaluations.

Table 3. Roughly the error rates that can be found in the literature, based on scenario (S) and technology (T) evaluations

	False reject / (FN)	False accept / (FP)	Evaluation method
Fingerprint	3 to 7 in 100 (3–7%)	1 to 10 in 100,000 (0.001–0.01%)	T
Face	10 to 20 in 100 (10–20%)	100 to 1,000 in 100,000 (0.1–1%)	T (S)
Voice	10 to 20 in 100 (10–20%)	2,000 to 5,000 in 100,000 (2–5%)	T
Iris	2 to 10 in 100 (2–10%)	$\geq 10^{-5}$ ($\geq 0.001\%$)	S
Hand	1 to 2 in 100 (1–2%)	10 to 20 in 1000 (1–2%)	S (T)
Signature	10 to 20 in 100 (10–20%)	2 to 5 in 100 (2–5%)	T & S

The problem in general with any biometric authentication system, again, is of *volume*, especially if using one attempt identification protocols. The more matching attempts for verification the more false rejects. But what is worse, the higher the number n of terrorists in the most-wanted list (the negative database **N**), the more false positives. This carries through to (positive) identification of m enrolled identities in positive database **M**. In an identification application a false positive is like a false accept for security purposes. Hence, when security is involved, the immediate conclusion is that it is *never* a good idea to use "pure identification" because both empirical and theoretical error rates of biometric identification ($1:N$ matching) are high, in which case the exception handling needs much attention [19].

However, when using any of the biometrics in Table 3 for screening (or negative identification), the only acceptable FPR (if any of the FP rates are acceptable) is obtained by running the authentication systems at (roughly) the FNR in the table. This means that fingerprint will then run at 3%-7% and face and voice run at 10%-20%. This means that a person in database **N**, the screening database, has anywhere from a 3% to 20% chance of *not getting caught*.

Finally note that the tabulated values were measured at operating points that might not be suitable for a particular application (decreased FAR can be traded for increased FRR to some extent). As a rule of thumb, an authentication system would in practice be run with a FRR around 5% (merely inconveniences the user), while a screening system would typically require a FRR of 0.1% (subjects who require exception handling).

9   Conclusions

In this paper, we have provided an overview of the overview of 1 : 1 biometric match engines both in positive as well as negative authentications contexts. The focus of the paper was to present basics of the performance evaluations of 1 : 1 match engines and their implications to the a biometric applications. We also defined and discussed various prevalent accuracy performance metrics. Further, we presented some of the methods for measuring biometric match engines and the issues related to such evaluations. Finally, we summarized the state of the art of biometric 1 : 1 engine performance for various technologies.

The accuracy performance of 1 : 1 biometric engines in primarily affected by various factors: (i) the intrinsic discriminatory information in the biometric identifiers (also referred to as individuality); (ii) the sensing technology; (iii) machine representation; (iv) the matching algorithm; (v) operating point; (iv) target population; and (v) impostor population. It is clear that biometrics is an emerging pattern recognition technology and is ridden with many challenging performance evaluations problems because our lack of understanding of how to realistically model these factors. There are also some difficult research issues to be addressed such as (i) meaningful metrics for performance evaluations; (ii) summarizing statistical variations in performance; and (iii) practical methods of independently comparing applications, biometric data sets, matchers, populations, system costs. Finally, there are some fascinating problems extrapolating the performance metrics gained from one scenario application to another.

References

1. Bolle, R., Connell, J., SharathPankanti, Ratha, N., Senior, A.: Guide to Biometrics. Springer Professional Computing, New York (2004)
2. Wayman, J.: A scientific approach to evaluating biometric systems using mathematical methodology. In: Proceedings of CardTech/SecureTech., Orlando, FL (1997) 477–492
3. Peterson, W., Birdsall, T., Fox, W.: The theory of signal delectability. Transactions of the IRE **PGIT-4** (1954) 171–212
4. Biometrics Working Group: Best practices in testing and reporting performance of biometric devices. http : //www.afb.org.uk/bwg/bestprac.html (2000)

5. Germain, R.: Large scale systems. In Jain, A., Bolle, R., Pankanti, S., eds.: Biometrics: Personal Identification in Networked Society. Kluwer Academic Press, Norwell, Mass (1999) 311–326
6. Daugman, J., Williams, G.: A proposed standard for biometric decidability. In: CardTechSecureTech, Atlanta, GA (1996) 223–234
7. NIST Speech Group: NIST Year 2003 Speaker Recognition Evaluation Plan. http://www.nist.gov/speech/tests/spk/2003/doc/2003-spkrec-evalplan-v2.2.pdf. (2003)
8. Mansfield, T., Wayman, J.: Best practices in testing and reporting performance of biometric devices, For biometrics working group. Technical Report Issue 2 Draft 9, Centre for Mathematics and Scientific Computing, National Physics Laboratory, Middlesex, UK (2002)
9. Phillips, P., Grother, P., Micheals, R., Blackburn, D., Elham, T., Bone, J.M.: FRVT 2002: Facial recognition vendor test. Technical report, DoD Counterdrug Technology Development Office, Defence Advance Research Project Agency, National Institute of Justice, Dahlgren, VA; Crane, IN; Arlington, VA (2003)
10. Blackburn, D., Bone, M., Phillips, P.: FRVT 2000: Facial recognition vendor test. Technical report, DoD Counterdrug Technology Development Office, Defence Advance Research Project Agency, National Institute of Justice, Dahlgren, VA; Crane, IN; Arlington, VA (2000)
11. Phillips, P., Moon, H., Rauss, P., Rizvi, S.: The FERET September 1996 database and evaluation procedure. In Bigün, J., Chollet, G., Borgefors, G., eds.: Proceedings of the First International Conference on Audio and Video-based Biometric Person Authentication. Number Lecture Notes in Computer Science 1206, Springer (1997)
12. Biometric Systems Lab, Pattern Recognition and Image Processing Laboratory, U.S. National Biometric Test Center: (FVC2002: Fingerprint verification competition)
13. Maio, D., Maltoni, D., Cappelli, R., Wayman, J., Jain, A.: FVC2000: Fingerprint verification competition. IEEE Transanctions on Pattern Analysis and Machine Intelligence 24 (2002) 402–412
14. Przybocki, M., Martin, A.: The 1999 NIST Speaker Recognition Evaluation Speaker Detection and Speaker Tracking. EUROSPEECH 99 6th European Conference on Speech Communication and Technology, Budapest, Hungary (1999)
15. Campbell, J.: (Ed.) NIST 1999 Speaker Recognition Workshop. Digital Signal Processing 10(1-3) (2000)
16. Duda, R., Hart, P.: Pattern classification and scene analysis. John Wiley & Sons, Inc., New York, NY (1973)
17. Mansfield, T., Kelly, G., Chandler, D., Kane, J.: Biometric product testing final report. Technical Report CESG Contract X92A/4009309, Centre for Mathematics and Scientific Computing, National Physics Laboratory, Middlesex, UK (2001)
18. Cochran, W.: Sampling Techniques. 3rd edn. Wiley Series In Probability and Mathematical Statistics. John Wiley & Sons,, New York (1977)
19. O'Gorman, L.: Seven issues with human authentication technologies. In: Proc. IEEE AutoID 2002, Tarrytown, NY, USA (2002) 185–186

Discussions on Some Problems in Face Recognition

Xiaoqing Ding and Chi Fang

Dept. of Electronic Engineering, Tsinghua University, Beijing 100084, P.R. China
{dxq, fangchi}@ocrserv.ee.tsinghua.edu.cn

Abstract. Face identification and verification have received more attention in
biometric person authentication as their non-invasive, broad useful, and
user-friendly. In the Face Authentication Test (FAT2004) held in conjunction
with the 17th International Conference on Pattern Recognition, Tsinghua
University won the Awards of Best Overall Performance Face Verification Algorithm. In this paper, we will discuss about some problems about improving
the face recognition performance. Imitating human face identification through
discriminating the face observation is very important for face recognition. Key
technologies for distinguishing persons based on face appearances of different
position, size, illumination, pose and age: face detection, feature location, size
and grey level of face appearance normalization. Also, feature extraction and
classification should be the focuses of face recognition research. Dealing with
3D pose variation and aging is the most difficult problem and needs more attention to obtain better face recognition performance.

1 Introduction

In recent years, the biometric person's authentication has been paid more attention on
since a growing trend towards e-commerce, e-banking has emerged and people's atti-
tude to security since September 11th has shifted [1]. Comparing with other biometric
authentication methods, face recognition has recently received significant attention
since they are non-intrusive and user-friendly. As a result they are so urgent concerned and rapid increased.

Even though current face recognition systems have reached a certain level of ma-
turity, their success is limited by the conditions imposed by many real applications.
For example, recognition of face images acquired in an outdoor environment and/or
large pose variations remain a far unsolved problem. In other words, current systems
are still far away from the capability of the human perception system.

In this year, a Face Authentication Test (FAT2004) [1][4] was held in conjunction
with the 17th International Conference on Pattern Recognition (ICPR2004), in which
Tsinghua University team won the award of "Best Overall Performing Face Verification Algorithm in the 2004 Face Authentication Test". This paper we will discuss
some problems about improving the face recognition performance based on our ex-
periences of participating in this competition.

The rest of this paper is organized as follows. Section 2 will introduce the
FAT2004. Next our principle methods for face recognition are addressed. In section 4

S.Z. Li et al. (Eds.): Sinobiometrics 2004, LNCS 3338, pp. 47–56, 2004.

is the state-of-the-art of face recognition. Section 5 illustrates the principle difficulties of face recognition in the future development. Last some conclusions are made.

2   Face Authentication Test on the BANCA Database [1]

The FAT2004 was on a new publicly available database known as BANCA according to a defined protocol [2][3]. Moreover, the competition also used a sequestered BANCA data for independent testing. There were 3 separate parts of the competition: pre-registered, automatic and sequestered. 13 different verification algorithms from 10 institutions submitted their results. Our Tsinghua University team won all of three parts of the competition [1].

2.1   The BANCA Database [2][3]

The BANCA database is a new large, realistic and challenging multi-modal (face and voice) database intended for training and testing multi-modal verification systems. The BANCA database was captured in four European countries. But in the FAT2004, only the English face images were used. Therefore, we will concentrate on this part of data and the BANCA database is only referring to this part of data in the followings.

The BANCA database includes 52 subjects (26 males and 26 females). Each subject was asked to record face images of 12 different sessions in three different scenarios (controlled, degraded and adverse) spanning three months. For recording, a cheap analogue web camera was used in the degraded scenario and a high quality digital camera was used in the controlled and the adverse scenarios. Fig. 1 shows some examples from this database.

 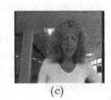

(a)   (b)   (c)

Fig. 1. Examples of the BANCA database   images. (a)   Controlled;   (b) Degraded;   (c) Adverse [1]

In the BANCA database, Sessions 1-4 contain data under Controlled conditions while sessions 5-8 and 9-12 contain Degraded and Adverse scenarios respectively. Each session contains two recordings per subject, a true client access and an informed impostor attack. For each recording, 5 frontal face images have been extracted from each video, which are supposed to be used as 5 client images and 5 impostor ones respectively.

The BANCA protocol is a difficult open-set verification protocol, which means that we can not adjust the face model and the system parameters such as threshold etc. on the evaluation set. The 52 subjects in the BANCA database are equally divided into two groups: G1 and G2, which are used alternatively as the development set and the evaluation set. The development set is used to calibrate and adjust those system parameters such as threshold etc.. Once the development phase is finished, the system performance can then be assessed on the evaluation set.

There are 7 different distinct experimental configurations have been specified in the BANCA protocol, namely, Matched Controlled (MC), Matched Degraded (MD), Matched Adverse (MA), Unmatched Degraded (UD), Unmatched Adverse (UA), Pooled test (P) and Grand test(G). The goal of these configurations is to test the different performances under training and testing of different scenarios. More details about the database and experimental protocols can be found in [2].

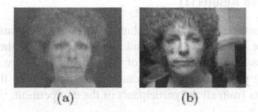

(a)   (b)

Fig. 2. Examples of the sequestered BANCA database images. (a) Controlled; (b) Degraded [1]

In addition, the sequestered BANCA data set in FAT2004 consists of 21 of the original 52 database subjects, 11 men and 10 women. It was captured over 24 months after the original recordings. Five images of each client were captured under two scenarios, controlled and degraded. Also, images of 22 non BANCA subjects were captured under these two conditions. These images were used to simulate impostor attacks. The cameras used to capture the images were both different to those used in the original recordings. Fig.2 shows some examples of the sequestered BANCA data.

2.2 The Competition [1][4]

The FAT2004 were carried out according to the most challenging Pooled (P) configuration of the BANCA database, i.e., only the 5 images from the session 1 were used in the enrollment, and the test are then performed across all other sessions. As no image data from the degraded and adverse conditions has been used in client enrolment, this makes BANCA protocol P very challenging. The environment, subject pose and camera sensor have all changed.

There were three separate parts to the competition: pre-registered, automatic and sequestered. In the pre-registered part, the eyes localizations of both training and testing images were supplied. But in the automatic part, the participants should use an automatic method of localization for at least the testing images, but manual localization for the training phase was allowed. Last, in the sequestered part, the entrants had to submit a trained automatic face verification system so that the performance could be evaluated on the sequestered dataset.

For the pre-registered and automatic parts of the competition, the entrants were requested to submit the Weighted Error Rate (*WER*) of both G1 and G2 for 3 specific operating conditions, which corresponded to 3 different values of the Cost Ratio R of the False Acceptance Rate (FAR) and the False Rejection Rate (FRR), namely, R = 0.1, R = 1, R = 10. And the *WER* is defined as:

$$WER(R) = (FRR + R \times FAR)/(1 + R).$$
(1)

The *WER* could be minimized on the development set by selecting a specified decision threshold. But for the sequestered part of the test, since the decision threshold of the submitted system was fixed, only the half-total error rate is reported (HTER), which is simply the average of the FAR and FRR.

2.3 The Competition Results [1]

There are 13 different verification algorithms from 10 institutions participated into this competition. For the pre-registered and automatic parts of the competition, the average *WER*s across both groups and all of three cost ratios were also reported. Table 1 shows the best performance, the average performance and the worst performance of the three parts from all the participants of the competition.

Table 1. The worst *WER*, the average *WER* and the best *WER* of all the participants in the FAT2004

	Worst *WER*	Average *WER*	Best *WER**
Pre-Registered	13.85%	8.59%	1.39%
Automatic	15.49%	9.85%	2.21%
Sequestered	51.11%	31.13%	13.47%

* All of best *WER*s were got by Tsinghua University Team.

From Table 1 we may know that although the P Test of the BANCA database is very challenging and the environment, subject pose and camera sensor have all changed, the best *WER*s were only 1.39% and 2.21% for the pre-registered part and the automatic part respectively, which may be practical performance in some applications. And it is noted that the best two algorithms of these two parts rely on the Gabor filters for the feature extraction. In general, the *WER*s of the automatic part are somewhat higher than those of the pre-registered part. Therefore, it is clear that the accurate localization is critical to get good verification performances.

Table 1 also shows that the *WER*s of the sequestered part are much higher than those of the other two parts. And it is reported that this trend is seen across all institutions that entered this part of the competition. There are some reasons resulting in the drops, such as over tuning of the system on the BANCA database, incorrect decision threshold on the sequestered data etc., but the most important reason is that the images of the subjects were taken over 24 months after the images used for the enrollment. Therefore, age variation is still the most difficult problem for a practical face recognition system.

3 Principle Methods for Face Recognition

Although the researches for face recognition have been long time and a lot of algorithms and methods have been proposed, also great progresses have been achieved recently, but face recognition technology is still developing and many papers on new face verification and recognition algorithms are being published almost daily. This is because some most difficult problems still exist, which are hardly against the big illumination variation, large angle pose turnabout and long time age variation, etc.. All of these variations on the face images make face recognition so difficult to be improved; also force people comprehensively think how we should study about the face recognition problem and what should we do for further solving the real face recognition problems.

Face recognition is a special 3D object problem from its 2D images, which is different with other object recognition problems. Such as face recognition is different with 2D character recognition; and different person's faces having near the same image structure is different with characters and other objects. Therefore, we should consider the face recognition problem, and what strategy should be adopted for solving the difficult face recognition problems? It is well known that the small differences in different person's face appearances but larger variations in the same person's appearance, including 3D pose and different viewpoint variances.

From statistical pattern recognition point of view, face features are represented with a very large within-class variation and a small between-class variation, and make so difficult to identify the face authentication stably and accurately.

Fortunately, we have noted that human can easily identify the familiar person from their face observation, which greatly enlightens us on the face recognition:

1. People easily identify the familiar person from his/her face observations which have been remembered before, but often hardly to say clearly how they can be recognized;

2. People can identify the person independent with the viewpoint, pose, illumination, express and time intervals;

3. People identify person depend on the learning, since he/she was born, he/she has learned from a lot of person observations in different pose, different viewpoint, different facial expressions, different illumination and different ages. It is obviously, for example, people can easily identify the perpendicularity person but headstand person.

4. Some features are more important than others in person identification, but the most important one is the holistic face features, which is much more important than the local organ features in face recognition;

5. Appearance on photographs contains much more information than the Caricatures of line drawings, which is useful for person face representation only depending on the human perception.

Imitating human face identification through discriminating the face observation is very helpful for us to research the face recognition, that is discriminating person mainly based on face appearances; the face recognition abilities the same as human are also dependent on the learning from face image samples, etc. Therefore, the better strategy for face recognition is simulating human identification person by face. We can see that human identification person authorization mainly depends on the person's face image. But what information do they use for human person authentication? Is it based on face contour and/or organic contours? Or based on the holistic face image? From these two kinds of face information, two kinds of methods are oriented: one is that face outline and organic contours are very important for face recognition, since they can simply represent different person by portraits [5]. Therefore, extracting the face outline and organic contour is the first problem, then the face representation and comparison are also should be solved. But serious problems have been met in implementation, they can hardly extract and locate the face outliner and organic contours correctly and exactly from face image. Even can hardly compare two contours for discriminate the different persons.

The other way is that the face information is on the holistic face image and different information between different persons are also on the holistic face images as human look at them, in the face images there contain so rich and enough information to identify even more than hundred thousands of persons. It is obvious that the enough information to discriminate different persons exist in the holistic face images. Therefore, the key problem is how to extract the discriminating features from holistic face image for face identification and verification.

Based on the discriminating features extracted from different person's face image, to identify different persons is the nature way for face recognition. The fundamental principles of face feature extracting are to make the same person's face features are as closer as possible, but different person's face features are as far away as possible. In other words, we should make the within-class variation as small as possible and the between-class variation as large as possible.

In order to extract face image features for the same person as close as possible whatever in the different pose, different expression, complex background and illumination, etc. a lot of methods could be adopted: first is face detection and face position normalization, face size normalization and gray scale normalization, etc.; the others are like pose normalization.

The position normalization and the size normalization are so important because face image matching and comparisons need to be implemented in the correspondent pixel positions. In general to find and locate two eye's central points are the possible and easier way, which can give a standard coordinates to locate the correspondent points of face image and give the normalization size of different face images. Also accurately locating of two eye's central points is very important to weaken the variation of face size, position, and pose. In doing so we need to develop special face detection and localization, eyes localization algorithms.

Face images are gray scale images, even are color images. The levels of face gray scale or color are great variation in the different light illumination in door or different sun-shine in out door. How to weaken the effect of different grey scale? The simplest way is to normalize face gray level. For the color information, it is useful to face detection, even for the face recognition, but the bigger variation in color information than in gray scale causes unstable for face detection and recognition. In order to avoid the compromise by unstable color information, the gray scale information is often only chosen for face detection and recognition in general. There also are many image enhancement methods could be adopted to face gray scale image normalization, such as histogram equalization, etc.

The discriminating feature extracted from the normalized face image is to find the discriminating information among different person's features. This is the most important step in face recognition, because it crucially determines the performance of face recognition.

From face image pixels we can get features with high dimension, in which many information redundancies exist: such as close related pixels, and similar face structure information in different face image. Compress and reduce this redundant information are necessary for effective face recognition. On the other hand it is also necessary to reduce the problem of the curse of dimensionality in pattern recognition.

Reducing the redundant information to get effective discriminating information is the effective step in face recognition. The often used method is principle component analysis (PCA), it can get optimum de-correlation and data compress from face representation, but it is not optimum discriminating feature extraction from different person. So a better method is PCA+LDA, which is broadly used in a lot of face recognition systems [5][9].

PCA and LDA are implemented on the original image features, and the performance heavily depends on the original features. The better way for optimum discriminating feature extraction is to improve the original features: that is the original features come from image pixels to form some optimized transformation image features. Some effective transforms have been proposed and adopted in many face recognition researches and systems to improve the face features. Such as appearance-based Harr transformation methods used in face detection, wavelet transformation used in face feature extraction. Especially, Gabor transformation has used in the face recognition and has got better performance by now [6].

4 The State of the Art of Face Recognition

After some intensive research of past more than ten years, the face recognition technology is greatly improved. Many algorithms were proposed, such as Eigenfaces [7], Fisherfaces [8][9], Local Feature Analysis (LFA) [10] and Elastic Bunch Graph Matching (EBGM) [11] etc.. Based on these technologies, some commercial systems are available for various applications, for examples, FaceIt from Identix, Cognitec Systems and Eyematic Interfaces Inc. etc.. Therefore, it seems that the face recognition is a mature technology. But in practice it is known that the face recognition still suffers from many difficulties in some applications. So we want to answer such a question, in what extend the face recognition is practical?

With the development of face recognition technology, it is clear that the evaluations of these algorithms are very important. Therefore, during the past several years, many evaluations of the face recognition were held, such as the serious of FERET evaluation [12][13], FRVT 2000 [14], FRVT 2002 [15] and the FAT2004 [1][4] etc.. Since the organizers were convinced that the evaluation should be based as closely as possible on a specific application, we may learn many lessons about the application's status of face recognition technology.

The serious of FERET evaluation tests were held in 1994, 1995 and 1996 respectively. Although the FERET database is not so realistic, the FERET evaluation tests did have a significant impact on the development of face recognition. They quantified the performance improvements of face recognition, and revealed three major problems of face recognition: age variations, illumination variations and pose variations [12][13].

Since there emerged many commercial face recognition systems after 1997, FRVT2000 was organized to assess the performance of them. Many lessons were learned from the FRVT2000 [14]: (1) the effects of compression and recording media don't affect performance; (2) pose doesn't significantly affect the performance up to $\pm 25°$, but do significantly affect the performance when reaching $\pm 40°$; (3) the indoor change of lighting don't significantly affect the performance, but moving from indoor to outdoor lighting significantly affect the performance; (4) the age variations was still a difficult problem for face recognition, but the performance was improved since the last FERET evaluation test.

The primary goal of FRVT2002 was to assess the ability of face recognition technology to meet the real-world requirements. The main database used in the FRVT2002 was 121,589 images of 37,437 people that were collected from the U.S. Department of State's Mexican nonimmigrant Visa archive. FRVT2002 found that [15]: (1) for normal indoor lighting, the performance of top system was about 90% verification rate at a false accept rate of 1%, but it is only 50% verification rate at a false accept rate of 1% for outdoor lighting; (2) the performance of top system degraded at approximately 5% as time increases one year; (3) the use of morphable models can significantly improve non-frontal face recognition.

Last, the FAT2004 has been introduced in quite detail in section 2. Although the P configuration of BANCA database suffers from the variations of indoor environment, subject pose (almost all in the vertical direction) , three months capturing interval and camera senor, the Equal Error Rate (EER) for the best automatic face verification system is only a few more than 3% [1]. But as the sequestered data was captured over 24 months after the original recording, the HTER dropped significantly to about 14% for the best face verification system in the sequestered part of the competition [1].

We learn from the above evaluations that face recognition technology continued to be improved. And we may draft the state-of-the-art of face recognition especially based on the last two evaluations. The face recognition technology may be practical (EER will be about 4% for face verification) in indoor environment, with slightly cooperation of the user, and by renewing/adapting the templates after per period of time. Some examples of such face recognition based applications are computer login system, gate access control system and registration system etc.. However, recognizing face with outdoor illumination variations, more than $\pm 40°$ pose variations and age interval variations are still the most difficulty research areas.

5 Principle Difficulties of Face Recognition in the Future Development

Up to now, great progresses have achieved and many commercial products have been emerged in world market, but some challenging research topics still unsolved in the face recognition. The age interval, illumination and pose problems are three prominent issues for appearance- or image-based approaches. Many approaches have been proposed to handle these issues with the majority of them exploring domain knowledge. Because in most face recognition applications the images are available only in the form of single or multiple views of 2D intensity data, so that the inputs to computer face recognition algorithms are visual only, and also appearance- or image-based approaches have achieved better results.

Face recognition is a special 3D object recognition problem from 2D image, because they have common face organs structure in face images, also have nearly the same pose variation for pose various face images. Therefore, the knowledge for the face images in different pose could be cached from various face images, and could be used in face recognition in various pose. Also some researchers have used 3D models of head for face recognition in various poses, they may be good approaches.

For the illumination problems, intelligent and adaptive image enhancement approaches should be developed and effective feature extraction and selection should be researched, such as Gabor filter based features are more robust for illumination variation.

For the age variation there is few method to solve this problem, the same as human, sometimes people also hard to distinct the authentication by photographs between longer time intervals. Therefore, the photographs are required in a short interval, such as within 3 months, in VISA application for some countries.

In general, for the unsolved perfectly face recognition problem we need to continue full efforts to mimic the visual perception of humans, to research new theory and approaches, to overcome the difficulties in face recognition, and to develop face recognition systems more like the remarkable face recognition ability of humans.

6 Conclusion

Face recognition is a special image recognition problem, and special 3D object recognition problem based on its 2D view images. Face recognition also is a more difficult image recognition problem for its pose and illumination variations, which cause much larger variance of face image for the same person and more similar face images for different persons.

Especially, the model and distribution of face feature variations has not been researched clearly, the reason also come from hardly to collect enough samples of all variations to count them for learning.

Face recognition has become one of the most active applications of pattern recognition, image analysis and understanding. Future researches will bring more accurate and more robust face recognition approaches and develop more useful face recognition systems in the authentication application.

References

1. Messer, K., Kittler, J. etc.: Face Authentication Test on the BANCA Database. Proc. of ICPR'2004. Vol.4. Cambridge (2004) 523-532
2. Bailly-Bailliere, E., Bengio, S. etc.: The BANCA database and evaluation protocol. Proc. Audio- and Video-Based Biometric Person Authentication. Berlin (2003) 625-638
3. The BANCA Database: http://www.ee.surrey.ac.uk/banca
4. The ICPR FAT2004 Home page: http://www.ee.surrey.ac.uk/banca/icpr2004
5. Zhao, W., Chellappa, R. etc.: Face recognition: a literature survey. ACM Computing Surveys. Vol. 35. No. 4 (2003) 399-458
6. Liu, Chengjun and Wechsler, H.: Gabor feature based classification using the enhanced fisher linear discriminant model for face recognition. IEEE Trans. on Image Processing. Vol. 11. No. 4 (2002) 467-476
7. Turk, M. and Pentland, A.: Eigenfaces for recognition. J. Cogn. Neurosci.. 3 (1991) 72-86
8. Belhumeur, P.N., Hespanha, J.P.etc.: Eigenfaces vs. Fisherfaces: recognition using class specific linear projection. IEEE Trans. on PAMI. Vol. 19 (1997) 711-720
9. Zhao, W., Chellappa, R. etc.: Discriminant analysis of principal components for face recognition. Proc. of AFGR (1998) 336-341
10. Penev., P. and Atick, J.: Local feature analysis: A general statistical theory for object representation. Netw.: Computat. Neural Syst.. Vol. 7 (1996) 477-500
11. Wiskott, L., Fellous, J.M. etc.: Face recognition by elastic bunch graph matching. IEEE Trans. on PAMI. Vol. 19 (1997) 775-779
12. Phillips, P.J., Wechsler, H. etc.: The FERET database and evaluation procedure for face-recognition algorithm. Image and Vision Computing. 16 (1998) 295-306
13. Phillips, P.J., Moon H. etc.: The FERET evaluation methodology for face recognition algorithms. IEEE Trans. on PAMI. Vol.22 (2000)
14. Blackburn, D. M., Bone M. etc.: Face recognition vendor test 2000. Tech. Rep.. http://www.frvt.org (2001)
15. Phillips, P.J., Grother P.J. etc.: Face recognition vendor test 2002: Evaluation report. NISTIR 6965. http://www.frvt.org (2003)

Improving Fingerprint Recognition Performance Based on Feature Fusion and Adaptive Registration Pattern

Jie Tian[1,2,*], Yuliang He[1,2], Xin Yang[1,2], Liang Li[1,2], and XinJian Chen[1,2]

[1] Biometrics Research Group, Key Laboratory of Complex Systems and Intelligence Science
Institute of Automation, CAS, P.O.Box 2728, Beijing, 100080, China
[2] Graduate School of the Chinese Academy of Science Beijing, 100039, China
tian@doctor.com

Abstract. This paper proposes an adaptive registration pattern based fingerprint matching method dealing with the non-linear deformations in fingerprint. The *"registration pattern"* between two fingerprints is the optimal registration of every part of one fingerprint with respect to the other fingerprint. *Registration patterns* generated from imposter's matching attempts are different from those patterns from genuine matching attempts, although they share some similarities in the aspect of minutiae. In this paper, we combine minutiae, associate ridges and orientation fields to determine the *registration pattern* between two fingerprints and match them. The proposed matching scheme has two stages. An offline, training stage, derives a *genuine registration pattern base* from a set of genuine matching attempts. Then, an online matching stage registers the two fingerprints and determines the *registration pattern*. A further fine matching is conducted. In addition, the block orientation field is used as the global feature of a fingerprint to improve the performance of this method. And 2nd and 3rd relational structures between minutiae are applied to promote the fingerprint matching method. Experimental results evaluated by FVC2004 demonstrate that the proposed algorithm is an accurate one.

Keywords: adaptive registration pattern, relational structure between minutiae, fingerprint identification.

1 Introduction

A fingerprint, a pattern of ridges and valleys on the surface of a finger, has been used for individual identification upon legal purpose. With the increasing volume of information technology, automatic fingerprint identification becomes more popular in civilian applications, such as access control, financial security and verification of

* This paper is supported by the Project of National Science Fund for Distinguished Young Scholars of China under Grant No. 60225008, the Key Project of National Natural Science Foundation of China under Grant No. 60332010, the Project for Young Scientists' Fund of National Natural Science Foundation of China under Grant No.60303022.
Corresponding author: Jie Tian ; Telephone: 8610-62532105; Fax: 8610-62527995.

S.Z. Li et al. (Eds.): Sinobiometrics 2004, LNCS 3338, pp. 57–66, 2004.
© Springer-Verlag Berlin Heidelberg 2004

firearm purchasers, etc. A fingerprint is becoming an identity of human being. Automatic Fingerprint Identification Systems (AFISs) have been performed very well for years in ideal circumstances. However, limited memory is in an off-line AFIS, such as Personal Digital Assistant (PDA) and IC Card systems. It is important to design a reliable fingerprint identification method for AFISs.

A lot of work in fingerprint identification proposed a wide range of algorithms with different techniques. Fingerprint matching techniques can be broadly classified as minutiae-based or correlation-based technologies. Minutiae-based techniques attempt to align two sets of minutiae points and determine the total number of matched minutiae [1, 2, 3, 4]. Correlation-based techniques compare the global pattern of ridges and furrows to see if the ridges in two fingerprints align [5, 6, 7, 8]. The performance of minutiae-based technologies relies on the accurate detection of minutiae points and the use of sophisticated matching methods to compare two minutiae sets which undergo non-rigid transformations. However, for correlation-based techniques, the performance is affected by non-linear distortions and the presentation of noise present in image. It is usually known that minutiae-based techniques perform better than correlation-based ones. Correlation-based techniques involve several problems [9]: (a) A fingerprint image may contain non-linear warping because of the effect of pressing a convex elastic surface (the finger) on at surface (the sensor). Moreover, various sub-regions in the sensed image are distorted differently due to the non-uniform pressure applied by the user. It is difficult to compare two such distorted prints, even if with consideration of translation and rotation effects. (b) Based on the moisture content of the skin, the acquired image may vary with different sensor time to time and therefore making more complicated correlation process.

In this paper, we introduce a novel fingerprint verification algorithm based on adaptive registration pattern for alignment in matching and combined comprehensive minutiae and global texture feature, block orientation field. The algorithm first coarsely aligns two fingerprints and determines the *possible RP* by optimally registering each part of the two fingerprints. Next, inspects the *possible RP* with a *genuine RP space*. A further fine matching is conducted if the *RP* makes a genuine one. The multiply rules as a principle of fusion are exploited in fingerprint matching. The matching performance is greatly improved by these strategies.

This paper is organized as follows. First, the feature representation and extraction method is introduced. Next, the matching algorithm is explained. Experimental result of the algorithm and its applications are given in Section 4. Section 5 contains discussion and further work.

2   Fingerprint Presentation

The uniqueness of a fingerprint is determined by the topographic relief of its ridge structure and the presence of certain ridge anomalies termed as minutiae points. Typically, the global configuration defined by the ridge structure is applied to determine the class [10] of the fingerprint, while the distribution of minutiae points is used to match and to establish the similarity between two fingerprints [11, 1]. Automatic fingerprint identification systems, that match a query print against a large database of prints (which may consist of millions of prints), rely on the pattern of ridges in the query image to narrow the search in the database (fingerprint index), and on the minutiae points to determine an exact match (fingerprint matching). The ridge flow pattern itself is seldom used for matching fingerprints.

A good quality fingerprint usually contains about 60 minutiae which is enough for its uniqueness. However, a bad quality fingerprint may have very narrow foreground area without enough reliable minutiae to indicate its uniqueness. To the best of our knowledge, local fingerprint texture (ridges or valleys) features can improve the identification performance. Therefore, we use minutiae and associated local texture in our method. All local comprehensive minutiae in fingerprint F are denoted by a vector set $M^F = \{M^F_i = (x_i, y_i, \alpha_i, \beta_i, \varphi_{i1,...}, \varphi_{iT}); T \geq 2, i=0, ..., m^F\}$, where: m^F is the number of minutiae in fingerprint F. For clarity, M^F_i denotes the ith minutia, presented by a feature vector $(x_i, y_i, \alpha_i, \beta_i, \varphi_{i1,...}, \varphi_{iT})$ $(T \geq 2, 1 \leq i \leq m^F$, where 1) x_i and y_i are its coordinates respectively. α_i is the local ridge direction at M^F_i in the anticlockwise direction. β_i is the local grey variation of an area centred by M^F_i. 2) (x_{ik}, y_{ik}) $(k=1, 2, \cdots, T)$, see Figure 1, are the points extracted from a ridge, which M^F_i locates, in equal step from its beginning point to its end. To represent local texture features of a local region centred at M^F_i, $\varphi_{ik} = \text{actan}((y_{ik} - y_i)/(x_{ik} - x_i))(k\ 1, 2, \cdots, T)$, the directions from M to (x_{ik}, y_{ik}) $(k=1, 2, \cdots, T)$ in the anticlockwise direction, are introduced to describe the curvature of the ridge. β_i and $\varphi_{ik} (k=1, 2, \cdots, T)$ describe the local texture properties of the local region associated with M^F_i, which accelerate aligning features during fingerprint matching.

The above defined comprehensive minutiae include local texture features and are dependent on their associated minutiae. It is hard to ensure their reliability although they enhance the uniqueness of a fingerprint. Therefore, it is feasible to use global feature for matching bad quality fingerprints to enhance performance of the matching method. In our experiments, we test a method using block orientation field [12] of a fingerprint as its global feature and to get inspiring results.

Comprehensive minutiae are combined with minutiae's nth relative structures [13]. 3rd order relational structures such as minutia-triangle employed in many methods [11, 2] require more computation expense than 2nd order relative structures. Both structures are enough to represent the Euclidean distance-based relations among minutiae. With comparison to 2nd order relative structures, 3rd order relational structures have more features to represent the uniqueness of a fingerprint although more memory and time are needed. These relational structures combine isolated comprehensive minutiae as an aspect for matching.

3 Fingerprint Matching Based on Adaptive Registration Pattern

3.1 Coarse Matching

The task of the coarse global registration is to align the two fingerprints and find the possible corresponding point pairs between the two feature sets. We revised the registration method as described in [14] and introduce an *orientation field matching degree* feedback mechanism to improve the robustness of global alignment.

To estimate the registration parameter, we use the minutiae set to construct the local structure set: $\{Fl_1, Fl_2, ..., Fl_n\}$. Each local structure in the input fingerprint is compared with each local structure in the registration fingerprint. Each comparison generates a registration parameter and a similarity score:

$$MFl_{p,q} = (Fl_p^t, Fl_q^i, (dx, dy, rot, s_x, s_y), s_{p,q}),$$ (1)

where the definition of the similarity score s_{pq} is the same with [15]. These comparisons give a possible correspondence list of feature points in two sets:

$$L_{corr} = \{(p_a^t, p_b^i, MFl_{p,q}) \mid p_a^t \in Fl_p^t, p_b^i \in Fl_q^i\}.$$ (2)

We cluster those registration parameters in $\{MFl_{p,q}\}$ into several candidate groups. Parameters in each group are averaged to generate a candidate global registration parameter. And the summation of similarity scores in each group becomes the power of each candidate registration parameter. The candidate parameters are sorted by their power and verified one by one using the orientation field information to choose the best global registration parameter.

3.2 Registration Pattern Determination

The next step is the determination of the *RP* that optimally registers each part of the two fingerprints. We take the input image as *"standard image"*, and take the registration fingerprint "a distorted image" versus standard one.

The feature set of the registration fingerprint is first aligned with the input fingerprint using the global alignment parameter we get in the last step. Next, we tessellate the overlap portion of the input image into seven non-overlap hexagons with radius=*R*. Then, we compute the optimal alignment parameter of the registration image with respect to each hexagon in the input image. The registration method is the same with that described in Section 3.1 except that: first, the searching space is greatly reduced, since the search region is restricted to the hexagon and its neighborhoods; second, sample points on associate ridges are utilized to provide more information for registration. The possible correspondence list is extended by the possible correspondences of sampled feature points. The illustration of the orientation and the type of the sample points are shown in Figure 1.

Fig. 1. Orientation and type of sample points on associate ridges

The registration parameters as a whole describe the *RP* between the two images:

$$RP = \{(dx_i, dy_i, rot_1, s_{xi}, s_{yi}); i = 1,..7\}$$ (3)

3.3 Learning Genuine Registration Patterns

Some different fingers may have similar flow patterns and many of their minutiae can be matched if we use a loose bounding box allowing the large distortion. However, when analyzing the two fingerprints in detail, we found that the *RP* was different from those from true matching. To learn the *genuine RPs*, we applied a set of distorted fingerprint images to derive a *genuine RP base (GRPB)*. This set of images was extracted from NIST Special DB24 [16]. The database contains 100 MPEG-2 compressed digital videos of live-scan fingerprint data. Users are required to place their finger on the sensor and distort their finger exaggeratedly once the finger touched the surface.

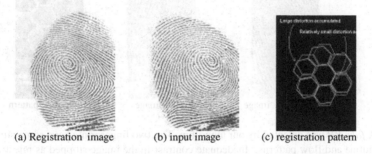

(a) Registration image   (b) input image   (c) registration pattern

Fig. 2. A *genuine RP* derived from a true matching attempt

Those images from the same finger were matched to one to one and RPs were computed. These *RPs* formed our *GRPB*. In an experiment, we choose seven fix-sized hexagons with *R*= 45 pixels. In most cases, they cover most of the overlap portion. And the alignment parameters of these hexagons can well represent the whole *RP*. Figure 2 shows a *genuine RP* calculated by our algorithm from two images in NIST Special DB24.

3.4 Registration Pattern Inspection

We define the distance between two *RPs*:

$$d(RP_i, RP_j) = \sum_k \sqrt{\left[\left(\frac{\left| dx_k^i - dx_k^j \right|}{s_d} \right)^2 + \left(\frac{\left| dy_k^i - dy_k^j \right|}{\lambda_d} \right)^2 + \left(\frac{\left| ds_{xk}^i - ds_{xk}^j \right|}{\lambda_x} \right)^2 + \left(\frac{\left| ds_{yk}^i - ds_{yk}^j \right|}{\lambda_y} \right)^2 + \left(\frac{\left| rot_k^i - rot_k^j \right|}{\lambda_r} \right)^2 \right]} \quad (4)$$

And a *genuine RP space*:

$$S_{GRP} = \{RP \mid \exists RP_i \in GRPB, d(RP, RP_i) < Thr_{gspace}\}. \tag{5}$$

In our algorithm, each matching attempt generates a *possible RP*. If the *possible RP* belongs to S_{GRP}, a further fine matching is conducted. Otherwise, the matching attempt is rejected. Figure 3 shows a *fake RP* detected by our algorithm.

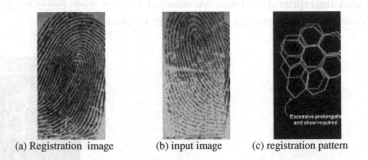

(a) Registration image   (b) input image   (c) registration pattern

Fig. 3. A *fake RP* was detected by our algorithm. The two fingerprints have some similarities in both minutiae and flow patterns. Inadequate contrast in the image stopped as rejecting it in the stage of coarse global registration, all those two fingerprints in fact belong to different types

3.4 Fine Matching

From the list of possible corresponding point pairs refined in the stage of *RP* determination, each feature point in the overlap portion of the registration fingerprint may have one or more corresponding feature points with the input fingerprint. The confliction of one feature point corresponding to more than one feature points can be solved by a simple rule: assign this feature point to the point which has the largest sum of similarity score with it. All the other correspondences are deleted. Then compute the matching score:

$$M = \frac{m}{\max(n_{input}, n_{template})} \times \sum s_i \tag{6}$$

where m is the number of matching feature points, n_{input} and $n_{Registration}$ are the numbers of feature points in the overlap portion of the input fingerprint and registration fingerprint respectively, and s_i is the similarity score in the final correspondence list.

For global texture feature, block orientation field, in this method, the mutual information (*MI*) method [18] is used to calculate the similarity between two fingerprints. However, the speed of this MI method is limited by the accuracy of the detected deformation model although it greatly increases the matching performance. Assume E denote the similarity between two fingerprints calculated with MI method. Their final similarity is obtained by fuse the relational structures and block orientation field, that is, a multiply rule, $F = M * E$, is used to estimate the final similarity.

4 Experimental Results

Feature selection and fusion play important role in matching. Two methods based on these schemes are proposed: the first one, denoted by "light" method, uses 2nd order relational minutia structures for local similarity measurement; another, denoted by "open" method, uses 3rd order relational minutia structures. In addition, the "open" method also use global feature, block orientation field, for matching. The two methods were submitted to FVC2004 [17] and tested by FVC2004. And their results were showed in Fig. 5 and Fig. 6. The "light" method is in the light team of FVC2004, and the "open" method is in the open team of FVC2004. The "open" method for the global features need more memory and time expenses in matching. Their testing results show that "light" method races 7 of the "light" team and the "open" method races 3 of the "open" team. Now the "light" method has been applied to the off-line AFISs, such as PDA, Mobile, lock, and so on. The demos of an off-line AFISs are showed in Fig.7.

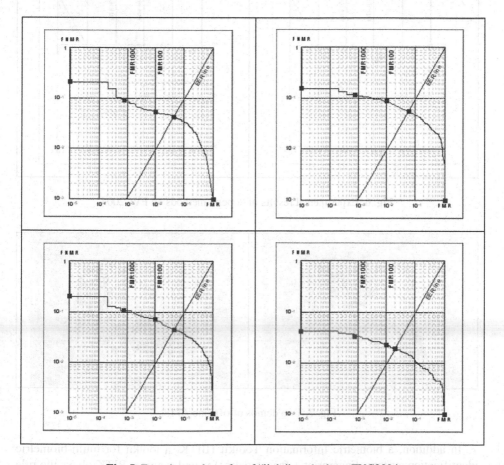

Fig. 5. Experimental results of "light" methods on FVC2004

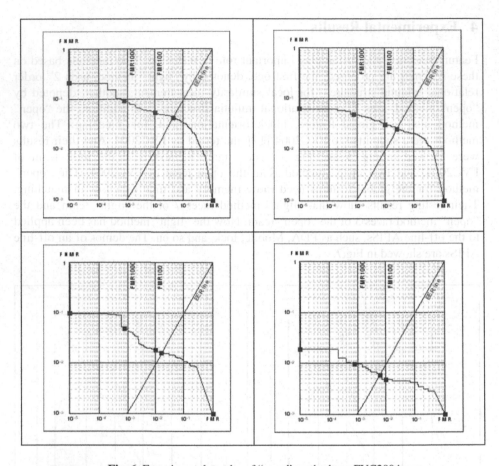

Fig. 6. Experimental results of "open" methods on FVC2004

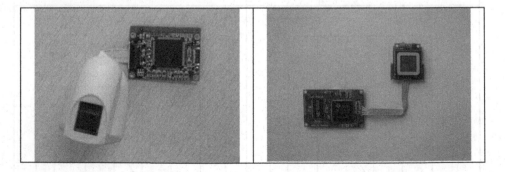

Fig. 7. Two demos of off-line AFISs

In addition, a biometric Information Toolkit (BITK, a toolkit for multi-biometric identification system (fingerprint + face + palm)) is under going. BITK obeys the rule of data flow, a principle of objective development. And BITK consists of source model, filter model and target model. The Source model is the beginning of data processing which only contains input without output. The functions are to read data from files, or other systems and devices storage. Filter model is the middle node of data processing. Its functions are to obtain data and output the processed results to the target model. All biometric data algorithms are included in this model, such as fingerprint enhancement, fingerprint matching, and so on. The target model is the ending step of data processing and it outputs or shows the results from the filter model.

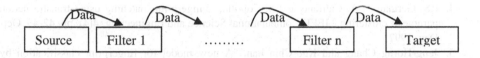

Fig. 8. Data Flow Model of BITK

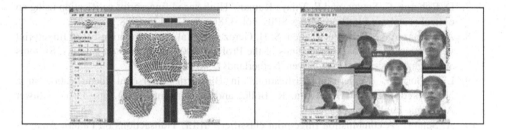

Fig. 9. Multi-biometric identification system based on BITK

5 Conclusion and Future Work

We have introduced a novel fingerprint verification algorithm based on feature fusion and adaptive registration pattern. The inspection of *possible RP* successfully detected many dangerous imposter's matching attempts, which had similar flow pattern and minutiae configuration with the registration images. In addition, global feature of a fingerprint, triangular relational structures, and multiply rule of fusion, are applied to matching, which improves the performance of the method.

Our further works in biometric recognition will be done in the following fields: First, we'll improve false match in our match which sometimes occurs if there are lot of non-linear deformations and distortions caused by incorrect finger placement. Such situations are also the main cause for the high false matching rates (FMR) in traditional matching algorithms. Currently, a *possible RP* is inspected one by one check with the *genuine RPs*. We are deriving a knowledge base from these patterns. Second, sensitivity of our method is to bad quality fingerprints will be improved in terms of those with many false minutiae. For example, it is hard for these dry fingerprints to extract enough minutiae. Other novel global features should be further exploited into our methods. In addition, a multi-resolution search strategy will be employed as well to calculate the optimal deformations in the deformation space.

References

1. Anil Jain, Hong Lin and R. Bolle, "On-line Fingerprint Verification," IEEE Transactions on Pattern Analysis and Machine Intelligence, Vol.19 No.4, pp.302-314, 1997.
2. Xudong Jiang and W.Y. Yau, "Fingerprint minutiae matching based on the local and Global Structures," Proceedings of the 15th International Conference on Pattern Recognition (ICPR 2000), Vol.2, pp.1042-1045, 2000.
3. Yuliang He, Jie Tian, Xiping Luo and Tanghui Zhang, "Image Enhancement and Minutiae Matching In Fingerprint Verification," Pattern Recognition Letters, Vol. 24/9-10 pp. 1349 - 1360, 2003.
4. RS. Germain, , A. Califano and S. Colville, "Fingerprint matching using transformation parameter clustering," IEEE Computational Science and Engineering, 4(4), pp. 42-49, Oct-Dec, 1997.
5. Jeng-Horng Chang and Kuo-Chin Fan, "A new model for fingerprint classification by ridge distribution sequences," Pattern Recognition, Vol.35, pp.1209-1223, 2002.
6. Alex Stoianov, Colin Soutar, and Allan Graham, "High-speed fingerprint verification using an optical correlator," in Proceedings SPIE, vol. 3386, pp. 242-252, 1998.
7. D. Roberge, C. Soutar, and B. Vijaya Kumar, "High-speed fingerprint verification using an optical correlator," in Proceedings SPIE, vol. 3386, pp. 123-133,1998.
8. A. M. Bazen, G. T. B. Verwaaijen, S. H. Gerez and et al, "A correlation-based fingerprint verification system," in Proceedings of the ProRISC2000 Workshop on Circuits, Systems and Signal Processing, (Veldhoven, Netherlands), Nov 2000.
9. L. O'Gorman, "Fingerprint verification," in Biometrics: Personal Identification in a Networked Society (A. K. Jain, R. Bolle, and S. Pankanti, eds.), pp. 43-64, Kluwer Academic Publishers, 1999.
10. A. Senior, "A combination fingerprint classifier," IEEE Transactions on Pattern Analysis and Machine Intelligence, vol.23, pp.1165-1174, Oct 2001.
11. Z. M. Kovács-Vajna, "A fingerprint verification system based on triangular matching and dynamic time warping," IEEE Transactions on Pattern Analysis and Machine Intelligence, vol. 22, pp. 1266-1276, Nov 2000.
12. Hong Lin, Yifei Wang, Anil Jain, "Fingerprint Image Enhancement: Algorithm and Performance Evaluation. IEEE Transactions on Pattern Analysis and Machine Intelligence, Vol.20, pp.777-789, 1998.
13. Stan Z Li, "Markov Random Field Modeling In Image Analysis," Springer-Verlag Tokyo, 2001.
14. Chen Hong, Jie Tian and Xin Yang, "Fingerprint Matching with Registration Pattern Inspection," In proceeding of the 4th International Conference of Audio-and Video-Based Biometric Person Authentication, pp.327-334, 2003.
15. Kuo Chin Fan, ChengWen Lee and Yuan Kai Wang, "A randomized approach with geometric constraints to fingerprint verification," Pattern Recognition, Vol. 33, pp. 1793-1803, 2000.
16. C.I. Watson, "NIST Special Database 24 Digital Video of Live-Scan Fingerprint Data," U.S. National Institute of Standards and Technology, 1998.
17. FVC2004-Third International Fingerprint Verification Competition, http://bias.csr.unibo.it/fvc2004/.
18. P.A.Viola, "Alignment by maximization of mutual information," Ph.D. thesis, Massachusetts Institute of Technology, Boston, MA, USA, 1995.

Iris Recognition Based on Non-local Comparisons

Zhenan Sun, Tieniu Tan, and Yunhong Wang

Center for Biometric Research and Testing,
National Laboratory of Pattern Recognition, Institute of Automation,
Chinese Academy of Sciences, P.O. Box 2728, Beijing, 100080, P.R. China
{znsun, tnt, wangyh}@nlpr.ia.ac.cn

Abstract. Iris recognition provides a reliable method for personal identification. Inspired by recent achievements in the field of visual neuroscience, we encode the non-local image comparisons qualitatively for iris recognition. In this scheme, each bit iris code corresponds to the sign of an inequality across several distant image regions. Compared with local ordinal measures, the relationships of dissociated multi-pole are more informative and robust against intra-class variations. Thus non-local ordinal measures are more suited for iris recognition. In our early work, we have built a general framework "robust encoding of local ordinal measures" to unify several top iris recognition algorithms. Therefore the results reported in this paper improve state-of-the-art iris recognition performance essentially as well as evolve the framework from pair-wise local ordinal relationship to non-local ordinal feature of multiple regions. Our ideas are proved on CASIA iris image database.

1 Introduction

After September 11th event, people realized that security is an important problem but it has not been well resolved. Because security rules are user dependent, reliable personal identification is a key issue of security. Traditional human authentication methods such as token-based and password-based are not reliable enough to meet the requirements of high level security situations. In response to the urgent demanding, biometrics is emerging as an alternative personal identification method [1,2]. Biometrics makes use of physiological or behavioral characteristics of people such as fingerprint, iris, face, palmprint, gait, voice, etc. to identify a person. Attracted by the promising application of biometrics in many important areas, many scientific researchers and engineers are working to make the biometric systems more reliable and more robust, as well as cost less computational and storage resources.

Iris image is a unique pattern and is informative for recognition. In addition, it is stable during the life and non-intrusive. Therefore iris pattern is regarded as "digital passport" and has been successfully applied for large population identification [3]. Of course the discriminating power of iris image comes from the random texture pattern, but how to model the randomness of iris signal efficiently? This is a very important problem in the field of iris recognition but it has not a clear and unified answer. Our newly publication [4] made an attempt to this problem. We found that several accurate

S.Z. Li et al. (Eds.): Sinobiometrics 2004, LNCS 3338, pp. 67–77, 2004.

iris recognition algorithms share a same idea—local ordinal encoding, which is a representation of iris image well-suited for recognition. After further analysis and summarization, a general framework of iris feature extraction is formulated. As a continuous work, in this paper we want to update this model from local comparisons to non-local comparisons, from pair-wise ordinal contrast to multiple regions' ordinal relationship. The motivation of this work comes from Sinha lab's [5] research on image representation via non-local comparisons [6]. In their experiments, non-local measurements appear to be more stable against a range of common image degradations than purely local ones. As we mentioned in [4] that iris feature extraction can be regarded as a procedure of robust parameter estimation and the main issue in iris recognition is to obtain a representation insensitive to various intra-class variations. Non-local ordinal measures are just for this purpose. So we decided to develop an iris feature extractor based on non-local comparisons.

The remainder of this paper is organized as follows. Section 2 gives a brief review of the general framework of iris recognition. The novel iris recognition method based on non-local comparisons will be introduced in Section 3. Section 4 reports the experimental results. In Section 5, we will discuss the method and figure out some meaningful works in the future. At last, we conclude the paper in Section 6.

2 Robust Encoding of Local Ordinal Measures

The acquired iris signal typically varies significantly from presentation to presentation. The sources causing intra-class iris variations include different illumination settings, occlusions of eyelids and eyelashes, nonlinear iris deformations, dust on the eyeglasses, specular reflections and iris alignment errors. Therefore the iris image representation should be robust against all sources of noises or variations without compromising discriminating power. Although absolute intensity values of image regions are not reliable for recognition, their mutual ordinal relationships are stable under different conditions of capture. In addition, the complex iris texture provides a rich source of local sharp variations. Therefore local ordinal measure [7] is a good candidate to represent iris image contents. In fact, many existing iris recognition methods used this information implicitly. A common practice to compare local regions is based on differential filters. After filtering, the local region covered by the operator is coded as 1 or 0 based on the sign of the filtering result. For example, Daugman [8] employed the Gabor filters (Figure 1a and 1b) to obtain 256 Bytes iris code, i.e. 2048 ordinal relationships. Noh et al. [9] used the Haar wavelet transform (Figure 1c) to obtain the relative information along the columns of the normalized iris image. Tan et al. [10] thresholded the spline wavelet transform's (Figure 1d) results to encoding the local ordinal information. These methods [8,9,10] all achieved good recognition performance.

Based on above observations, a general framework of iris recognition [4] is formulated in Figure 2. With the guidance of this framework, a novel iris recognition method based on robust estimating the direction of image gradient vector is developed [11]. The direction of image gradient vector also denotes a kind of local ordinal relationship, providing the information along which direction the intensity contrast is the most sharp.

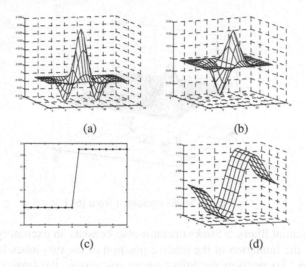

(a)   (b)

(c)   (d)

Fig. 1. Differential filters employed by different iris recognition algorithms; (a) Even Gabor filter; (b) Odd Gabor filter; (c) Discrete Haar wavelet; (d) Quadratic spline wavelet

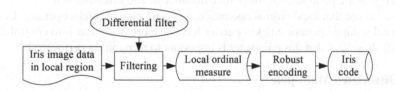

Fig. 2. Robust encoding of local ordinal measures

3 Non-local Comparisons for Iris Recognition

3.1 Dissociated Dipole

It is obvious existing iris recognition methods only used the local relative relationships, ignoring the rich ordinal information between the long-distance regions. Because the adjacent regions are dependent each other, the probability that two distant regions in an iris image will differ is much greater than that of two adjacent regions [6]. Therefore long-distance comparisons are more tolerant to common image degradations than purely local ones. In addition, adjacent image regions are information redundant so comparing distant image regions will increase single iris code's information capacity. But the differential filters are not able to compare distant small image regions due to the conflation of the size of the differential filter's lobes with the distance spanned by that operator [6].

So Balas and Sinha proposed a kind of novel operator, named as "Dissociated Dipole" or "Sticks" (See Figure 3), to encode the non-local image relationships [6].

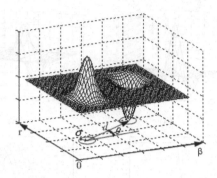

Fig. 3. Sticks operator (from [6])

Like differential filters, a Sticks operator also consists an excitatory and an inhibitory lobe. But the limitation of the relative position of the two lobes is removed from common filters. To perform the Sticks on an iris image, the image should be pre-processed first. The details of iris image pre-processing can be found in [8,10].

In the coordinates shown in Figure 3, there are three parameters in Sticks operator for tuning: scale parameter σ, inter-lobe distance d, and orientation θ.

We can see that local ordinal operator is a special case of Sticks operator. Compared with local ordinal operator, Sticks operator has one more parameter d to control the filter. We will show later that this parameter is important to recognition performance.

3.2 Dissociated Multi-pole

In this subsection, we want to extend Balas and Sinha's non-local filter "Dissociated Dipole" to "Dissociated Multi-Pole". Different from Dissociated Dipole, Dissociated Multi-Pole may be combined by many spatial randomly distributed lobes. The shape of these lobes also may be different. The motivation is straightforward. When more than two image regions are compared, the derived ordinal measure should be more robust. In addition, an ordinal measure extracted by Dissociated Multi-Pole can represent more complex image micro-structures. Comparatively, Dissociated Dipole can only tell us a slope edge's orientation. An example of Dissociated Multi-Pole is shown in Figure 4.

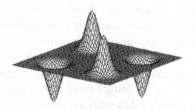

Fig. 4. Dissociated Multi-Pole

To be effective for iris recognition or image representation, there are three rules in development of Dissociated Multi-Pole (DMP):

1) Each lobe of DMP should be a low-pass filter. On one hand, intensity information of the region covered by the lobe can be statistically estimated; on the other hand, the image noises are attenuated by low-pass filtering.
2) To obtain the locality of the operator, the coefficients of each lobe should be such arranged that the weight of a pixel is inverse proportional to its distance from the lobe center. Gaussian mask satisfies this rule well, but it is not the only one.
3) The sum of all lobes' coefficients should be zero, so that the iris code of a non-local comparison has equal probability being one or zero. Thus the entropy of single iris code is maximized. In the example shown in Figure 4, the sum of two excitatory lobes' weights is equal to the inhibitory lobes' total absolute weights.

Compared with Sticks operator, DMP is a more general concept. So all ideas of ordinal measures could be unified into the framework of DMP. Similar to the framework illustrated in Fig. 2, the block diagram of iris recognition based on non-local comparisons is demonstrated in Figure 5.

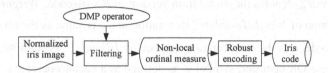

Fig. 5. Block diagram of iris recognition based on non-local comparisons

The DMP operator slides across the whole normalized iris image, and each non-local comparison is encoded as one bit, i.e. 1 or 0 according to the sign of the filtering result. All the binary iris codes constitute a composite feature of the input iris image. The dissimilarity between two iris images is determined by the Hamming distance of their features [8]. In order to complement the possible rotation difference between the two iris images, the input iris code is circularly rotated at different starting angles to match the template iris code. And the minimum Hamming distance of all matching results is the measure describing the dissimilarity between the two iris images. Because the preprocessing has complemented the position and scale differences between two iris images, the whole procedure of iris matching is insensitive to the iris data's position, scale and rotation variance.

In conclusion, iris feature based on non-local comparisons (Fig. 5) represents iris image contents in three levels of locality: each iris feature element (iris code) describes the ordinal information of an image region covered by the DMP, which is localized by the central *pixel* of the image region; and each ordinal measure is jointly determined by several *regions'* averaged intensities; in the end all ordinal measures are concatenated to build a *global* description of the iris.

3.3 Weighted Ordinal Measures

For the normalized iris image, the importance of each iris code may be different because some image regions have higher possibility to be occluded by eyelids or eyelashes. Because it is not efficient to detect all occlusions of iris images in practice, we
want to establish a general weighting template to alleviate the influence of these occlusions. The weighting template is learned from thousands of intra-class matching
results. Recognition performance of each bit iris code is individually measured.
Higher recognition rate, more weight is assigned to the iris code. After coarsely quantization, all weights constitute a composite weighting template. Based on the weighting template, the dissimilarity between two iris images A and B is measured by their
weighted Hamming distance:

$$HD_{AB} = \min\{HD^i_{AB}(Iriscode_A, Iriscode^i_B), i = 1, 2, \cdots, n\} \tag{1}$$

$$HD^i_{AB}(Iriscode_A, Iriscode^i_B) = \frac{Sum[(Iriscode_A \otimes Iriscode^i_B) \times (WeightTemplate \times WeightTemplate^i)]}{Sum(WeightTemplate \times WeightTemplate^i)} \tag{2}$$

where $Iriscode^i_B$ denotes the ith rotation version of B's iriscode, $WeightTemplate^i$ is a
rotation version of $WeightTemplate$, its rotation angle is same as the ith rotation angle
of B's iriscode, n is the total rotation number of $Iriscode_B$, symbol $\otimes$ denotes Boolean Exclusive-OR operator, symbol $\times$ is defined as a vector operator :

$$(x_1, x_2, \cdots, x_m) \times (y_1, y_2, \cdots, y_m) = (x_1 y_1, x_2 y_2, \cdots, x_m y_m) \tag{3}$$

$$sum(X(x_1, x_2, \cdots x_m)) = \sum_{j=1}^{m} x_j \tag{4}$$

HD_{AB} ranges from 0 (absolute matched) to 1 (absolute not matched), providing a
quantitative distance for identity verification. If HD_{AB} is lower than some threshold, A
and B are determined from same eye, or else they are regarded as inter-class samples.

4 Experiments

In order to evaluate the recognition performance of various methods, CASIA Iris
Image Database is used as the test dataset, which has been worldwide shared for research purposes [12]. The database includes 2,255 iris image sequences from 306
different eyes (hence 306 different classes) of 213 subjects. To satisfy requirement of
using images captured in different stages for training and testing respectively, 100
sequences taken at the early time are not used in the experiments. The images are
separated to two sets: a training set of 918 template sequences (Three sequences per
eye) and a testing set of 1,237 sequences of all people. For the images of the same eye,
the time interval between the samples in the training set and the instances of testing set

is more than one month and the longest interval is about six months. The format of the data is 8-bits gray level image with resolution 320×280. Ten images in each sequence are automatically selected by image quality assessment module [13], but there are still some poor quality iris images used. In order to test our scheme in a low Failure to Enrollment Rate (FTE) situation, we randomly select an image from the ten qualified images of each sequence to construct a challenging dataset. All possible comparisons are made between the data collected at two different times. So there are a total of 918×1,237= 1,135,566 comparisons between the test images and the model data, including 3,711 intra-class comparisons and 1,131,855 inter-class comparisons.

Sticks operator is the simplest Dissociated Multi-Pole operator, which will be tested on CASIA dataset. Because the most discriminating information of iris image is along the angular direction, the orientations of tested Sticks operators are all set to be parallel with angular direction in normalized iris image. To investigate the influence of inter-lobe distance on recognition performance, two versions of Sticks operators with same parameters but different d are evaluated. The size of basic lobe is 5 by 5, we choose $d=5$ and $d=9$ to represent local ordinal operator and non-local operator. For simplicity, we take Dissociated Tripole (DTP) as an example of Dissociated Multi-Pole. To capture the most distinctive iris features, a DTP operator is also designed along the angular direction in the normalized iris image. Three lobes are arranged in a line and the inhibitory lobe is located between two excitatory lobes (Figure 6).

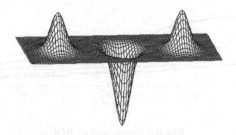

Fig. 6. Dissociated Tripole used for testing

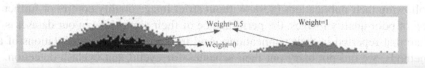

Fig. 7. Iris code weighting template

The weight template learned from another dataset (randomly resample the 2155 iris image sequences again) is shown in Figure 7. The weights are quantified to three levels based on the average Hamming distance of 3,711 intra-class comparisons in training set. The weights of iris codes in white region is set to 1.0 because the average Hamming distance in this region is smaller than 0.3; the weights of iris codes in gray region is set to 0.5 because the average Hamming distance in this region is smaller than 0.5 but larger than 0.3. Even though inter-class iris matching's average Hamming distance is 0.5, so the weights of black region are set to 0 because the average Hamming distance in this region is less than 0.5. We can see that the iris regions whose weights are not equal to one are often occluded by eyelids and eyelashes. The experimental results are consistent with our observations. Despite the weighting strategy has not been optimized, the improvement of recognition accuracy is significant.

For the purpose of comparison with the state-of-the-art iris recognition methods, the recognition performance of several typical local ordinal measure filters ([8-11], Sticks operator with d=5) as well as some non local operators (Sticks operator with d=9, Dissociated Tripoles) are shown in Fig. 8.

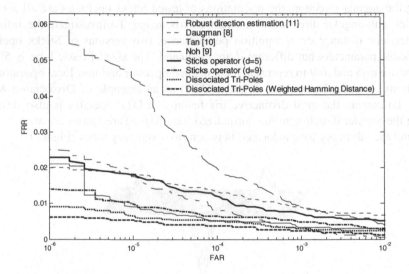

Fig. 8. Comparison of ROCs

It should be pointed out that both Daugman's and Noh's algorithms are coded following their publications [8,9]. Without strict image quality control or further filtering of poor quality images, the performance of their algorithms in our dataset is worse than that reported in their publications. And in our current implementations of all the methods, we did not carry out their schemes for eyelid and eyelash detection. However, this should not influence comparison experiments and the resulting conclusions in this paper.

5 Discussions and Future Work

Based on the above experimental results, we can draw a number of conclusions as well as find that some issues need to be further investigated.

1. The recognition performance of local comparisons (Sticks operator with d=5) is similar to the state-of-the-art iris recognition algorithms' results [8-11], which is determined by the nature of their internal representations of iris image structure because they are all based on local ordinal measures. This evidence supports the previously established general framework of iris recognition [4].

2. From Fig. 8, we can see that non-local ordinal features are more discriminative than local ordinal features for iris recognition, this conclusion is consistent with Sinha's discovery [6] that non-local comparison is more robust for image content representation; non-local comparison of three regions is more effective for recognition than Dissociated Dipole; weighted Hamming distance can improve recognition accuracy. Because existing iris recognition methods only used local ordinal features, our methods based on non-local comparisons are in leading position of iris recognition field.

3. Local and non-local ordinal measures are complementary each other, so we can improve the iris recognition performance by information fusion. And integration of Sticks operators with different inter-lobe distances, orientations and scales can further improve the accuracy of iris recognition.

4. Balas and Sinha's psychophysical experiments [6] proved the plausibility of long-distance comparison of two regions. It still needs an experiment to verify the plausibility of subjects' ability to compare three or more distant image regions simultaneously. Another question deserving of further research is the possibility that neural systems in the mammalian visual pathway execute Dissociated Multi-Pole operator.

5. Mukherjee et al. [14] have developed a regularization approach for image reconstruction from local ordinal measures. How to reconstruct images from Dissociated Multi-Pole operator's results? Although the reconstruction is not necessary for recognition, image compression based on the Dissociated Multi-Pole operator is possible if the answer is "yes".

6. The main computational costs of our methods are paid on low-pass filtering. There are many fast algorithms available for this purpose, such as Sum-box technique [15] or integral image [16]. We can simplify the feature extraction procedure to additions and subtractions. This work will facilitate the realization of iris recognition algorithms via hardware and make real-time iris recognition possible in the embedded systems, such as PDA and cell phone.

6 Conclusions

In this paper, non-local ordinal measures are utilized for iris recognition. The experimental results are very encouraging, showing that the novel method is superior to existing algorithms in terms of accuracy. Since Dr. Daugman's pioneer work in 1993 [8], iris recognition accuracy has never been substantially improved because all the algorithms proposed before are limited in local comparisons. Compared with local ordinal measures, well-developed non-local ordinal measures are more suited for iris recognition. The works in this paper greatly enrich the previous general framework of iris recognition from local comparisons to non-local comparisons. Because the local relationships are the special cases of non-local comparisons, the framework can be updated as "robust encoding of non-local ordinal measures" (See Fig. 5). This is a revolution of iris recognition since this paper discovers that there are many useful contents of iris images have been ignored for recognition. With the guidance of this novel framework, new and improved iris recognition systems are expected to be developed. Although the method based on non-local comparisons is developed in the context of iris recognition, we think this is a general scheme for image representation applicable to many other detection or recognition tasks.

Acknowledgement

This work is funded by research grants from the Natural Science Foundation of China (Grant No. 60335010, 60121302, 60275003, 60332010, 69825105) and the Chinese Academy of Sciences.

References

1. A. Jain, R. Bolle, and S. Pankanti, Biometrics: Personal Identification in a Networked Society, Norwell, MA: Kluwer, 1999.
2. D. Zhang, Automated Biometrics: Technologies and Systems, Norwell, MA: Kluwer, 2000.
3. http://www.iridiantech.com
4. Zhenan Sun, Tieniu Tan, Yunhong Wang, "Robust Encoding of Local Ordinal Measures: A General Framework of Iris Recognition", in D. Maltoni and A.K. Jain (Eds.): Proceedings of the ECCV 2004 International Workshop on Biometric Authentication (BioAW), Lecture Notes in Computer Science, Vol.3087, pp. 270–282, Springer-Verlag Berlin Heidelberg, 2004.
5. The Sinha Laboratory for Vision Research at MIT, http://web.mit.edu/bcs/sinha/home.htm.
6. B. Balas and P. Sinha, "Dissociated Dipoles: Image Representation via Non-local Comparisons", CBCL Paper #229/AI Memo #2003-018, Massachusetts Institute of Technology, Cambridge, MA, 2003.
7. P. Sinha, "Qualitative Representations for Recognition". In: H.H. Bülthoff, S.-W. Lee, T.A. Poggio, C. Wallraven (Eds.): Biologically Motivated Computer Vision. Lecture Notes in Computer Science, Vol. 2525. Springer-Verlag, Heidelberg, pp.249–262, 2002.
8. J. Daugman, "High Confidence Visual Recognition of Persons by a Test of Statistical Independence", IEEE Trans. Pattern Analysis and Machine Intelligence, Vol.15, No.11, pp.1148–1161, 1993.
9. S. Noh, K. Bae, and J. Kim, "A Novel Method to Extract Features for Iris Recognition System", Proc. the 4th International Conference on Audio- and Video-Based Biometric Person Authentication, pp.862–868, 2003.
10. L. Ma, T. Tan, Y. Wang, and D. Zhang, "Efficient Iris Recognition by Characterizing Key Local Variations", IEEE Trans. Image Processing, Vol. 13, No. 6, pp.739–750, 2004.
11. Zhenan Sun, Yunhong Wang, Tieniu Tan, Jiali Cui, "Robust Direction Estimation of Gradient Vector Field for Iris Recognition", Proceedings of the 17th International Conference on Pattern Recognition, Vol.2, pp.783–786, IEEE Computer Society Press, 2004.

12. CASIA Iris Image Database, Chinese Academy of Sciences, Institute of Automation, http://www.sinobiometrics.com/casiairis.htm.
13. L. Ma, T. Tan, Y. Wang, and D. Zhang, "Personal Identification Based on Iris Texture Analysis", IEEE Trans. PAMI, Vol. 25, No.12, pp.1519-1533, 2003.
14. S. Mukherjee, S. Thoresz, P. Sinha, "The Fidelity of Local Ordinal Encoding", In T. Dietterich, S. Becker & Z. Ghahramani (Eds.), Advances in Neural Information Processing Systems (14). MIT Press: Cambridge, MA, 2002.
15. Jun Shen, Wei Shen, Serge Castan, and Tianxu Zhang, "Sum-box technique for fast linear filtering", Signal Processing, Vol. 82, pp.1109–1126, 2002.
16. P. Viola and M. Jones, "Rapid Object Detection Using a Boosted Cascade of Simple Features", Proc. Conf. Computer Vision and Patter Recognition, pp.511–518, 2001.

Palmprint Authentication Technologies, Systems and Applications

David Zhang[1], Guangming Lu[2], Adams Wai-Kin Kong[1, 3], and Michael Wong[1]

[1] Biometric Research Centre, Department of Computing,
The Hong Kong Polytechnic University, Kowloon, Hong Kong
{csdzhang, csmkwong}@comp.polyu.edu.hk
http://www.comp.polyu.edu.hk/~biometrics
[2] Biocomputing Research Lab,
School of Computer Science and Engineering,
Harbin Institute of Technology, Harbin, China
Luguangm@hit.edu.cn
[3] Electrical and Computer Engineering,
University of Waterloo, Ontario, Canada N2L 3G1
adamskong@ieee.org

Abstract. This paper presents a novel personal authentication system using palmprints. The technology uses the unique information extracted from palmprints (such as principal lines, wrinkles, and textures) during the authentication process to eliminate possible frauds that cannot be avoided by traditional methods (using password or cards). The uniqueness of features and robustness of algorithm make the system far superior to existing biometric systems. This paper first presents the system architecture construction and the algorithm design. Being a robust and reliable system, it was tested by more than 8,000 palmprint images with very low false acceptance rate (0.02%), and a relative high genuine acceptance rate (98.83%). The whole process time for once authentication is less than 1 second. Finally some possible applications are discussed which could be benefited by using palmprint technology.

1 Introduction

Personal authentication plays a critical role in our society. e-Commerce applications such as e-Banking or security applications such as building entrance demand fast, real time, and accurate personal identification. Knowledge-based approaches use "something that you know" (such as passwords and personal identification numbers [1]) for personal identification; token-based approaches, on the other hand, use "something that you have" (such as passports or credit cards) for the same purpose. Tokens (e.g. credit cards) are time consuming and expensive to replace. These approaches are not based on any inherent attribute of an individual in the identification process made them unable to differentiate between an authorized person and an impostor who fraudulently acquires the "token" or "knowledge" of the authorized person. This is why biometrics identification or verification system started to be more focused in the recent years.

S.Z. Li et al. (Eds.): Sinobiometrics 2004, LNCS 3338, pp. 78–89, 2004.

Biometrics involves identifying an individual based on his/her physiological or behavioral characteristics. Using biometrics for personal authentication is not new, which has been implemented over thousands years. Undoubtedly, face recognition is a direct and intuitive approach for human beings as the most common biometric. But fingerprint and signature are regarded as the two most important biometrics technologies which have been used to approbate the contents of a document or to authenticate a financial transaction with long history. Other biometric technologies such as iris, hand geometry and voice recognition systems have also been deployed for various applications in recent years [1]. After the 911 terrorist attacks, the interest on biometrics-based security solutions and applications has increased dramatically. This further pushes the demand on the development of different biometrics products.

Among all biometric technologies, hand-based biometric including, hand geometry and fingerprint is the most popular biometrics gaining about 60% of market shares in 2004 [2]. The proposed palmprint authentication system is a hand-based biometric technology exploiting the features in the inner surface of our palm for personal identification. We expect that the palmprint authentication system could receive a high user acceptance rate, similar to that of the fingerprint, hand geometry and hand vein technologies [3-6]. We believe that palmprints has enough stable and distinctive information for separating an individual from a large population because of its rich features (principal lines, wrinkles and palmprint texture). In addition, its large surface area and touchless acquisition method had a beneficial effect on the noise resistance for the effective feature extraction.

There have been some companies, including NEC and PRINTRAK, which have developed several palmprint systems for criminal applications [7-8]. On the basis of fingerprint technology, their systems exploit high resolution palmprint images to extract the detailed features like minutiae for matching the latent prints. Such approach is not suitable for developing a palmprint authentication system for civil applications. It requires a fast, accurate and reliable method for the personal identification. On the basis of our previous research work [9], we developed a novel palmprint authentication system to fulfill such requirements. This paper provides the whole picture on the implementation of a personal authentication system using palmprint, reveals the system architecture, and presents possible applications.

The rest of the paper is organized as follows. The system architecture is shown in Section 2. The recognition module is described in Section 3. Experimental results of verification, identification, robustness, and computation time are provided in Section 4. Some possible applications of personal authentication using palmprint are revealed in Section 5, and finally conclusions are given in Section 6.

2   System Architecture

The proposed palmprint authentication system has four major components: *User Interface Module, Acquisition Module, Recognition Module* and *External Module*. Fig. 1 shows the details of each module of the palmprint authentication system.

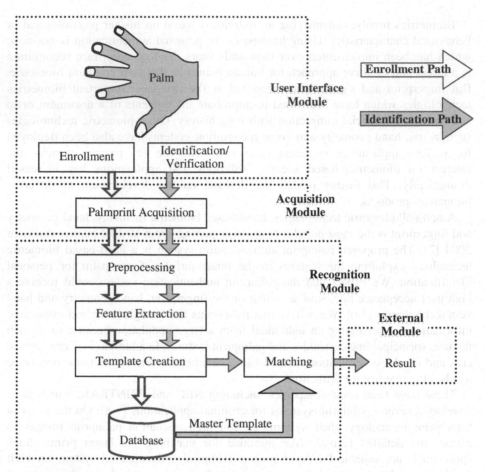

Fig. 1. The breakdown of each module of the palmprint authentication system

The functions of each component are listed below:

A) *User Interface Module* provides an interface between the system and users for the smooth authentication operation. It is crucial to develop a good user interface such that users are pleasure to use the device so that we designed a flat platen surface for the palm acquisition [10]. Also, there are some servicing functions provided for the administrator, such as enroll user, delete user, etc. A small LCD display will show appropriate message to instruct the users in the enrollment process and during/after the identification process.

B) *Acquisition Module* is the channel for the palm to be acquired for the further processing. It calls the frame grabber to transfer one frame of image to the processor, and then examines whether a hand has put on the device.

C) *Recognition Module* is the key part of our system, which determines whether a user is authenticated. It consists of image preprocessing algorithm to detect the key points of the hand for central part extraction, feature extraction algorithm to obtain some effective features, template creation to store the registered features (during enrolment), database updating to add the new user information (during enrolment), and matching to compare the input features and templates from the database (on the identification process).

D) *External Module* receives the signal come from the recognition module to allow some operations to be performed or denied the operations requested. This module actually is an interfacing component, which may be connected to another hardware or software components. Currently, our system uses a relay to control an electronic door lock for the physical access control. On the other hand, if the proposed system is used on an employee attendance system, it keeps track of the record on who has identified at what time, and finally sends this information to the respective accounting system.

The design methodology and implementation of the user interface module and the acquisition module have been described in detail in [10]. The external module is an interfacing component which is application dependent. In this paper, we are not intended to discuss these modules any more; we only concentrate on the discussion about the recognition module and the performance issues of the proposed system.

3   Recognition Module

After the palmprint images are captured by the *Acquisition Module*, they are fed into the recognition module for palmprint authentication. The recognition module is the key part of the palmprint authentication system, which consists of the stages of: image preprocessing, feature extraction, and matching.

3.1 Preprocessing

When capturing a palmprint, the position, direction and stretching degree may vary from time to time. The preprocessing algorithm is used to align different palmprints and extract the corresponding central part for feature extraction [9]. In our palmprint system, both the rotation and translation are constrained to some extent by the pegs on the user interface panel. We use the holes between fingers as the parameters to build a coordinate system for aligning different palmprint images by the following five steps:

Step 1: Apply a lowpass filter, $L(u, v)$, such as Gaussian, to an original image, $O(x, y)$. A threshold, T_p, is used to convert the convolved image to a binary image, $B(x, y)$, as shown in Fig. 2 (b).

Step 2: Obtain the boundaries of the holes, $(F_i x_j, F_i y_j)$ $(i=1, 2)$, between fingers using a boundary tracking algorithm (see Fig. 2 (c)). The boundary of the hole between ring and middle fingers is not extracted since it is not useful for the following processing.

Step 3: Compute the tangent of the two holes. Let (x_1, y_1) and (x_2, y_2) be any points on $(F_1 x_j, F_1 y_j)$ and $(F_2 x_j, F_2 y_j)$, respectively. If the line $(y=mx+c)$ passing though these two points satisfies the inequality, $F_i y_j \leq m F_i x_j + c$, for all i and j (see Fig. 2 (d)), then the line $(y = mx + c)$ is considered as the tangent of the two holes.

Step 4: Line up (x_1, y_1) and (x_2, y_2) to get Y-axis in palmprint coordinate system and make a line passing through the midpoint of the two points, which is perpendicular to this Y-axis to determine the origin of the system (see Fig. 2 (d)).

Step 5: Extract a sub-image with a fixed size on the basis of the coordinate system. The sub-image is located at a certain part of the palmprint image for feature extraction (see Figs. 2 (e)-(f)).

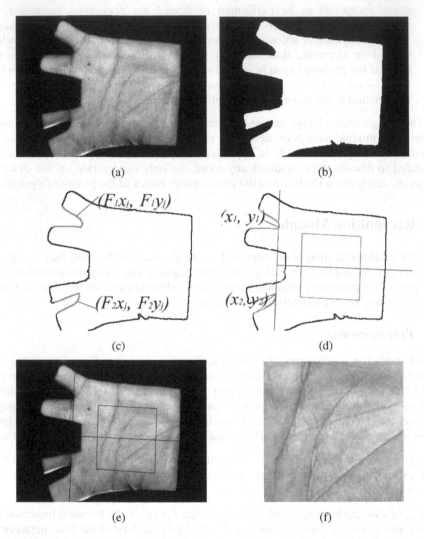

Fig. 2. The main steps of preprocessing. (a) Original image, (b) binary image, (c) boundary tracking, (d) building a coordinate system, (e) extracting the central part as a sub-image and (f) preprocessed result

3.2 Feature Extraction

The feature extraction technique implemented on the proposed palmprint system is modified from [9], where a single circular zero DC Gabor filter is applied to the preprocessed palmprint images and the phase information is coded as feature vector called PalmCode. The modified technique exploited four circular zero DC Gabor filters with the following general formula:

$$G_D = \frac{1}{2\pi\sigma^2} \exp\left\{-\frac{1}{2}\left[\frac{(x'-x_o)^2}{\sigma^2} + \frac{(y'-y_o)^2}{\sigma^2}\right]\right\}\left\{\exp(i2\pi\omega x') - \exp(-2\pi^2\omega^2\sigma^2)\right\} \quad (1)$$

where, $x' = x\cos\theta + y\sin\theta$ and $y' = -x\sin\theta + y\cos\theta$; (x_0, y_0) is the center of the function in the spatial domain of the function; ω is the frequency of the sinusoidal plane wave along the orientation, θ ; σ is the standard deviations of the circular Gaussian function; θ is the direction of the filter. The four Gabor filters share the same parameters, σ and ω, only different in θ. The corresponding values of θ are 0, $\pi/4$, $\pi/2$ and $3\pi/4$.

In the previous approach, only the phase information is exploited but the magnitude information is totally neglected. The proposed method is to use the magnitude to be a fusion condition to combine different PalmCodes generated by the four Gabor filters. Mathematically, the implementation has the following steps.

1. The four Gabor filters are applied to the preprocessed palmprint image, I described as G_j*I, where G_j (j=1, 2, 3, 4) is the circular zero DC Gabor filter and "*" represents an operator of convolution.

2. The square of the magnitudes of the sample point is obtained by $M_j(x,y) = G_j(x,y)*I \times \overline{G_j(x,y)*I}$, where "—" represents complex conjugate.

3. According to the fusion rule, $k = \arg\max_j(M_j(x,y))$, the phase information at point (x, y) is coded as the followings:

$$
\begin{array}{llll}
h_r = 1 & if & \operatorname{Re}[G_k * I] \geq 0, \\
h_r = 0 & if & \operatorname{Re}[G_k * I] < 0, \\
h_i = 1 & if & \operatorname{Im}[G_k * I] \geq 0, \\
h_i = 0 & if & \operatorname{Im}[G_k * I] < 0.
\end{array}
\quad (2)
$$

This coding method is named as Fusion Code. More discussion and comparisons between Fusion Code and PalmCode are given in [11]. It can be proved that Fusion Code is independent of the local contrast and brightness of the palmprint images.

3.3 Matching

The feature matching determines the degree of similarity between two templates – the authentication template and the master template. Since the format of Fusion Code and PalmCode are exactly the same, a normalized hamming distance implemented in PalmCode is still useful for comparing two Fusion Codes. Fusion Code is represented by a set of bits. Mathematically, the normalized hamming distance is represented by:

$$D_o = \frac{\sum_{i=1}^{N}\sum_{j=1}^{N} P_M(i,j) \cap Q_M(i,j) \cap \left((P_R(i,j) \otimes Q_R(i,j) + P_I(i,j) \otimes Q_I(i,j))\right)}{2\sum_{i=1}^{N}\sum_{j=1}^{N} P_M(i,j) \cap Q_M(i,j)}, \quad (3)$$

where P_R (Q_R), P_I (Q_I) and $P_M(Q_M)$ are the real part, imaginary part and mask of the Fusion Code $P(Q)$, respectively; $\otimes$ and $\cap$ are Boolean operators, XOR and AND, respectively. The ranges of normalized hamming distances are between zero and one, where zero represents perfect matches. Because of the imperfect preprocessing, one of the Fusion Code is vertically and horizontal translated to match the other again. The ranges of the vertical and the horizontal translations are defined from –2 to 2. The minimum D_0 value obtained from the translated matching is considered to be the final matching score.

4 Performance Evaluation

4.1 Testing Database

We collected palmprint images from 200 individuals using our palmprint capture device described in [9]. The subjects are mainly students and staff volunteers from The Hong Kong Polytechnic University. In this dataset, 134 people are male, and the age distribution of the subjects is: about 86% are younger than 30, about 3% are older than 50, and about 11% are aged between 30 and 50. In addition, we collected the palmprint images on two separate occasions. On each occasion, the subject was asked to provide about 10 images each of the left palm and the right palm. Therefore, each person provided around 40 images, resulting in a total number of 8,025 images from 400 different palms in our database. All the testing images used in the following experiments were 384 × 284 with 75 dpi.

4.2 Experimental Results of Verification

Verification refers to the problem of confirming or denying a claim of individuals and considered as one-to-one matching. Two groups of experiment are carried out separately. In the first experiment, each palmprint image is matched with all other palmprint images in the database. A correct matching occurs if two palmprint images are from the same palm; incorrect matching otherwise. Fig. 3 (a) shows the probability of genuine and imposter distributions estimated by the correct and incorrect matchings. Some thresholds and corresponding false acceptance rates (FARs) and false rejection rates (FRRs) are listed in Table 1 (a). According to Table 1 (a), using one palmprint image for registration, the proposed system can be operated at a low false acceptance rate 0.096% and a reasonably low false rejection rate 1.05%.

In the second experiment, the testing database is divided into two databases, 1) registration database and 2) testing database. Three palmprint images of each palm collected in the first occasion are selected for the registration database. Fig. 3 (b) shows the probability of genuine and imposter distributions estimated by the correct and incorrect matchings, respectively. Some threshold values along with its corresponding false acceptance and false rejection rates are also listed in Table 1 (a). According to Table 1 (a) and Fig. 3, we can conclude that using three templates can provide better verification accuracy. It is also the reason for those commercial biometric verification systems requiring more than one sample for registration.

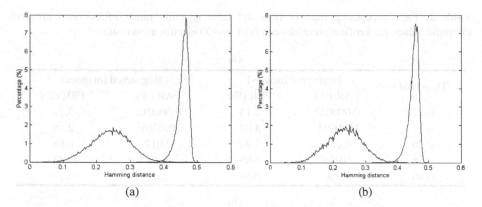

(a)   (b)

Fig. 3. Verification test results. (a) and (b) show the Genuine and imposter distributions for verification tests with one and three registered images per palm, respectively

4.3 Experimental Results of Identification

Identification test is a one-against-many, N comparison process. In this experiment, N is set to 400, which is the total number of different palms in our database. The registration database contains 1,200 palmprint images, three images per palm. The testing database has 6,825 palmprint images. Each palmprint image in the testing database is matched to all of the palmprint images in the registration database. The minimum hamming distances of correct matchings and incorrect matchings are regarded as the identification hamming distances of genuine and impostor, respectively. This experiment is also called a one-trial test since the user only provides one palmprint image in the test to make one decision. In fact, a practical biometric system collects several biometric signals to make one decision. Therefore, in this experiment, we implement one-, two- and three-trial tests. Fig. 4 shows ROC curves of the three tests and Table 1 (b) lists the threshold values along with its corresponding FARs and FRRs of the tests. According to Fig. 4 and Table 1 (b), more input palmprints can provide more accurate results.

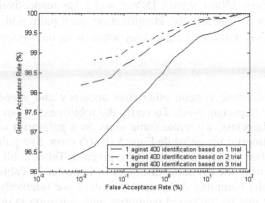

Fig. 4. The ROC curves on a 1-against-400 identification testing with different numbers of trials

Table 1. False acceptance rates (FARs) and false rejection rates (FRRs) with different threshold values, (a) verification results and (b) 1-to-400 identification results

(a)

Threshold	Registered image=1		Registered images=3	
	FAR (%)	FRR (%)	FAR (%)	FRR (%)
0.32	0.000027	8.15	0.000012	5.12
0.34	0.00094	4.02	0.0016	2.18
0.36	0.011	1.94	0.017	0.86
0.38	0.096	1.05	0.15	0.43
0.40	0.68	0.59	1.03	0.19

(b)

Threshold	Trial=1		Trial=2		Trial=3	
	FAR (%)	FRR (%)	FAR (%)	FRR (%)	FAR (%)	FRR (%)
0.320	0.0049	3.69	0.0098	1.80	0.020	1.17
0.325	0.0439	2.93	0.088	1.34	0.131	1.06
0.330	0.15	2.29	0.28	1.02	0.42	0.68
0.335	0.37	1.90	0.68	0.72	0.96	0.48
0.340	0.84	1.51	1.43	0.57	1.93	0.37
0.345	1.45	1.16	2.32	0.42	3.02	0.26

4.4 Response Time

Another key issue for a civilian personal authentication system is whether the system can run in real time. In other words, the system should response to the user quickly. The proposed method is implemented using C language and Assemble language on a PC embedded Intel Pentium IV processor (1.4GHz) with 128MB memory. The execution time for image collection, image preprocessing, feature extraction and matching are 340ms, 250ms, 9.8ms, 180ms, and 1.3μs respectively. That is, the total execution time for a 1-against-400 identification, each palm with 3 templates, is less than 1 second. Users will not feel any delay when using our system.

4.5 Robustness

As a practical biometric system, other than accuracy and speed, robustness of the system is another important issue. To verify the robustness of our proposed algorithm against noisy palmprints, we wrote some texts on a palmprint of a hand. Fig. 5 (a) shows a clear palmprint image while Figs. 5 (b)-(f) show five palmprint images, with different texts. Their hamming distances are given in Table 2; all of them are smaller than 0.29. Comparing the hamming distances of imposter in Tables 1 (a) and (b), it is ensured that all the hamming distances in Table 2 are relatively small. Figs. 5 and Table 2 illustrate that the proposed palmprint authentication system is very robust to the noise on the palmprint.

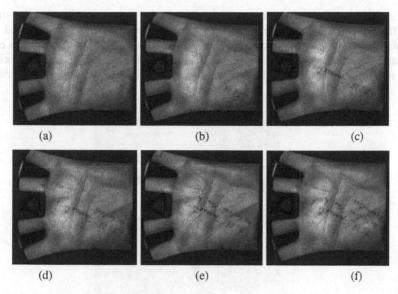

(a)   (b)   (c)

(d)   (e)   (f)

Fig. 5. Palmprint images with different texts for testing the robustness of the system

Table 2. The hamming distances of Fig. 5

Figs	5 (b)	5 (c)	5 (d)	5 (e)	5 (f)
5 (a)	0.19	0.21	0.27	0.29	0.28
5 (b)		0.18	0.27	0.26	0.27
5 (c)			0.27	0.28	0.28
5 (d)				0.23	0.19
5 (e)					0.19

5 Applications

Biometrics can be used in systems ranging from customer oriented to employee oriented applications to improve the work flow and eliminate frauds. Our system can be treated as a supplement of existing service or even a replacement of current method such as smart card or password based authentication systems. Our proposed system is an identification system, but it can also be used as a verification (authentication) system by adding a token such as smart card or PIN numbers.

One of the most popular biometric applications is the time and attendance system implemented to prevent frauds from buddy punching. In fact, our palmprint authentication system is most suitable to be used in this type of application because it can be operated in real time for identification/verification, has high accuracy rate and high user acceptance rate. In addition, our system has two modes of operations: identification and verification so that employees do not need to bring any card but their hand to identify their identity. Log files are stored on the file system and can be linked with external software for the automatic salary calculation.

Our system can be extended from a standalone system to a networked version. In addition, we provide different means of input methods such as barcode reader, smart card, and keyboard to allow the most flexible deployment arrangements for the need of different business organizations. In summary, our system can be used in the following applications: ATMs, credit card purchases, airports, building access control, time and attendance management, citizen ID program, biometric passport, voting and voter registration, etc. Fig. 6 shows a standalone version of our prototype system.

Fig. 6. A standalone version of our prototype system

6   Conclusions

In this paper, we have presented a novel personal authentication system using palmprints. The proposed system can accurately identify a person in real time, which is suitable for various civil applications such as access control and employee management systems. Experimental results show that the proposed system can identify 400 palms with very low false acceptance rate (0.02%), and a relative high genuine acceptance rate (98.83%). For verification, the system can operate at a false acceptance rate, 0.017% and a false rejection rate, 0.86%. The experimental results including accuracy, speed and robustness demonstrate that the palmprint authentication system is superior to other hand-based biometrics systems, such as hand geometry and fingerprint verification system [12-14] and is practical for real-world applications. The system has been installed at the Biometric Research Center, Department of Computing, The Hong Kong Polytechnic University since March 2003 for access control [10].

References

1. A. Jain, R. Bolle and S. Pankanti (eds.), Biometrics: Personal Identification in *Networked Society*, Boston, Mass: Kluwer Academic Publishers, 1999.
2. International Biometric Group's Biometric Market Report 2004-2008: http://www.biometricgroup.com/reports/public/market_report.html.

3. R. Sanchez-Reillo, C. Sanchez-Avilla and A. Gonzalez-Marcos, "Biometric identification through hand geometry measurements", *IEEE Transactions on Pattern Analysis and Machine Intelligence*, vol. 22, no. 10, pp. 1168-1171, 2000.

4. S.K. Im, H.M. Park, Y.W. Kim, S.C. Han, S.W. Kim and C.H. Kang, "An biometric identification system by extracting hand vein patterns", *Journal of the Korean Physical Society*, vol. 38, no. 3, pp. 268-272, 2001.

5. A. Jain, L. Hong and R. Bolle, "On-line fingerprint verification", *IEEE Transactions on Pattern Analysis and Machine Intelligence*, vol. 19, no. 4, pp. 302-314, 1997.

6. A.K. Jain, A. Ross and S. Prabhakar, "An introduction to biometric recognition", *IEEE Transactions on Circuits and Systems for Video Technology,* vol. 14, no. 1, January 2004.

7. NEC Solutions (America), Inc., 2002. *Automated Palmprint Identification System*, http://www.necsam.com/idsolutions/download/palmprint/palmprint.html

8. Omnitrak AFIS/Palmprint Identification Technology, http://www.motorola.com/LMPS/RNSG/pubsafety/40-70-10.shtml

9. D. Zhang, W.K. Kong, J. You and M. Wong, "On-line palmprint identification", *IEEE Transactions on Pattern Analysis and Machine Intelligence*, vol. 25, no. 9, pp. 1041-1050, 2003.

10. D. Zhang, *Palmprint Authentication*, Kluwer Academic Publishers, USA, 2004.

11. W.K. Kong and D. Zhang, "Feature-level fusion for effective palmprint identification", *Proceedings International Conference on Biometric Authentication*, Hong Kong, 15-17, July, 2004.

12. A.K. Jain, S. Prabhakar, L. Hong and S. Pankanti, "Filterbank-based fingerprint matching", *IEEE Transactions on Image Processing*, vol. 9, no. 5, pp. 846-859, 2000.

13. A.K. Jain, L. Hong and R. Bolle, "On-line fingerprint verification", *IEEE Transactions on Pattern Analysis and Machine Intelligence*, vol. 19, no. 4, pp. 302-314, 1997.

14. R. Sanchez-Reillo, C. Sanchez-Avilla and A. Gonzalez-Marcos, "Biometric identification through hand geometry measurements", *IEEE Transactions on Pattern Analysis and Machine Intelligence*, vol. 22, no. 18, pp.1168-1171, 2000.

Novel Face Detection Method Based on Gabor Features

Jie Chen[1], Shiguang Shan[2], Peng Yang[2], Shengye Yan[2], Xilin Chen[2], and Wen Gao[1,2]

[1] School of Computer Science and Technology,
Harbin Institute of Technology, 150001, China
[2] ICT-ISVISION JDL for AFR, Institute of Computing Technology,
CAS, Beijing, 100080, China
{jchen, sgshan, pyang, syyan, xlchen, wgao}@jdl.ac.cn

Abstract. Gabor-based Face representation has achieved great success in face recognition, while whether and how it can be applied to face detection is rarely studied. This paper originally investigates the Gabor feature based face detection method, and proposes a coarse-to-fine hierarchical face detector combining the high efficiency of Harr features and the excellent discriminating power of the Gabor features. Gabor features are AdaBoosted to form the final verifier after the cascade of Harr-based AdaBoost face detector. Extensive experiments are conducted on several face databases and verified the effectiveness of the proposed approach.

1 Introduction

Over the past ten years, face detection has been thoroughly studied in computer vision research for its interesting applications, such as video surveillance, human computer interface, face recognition, and face image database management etc. Face detection is to determine whether there are any faces within a given image, and return the location and extent of each face in the image if one or more faces present [20]. Recently, the emphasis has been laid on data-driven learning-based techniques, such as [5], [8], [9], [10], [12], [13], [14], [15] and [19]. All of these schemes can be found in the recent survey by Yang [20]. After the survey, the methods based on boosting are much researched. Viola described a rapid object detection scheme based on a boosted cascade of simple features. It brought together new algorithms, representations and insights, which could broader applications in computer vision and image processing [16]. Boosting is simple and easy to implement. It has been proven that Boosting minimizes an exponential function of the margin over the training set. However, a strong classifier learnt by AdaBoost is suboptimal for the applications in terms of the error rate [1]. Therefore, some improved versions are developed. Li et al. proposed a FloatBoost-based algorithm to guarantee monotonicity of the sequential AdaBoost learning and developed a real-time multi-view face detection system [7]. C. Liu et.al developed a general classification framework called Kullback-Leibler Boosting [6]. Xiao et.al proposed a boosting chain algorithm, which can combine the boosting classifiers into a hierarchy "chain" structure [18].

In face recognition, the Elastic Bunch Graph Matching (EBGM) has attracted much attention because it firstly exploited the Gabor transform to model the local features

S.Z. Li et al. (Eds.): Sinobiometrics 2004, LNCS 3338, pp. 90–99, 2004.

of faces [17]. However, EBGM takes the complete set of Gabor features and then most of them are redundant for classification. For examples, Fasel pointed out in [3] that the Gabor features used in [17] are not the best ones for the representation of facial landmarks. In [4], Huang et.al proposed a classification-based face detection method using Gabor filter features. But they utilized only the Gabor features. It would decrease the detection speed of the resulting detector.

This paper is an attempt to solve this question by introducing the AdaBoost method into the Harr+Gabor feature-based face detection detector. That is to say, the resulting detector will consist of weak classifiers based on the Harr and Gabor features and is boosted by AdaBoost. AdaBoost selects a set of Harr features as the first part of the cascade detector to increase the speed and a small set of available Gabor features from the extremely large set as the second part of the cascade detector to decrease the false alarms of the detector. The final strong classifier, which combines a few hundreds of weak classifiers (Harr+Gabor features), is evaluated on the test set.

The remaining part of this paper is organized as following: In section 2, the Gabor representation of faces is introduced. Section 3 describes the boosting learning for features selection and classifiers construction. Experiments and analyses are demonstrated in section 4, followed by a small discussion. Conclusions and future work are presented in section 5.

2 Gaborface

Gabor filter can capture salient visual properties such as spatial localization, orientation selectivity, and spatial frequency characteristics. Considering these excellent capacities and its great success in face recognition [11], we choose Gabor features to represent the face image besides the Harr-like features. Gabor filters are defined as following:

$$\psi_{u,v}(z) = \frac{\|k_{u,v}\|^2}{\sigma^2} e^{\left(-\frac{\|k_{u,v}\|^2\|z\|^2}{2\sigma^2}\right)} \left[e^{i\vec{k}_{u,v}z} - e^{-\frac{\sigma^2}{2}} \right], \tag{1}$$

where $k_{u,v} = k_v e^{i\phi_u}$; $k_v = \frac{k_{max}}{f^v}$ gives the frequency; $\phi_u = \frac{u\pi}{8}$, $\phi_u \in [0,\pi)$ gives the orientation; and $z = (x, y)$;

$$k_{u,v} = k_v e^{i\phi_u}, \tag{2}$$

where $e^{i\vec{k}_{u,v}z}$ is the oscillatory wave function whose real part and imaginary part are cosine function and sinusoid function, respectively. In equation 1, v controls the scale of Gabor filters, which mainly determines the center of the Gabor filter in the frequency domain; u controls the orientation of the Gabor filter.

In our experiment we use the Gabor filters with the following parameters [7]: five scales $v \in \{0,1,2,3,4\}$ and eight orientations $u \in \{0,1,2,3,4,5,6,7\}$ with $\sigma = 2\pi$, $k_{max} = \pi/2$, and $f = \sqrt{2}$.

The Gaborface, representing one face image, is computed by convoluting it with corresponding Gabor filters. Figure 1 shows the Gaborface representation of a face image.

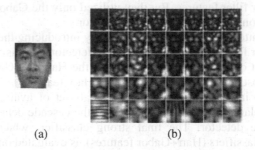

(a)   (b)

Fig. 1. Gaborface representation for one face

3 AdaBoost-Based Detector Training

As we know, boosting learning is a strong tool to solve two-class classification problems. Noticing the great success of AdaBoost in face detection area, we exploited it in our method to combine weak classifiers into a final strong one.

We use AdaBoost to select a small set of Harr or Gabor features (or weak classifiers) from the original extremely high dimensional Harr or Gabor feature space to form a strong classifier. A strong classifier learned by AdaBoost, is formed by:

$$S(x) = \sum_{t=1}^{T} \alpha_t h_t(x),$$

(3)

where α_m is the combining coefficient and $h_t(x)$ is a threshold function. How to derive α_m and $h_t(x)$ will be discussed in the following section.

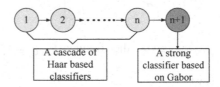

Fig. 2. A cascade classifier, combined by AdaBoost, has n+1 stages. The first n stages are n strong classifiers and each are composed of several weak classifiers based on Harr features. The $(n+1)^{st}$ stage is also a strong classifier and is composed of several weak classifiers but based on Gabor features

A large number of experimental studies have shown that classifiers combination can exploit the discriminating power of individual feature sets and classifiers. With the success of boosting in the application of face detection, boosting, as one of the most commonly used methods of combining classifiers based on statistical re-sampling techniques, boosting has shown its strong ability to discriminate the two-class problem. AdaBoost, a version of the boosting algorithm, is taken to solve this two-class problem. Herein, we use AdaBoost to train a strong classifier. A strong classifier is formed by AdaBoost, which combines a number of weak classifiers as shown in Fig.2.

Table 1. The AdaBoost algorithm for classifier learning

Given labeled examples set S and two threshold, δ_1, δ_2 :

- $i = 1$; The first stage error rate $F_1 = 1$;
- Train the first n-stage strong classifier based on the Harr feature.
  - ❈ While the first i stages error rate $F_i > \delta_1$
    1) Train a strong classifier by AdaBoost based on the Harr features;
    2) Calculate the $(i+1)^{st}$ stage error rate e_{i+1} ;
    3) The first $(i+1)^{st}$ stages error rate $F_{i+1} = F_i \times e_{i+1}$ and $i = i+1$;
  - ❈ Combine these n stages into a cascade detector
- Train the $(n+1)^{st}$ stage strong classifier based on the Gabor features.
  - ❈ While the $(n+1)^{st}$ stage error rate e_{n+1}, and $e_{n+1} \times \delta_1 > \delta_2$
    1) For each Gabor feature, k, train a classifier h_k with respect to the weighted samples as based on the Harr-like features;
    2) Calculate error rate
  - ❈ Combine all of these weak classifiers based on the Gabor features into a strong classifier.
- Combine the first n stages and the $(n+1)^{st}$ stage strong classifier into a resulting cascade detector.

The AdaBoost process is described in table 1. $S(x) = \sum_{t=1}^{T} \alpha_t h_t(x)$ of table 1 is demonstrated as equation (3), where $\alpha_m \geq 0$ is the combining coefficient which is learned as in the table 1.

4   Experiments and Analyses

4.1   Performance Comparison

To compare the representative ability of Harr and Gabor features for discriminating face and non face, we use two group feature sets. The first group consists of only Harr features while the second is composed of only Gabor features. The data set consists of a training set of 6,977 images (2,429 faces and 4,548 non-faces) and a test set of 24,045 images (472 faces and 23,573 non-faces). The images are 19×19 grayscale and re-normalized to 20×20. The data are available on the CBCL webpage [22]. Two different classifiers based on different feature set are trained on this training set as demonstrate in [16]. The detection performances on this test set are compared in Fig. 3. From the ROC curves one can find that the classifier based on the Gabor features outperforms the one based on the Harr distinctly. That is to say the Gabor features can describe the difference between the faces and non-faces more efficient than the Harr features.

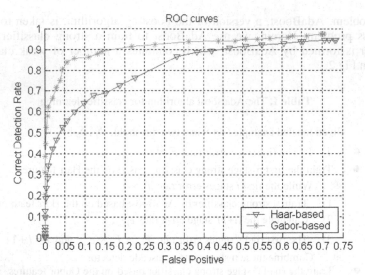

Fig. 3. The ROC curves for our detectors on the MIT face test set which are available on the CBCL webpage

4.2 Training the Detector

To compare the detector's performance improvement based on different feature set further, we use two group feature sets. The first group consists of only Harr features while the second is composed of both Harr and Gabor features. The first classifier is trained as described in [16] and the second is trained as shown in table 1. The face-image database consists of 6,000 faces (collected form Web), which cover wide variations in poses, facial expressions and lighting conditions. After the preprocessing by GA operations [2], we get 100,000 face images. For negative examples we start with 100,000 non-face examples from 16,536 images of landscapes, trees, buildings, etc. Although it is extremely difficult to collect a typical set of non-face examples, the bootstrap [15] is used to include more non-face examples during training.

In our experiment, all of the face samples are normalized to 20×20 and we use the Gabor filters with five scales and eight orientations. The number of Gabor features of each sample is $20 \times 20 \times 5 \times 8 = 16000$, from which the training algorithm would select tens of the most discriminant ones to form the last stage of the cascade detector as demonstrated in Fig 2 and table 1. To the second classifier, we run AdaBoost in 22 stages, a total of 4231 rounds, and got 4231 features. In this cascade, the first 21 stages are composed of weak classifiers based on Harr features with 4135 features while the last stage consists of 96 weak classifiers based on Gabor features.

4.3 Detection Results

The resulting detectors, trained on different features, are evaluated on the MIT+CMU frontal face test set, which consists of 130 images showing 507 upright faces [12]. The detection performances on this set are compared in Fig. 4. From the ROC curves one can find that we get the detection rate of 90.37% and 8 false alarms with the detector trained based on the Harr+Gabor feature set. P. Viola reported a similar detection capability of 89.7% with 31 false detects (by voting) [16]. However, different criteria (e.g. training time, number of training examples involved, cropping training set with different subjective criteria, execution time, and the number of scanned windows in detection) can be used to favor one over another, which will make it difficult to evaluate the performance of different methods even though they use the same benchmark data sets [20]. Some detected results on these test sets are shown in Fig. 5.

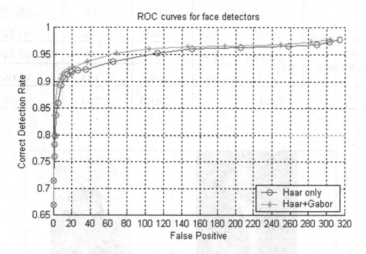

Fig. 4. The ROC curves for our detectors on the MIT+CMU frontal face test set

From the ROC curves we can also conclude that the detector trained on the Harr+Gabor feature set outperforms the detector trained only on the Harr feature set. The possible reason is that the Gabor feature can represent the difference between the face and non-face more efficient than the Harr feature only. Therefore, some false alarms by the classifier based on the Harr features in first part of the cascade are corrected by the classifier based on the Gabor features in the last stage.

The detector trained on the Harr+Gabor feature set is also tested on the other test set except that on the MIT+CMU frontal face test set. This test set is selected from the CAS-PEAL Face Database, which includes large-scale face images with different sources of variations, especially poses, expressions, accessories, and lighting [21]. The CAS-PEAL face database contains 99,594 images of 1,040 individuals (595 males and 445 females) with varying Pose, Expression, Accessory, and Lighting (PEAL). For each subject, 9 cameras spaced equally in a horizontal semicircular shelf are mounted to simultaneously capture images across different poses in one shot. Each subject is also asked to look up and down to capture 18 images in another two shots. It also considered 5 kinds of expressions, 6 kinds accessories (3 glasses, and 3 caps), and 15 lighting directions. A subset containing 24,018 images of 1,040 subjects is selected from this database because our detector is a frontal face detector. The detection results are listed in table 2. The frontal sub-directory consists of those images with only one frontal face in each image. The pose sub-directory is composed of those images with one face in multi-view but within 30° in each image. The sub-directory PD is those images with one face looking down; the sub-directory PM is those images with one face looking horizontally; the sub-directory PU is those images with one face looking up.

Table 2. Detection rates from various sub-directory on Set1

Data Set			Faces	False alarms	Detection rates
Results in each sub-directory	Frontal		9029	66	96.42%
	POSE (within 30°)	PD	4998	18	94.74%
		PM	4993	35	99.78%
		PU	4998	135	98.06%
Total			24018	254	97.08%

Fig. 5. Face detection on the MIT+CMU frontal face test set

From the table 2, one can find that the detector successfully detects 23,324 faces from the 24,018 images (each image contains only one face) with only 254 false detects. The highest hit rate is in the PM sub-directory because all faces in this file are frontal and have fewer variations than that of the frontal sub-directory, which has more poses, expressions, accessories, and lighting variations. It is these variations that lead to more false alarms and less hit rates in the frontal sub-directory. From this table, one can also find the images with looking-down faces are a little harder for the detector to locate than the images containing looking-up faces. It may be that the looking-down faces have more effect on the eyes and therefore make it difficult to distinguish these faces from the background. Fig. 6 shows examples of the detected faces, where a square indicates a face region successfully detected. Note that the resolution of the images is 640×480, and the faces are detected at different scales.

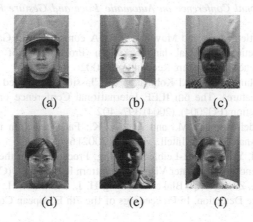

(a)   (b)   (c)

(d)   (e)   (f)

Fig. 6. Face detection results on some images from CAS-PEAL. (a) Accessories. (b), (c), (d), (e): lighting, multiple lamps and lanterns are used to cover varying lighting conditions, (f): pose

5 Conclusion

This paper originally investigates the possibility to apply Gabor features to face detection motivated by the success of Gabor feature in face identification and verification area. Our experiments have shown that Gabor feature-based representation does have more powerful discriminating capability. However, Gabor feature is too high dimensional and its computation is too time-consuming. Therefore, we further proposed a coarse-to-fine hierarchical face detector by combining the popular Harr features and Gabor features using the cascade AdaBoosting method, in which the time-consuming Gabor-based face verifier accomplishes the final validation of few candidates. Extensive experiments are conducted on CMU+MIT face database to evaluate the efficiency and effectiveness of the framework, which shows that only tens of Gabor features are enough for decreasing the false alarm rate with an acceptable detection speed.

Our future work will focus on how to improve the face detection framework based on Harr+Gabor by trading off the efficiency and accuracy. Also, how to extract the few Gabor feature rapidly should also be considered.

Acknowledgement

This research is partially sponsored by Natural Science Foundation of China under contract No.60332010, National Hi-Tech Program of China (No. 2001AA114190, 2002AA118010 and 2003AA142140), and ISVISION Technologies Co., Ltd.

98   J. Chen et al.

References

1. Buhlmann P. and Yu B.: Invited discussion on Additive logistic regressions: a statistical view of boosting (Friedman, Hastie and Tibshirani). *The Annual of Statistics*, 28(2): (2000) 377-386
2. Chen J., Gao W.. Expand Training Set for Face Detection by GA Re-sampling. *The 6th IEEE International Conference on Automatic Face and Gesture Recognition (FG2004).* (2004) 73-79
3. Fasel I. R., Bartlett M. S, and Movellan J. R: A comparison of Gabor filter methods for automatic detection of facial landmarks. In Proceedings of the 5th International Conference on Face and Gesture Recognition, 2002
4. Huang L.-L., Shimizu A., and Kobatake H.: Classification-Based Face Detection Using Gabor Filter Features. The 6th IEEE International Conference on Automatic Face and Gesture Recognition (FG2004). (2004) 397- 402
5. Hsu R. L., Abdel-Mottaleb M., and Jain A. K.: Face detection in color images. IEEE Trans. Pattern Anal. Machine Intell., vol. 24, (2002).696–706
6. Liu C., Shum H. Y.: Kullback-Leibler Boosting. Proceedings of the 2003 IEEE Computer Society Conference on Computer Vision and Pattern Recognition (CVPR'03). 2003.
7. Li S. Z., Zhu L., Zhang Z.Q., Blake A., Zhang H. J., and Shum H.: Statistical Learning of Multi-View Face Detection. In Proceedings of the 7th European Conference on Computer Vision. 2002.
8. Liu C. J.: A Bayesian Discriminating Features Method for Face Detection. IEEE Trans. Pattern Analysis and Machine Intelligence, vol. 25, June (2003) 725-740.
9. Osuna E., Freund R., and Girosi F.: Training support vector machines: An application to face detection. Proc. IEEE Computer Soc. Conf. on Computer Vision and Pattern Recognition, June 1997, pp. 130–136.
10. Papageorgiou C. P., Oren, M. and Poggio T.: A general framework for object detection. in Proc. 6th Int. Conf. Computer Vision, Jan. 1998, pp.555–562.
11. Phillips P. J., Moon H., Rauss P., and Rizvi. SA.: The FERET Evaluation Methodology for Face-Recognition Algorithms. Proceedings of Computer Vision and Pattern Recognition, Puerto Rico, (1997) 137-143
12. Rowley H. A., Baluja S., and Kanade T.: Neural Network-Based Face Detection. IEEE Tr. Pattern Analysis and Machine Intel. vol. 20, (1998) 23-38.
13. Rowley H. A., Baluja S., and Kanade T.: Rotation Invariant Neural Network-Based Face Detection. Conf. Computer Vision and Pattern Rec., (1998) 38-44.
14. Schneiderman H. and Kanade T.: A Statistical Method for 3D Object Detection Applied to Faces. Computer Vision and Pattern Recognition, (2000) 746-751.
15. Sung K. K., and Poggio T.: Example-Based Learning for View-Based Human Face Detection. IEEE Trans. on PAMI Vol.20. , No. 1, (1998) 39-51.
16. Viola P. and Jones M.: Rapid Object Detection Using a Boosted Cascade of Simple Features. Conf. Computer Vision and Pattern Recognition, (2001) 511-518.
17. Wiskott L., Fellous J., Kruger N., von der Malsburg C.: Face recognition by elastic bunch graph matching. IEEE Trans. PAMI, vol. 19, no. 7, (1997) 775-669,.
18. Xiao R., Li M. J., Zhang H. J.: Robust Multipose Face Detection in Images. IEEE Trans on Circuits and Systems for Video Technology, Vol.14, No.1 (2004) 31-41.
19. Yang M. H., Roth D., and Ahuja N.: A SNoW-Based Face Detector. Advances in Neural Information Processing Systems 12, MIT Press, (2000) 855-861.

20. Yang M. H., Kriegman D., and Ahuja N.: Detecting Faces in Images: A Survey. IEEE Tr. Pattern Analysis and Machine Intelligence, vol. 24, Jan. (2002) 34-58.
21. http://www.jdl.ac.cn/peal/index.html
22. http://www.ai.mit.edu/projects/cbcl/ software-dataset / index.html.

Optimal Shape Space and Searching
in ASM Based Face Alignment

Lianghua He[1], Stan Z. Li[2], Jianzhong Zhou[3], Li Zhao[1], and Cairong Zou[1]

[1] Southeast University, Dept. of Radio Eigneering, SiPaiLou 2#, Nanjing, P.R. China
[2] Microsoft Research Asia, Beijing Sigma Center, Beijing, 100080, P.R. China
[3] Southeast University, Research Center of Learning Science, SiPaiLou 2#, Nanjing P.R. China

Abstract. The Active Shape Models (ASM) is composed of two parts: the ASM shape model and the ASM search. The standard ASM, with the shape variance components all discarded and searching in image subspace and shape subspace independently, has blind searching and unstable search result. In this paper, we propose a novel idea, called Optimal Shape Subspace, for optimizing ASM search. It is constructed by both main shape and shape variance information. It allows the reconstructed shape to vary more than that reconstructed in the standard ASM shape space, hence is more expressive in representing shapes in real life. A cost function is developed, based on a careful study on the search process especially regarding relations between the ASM shape model and the ASM search. An Optimal Searching method using the feedback provided by the evaluation cost can significantly improve the performance of ASM alignment. This is demonstrated by experimental results.

1 Introduction

Accurate alignment of faces is very important for extraction of good facial features for success of applications such as face recognition, expression analysis and face animation. Active Shape Models (ASM)[1] proposed by Cootes et al is one successful shape models for object localization. In it, the local appearance model, which represents the local statistics around each landmark, efficiently finds the best candidate point for each landmark in searching the image. The solution space is constrained by the properly trained global shape model. Based on the accurate modeling of the local features, ASM obtains nice results in shape localization.

Usually, the dimensionality of the principal shape model is chosen to explain as high as 95%~98% of variation in the tangent shape space (TSS) so that the ASM model could approximate any shape in TSS accurately. The underlying assumption is that if the reconstruction error is small, the overall error of ASM search will also be small. This underlying assumption was taken for granted by previous works without any justification. However, our analysis of optimal shape subspace and optimal search processing for ASM shows that this is inadequate.

In standard ASM search, each point is first searched in ISS according to the profiles perpendicular to the object contour around it. Then shape mode constrain is

S.Z. Li et al. (Eds.): Sinobiometrics 2004, LNCS 3338, pp. 100–109, 2004.

performed to adjust the search result. These two steps are done alternatively and independently. If no evaluation is given to the search result and no direction constrain is given to the search process, the search will never stop and the result is very sensitive to the patch noise. Several evaluation methods are proposed [1],[2],[3],[4],[5], especially [4] can be used in a new image searching, but it needs to build the model of Active Appearance Model (AAM). As for shape model constraints, no discussion about it appears in previous works.

In this paper, The Optimal Shape Subspace (OSS) is proposed after analyzing the properties of ASM search subspace. The idea is the following: To minimize the error between the search result and the input, we should construct a search subspace which not only constrains the search in the principal shape space, but also allows the shape to vary as much as possible. The OSS allows good variations of shape information with minimal dimension. On the other hand, a simple evaluation method based on the point searching cost value in ISS is present to measure the quality of ASM search, to produce reliable search results. We also proposed a method to constraint the search actions according to the shape adjusted in OSS. At last, combining the evaluation and the constraints, we get an Optimal Searching method with the information from both image subspace (ISS) and OSS.

The rest of the paper is arranged as follows: In section 2, after describing ASM algorithm briefly, the optimal searching subspace is analyzed. In the end, we proposed the algorithm of construction. In Section 3, we focus on the question of ASM searching and give an optimal searching method. Experimental results are provided in Section 4 before conclusions are drawn in Section 5.

2 Optimal Shape Subspace in ASM

2.1 Traditional ASM Modeling

To train ASM model, shapes in image shape space (ISS) should first be annotated in the image domain, Then these shapes in ISS are aligned into those in tangent shape space (TSS), When a training set of the tangent shapes in TSS is given, the basis functions for the KLT are obtained by solving the eigenvalue problem $\Lambda = \Phi^T \Sigma \Phi$, where Σ is the covariance matrix, Φ is the eigenvector matrix of Σ, and Λ is the corresponding diagonal matrix of eigenvalues. The ASM model is trained by PCA, which can be seen as a linear transformation extracting a lower-dimensional subspace of the KL basis corresponding to the maximal eigenvalues. The ASM model can be written as: $x = \bar{x} + \Phi_t b$, where $\bar{x}$ is the mean tangent shape vector, $\Phi_t = \{\phi_1 | \phi_2 | \cdots | \phi_t\}$ which is a submatrix of Φ, contained the principle eigenvectors corresponding to the largest eigenvalues (sorted so that $\lambda_i \geq \lambda_{i+1}$), and b is a vector of shape parameters. For a given shape, its shape parameter is given by: $b = \Phi_t^T (x - \bar{x})$. The number of eigenvectors (t) to retain can be chosen in several ways [8]: The usual way is to choose so as to explain a given proportion (e.g. 98%) of the variance exhibited in the training data. We call this proportion the (subspace) explanation proportion. The total variance in the training data is the sum of all the eigenvalues $V_T = \sum \lambda_i$. We can then choose the t largest eigenvalues such that $\sum_{i=1}^{t} \lambda > \alpha V_T$, where α defines the explanation proportion of the total variation (for instance, 0.98 for 98%). Another way is to choose t so that the residual terms can be considered as noise. And an alternative approach is to choose enough modes that the model can approximate any training example to within a given accuracy. These ways are all based the reconstruction error which Zhao et al. [5] thought is not enough. They proposed a P-TSS shape subspace and get some better results.

2.2 The Optimal Shape Subspace (OSS)

We can see from above that the TSS in standard ASM and Zhao et al.[5] is constructed only considered the principal shapes and discarded all others components. This is some inadequate since every model to be described has much variance and we could not express them all in a given model space. Thus, we should consider the shape variance except the shape itself. As an optimal TSS, we think, it should have such properties: First, it can allow the shape it reconstructed varies as much as possible. When reconstructing a shape in it, we have the minimal reconstruction error. Second, its dimension should be as few as possible. Not only can it reduce the computation, but also the constraint when reconstructing is small. Third, which is the most important; the total changes between the search result and its reconstruction must be as small as possible, for we believe in some degree that the points after search are the best candidates in that iteration. The aim of reconstruction is to adjust the points, which deviate too much, but not to reconstruct a new shape. We call the shape subspace satisfied such three properties the Optimal Shape Subspace (OSS).

Among the three points, the last is the basic and others two can be deduced from it. If we want to move as few as possible points in shape adjusting, the reconstructed shape should vary very much, because every kind of shape could have much variance in real life, which means that the basis of OSS is variable as much as possible. This is consistence with the first. Certainly, if we use the whole shape space, we can get every possible linear combinatorial shape of training shapes. However, we should make more calculation, which would affect the efficiency. So the OSS should satisfy the second rule.

For the first one, the larger is the t , the more shapes this subspace can reconstruct. While for the second, the fewer the better. Considering the first and the second together, we decompose OSS into two parts: the principal shape subspace (PSSS) which control the shape in searching and the principal variance shape subspace (PVSS) to control the shape variance in searching. They are both the subspace of Φ with orthogonality: $OSS = PSSS \oplus PVSS$.

When constructing, the PSSS shares the same meaning of TSS and could be constructed like Φ_t in standard ASM. In this paper, we adopt the rule of Zhao et al. [5]; about 72% proportion of the variance exhibited in the training data is selected. But for PVSS, the construction suffers some difficulties. We should find a parameter to stand for the shape variance for every eigenvector. Supposed that every element of a given eigenvector is same and its projection coefficient changes, the whole shape will only transforms in shift, but will not change in itself (Shown in Figure 1 the last row). That is, only the variance of eigenvector itself controls the shape transformation. Thus, to select the eigenvectors with largest variance to construct PVSS is some reasonable. From Figure1 with the mouth model, we can see the larger the variance of the eigenvector is, the more deformable it can be. But it is necessary to get correlation of all candidates before constructing the PVSS, since maybe two or more eigenvectors express the same deformation with the difference only in the magnitude and sign, just like the 2nd and 3rd rows in Figure1. In order to satisfy the second point in OSS, one of them should be excluded.

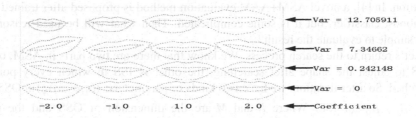

Fig. 1. The relationship between the eigenvectors variance and its deformability

In total, the steps of the proposed algorithm to construct the OSS are as follows:

1. Select the eigenvectors with 72% proportion of the variance in the training data.
2. Get the correlation matrix of the left eigenvectors.
3. Get the variance for the left eigenvectors.
4. Select the largest variance eigenvectors with least correlation coefficient. The number can be chosen in many ways, one can set the threshold of total number or the value of the variance. In this paper, we select the number half-auto, that is, we manually select the principal deformations in all the eigenvector candidates after printing.

There are two main improvements in constructing OSS. First, the major shape and shape variance are considered, So, It not only can reconstruct the shape similar to the training with least reconstruction error, but also it can approximate the shape, which has much difference from the training as much as possible. Second, the basis to control shape variance is selected after removing correlation, which would make the space more compressive.

3 Optimal Search Processing in ASM

After the OSS is constructed, the next work is searching. In traditional way or others [2,3,5], searching is performed in ISS and TSS alternately. No evaluation is given to the temporary search result and no discussion is made about the relation between the

ISS and TSS when searching. The underlying assumption is that the result after iteration in ISS and TSS is completely right. Obviously this assumption is not always right, for example, if we search a face in the image without one, the result is not right one any more. Thus, we can not get a stable result. It can be oscillatory when most of the points in right place in searching or wrong on the contrary. If we can evaluate the search result right away, we will know the result situation and decide whether it is right, so that we can select the best candidates to make further iteration. If we know the relation between ISS and TSS, we can search with more robust and more controllable by using the constraints from the information of ISS and TSS together.

The point-to-point error was used by most researchers to evaluate the searching result shape [1],[2],[3],[5]. But it could not be used because we do not know the true position. In [4], a novel ASM+AAM evaluation method is proposed after trained with Adaboost classifier, but it is some complicated. Then what will be used reasonable and simple to evaluate the result?

Let's return to the search process. We know that there are two parts in ASM, one is OSS to adjust the shape after searching, the other is ISS in which every point is searched. So after iteration, we have two kinds of parameters: $(\alpha_1, \alpha_2, ... \alpha_N)$ in OSS and $(\beta_1, \beta_2, ... \beta_M)$ in ISS. Where N and M are the dimension of OSS and the point number of the model. β_i is the projection error in ISS of ith point. Its value shows the possibility that the point i is the right ith point. If it is large, the possibility will be small and maybe the search result is wrong. Homoplastically, for the whole model, if the total error $\sum \beta_i$ is small, it dedicates that there are more points with large possibility in its right place. The experimental results (Figure 2) show that around the right shape, the larger the total error is the further from the right shape the searching shape is. In other words, it means that this total error value can evaluate the search result. So, in this paper, $\sum \beta_i$ is used as the cost value to evaluate the search result.

α_i is the projection coefficient in the OSS. As analyzed in section 2, its value denotes the shape transformation along the ith basis. In PSSS, every basis is for main shapes, if the projection coefficient is larger or smaller than the threshold, it shows that the search result did not like the shape any more, which means that most of points are in the wrong places. The reasonable explanation for this is the initial shape is far from the corresponding true position. Maybe the initial scale is too large or too small and maybe the shift of X or Y is too much. The shifting can be omitted because of the detection before. So the initial scale is the key point. Now we can conclude that if the α_i in PSSS is out of range, we can believe in some extent that it is the reason of initial shape scale. This is very useful in forecasting the search direction in the next iteration.

In PVSS, if α_i is out of range, the searching result will transform too much in ith rotation direction. This can be brought by wrong searching completely or some points searching with right, others are wrong. Just like in PSSS, the possibility of the whole shape wrong searching is small. So it is mainly because of unbalance searching. A logical reason for this unbalance is that some points are near the right place, some is far from the right place which can appear when the initial shape intersect with the right. This is the second conclusion.

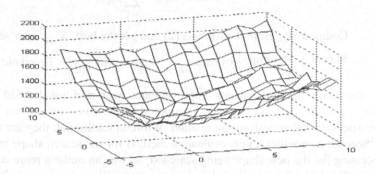

Fig. 2. Model Cost Value in X and Y shift

According to the analysis above, after iteration, we get the out of range coefficients $\alpha_{11}\alpha_{12}\cdots\alpha_{1n_1}, \alpha_{21}\alpha_{22}\cdots\alpha_{2n_2}$ and the total cost value $\cos tvalue = \sum_{i=1}^{M}\beta_i$, n_1 is the number in PSSS and n_2 is the number in PVSS. According to the analysis above, we can forecast the distortion between the right shape and the search result in scale and shift in such way:

$$\Delta_S = X_{old}*\prod_{i=1}^{n_2}(\frac{\alpha_{2i}}{Threshold}-1) \quad \Delta_O = \delta*\prod_{i=1}^{n_1}(\frac{\alpha_{1i}}{Threshold}-1) \tag{1}$$

where $Threshold_i$ and δ are the const value. But the former of $Threshold_i$ should be selected very carefully, for it not only contains the value information, but also contains the scale or shift direction information. The final initial shape position for the next iteration we used is

$$X_{new} = X_{old}(1+\prod_{i=1}^{n_1}\frac{a_{1i}}{Threshold_i})+\lambda*\prod_{j=1}^{n_2}\frac{a_{2j}}{Threshold_j} \tag{2}$$

From the analysis above, we know that the initiate shape before searching is more similar to the right after preprocessing in such way. Considered the performance of robust, we search the shape around X_{new} (±5 Pixels in X and Y direction) through few steps circulation in scale and shift and choose the one as X'_{new} with least $\cos tvalue$.

In total, the method for the optimal searching is:

1. Initiate the shape with the detection algorithm [6] for the first time.

2. Calculate $\cos tvalue_{old} = \sum_{i=1}^{M}\beta_{oldi}$

3. Search as the traditional ASM.

4. Get the parameters of $\alpha_1\alpha_{12}\cdots\alpha_{n_1}$, $\alpha_{21}\alpha_{22}\cdots\alpha_{2n_2}$ and the total cost value

$$costvalue_{new} = \sum_{i=1}^{M} \beta_{newi}$$

5. Compute X_{new} from the formula (2) and get the best X'_{new} after searching.

6. Repeat $3-5$,untill $\left| \cos tvalue_{new} - \cos tvalue_{old} \right| < Threshold$

This algorithm has three major improvements over traditional ASM searching methods. First, the ISS and OSS are considered at the same time when searching. They restrict each other with strong relation. While in traditional, they are used separately. Second, it provides a new evaluation method for the search shape and a set of preprocessing for the new shape being searched, so we can make a more controllable searching. Third, the final result is determinate, not oscillatory any more. This is very important because we do not know exactly how many times of searching are enough for a new image in traditional, but now, no such question.

4 Experiments and Results

The database used consists of 1406 face images from the FERET[7], the AR[8]databases and other collections. 87 landmarks are labeled on each face. We randomly select 703 images as the training and the other 703 images as the testing images. Multi-resolution search is used, using 4 levels with resolution of 1/8, 1/4, 1/2, 1 of the original image in each dimension. At most 10 iterations are run at each level. The ASM uses profile models of 11 pixels long (5 points on either side) and searches 2 pixels either side.

4.1 OSS

On each test Image, we make two kinds of tests with different ways to initialize the start mean shape. In the first method, we initialize it after face detection. In the second, we initialize the starting mean shape with displacements from the true position by ± 10 pixels in both x and y. Point location accuracy is used to give the evaluation for every search subspace in two categories. The comparison results are shown in Figure 3. The X coordinate is point-to-point error and the Y coordinate is the percentage of the samples whose point-to-point errors are less than the given point-to-point errors value. We can see that in the first situation, the search error is mainly around 5 pixels for OSS, much better than the other two methods with nearly the same error of about 20 pixels. In the second experiment, although the difference among three methods is very small, searching with OSS is still the best.

4.2 Optimal Searching

In this experiment, optimal searching, the traditional ASM searching and Zhao et al's searching are compared using the initialization of a face detection method [6]. Like the experiment in testing OSS, point location accuracy is also computed to evaluate their performance. The result is shown in Figure 4. It can be seen that the optimal

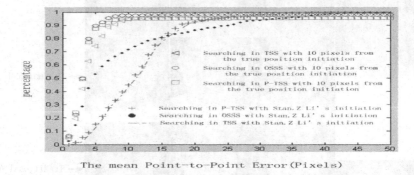

Fig. 3. The percentage of located shapes whose point-to-point errors are less than a threshold in different searching subspace with initiating mean shape using a face detection algorithm [6] and ±10 pixels from the true position

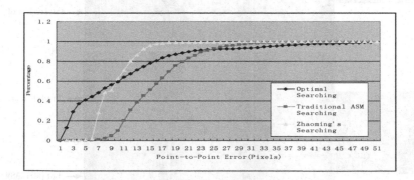

Fig. 4. The percentage of located shapes whose point-to-point errors are less than a threshold in different search way

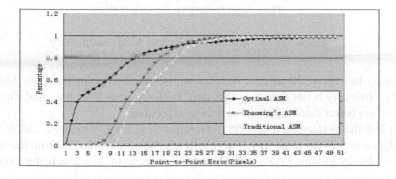

Fig. 5. The percentage of located shapes whose point-to-point errors are less than a threshold in different kind of ASM

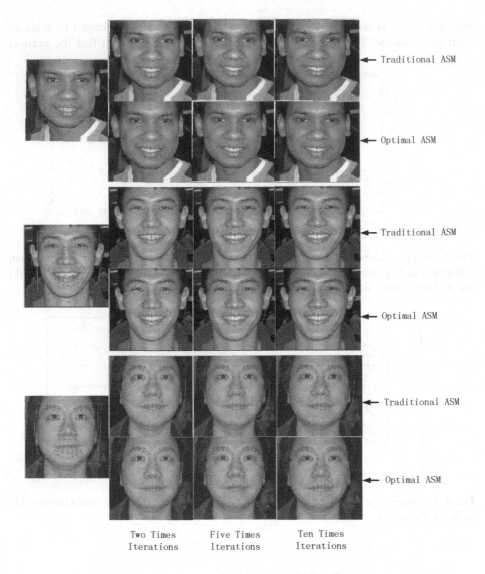

← Traditional ASM

← Optimal ASM

← Traditional ASM

← Optimal ASM

← Traditional ASM

← Optimal ASM

| Two Times Iterations | Five Times Iterations | Ten Times Iterations |

Fig. 6. Traditional ASM and Optimal ASM search results

searching has about 50 percent samples whose point-to-point error are less than 5 pixels, obviously better than the other two. Both Optimal Searching and Zhao et al's method are better than traditional searching algorithm.

At last the performance of OSS + Optimal Searching, which we call is Optimal ASM, is tested in the same way. The results are shown in figure 5. From the figure we can see that by jointing OSSS with Optimal Searching, the result is better overwhelmingly.

Some search results with Optimal ASM compared with Traditional ASM are shown in Figure 6. We select three kinds of samples: good initial condition, bad initial condition with expression and bad initial condition without expression. The first column is the three samples with face detection result and initial ASM. Every sample has two kinds of ASM search results: traditional ASM search result and Optimal search results, in different rows with different iterations. We can see from Figure 6 that after a number of iterations, there is no much difference when initial conditional is good. But on the contrary when initial ASM is far from the true, Optimal ASM proposed in this paper has better performance than Traditional ASM.

5 Conclusion

In this paper, we have discussed Optimal Shape Subspace (OSS) in ASM training and Optimal Searching in ASM searching. With the best experimental results, it can vary very much and the subspace to describe them should give enough shape information. We call this kind of shape subspace the Optimal Shape Subspace (OSS). Because of using evaluation and constraints in search process in the proposed method which is never done by all the work before, not only a more reliable and accurate result but also a controllable search process are acquired, which is why we call this as Optimal Searching. Every kinds of experiments results all show that search with OSS and/or optimal searching has much more efficiency and accuracy.

References

1. Cootes, T.F., Taylor, C.J., Cooper, D.H., Graham, J.: "Active shape models: Their training and application". CVGIP: Image Understanding 61 (1995) 38–59
2. Yan, S.C., Liu, C., Li, S.Z., Zhu, L., Zhang, H.J., Shum, H., Cheng, Q.: "Texturecon-strained active shape models". In: Proceedings of the First International Workshopon Generative-Model-Based Vision (with ECCV), Copenhagen, Denmark(2002)
3. Rogers, M., Graham, J.: Robust active shape model search. In: Proceedings of the European Conference on Computer Vision. Number IV, Copenhagen, Denmark (2002) 517–530
4. Xiangsheng Huang, Stan Z. Li , Yangsheng Wang. "evaluation of Face Alignment Solutions Using Statistical Learning", The 6th International Conference on Automatic Face and Gesture Recognition. Seoul, Kourea. May, 2004
5. Ming Zhao, Stan.Z.Li Chun Chen,"Subspace analysis and optimization for AAM based face alignment". The 6th International Conference on Automatic Face and Gesture Recognition , Seoul, Korea,May,2004
6. Stan Z. Li , ZhenQiu Zhang."FloatBoost Learning and Statistical Face Detection". IEEE Transactions on Pattern Analysis and Machine Intelligence. Vol.26,No.9,September,2004.
7. Phillips, P.J., Moon, H., Rizvi, S.A., Rauss, P.J.: The FERET evaluation methodology for face-recognition algorithms. IEEE Transactions on Pattern Analysis and Machine Intelligence 22 (2000) 1090–1104
8. Martinez, A., Benavente, R.: "The AR face database". Technical Report 24, CVC(1998)

Gabor Wavelet-Based Eyes and Mouth Detection Algorithm

Xiangping Wang and Xingming Zhang

Department of Computer Engineering and Science,
South China University of Technology,
GuangZhou, China 510640
scut_wxp@yahoo.com.cn, cszxm@scut.edu.cn

Abstract. A Gabor wavelet-based eyes and mouth detection system is presented. To extract the potential feature points in face organs, this approach combines the skin color model, grayscale gradient clue and motion model. And then the position-pair of highest likelihood, which is determined from a set of rules, is taken into account. We can verify all of the probable eyes-pairs by Gabor wavelet and support vector machine (SVM) as well. Finally, the position of mouth has been detected according to the position of eyes. The result of experiment shows, the proposed system provided higher right detection rate of right eyes and mouth. In addition, the performance of system can be improved by further learning.

1 Introduction

Eyes and mouth detection is very important for face recognition, it's the first step of our works. Based on them you can easily and accurately extract the face feature and analyze them. Eyes and mouth detection is very easy for human beings, however, for computer, it's not easy at all. In order to detect the human face, computer should accomplish the task as follow: Given a static image or a segment of dynamic video, it can detect and locate the position of eyes and mouth. To archive this aim, the system will come down to segment, extract and verify the eyes and mouth under arbitrary background. This paper proposes a new way for eyes and mouth detection in details. Firstly, to extract the potential feature points in face organs, this approach combines the skin color model, grayscale gradient clue and motion model. And then the position-pair of highest likelihood, which is determined from a set of rules, is taken into account, and verify the probable eyes-pairs by Gabor wavelet and SVM. Finally, it can detect the position of mouth by the position of eyes. The result of experiment shows, the proposed system has achieved higher right detection rate of right eyes and mouth. The structure of this paper will arrange as follow: In section 2 the process of eyes-pair extraction and verification has been illuminated in details. In section 3 the process of mouth detection has been described. And the result of experiment and analysis are presented in section 4. At last we will conclude the problems of our system and future work.

S.Z. Li et al. (Eds.): Sinobiometrics 2004, LNCS 3338, pp. 110–117, 2004.
© Springer-Verlag Berlin Heidelberg 2004

2 Eyes-Pair Extraction and Verification

2.1 Feature Points Extraction

In the face image the intensities of eyes are usually smaller than their surroundings, utilizing this character we can extract feature points by the way of mathematics morphologic. And combine it with several other methods to eliminate the influence of background and intensify feature points.

- a). Using skin color probability model to eliminate the shadow of face.
- b). Using skin area to eliminate the affect of background.
- c). Binarizing feature points object image.

2.2 Rule Module

In the final image (After Section 2.1), almost all of the areas are similar to eyes. So we try to find out the highest likelihood pair from all eyes-pairs. We establish a series of rules based on right and left eyes-pair feature. At first, we remove some impossible eyes feature points and feature-pair, and then regulate the remainder feature-pairs with reliability according as those rules, finally the highest reliability among them will be made pairs by way of eyes-pairs to verify.

2.3 Verification Module

2.3.1 The Retinotopic Grid

In our experiments we used a grid which consisted of 50 points arranged in five concentric circles (Fig.1). We set the radius of the innermost circle to three pixels and that of the outermost circle to 30 pixels, which is about the average inter-eye distance in the images we used for training and testing. Receptive fields are modeled by computing a vector of 30 Gabor filter responses at each point of the retina. The filters are organized in five frequency channels. Filter wavelengths span the range from to 16 pixels in half-octave intervals.

By the retinotopic grid[1], we can use the information of eyes surrounding to verify eyes-pairs.

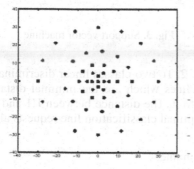 

Fig. 1. Left: the retinotopic grid (axes graded in pixels). Right: the specific effect image

2.3.2 The Modified Gabor Filter

In our experiment, we use a modified Gabor filter[1]. That is, for a filter tuned to orientation ϕ_0 and angular $\omega_0 = \exp(\xi_0)$:

$$\hat{G}(\xi, \phi) = A \exp\left\{-\frac{(\xi - \xi_0)^2}{2\sigma_\xi^2}\right\} \exp\left\{-\frac{(\phi - \phi_0)^2}{2\sigma_\phi^2}\right\} \tag{1}$$

Where A is a normalization constant and (ξ, ϕ) are the log-polar frequency coordinates:

$$(\xi, \phi) = \left(\log\|(\omega_x, \omega_y)\|, \tan^{-1}(\omega_y / \omega_x)\right) \tag{2}$$

2.3.3 Support Vector Machine (SVM)

Support vector machine[2] was named support vector network previously. And it is the brand-new part of the statistics learning theory. SVM can apply to learn in high dimension and small examples. SVM is based on the discipline of structure venture minimum. And the object wants to minimize the upper limit of expectation venture or practice venture, and to find out optimal hyperplane under linear discriminable. Due to the problem of linear undiscriminable, it projects the input vector into high dimension feature space with nonlinear projecting, and find the optimal hyperplane.

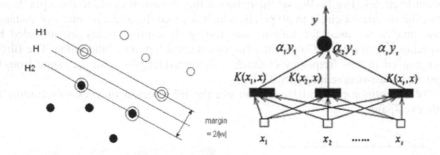

Fig. 2. Optimal hyperplane   Fig. 3. Support vector machine

Optimal hyperplane has been showed as Fig. 2. To two-classes linear discriminable situation, H1 and H2 are respectively the beelines which are the minimal distance points to the classification line H and parallel to it. The distance between H1 and H2 are named two-classes classification margin. Optimal classification line requests all of examples in the example gallery

(1) can be partitioned off by this classification line.
(2) the maximal classification margin.

and extends to high dimension, the optimal classification line will be instead of optimal hyperplane. The classification function computed by SVM is similar to neural network (see Fig. 3).

2.3.4 Modelling Eyes and Mouth Landmarks

The eyes and mouth finer or extended model: the model is obtained by placing the whole retinotopic grid at the location of the facial landmark on the training images and collecting the set of Gabor filter responses from all of the retinal points. These Gabor features are then arranged into a single vector, and then throw them to SVM for training the model. Through this training method, the eyes and mouth extended model can be built.

In the process of training, a training set of 200 frontal images has been extracted from our gallery. It provides 200 positive examples for each landmark. Negative examples are collected by extracting Gabor vectors at 10 random locations in each image. Right eyes and mouths have been included as negative examples in the model of the left eye as well.

2.3.5 Eyes-Pairs Verification

Using skin probability model, grayscale gradient clue and motion model we can extract the potential feature points in face organs. And then the position-pair of highest likelihood, which is determined from a set of rules, is taken into account, finally we apply the eyes extend model to verify all of probable eyes-pairs. In the course of verification, we find out eyes-pair with the maximal SVM return value among all probable eyes-pairs. And we judge them by the threshold. If the probable eyes-pair is bigger than the threshold, it will be located as eyes-pair, otherwise there is no eyes-pair will be located i.e. the system consider there is no eye-pair found among all of the feature-pairs.

3   Mouth Detection

Through extracting and verifying eyes landmarks, we got the eyes position. In this approach, the mouth location is based on the position of eyes.

The detail as follows:

1) We gain the mouth extended model by the training method mentioned in section 2.3.4.
2) Taking advantage of the triangle relationship between both eyes (right and left eyes) and mouth positions (Fig 4.B), we get the position area mainly (Fig 4.A).
3) Then we will put the A(Fig 4.A) area to mouths verification, and find out the point position that has the maximal SVM return value, so that point is the mouth point what we want.

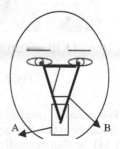

Fig. 4. Evaluate the mouth area

4   Experiment Result

To test the algorithm we proposed, we use a testing set of 306 images of 106 subjects. Every image in the testing gallery has a resolution of 320×240, and the background is very complex. The camera of Intel PC430 is used as the capture device in the test, we make out some limitation to face pose when taking images, the angle of horizontal rotating and depth rotating is small than 30^0. We adopt three different illumination conditions, in order to evaluate the adaptability to illuminant variance. Three illumination condition have been set:

A: Face frontage has a lamp-house, and up-side has three lamp-houses, the illumination irradiates uniformly to the face area, and the illumination intensity is bright.

B: Face frontage also has a lamp-house, the illumination irradiates slightly and nonuniformly to the face area, and the illumination intensity is middle.

C: There is only the outside natural illumination, the illumination on face area is nonuniformity, and the illumination is some dark.

The effect of the experiment is presented as in Fig. 6. In addition, the detection results under corresponding A, B, C illumination conditions are shown on Table1.

From the experimental result you can see the relationship between the right detection rate on eyes and mouth and different illumination condition. In the normal illumination condition (Fig 5-A) the algorithm we proposed has achieved good detection result, and in the colored illumination condition (Fig 5-B) the right detection rate was affected a little. And what's more, in the side illumination condition (Fig 5-C), because facial right and left area have different illumination, it will be difficult to extract the feature by fixed threshold, so we extracted the feature by dynamic threshold. At the same time the frequency domain information around the eyes and mouth will be affected in C illumination condition.

(A illumination)   (B illumination)   (C illumination)

Fig. 5. Three different testing illumination conditions

The criterion used to evaluate the results is a relative error measure based on the distances between the expected and the estimated eye and mouth positions. Let E1, E2 and M1 be the manually extracted left and right eye and mouth positions of a face image, E1', E2' and M1' be the estimated positions by the proposed detection method. D1 be the distance between E1 and E1', D2 be the distance between E2 and E2', and D3 be the distance between M1 and M1'. If both of D1 and D2 are less than

2 pixels, we think the eye detection is considered to be correct. If D3 is less than 2 pixels, we think the mouth detection is considered to be correct. Through this criterion, the evaluation of right detection rate (DR) is defined:

DR = ND (the numbers of right detection) / TN (the total numbers of faces).

Table 1. The final testing result

The testing illumination	Face numbers	The result of eyes detection			The result of mouth detection		
		False positive	Missed detections	Right detection rate	False positive	Missed detections	Right detection rate
A	106	5	1	94.3%	5	0	95.3%
B	106	7	1	92.5%	8	0	92.5%
C	106	10	0	90.6%	10	0	90.6%
Total	318	22	2	92.5%	23	0	92.8%

Fig. 6. Detecting the eyes and mouth in A,B,C illumination condition

5   Conclusions

In this paper, a Gabor wavelet-based eyes and mouth detection system is presented. To extract the potential feature points in face organs, this approach combines the skin color model, grayscale gradient clue and motion model. And then the position-pair of highest likelihood, which is determined from a set of rules, is taken into account. And we can verify all of the probable eyes-pairs by Gabor wavelet and SVM. Finally, the position of mouth has been detected according to the position of eyes. Because using the information around eyes and mouth, this proposed system provided higher right detection rate of eyes and mouth.

However, this algorithm need be further improved on some place. Because we use the skin colored information, so the algorithm will be affected by the illumination condition. For example, there are some false positives through this detector under colored illumination condition (like red light). And due to more maximal grayscale difference, it will affect the right rate of feature extracting to a certain extent. Otherwise, due to the effect of the facial deeper rotating in mouth detection phase, thereby it's hard to gain the probable mouth area accurately, so the final mouth right detection rate will be a little bit lower.

Acknowledgements

This work is supported by the GuangZhou Science and Technology Program Foundation under Grant 2002X GP16 (Person movement, Track, Recognition and Surveillance System), and also supported by TianHe district Science and Technology Program Foundation under Grant 2002X GP11 (Dynamic Face Recognition-based Identity Authentication System).

References

1. F.Smeraldi*, J.Bigun. : Retinal vision applied to facial features detection and face authentication. Pattern Recog. 23 (2003) 463–475
2. Bian Zhaoqi, Zhang Xuegong. : Pattern recognition. Tsinghua University Press, Beijing, China (2001.5)
3. Bigun,J. : Gabor phase in boundary tracking and region segregation. In: Proc. DSP & CASES Conf., Nicosia,Cyprus.University of Nicosia (1993) 229–234
4. Mao Mingfeng, Zhang Xingming, Guo Yucong. : fast rule-based eyes location algorithm. Computer engineer, Shanghai, China (2003)
5. D.Maio and D.Maltoni. : Real-time face location on gray-scale static images. Pattern Recog. 33 (2000) 1525–1539
6. M. Propp and A.Samal. : Artificial neural network architecture for human face detection. Intell. Eng. Systems Artificial Neural Networks. 2 (1992) 535–540
7. Rein-Lien Hsu, Mohanmed Abdel-Mottaleb, Anil K.Jain. : Face Detection in Color images. In IEEE Transaction on pattern analysis and machine intelligence. 24 (2002.5) 5
8. Jianxin Wu, Zhi-Hua Zhou. : Efficient face candidates selector for face detection. In Pattern Recognition (2003) 1175–1186
9. R.Chellappa, C.L.Wilson, S.Sirohey. : Human and machine recognition of faces: a survey. Proc. IEEE. 83 (5) (1995) 705–741
10. Arleo, A., Smeraldi, F., Hug, S., Gerstner, W. : Place cells and spatial navigation based on vision, path integration, and reinforcement learning. In: Advances in Neural Information Processing Systems. 13, MIT Press, Cambridge, MA 89–95
11. Bigun, J., Duc, B., Fischer, S., Makarov, A., Smeraldi, F. : Multiple modal person authentication. In: Wechsler, H., et al. (Eds.), Nato-Asi Advanced Study on Face Recognition. F-163, Springer, Berlin (2000) 26–50
12. Cortes, C., Vapnik, V. : Support-vector networks. Machine Learning. 20 (1995) 273-297
13. Lades, M., Vorbruggen, J.c., Buhmann, J., Lange, J., von der Malsbury, C., Hurtz, R.P., Konen, W. : Distortion invariant object recognition in the dynamic link architectures. IEEE Trans. Comput. 42(3) (1993) 300–311
14. Osuna, E., Freund, R., Girosi, F. : Improved training algorithm for support vector machines. In: Proc. IEEE NNSP'97. (1997) 276–285

15. Orban, G.A. : Neuronal Operations in the Visual Cortex Studies of Brain Functions. Springer, Berlin (1984)
16. Schwartz, E.L. : Computational anatomy and functional architecture of striate cortex: a spatial mapping approach to perceptual coding. Visual Res. 20 (1980) 645–669
17. Smeraldi, F. : Attention-driven pattern recognition. Ph.D. Thesis. Swiss Federal Institute of Technology, Lausanne, Switzerland . 2153 (200) (2000)
18. Matas, J., Jonsson, K., Kittler, J. : Fast face localization and verification. In: Clark, A.F. (Ed.), Proc. British Machine Vision Conf. (BMVC97) (2000)

An Entropy-Based Diversity Measure for Classifier Combining and Its Application to Face Classifier Ensemble Thinning

Wenyao Liu, Zhaohui Wu, and Gang Pan

Department of Computer Science and Engineering,
Zhejiang University, Hangzhou, 310027, P.R. China
{liuwy, wzh, gpan}@cs.zju.edu.cn

Abstract. In this paper, we introduce a new diversity measure for classifier combining, called Entropy-based Pair-wise Diversity Measure (EBPDM). Its application to help removing redundant classifiers from a face classifier ensemble is conducted. The preliminary experiments on UC Irvine repository and AT&T face database demonstrate that, compared with other diversity measures, the proposed measure is comparable at predicting the performance of multiple classifier systems, and is able to make classifier ensembles smaller without loss in performance.

1 Introduction

Classifier combining has appealed more and more attention because of its potential ability in boosting the overall accuracy[1]. This technique is now being used in a variety of fields, particularly in multiple biometric modality fusion. It has been proved that combining multiple biometric modalities can lead to better performance than using a single modality[2].

In the research of classifier combining, it's widely accepted that base classifiers to be combined should be *diverse* (negative dependent, independent, or complementary) [3-5]. We can imagine it meaningless to combine several *identical* classifiers.

Sometimes, altering diversity among classifiers can be the key to the success (or failure). For example, classifier ensemble methods such as bagging, boosting, and arcing[6] are all based on the idea of promoting diversity[7].

Diversity measures aim to describe the diversity among classifiers in multiple classifier systems. However, up to now, there hasn't been many achievements in the research of diversity measures, for the existing measures are always not able to show strong correlation between diversity and classifier combining accuracy boosting[8].

In this paper, we propose a pair-wise diversity measure based on entropy, and use it to remove redundant classifiers in an ensemble of face classifiers. Our new diversity measure is introduced in Section 2. The experiments, which compare the measures by computing the correlation between diversity measures and accuracy boosts, are described in Section 3. The application to face classifier ensemble thinning is illustrated in Section 4.

S.Z. Li et al. (Eds.): Sinobiometrics 2004, LNCS 3338, pp. 118–124, 2004.

Diversity Measures.
The start point of diversity measures is the Dietterichs' Kappa statistic[6], which bases on the degree of similarity between two classifiers. They measured the diversity by computing a degree-of-agreement statistic for each pair of classifiers, and the average of all paired values was regarded as the diversity of the ensemble.

Kuncheva and Whitaker[9] compared ten diversity measures by experiments, including four pair-wise measures and six non-pair-wise ones. Since they found the effect of diversity measures unclear, they recommended the pair-wise Q statistic for it's simple and understandable. So we choose it to compare with our measures in Section 3.

We also choose a non-pair-wise measure from Kuncheva's paper to compare with, which is Inter-rater Agreement function. It's also referred to as Kappa except that it is non-pair-wise, so we will call it k for short at following sections.

The algorithms of above two measures can refer to Figure 1. It's interesting that both of this two diversity measures only consider whether the classification is correct or not instead of taking into account the real classification.

$$\overline{Q} = \frac{2}{L(L-1)} \sum_{i=1}^{L-1} \sum_{k=i+1}^{L} \frac{p^{11} p^{00} - p^{01} p^{10}}{p^{11} p^{00} + p^{01} p^{10}}$$

L = Number of classifiers

p^{00} = p(Classifier i is incorrect, Classifier k is incorrect)

p^{01} = p(Classifier i is incorrect, Classifier k is correct)

p^{10} = p(Classifier i is correct, Classifier k is incorrect)

p^{11} = p(Classifier i is correct, Classifier k is correct)

$$k = 1 - \frac{\frac{1}{L} \sum_{i=1}^{N} l(z_i)(L - l(z_i))}{N(L-1)p(1-p)}$$

N = Number of samples

L = Number of classifiers

p = Average classifier accuracy

$l(z_i)$ = Correct classifications for classifier i

Fig. 1. Algorithms of Q statistic and Inter-rater Agreement function

Entropy is the best-known measure of uncertainty[10], the definition of it is as following:

$$H(x) = -\sum p_i \log_2 p_i \tag{1}$$

In which p_i means the probability of a given symbol.

We use (1) to construct our entropy-based pair-wise diversity measure (also called EBPDM). The algorithm can refer to Figure 2 (The meaning of each symbol is the same as above algorithm of Q statistic).

$$\overline{SE} = \frac{2}{L(L-1)} \sum_{i=1}^{L-1} \sum_{k=i+1}^{L} -(p^{00} \log_2 p^{00} + p^{01} \log_2 p^{01} + p^{10} \log_2 p^{10} + p^{11} \log_2 p^{11})$$

Fig. 2. The algorithm of EBPDM

Like Kappa statistic, our measure also aims to point out the relationship between each pair of classifiers and then calculate the average. We calculate the entropy for each pair of classifiers, and then average all the paired entropies.

EBPDM has following advantages: firstly, it's easy to understand and implement. Secondly, since it's pair-wise, it can make the best of as much information from the ensembles as possible. Thirdly, it makes full use of entropy's superiority in measuring uncertainty of classifiers.

2   Diversity Experiments

In this section, we perform some experiments on two data sets from the UCI Repository of Machine Learning Database[11]: the Pima Indian Diabetes data and the Sonar data. Both data sets and the experimental protocol are summarized in Table 1.

Table 1. Summary of the data sets and experimental protocol(c: number of classes; N: number of the samples in the data set; n: number of features used in our experiments; [n1, n2, n3]: partition method-how many features in each classifier)

Name	c	N	n	[n1, n2, n3]	Number of ensembles	Training/testing
Pima	2	768	8	[3, 3, 2]	560	10-folder cross-validation
Sonar	2	208	10	[4, 4, 2]	3150	Holdout (random halves)

Table 2. Correlation between combining and diversity

(a) Pima Data

Diversity / Combining	Q	k	EBPDM
Vote	**-0.6039**	0.0192	0.5010
NB	0.1151	0.0675	**0.2828**
Max	-0.0910	0.0781	**0.4975**
Average	-0.3692	0.0453	**0.6759**
Product	-0.3217	0.0391	**0.6549**
Min	-0.0910	0.0781	**0.4975**
DT	-0.0607	0.0413	**0.4642**

(b) Sonar Data

Diversity / Combining	Q	k	EBPDM
Vote	-0.0025	-0.0193	**-0.0910**
NB	0.0012	0.0002	**-0.0046**
Max	-0.0649	-0.0107	**0.2788**
Average	-0.0984	-0.0155	**0.2793**
Product	-0.0958	-0.0155	**0.2800**
Min	-0.0649	-0.0107	**0.2788**
DT	-0.1285	0.0118	**0.2750**

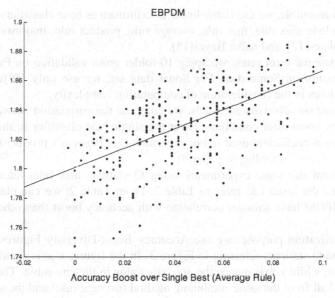

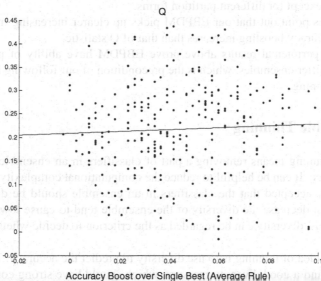

Fig. 3. Accuracy Boost-Diversity figures on Pima Data

We partition the features of each data set into three parts, thus we are able to run an exhaustive experiment with all possible partitions. Referring to Table 1, we use [n1, n2, n3] to describe the partition form $(n1+n2+n3 = n)$, so the total number of ensembles is $C_n^{n1} \cdot C_{n-n1}^{n2} \cdot C_{n-n1-n2}^{n3}$, and each ensemble includes three base classifiers.

For each ensemble, we use fisher linear discriminant as base classifiers. Combining methods include max rule, min rule, average rule, product rule, majority vote[1], decision templates[12], and naïve Bayes[13].

To compute the error rates, we apply 10-folder cross-validation on Pima data and holdout measure on Sonar data. For Sonar data set, we use only 10 features from original features in the consideration of computation complexity.

To evaluate our diversity measures, we compute the correlation between EBPDM and accuracy boost after combining (over the single best classifier in the ensemble). The correlation coefficient used in our experiments is Pearson's product moment correlation coefficient according to paper[8].

We perform the same experiments using Q statistic and Inter-rater Agreement function, and the result can refer to Table 2. From Table 2, we can clearly observe that our EBPDM have stronger correlation with accuracy boost than other two measures.

For visualization purpose, we use Accuracy Boost-Diversity Figures to compare EBPDM and Q statistic, referring to Figure 3. In the figure, x-axis stands for the accuracy boost, while y-axis means the diversity value in the ensemble. The data points are obtained all from the same combining method (average rule) and the same data set (Pima data), except for different partition forms.

The figures point out that our EBPDM picks up clearer increasing trend of diversity while accuracy boosting increases than that of Q statistic.

All the experimental results above prove EBPDM have ability of predicting the trend of classifier ensembles, which is the precondition of our following application to ensemble thinning.

3   Ensemble Thinning

Ensemble thinning means removing a part of classifiers in an ensemble without loss in performance. It can be helpful to reduce the computational complexity.

It's widely accepted that the classifiers in an ensemble should be diverse. Those classifiers that decrease the diversity of the ensemble tend to cause lower combining accuracy. Thus, diversity can be regarded as the criterion to decide whether to remove a classifier.

The basic idea of thinning is to use diversity to predict the accuracy. The main difficulty is to find a good diversity measure, which should have strong correlation with accuracy boost in the ensemble. We apply our diversity measure EBPDM to the thinning algorithm, shown in Figure 4. Each time we remove one classifier, without which the ensemble can be of the strongest diversity, and get the new ensemble. We repeat the procedure until the ensemble is small enough.

We perform face recognition experiments on AT&T face database[14]. It includes 400 gray scale face images of 40 persons, taken at different time, under various illuminations and with diverse expression. All of the images are of size 92×112. Figure 5 shows some examples taken from the database. We separate the images into two sessions of same size, then use one session to train the ensemble and the other one to evaluate the error rates.

> While (number removed <= maximum number to remove)
> For (each classifier Ci in the ensemble)
>   Calculate EBPDM of ensemble without Ci
> Remove Ci causing the highest EBPDM

Fig. 4. The algorithm of ensemble thinning

Fig. 5. Examples taken from AT&T face database

The first step of face recognition is preprocessing the face image. We resize the image into size 36×44. At the second step, we use principal component analysis (PCA) to build the feature space and choose the nearest neighbor as base classifier, and apply bagging method (random select a part of samples in the data set to be training patterns repeatedly, then combining the result) to construct an ensemble of twenty classifiers. We don't perform much preprocessing or use complicate classifiers because we don't focus on constructing excellent face recognition systems. Our purpose is to prove it appropriate of EBPDM to perform ensemble thinning.

In consideration of comparability, we first compute the error rates of combining the ensemble with twenty classifiers without thinning, and then compute the error rates after removing ten classifiers from the ensemble. Combining methods here include max rule, min rule, average rule, product rule, and majority vote.

The error rates of different combining methods before and after thinning are both shown in Table 3.

Table 3. Experimental result of ensemble thinning

Combining method	Before thinning	After thinning
Max	8.00%	**7.00%**
Min	8.50%	**7.50%**
Sum	7.50%	7.50%
Product	8.00%	**7.50%**
Majority vote	7.50%	7.50%

Observed from Table 3, after thinning, three in the five combining methods can achieve boost in accuracy though the number of classifiers is only half. The other two methods maintain the same error rates as before. Through the result, we can conclude that our thinning method based on EBPDM can improve or at least maintain the performance of the ensemble while reducing the complexity of computation.

4   Conclusion

This paper presents our preliminary work on diversity. Diversity among classifiers can obviously affect the accuracy of classifier ensembles. However, the measures to quantify diversity are not yet well defined. Our measure based on entropy can show stronger correlation with the accuracy boosting compared to Q statistic and Inter-rater Agreement function. At the same time, the measure is easy to understand and implement.

Since the increasing in accuracy can be expected by increasing the diversity in ensembles, the EBPDM can be used to perform ensemble thinning. The experiments on AT&T face database prove our method can reduce the computing complexity of combining and remove sub optimal classifiers to gain better performance.

References

1. Kittler, J., Hatef, M., Duin, R., Matas, J.: On Combining Classifiers. IEEE Transactions on Pattern Analysis and Machine Intelligence, 1998, **20**(3): 226-239.
2. Brunelli, R., Falavigna, D.: Person Identification Using Multiple Cues. IEEE Transactions on Pattern Analysis and Machine Intelligence, 1995, **17**(10):955-966.
3. Lam., L.: Classifier Combinations: Implementations and Theoretical Issues. In: *Proc. the 1st Int'l Workshop on Multiple Classifier Systems (MCS2000)*, Cagliari, Italy, 2000: Springer-Verlag. 78-86.
4. Kuncheva, L.I., Whitaker, C.J., Shipp, C.A.: Is Independence Good for Combining Classifiers? In: *15th Int'l Conf. Pattern Recognition*, 2000. 168-171.
5. Kuncheva, L.I., Whitaker, C.J., Shipp, C.A.: Limits on the Majority Vote Accuracy in Classifier Fusion. Pattern Analysis and Application, 2003, **6**(1): 22-31.
6. Dietterich, T.: An Experimental Comparison of Three Methods for Construction Ensembles of Decision Trees: Bagging, boosting, and randomization. Machine Learning, 2000, **40**(2): 139-158.
7. Melvill, P., Mooney, R.J.: Creating Diversity in Ensembles Using Artificial Data. Information Fusion: Special Issue on Diversity in Multi-classifier Systems, 2004, **to appear**.
8. Shipp, C.A., Kuncheva, L.I.: Relationships between Combination Methods and Measures of Diversity in Combining Classifiers. Information Fusion, 2002, **3**(2002): 135-148.
9. Kuncheva, L.I., Whitaker, C.J.: Measures of Diversity in Classifier Ensembles. Machine Learning, 2003, **51**: 191-207.
10. Shannon, C.E.: A Mathematical Theory of Communication. Bell System Technical Journal, 1948, **27**(3): 379-423,623-656.
11. http://www.ics.uci.edu/~mlearn/MLRepository.html.
12. Kuncheva, L.I., Bezdek, J., Duin, R.: Decision Templates for Multiple Classifier Fusion: An Experimental Comparison. Pattern Recognition, 1999, **34**(2): 299-314.
13. Dietrich, C., Schwenker, F., Riede, k., Palm, G.: Classification of Bioacoustic Time Series Utilizing Pulse Detection, Time and Frequency Features and Data Fusion. 2001.
14. http://www.uk.research.att.com/facedatabase.html.

Estimating the Visual Direction with Two-Circle Algorithm

Haiyuan Wu, Qian Chen, and Toshikazu Wada

Faculty of Systems Engineering, Wakayama University, Japan

Abstract. This paper describes a novel method to estimate visual direction from a single monocular image with "two-circle" algorithm. We assume that the visual direction of both eyes is parallel and iris boundaries are circles in 3-D space. Our "two-circle" algorithm can estimate the normal vector of the supporting plane of two iris boundaries, from which the direction of the visual direction can be calculated. Most existing gaze estimation algorithms require eye corners and some heuristic knowledge about the structure of the eye as well as the iris contours. In contrast to the exiting methods, ours does not use that additional information. Another advantage of our algorithm is that it does not require the focal length, therefore, it is capable of estimating the visual direction from an image taken by an active camera. The extensive experiments over simulated images and real images demonstrate the robustness and the effectiveness of our method.

1 Introduction

Visual direction provides several functions such as giving cues of people's interest, attention or reference by looking at an object or person. It also plays an important role in many human computer interaction applications. So, visual direction estimation is a very important task.

According to anatomy, the visual direction is the direction of straight line passing through the object of fixation, the nodal point and the fovea. Because the nodal point and the fovea are inside the eyeball, they cannot be observed with a normal video camera. Therefore the visual direction cannot be estimated directly. However, since the visual direction is equivalent to the line connecting the eyeball center and the pupil center, or the normal vector of the supporting plane of the iris boundary form a (approximately) constant angle, it can be calculated indirectly from the 3D position of the eyeball center and the pupil center, or the normal vector of the supporting plane of the iris boundaries.

Most of the gaze researches are focused on the eye detection or gaze tracking, which only give the position of eyes on input image planes[3]-[10]. Many of them assumed that the iris contours in the image are circles, but it is not always right.

Matsumoto *et al* proposed a gaze estimation method[6]. They assumed that the position of the eyeball center related to the two eye corners is known (manually adjusted), and the iris contour on the image is a circle. They located the eye corners by using a binocular stereo system, and estimated the iris center by applying Hough Transformation to the detected iris contours. Then, they *calculated* the 3D position of the eyeball center from the head pose and two eye corners. The visual direction is calculated from the iris center and the eyeball center.

S.Z. Li et al. (Eds.): Sinobiometrics 2004, LNCS 3338, pp. 125–136, 2004.

Wang *et al* presented a "one-circle" algorithm to estimate the visual direction using a monocular camera with known focal length[3]. They detected the elliptical iris contour and used it to calculate the normal vector of the supporting plane of the circular iris boundary. In order to resolve the ambiguity of the multi-solutions, they assumed that the *3D distances* between the eyeball center and each of the two eye corners are equal. However, they did not show how to obtain the *3D positions* of the two eye corners.

There are two kinds of approaches to estimate the visual direction. The first one uses elliptical iris contour to estimate the normal vector of the supporting plane of the iris boundary. The other is to estimate the invisible eyeball center, and then to use it to calculate the visual direction together with the detected iris center.

We consider that the former is a more useful and more reliable approach because it depends on less image features and knowledge about the eyes than the eyeball center based algorithms. The accuracy of the conic-based algorithm depends on the precision of the elliptical iris contour detected from an input image. In order to obtain satisfying results, the size of the iris contour in the image should be big enough. We consider that this requirement is acceptable because

1. High-resolution cameras are becoming popular and less expensive nowadays.
2. We are developing an active camera system for observing human faces and eyes, which uses a camera mounted on a pan-tilt unit. The camera parameters including focal length and the viewing direction are controlled by a computer. (see Fig.1).

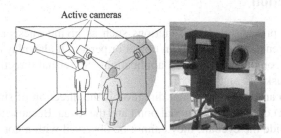

Fig. 1. Our active camera system and used pan-tilt camera

By using aforesaid provisions together with real-time face detecting/tracking method, image containing big enough face and eyes can be obtained continuously.

We have presented a "two-circle" algorithm recently. Compared with the "one-circle" algorithm, our "two-circle" algorithm has two advantages:

1. It can give an unique answer of the visual direction without using eye corners.
2. It does not require a known focal length of the camera, and it does not use the orthographical projection approximation.

In this paper, we present a method for estimating the visual direction from two iris contours detected from one monocular image by using the "two-circle" algorithm Our "two-circle" algorithm does not require the whole irises or their centers to be viewable, or their radius. It also allows our algorithm to use a camera with unknown focal length. The second feature is that no orthographical approximation is required, which is not always correct because the eyes are not always far from the camera.

The extensive experiments over simulated images and real images demonstrate the robustness and the effectiveness of our method.

2 "Two-Circle" Algorithm

When people look at a place that is not so near, the visual directions of the both eyes are approximately parallel, thus the supporting planes of the both iris boundaries are also parallel. We have presented a algorithm called as "two-circle" algorithm[1], it can estimate the normal vector of the supporting plane(s) from an image containing two circles on the same plane or on two different but parallel planes taken by a camera with unknown focal length. So, we can use the "two-circle" algorithm to estimate the visual direction. Hereafter, we describe the algorithm briefly.

2.1 Elliptical Cone and Circular Cross Section

Here, we discuss a problem of estimating a plane direction from one image containing one circle, which is provided that the image was taken by a camera with known focal length. M.Dhome[11] addressed it in a research about the pose estimation of an object of revolution.

When a circle is projected onto an image plane by perspective projection, it shows an ellipse in general case. Considering a camera coordinate system that the origin is the optical center and the Z-axis is the optical axis, then the oblique elliptical cone defined by the optical center and the ellipse on the image plane $z = -f$ (f is the focal length) can be described by the following equation in quadric form,

$$\mathbf{P}^T \mathbf{Q} \mathbf{P} = 0, \tag{1}$$

where

$$\mathbf{Q} = \begin{pmatrix} A & B & -\frac{D}{f} \\ B & C & -\frac{E}{f} \\ -\frac{D}{f} & -\frac{E}{f} & \frac{F}{f^2} \end{pmatrix}. \tag{2}$$

$\mathbf{Q}$ can be expressed by its normalized eigen-vectors ($\mathbf{v}_1$, $\mathbf{v}_2$, $\mathbf{v}_3$) and eigen-values (λ_1, λ_2, λ_3) as following:

$$\mathbf{Q} = \mathbf{V} \mathbf{\Lambda} \mathbf{V}^T, \tag{3}$$

where

$$\begin{cases} \mathbf{\Lambda} = \text{diag}\{\lambda_1, \lambda_2, \lambda_3\} \\ \mathbf{V} = \begin{pmatrix} \mathbf{v}_1 & \mathbf{v}_2 & \mathbf{v}_3 \end{pmatrix} \end{cases}. \tag{4}$$

Considering a supporting plane coordinate system that the origin is also the optical center, but the Z-axis is defined by the normal vector of the supporting plane of the circle to be viewed. If the center and the radius of the circle is given by (x_0, y_0, z_0) and

r respectively, the oblique circular cone dis efined by the optical center and the circle is given by,

$$P_c{}^T Q_c P_c = 0, \tag{5}$$

where

$$Q_c = \begin{pmatrix} 1 & 0 & -\frac{x_0}{z_0} \\ 0 & 1 & -\frac{y_0}{z_0} \\ -\frac{x_0}{z_0} & -\frac{y_0}{z_0} & \frac{x_0^2+y_0^2-r^2}{z_0^2} \end{pmatrix}. \tag{6}$$

Since Q_c and Q describe the same cone surface, there is a rotation matrix R_c that transforms P_c to P as follows,

$$P = R_c P_c. \tag{7}$$

Since kQ_c describes the same cone as Q_c for any non-zero k, we obtain the following equation from Eq.(7), Eq.(5), Eq(3) and Eq.(1),

$$(V^T R_c)^T \Lambda (V^T R_c) = k Q_c. \tag{8}$$

Because $VV^T = R_c R_c^T = I$, we have

$$(V^T R_c)(V^T R_c)^T = I. \tag{9}$$

Without losing generality, we assume that

$$\lambda_1\lambda_2 > 0, \quad \lambda_1\lambda_3 < 0, \quad |\lambda_1| \geq |\lambda_2|. \tag{10}$$

Solving Eq.(8) and Eq.(9), we obtain,

$$V^T R_c = \begin{pmatrix} g\cos\alpha & S_1 g\sin\alpha & S_2 h \\ \sin\alpha & -S_1\cos\alpha & 0 \\ S_1 S_2 h\cos\alpha & S_2 h\sin\alpha & -S_1 g \end{pmatrix}, \tag{11}$$

where α is a free variable, S_1 and S_2 are undetermined signs, and

$$g = \sqrt{\frac{\lambda_2-\lambda_3}{\lambda_1-\lambda_3}}, \quad h = \sqrt{\frac{\lambda_1-\lambda_2}{\lambda_1-\lambda_3}}, \tag{12}$$

Thus R_c can be calculated as following from Eq.(9):

$$R_c = V(V^T R_c). \tag{13}$$

Then the normal vector of the supporting plane can be calculated as follows,

$$N = R_c \begin{pmatrix} 0 \\ 0 \\ 1 \end{pmatrix} = V \begin{pmatrix} S_2\sqrt{\frac{\lambda_1-\lambda_2}{\lambda_1-\lambda_3}} \\ 0 \\ -S_1\sqrt{\frac{\lambda_2-\lambda_3}{\lambda_1-\lambda_3}} \end{pmatrix}. \tag{14}$$

However, since the two undetermined signs S_1 and S_2 are left, we have four possible answers for N. If we define the normal vector of the supporting vector to be the one directing to the camera, we have the constraint, $N \bullet (0\ 0\ 1)^T > 0$. Then at least one of S_1 and S_2 can be determined, thus the number of the possible answers of N and C is reducible to two or less.

2.2   The "Two-Circle" Algorithm

As described in the section 2.1, the normal vector of the supporting plane and the center of the circle can be determined from one perspective image, when the focal length is known. But, when the focal length is unknown, we can not form unique oblique elliptical cone, and accordingly we can not determine the normal vector.

In order to solve this problem, we consider using two circles. After contours of two circles are detected and fitted with ellipses, according to section 2.1, two oblique elliptical cones can be formed from the each of the detected ellipses *if we give a focal length*. From each of them, the normal vector of the supporting plane can be estimated independently. If we have given a wrong focal length, the formed cones will be deformed from the real ones, and the estimated normal vectors of the supporting plane(s) from each of the two cones will be different from each other. If and only if we give the correct focal length, the normal vectors estimated from each of the detected ellipses will become parallel, and the angle between the two normal vectors θ will be near to zero (see Fig.2).

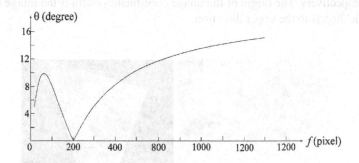

Fig. 2. The relation between the focal length f and the angle between the two normal vectors

Let $N_1(f)$ denote the normal vector estimated from one of the two ellipses and $N_2(f)$ denote the normal vector estimated from the other. Because the supporting planes of the two circles are parallel, $N_1(f)$ and $N_2(f)$ are also parallel. This constraint can be expressed by the following equation,

$$N_1(f) \times N_2(f) = 0. \tag{15}$$

Thus by minimizing the following expression, the normal vector as well as the focal length f can be determined. The undermined signs remained in Eq.(14) can also be determined at the same time.

$$\left(N_1(f) \times N_2(f)\right)^2 \rightarrow \min. \tag{16}$$

Therefore, by taking a face image where two eyes are big enough, the normal vector of the supporting planes of the both circular iris boundaries can be estimated, from which the visual direction can be calculated. Here, the iris center, the eyeball center, the iris radius and other facial features except the iris contour are not used.

3   Experimental Results

We first tested our algorithm on some simulated images to exame the estimation error caused by the quantification error. We noticed that if the minor axis is bigger than 30 pixels, the estimation error will become small enough[1].

3.1   Experiment with Real Images

We tested our method with a real image shown in Figure 3(a). The detected and fitted ellipses are superimposed in the original image. It contains three circular objects: CD1 (the big CD on the table), CD2 (the big CD on the book) and CD3 (the small CD on the table). CD1 and CD3 are coplanar, and CD2 is on another plane that is parallel to the supporting plane of CD1 and CD3. The image size is 1600×1200[Pixel]. The parameters of the detected ellipses are shown in Table 1, where a, b, θ and (x_0, y_0) is the major axis, minor axis, the angle between the major axis and the X-axis, and the center of the ellipse, respectively. The origin of the image coordinate system is the image center, and the Y axis directs to the upper direction.

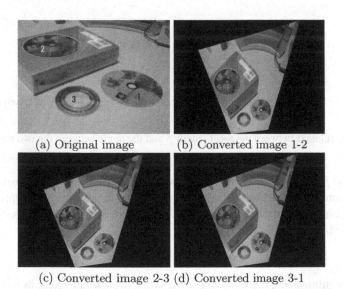

(a) Original image   (b) Converted image 1-2

(c) Converted image 2-3 (d) Converted image 3-1

Fig. 3. Original image and converted images

The normal vector of the supporting plane (a table) and the focal length of the camera can be estimated using any two of the three circles (CD discs). The results are summarized in Table 2. Since the true answer is not available, we used the estimation results to convert the original image to a vertical view of the table to see whether it resembles the real scene or not. The three results obtained by using different circle pairs

Table 1. Estimated parameters of the ellipses

No.	CD1	CD2	CD3
a(pixel)	332	307	242
b(pixel)	180	127	162
θ(degree)	13.2	-1.1	3.5
x_0(pixel)	400	-440	-162
y_0(pixel)	-115	325	-252

are shown in figure 3 (b), (c) and (d). In the converted images, each circular object shows a circle and the book shows a rectangle. This indicates that the "two-circles" algorithm could give correct results for real images.

Table 2. Estimated extrinsic parameters from the image shown in Figure 3(a)

No.	θ (degree)	β (degree)	Normal Vector	f (pixel)
1-2	33.3	4.9	(0.07 0.83 0.55)	1998
2-3	34.2	6.1	(0.09 0.82 0.56)	1893
3-1	33.7	6.3	(0.09 0.83 0.55)	2007

3.2 Experiment with Real Face Images

In order to test facial image recognition algorithms including the proposed visual direction estimation in this paper, we have built a eye gaze image database. All the images were taken in a indoor environment where the lighting condition, the camera setting, etc. are controllable. For each person, we let him/her show 15 different head poses and gaze directions by giving instructions. Figure 7 shows a sample image set of one person in the database. Currently, we have 92 × 15 images in the database.

We tested our method by applying it to many real face images taken by a digital still camera (Canon EOS DigitalKiss) with a zoom lens (f=18-55[mm] or f=2450-7500[Pixel]). The image size is 3072 × 2048[Pixel]. Some of the images used in the experiment are shown in Figure 6. The experimental environment for taking the images No.1-No.6 is shown in figure 4, where We let a user look at a marker far away from him/her in the frontal direction. The image No.1-No.2 were taken by camera C1, and No.3-No.6 were taken by camera C2. The images No.7-No.9 were taken in a uncontrolled environment.

For each image, the eye regions are detected[2]. Some sample images enhancement processings are applied to the eye region to make the iris clear. Then the iris contours are detected and fitted with ellipses, which are used to calculate the normal vector of the supporting plane of the iris boundaries with the "two-circles" algorithm. The direction of the visual direction is obtained from the estimated normal vector. Figure 5 shows the procedure of visual direction estimation.

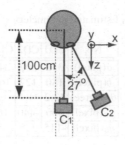

Fig. 4. The test environment for the visual direction estimating experiment

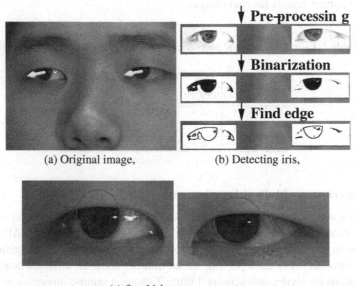

| Image size | a_l: b_l: θ_l: x_{0l}: y_{0l} | visual direction direction |
(Pixel)	a_r: b_r: θ_r: x_{0r}: y_{0r}	
720×480	33: 33: -35.9: 190: 63	(-0.35 -0.07 0.94)
	34: 30: 83.3: -178: 56	

(d) The fitted ellipse parameters and estimated visual direction.

Fig. 5. The procedure of the visual direction estimation

Figure 6 and 7 show some experimental results of visual direction estimation. The experimental results obtained from the images shown in Figure 6 are summarized in Table 3, and estimated visual direction was showed by arrows superimposed on iris in each face image.

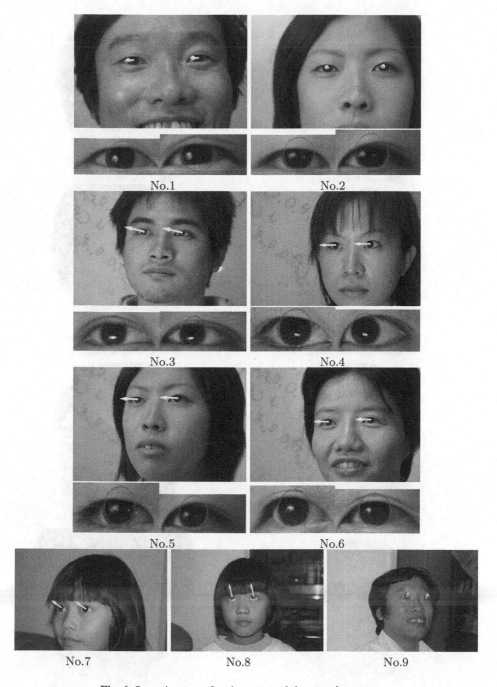

No.1   No.2

No.3   No.4

No.5   No.6

No.7   No.8   No.9

Fig. 6. Some images of real scene used the experiment

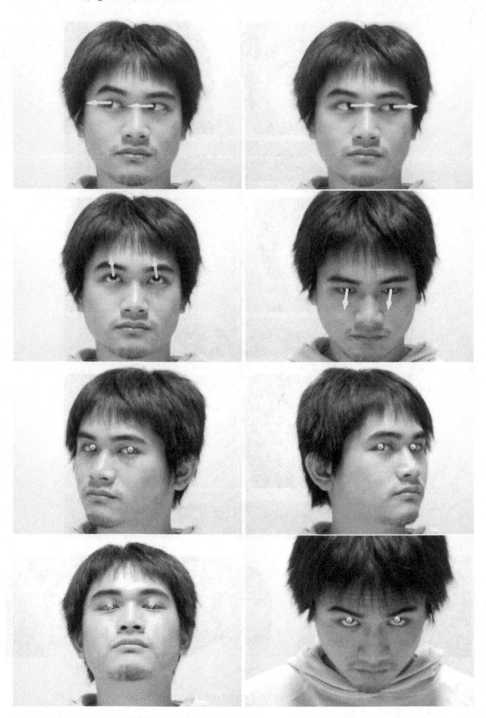

Fig. 7. A sample experimental results using our face images in our database

Table 3. Experimental results estimated from the images shown in Figure 6

No.	Elliptical iris contours left: a_l: b_l: θ_l: x_{ol}: y_{ol} right: a_r: b_r: θ_r: x_{or}: y_{or}	visual direction direction
1	112: 100: 84.5: 672: 243 109: 103: -79.7: -477: 195	(-0.28 -0.00 0.96)
2	102: 99: 38.9: 861: 102 100: 98: -83.4: -146: 84	(-0.07 0.02 0.99)
3	69: 56: -73.9: 390: 291 63: 52: -79.4: -277: 313	(-0.57 0.13 0.81)
4	68: 63: -89.4: 635: 89 74: 59: -85.9: 14: 78	(-0.61 -0.01 0.79
5	88: 75: -76.5: 324: 492 78: 60: -81.5: -375: 469	(-0.56 0.02 0.83)
6	73: 70: 86.0: 647: 97 73: 62: -83.6: -109: 54	(-0.49 -0.00 0.87)
7	62: 55: -63.0: -98: -175 59: 46: -68.4: -588: -160	(-0.36 0.26 0.89
8	46: 37: -5.3: 107: 79 47: 35: -26.2: -325: 66	(-0.13 0.55 0.83)
9	35: 33: 62.8: 456: 53 36: 34: 22.7: 43: 77	(0.13 0.20 0.97)

4   Conclusion

This paper has presented a new method to estimate visual direction from a single monocular image. This method only uses the iris contours and does not require the whole wiew
of the iris boundaries, and it does not use the information about the iris centers. Compared
with existing method, our method does not use either the eye corners or the heuristic
knowledge about the eyeball. Another advantage of our algorithm is that a camera with
an unknown focal length can be used without assuming the orthographical projection.
The extensive experiments over simulated images and real images demonstrate the robustness and the effectiveness of our method.

Acknowledgments

This research was partially supported by the Ministry of Education, Culture Sports
Science and Techmology, Grant-in-Aid for Scientific Research (A)(2), 16200014, and
(C), 16500112, 2004.

References

1. Q.Chen, H.Wu and T.Wada, Camera Calibration with Two Arbitrary Coplanar Circles, ECCV, pp.521-532, 2004.
2. H. WU, *et al*, Automatic Facial Feature Points Detection with SUSAN Operator, SCIA, pp.257-263, 2001.
3. J.G. Wang, E. Sung and R. Venkateswarlu, Eye Gaze Estimation from a Single Image of One Eye, ICCV'03.
4. A.Criminisi, J. Shotton, A. Blake and P.H.S. Torr, Gaze Manipulation for One-to-one Tele-conferencing, ICCV'03.
5. D.H. Yoo, *et al*, Non-contact Eye Gaze Tracking System by Mapping of Corneal Reflections, FG, 2002
6. Y. Matsumoto and A. Zelinsky, presented An Algorithm for Real-time Stereo Vision Implementation of Head Pose and Gaze Direction Measurement, FG, pp.499-504, 2000.
7. J. Zhu and J. Yang, Subpixel Eye Gaze Tracking, FG, 2002
8. Y.l. Tian, K. Kanade and J.F. Cohn, Dual-state Parametric Eye Tracking, FG, pp.110-115, 2000
9. A. Schubert, Detection and Tracking of Facial Feature in Real time Using a Synergistic Approach of Spatio-Temporal Models and Generalized Hough-Transform Techniques, FG, pp.116-121, 2000.
10. F.D.l. Torre, Y. Yacoob and L. Davis, A Probabilistic Framework for Rigid and Non-rigid Appearance Based Tracking and Recognition, FG, pp.491-498, 2000.
11. M.Dhome, J.T.Lapreste, G.Rives and M.Richetin, Spatial Localization of Modeled Objects of Revolution in Monocular Perspective Vision, *ECCV 90*, pp. 475–485, 1990.
12. K.Kanatani and L.Wu, 3D Interpretation of Conics and Orthogonality, *Image Understanding*, Vol.58, Nov, pp. 286-301, 1993.
13. L.Wu and K.Kanatani, Interpretation of Conic Motion and Its Applications, *Int. Journal of Computer Vision* , Vol.10, No.1, pp. 67–84, 1993.

Multiple Face Contour Detection Using Adaptive Flows

Fuzhen Huang and Jianbo Su

Institute of Automation & Research Center of Intelligent Robotics,
Shanghai Jiaotong University, Shanghai, 200030, China
{fzhuang0015, jbsu}@sjtu.edu.cn

Abstract. A novel method based on a curve evolution approach using adaptive flows is presented for multiple face contour detection in grayscale images. Assuming that the image consists of an arbitrary unknown number of separated faces and a uniform background region, the proposed method adaptively estimates mean intensities for each separated region and use a single curve to capture multiple regions with different intensities. The adaptive flow developed in this paper is easily formulated and solved using level set method. Experiments are performed on a large test set and show the efficiency of our method.

1 Introduction

Face contour detection is important in facial feature extraction [1] and in model-based coding [2]. The inner face boundary (the border of the chin, cheeks and lower hairline) has also been used in face recognition studies, as part of an extended feature vector [3]. For the face boundary, classical edge detection techniques are limited by their inability to provide an implicit description and can fail to exploit the inherent continuity of the face boundary. As such, curve evolution methods especially active contours are probably the best choice.

One of the first active contours, snakes, was designed to model the continuity and smoothness in curves, and at the same time provides sufficient flexibility and deformability to cope with shapes of curves. Huang and Chen [1], Lam and Yan [4], Sobottka and Pitas [5] have all used snakes to extract or track face contours in images. Their successes have demonstrated that snakes are indeed a good choice for detecting the head boundary. However, as there are no estimation of the head's position in the image, the search is performed inwards from the edge of the image leading to the snake converge to strong image features in the background at times.

Another class of active contour, active shape models [6], exploits shape information based statistics obtained from training data. Cootes and Taylor [6] have provided a suitable initialization method and demonstrated very accurate extraction of the facial features and face boundary. However, this method has so far been demonstrated only for a small range of viewpoints against a simple background. Moreover, active shape models can only deform to allowed variations of a basis shape.

Geometric active contours [7] were introduced more recently. Based on the theory of curve evolution implemented via level set techniques [8], they have several important advantages over the above two kinds of models, such as numerical

S.Z. Li et al. (Eds.): Sinobiometrics 2004, LNCS 3338, pp. 137–143, 2004.

computation stability and the ability to change topology during deformation. In [9] Harper and Reilly proposed a method based on level set to segment face regions in color video sequence. However, their level set approach is very simple and use of color alone cannot separate face from other skin-like regions such as arms or hands.

Unfortunately, all the above successes in face contour detection are currently limited only to single face contour detection with front-parallel viewpoints. In this paper, we will describe a method using geometric active contours based on adaptive flows to detect multiple face boundaries in grayscale images. Assuming that the image consists of an arbitrary unknown number of separated faces and a uniform background region, the proposed method adaptively estimates mean intensities for each separated region and use a single curve to capture multiple regions with different intensities.

The remainder of this paper is arranged as follows: Section 2 briefly introduces the geometric active contours, Section 3 presents our multiple face contour detection algorithm based on adaptive flows, Section 4 shows some experimental results and discussions, Section 5 is the concluding remarks.

2   Geometric Active Contours

Geometric active contours are based on the theory of curve evolution implemented via level set techniques. Its central idea is to follow the evolution of a function ϕ whose zero level set always corresponds to the position of a closed curve C, i.e.:

$$C(t) = \{\bar{x} \mid \phi(\bar{x},t) = 0\}. \tag{1}$$

The original geometric active contour formulation is given by [7]:

$$\frac{\partial \phi}{\partial t} = g(|\nabla I|)(\kappa + v)|\nabla \phi|, \tag{2}$$

where $|\nabla \phi|$ denotes the gradient norm of ϕ, $\kappa = \text{div}(\nabla \phi / |\nabla \phi|)$ is the curvature, v is a constant, $g(|\nabla I|)$ is an edge potential derived from the image I and defined as:

$$g(|\nabla I|) = \frac{1}{1 + |\nabla G_\sigma * I|^p}, \tag{3}$$

where G_σ is the Gaussian function, $p = 1\, or\, 2$. In (1), the product $g(\kappa + v)$ determines the overall evolution speed of level sets of ϕ along their normal direction.

The original geometric active contour model works well for objects that have good contrast. When the object boundary is indistinct or has gaps, however, the contour tends to leak through the boundary. The reason may be that the models rely on the image gradient $|\nabla I|$ to stop the curve evolution. So it can only detect objects with edges defined by gradients. To address this problem, Chan and Vese [10] proposed a novel model without a stopping edge function. Assume that the image I consists of two regions with approximately piecewise constant intensities: a foreground region R with a constant intensity u_0, and a background region with a different intensity v_0. Their model is developed to minimize a fitting energy with some regularization terms, of the form

$$E_{MS}(C,c_1,c_2) = \lambda_1 \int_{inside(C)} (I-c_1)^2 \, dA + \lambda_2 \int_{outside(C)} (I-c_2)^2 \, dA + \mu \int_C ds \,, \qquad (4)$$

where $\mu \geq 0$, $\lambda_1, \lambda_2 > 0$ are fixed parameters, C is a closed curve to be determined, and c_1, c_2 are two unknown parameters to be chosen inside and outside C respectively. A binary flow that evolves the curve along the steepest descent for the energy is

$$C_t = \left(-\lambda_1 (I-c_1)^2 + \lambda_2 (I-c_2)^2 \right) \vec{N} - \mu \kappa \vec{N} \,, \qquad (5)$$

where $\vec{N}$ is the outward normal of C, and κ is the local curvature of C. The final model can be easily expressed in a level set form as

$$\frac{\partial \phi}{\partial t} = \delta(\phi) \left[\mu \kappa - \lambda_1 (I-c_1)^2 + \lambda_2 (I-c_2)^2 \right]. \qquad (6)$$

And the parameters c_1, c_2 are computed as:

$$c_1 = \frac{\int_\Omega I(x,y) H(\phi) dxdy}{\int_\Omega H(\phi) dxdy} \,, \quad c_2 = \frac{\int_\Omega I(x,y)(1-H(\phi)) dxdy}{\int_\Omega (1-H(\phi)) dxdy}. \qquad (7)$$

The Heaviside function H in (7) and the one-dimensional Dirac measure δ in (6) are defined respectively by

$$H(z) = \begin{cases} 1, & \text{if } z \geq 0 \\ 0, & \text{if } z < 0 \end{cases}, \quad \delta(z) = \frac{d}{dz} H(z). \qquad (8)$$

This model can detect objects with smooth boundaries or discontinuous boundaries. Moreover, even if the initial image is very noisy, the boundaries can very well detected and preserved. However, using only one level set function, it can represent only two phases or segments in the image.

3 Adaptive Flows for Multiple Face Contour Detection

When working with level sets to represent more than two segments, the general idea is to use more than one level set function. For example, Zhao et al. [11] use one level set to represent each region. Thus, if N regions need to be segmented, then N level set functions are needed. Chan and Vese also proposed a multi-phase level set representation in [12]. Based on the Four Color Theorem, they assume that in general, at most two level set functions are sufficient to detect and represent distinct objects of distinct intensities in the piecewise smooth case. However, as the evolutions of multiple level set functions are coupled each other in all these multi-phase models, the convergence is very time-consuming and the algorithm may not converge to a global minimum.

In this section, we will develop a single curve evolution method using adaptive flows that can handle images with multiple non-overlapping regions and use the new model for multiple face contour detection. Our model is derived from [13] and is an extension of the two-phase model proposed by Chan and Vese in [10] as described in the last section. The basic idea of our method is to capture multiple face contours using a single curve, i.e., our algorithm is implemented using a single level set function to segment the image into n separated foreground regions and a background region, assuming that there are n separated faces in the image.

Given a closed curve C, which consists of N_c multiple closed curve segments and each segment encloses a separated region. Let χ_i denote the characteristic function over the region enclosed by the i th curve segment C_i, defined as

$$\chi_i(\vec{r}) = \begin{cases} 1 & if\ \vec{r} \in ith\ region \\ 0 & otherwise \end{cases}. \tag{9}$$

Let c_i denote the mean intensity of the i th region enclosed C_i, and c_b denote the mean intensity of the region outside the curve C. Then to obtain the desired gradient flow, we want to minimize the following energy functional

$$E = \lambda_1 \int_{inside(C)} \left(I - \sum_{i=1}^{N_c} c_i \chi_i \right)^2 dA + \lambda_2 \int_{outside(C)} (I - c_b)^2 dA + \mu \int_C ds. \tag{10}$$

In the above energy functional, the foreground region can have an arbitrary number of distinct regions, each of which has a constant intensity value inside the region. Thus, it is a generalization of the energy functional of the Chan-Vese model as in (4). Note also that the number of regions N_c can change as the curve C evolves, thereby determining the number of distinct piecewise constant intensity values as part of the optimization.

The resulting gradient flow that evolves curve C along the steepest descent of the energy functional (10) is

$$C_t = \left[-\lambda_1 \left(I - \sum_{i=1}^{N_c} c_i \chi_i \right)^2 + \lambda_2 (I - c_b)^2 \right] \vec{N} - \lambda \kappa \vec{N}. \tag{11}$$

The above equation allows any point on a closed curve segment to evolve according to the gradient force jointly determined by the intensity of the original image at that point, the mean intensity of the region enclosed by the curve segment, and the mean intensity of the background region. This gradient force varies from one separated region to the other, marking the resulting flow for curve evolution adaptive to the image domain, so we call it adaptive flows. Note that in the case where there is only one closed curve segment, i.e., $N_c = 1$, the above curve is the same as the binary flow equation in (5).

For effective computation, the gradient flow in (10) can be implemented using level set techniques, by representing the curve C as the zero level set of a scalar function ϕ. The final model is as follows:

$$\frac{\partial \phi}{\partial t} = \delta(\phi)\left[\mu\kappa - \lambda_1\left(I - \sum_{i=1}^{N_c} c_i \chi_i\right)^2 + \lambda_2\left(I - c_b\right)^2\right]. \tag{12}$$

The function ϕ can be used to determine the number of isolated closed curve segments efficiently, by finding connected components where ϕ has the same sign. The parameters c_i ($i = 1, \cdots, N_c$) and c_b can be computed as

$$c_i = \frac{\int_\Omega I \chi_i \mathrm{d}A}{\int_\Omega \chi_i \mathrm{d}A}, \quad c_b = \frac{\int_\Omega I(1 - \sum_{i=1}^{N_c} \chi_i)\mathrm{d}A}{\int_\Omega (1 - \sum_{i=1}^{N_c} \chi_i)\mathrm{d}A}. \tag{13}$$

The corresponding numerical algorithm used in our implementation is summarized as follows:

(1) Initialize contour $C(t = 0)$, and determine the number of separated region N_c enclosed by $C(t = 0)$. Initialize the level set function ϕ using the signed distance function of $C(t = 0)$.

(2) For each separated region, estimate its local mean intensity c_i and the background intensity c_b according to equation (13).

(3) Evolve the level set function ϕ according to equation (12) and obtain a new contour $C(t)$ as the zero level set of ϕ.

(4) Estimate the number of separated regions N_c enclosed by the new contour $C(t)$.

(5) Repeat step (2) to (4) until the contour converges.

4   Experimental Results and Discussions

In our experiment we have collected a large set of real face images with different size from the Internet, each of which contains multiple faces with various sizes and different backgrounds. Most of the faces in the face database are separated from each other. The algorithm is implemented in Matlab and based on a Pentium IV 1.8G PC. The average speed is about 10 second. In all our experiment, we set the initial parameters as follows: $\lambda_1 = \lambda_2 = 1$, $\mu = 0.02 * 255^2$.

Fig. 1 gives an example to demonstrate how our algorithm works. Fig. 1 (a) is an original image from our dataset. Fig. 1 (b) is the image added with initial curves, where white curves denote the initialize curves. It is natural to consider different initial conditions for the same image with the same parameters and the initial conditions do influence the convergence of the algorithm. But from our experiment, we find that for real images the initial condition of generating multi-component initial curve with a large number of small spoiled sub-regions as in (b) has the tendency of computing a global minimum. Fig. 1 (c) shows the final result, where the white curves are the detected face contours. To speed up the curve evolution convergence procedure, the number of faces in the image is used as a prior and validated the final results, i.e., the algorithm is ended when the number of separated region N_c equals to the number of faces a priori.

Fig. 2 shows some other multiple face contour detection results. From these results we can see that almost all faces in our test images can be detected satisfactorily. But since we use the number of faces as the convergent condition, the final face contours are not so accurately, especially those in hairlines, ears, or chins due to the poor contrast in these regions.

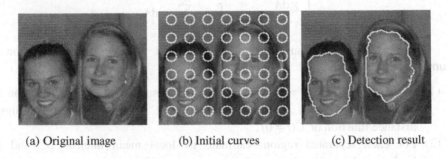

(a) Original image   (b) Initial curves   (c) Detection result

Fig. 1. Segmentation result of extended Chan-Vese model

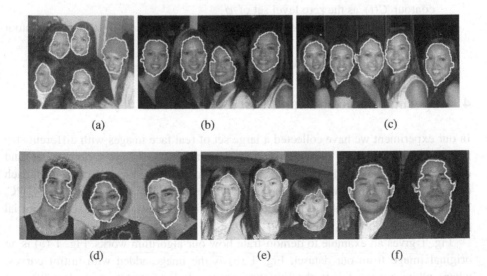

(a)   (b)   (c)

(d)   (e)   (f)

Fig. 2. Some multiple face contour detection results

5 Conclusions

In this paper, a multiple face contour detection method based on a curve evolution approach using adaptive flows is proposed. Assuming that there are n separated faces in the image, our goal is to use a single curve which consists of n separated multiple closed curve segments and each segment encloses a separated face region. To speed up the curve converge process, the number of faces in the image is used as a priori and validated the final results. Experiments on a large dataset show that our method can detect multiple face contours in images quite exactly. However, our method still has difficulty in extracting face contours that are occluded by other objects. And we do not test our model on overlapped face images. Our future work will be conducted to deal with partially occluded or overlapped face contour detection problems.

References

1. Huang, C.L., Chen, C.W.: Human facial feature extraction for face interpretation and recognition. Pattern recognition 12 (1992) 1435–1444
2. Welsh, W.J., Searby, S., Waite, J.B.: Model-based image coding. British telecom technology Journal 3 (1990) 94–106
3. Jia, X., Nixon, M.S.: Extending the feature vector for extraction for automatic face recognition. IEEE Transactions on Pattern Analysis and Machine Intelligence 12 (1995) 1167–1176
4. Lam, K.M., Yan, H.: Location head boundary by snakes. International Symposium on Speech, Image Processing and Neural Networks (1994) 17–20
5. Sobottka, K., Pitas, I.: Segmentation and tracking of faces in color images. Proceedings of the International Conference on Automatic Face and Gesture Recognition (1996) 236–241
6. Cootes, T.F., Taylor, C.J., Cooper, D.H., et al.: Active shape models – their training and application. Computer Vision and Image Understanding 1 (1995) 38–59
7. Caselles, V., Catte, F., Coll, T., et al.: A geometric model for active contours in image processing. Numerische Mathematik 1 (1993) 1–31
8. Sethian, J.A.: Level Set methods and Fast Marching Methods: Evolving interfaces in computational geometry, fluid mechanics, computer vision, and materials science. Cambridge University Press (1999)
9. Harper, P., Reilly, R.B.: Color based video segmentation using level sets. International Conference on Image Processing (2000) 480–483
10. Chan, T.F., Vese, L.A.: Active contours without edges. IEEE Transactions on Image Processing 2 (2001) 266–277
11. Zhao, H.K., Chan, T.F., Merriman, B., Osher, S.: A variational level set approach to multiphase motion. Journal of Computational Physics 1 (1996) 179–195
12. Vese, L.A., Chan, T.F.: A multiphase level set framework for image segmentation using the Mumford and shah model. International Journal of Computer Vision 3 (2002) 271–293
13. Feng, H., Castanon D.A., Karl W.C.: A curve evolution approach for image segmentation using adaptive flows. Proceedings of the 8th International Conference on Computer Vision (2001) 494–499

Pose Normalization Using Generic 3D Face Model as a Priori for Pose-Insensitive Face Recognition

Xiujuan Chai[1], Shiguang Shan[2], Wen Gao[1,2], and Xin Liu[1]

[1] School of Computer Science and Technology, Harbin Institute of Technology,
150001 Harbin, P.R. China
{xjchai, wgao, xin_liu}@jdl.ac.cn
[2] ICT-ISVISION Joint R&D Laboratory for Face Recognition, CAS,
100080 Beijing, P.R. China
{sgshan}@ict.ac.cn

Abstract. Abrupt performance degradation caused by face pose variations has been one of the bottlenecks for practical face recognition applications. This paper presents a practical pose normalization technique by using a generic 3D face model as a priori. The 3D face model greatly facilitates the setup of the correspondence between non-frontal and frontal face images, which can be exploited as a priori to transform a non-frontal face image, with known pose but very sparse correspondence with the generic face model, into a frontal one by warping techniques. Our experiments have shown that the proposed method can greatly improve the recognition performance of the current face recognition methods without pose normalization.

1 Introduction

The face recognition (FR) technique can be applied in many fields including human-machine interface, commercial and law enforcement, such as face screen saver, access control, credit card identity and mug-shot database matching, etc. In the past few years, FR has been developing rapidly, which makes the above applications feasible. However the pose and illumination are still the bottlenecks in the study and practice of FR [1]. This paper focuses on the pose problem in FR.

Pose-invariant face recognition is to perform the recognition of the face image, whose pose is different from the images in gallery. The difference between poses, to a great extent, will induce the intensity variation even for the same person. The distinction is often more remarkable than that caused by the difference of persons under the same pose. So the performance of the conventional appearance-based method, such as eigenface, will decrease dramatically when the input image is non-frontal.

Many approaches have been proposed to recognize faces under various poses. Among them, view-based subspace methods are most famous [2,3,5,6]. These techniques need lots of face images in all pose classes. And the performance of the recognition has great relation to the sampling density. Similarly, Murase and Nayar

S.Z. Li et al. (Eds.): Sinobiometrics 2004, LNCS 3338, pp. 144–152, 2004.

[4] projected the multiple views of the object into an eigenspace and the projections fell on a 2D manifold in that eigenspace. Modeling the manifold makes the recognition of the faces feasible under arbitrary pose. Neural networks are also applied to multi-views face recognition. In [9], several neural networks are trained each for an eigenspace of different poses, and their results are combined with another neural network so as to perform face recognition. Another approach to tackle the pose-invariant face recognition is the eigen light-fields proposed by Gross and Matthews [10,11]. This algorithm operates by estimating the eigen light-fields of the subject's head from the input gallery or probe images. Matching between the probe and gallery is then performed by means of the eigen light-fields. But the precise computation of the plenoptic function is difficult, and in [8,10], the authors substitute the plenoptic function approximately by concatenating the normalized images vectors under many poses.

Another mainstream way is to synthesize the frontal view from the given non-frontal pose image by using the rendering methods of computer graphics. The view-based Active Appearance Models proposed by Cootes and Walker [8] and the 3D Morphable Model technique put forward by V. Blanz and T. Vetter are representative methods [7,13]. But the good results of these methods depend on the time-consuming optimization, which is the reason why these algorithms do not fit the real-time tasks.

Our motivation is to find a fast and effective algorithm to do pose-insensitive face recognition. In this paper, we proposed a novel pose normalization strategy, and the normalized frontal face images can be used as the input of the frontal face recognition system to perform the recognizing. First, we investigate the relationship between the 3D face model and the 2D face image. Thus the correspondence of some feature points locations between the non-frontal face and the frontal face can be obtained easily. The corresponding feature points share the same semantic meaning. Therefore the shape vectors used to do warping are formed by concatenating the coordinate values of the points. After triangulating the feature points, gray texture mapping is performed from the non-frontal image to fontal one. Finally, for the region, which is visible in the frontal view but invisible in the non-frontal view, the symmetry of the face is exploited to make compensation.

The remaining part of the paper is organized as follows: in Section 2, we introduce the generic 3D face model and the process of labeling the feature points. Section 3 describes the pose normalization algorithm in details. Pose-invariant face recognition framework and experiments are presented in Section 4, followed by short conclusion and discussion in the last section.

2 The Generic 3D Model

An intuitional way to do pose normalization is using the affine transformation between the images under non-frontal and frontal poses recurring to the sparse correspondence. This can be illustrated in Figure 1.

(a) Frontal pose   (b) Left pose

Fig. 1. Example face images with landmarks under two different poses

But in fact, the pair of landmarks in (a) and (b) is not corresponding to each other absolutely in semantic. The head rotation causes the invisibility of some contour points in frontal pose. In non-frontal image, the corresponding points with the same semantic meaning cannot be found (take the Fig.1. as the example). So the corresponding relation of landmarks between different poses cannot be established easily. For example, in the Figure 1, we usually think that the red dot in (a) and (b) are the same point, but in fact they are not. The real corresponding point in (a) to the red dot in (b) is the blue rectangle point. And actually, most points at left profile contour in frontal view will disappear when the face rotates to left pose. Therefore the key of affine transformation based on feature points is to find the proper correspondence between the feature points under different poses.

To define the corresponding feature points at different poses precisely, we hereby import the generic 3D face model. The mesh structure is used to construct the 3D face model [12]. Our 3D model is formed by totally 1143 space vertices and 2109 triangles. Based on this 3D face model, we can rotate the model with any rotation angle and project it to 2D image. Therefore it is easy to obtain the locations of the corresponding feature points. First by setting the view point to frontal, we label 60 feature points marking the organs and contour in frontal, then we set the view point to the specific angle of view and again label the feature points marking the face edges. When completing the label process, we compute all the feature points coordinate values under multi-poses. Thus the correspondence of sparse landmarks between frontal and the appointed rotated pose will be found out. Figure 2 presents the examples of some face images with feature points labeled on the generic 3D face model.

Consequently the corresponding shape vectors between arbitrary two poses can be erected according to this method. When computing the affine transformation between the shape vectors under two poses, we selected proper feature points to compose the shape vector. We also take the Figure 2 (a) and (b) as an example to explain. If we want to erect the correspondence between the shape vectors of frontal and left 15-degree pose, the landmarks in (b) are regarded as the shape vector under left. We should find the corresponding landmarks in (a) to the left contour key points. So the 11 red points rather than the blue contour points are selected to represent the shape vector of the frontal face. The feature points selection strategy can insure the consistence of these two shape vectors under two poses. Following the affine transformation between the two vectors, we compensate the region invisible under the given left pose, but visible under frontal pose. The region is shown in the (d). There are two connected region in (d), in the case of above, we can obviously know that the left connected region in (d) is the region need to do compensation.

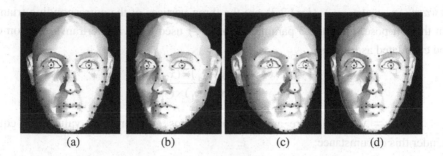

(a)   (b)   (c)   (d)

Fig. 2. Face samples with feature points marked under 3D condition

By rotating the 3D model, 2D model images under any pose can be gotten and the corresponding landmarks can be pre-determined. For a given face image, whose pose is determined first, we normalize its size to 92×112 according to the coordinates of its two eyes in the facial image and those in the model image under the same pose. Then a rude alignment between the given image and the model image is realized and the approximate locations of the landmarks in the given image are gotten to do pose normalization. Although this alignment is an approximation and may affect the synthesis, our target is to do recognition with the normalization frontal image rather than vivid synthesis. The landmarks are hard to be located precisely, and this process usually takes long time. Based on these considerations, we import this easy-applied landmarks alignment strategy as mentioned above.

3   The Pose Normalization Algorithm

By labeling the 3D face images manually, we can get some fiducial feature points (x_i, y_i) , some of which are selected to compose the shape vector $S = (x_1, y_1, \cdots, x_n, y_n)$. In our implementation, $n = 60$. In addition, another 10 feature points are concatenated with the corresponding points in the shape vector so as to compose the region to be compensated. See Figure 2 for reference. Through the generic 3D face model, we can obtain the universal shape vector to carry out the pose normalization.

The description of this algorithm is as follows. Here we take the transforming from left pose to frontal pose for example:

1.   Triangulate the shape vector of left pose, and then partition the face region into many triangles. Rationally, we assume that the pixels in one triangle have the similar transformation trend when the pose changed.
2.   The frontal face should do the same triangle partition. The corresponding feature points to the left pose face constitute the corresponding triangles.

3. For every pixel (x, y) in the triangle in the frontal face, the corresponding location in the triangle of the left face can be easily computed:

Let $(x_i, y_i)(i = 1,2,3)$ denote the three vertices of a triangle in the frontal pose, $(warp\_x_i, warp\_y_i)$ $(i = 1,2,3)$ are the three vertices of the corresponding triangle in the left pose. First, the 3 parameters α, β, γ used to do affine transformation can be calculated as follows:

$$\gamma = \frac{(y_2 - y_1) \times (x - x1) - (y - y_1) \times (x_2 - x_1)}{(x_3 - x_1) \times (y_2 - y_1) - (x_2 \quad x_1) \times (y_3 - y_1)} \tag{1}$$

If $x_2 = x_1$, then there are 2 vertices whose x coordinate values are equal. Under this circumstance:

$$\beta = \frac{(y - y_1) - \gamma(y_3 - y_1)}{(y_2 - y_1)} \tag{2}$$

Otherwise: $$\beta = \frac{(x - x_1) - \gamma(x_3 - x_1)}{(x_2 - x_1)} \tag{3}$$

The last parameter: $\alpha = 1 - \gamma - \beta$ $\qquad$ (4)

Having decided the three parameters, the transformed value $(warp\_x, warp\_y)$ in the left pose can be calculated through the following formula:

$$warp\_x = \alpha \times warp\_x_1 + \beta \times warp\_x_2 + \gamma \times warp\_x_3$$
$$\tag{5}$$
$$warp\_y = \alpha \times warp\_y_1 + \beta \times warp\_y_2 + \gamma \times warp\_y_3$$

4. So the intensity value $f(x, y)$ of the pixel in the virtual frontal face image can be computed by:

$$f(x, y) = f'(warp\_x, warp\_y) \tag{6}$$

Where $f'(x, y)$ is the intensity of point in the given non-frontal face image.

5. Let: $\begin{cases} x1 = int(warp\_x) \\ y1 = int(warp\_y) \end{cases}$, and $\begin{cases} dx = warp\_x - x1 \\ dy = warp\_y - y1 \end{cases}$, then:

$$f(x, y) = (1 - dx) \cdot [(1 - dy) \cdot f'(x1, y1) + dy \cdot f'(x1, y1 + 1)] +$$
$$dx[(1 - dy) \cdot f'(x1 + 1, y1) + dy \cdot f'(x1 + 1, y1 + 1)] \tag{7}$$

6. For the invisible region in the non-frontal face image, we can compensate the intensity values by using the symmetrical pixels. But this symmetrical compensation strategy will be seriously affected by the illumination. So we adopt a simple but

effective strategy to approximate the invisible pixel gray value with the intensity of the nearest pixel horizontal in face region.

4 Pose-Invariant Face Recognition Framework and Experiments

In this paper, we utilize the pose normalization strategy to tackle the pose problem in face recognition. For a given non-frontal image, we use the above-mentioned 3D-model-based pose normalization algorithm to convert it to frontal image. Then take the normalized frontal image as the input of the general frontal face recognition system to perform recognizing. Our pose-invariant FR system framework is shown in Figure 3. In this paper, the pose estimation is not our main study content, so we make the assumption that the poses of the input images are known.

First, we make an experiment on a subset of the Facial Recognition Technology (FERET) database, including five different poses, with 200 face images for each pose. In our case, the five basic poses are rotation left for 15 degree and 25 degree, frontal, rotation right for 15 degree and 25 degree respectively. Prior to obtaining the shape vectors for triangulation and affine transformation, we have to label the shape feature points manually in the generic 3D model uppermost to gain the five shape vectors for the corresponding five poses.

Fig. 3. The pose-invariant face recognition system framework

Before performing face pose normalization, input facial image must be normalized to the same size of 92×112 by the irises locations. And the standard two irises locations are varied according to the specific pose class.

How can we evaluate the performance of the pose normalization algorithm? One intuitive way is looking over the frontal face image, converted from the pose image, and giving evaluation experimentally. To obtain more objective quantitative evaluation measure, we use the virtual frontal face images, generated by our pose normalization algorithm, as the input of the general frontal face recognition system. Then the recognition ratio is compared with that taking the original posed images as the input.

The recognition strategy used in this experiment is to compute the cosine distance between the test image vector to be recognized and each normalized image vector in training set. The nearest neighbor method is used to get the identity class information. To eliminate the impact of the hair and the background when recognizing, a mask is added to the input image of the FR system.

Experimental results show that our pose normalization algorithm based on generic 3D face model has a good performance on pose normalization. The performance test results are presented in Table 1. Some original masked images and the masked frontal face images after pose normalization used to do face recognition are displayed in Figure 4. The first row in Fig. 4 is the two example persons' masked original face images under non-frontal poses. The bottom row is the corrected views after pose normalization with our algorithm corresponding to the above pose. In Table 1, it is clear that the recognition ratio has increased averagely 24.4%, which is much better than that only using the non-frontal face image without pose normalization.

Table 1. Evaluate the performance of the pose normalization algorithm in subset of FERET Database

	Left 25	Left 15	Right 15	Right 25
Recognition rate no pose alignment	27%	63%	47%	26%
Recognition rate after pose alignment	55.5%	77.5%	77.5%	50%
Increased rate	28.5%	14.5%	30.5%	24%

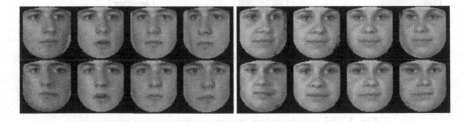

Fig. 4. The masked face images used as the input for the frontal face recognition system

We take experiments on another large database called CAS-PEAL database to test the validity of this pose normalization algorithm [14]. We classify the test images into three sets according to the pitching variation, called PM, PU and PD respectively. PM is composed by the images which only having the rotation in left or right, but without pitch rotation, including 4993 test samples. PD is composed by the images that are in looking down pose combined turning left or right, including 4998 test samples. Similarly, PU is composed by the images that are in looking up pose combined turning left or right, including 4998 tests samples. In this experiment, our frontal face recognition system uses the PCA plus LDA algorithm based on 2D Gabor features. We also use the virtual frontal face images, which have been done pose normalization to do face recognition. Comparing the recognition ratio with what is get from using the masked original images not doing pose normalization to do recognizing, we can find that there is greater increasing as shown in Figure 5. For the PM pose, we achieve 15.8% increasing in right recognition rate. 8.6% and 13.7% increasing are gained for the PU and PD pose respectively.

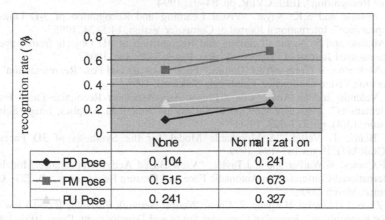

	None	Normalization
—◆— PD Pose	0. 104	0. 241
—■— PM Pose	0. 515	0. 673
—▲— PU Pose	0. 241	0. 327

Fig. 5. The performance evaluation of pose normalization for pose-invariant face recognition in the subsets of CAS_PEAL Database

5 Conclusion

In this paper we discuss the face pose normalization and erect a pose-invariant face recognition framework. A simple triangulation and affine transformation method is used to correct the non-frontal face to frontal face image by warping the shape vector under any appointed pose to frontal. The landmarks under appointed poses are gained from a generic 3D face model, which makes the correspondence between the different poses shape vectors found easily. To correct the non-frontal images, if the poses of images are known, then the shape vectors used to do transformation are definite. Finally, through shape warping and gray texture mapping, the frontal image is generated. Our experiments demonstrate the good performance and low complexity of such a generic 3D face model based method.

Whereas, the face rotation is not the simple linear transformation, affine transformation cannot model the sophisticated varieties precisely. This causes our algorithm less effective when the head rotation is greater than 35 degree. So erecting the elaborate 3D model for the specific person is an orientation in our future work.

Acknowledgements

This research is partially sponsored by Natural Science Foundation of China under contract No.60332010, National Hi-Tech Program of China (No. 2001AA114190 and 2002AA118010), and ISVISION Technologies Co., Ltd. The authors would also give thanks to those who provided the public face databases.

References

1. R.Brunelli and T.Poggio, "Face Recognition: Features versus Template", TPAMI, 15(10), pp. 1042–1052, 1993
2. A. Pentland, B. Moghaddam and T. Starner. "View-based and Modular Eigenspace for Face Recognition", IEEE CVPR, pp. 84–91, 1994
3. H. Murase and S.K. Nayar. "Visual Learning and Recognition of 3-D Objects form Appearance", International Journal of Computer Vision, 14:5–24, 1995
4. H.Murase and S. Nayar. "Learning and Recognition of 3D Objects from Appearance", International Journal of Computer Vision. Pages 5–25, Jan. 1995.
5. SmMcKenna, S. Gong and J.J. Collins. "Face Tracking and Pose Representation", British Machine Vision Conference, Edinburgh, Scotland, 1996.
6. D. Valentin and H. Abdi. "Can a Linear Autoassociator Recognize Faces From New Orientations", Journal of the Optical Society of American A-optics, Image Science and Vision, 13(4), pp. 717–724, 1996.
7. V. Blanz, T. Vetter. "A Morphable Model for the Synthesis of 3D Faces", Proc. SIGGRAPH, Pages 187–194, 1999.
8. T.F.Cootes, K.Walker and C.J.Taylor. "View-Based Active Appearance Models", IEEE International Conference on Automatic Face and Gesture Recognition . pp. 227– Grenoble, France, March. 2000.
9. Z. Zhou, J.HuangFu, H.Zhang, Z. Chen. "Neural Network Ensemble Based View Invariant Face Recognition", Journal of Computer Study and Development. Pages 1061–1065. 38(9) 2001.
10. R. Gross, I. Matthews, and S. Baker. "Eigen Light-Fields and Face Recognition Across Pose", In Proceedings of the Fifth International Conference on Face and Gesture Recognition. 2002.
11. R. Gross, I. Matthews, and S. Baker. "Appearance-Based Face Recognition and Light Fields", Tech. Report CMU-RI-TR-02-20, Robotics Institute, Carnegie Mellon University, August, 2002.
12. D.L. Jiang, W. Gao, Z.Q. Wang, Y.Q. Chen. "Realistic 3D Facial Animation with Subtle Texture Changes", ICICS-PCM2003, Singapore, Dec. 2003
13. V. Blanz and T. Vetter. "Face Recognition Based on Fitting a 3D Morphable Model", IEEE Transactions on PAMI. Vol. 25. pp.1063-1074, 2003
14. W. Gao, B. Cao, S.G. Shan, D.L. Zhou, X.H. Zhang and D.B. Zhao. "The CAS-PEAL Large-Scale Chinese Face DataBase and Evaluation Protocols", Technique Report No. JDL-TR_04_FR_001, Joint Research & Development Laboratory, CAS, 2004 (http://www.jdl.ac.cn)

Gabor-Based Kernel Fisher Discriminant Analysis for Pose Discrimination

Jiada Chen, Jianhuang Lai, and Guocan Feng

Center of Computer Vision, Sun Yat-sen University
Reis_chen@163.com, {stsljh, mcsfgc}@zsu.edu.cn

Abstract. This paper presents a novel Gabor-based Kernel Fisher Discriminant Analysis (KFDA) method to determine human pose under depth rotation (out of the image plane). Specially, the capability of different orientation and size of Gabor Filter is discussed and the optimal one is selected for feature representation. Then KFDA with fractional power polynomial models leads to a non-linear projection to meet the non-linear depth rotation of human face. In the experiment section, we can see that, the correct classification rate of 93.5% is achieved in MIT database.

1 Introduction

Human face recognition is a hot research spot in many areas like artificial intelligence and pattern recognition. However, according the survey in FRVT 2002 [1], there are two main issues that are far from being solved, namely illuminant problem and pose problem. The pose problem, especially the depth rotation, induces non-linear transformations in the projected images of the face and then facial features become occluded and the outline of the face alters its shape causing interference with the background. Pose estimation is therefore a difficult task. To deal with the problem, pose invariants and the proper non-linear model must be found.

Basically, automatic face pose estimation can be divided into three approaches: appearance based approach, model based approach and the hybrid approach. Appearance based method, on the assumption that the number of face poses is countable, finds the mapping of the facial features from different 3D poses through the training data. These features can be skins color、 color saturation 、 gradient of brightness or transformation of the gray image. Motvani [2] used wavelet transformation to represent the facial feature and PCA was used to reduce dimension. J.Sherrah, S.Gong [4] discussed the capability of discriminating different poses of GWT and PCA. Yuan [5] formulated the mapping from 2D face to 3D pose through neural network and Jeffrey [6] used SVM to learning.

Model based approach assumes that there is a standard stable 3D face model and the correspondence of 3D and 2D features is already known. Then the pose can be formulated using traditional methods. Heinzmann [9] detected eyes and mouth in the image assuming that the two far eye corners and the center of mouth form an isoceles triangle. Wang [7] studied the relation between two eyes corners and two mouth cor-

S.Z. Li et al. (Eds.): Sinobiometrics 2004, LNCS 3338, pp. 153–161, 2004.

ners using vanishing point method and computed the accurate angle of slant and tilt. Gee and Cipolla [10] developed a human face model based on the ratio between facial features. Simple and easy to realize as it is, model based approach needs several hypotheses and the accuracy of estimation is depended by and large on the accuracy of feature detection.

The hybrid approach combines model, sometimes 3D model, and facial features and then minimizes an energy function after iterations. Volker Blanz and Thomas Vetter [3] built a 3D average model. Then Bayes Rule was applied to estimation the parameters of the illuminant model and texture and then a 3D face of certain person were synthesized. Lee [11] defined a deformable 3D face model with three sub-model named edge model, color model and a wire frame model (WFM). The main drawback of this kind of approaches is the high computation cost of the procedure to optimal the energy function.

In this paper, we select optimal Gabor feature as pose invariant across different face views. The capability of different size and orientation are discussed in section 2. In the section 3, Kernel Fisher Discriminant Analysis with fractional power polynomial models is introduced and used to build the projection of non-linear transformation. Finally, the experiment result and conclusion are presented in section 4 and section 5.

2   Gabor Feature Representation

2.1   Gabor Filter

Gabor wavelets were introduced to image analysis due to their biological relevance and computational properties. The Gabor wavelets, whose kernels are similar to the 2D receptive field profiles of the mammalian cortical simple cells, exhibit desirable characteristics of spatial locality and orientation selectivity, and are optimally localized in the space and frequency domains.

The Gabor filters can be defined as a convolution:

$$J_j(\vec{x}) = \int I(\vec{x}')\varphi_j(\vec{x} - \vec{x}')d^2\vec{x}' \tag{1}$$

with a family of Gabor kernels:

$$\varphi_j(\vec{x}) = \frac{k_j^2}{\sigma^2}\exp(-\frac{k_j^2 x^2}{2\sigma^2})\left[\exp(i\vec{k}_j\vec{x}) - \exp(-\frac{\sigma^2}{2})\right] \tag{2}$$

in the shape of plane wave vector $\vec{k}_j$, restricted by a Gaussian envelope function. σ is the deviation of Gaussian function, $\vec{x} = (x, y)$ is a given pixel while $I(\vec{x})$ the gray function of the image. $\exp(-\frac{\sigma^2}{2})$ makes the kernel DC-free, i.e. the integral $\int \varphi_j(\vec{x})d^2\vec{x}$ vanishes.

Wiskott [8] develops Gabor Jet which describes a small patch of the image around one pixel using 5×8 Gabor Filters. However, Gabor Wavelets cannot be implemented using Lifting Scheme and form a non-orthogonal set thus making the computation of wavelet coefficients difficult and expensive. So it is a heavy burden to the system using 5×8 Gabor Filters. Liu [12] downsamples the responses of convolution with interval $\rho = 64$, which reduce the dimension of the features to some extend. But it still needs 5×8 convolution operations since he does not reduce the number of the filters. On the other side, whether the capability of multi-Gabor filter is better than that of the single-Gabor filter needs further discussion.

2.2 Selection of Gabor Filter Size

As mentioned above, Gabor Wavelet is a sine wave enveloped by a Gaussian function. Due to the character of Gaussian function, the response of the convolution is smoother compared to the original image. The larger size the Filter has, the smoother the response is. That is to say, the edge information will be weakened while using Filters with large size. Furthermore, structure information around each pixel is also important to discriminate different poses. Different sizes will be discussed in the experiment section, and we can see that the Filter with size 3 has the best result.

2.3 Selection of Gabor Filter Orientation

There are two kinds of depth rotation, namely slant and tilt. Due to the shape of the plane wave of Gabor Filter, it is easy to formulate that Filters with horizon orientation (Horizontal Filters) contribute more to discriminate slant poses while Filters with vertical orientation (Vertical Filters) contribute more to discriminate tilt poses, especially in small angle rotation.

We choose two groups of poses with slant and tilt in MIT and FETET database, some of which are present in Figure 1 and Figure 2. The mean of each pose is filtered by 7×8 Filters (7 sizes and 8 orientations). Figure 2 and Figure 3 show the difference of the mean of each orientation. We use the following expression to demonstrate our selection of orientation:

$$\frac{1}{7} \sum_i \left\| O(\varphi_j^i(\overline{y}^{(m)})) - O(\varphi_j^i(\overline{y}^{(n)})) \right\| \qquad (j=1,2,\ldots,8) \qquad (3)$$

where $\varphi_j^i(y)$ denotes the filter with size i (i =3,5,7,9,11,13,15) and orientation $j/8$ pi, $O(x) = (x - \overline{x})/v$ ($\overline{x}$ is the mean of all pixels and v is the standard deviation) normalizes x to zero mean and unit variance, $\overline{y}^{(m)}$ and $\overline{y}^{(n)}$ the mean of pose m, n. (m, n = 1,2,…,K, K is the class number of poses)

A conclusion can be draw from Figure 1 and Figure 2 that, Horizontal Filters magnify the difference between slant poses and Vertical Filters magnify the difference between tilt poses. That means, it is more efficient to use Horizontal Filters to discriminate slant poses while Vertical Filters to discriminate tilt poses.

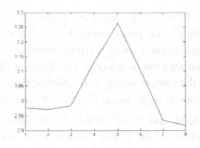

(a) Two groups of images with tilt rotation in MIT database.

(b) Difference of mean of each orientation, e.g. (0,1,2,3,4,5,6,7)*1/8*Pi, which the abscissa denotes.

Fig. 1. Selection of orientation for tilt rotation poses

(a) Two groups of images with slant rotation in MIT database

(b) Two groups of images with slant rotation in MIT database

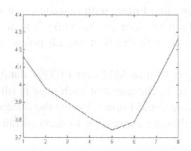

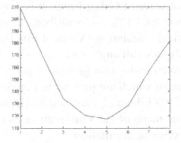

(c) Difference of mean of each orientation, e.g. (0,1,2,3,4,5,6,7)*1/8*Pi, which the abscissa denotes

(d) Difference of mean of each orientation, e.g. (0,1,2,3,4,5,6,7)*1/8*Pi, which the abscissa denotes

Fig. 2. Selection of orientation for slant rotation poses in MIT and FERET database

3 KFDA with Fractional Power Polynomial Models

Fisher Discriminant Analysis (FDA) finds an optimal linear projection of training data that maximizes the ratio between within-class scatter matrix and scatter matrix of all data. As mention in reference [4], depth rotation of human face produces a non-linear transformation from frontal view space to profile view space. Therefore, FDA is no longer the optimal projection for this situation.

Since we cannot use linear projection to represent the non-linear data, here Kernel Fisher Discriminant Analysis is introduced [13] to firstly map the data non-linearly to a new space and computer the Fisher linear discriminant there.

We assume we have l classes and each class has n_i data samples and the total number of data samples is n.

Let $x \in \chi$ be the original image vector, we have

$$y = \varphi(x) \tag{4}$$

$\varphi(x)$ is the response of the optimal Gabor Filter. Therefore, $y \in Y$ be the data of the new input space and the Fisher criterion is:

$$J(w) = \frac{\left| w^T S_b w \right|}{\left| w^T S_w w \right|} \tag{5}$$

where

$$S_b = \sum_{i=1}^{l} \frac{n_i}{n} (m_i - m)(m_i - m)^T$$

$$S_w = \sum_{i=1}^{l} \frac{1}{n} \sum_{y \in Y_i} (y - m_i)(y - m_i)^T$$

m_i is the mean of i class pose and m is the mean of the whole training samples and $Y = \{Y_1, Y_2, ..., Y_l\}$.

Let ϕ be a non-linear mapping to some feather space γ. To find the linear discriminant in γ, we need to maximize:

$$J(w) = \frac{\left| w^T S_b^\phi w \right|}{\left| w^T S_w^\phi w \right|} \tag{6}$$

now $w \in \gamma$ and S_h^ϕ and S_w^ϕ are corresponding matrix in γ i.e.

$$S_b^\phi = \sum_{i=1}^{l} \frac{n_i}{n} (m_i^\phi - m^\phi)(m_i^\phi - m^\phi)^T$$

$$S_w^\phi = \sum_{i=1}^{l} \frac{1}{n} \sum_{y^\phi \in \gamma_i} (y^\phi - m_i^\phi)(y^\phi - m_i^\phi)^T$$

where

$$m_i^\phi = \frac{1}{n_i}\sum_{j=1}^{n_j}\phi(y_j)$$

$$m^\phi = \frac{1}{n}\sum_{j=1}^{n}\phi(y_j)$$

The dimension of γ is always very high even indefinite and cannot be solved directly. Then instead of mapping the data explicitly, we formulate an algorithm, which only uses dot-product $(\phi(x)\cdot\phi(y))$ of the training data, so called kernel function $k(x,y)$ [13]. Different kernel function used, different mapping represents the relation of the original data and the feature space. In this paper we adopt the kernel of fractional power polynomial models mentioned in [12] where the author extended the polynomial kernels to include fractional power polynomial models, namely, $k(x,y) = (x\cdot y+\eta)^d \quad 0<d<1$. Conclusion was draw there that the smaller integer parameter d was, the better the result was. We adopt the parameters used in [12], $d=0.6$ and $\eta=0$.

From the theory of reproducing kernels [13] we know that any solution $w\in\gamma$ must lie in the span of all training samples in γ. Therefore we can find an expansion for w of the form

$$w = \sum_{j=1}^{n}\alpha_j\phi(y_j) \tag{7}$$

Let $\psi = (\phi(y_1),\phi(y_2),...,\phi(y_n))$, $\alpha = (\alpha_1,\alpha_2,...,\alpha_n)^T$, Then we have $w=\psi\alpha$. Substituting $w=\psi\alpha$ into $J(w)$ and after some mathematical manipulations, we get the final discriminant $J(\alpha)$ writtern as:

$$J(\alpha) = \frac{\alpha^T M\alpha}{\alpha^T N\alpha} \quad \alpha = (\alpha_1,\alpha_2,...,\alpha_n)^T \tag{8}$$

where

$$M = \sum_{i=1}^{l}\frac{n_i}{n}(M_i-M_0)(M_i-M_0)^T$$

$$(M_i)_j = \frac{1}{n_i}\sum_{k=1}^{n_i}k(y_j,y_k^i), j=1,2,...,n$$

$$(M_0)_j = \frac{1}{n}\sum_{k=1}^{n}k(y_j,y_k), j=1,2,...,n$$

$$(K_i)_{pq} = k(y_p, y_q^i), p = 1,2,...,n; q = 1,2,..,n_i$$

$$N = \sum_{i=1}^{l} \frac{1}{n} K_i (I_{n_i} - 1_{n_i}) K_i^T$$

4 Experimental Results

In the experiment procedure, we use MIT database which includes 62 objects with 15 poses, made up of 5 slant poses and 3 tilt poses. Some of them are presented in Figure 2 and Figure 3. 31 objects are used for training and the remained for testing. For the 5 slant poses, the correct classification rate of our method reaches 93.5%. Table.1 lists the results of some methods of feature representation.

Table 1. Rates of classification of some methods

Motvani [2]	83.3%
Liu [12]	80.6%
40 Gabor +KFDA (downsamples with interval 64)	92.2%
Our method (single optimal Gabor +KFDA)	93.5%

4.1 Result of Different Size of Gabor Filters

In order to compare the capability of Filters with different sizes, we convolute the 5 slant poses with 7×8 Filters and Figure 3 shows the result of the correct classification rate and it is clear that the smaller size the Filter is with, the higher rate reaches.

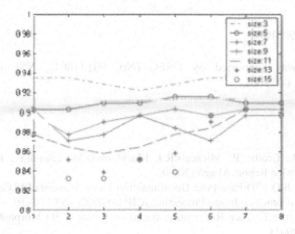

Fig. 3. The correct classification rate of different Gabor Filters (7×8)

4.2 Result of Different Orientation of Gabor Filters

We focus on the 5 slant poses and 3 tilt poses in MIT to illuminate different influence of Filter orientations. Mean of each orientation is computed and the result is showed in Figure 4. As we can see, when discriminating 3 tilt poses, the peak of rate appears right in the middle which denotes that the Vertical Filter have a higher rate than Horizontal Filters. When it comes to 5 slant poses, the Horizontal Filters is better.

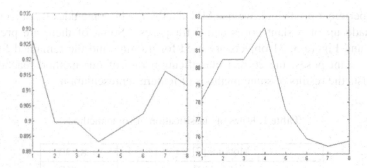

Fig. 4. The mean rate of the different orientations (0,1,2,3,4,5,6,7)*1/8*Pi, which the abscissa denotes. The left is for 5 slant poses and the right for 3 tilt poses

5   Conclusion

As the conclusion, Gabor wavelets have the excellent ability to represent human faces, especially discriminate different kinds of depth rotation when proper size and orientation is selected. We also can conclude that, it is not necessary to combine Gabor Filters of all sizes and orientations. In fact, single Gabor selected corresponding to the rotation kind gains enough information for classification.

Acknowledgement

This project was supported by NSFC (No. 60144001), NSF of GuangDong, P.R.China (No. 021766).

References

1. Phillips ,P.J., Grother,P., Micheals,R.J, Blackburn,D.M. Tabassi,E., Bone,J.M.: FRVT 2002: Evaluation Report. March (2003).
2. Motvani,C., Ji,Q.: 3D Face Pose Discrimination Using Wavelets [A].Greece. IEEE International Conference on Image Processing(ICIP'2002)[C] (2001) 7~10.
3. Blanz,V., Vetter,T.: Face Recognition Based on Fitting a 3D Morphable Model. PAMI Vol.25(9) (2003).

4. Sherrah,J., Gong,S.: Face Distributions in Similarity Space under Varying Head Pose. Image and Vision Computing. Vol(12) (2001) 807–819.
5. Yuan,C., Niemann,H.: Neural Networks for the Recognition and Pose Estimation of 3D Objects from a Single 2D Perspective View[J]. Image and Vision Computing. Vol.19(9~10) (2002) 585~592.
6. Huang,J., Shao,X.H., Wechsler,H.: Face Pose Discrimination Using Support Vector Machines(SVM). Computer and Systems Sciences. Vol.(163) Springer Berlin (1997) 528-535.
7. Wang,J.G., Sung,E.: Pose Determination of Human Faces by Using Vanishing Points. Pattern Recognition. 34 (2001) 2427–2445.
8. Wiskott,L., Fellous,J., Kruger,N., Masberg,C.: Face Recognition by Elastic Bunch Graphic Matching. International Conference on Image Processing (ICIP '97). Vol.3(10) (1997).
9. Heinzmann, Zelinsky: 3-D Facial Pose and Gaze Point Estimation Using a Robust Real-Time Tracking Paradigm [A]. Proc.of the 3rd. International Conference on Face & Gesture Recognition[C]. (1998) 142~147.
10. Gee,A.H., Cipolla,R.: Determining the Gaze of Faces in Images[J]. IEEE Transactions on Systems, Man, and Cybernetics. Vol.25(4) (1995) 449~677.
11. Lee, Ranganath: 3D Deformable Face Model for Pose Determination and Face Synthesis[A]. Proc.of International Conference on Image Analysis and Processing[C] (1999) 260~265.
12. Liu,C.J.: Gabor-Based Kernel PCA with Fractional Power Polynomial for Face Recognition, IEEE PAMI Vol.28(5) (2004).
13. Larsen,J., Wilson,E., Douglas,S.: Fisher Discrimination Analysis with Kernels. Neural Networks for Signal Processing IX IEEE. (1999) 41–48.

Robust Pose Estimation of Face Using Genetic Algorithm

Chao Zhang, Guocan Feng, and Jianhuang Lai

Center of Computer Vision, School of Mathematics and Computing Science,
Sun Yat-sen University, 510275, Guangzhou, China
zczsu@sina.com, {mcsfgc, stsljh}@zsu.edu.cn

Abstract. This paper focuses on the problem of human face pose estimation using single image. Because the traditional approaches for 2D-3D feature-based pose estimation problem requires two inputs, they can not work very well due to lack of correspondences of the input image. In this paper, we propose pose estimation algorithm for human face based on genetic algorithm. The proposed method overcomes the shortcomings by using a general 3D point-feature template as the correspondences and some more constraints onto the optimizing function. The experiments show the proposed method gives good performance in accuracy and robustness.

1 Introduction

Face recognition researches have been a very hot field of computer vision and pattern recognition for decades. Since the pose variation of the faces leads the reduction of the recognition accuracy, pose estimation or face orientation determination is a fundamental problem in human face recognition research [1]. As a basic problem in computer vision, the pose estimation can be formulated as the process of determining the object reference frame with respect to the camera reference frame, giving some certain measurements of the object in both frames. These measurements can be some 3D points on the surface of the probed object or the 2D points on images [2] as shown in Figure 1. With the correspondences measurements of the same point in two frames, we can get the pose solution by solving constraint equations [3-4]. Pose estimation problem is also named the exterior camera calibration problem and it has many important applications in object recognition, vision-based navigation, auto human face recognition, human computer interaction (HIC) and cartography [5].

There are a lot of literatures that focused on the topic and fall into two categories. The first is feature-based approach, and the most of the existing algorithms belongs this category. In those algorithms, several pairs of corresponding point, lines or curves and usually are employed to approximate solution by iteration. One of most classical algorithm is the Perspective N-Point problem, where N is the number of points used and often takes 3, or 4, or 5 or more [9,10,14]. This idea can be described as: given a set of points with their coordinates in an object-centered frame and their corresponding projections onto an image plane and given the intrinsic camera parameters, find the transformation matrix between the object frame and the camera frame [5].

The second is appearance-based approach. In these category, the oriented face image is regarded as a whole input instead of feature points extracted from it to estimate the pose. The manifold method proposed by H. Murase and S. K. Nayar [11] is one the most important in these category [11]. Louis-Philippe and Patrik [12] proposed 3D View-Based Eigenspaces to estimate the head pose. Hattori [13] estimated the face pose by using the symmetry plane of face and a 3D face model from 3D laser scanner. This method has a fast and accurate result for certain people's face pose, but some complicated equipment is needed. Kwang exploited 3D face template to fit the image points of face to be estimated, the feature points were localized by a Fourier domain matched filter technique and the iteration is executed by using a EM algorithm.

1.1 Feature-Based 2D-3D Pose Estimation

The transform between two frames can be presented by rotation transform **R** and translation transform T. The relationship between object space and image space is given by equation (1) and (2), where **R** is the 3×3 rotational matrix, **T** is the 3D translation vector and f is the focal length of the camera. $(x \quad y \quad z)^T$ and $(u \quad v)^T$ represent a feature point of object and is corresponding image respectively.

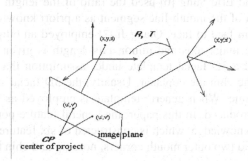

Fig. 1. The pose problem in perspective image model

$$\begin{pmatrix} x' \\ y' \\ z' \end{pmatrix} = R \begin{pmatrix} x \\ y \\ z \end{pmatrix} + T - \begin{pmatrix} r_{11} & r_{12} & r_{13} \\ r_{21} & r_{22} & r_{23} \\ r_{31} & r_{32} & r_{33} \end{pmatrix} \begin{pmatrix} x \\ y \\ z \end{pmatrix} + \begin{pmatrix} t_1 \\ t_2 \\ t_3 \end{pmatrix} \cdot \qquad (1)$$

$$(u \quad v)^T = \left(f \frac{x'}{z'} \quad f \frac{y'}{z'} \right)^T \cdot \qquad (2)$$

The rotation transform **R** can be decomposed to three sub-rotations:

$$R = R_x(\theta_x) R_y(\theta_y) R_z(\theta_z) \cdot \qquad (3)$$

where θ_x, θ_y and θ_z are three Euler angles, while the three matrices rotated along with z-axis, y-axis and x-axis can be written as follows respectively:

$$R_z(\theta_z) = \begin{pmatrix} \cos(\theta_z) & -\sin(\theta_z) & 0 \\ \sin(\theta_z) & \cos(\theta_z) & 0 \\ 0 & 0 & 1 \end{pmatrix}. \tag{4}$$

$$R_y(\theta_y) = \begin{pmatrix} \cos(\theta_y) & 0 & \sin(\theta_y) \\ 0 & 1 & 0 \\ -\sin(\theta_y) & 0 & \cos(\theta_y) \end{pmatrix}. \tag{5}$$

$$R_x(\theta_x) = \begin{pmatrix} 1 & 0 & 0 \\ 0 & \cos(\theta_x) & -\sin(\theta_x) \\ 0 & \sin(\theta_x) & \cos(\theta_x) \end{pmatrix}. \tag{6}$$

Pose estimation for human face can be described as: For a given face image, how to get the orientation (presented by the 3 rotation angles) of the face with respect to his (or her) own 'front face image'. That is to say the input is only one. But the most of traditional approaches always needs two corresponding face images just as the inputs at both sides of equation (1). Therefore, another images are required, such as Jian-Gang Wang and Eric Sung [6] used the ratio of the length of the eye-line segment and the length of the mouth-line segment as a priori knowledge for this ratio is relatively stable from face to face. Qiang Ji [7] employed an ellipse as face template and the ratio of the major axis and minor axis' length is given. While Kwang and Marco [8] exploited a 3D facial template under assumption that the left eyes, right eyes, the lips and the chin are coplanar. Usually, the 3D facial structure of different person is not the same. When generic template is employed as the correspondence, the error will be introduced. In this paper, the general feature points template is utilized as the a priori knowledge, which is constructed of six feature points on face: two outer-eye corners and two outer mouth corners, nose tip and chin tip.

2 Genetic Algorithms

Genetic algorithms (GAs) are a part of evolutionary computing, which is a rapidly growing area of artificial intelligence. GAs, inspired by Darwin's theory of evolution [15,16], are searching algorithms based on the mechanics of natural selection and natural genetics. GAs apply not deterministic rules, but probabilistic transition. In GAs, a solution of a problem is coded to a string or a chromosome. By using operations such as reproduction, crossover and mutation, the string which is fitter than the others get better chance to reproduce.

A canonical GA is composed of three operators: reproduction (selection), crossover and mutation. Reproduction (selection) is a process in which individual strings are copied according to the fitness given by a fitness function. Following is the typical genetic algorithm:

Step 1.   code the given problem by gene string;

Step 2.   initialize a population pop(n) and let n=0;

Step 3.   evaluate the fitness function value fit(n) of
           each string in the population pop(n). From
           the fit(n), see which individual is solution
           what we want. if we find a satisfied solution,
           we may cease the process, else let n++ and
           continue;

Step 4.   select descendant pop(n) from the older
           generation pop(n-1);

Step 5.   crossover and mutate pop(n) according to cer-
           tain strategy;

Step 6.   go to step3

In a face recognition system, the robustness of the pose estimation is essential, because the probed images will have various scale, illumination and expression. The
feature-based least-square error methods are very sensitivity to the accuracy of the
corresponding points, while GAs have the advantages over other searching techniques
of robust and adaptive. Therefore GA is applied as the optimizer in our parameters
searching in our algorithm for this reason.

3 The Proposed Method

To adjust an oriented face image to corresponding front view face image, give notations of the pose parameters 3 rotation angles as $\theta_x, \theta_y, \theta_z$ and translation vector as
$\mathbf{T}(t_x, t_y, t_z)$. In face recognition system, the face images are always segmented from
the picture, and though the information about translation can hardly be retrieved.
Assume the face is positioned at center of images, so the two translation parameters
t_x, t_y can be set to 0 and will not introduce big error. Then we can simplify the face
pose estimation problem as: given a human face image, get the orientation presented
by angle $(\theta_x, \theta_y, \theta_z)$ relative to his or her 'front face'.

3.1 Definition of 'Front Face'

To define the front face uniformly, the 3D Cartesian coordinate system is introduced
as shown in figure 2.

Six points on face surface are chosen as the template. They are two outer eye corners, two outer mouth corners, nose tip and chin tip, which are marked 1, 2, ..., 6;

(refer to Figure (2). The origin of the coordinates is located at the nose tip position, and the plane defined by point 1,2 and 3 is regarded as the face plane, while yz-plane is perpendicular to face plane and cross nose tip point and center-point of two eyes. Then z-axis is through nose tip and determined by normal of face plane. Therefore each face can define its own coordinates like this, while three angles $(\theta_x, \theta_y, \theta_z)$ just present the face's pose.

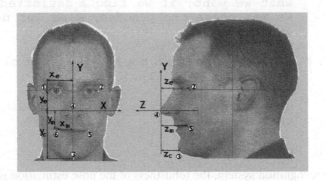

Fig. 2. The coordinates attached to the face by the feature points on face

Once the coordinates is defined, the 3D coordinate of each point $p_i (i = 1, 2, ..., 6)$ can be expressed as follows:

$$(p_1, p_2, ..., p_6) = \begin{pmatrix} -x_e & x_e & 0 & 0 & x_m & -x_m \\ y_e & y_e & -y_c & 0 & -y_m & -y_m \\ z_e & z_e & z_c & 0 & z_m & z_m \end{pmatrix}. \tag{7}$$

The points $q_i (i = 1, 2, ..., 6)$ on its corresponding image can be obtained by the perspective camera model which described by equation (1) and (2). Here, we use a given six coordinates $(p_1, p_2, ..., p_6)$ as a template and then project them to the image plane we get six image points $q_i' (i = 1, 2, ..., 6)$:

$$q_{i1}' = f \frac{r_1 x_i + t_1}{r_3 x_i + t_3}, \quad i = 1, 2, ..., 6 . \tag{8}$$

$$q_{i2}' = f \frac{r_2 x_i + t_1}{r_3 x_i + t_3}, \quad i = 1, 2, ..., 6 . \tag{9}$$

Where r_1 , r_2 and r_3 is the row vectors of rotation matrix **R** and $t = (t_1, t_2, t_3)'$, here t_1, t_2 are both 0, f is the focal length of the camera and is a given fixed value.

Now, define a distance function:

$$d(q_i, q_i') = \sum_i^6 |q_i - q_i'| \cdot \tag{10}$$

Where q_i is the points on face to be estimated and they all be labeled manually, because the topic of feature points extraction has been discussed in many literatures[1,9]. This paper mainly focuses on estimation of rotation angles.

A lot of research have focused on minimize this distance function $d(q_i, q_i')$ to get the **R** and **t** pose parameters, such as [14,17], but these approaches are sensitive to points selected. In the face recognition system, it is difficult to meet the requirement of system for both the number of points and noise level, This means the existing methods do not work well here.

Actually, if two faces are of the same pose, the line determined by tow far-eye corners are parallel. So a new function which measure the distance of poses is given by:

$$f(p)=k_1 \times g(v_1, \hat{v}_1)+k_2 \times g(v_2, \hat{v}_2)-d(p_i, \hat{p}_i) \tag{11}$$

which is also the fitness function used by GA and where

$$g(v_1, \hat{v}_1) = \cot(\arccos(v_1, \hat{v}_1)) \tag{17}$$

and $V_1 = q_2 - q_1$, $\hat{V}_1 = q_2' - q_1'$; $v_2 = q_5 - q_6$, $\hat{v}_2 = q_5' - q_6'$; look at fig. 3

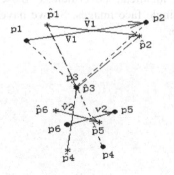

Fig. 3. Definition of v_1, $\hat{v}_1$, v_2, $\hat{v}_2$

3.2 Implementation of the GA

We use the canonical GA as the optimizer in this paper. A chromosome is a sequence of binary digits with a cardinality of 2, and there have 3 parameters need to be found in our approach there are 3 genes in the chromosome. Each gene is associated with a real number set representing the interval over which a parameter can assume values.

Thus 3 real parameter sets together constitute the pose space and the search space of GA. The parameters configuration is in table 1.

Table 1. Parameters of GA

No. of chromosomes	50
Length of each gene	12 bits
Crossover rate	0.89
Mutation rate	0.01
max generation	50

4 Result and Discussion

The accuracy: A lot of images of the template with various poses were generated as test images. Using the test images, we get the performance of the proposed algorithm based GA in the favorable circumstance while the input data without noise. The average errors on three rotations for 58 different pose images through three times experiments is $(\Delta\theta_x, \Delta\theta_y, \Delta\theta_z)$ =(1.1861, 2.5908, 3.8977).

The robustness: Firstly, we compare the difference between individual 3D data and template used. Because for different individual, these six points $(p_1, p_2, ..., p_6)$ are not identical, nevertheless, these six coordinates can't be found correctly from a single face images. So we have to use a general template, which will introduce error.

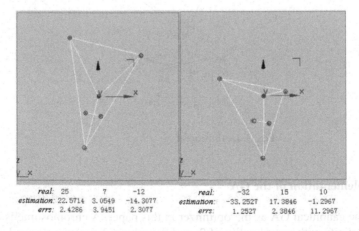

real:	25	7	-12	*real:*	-32	15	10
estimation:	22.5714	3.0549	-14.3077	*estimation:*	-33.2527	17.3846	-1.2967
errs:	2.4286	3.9451	2.3077	*errs:*	1.2527	2.3846	11.2967

Fig 4. The estimation result of template's own images, blue circle is the input image point coordinate, '*' is the image of template point project to image plane by the estimation rotation parameter

Experiment has been done to explore the error when the length of eye line segment and length of segment between nose tip and chin tip change. Figure 5 shows when these two parameters of probed faces are less variance from the template the error increases little.

Secondly, we explore the effect by noise while locating the six points by manually or automation. Figure 6 shows the average error against the input noise. The results demonstrate the error for estimation of angles is less than 5.

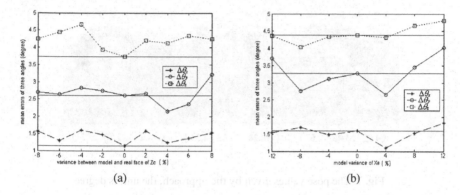

(a)   (b)

Fig. 5. Average rotation angle errors against percent of deference. (a) the length of eye line difference from –12% to 12%. (b)distance of nose tip to chin tip difference between –8% to 8%

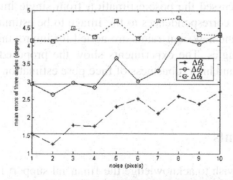

Fig. 6. Average error against input noise

Face pose estimation: The performance of real face pose estimation was show in figure 7. Given an arbitrary face image with appropriate size and hand-labeled six points on it, the three angels then can be given by the algorithm proposed. The little circle 'o' presents the points manually labeled and the asterisk '*' represents the correspondent template points which are projected to the image plane with estimated pose, the accuracy can be estimated by the distance of the corresponding points pair.

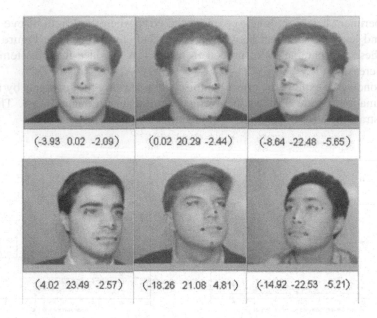

(-3.93 0.02 -2.09)   (0.02 20.29 -2.44)   (-8.64 -22.48 -5.65)

(4.02 23.49 -2.57)   (-18.26 21.08 4.81)   (-14.92 -22.53 -5.21)

Fig. 7. The pose values given by the approach, the unit is degree

5 Conclusion

In this paper we discussed the pose estimation from single image, just using a six-point template as the correspondences to the image to be estimated. GA is utilized as the optimizer and some new constraints are added for improving estimation accuracy in searching the 3 angles. The experiments show the proposed algorithm gets good estimation accuracy and high robustness of face pose estimation using single image.

Acknowledgements

Finally, the authors wish to acknowledge the financial support from Ministry of Education, China under the key project grant No. 104145, and partial support from NSFC (No. 60144001) and Guangdong NSFC (No. 031609).

References

1. Zhao, W., Chellappa, R., Rosenfeld, A., and Phillips, P.J. : Face Recognition: A Literature Survey. UMD CfAR Technical Report CAR-TR-948, (2000)
2. Xu, W., L., Zhang, L., H. : Pose estimation problem in computer vision. IEEE TENCON '93/BeiJing. (1993)

3. Huang, T. S. and Netravali, A. N. : Motion and Structure from Feature correspondences: A review. Proceedings of the IEEE, Vol.82(2) (1994).
4. Haralick, R. M., Lee, C. N. : Analysis and Solutions of the Three Point Perspective Pose Estimation Problem. Proceedings of the IEEE Conference on Computer Vision and Pattern Recognition. Hawaii (1991) 592–598
5. Horaud, R., Conio, B. and Leboulleux, O. : An Analytic solution for perspective 4-point problem. Computer vision, Graphics and image processing, Vol. 47 (1989) 33–44
6. Wang, J.G. and Sung, E. : Pose determination of human faces by using vanishing points. Pattern Recognition, Vol.34 (2001) 2427–2445
7. Ji Qiang and Hu Rong. : Face Pose Estimation From a Face Ellipse. http://www.cs.unr.edu/~rong /Pose/Pose.html
8. Choi, K. N., Carcassoni, M. and Hancock, E. R. : Recovering facial pose with the EM algorithm. Pattern Recognition, Vol. 35 (2002) 2073-2093
9. Feng, G. C., and Yuen, P. C. : Recognition of head-&-shoulder face image using virtual frontal-view image. IEEE Trans, System Man and Cybernetics. Vol. 30(6), (2000) 871–882
10. Hancock, E. R., Lee, C. N. Ottenberg, K. and Nolle, M. : Review and analysis of solutions of the three point perspective pose estimation preblem. International Journal of computer vision. Vol.13(3) (1994) 331–356
11. Murase, H. and Nayar, S. K. : Visual learning and recognition of 3-D objects from appearance. International Journal of Computer Vision, Vol. 14 (1995) 5–24
12. Morency, L.P., Sundberg, P. and Darrell, T. : Pose Estimation using 3D View-Based Eigenspaces. Proceedings of the IEEE International Workshop on Analysis and Modeling of Faces and Gestures(AMFG'03)
13. Hattori, K., Matsumori, S., Sato, Y., : Estimating pose of human face based on symmetry plane using range and intensity image. Internat. Conf. on Pattern Recognition., (1998)1183–1187
14. Haralick, R. M., Joo, H. : 2D-3D Pose stimation. ICPR'88 (1988) 385–391
15. Lu, J. G., Li, Q. : The theory and application of genetic algorithm. China university of mining and technology Press.
16. Zhang, W. X. Liang, Y. : Mathematic basis of genetic algorithm, Xi'an Jiaotong University Press
17. Moshe Ben-Ezra, Peleg, S., Werman M. : Model Based Pose Estimator Using linear-Programming
18. Wu Lifang, Sheng Kai, Zhang Sicong, Liu Xun. : Representation and estimation of facial pose. The 1st Chinese Conference on Affective Computing and Intelligent Interaction. Beijing China (2003) 8–9

Facial Pose Estimation Based on the Mongolian Race's Feature Characteristic from a Monocular Image*

Huaming Li, Mingquan Zhou, and Guohua Geng

Institute of visualization technology,
Department of Computer Science,
Northwest University, Xi'an 710069, P.R. China
huaminglcc@hotmail.com

Abstract. Pose estimation plays an important role in the field of face recognition. This paper presents a fast method to estimate the pose of human head from a monocular image, combining with the research result of the anthropometry in the Mongolian race's feature we had obtained, and cooperating with the theory of the projective geometry. The realization of our method uses only five points in the human face, and does not need any auxiliary equipment. So it can be practiced and popularized very well. It has been proved by experiment that the results of estimation are very close with actual rotational angles of human face. Especially when facial rotation in a naturally small angle, less than $30°$, we can obtain the approximate accurate value of rotational angles by using this method.

1 Introduction

Pose estimation of human faces plays an important role in Computer vision, Face recognition and Human-computer interaction. It can be used in such as videophone, automatic control based on video, 3D face recognition and virtual movie-production etc. Presently, a large amount of research [1] [2] [3] has been performed on this field, and some methods have been proposed. All these methods can classify into two kinds - one based on facial model, the other based on facial appearance. The methods based on model mainly use the 3D or 2D geometrical model of human face, estimates facial pose by establish the relationship between the shape of model and 3D facial pose. This kind of methods always starts with facial feature detection and extraction, and the features that are mostly frequent used are eyes, mouth and nose [1]. The methods based on facial appearance think that the difference of facial appearance of a same people in photos is cause by different facial pose, and the regulation existed in the change can be studied. So we can use this regulation to analyze the input image, estimate approximately facial pose. The techniques that are mostly used in these methods are Eigenspace, Principal component analysis and Neural network etc [5].

---

* This paper was funded by National Natural Science Foundation of China, and granting No. is 60271032.

In this paper, we improve the traditional geometrical model method [6] with our research in the Mongolian race's feature characteristic; present a novel pose estimate method that can be used in China. The theoretical bases of our method are the principle of monocular imaging, projective invariants and statistical knowledge from anthropometry. With this method, we compute the real pose of face through an isosceles triangular model of face that is composed of the four eye-corners (two endocanthions and two exocanthions) and subnasale. Because only five points used in computation, this method is fast and real-time, requires no prior information, requires no extra equipment and almost not be influenced by face expression etc. We have got the anticipative results from the experiment.

2 The Analysis of the Mongolian Race's Feature Characteristic

The difference of Races is obvious, and it is the core field of the research of anthropology. Anthropometry is a key technique to find out this difference and abstract the regulation from this difference. The combination of computer technology and anthropometry has a lot of typical precedents early, for example, face statistical information is often used in face feature detection. The Mongolian race is regarded as the main race of China, the statistical information of its feature has very important scientific meaning to our research in the fields such as facial pose estimate and face recognition, etc. Because the research of us focuses on the four eye-corners and subnasale of human face, we mainly analyze the following two contents when we measure the facial information of the Mongolian race.

1. The width of eye fissure (the distance between endocanthion and exocanthion)
2. The length of nose (the distance between subnasale and the line of two endocanthions)

Table 1. Face statistical information form 224 cases

	Average length (mm)	Standard deviation (mm)
The width of eye fissure (male, n=100)	31.40	1.53
The length of nose (male, n=100)	45.64	1.84
The width of eye fissure (female, n=124)	30.37	2.16
The length of nose (female, n=124)	42.51	1.52
The width of eye fissure (average, n=224)	30.885	
The length of nose (average, n=224)	44.075	

Table 1 shows the statistical information of face measurement from 100 males and 124 females who we choose randomly. Let L_e denote the average width of eye fissure and L_n denote the average length of nose. Through analyzing, we can find out that the relationship surely exists between L_e and L_n. We use a formula to figure out this relationship as follows:

$$L_e = 0.7L_n \qquad (1)$$

3 Facial Triangular Model

Facial computational triangular model that we use is based on the statistical experience knowledge from anthropometry. Though there are numerous feature points in human face, we only choose endocanthions, exocanthions and subnasale to build our model. It is because that the positions of these points at the face are independent toward face expression; namely while people makes various kinds of expressions, the positions of these five points have no obvious change. And the detection of these points is in comparative stable state even when the facial appearance is changed, for example, the change produced by hairdo, glasses, beard, etc. Finally, the geometrical shape formed by these points is an isosceles triangle that benefits our calculation.

We employ a coordinates system to realize our algorithm. This system's origin point is the focal point of the camera. Let X-Y plane denote the image plane and the viewing direction coincides with the Z-axis. We use α, β, γ denote the three rotation angles of head about the X,Y and Z axis, respectively. Each point in the coordinate system is expressed as (X_i, Y_i, Z_i).

The whole model is set up based the assumed foundations as follows:

1. Two endocanthions and two exocanthions are approximately co-liner in three-dimension. And this line is parallel with X-axis in a front facial image (when α=β=γ=0).
2. Based on statistical knowledge from anthropometry, we know the width of two eyes is equal.
3. All these five points in the image are seeable.

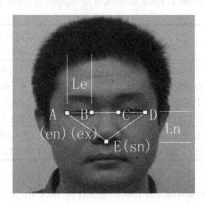

Fig. 1. Facial triangular model. This shows an example of our model, we denote the four eye corners with A, B, C and D; denote the subnasale with E. As talked above, we know $AB = CD$

4 The Method of Pose Estimation

The purpose of pose estimation is to calculate the rotational angles of head corresponding with three coordinate axes approximately. Consulted with the method that Horprasert [6] presented, we improve this geometric method with our research talked above. We calculate each angle in the different coordinate environment, respectively, and the different points involved in calculation of each angle.

4.1 The Estimation of γ (Roll, the Rotation Angle of Z Axis)

γ can be straightforward estimated by the position of two endocanthions in the image plane. Let a (x_a, y_a, z), d (x_d, y_d, z) denote these two outer eye-corners in the image. We calculate this angle with the formula as follows:

$$\gamma = \arctan \frac{y_a - y_d}{x_a - x_d} \qquad (2)$$

4.2 The Estimation of β (Yaw, the Rotation Angle of Y Axis)

To calculate β, we let a, b, c, d denote the four eye-corners in the image plane (see Fig. 2). Each point is expressed as (x_i, y_i, z). Let f denote the focus of the camera. Let D denote the actual width of eye; D1 denote half of the distance between the two inner eye-corners. From the projective invariance of the cross-ratios, we have

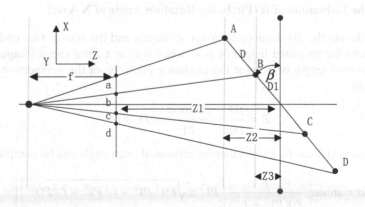

Fig. 2. The perspective projection of eye-corners while the head is rotating about Y axis

$$I = \frac{(x_a - x_b)(x_c - x_d)}{(x_a - x_c)(x_b - x_d)} = \frac{D^2}{(2D1 + D)^2} \qquad (3)$$

From the theory of perspective projection, we obtain

$$x_a = \frac{f(D+D1)\cos\beta}{Z1-(D+D1)\sin\beta+f} \quad (4) \qquad x_b = \frac{fD1\cos\beta}{Z1-D1\sin\beta+f} \quad (5)$$

$$x_c = \frac{fD1\cos\beta}{Z1+D1\sin\beta+f} \quad (6) \qquad x_d = \frac{f(D+D1)\cos\beta}{Z1+(D+D1)\sin\beta+f} \quad (7)$$

From (4) we obtain $Z1 = Z2\times S - f$ (8) where $S = \dfrac{f}{x_a\tan\beta}+1$ (9). From (9), we

can determine the head yaw $\beta = \arctan\dfrac{f}{(S-1)x_a}$ (10). However, we need to deter-

mine S and xa first. From (3) – (8), we obtain a quadratic equation in S:

$$\frac{x_a - x_b}{x_c - x_d} = -\frac{(Z2S+D1\sin\beta)[Z2S+(D1+D)\sin\beta]}{(Z2S-D1\sin\beta)[Z2S-(D1+D)\sin\beta]} = -\frac{(S+1)(S+\dfrac{Q}{2+Q})}{(S-1)(S-\dfrac{Q}{2+Q})} \quad (11)$$

To determine x_a, we employ anther two cross-ratio invariants

$$\frac{(x_a-x_b)x_c}{(x_b-x_c)x_d} = \frac{DD1}{2D1(D+D1)} = -\frac{1}{2+Q} = M = \frac{(x_c-x_d)x_b}{(x_b-x_c)x_d} \quad (12)$$

By replacing the result of (11) and (12) in (10), we can determine the degree of β.

4.3   The Estimation of α (Pitch, the Rotation Angle of X Axis)

Let D denote the 3D distance between subnasale and the line of two endocanthions, P0 denote the projected length of nose when it is in a front facial image, P1 denote the observed length of nose at the unknown pitch. From the perspective projection, we obtain

$$Z = \frac{fD}{P0} = \frac{fD\cos\alpha}{P1} + D\sin\alpha \quad (13)$$

From (13) it can be known that the estimated pitch angle can be computed by:

$$\alpha = \arcsin\left[\frac{f}{P0(P1^2+f^2)}\left[P1^2 \pm \sqrt{P0^2 P1^2 - f^2 P1^2 + f^2 P0^2}\right]\right] \quad (14)$$

From (14) we know the calculation of α depend on P0 that we do not know before. To solve this problem, Yilmaz [4] emphasizes that we should obtain a front facial image in the image sequences at first, and use this front image as the basal criterion. If we only use a single image, we must estimate P0 from this unknown postural image. As we talk in stage 2, we can determine P0 with the projected width of eye fissure in a front facial image (use the formula (1)). And the projected width of eye fissure in a front facial image can be calculated with the observed eye's width in the unknown postural image and γ that we obtained in 4.1.

5   Experimental Results

Considered with reality, we limit the degree of these three angles in [-90, 90]. Using the Olympus E-20P camera, we get a set of data in the state of 50mm focus to experiment our method. These images include front facial image and the images while face is rotated according X, Y, Z-axes.

The result shows that the degree that we estimated is very close to the real degree of the rotation and our method is practicable. The errors in the course of experiment mainly are brought from three reasons as follows:

1. The quality of the image: Such as too many noises will disturb the detection of features.
2. The inevitably errors of the localization of features: When the rotational angle of face is too large, the features will be detected inaccurate. This kind of errors can be reduced by using the more accurate method (like AAM) to detect the facial features.
3. The approximate characteristic of our face model: Because the variety of face, facial model, the foundation of our method, is based on the statistical information, so this model just express the characteristic of face approximately. This slight disparity between model and actual facial data is the reason why the certain estimated error is existed in our experiment.

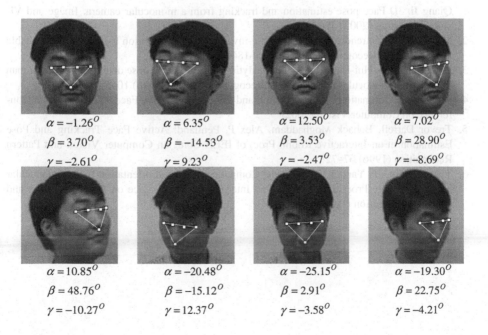

$\alpha = -1.26^{o}$ $\alpha = 6.35^{o}$ $\alpha = 12.50^{o}$ $\alpha = 7.02^{o}$
$\beta = 3.70^{o}$ $\beta = -14.53^{o}$ $\beta = 3.53^{o}$ $\beta = 28.90^{o}$
$\gamma = -2.61^{o}$ $\gamma = 9.23^{o}$ $\gamma = -2.47^{o}$ $\gamma = -8.69^{o}$

$\alpha = 10.85^{o}$ $\alpha = -20.48^{o}$ $\alpha = -25.15^{o}$ $\alpha = -19.30^{o}$
$\beta = 48.76^{o}$ $\beta = -15.12^{o}$ $\beta = 2.91^{o}$ $\beta = 22.75^{o}$
$\gamma = -10.27^{o}$ $\gamma = 12.37^{o}$ $\gamma = -3.58^{o}$ $\gamma = -4.21^{o}$

Fig. 3. The experimental result

It should be noticed that the experimental result is most accurate when the degrees of face rotation according three axes are all less than 30°. The experiment has proved that our method can be used in most practical application and can achieve the anticipated goal. Fig.3 shows the final data that we obtained from estimating as follows.

6 Conclusions

Through the theoretical analysis of the monocular imaging environment, we can know that we cannot estimate all the rotational degrees just based on a single image. This paper presents a novel method which theoretical bases are the principle of monocular imaging, projective invariants of the cross-ratios and statistical knowledge from anthropometry. As a result of using the statistical information of the Mongolian Race's feature, our method is suitable to be used in the north of China. With the constant improvement of the feature detection's method, our method can become more and more accurate. Because of the convenience and real-time character of our method, it can be applied in many kinds of applications, and has the high practical value.

References

1. Qiang Ji: 3D Face pose estimation and tracking from a monocular camera. Image and Vision Computing (2002) 499–511
2. Mun Wai Lee, Surendra Ranganath: Pose-invariant face recognition using a 3D deformable model. Pattern Recognition (2003) 1835–1846
3. Shinn-Ying Ho, Hui-Ling Huang: An analytic solution for the pose determination of human faces from a monocular image. Pattern Recognition Letters (1998) 1045–1054
4. A. Yilmaz: Automatic Feature Detection and Pose Recovery for Faces. The 5th Asian Conference on Computer Vision (2002)
5. Trevor Darrell, Baback Moghaddam, Alex P. Pentland: Active Face Tracking and Pose Estimation in an Interactive Room. Proc. of IEEE Conf. on Computer Vision and Pattern Recognition (1996) 67–72
6. T. Horprasert, Y. Yacoob, L. S. Davis: Computing 3-D head orientation from a monocular image sequence. Proceedings of the 2nd International Conference on Automatic Face and Gesture Recognition (1996)

Boosting Local Binary Pattern (LBP)-Based
Face Recognition

Guangcheng Zhang[1], Xiangsheng Huang[2], Stan Z. Li[2],
Yangsheng Wang[2], and Xihong Wu[1]

[1]Center of Information Science, Peking University, Beijing 100871, China
[2]Institute of Automation, Academy of Chinese Sciences, Beijing 100080, China
xiangshenghuang@hotmail.com

Abstract. This paper presents a novel approach for face recognition
by boosting statistical local features based classifiers. The face image is
scanned with a scalable sub-window from which the Local Binary Pattern
(LBP) histograms [14] are obtained to describe the local features of a face
image. The multi-class problem of face recognition is transformed into
a two-class one by classifying every two face images as intra-personal or
extra-personal ones [9]. The Chi square distance between corresponding
Local Binary Pattern histograms of two face images is used as discriminative feature for intra/extra-personal classification. We use AdaBoost
algorithm to learn a similarity of every face image pairs. The proposed
method was tested on the FERET FA/FB image sets and yielded an
exciting recognition rate of 97.9%.

1 Introduction

Face recognition has attracted much attention due to its potential values for
applications as well as theoretical challenges. As a typical pattern recognition
problem, face recognition has to deal with two main issues: (i)what features
to use to represent a face, and (ii)how to classify a new face image based on
the chosen representation. Up to now, many representation approaches have
been introduced, including Principal Component Analysis (PCA) [15], Linear
Discriminant Analysis (LDA) [3], independent component analysis(ICA) [1, 8],
and Gabor wavelet features [18]. It computes a reduced set of orthogonal basis
vector or eigenfaces of training face images. A new face image can be approximated by weighted sum of these eigenfaces. PCA provides an optimal linear
transformation from the original image space to an orthogonal eigenspace with
reduced dimensionality in the sense of the least mean square reconstruction error. LDA seeks to find a linear transformation by maximising the between-class
variance and minimising the within-class variance. ICA is a generalization of
PCA, which is sensitive to the high-order relationships among the image pixels.
Gabor wavelets capture the local structure corresponding to spatial frequency
(scale), spatial localization, and orientation selectivity.

While regarding classification methods, nearest neighbor [15], convolutional
neural networks [6], nearest feature line [7], Bayesian classification [9] and Ad-

S.Z. Li et al. (Eds.): Sinobiometrics 2004, LNCS 3338, pp. 179–186, 2004.
© Springer-Verlag Berlin Heidelberg 2004

aBoost method have been widely used. The Bayesian inra/extra-person classifier (BIC) [9] uses the Bayesian decision theory to divide the difference vectors between pairs of face images into two classes: one representing intra-personal differences (i.e. differences in a pair of images of the same person) and extra-personal differences. Adaboost method, introduced by Freund and Schapire [4], which provides a simple yet effective stage-wise learning approach for feature selection and nonlinear classification at the same time, has achieved great success in face detection [16] and other applications [12, 17].

Timo ct al recently proposed a novel approach for face recognition, which takes advantage of the Local Binary Pattern (LBP) histogram that is proved to be an effective texture description [14]. In their method, the face image is equally divided in to small sub-windows from which the LBP features are extracted and concatenated to represent the local texture and global shape of face images. Weighted Chi square distance of these LBP histograms is used as a dissimilarity measure of different face images. Experimental results showed that their method outperformed other well-know approaches such as PCA, EBGM and BIC on FERET database.

However, there are obviously two aspects could be improved in Timo's method. First, in their method, a face image is equally divided into sub-regions from which LBP histograms are extracted, which means the variety of the size and position of the obtained features are limited. By shifting and scaling a sub-window much more features could be obtained, which yields a more complete and agile description of face images. Second, the weight of Chi square distance is chosen in a somehow coarse way. And it would be more reasonable if some statistical learning algorithm is utilized to get the value of weight.

In this work, we present a novel approach for face recognition which uses boosted statistical local feature based classifiers. First, by scanning the face image with a scalable sub-window, over 7,000 sub-regions are obtained, from which corresponding Local Binary Pattern histograms are extracted. The face recognition task is considered as a two-class problem by classifying every two face images as intra-personal or extra-personal ones and outputting a similarity describing how confident two face images are of one person. The Chi square distance between corresponding LBP histograms are used as discriminative features for this intra/extra-personal classification. By applying AdaBoost learning algorithm, a few of most efficient LBP features were selected, and a similarity function was obtained in the form of linear combination of LBP feature based weak learners. Experimental result on FERET FA/FB image sets shows that the proposed method yields a better recognition rate of 97.9% by utilizing much less features than Timo's approach.

The rest of this paper is organized as follows: In section 2, the Local Binary Patterns are introduced, and the features which discriminate intra/extra personal face images are constructed. In section 3, the AdaBoost learning for weak classifiers selection and classifier construction are proposed. And the experiment results on the FERET database is given in section 4. In section 5, we present the conclusion and future work.

2   Local Binary Patterns

2.1   Local Binary Pattern

The original LBP operator, introduced by Ojala [10], is a powerful method of texture description. The operator labels the pixels of an image by thresholding the 3×3-neighborhood of each pixel with the center value and considering the result as a binary number. Then the histogram of the labels can be used as a texture descriptor. An illustration of the basic LBP operator is shown in Fig.1.

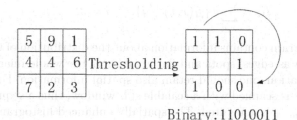

Binary:11010011

Fig. 1. The basic LBP operator

The most prominent limitation of the LBP operator is its small spatial support area. Features calculated in a local 3×3 neighborhood cannot capture large scale structure that may be the dominant features of some textures. Later the operator was extended to use neighborhoods of different size [11]. Using circular neighborhoods and bilinearly interpolating the pixel values allow any radius and number of pixels in the neighborhood. See Fig.2 for an example of these kind of extended LBP.

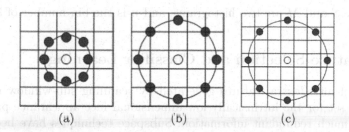

(a)   (b)   (c)

Fig. 2. Three examples of extended LBP. (a) The circular (8,1) neighborhood.(b)The circular (8,2) neighborhood. (c)The circular (8,3) neighborhood. The pixel values are bilinearly interpolated whenever the sampling point is not in the center of a pixel

Another extension to the original operator is to use so called uniform patterns [11]. A Local Binary Pattern is called uniform if it contains at most two bitwise transitions from 0 to 1 or vice versa when the binary string is considered circular. Ojala noticed that in their experiments with texture images, uniform patterns account for a bit less than 90% of all patterns when using the (8,1) neighborhood and for 70% in (16,2) neighborhood. We use the following notation for the LBP operator: $LBP_{P,R}^{u2}$ means using the operator in a neighborhood of P sampling points on a circle of radius R. Superscript ^{u2} stands for using uniform patterns and labelling all remaining patterns with a single label.

2.2 Measurement of Likelihood

A histogram of the labelled image $f_l(x, y)$ can be defined as

$$H_i = \sum_{x,y} I\{f_l(x, y) = i\}, \quad i = 0, \ldots, n - 1 \tag{1}$$

This histogram contains information about the distribution of the local micro-patterns, such as edges, spots and flat areas, over the whole image. For efficient face representation, one should retain also spatial information. For this purpose, the face image is scanned with a scalable sub-window, thus a sequence of regions $R_0, R_1, \ldots, R_{m-1}$ is generated. The spatially enhanced histogram is defined as

$$H_{i,j} = \sum_{x,y} I\{f_l(x, y) = i\}I\{(x, y) \in R_j\} \tag{2}$$

In this histogram, we effectively have a description of the face on two different levels of locality: the labels for the histogram contain information about the patterns in pixel-level, the labels are summed over a small region to produce information on regional level [14]. Several possible dissimilarity measures are available. In this work, Chi square statistic (χ^2) is adopted:

$$\chi^2(S, M) = \sum_i^n \frac{(S_i - M_i)^2}{(S_i + M_i)} \tag{3}$$

Where S and M are two histograms, and n is the bin number of histogram.

3   Feature Selection and Classifier Learning

The set of intra/extra features generated by scanning sub-window is an over-complete set for the intrinsically low dimensional face appearance pattern and contains much redundant information. Subspace techniques have been used to reduce the dimensionality [2, 19]. We propose to use Adaboost to select most significant intra/extra features from a large feature set.

Therefore, AdaBoost is adopted to solve the following three fundamental problems in one boosting procedure: (1) learning effective features from a large feature set, (2) constructing weak classifiers each of which is based on one of the selected features, and (3) boosting the weak classifiers into a stronger classifier.

The basic form of (discrete) AdaBoost [4] is for two class problems. A set of N labelled training examples is given as $(x_1, y_1), \ldots, (x_N, y_N)$, where $y_i \in \{+1, -1\}$

is the class label for the example $x_i \in R^n$. AdaBoost assumes that a procedure is available for learning sequence of *weak classifiers* $h_m(x)$ $(m = 1, 2, \ldots, M)$ from the training examples, with respect to the distributions $w_i^{(m)}$ of the examples. A *stronger classifier* is a linear combination of the M weak classifiers

$$H_M(x) = \sum_{m=1}^{M} h_m(x) \tag{4}$$

---

0. (Input)
   (1) Training examples $\{(x_1, y_1), \ldots, (x_N, y_N)\}$,
   where $N = a + b$; of which a examples have $y_i = +1$
   and b examples have $y_i = -1$;
1. (Initialization)
   $w_{0,i} = \frac{1}{2a}$ for those examples with $y_i = +1$ or
   $w_{0,i} = \frac{1}{2b}$ for those examples with $y_i = -1$.
2. (Forward Inclusion)
   For $t = 1, \ldots, T$
   (1) Train one hypothesis h_j for each feature j with w_t,
       and error $e_j = Pr_i^{w_t}[h_j(x_i) \neq y_i]$
   (2) Choose $h_t(x) = h_k(x)$, such that $\forall j \neq k$, $e_k < e_j$.
       Let $e_t = e_k$.
   (3) Update $w_{t+1,i} \leftarrow w_{t,i}\beta_t^{I_i}$, where $I_i = 1$ or 0 for
       example x_i classified correctly or incorrectly respectively
       and $\beta_t = e_t/(1 - e_t)$, normalize to $\sum_i w_{t+1,i} = 1$;
3. (Output)
   $$H(x) = \begin{cases} 1, & if \ \sum_{t=1}^{T} \alpha_t h_t(x) > \sum_{t=1}^{T} \alpha_t \\ 0, & otherwose \end{cases}$$
   where $\alpha_t = \log \frac{1}{\beta_t}$

Fig. 3. AdaBoost Algorithm

The AdaBoost algorithm based on the descriptions from [13, 5] is shown in Fig. 3. The AdaBoost learning procedure is aimed to derive α_t and $h_t(x)$.

4   Experiments

The proposed method was tested on the FERET fa/fb image sets. There are totally 3,737 images in the training CD set of FERET database, and we used images in the training CD that are from fa and fb set as training images. Thus, our training image set consists of 540 images of 270 subjects. All images are rectified, cropped and scaled to 142 pixels high by 120 pixels wide according to the eye positions the FERET database provided. The preprocessed images are

Fig. 4. Some examples of preprocessed face images

illustrated in Fig.4. The training set yields 270 intra-personal image pairs and 145,260 extra-personal image pairs.

By shifting and scaling the sub-window, 7,350 LBP histograms are extracted from each face image. And we got 7,350 candidate features for the intra-extra personal classification by computing the Chi square distance between corresponding LBP histograms of each image pairs. AdaBoost was applied on the positive sample set of 270 intra-personal image pairs and the negative sample set of 145,260 extra-personal image pairs. Finally, AdaBoost ran 23 rounds and 23 Chi Square distances of 23 corresponding LBP histograms pairs were selected. The first four sub-windows learned, from which the LBP histograms are extracted, are shown in Fig.5.

Fig. 5. The first four sub-windows from which the Chi square distance between corresponding LBP histograms are obtained

To test the efficiency of our proposed method, several comparative experiments were tested on the probe set fb with the gallery fa of the FERET database. There are 1196 images in fa, 1195 images in fb, and all exactly the subjects have exactly one image in both fa and fb. The rank curves of the final

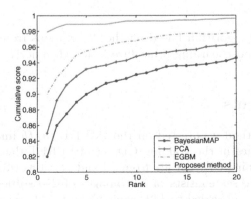

Fig. 6. Rank curves for the fb probe sets

recognition results are plotted in Fig.6. It should be noted that the CSU implementations of the algorithms whose results we introcued here do not achieve the same figures as in original FERET test due to some modifications in the experimental setup. Our approach has achieved the upper bound recognition performance shown in Fig.6. While Timo's method uses a feature vector length of 2301(59*39) and gets a recognition rate of 97% on FERET FA/FB image sets[16], our approach uses only 1357 (59 * 23) features yet delivers a slightly better recognition rate of 97.9%. Thus, the presented method has a faster recognition speed and consumes less disk space without depressing the recognition accuracy.

5   Conclusion

This paper presents a new method for face recognition by effectively combining some of the previously published approaches. The two-class problem of face verification and the multi-class problem of face recognition are solved in one framework, by learning a similarity function describing how confident every two face images are of the same person, as in [9]. AdaBoost learning algorithm is used to select the Local Binary Patterns based features [14], as well as to obtain the similarity function. Experimental results on FERET FA/FB image set show that our method achieves a better recognition rate of 97.9% yet utilizes much less features than Timo's approach [14].

References

1. Marian Stewart Bartlett, H. Martin Lades, and T. J. Sejnowski. Independent component representations for face recognition. *Proceedings of the SPIE, Conference on Human Vision and Electronic Imaging III*, 3299:528–539, 1998.
2. T. F. Cootes, C. J. Taylor, D. H. Cooper, and J. Graham. "Active shape models: Their training and application". *CVGIP: Image Understanding*, 61:38–59, 1995.
3. K. Etemad and R. Chellapa. "Face recognition using discriminant eigenvectors". In *Proceedings of the International Conference on Acoustic, Speech and Signal Processing*, 1996.
4. Y. Freund and R.E. Schapire. "A decision-theoretic generalization of on-line learning and an application to boosting". *Journal of Computer and System Sciences*, 55(1):119–139, August 1997.
5. J. Friedman, T. Hastie, and R. Tibshirani. "Additive logistic regression: a statistical view of boosting". *The Annals of Statistics*, 28(2):337–374, April 2000.
6. Steve Lawrence, C. Lee Giles, A.C. Tsoi, and A.D. Back. "Face recognition: A convolutional neural network approach". *IEEE Transactions on Neural Networks*, 8(1):98–113, 1997.
7. S. Z. Li and J. Lu. "Face recognition using the nearest feature line method". *IEEE Transactions on Neural Networks*, 10(2):439–443, March 1999.
8. C. Liu and H. Wechsler. "Independent component analysis of gabor features for face recognition". In *3rd International Conference on AUDIO- and VIDEO-BASED BIOMETRIC PERSON AUTHENTICATION*, Halmstad, Sweden, June 6-8 2001.

9. B. Moghaddam, C. Nastar, and A. Pentland. "A Bayesain similarity measure for direct image matching". *Media Lab Tech Report* No. 393, MIT, August 1996.
10. T. Ojala, M. Pietikainen, and D. Harwood. "A comparative study of texture measures with classification based on feature distributions". *Pattern Recognition*, 29(1):51–59, January 1996.
11. T. Ojala, M. Pietikainen, and M. Maenpaa. "Multiresolution gray-scale and rotation invariant texture classification width local binary patterns". *IEEE Transactions on Pattern Analysis and Machine Intelligence*, 24(2002):971–987.
12. L.Zhang S.Z.Li Z.Y. Qu and X.S.Huang. "Boosting local feature based classifiers for face recognition". In *The First IEEE Workshop on Face Processing in Video*, Washington D.C, June 2004.
13. R. E. Schapire and Y. Singer. "Improved boosting algorithms using confidence-rated predictions". In *Proceedings of the Eleventh Annual Conference on Computational Learning Theory*, pages 80–91, 1998.
14. M.Pietikainen T.Ahonen, A. Hadid. "Face recognition with local binary patterns". In *Proceedings of the European Conference on Computer Vision*, pages 469–481, 2004.
15. Matthew A. Turk and Alex P. Pentland. "Eigenfaces for recognition". *Journal of Cognitive Neuroscience*, 3(1):71–86, March 1991.
16. P. Viola and M. Jones. "Robust real time object detection". In *IEEE ICCV Workshop on Statistical and Computational Theories of Vision*, Vancouver, Canada, July 13 2001.
17. P.Yang S.G.Shan W.Gao and S.Z.Li D.Zhang. "Face recognition using ada-boosted gabor features". In *The Sixth International Conference on Automatic Face and Gesture Recognition*, pages 356–361, Seoul, Korea, May 2004.
18. L. Wiskott, J.M. Fellous, N. Kruger, and C. Vonder malsburg. "face recognition by elastic bunch graph matching". *IEEE Transactions on Pattern Analysis and Machine Intelligence*, 19(7):775–779, 1997.
19. S. C. Yan, M.J.Li, H.J.Zhang, and Q.S.Cheng. "Ranking prior likelihood distributions of bayesian shape localization framework". In *ICCV 2003*, pages 524–532, Mediterranean coast of France, October 2003.

Gabor Features Based Method Using HDR (G-HDR) for Multiview Face Recognition[1]

Dan Yao, Xiangyang Xue, and Yufei Guo

FuDan University, Dept. of Computer Science and Engineering,
220 HanDan Road, Shanghai, China
022021227@fudan.edu.cn

Abstract. This paper introduces a novel algorithm named G-HDR, which is a Gabor features based method using Hierarchical Discriminant Regression (HDR) for multiview face recognition. Gabor features help to eliminate the influences to faces such as changes in illumination directions and expressions; Modified HDR tree help to get a more precise classify tree to realize the coarse-to-fine retrieval process. The most challenging things in face recognition are the illumination variation problem and the pose variation problem. The goal of Our G-HDR is to overcome both difficulties. We conducted experiments on the UMIST database and Volker Blanz's database and got good results.

1 Introduction

Face recognition is a subject of great interest in recent years due to its wide applications in digital video management, surveillance, law enforcement, banking and security system access authentication etc.

There are large numbers of existing works in face recognition. The typical techniques are PCA, Neural Network, LDA and deformable template etc [7]. Although significant progress has been made recently in this area, how to handle face recognition robustly still is a big problem due to at least two major challenges – the illumination variation problem and the pose variation problem. Most existing systems which follow several basic recognition techniques can't perform well when facing either of these problems.

The changes induced by illumination are often larger than the differences between individuals. To solve this problem, many approaches have been proposed such as discarding the principal components which vary mainly due to lighting, model-based and image comparison and so on.

When poses changes, the performance of face recognition systems decrease dramatically. How to solve the rotation-in-depth problem is a major research issue. As it is said in [7], existing methods can be divided to three types: 1) methods in which

---

[1] This work was supported in part by Natural Science Foundation of China under contracts 60003017 and 60373020, China 863 Plans under contracts 2002AA103065, and Shanghai Municipal R&D Foundation under contracts 03DZ15019 and 03DZ14015, MoE R&D Foundation under contracts 104075.

S.Z. Li et al. (Eds.): Sinobiometrics 2004, LNCS 3338, pp. 187–195, 2004.
© Springer-Verlag Berlin Heidelberg 2004

multiple database images of each pose are available, 2) hybrid methods when multiple images are available during training but only one database image person is available during recognition, 3) single image based methods. The third approach has been realize by [6] via 3-D modeling.

Although these methods towards the two challenges are popular, they have one or several of the following drawbacks: 1) they need multiple samples in any kind of poses or lighting conditions; 2) the illumination problem and pose problem are solved separately; 3) the time costs are expensive.

Our G-HDR system is designed to try to solve these drawbacks. The algorithm is based on Gabor features. It can overcome the challenge due to illumination and expressions since the excellent properties of Gabor wavelets [2], [9]. The G-HDR algorithm needs only one sample in each pose direction. And the algorithm builds a tree after training so it can do fast retrieval and recognition and the time cost is low.

This paper is organized as follows: section 2 introduces Gabor wavelets; the HDR algorithm is described in section 3; section 4 presents our novel G-HDR algorithm; section 5 provides the experiments and results; and conclusions are drawn in section 6.

2   Gabor Wavelets

Gabor wavelets are one kind of the most widely used complex wavelets and almost the best methods for image representation [2], [3], [4]. Gabor wavelets have optimal localization properties in the spatial and frequency domains since their kernels are similar to the 2-D receptive field profiles of the mammalian cortical simple cells. So in addition to changes in illumination directions, Gabor wavelets can extract desirable texture features from images, which are important for image analysis and segment, pattern recognition, motion estimation and so on.

Gabor transform is a kind of Fourier transforms which use any Gaussian function as the window function. Daughman [5] extended the 1-D Gabor proposed by Gabor to 2-D form to model the receptive fields of the orientation-selective simple cells:

$$G(x, y) = \frac{1}{2\pi\sigma\beta} e^{-\pi\left[\frac{(x-x_0)^2}{\sigma^2} + \frac{(y-y_0)^2}{\beta^2}\right]} e^{i[\xi_0 x + v_0 y]} \tag{1}$$

where (x_0, y_0) is the center of the receptive field in the spatial domain and (ξ_0, v_0) is the optimal spatial frequency domain. σ and β are the standard deviations of the elliptical Gaussian along X and Y.

The detail presentation of Gabor Feature in our G-HDR method will be introduced in section 4.

3   Hierarchical Discriminant Regression (HDR)

Juyang Weng et al proposed a new classification and regression algorithm [1] for high dimensional data. Our G-HDR is based on the algorithm.

3.1   HDR Algorithm

This algorithm casts classification problems and regression problems into a regression problem, namely, the outputs are numeric values. According to [1], the clustering is a doubly clustered progress that is done in both output-space and input-space at each node. The labels of clusters in the input-space are from the clustering of output-space, that is to say, the clustering in input-space is according to the clustering result in output-space.

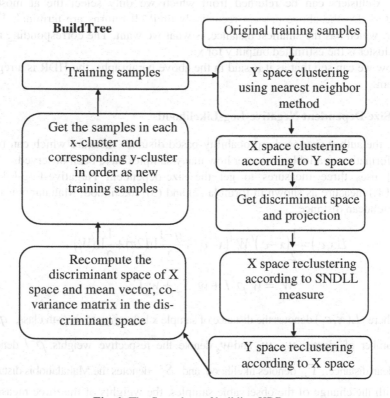

Fig. 1. The flow chart of building HDR tree

The algorithm can automatically derive discriminant features. In each inter node exists a discriminant space. The projection on the space can help to reduce the dimensions of data and find the discriminant features.

It is also a hierarchical statistical modeling progress. After being executed, the algorithm recursively builds a tree from the training set. Every cluster of each node is modeled as a multidimensional Gaussian to realize the coarse-to-fine retrieval. To be noted, here each node has two types of clusters: x-clusters and y-clusters since the clustering is done in both spaces.

Considering compute efficiency and limit memory, the HDR tree doesn't keep the actual input samples. Each cluster only keeps the mean vector and covariance matrix.

Fig. 1 is the flow chart of the algorithm in the building tree part.

The clustering in Y space is done using nearest neighbor cluster method and measured by Euclidean distance. Here the values in Y space are all numeric values.

The retrieval process is easy to understand. Given an HDR tree and a test example x to estimate the output vector y. The process starts from the root. According to the probability-based distance to each cluster in the node, we select at most top k x-clusters named active x-cluster which have smaller distances. If an active x-cluster has child nodes, then find top k x-clusters in each child nodes like above. At most k^2 active x-clusters can be returned from which we only select the at most top k x-clusters. Do the above process recursively until all returns are terminal. Then the cluster, which has the smallest distance, is what we want. The corresponding mean of its y-cluster is the estimated output y for x.

Now we can see that as it is said in the above paragraphs, the HDR is a regression problem.

3.2 Size-Dependent Negative-Log-Likelihood

In [1], the author proposed a probability-based distance measure which can fully use the information available no matter how many samples have been observed.

[1] uses three measures to get the size-dependent Negative-Log-Likelihood (SDNLL) measure as shown in formula (2) and (3): likelihood, Mahalanobis distance and Euclidean distance.

$$L(x,c_i)=\frac{1}{2}(x-c_i)^T W_i^{-1}(x-c_i)+\frac{q-1}{2}\ln(2\pi)+\frac{1}{2}\ln(W_i) \tag{2}$$

$$W_i = w_e\rho^2 I + w_m S_w + w_g \Gamma_i \tag{3}$$

Where $L(x,c_i)$ denotes the distance of sample x belonging to the i-th class, q denotes the number of classes, w_e, w_m and w_g denote the respective weights. $\rho^2 I$ denotes the Euclidean distance, Γ_i denotes likelihood, and S_w denotes the Mahalanobis distance.

With the change of the observable samples, the weights of the three measures are changed. So based on HDR algorithm, our G-HDR can handle unbalanced samples well.

However, our G-HDR algorithm reverts to the classification problem to gain better performance which will be introduced in the following section.

4 G-HDR Method

We describe in this section our novel G-HDR method for multiview face Recognition.

4.1 Gabor Feature Representation

We choose the Gabor wavelets expressed by the following function [2]:

$$\Psi_{\mu,v}(z) = \frac{\|k_{\mu v}\|^2}{\sigma^2} e^{-\left(\|k_{\mu v}\|^2 \|z\|^2 / 2\sigma^2\right)} \left[e^{izk_{\mu v}} - e^{-\left(\sigma^2 / 2\right)} \right] \tag{4}$$

Where $z = (x, y)$, μ and v denote the orientations and scales of the Gabor wavelets. $k_{\mu,v} = k_v e^{i\phi_\mu}$, $k_v = k_{\max} / f^v$, $\phi_\mu = \pi \mu / 8$, $k_{\max}$ is the maximum frequency and f is the spacing factor between wavelets in the frequency domain. Like most cases, our Gabor wavelets consist of eight orientations and five scales. Different Gabor wavelet extracts different poses and scale information. And we choose the following parameters: $\sigma = 2\pi$, $k_{\max} = \pi / 2$, and $f = \sqrt{2}$.

Define $I(x, y)$ to be an intensity image, then the Gabor feature representation of the image is expressed as:

$$O_{\mu,v}(x, y) = I(x, y) * \psi_{\mu,v}(x, y) \tag{5}$$

$*$ denotes the convolution operator. The image can be expressed by the set: $S = \{O_{\mu v}(x, y) : \mu \in \{0,...,7\}, v \in \{0,...,4\}\}$ In our paper, we compute $O_{\mu,v}(x, y)$ using FFT and inverse FFT (here $\Im$ denotes FFT operator):

$$O_{\mu,v}(x, y) = \Im^{-1}\left\{\Im\{I(x, y)\} \Im\{\psi_{\mu,v}(x, y)\}\right\} \tag{6}$$

Via this function, we can get coarse high-frequency features similar to faces in different orientations and scales, and ignore the low-frequency features such as the changes in illumination directions.

From the above description about Gabor features we know that the Gabor features result in the Eigen space largely exceed the original image in dimensions. So we must subsample the original big image to small image. In our algorithm, we downsample a 128*128 image to 16*16, then, after the Gabor transform, we can get a 10240 vector as the feature of the image whose dimension is reduced largely.

4.2 Gabor Feature Based HDR Tree (G-HDR)

Fig. 2 is the simple frame of our G-HDR algorithm.

As mentioned in section 3, Based on the HDR algorithm in [1], our algorithm reverts to the classification problem. Because it can reduce the time cost and gets better performance. This has been proved by the second experiment in section 5.

This is the difference with the HDR tree in [1]. The Y-Clustering of G-HDR clusters the labels of all classes, not the numeric values which are the mean vector of each class in HDR.

The Procedure of Clustering-Y Is Below

Given m classes and the goal is to cluster Y. n_i, is the number of the samples in class i (i = 1,2,······, m). The total number of samples is n.

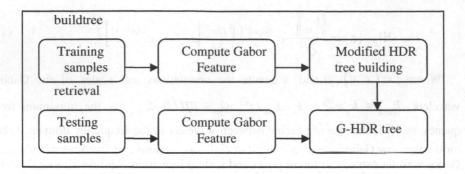

Fig. 2. Processes of tree building and retrieval in G-HDR

1. Let the labels of class i be the $\{ y_{i1}, y_{i2}, \cdots, y_{in_i} \}$, Of course, the labels in the same class are same.

2. Let the center of y-cluster 1 is y_{11}, named Y_1. Set j = 2;

3. To the rest n-1 samples, for j = 2 to n do

   • Compute the Euclidean distance $d = dist\left(y_j, Y_k \right)$, Cluster all the labels using the nearest neighbor method, where Y_k is the label of k-th class.

   • If $d > \delta$, a new cluster is born with y_j as its center.

Our process of clustering-Y is simpler and quicker compare with the process of clustering-Y of original HDR algorithm. The most important thing is that it can divide all the samples in different classes since the distances between labels are usually larger than that between the means of clusters. So we can get more precise results. The following experiments proved this.

One of essences of HDR is that it can cluster classes form coarse to fine recursively. So, even if the intra-difference of identical class is large, the HDR can cluster similar samples to one cluster, consequently, one class may be clustered to several clusters all that have the same labels. When doing retrieval, given a test example, no matter which leaf it reaches at last, the label corresponding to the samples in the leaf node is the label of the test example. Since the original class has been divided several clusters, the probability of the sample falling in one cluster of corresponding class is large. So HDR algorithm can handle this type of classification well.

Form foregoing analysis to the properties of HDR, we can see that our G-HDR, based on HDR, is appropriate to the classifications of which the intra-difference of one class is large. This has also been proved by the second experiment in section 5.

5   Experiments and Results

Two experiments were conducted using our G-HDR algorithm. First, we present the experiment results of the recognition for eleven poses of face. Then, we show the experiment results of recognition for multiview faces.

5.1   Recognition for Poses of Multiview Face

We applied the G-HDR algorithm to Blanz, V's database. There are 200 people in this database, including 100 females and 100 males. Each of them has 7 poses rotated-in-depth from one profile to another profile spacing by 30 degree. Then we rotated the frontal face to get four rotated-in-plane images corresponding to 30 and 60 degree in left and 30 and 60 degree in right. The different poses of one person are shown in Figure 3. Thus we get 11 classes of poses, and each class includes 100 samples.

Fig. 3. The eleven poses of one person

We use the female images as training images and the male images as testing images. We also do experiments by other popular method to do a comparison. The results of the experiments are in Table 1.

Table 1. The results of recognition for poses. G-HDR means our method; while HDR(n) means the unmodified HDR algorithm. From Table 1, we can see that our method is better than the other methods

method	G-HDR	HDR(n)	PCA
Error number	0	7	85

5.2   Recognition for Multiview Face

In the second experiment, we applied the new algorithm to UMIST database [8], The UMIST Face Database consists of 564 images of 20 people. Each covers a range of poses from profile to frontal views. Subjects cover a range of race/sex/appearance. The files are all in PGM format, approximately 220 x 220 pixels in 256 shades of grey. And these samples also include some moderate changes of illuminations. Besides, the numbers of samples of every class aren't equal, which are from 84 to 24 per class. Some samples of one person in UMIST database are shown in Fig. 4.

From the comparison between G-HDR(n) and HDR(n), we can see that the Gabor features help to get better discriminant feature eliminating the illuminations and expressions, and the dimension of Gabor features is smaller than that of images, so the retrieval time is less. From the comparison between G-HDR(n) and G-HDR, we can conclude that modified HDR is better than original HDR when applying it to this kind of classification problem since our method can build the G-HDR tree more compact so the tree may be shorter than HDR tree in [1] to spend less retrieval time.

Fig. 4. Some samples of one person in UMIST database

Table 2. The results of recognition for multiview face. The G-HDR(n) means the method of Gabor feature based using unmodified HDR; the HDR(n) means the method of no Gabor feature based using unmodified HDR and the G-HDR means our method that is Gabor feature based using modified HDR. The last row includes retrieval times, which are the time costs of one test sample using different methods. The rest elements of this table are the error numbers. Every experiment was done five turns and got the results

Error number		HDR(n)	G-HDR(n)	G-HDR
The number of test samples per class	5	7	5	0
	10	16	12	3
Retrieval time		1.375	1.109	0.235

Because existing approaches for multiview face recognition need multi samples in each poses or need to know the precise degree of each pose, the UMIST database is not appropriate. Therefore we didn't do other experiments to make comparisons. However, since the G-HDR needs to extract Gabor features the time cost of which is very high, so our algorithm takes more time than original HDR algorithm to train. We will do more work to enhance the efficiency.

6   Conclusions

We proposed a novel algorithm named G-HDR, which is a Gabor features based method using Hierarchical Discriminant Regression (HDR) for multiview face recognition. It uses Gabor Feature to avoid the influences due to lighting changes and expressions. It realizes a coarse to fine retrieval process to get precise results and low time cost. However, the change of illumination in our experiments is not too much; otherwise, more works need to be done to get better Gabor Features to overcome the challenge. And the poses in UMIST are continuous, that is to say, the neighboring poses are similar. If not, assume we only have rotated 10, 30, 60 degree samples in training dataset and want to recognize a rotated 50 degree image, the result will be bad.

More works will be put on these two aspects to gain better performance.

References

1. Hwang, Wey-Shiuan and Weng, Juyang : Hierarchical Discriminant Regression. IEEE Transactions on Pattern Analysis and Machine Intelligence. Vol. 22(11) (2000)
2. Liu, Chengjun and Wechsler, H. : Gabor feature based classification using the enhanced fisher linear discriminant model for face recognition. IEEE Transactions on Image Processing. Vol. 11 (4) (2002) 467–476
3. Fazel-Rezai, R. and Kinsner, W. : Image analysis and reconstruction using complex Gabor wavelets. Canadian Conference on Electrical and Computer Engineering2000. Vol. 1 (2000) 440–444
4. Tao, Liang and Kwan, H.K. : Real-valued discrete Gabor transform for image representation. IEEE International Symposium on Circuits and Systems. ISCAS 2001. Vol. 2 (2001) 589–592
5. Daugman, J. G. : Uncertainly relation for resolution in space, spatial frequency, and orientation optimized by two-dimensional visual cortical filters. J.Opt.Soc.Amer.A. Vol. 2 (1985) 1160–1169
6. Blanz, V. and Vetter, T. : Face Recognition Based on 3D Shape Estimation from Single Images. Computer Graphics Technical Report No.2, University of Freiburg. 2002
7. Zhao, W., Chellappa, R., Phillips, P.J., and Rosenfeld, A. : Face Recognition: A Literature Survey. ACM Computing Surveys (CSUR). Vol.35 (4) (2003) 399–458
8. Daniel B. Graham and Nigel M. Allinson. : in Wechsler, H., Phillips, P. J., Bruce, V., Fogelman-Soulie, F. and Huang, T. S. (eds): Face Recognition: From Theory to Applications. NATO ASI Series F. Computer and Systems Sciences. Vol. 163. (1998) 446–456
9. Schiele, B. and Crowley, J. L. : Recognition without correspondence using multidimensional receptive field histograms. Int. J. Comput.Vis. Vol. 36(1) 2000 31–52

Face Recognition Under Varying Lighting Based on Derivates of Log Image

Laiyun Qing[1,2], Shiguang Shan[2], and Wen Gao[1,2]

[1] Graduate School, CAS, Beijing, 100039, China
[2] ICT-ISVISION Joint R&D Laboratory for Face Recognition, CAS,
Beijing 100080, China
{lyqing, Sgshan, wgao}@jdl.ac.cn

Abstract. This paper considers the problem of recognizing faces under varying illuminations. First, we investigate the statistics of the derivative of the irradiance images (log) of human face and find that the distribution is very sparse. Based on this observation, we propose an illumination insensitive distance measure based on the *min* operator of the derivatives of two images. Our experiments on the CMU-PIE database have shown that the proposed method improves the performance of a face recognition system when the probes are collected under varying lighting conditions.

1 Introduction

Face recognition has attracted much attention in the past decades for its wide potential applications in commerce and law enforcement, such as mug-shot database matching, identity authentication, access control, information security, and surveillance. Much progress has been made in the past few years [20].

However, face recognition remains a difficult, unsolved problem in general due to several bottlenecks, among which illumination change is one of the most challenging problems. It has been argued that the variations between the images of the same face due to illumination and viewing direction are almost always larger than the image variations due to the change in face identity [11]. These observations have been further verified by the evaluation of the state-of-the-art systems as well. The FERET tests [12] and the recent FRVT 2002 [13] revealed that the recognition performances of the best systems degraded significantly when the illuminations changed.

There has been much work dealing with illumination variations in face recognition. Generally, these approaches can be categorized into three fundamental categories: the invariant features based approaches, the statistics-based approaches and the model-based approaches [14].

The invariant features based approaches seek to utilize features that are invariant to the changes in appearance. Examples of such representation considered by early researchers are edge maps, image intensity derivatives, and images convolved with 2D Gabor-like filers. However, Adini's empirical study [1] had shown that "None of the representations considered is sufficient by itself to overcome image variations

S.Z. Li et al. (Eds.): Sinobiometrics 2004, LNCS 3338, pp. 196–204, 2004.

because of a change in the direction of illumination". Chen et al [4, 6] had drawn the conclusion that even for diffuse objects, there were no discriminative functions that are invariant to illumination. But they provided two illumination insensitive measures based on probabilistic information: the ratio image [4] and the distribution of the image gradient [6].

The statistics-based approaches learn the distribution of the images collected under varying lighting conditions in some suitable subspace/manifold by statistical analysis of a large training set. Recognition is then conducted by choosing the subspace/manifold closest to the novel image. Eigenface [15], Fisherface [3], and Bayesian method [10] are the typical methods belonging to this category. In this context, one of the most important observations is that the images of a convex Lambertian surface caused by varying illuminations lie in a low-dimensional subspace embedded in the image subspace. Especially, Hallinan [9] reported that 5-D subspace would suffice to represent most of the image variations due to illumination changes including extreme cases.

The model-based approaches are based on the reflectance equation and model the functional role of the extrinsic imaging parameters (such as lighting and view direction) explicitly. These methods build a generative model of the variations of the face image. 3D Linear subspace [17], Quotient Image method [18], Illumination Cones [8] and 3D Morphable model [5] are the successful methods belonged to this kind of approaches. Recently, the 9-D linear subspace [2, 16] using spherical harmonics was proposed, which facilitated the modeling of the more generic illuminations.

All the above approaches have their advantages and disadvantages. The invariant features need little *prior* knowledge and they are suitable for preprocessing, though the performances are not the best. The performances of the statistics-based approaches depend on the images used for training. If the illuminations of the images for training are sampled well enough, the performance is satisfying. The model-based methods are generative but they need several images per object or the class information. And the assumption of Lambertian surface is not strictly satisfied in real applications.

In this paper, we propose an illumination insensitive similarity measure for face recognition under varying lighting. The measure is based on the observation that the partial derivatives of the log irradiances are very sparse.

The rest of the paper is organized as follows. The statistics of the derivates of the log of the face irradiances and the measure of the *min* operator based on the statistics are described in section 2. We show the experimental results of the proposed measure in section 3, followed by some concluding remarks in section 4.

2 The Illumination Insensitive Measure

Assuming the face is Lambertian surface, denoting by $I(x, y)$ the input face image, $R(x, y)$ the reflectance image and $E(x, y)$ the irradiance image, the three images are related by

$$I(x, y) = R(x, y)E(x, y).$$ (1)

Rewriting Eq. (1) in log domain, it is

$$\log I(x, y) = \log R(x, y) + \log E(x, y).$$ (2)

If we apply a derivative filter to Eq. (2), we can get

$$\nabla \log I(x, y) = \nabla \log R(x, y) + \nabla \log E(x, y).$$ (3)

That is, the resulting filter output of a face image is the sum of that of the reflectance image and the irradiance images. We then check the statistical properties of the outputs of the filter of the irradiance images in the next subsection.

2.1 The Statistics of the Derivates of Face Irradiances

Assuming the human surface is a convex Lambertian surface and according the spherical harmonic images model proposed in [2, 16], the irradiance images is determined by the low frequency components of the illumination environment and the shape of the face, i.e.

$$E(x, y) = \sum_{l=0}^{2} \sum_{m=-l}^{l} A_l L_{lm} Y_{lm} (\alpha, \beta),$$ (4)

where $A_l (A_0 = \pi, A_1 = 2\pi/3, A_2 = \pi/4)$ [2, 16] are the spherical harmonic coefficients of Lambertian reflectance, L_{lm} are the coefficients of the incident light, and Y_{lm} are the spherical harmonic functions. (α, β) is the normal of the point (x, y) in the input image.

We analyze the distribution of the derivates of the irradiance maps from a training set. Human faces can be assumed rationally to have the similar shapes. Therefore the training sets are constructed by the irradiance images of an average face shape under varying illuminations.

We select two sets of illumination environments. One set consists of 9 maps in Debevec's Light Probe Image Gallery (http://www.debevec.org/Probes/), which can be regards as the representatives of the natural illuminations. Debevec's maps represent diverse lighting conditions from 4 indoor settings and 5 outdoor settings. Because illumination statistics vary with elevation [7], we rotate each light probe horizontally per $30°$, resulting 12 different light conditions from one light probe. The other set is a point light source of different directions. The 64 directions of the flash are the same as the geodesic dome in the Yale B database [8].

We compute the nine low spherical harmonic coefficients L_{lm} ($0 \le l \le 2, -l \le m \le l$), for every illumination map as

$$L_{lm} = \int_{\theta_i=0}^{\pi} \int_{\phi_i=0}^{2\pi} L(\theta_i, \phi_i) Y_{lm}^* \sin \theta_i d\theta_i d\phi_i,$$ (5)

where $L(\theta_i, \phi_i)$ is the illumination intensity of the direction (θ_i, ϕ_i). Then the irradiance image is computed with Eq. (4) using the average face shape. Finally, the derivate filter is applied to the log of the irradiance image to get the $\nabla \log E(x, y)$.

Fig. 1 shows some examples of the varying illuminations and the corresponding filtered irradiance images. All the illuminations are scaled as $L_{00} = 60$ for better visualization. It can be seen that the filtered irradiances are almost zero (black pixels). Fig. 2 shows the distributions of the vertical derivatives for the two datasets. Though the illuminations vary very much, the two distributions have similar shape that are peaked at zero and fall off much faster than Gasussian, i.e., the outputs of the derivative filtered irradiances are very sparse. The statistics are similar with those of the natural images [7] and the natural illuminations [20]. Though human face is not convex strictly, the distribution does not change much.

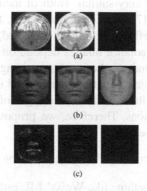

(a)

(b)

(c)

Fig. 1. Some examples of the filtered face irradiance images. (a) The varying illuminations. (b) The irradiance images under the varying illuminations. (c) The corresponding vertical derivative filtered irradiance images

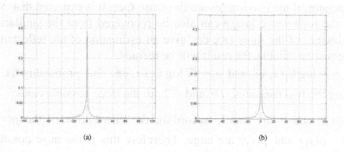

(a)   (b)

Fig. 2. The distributions of the vertical derivative of the face irradiance images. (a) Natural illuminations. (b) Point light sources

2.2 The Illumination Insensitive Measure

The above-mentioned observations that the filtered irradiance images are very sparse mean that the energy of the most of the pixels of the irradiance images is small. According to Eq. (3), at these pixels, the energy of the filtered image $\nabla \log I(x, y)$ is mostly caused by $\nabla \log R(x, y)$, i.e., $\nabla \log I(x, y) \approx \nabla \log R(x, y)$. The filtered reflectance image is invariant with illumination. Therefore, the filtered image

$\nabla \log I(x, y)$ can be used as an illumination insensitive measure for face recognition. This measure had been used in [4], which were derived from the connection between the $\nabla \log I(x, y)$ and the gradient of the ratio of the two images. Then, the *Euclidean* distance map between the two images based on the feature $\nabla \log I(x, y)$ can be defined as

$$D1_{I_1, I_2}(x, y) = \left| \nabla \log I_1(x, y) \right| - \left| \nabla \log I_2(x, y) \right|, \tag{6}$$

and used as distance of two images in face recognition in [4].

Actually, the distribution of the filtered face irradiance images and the filtered face reflectance images are very similar. Both of them have distribution similar with that of the natural images [7]. But for human faces, the locations of the pixels with larger intensity in filtered reflectance images are fixed, such as in the region of mouth, mustache and eyes. The irradiance images depend on the shape and the illumination. As the illuminations are random, the irradiance images are random, resulting in the random locations of the large intensity in the filtered irradiance images. Then the *min* operator on two or more filtered irradiance images of the same face can weaken the effect of varying illuminations. Therefore, we propose a new similarity map of two images based on the *min* operator as

$$S2_{I_1, I_2}(x, y) = \min\left(\left| \nabla \log I_1(x, y) \right|, \left| \nabla \log I_2(x, y) \right| \right). \tag{7}$$

The *min* measure is something like Weiss' ML estimation of the reflectance image in [20]. In Weiss's ML estimation, the filtered reflectance image is the *median* of the filtered image sequences. Then the reflectance image can be recovered from the estimation of filtered reflectance image. However, the *median* operator needs at least three images per subject, which is not satisfied by many face recognition systems. In our *min* operator, if the two images are the same face, it is expected that $S2 \approx \nabla \log R$. Therefore the reflectance image can also be recovered from the similarity map $S2$. Only two images of the same face can give an estimation of the reflectance image. If more images are available, the result will be refined.

Let $v_1 = \left| \nabla \log E_1(x, y) \right|$ and $v_2 = \left| \nabla \log E_2(x, y) \right|$, the probability is $p(v_1)p(v_2)$. We compare the two measures, $D1$ and $S2$, in the three possible cases:

1. Both v_1 and v_2 are small. According the distribution of the $p(v)$ in section 2.1, $p(v_1)$ and $p(v_2)$ are large. Therefore this is the most possible case. In this case, both the two measures, $D1$ and $S2$ are insensitive to the variations in illuminations.

2. v_1 is small and v_2 is large. Then $p(v_1)$ is large and $p(v_2)$ is small. This is the less possible case. The difference $\left| v_1 - v_2 \right|$ is large and then the measure $D1$ is large. The result of the *min* operator, $\left| \min(v_1, v_2) \right|$, is small and the measure $S2$ is more insensitive to illumination. The same is for the case of v_1 is large and v_2 is small.

3. Both v_1 and v_2 are large. $p(v_1)$ and $p(v_2)$ are small and this is the least possible case. In this case, $|v_1 - v_2|$ is small and $|\min(v_1, v_2)|$ is large. Therefore the measure $D1$ is more insensitive to illumination than the measure $S2$. But this case is little possible and then the measure $S2$ is more invariable to illumination in total.

For face recognition, we define the similarity score of two images as

$$s2(I_1, I_2) = \sum_{x,y} S2_{I_1, I_2}(x, y).\qquad(8)$$

If the two images are of the same face, it is expected that $S2 \approx \nabla \log R$ and $s2 \approx \sum_{x,y} |\nabla \log R(x, y)|$, i.e., the intrapersonal similarity maps are just like the filtered reflectance image of faces. If the two images are from different faces, the similarity map $S2$ is more random and $s2$ is smaller.

3 The Experimental Results

The publicly available face database, the CMU-PIE database [19], is used in our experiments. We select the frontal images with lighting variations for the experiments. There are total 68 persons included in the database. There are 21 flashes and the room lights to illuminate the face. The images were captured with the room lights on and off, resulting in 43 different conditions. Some examples of the images under different illuminations are shown in Fig. 3.

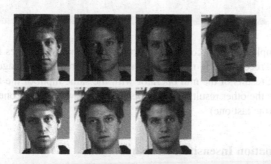

Fig. 3. Some examples of the images in the CMU-PIE database. The first three images in the first row are from "illum" set and the images in the second row are from "lights" set. The last image in the first row is taken with just the room light (f01 in "lights" set)

The images in CMU-PIE database under the 43 illuminations classified into two subsets: "illum" and "lights". There are some differences between the two subsets. In the "illum" subset, the room lights is turned off and the subject is not wearing glasses. While in the "lights" subset, the room lights is turned on. And the subject is wearing glasses if and only if they normally do. The flash numbers are 02-21. The flash number "01" corresponds to no flash (only for the "lights" subset). See the reference [19] for more details of the meaning of the flash number.

3.1 The Recovered Reflectance Images

We compare the reflectance images recovered by Weiss's *median* operator and our *min* operator in this subsection. In this experiments, two filters: horizontal and vertical derivative filters, are used. Fig. 4 shows the reflectance image using different number of input images recovered by the *median* operator and the *min* operator. The input images are given in Fig. 3. Note that the *min* operator needs at least two images while the *median* operator needs at least three images and the number of the images needs to be odd.

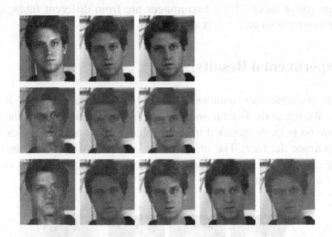

Fig. 4. Some examples of the recovered reflectance images. The images in the first row is the reflectance images recovered by median operator with three input images, the images in the second row are the results of the min operator with the same input of the first row. The images in the third row are the other results of min operator with two (the first one to the third one) and four input images (the last one)

3.2 The Illumination Insensitive Measure

To test the variations in illuminations only, both the gallery and probe are from the same subsets. In the experiments, we select the flash "11" in each subset as galleries for the both subsets. As the illumination of the gallery released by the CMU-PIE database is the same as that of the flash "01" in subset "lights", the results on the subset "lights" with the gallery flash "01" is also given.

Our experiments compare the three measures: the correlation of the image intensity I, $L2(|\Delta \log I|)$ and $Min(|\Delta \log I|)$. Face recognition is achieved by finding a nearest neighbor based on the image similarity or distance. As many facial features such as eyes, mouth, and eyebrows are horizontal, we use the vertical derivate in the recognition experiments only.

The experimental results of face recognition on the CMU-PIE database are listed in Table 1. Both the measure $L2(\ |\Delta \log I|\ )$ and $Min(\ |\Delta \log I|\ )$ improve the performances of face recognition much when the probes are taken under different illuminations. And the error rates using the measure $Min(|\Delta \log I|)$ are the lowest.

Table 1. Error rate comparisons between different measures on the CMU-PIE database

Gallery	Probe	Measure	Error rate (%)
"illum" (f11)	"illum"	Correlation (I)	47.1
		$L2(|\Delta \log I|)$	12.6
		$Min(|\Delta \log I|)$	9.6
"lights" (f11)	"lights"	Correlation (I)	14.3
		$L2(|\Delta \log I|)$	0.4
		$Min(|\Delta \log I|)$	0.4
"lights" (f01)	"lights"	Correlation (I)	18.5
		$L2(|\Delta \log I|)$	3.2
		$Min(|\Delta \log I|)$	0.3

4 Conclusions

In this paper, we investigate the statistics of the derivative of the log irradiance images of human face and find that the distribution is very sparse. Based on this observation, we propose an illumination insensitive measure for face recognition based on the *min* operator of the derivatives of log of two images. We compare the proposed measure for reflectance images recovering with the *median* operator proposed by Weiss [20]. When the probes are collected under varying illuminations, our experiments of face recognition on the CMU-PIE database show that the proposed measure are much better than the correlation of image intensity and a little better than the Euclidean distance of the derivate of the log image used in [4].

Acknowledgement

This research is partly sponsored by Natural Science Foundation of China (under contract No. 60332010), National Hi-Tech Program of China (No.2001AA114190 and No. 2002AA118010), and ISVISION Technologies Co., Ltd. Portions of the research in this paper use the CMU-PIE database. The authors wish to thanks everyone involved in collecting these data.

References

1. Y. Adini, Y. Moses and S. Ullman: Face Recognition: The Problem of Compensting for changes in illumination Direction. IEEE Trans. On PAMI. Vol. 19(7) (1997) 721–732
2. R. Basri and D. Jacobs: Lambertian Reflectance and Linear Subspaces. Proc. ICCV'01. (2001) 383–390
3. P.N. Belhumeur, J.P. Hespanha and D.J. Kriegman: Eigenfaces vs Fisherfaces: recognition using class specific linear projection. IEEE Trans. On PAMI. Vol. 20(7) (1997)
4. P.N. Belhumeur and D.W. Jacobs: Comparing images under variable illumination. Proc. CVPR'98. (1998)
5. V. Blanz and T. Vetter: Face Recognition Based on Fitting a 3D Morphable Model. IEEE Trans. on PAMI. Vol. 25(9) (2003) 1–12
6. H.F. Chen, P.N. Belhumeur and D.W. Jacobs: In Search of Illumination Invariants. Proc. CVPR'00. Vol.1 (2000) 1254–1261
7. R.O. Dror, T.K. Leung, E.H. Adelson, and A.S. Willsky: Statistics of real-world illumination. Proc. CVPR'01. (2001)
8. A.S. Georghiades, P.N. Belhumeur and D.J.Kriegman: From Few to Many: Illumination Cone Models for Face Recognition under Differing Pose and Lighting. IEEE Trans. On PAMI. Vol. 23(6) (2001) 643–660
9. P. Hallinan: A Low-Dimensional Representation of Human Faces for Arbitrary Lightening Conditions. Proc. CVPR'94. (1994) 995–999
10. B. Moghaddam, T. Jebara, and A. Pentland: Bayesian Face Recognition. Pattern Recognition. Vol. 33 (2000) 1771–1782
11. Y. Moses, Y. Adini and S. Ullman: Face Recognition: the Problem of Compensating for Changes in Illumination Direction. Proc. ECCV'94. Vol. I (1994) 286–296
12. P.J. Phillips, H. Moon, et al.: The FERET Evaluation Methodology for Face-Recognition Algorithms. IEEE Trans. On PAMI. Vol. 22(10) (2000) 1090–1104
13. P.J. Phillips, P. Grother, R.J Micheals, D.M. Blackburn, E. Tabassi, and J.M. Bone: FRVT 2002: Evaluation Report. http://www.frvt.org/DLs/FRVT_2002_Evaluation_Report.pdf, March 2003
14. S. Shan, W. Gao, B. Cao, D. Zhao: Illumination Normalization for Robust Face Recognition against Varying Lighting Conditions. IEEE International Workshop on Analysis and Modeling of Faces and Gestures. (2003) 157–164
15. M. Turk and A. Pentland. Eigenfaces for Recognition. Journal of cognitive neuroscience. Vol. 3 (1991) 71–86
16. R. Ramamoorthi and P. Hanrahan: An efficient representation for irradiance environment maps. Proc. SIGGRAPH'01. (2001) 497–500
17. Shashua: On photometric issues in 3D visual recognition from a single 2D image. IJCV. Vol. 21(1-2) (1997) 99–122
18. Shashua and T. Riklin-Raviv: The Quotient Image: Class-Based Re-Rendering and Recognition With Varying Illuminations. IEEE Trans. on PAMI. (2001) 129–139
19. T. Sim, S. Baker and M. Bsat: The CMU Pose, Illumination, and Expression (PIE) Database. Proc. FG'02 (2002)
20. Y. Weiss: Deriving intrinsic images from image sequences. Proc. ICCV'01. Vol. II (2001) 68–75
21. W.Y. Zhao, R. Chellappa, A. Rosenfeld, et al.: Face recognition: A literature survey. UMD CfAR Technical Report CAR-TR-948 (2000)

A Fast Method of Lighting Estimate Using Multi-linear Algebra

Yuequan Luo and Guangda Su

The State Key Laboratory of Intelligent Technology and System,
Electronic Engineering Department, Tsinghua University, Beijing, 100084, China
luo-yq02@mails.tsinghua.edu.cn, sugd@ee.tsinghua.edu.cn

Abstract. Natural facial images are the composite consequence of multiple factors and illumination is an important one. In many situations, we must normalize the facial image's illumination or simulate the similar lighting condition; therefore, accurate estimation of the facial image's lighting is necessary and can help get a good result. Because of its richer representational power, multi-linear algebra offers a potent mathematical framework for analyzing the multifactor structure of image ensembles. We apply multi-linear algebra to obtain a parsimonious representation of facial image ensembles which separates the illumination factor from facial images. With the application of multi-linear algebra, we can avoid not only the use of 3D face model, but also that of the complicated iterative algorithm, thus we obtain a fast and simple method of lighting estimation.

Keywords: Lighting estimate; multi-linear algebra.

1 Introduction

It has been observed that "the variations between the images of the same face due to illumination are almost larger than the images variations due to change in face identity" [1]. People possess a remarkable ability to recognize faces when confronted by a broad variety of lighting conditions. Developing a robust computational model of face recognition under various illuminations remains a difficult problem. Unfortunately, natural facial images are often taken under various illuminations, which depress the recognition rate to an unacceptable level.

Although no revolutionary practical solutions are available for the problem of illumination variation by far, some solutions to the illumination problem have emerged. These solutions include EigenFace and edge image [9], Higher order PCA [10] and kernel analysis [11,12], Gabor Wavelet Basis [13,14], Quotient image [5,27], illumination cone [2,3,16], Symmetric Shape from Shading(SSFS) [4,15], Multi-linear subspace analysis [6-8], Spherical Harmonic Analysis [17-24]. Direct or indirect estimation of the lighting of images is required in many of those algorithms. In some situations, we must de-lighting or re-lighting the facial image to get a desirable image. Thus accurate estimation of the facial image's lighting is necessary and can help get a good result. Lee and Rosenfeld(1989), Zheng and Chellappa(1991), Pentland (1982) respectively present three similar algorithms of lighting estimation,

S.Z. Li et al. (Eds.): Sinobiometrics 2004, LNCS 3338, pp. 205–211, 2004.
© Springer-Verlag Berlin Heidelberg 2004

which are named source from shading. But none of the three algorithms produced satisfactory estimates for the slant angle. Based on those three algorithms, literature [15] proposes a new model-based method to estimate the slant angle more reliably. The algorithm uses a simple 3D face model to help in the determination of the slant angle and tilt angle. The algorithm gets an image generated from the 3D face model by a given hypothesized slant angle and tilt angle, compares it to the source image, and then searches all ranges of slant angle and tilt angle for minimal MSE to get the estimation of them. Literature [25,27] consider the lighting estimation as a consecutive classify problem, and use kernel regression estimation to estimate the lighting direction. However, one disadvantage of those algorithms is computationally complicated and time consuming.

Multi-linear algebra, the algebra of higher-order tensors, offers a potent mathematical framework for analyzing the multifactor structure of image ensembles and has recently attracted attention because of its richer representational power. M. Alex etc. used it in face recognition directly to solve the problem of illumination, viewpoint and expression [6-8]. In our method of lighting estimation, we consider lighting variation as one factor of facial images and apply multi-linear algebra to obtain a fast and simple method of lighting estimation.

The remainder of this paper is organized as follows: Section 2 covers the foundations of tensor algebra that are relevant to our approach. Section 3 applies multi-linear analysis algorithm to the lighting estimation. Section 4 introduces the experiment and concludes result of our method.

2   Relevant Multi-linear Algebra

A *tensor* is a higher order generalization of a vector (first order tensor) and a matrix (second order tensor). Tensors are multi-linear mappings over a set of vector spaces. The order of tensor $A \in \mathbb{R}^{I_1 \times I_2 \times \cdots \times I_N}$ is N. An element of A is denoted as $a_{i_1 \ldots i_n \ldots i_N}$, $1 \le i_n \le I_n$. In tensor terminology, the *mode-n vectors* of an Nth order tensor A are the I_n–D vectors obtained from A by varying index i_n while keeping the other indices fixed.

Mode-n flattening: an Nth order tensor A can be flattened by N directions. Mode-n flatten a tensor A generate a matrix $A_{(n)} \in \mathbb{R}^{I_n \times (I_{n+1} \ldots I_N I_1 \ldots I_{n-1})}$ which column vectors are the mode-n vectors of tensor A.

The *mode-n product* of a tensor $A \in \mathbb{R}^{I_1 \times I_2 \times \cdots \times I_n \times \cdots \times I_N}$ by a matrix $M \in \mathbb{R}^{J_n \times I_n}$ is a tensor $B \in \mathbb{R}^{I_1 \times I_2 \times \cdots \times J_n \times \cdots \times I_N}$ and can be denoted as $B = A \times_n M$ in tensor notation or as $B_{(n)} = M \times A_{(n)}$ in terms of flattened matrices. The mode-n product has two properties:

$$A \times_m U \times_n V = A \times_n V \times_m U \qquad (1)$$

$$(A \times_n U) \times_n V = A \times_n (VU) \qquad (2)$$

The *mode-n SVD* is a generalization of matrix SVD. It decomposes a tensor as the mode-n product of N-orthogonal spaces and expressed as follows:

$$A = Z \times_1 U_1 \times_2 U_2 \ldots \times_n U_n \ldots \times_N U_N \qquad (3)$$

The mode-n SVD can be computing recur to conventional matrix SVD: U_n is the left matrix of SVD of matrix $A_{(n)}$. Tensor Z in the formula (3) called as *core tensor*, it's satisfy follow formula:

$$Z = A \times_1 U_1^T \times_2 U_2^T ... \times_n U_n^T ... \times_N U_N^T \qquad (4)$$

For further discussion on the tensor, see [8,26].

3 Lighting Estimation Using Multi-linear Algebra

Collect facial image under some appointed illuminations and expression for every individual to form bootstrap database. With multi-linear algebra, we can decompose bootstrap facial image by N-mode SVD as follows:

$$T = Z \times_1 U_{pixels} \times_2 U_{peoples} \times_3 U_{illums} \times_4 U_{express} \qquad (5)$$

In the upper formulation, the mode matrix $U_{peoples}, U_{illums}, U_{express}$ respectively spans the spaces of people, illumination, expression parameters, the mode matrix U_{pixels} span the spaces of images. The core tensor Z governs the interaction between these factors and this is an advantage of multi-linear analysis beyond linear PCA which represents only the principal axes of variation over all images. Since each column of U_{pixels} is an eigenface, multi-linear analysis subsumes linear PCA analysis.

Regardless of illumination and expression, we can represent each person with the same coefficient vector. This can be express as $T = B \times_2 U_{peoples}$, where the tensor $B = Z \times_1 U_{pixels} \times_3 U_{illums} \times_4 U_{express}$ defines different bases for each combination of illumination and expression and the mode matrix $U_{peoples}$ contains the coefficient. It should be noted that, different from PCA, the bases in tensor B are not orthogonal basis. Since the tensor B contains different bases for each combination of illumination and expression, we index into basis tensor B for a particular illumination i, and expression e to obtain a subtensor $B_{i,e}$, then flatten the subtensor along people direction to get matrix $B_{i,e(peoples)}$, which column vectors span the space of images under particular illumination i, and expression e. While estimate lighting, given a facial image under unknown illumination, we project the image onto subtensor $B_{i,e}$ for every illumination i and expression e, and identifies the image's lighting as the illumination i relative to the max projection.

For accurate estimate lighting of image, the algorithm needs a lot of illuminations to form bootstrap database to ensure that these illuminations can cover the lighting space equably. For example, if we expect the estimation accuracy of azimuth and elevation less than 5 degree, we need more than 300 illuminations. This not only adds difficulty to form bootstrap database, but also is computationally time assuming. As we estimate azimuth and elevation respectively, we need only about 36 illuminations. To reduce computation in lighting estimation, we apply optimal dimensionality reduction to tensor, for further discussion see literature [7].

4   Experiments and Conclusion

In our experiments, we employed a portion of the Yale Face Database B [3]. Since the Yale Face Database B contains only one expression, we removed expression factor in multi-linear analysis. We picked up the face in the image and resized the face to 85×90. We used 9 people's images to form bootstrap and the others for test. We prepared two experiments, one was to estimate the lighting direction directly and the other was to estimate the azimuth and elevation respectively. Because of the symmetry of face, we select only half illuminations of azimuth for the experiments. Some face images are shown in fig 1.

Fig. 1. Some of face images using in our experiments

In the first experiment, we select all 35 illuminations for training. The result is satisfactory, each of the test images accurately vest in its corresponding lighting condition. But as mentioned before, it's impossible to cover all the half space (left or right) with just only 35 illuminations. It at least needs 190 illuminations for less than 5 degree error. Both computation and the forming of image database are difficult. So we did not focus on this method.

In the second experiment, we firstly select 11 illuminations for azimuth and 6 illuminations for elevation. Although the illuminations of azimuth in the Yale Face Database B at special elevation are not sufficient to get accurate estimation, we can compensate this by interpolation. The similar situation exists for elevation estimate. We presume that image changes because lighting is "continuous", i.e. the image change is small when the lighting change is little and large when lighting change is great. So we could interpolate to estimate the value at an appointed lighting angle and it's validated by the experiment results that the interpolated values are close to the true values. In the experiment, we interpolate at every times of 5 degree. When the azimuth is large, most part of the face is in shadow, which is similar to the case when elevation is large. Thus, the estimation of elevation will shift to large if the azimuth is great, which brings additional confusion to estimate. Adding sets of illumination at big azimuth would compensate the confusion, and this can be validated by the first experiment and the following results. Limited by the database, we additionally chose 4 elevation illuminations respectively at azimuth equal to 35 and 110 degree. Part of the results is shown in the following tables.

Table 1. Partial result of the estimation of azimuth (the bold-italic denotes the error estimation value and the value after '/' denotes the error)

Test	A000E+00	A000E+20	A015E+20	A020E+10	A025E+00
Estimate	00	00	15	20	25
Test	A020E-10	A010E-20	A000E-20	A035E+65	A070E+45
Estimate	20	10	00	35	70
Test	A060E+20	A070E+00	A060E-20	A050E-40	A110E+15
Estimate	60	70	60	50	110
Test	A120E+00	A110E-20	A070E-35	A085E-20	A095E+00
Estimate	120	110	70	85	95
Test	A110E+65	A000E+90	A020E-40	A035E-20	A050E+00
Estimate	*105/5*	*10/-10*	20	35	50
Test	A000E+45	A000E-35	A005E-10	A010E+00	A005E+10
Estimate	00	00	*00/5*	10	*00/5*

Table 2. Partial result of the estimation of elevation(the bold-italic denotes the error estimation value and the value after '/' denotes the error)

Test	A000E+00	A000E+20	A015E+20	A020E+10	A025E+00
Estimate	00	+20	+20	+10	00
Test	A020E-10	A010E-20	A000E-20	A035E+65	A070E+45
Estimate	-10	-20	-20	+65	*+50/-5*
Test	A060E+20	A070E+00	A060E-20	A050E-40	A110E+15
Estimate	*+25/-5*	00	-20	-35	+15
Test	A120E+00	A110E-20	A070E-35	A085E-20	A095E+00
Estimate	*-5/5*	-20	*-40/5*	-20	*-5/5*
Test	A110E+65	A000E+90	A020E-40	A035E-20	A050E+00
Estimate	+65	+90	-40	-20	*-5/5*
Test	A000E+45	A000E-35	A005E-10	A010E+00	A005E+10
Estimate	+45	-35	-10	00	+10

Table 1 shows the estimation results of azimuth. Although the results are satisfactory, error occurred under two situations, one is when the elevation is large (A000E+90) or both azimuth and elevation are large (A110E+65) and the other is the difference between the two illuminations is very small (A005E+10, A005E-10). The second error is usually very small and almost insignificant since the difference is small. But the effect of the first error could not be neglected and is usually more serious than the second. As suggested before, the error could be removed by adding a set of illuminations at large elevation.

The result of estimation for elevation is not as well as azimuth if only using one set illumination, especially when azimuth is large, the result will become unacceptable. Although we use three sets of illuminations, some error would occur at some place distant from samples, i.e. the error appears at place where the sample is sparse. This is because of the limitation of database. Since the elevations are sparse in the database, particularly when the azimuth is large, the interpolation is not credible and this is a big reason of error.

The accuracy of this lighting estimation method lies on the number and distribution of illumination in bootstrap. Thus the complexity of the forming of database and computation is in conflict with the accuracy of estimation. It's unworthy to seek for accuracy excessively. By using a 3D face model, the algorithm in literature [15] gets an image generated by every given slant and tilt angle, then it gets the estimation of slant angle and tilt angle through the iterative algorithm, the initial value of which is possible to be at any point within the whole space of slant angle and tilt angle. Different from it, our method needs only an operation of projection, therefore our method is much more simple and faster than the method in [15]. Although our algorithm is not an accurate method, it's a fast and simple method and can be used to speed up other complicated method. We use this method to get a coarse estimation of lighting for the initial value of other accurate method, for example, the method using in [15], and the result is that the range of searching is reduced. Thus, the combination of our method and that in literature [15] is as accurate as method in [15] but much faster than it. And experiment shows that its time consumption is only one sixth of the original method or even less.

References

1. Y.Moses, Y.Adini, and S.Ullman, "Face Recognition: The Problem of Compensating for Changes in Illumination Direction", Proc. European Conf. Computer Vision, pp. 286-296, 1994.
2. A.S.Georghiades, P.N. Belhumeur and D.J. Kriegman, "From Few to Many : Generative Models for Recognition Under Variable Pose and Illumination", IEEE Conf. on Automatic Face and Gesture Recognition, March 2000, oral presentation, pp. 277-284.
3. A. S. Georghiades, P.N. Belhumeur and D.J. Kriegman, "From Few to Many: Illumination Cone Models for Face Recognition under Variable Lighting and Pose", IEEE Trans. on Pattern Analysis and Machine Intelligence, June 2001, pp. 643-660.
4. Wenyi Zhao, Rama Chellappa, "Illumination-Insensitive Face Recognition Using Symmetric Shape-from-Shading", Computer Vision and Pattern Recognition (CVPR'00)-Volume 1. June 13 - 15, 2000. p. 1286
5. Amnon Shashua, Tammy Riklin-Raviv, "The Quotient Image: Class-Based Re-rendering and Recognition with Varying Illuminations", IEEE Transactions on Pattern Analysis and Machine Intelligence, vol.23, No.2, February 2001
6. M. Alex, O. Vasilescu, Demetri Terzopoulos, "Multilinear Image Analysis for Facial Recognition", Proceedings of the International Conference on Pattern Recognition (ICPR'02) 2002
7. M. Alex,O. Vasilescu, Demetri Terzopoulos, "Multilinear Subspace Analysis of Image Ensembles", CVPR03(II: 93-99).
8. M. Alex, O. Vasilescu, Demetri Terzopoulos, "Multilinear Analysis of Image Ensembles: TensorFaces", ECCV 2002, Lecture Notes in Computer Science, Vol. 2350, p447-460
9. Alper YILMAZ, Muhittin GOKMEN, "Eigenhill vs. Eigenface and Eigenedge", Pattern Recognition Journal, Vol. 34, 2001, pp. 181-184. 2000
10. Hyun-Chul Kim, Daijin Kim, Sung Yang Bang, "FACE RETRIEVAL USING 1ST- AND 2ND-ORDER PCA MIXTURE MODEL", pp. 605-608, Proc. International Conference on Image Processing (ICIP2002), Rochester, USA, September, 2002
11. Juwei Lu, Konstantions N.Plataniotis, Anastasios N.Venetsanopoulos, "Face Recognition Using Kernel Direct Discriminant Analysis Algorithms", IEEE Transactions on Neural Networks, Vol. 14, No. 1, Page: 117-126, January 2003.
12. Juwei Lu, Konstantions N.Plataniotis, Anastasios N.Venetsanopoulos, "Face Recognition Using LDA-Based Algorithms", IEEE Transactions on Neural Networks, Vol. 14, No. 1, Page: 195-200, January 2003

13. Xiaoling Wang, Hairong Qi, "Face Recognition Using Optimal Non-orthogonal Wavelet Basis Evaluated By Information Complexity", 16 th International Conference on Pattern Recognition (ICPR'02) Volume 1 August 11 - 15, 2002

14. Chengjun Liu, Harry Wechsler, "Independent Component Analysis of Gabor Features for Face Recognition", IEEE Transactions on Neural Networks, vol. 14, no. 4, pp. 919-928, 2003

15. Wenyi Zhao, R. Chellappa, "Robust Face Recognition using Symmetric Shape-from-Shading", Center for Automation Research, University of Maryland, College Park, Technical Report CAR-TR-919.

16. P. Belhumeur, D. Kriegman, "What Is the Set of Images of an Object under All Possible Illumination Conditions",Int'l J.Computer Vision, vol.28, no.3, pp.245-260, July 1998.

17. Peter Nillius,Jan-Olof Eklundh, "Low-Dimensional Representations of Shaded Surfaces under Varying Illumination", 2003 Conference on Computer Vision and Pattern Recognition (CVPR '03) - Volume II June 18 - 20, 2003 Madison, Wisconsin. p. 185

18. Lei Zhang, Dimitris Samaras, "Face Recognition Under Variable Lighting using Harmonic Image Exemplars", In Proc.CVPR2003, pp.I: 19-25

19. Haitao Wang, Yangsheng Wang, Hong Wei, "Face Representation and Reconstruction under Different Illunimation Conditions", Seventh International Conference on Information Visualization (IV'03) July16 - 18, 2003, p72

20. Ronen Basri, David W. Jacobs, "Lambertian Reflectance and Linear Subspaces", IEEE Transactions on Pattern Analysis and Machine Intelligence, vol25, No.2, February 2003

21. Ravi Ramamoorthi , "Analytic PCA construction for theoretical analysis of lighting variability, including attached shadows, in a single image of a convex Lambertian object", IEEE PAMI, vol. 24, no. 10, pp. 1322-1333, 2002

22. R. Epstein, P. Hallinan, A. Yuille, "5 plus or minus 2 eigenimages suffice: An empirical investigation of lowdimensional lighting models", In IEEE Workshop on Physics-Based Modeling in Computer Vision, pages 108–116, 1995.

23. P. Hallinan, "A low-dimensional representation of human faces for arbitrary lighting conditions", In CVPR 94, pages 995–999,1994.IJCV, 35(3):203–222, 1999.

24. Laiyun Qing, Shiguang Shan, Wen Gao, "Face De-lighting under Natural Illumination", Advances in Biometrics (2), p43

25. Sim T., Kanade T. "Combining Models and Exemplars for Face Recognition: an Illumination Example", Proc. Of Workshop on Models versus Exemplars in Computer Vision, CVPR 2001

26. T. G. Kolda. "Orthogonal tensor decompositions", SIAM Journal on Matrix Analysis and Applications, 23(1):243–255, 2001.

27. Laiyun Qing, Shiguang Shan, Wen Gao, "Illumination Alignment for Face Image with Ratio Image", Advances in Biometrics (2), p106

Face Recognition Using More Than One Still Image: What Is More?

Shaohua Kevin Zhou

Siemens Corporate Research,
Integrated Data Systems Department,
755 College Road East, Princeton, NJ 08540
kzhou@scr.siemens.com

Abstract. While face recognition from a single still image has been extensively studied over a decade, face recognition based on more than one still image, such as multiple still images or a video sequence, is an emerging topic. Using more than one image introduces new recognition settings. In terms of recognition algorithm, multiple still images or a video sequence can be treated as a single still image in a degenerate manner. However, this treatment neglects additional properties present in multiple still images and/or video sequences. In this paper, we review three properties, manifested in multiple still images and/or video sequence, and their implications to different recognition settings. We also list corresponding approaches proposed in the literature that utilize these properties.

1 Introduction

While face recognition from a single still image has been extensively studied over a decade, face recognition based on a group of still images (also referred as multiple still images) or a video sequence is an emerging topic. This is mainly evidenced by the growing increase in the literature. For instance, a research initiative called Face Recognition Grand Challenge [1] is organized. One specific challenge directly addresses the use of multiple still images that is reportedly to improve the recognition accuracy significantly [3]. Recently a new workshop jointly held with CVPR 2004 is devoted on face processing in video [2]. It is predictable that with the ubiquity of video sequences, face recognition based on video sequences will become more and more popular.

It is obvious that multiple still images or a video sequence can be regarded as a single still image in a degenerate manner. More specifically, suppose that we have a single-still-image-based face recognition algorithm $\mathcal{A}$ (or the base algorithm) by some means, we can construct an assembly recognition algorithm based on multiple still images or a video sequence by combining multiple base algorithms denoted by $\mathcal{A}_i$'s. Each A_i takes a different single image y_i as input, coming from the multiple still images or video sequences. The combining rule can be additive, multiplicative, and so on. Section 3 presents a detailed example of constructing an assembly recognition algorithm.

S.Z. Li et al. (Eds.): Sinobiometrics 2004, LNCS 3338, pp. 212–223, 2004.
© Springer-Verlag Berlin Heidelberg 2004

Even though the assembly algorithms might work well in practice, clearly, the overall recognition performance of the assembly algorithm is solely based on those of separate algorithms and hence designing the base algorithm $\mathcal{A}$ is of ultimate importance. Therefore, the assembly algorithms completely neglect additional properties possessed by multiple still images or video sequences.

Three additional properties are available for multiple still images and/or video sequences:

1. [*P1*: **Multiple Observations**]. This property is directly utilized by the assembly algorithm. One main disadvantage of the assembly algorithms is its *ad hoc* combining rule. However, theoretic analysis based on multiple observations can be derived as shown later.
2. [*P2*: **Temporal Continuity/Dynamics**]. Successive frames in the video sequences are continuous in the temporal dimension. Such continuity, coming from facial expression, geometric continuity related to head and/or camera movement, or photometric continuity related to changes in illumination, provides an additional constraint for modeling face appearance. In particular, temporal continuity can be further characterized using dynamics. For example, facial expression and head movement when an individual participates certain activity result in structured changes in face appearance. Depiction of such structured change (or dynamics) further regularizes face recognition.
3. [*P3*: **3D Model**]. This means that we are able to reconstruct 3D model from a group of still images and a video sequence. Recognition can then be based on the 3D model.

Clearly, the first and third properties are shared by multiple still images and video sequences. The second property is solely possessed by video sequences. We will elaborate these properties in Section 4.

The properties manifested in multiple still images and video sequences present new challenges and opportunities. On the one hand, by judiciously exploiting these features, we can design new recognition algorithms other than those of assembly nature. On the other hand, cares should be exercised when exploiting these properties. Generally speaking, the algorithms utilizing these properties are advantageous to the assembly ones in terms of recognition performance, computational efficiency, etc.

There are two recent survey papers [11, 42] on face recognition in the literature. In [11], face recognition is in its early age and none of the reviewed approaches was video-based. In [42], video-based recognition is identified as one key topic. Even though it had been reviewed quite intensively, all video-based approaches were not categorized. In this paper, we attempt to bring out new insights through studying the three properties. We proceed to the next section by recapitulating some basics of face recognition and introduce new recognition settings that use more than one image.

2   Recognition Setting

In this section, we address the concept of training, gallery, and probe sets and present various recognition settings based on different types of inputs used in the gallery and probe sets.

2.1   Gallery, Probe, and Training Sets

We here follow a face recognition test protocol FERET [28] widely observed in the face recognition literature. FERET assumes availability of the following three sets, namely one training set, one gallery set, and one probe set. The gallery and probe sets are used in the testing stage. The gallery set contains images with known identities and the probe set with unknown identities. The algorithm associates descriptive features with the images in the gallery and probe sets and determines the identities of the probe images by comparing their associated features with those features associated with gallery images.

According to the imagery utilized in the gallery and probe sets, we can define the following nine recognition settings as in Table 1. For instance, the *mStill-to-Video* setting utilizes multiple still images for each individual in the gallery set and a video sequence for each individual in the probe set. The FERET investigated the *sStill-to-sStill* recognition setting.

Table 1. Recognition settings based on a single still image, multiple still images and a video sequence

Probe \ Gallery	A single still image	A group of still images	A video sequence
A single still image	*sStill-to-sStill*	*mStill-to-sStill*	*Video-to-sStill*
A group of still images	*sStill-to-mStill*	*mStill-to-mStill*	*Video-to-mStill*
A video sequence	*sStill-to-Video*	*mStill-to-Video*	*Video-to-Video*

The need of a training set in addition to the gallery and probe sets is mainly motivated by that fact that the *sStill-to-sStill* recognition setting is used in the FERET. The purpose of the training set is provided for the recognition algorithm to learn the face space. For example, in subspace methods, the training set is used to learn the projection matrix for the face space. Typically, the training set does not overlap with the gallery and probe sets in terms of identity. This is based on that the face space characterization is applied for all individuals and generalization across the identities in the training and gallery sets is used. If more than one still image is used in the gallery set to represent one individual, the training set can be omitted provided that there are enough number of images.

3   Assembly Recognition Algorithm

Here is a concrete example of constructing an assembly recognition algorithm. Suppose that the still-image-based face recognition uses the nearest distance classification rule, the recognition algorithm $\mathcal{A}$ performs the following:

$$\mathcal{A} : \hat{n} = \arg \min_{n=1,2,...,N} d(\mathbf{y}, \mathbf{x}^{[n]}), \tag{1}$$

where N is the number of individuals in the gallery set, d is the distance function, $\mathbf{x}^{[n]}$ represents the nth individual in the gallery set, and $\mathbf{y}$ is the probe single still image. Equivalently, the distance function can be replaced by a similarity function s. The recognition algorithm becomes:

$$\mathcal{A} : \hat{n} = \arg \max_{n=1,2,...,N} s(\mathbf{y}, \mathbf{x}^{[n]}). \tag{2}$$

In this paper, we interchange the use of the distance and similarity functions if there is no confusion.

The common choices for d include the following:

– Cosine angle:

$$d(\mathbf{y}, \mathbf{x}^{[n]}) = 1 - cos(\mathbf{y}, \mathbf{x}^{[n]}) = 1 - \frac{\mathbf{y}^T \mathbf{x}^{[n]}}{||\mathbf{y}|| \cdot ||\mathbf{x}^{[n]}||} \tag{3}$$

– Distance in subspace:

$$d(\mathbf{y}, \mathbf{x}^{[n]}) = ||\mathbf{P}^T \{\mathbf{y} - \mathbf{x}^{[n]}\}||^2 = \{\mathbf{y} - \mathbf{x}^{[n]}\}^T \mathbf{P} \mathbf{P}^T \{\mathbf{y} - \mathbf{x}^{[n]}\}, \tag{4}$$

where $\mathbf{P}$ is a subspace projection matrix. The common subspace methods include principal component analysis (a.k.a. eigenface [37]), linear discriminant analysis (a.k.a Fisherface [7, 15, 41]), independent component analysis [6], local feature analysis [27], intra-personal subspace [26, 45] etc.
– 'Generalized' Mahanalobis distance:

$$d(\mathbf{y}, \mathbf{x}^{[n]}) = \{\mathbf{y} - \mathbf{x}^{[n]}\}^T \mathbf{W} \{\mathbf{y} - \mathbf{x}^{[n]}\}, \tag{5}$$

where the $\mathbf{W}$ matrix plays a weighting role. If $\mathbf{W} = \mathbf{P}\mathbf{P}^T$, then the 'generalized' Mahanalobis distance reduces to the distance in subspace. If $\mathbf{W} = \Sigma^{-1}$ with Σ being a covariance matrix, then the 'generalized' Mahanalobis distance reduces to the regular Mahanalobis distance.

Using the base algorithm $\mathcal{A}$ defined in (1) as a building block, we can easily construct various assembly recognition algorithms [14] based on a group of still images and a video sequence. By denoting a group of still images and a video sequence by $\{\mathbf{y}_t; \ t = 1, 2, ..., T\}$, the recognition algorithm $\mathcal{A}_t$ for $\mathbf{y}_t$ is simply

$$\mathcal{A}_t : \hat{n} = \arg \min_{n=1,2,...,N} d(\mathbf{y}_t, \mathbf{x}^{[n]}). \tag{6}$$

Some commonly used combining rules are listed in Table 2.

In the above, the nth individual in the gallery set is represented by a single still image $\mathbf{x}^{[n]}$. This can be generalized to use multiple still images or a video sequence $\{\mathbf{x}_s^{[n]}; \ s = 1, 2, \ldots, K_s\}$. Similarly, the resulting assembly algorithm is to combine the base algorithms denoted by $\mathcal{A}_{ts}$'s:

$$\mathcal{A}_{ts} : \hat{n} = \arg \min_{n=1,2,...,N} d(\mathbf{y}_t, \mathbf{x}_s^{[n]}). \tag{7}$$

Table 2. A list of combining rules. The J function used in majority voting is an indicator function

Method	Rule
Minimum arithmetic mean	$\hat{n} = \arg\min_{n=1,2,\ldots,N} \frac{1}{T} \sum_{t=1}^{T} d(\mathbf{y}_t, \mathbf{x}^{[n]})$
Minimum geometric mean	$\hat{n} = \arg\min_{n=1,2,\ldots,N} \sqrt[T]{\prod_{t=1}^{T} d(\mathbf{y}_t, \mathbf{x}^{[n]})}$
Minimum median	$\hat{n} = \arg\min_{n=1,2,\ldots,N} \{med_{t=1,2,\ldots,T}\ d(\mathbf{y}_t, \mathbf{x}^{[n]})\}$
Minimum minimum	$\hat{n} = \arg\min_{n=1,2,\ldots,N} \{\min_{t=1,2,\ldots,T}\ d(\mathbf{y}_t, \mathbf{x}^{[n]})\}$
Majority voting	$\hat{n} = \arg\max_{n=1,2,\ldots,N} \sum_{t=1}^{T}\ J[\mathcal{A}_t(\mathbf{y}) == n]$

4   Properties

The multiple still images and video sequence are different from one still image as they possess additional properties not cherished by a still image. In particular, three properties manifest themselves that motivated various approaches recently proposed in the literature. Below, we analyze the three properties one by one.

4.1   [*P*1: Multiple Observations]

This is the most commonly used feature of multiple still images and video sequence. If only this property is concerned, a video sequence reduces to a group of still images with the temporal dimension stripped. In other words, every video frame is treated as a still image. Another implicit assumption is that all face images are normalized before subjecting to subsequence analysis.

The assembly algorithms utilize this property in a straightforward fashion. However, as mentioned above, the combining rules are rather *ad hoc*, which leaves room for a systematic exploration of this property by using different representations of the multiple observations $\{\mathbf{y}_1, \mathbf{y}_2, \ldots, \mathbf{y}_T\}$. Once an appropriate representation is fixed, a recognition algorithm can be accordingly designed.

Various ways of summarizing multiple observations have been proposed. In terms of the summarization rule, these approaches can be roughly grouped into four categories.

One Image or Several Images. Multiple observations $\{\mathbf{y}_1, \mathbf{y}_2, \ldots, \mathbf{y}_T\}$ are summarized into one image $\hat{\mathbf{y}}$ or several images $\{\hat{\mathbf{y}}_1, \hat{\mathbf{y}}_2, \ldots, \hat{\mathbf{y}}_m\}$ (with $m < T$). For instance, one can use the mean or the median of $\{\mathbf{y}_1, \mathbf{y}_2, \ldots, \mathbf{y}_T\}$ as the summary image $\hat{\mathbf{y}}$. Clustering techniques can be invoked to produce the summary images $\{\hat{\mathbf{y}}_1, \hat{\mathbf{y}}_2, \ldots, \hat{\mathbf{y}}_m\}$. In terms of recognition, we can simply apply the still-image-based face recognition algorithm based on $\hat{\mathbf{y}}$ or $\{\hat{\mathbf{y}}_1, \hat{\mathbf{y}}_2, \ldots, \hat{\mathbf{y}}_m\}$. This applies to all nine recognition settings listed in Table 1.

Matrix. Multiple observations $\{\mathbf{y}_1, \mathbf{y}_2, \ldots, \mathbf{y}_T\}$ form a matrix[1] $Y = [\mathbf{y}_1, \mathbf{y}_2, \ldots, \mathbf{y}_T]$. The main advantages of using the matrix representation is that we can rely

---

[1] Here we assume that each image $\mathbf{y}_i$ is 'vectorized'.

on the rich literature of matrix analysis. For example, various matrix decompositions can be invoked to represent the original data more efficiently. Metrics measuring similarity between two matrices can be used for recognition.

This applies to the *mStill-to-mStill*, *Video-to-mStill*, *Video-to-mStill*, and *Video -to-Video* recognition settings. Suppose that the nth individual in the gallery set has a matrix $X^{[n]}$, we determine the identity of of a probe matrix Y as

$$\hat{n} = \arg \min_{n=1,2,\ldots,N} d(Y, X^{[n]}), \qquad (8)$$

where d is a matrix distance function.

Yamaguchi *el al.* [40] proposed the so-called *Mutual Subspace Method* (MSM) method. In this method, the matrix representation is used and the similarity function between two matrices is defined as the angle between two subspaces of the matrices (also referred as principal angle or canonical correlation coefficient). Wolf and Shashua [38] extended computation of the principal angles into a nonlinear feature spacec $\mathcal{H}$ called reproducing kernel Hilbert space (RKHS) [32] induced by a positive definite kernel function. Zhou [48] systematically investigated the kernel functions taking matrix as input (also referred to as matrix kernels). Two kernel functions using trace and determinant are proposed. Using them as building blocks, Zhou [48] constructed more kernels based on the column basis matrix, the 'kernelized' matrix, and the column basis matrix of the 'kernelized' matrix.

Probability Density Function (PDF). In this rule, multiple observations $\{y_1, y_2, \ldots, y_T\}$ are regarded as independent realizations drawn from an underlying distribution. PDF estimation techniques such as parametric, semi-parametric, and non-parametric methods [13] can be utilized.

In the *mStill-to-mStill*, *Video-to-mStill*, *Video-to-mStill*, and *Video-to-Video* recognition settings, recognition can be performed by comparing distances between PDF's, such as Bhattacharyya and Chernoff distances, Kullback-Leibler divergence, and so on. More specifically, suppose that the nth individual in the gallery set has a pdf $p^{[n]}(x)$, we determine the identity of a probe PDF $q(y)$ as

$$\hat{n} = \arg \min_{n=1,2,\ldots,N} d(q(y), p^{[n]}(x)), \qquad (9)$$

where d is a probability distance function.

In the *mStill to sStill*, *Video to sStill*, *sStill-to-mStill*, and *sStill-to-Video* settings, recognition becomes a hypothesis testing problem. For example, in the *sStill-to-mStill* setting, if we can summarize the multiple still images in query into a pdf, say $q(y)$, then recognition is to test which gallery image $x^{[n]}$ is mostly likely to be generated by $q(y)$.

$$\hat{n} = \arg \max_{n=1,2,\ldots,N} q(x^{[n]}). \qquad (10)$$

Notice that this is different from the *mStill-to-sStill* setting, where each gallery object has a density $p^{[n]}(y)$, then given a probe single still image y, recognition checks the following:

$$\hat{n} = \arg \max_{n=1,2,...,N} p^{[n]}(\mathbf{y}). \tag{11}$$

Shakhnoarovich *et al.* [33] proposed to use the multivariate normal density for summarizing face appearances and the Kullback-Leibler (KL) divergence or relative entropy for recognition. In [18, 19], Jebara and Kondon proposed probability product kernel function. In [47], Zhou and Chellappa computed the probabilistic distances such as the Chernoff and Bhattacharyya distances, the KL divergence, etc., in the RKHS space. Recently, Arandjelović and Cipolla [5] used resistor-average distance (RAD) for video-based recognition.

Manifold. In this rule, face appearances of multiple observations form a highly nonlinear manifold $\mathcal{P}$. Manifold learning has recently attracted a lot of attention. Examples include [30, 35].

After characterizing the manifolds, face recognition reduces to (i) comparing two manifolds if we are in the *mStill-to-mStill*, *Video-to-mStill*, *Video-to-mStill*, and *Video-to-Video* settings and (ii) comparing distances from one data point to different manifolds if we are in the *mStill-to-sStill*, *Video-to-sStill*, *sStill-to-mStill*, and *sStill-to-Video* settings.

For instance, in the *Video-to-Video* setting, galley videos are summarized into manifolds $\{\mathcal{P}^{[n]}; n = 1, 2, \ldots, N\}$. For the probe video that is summarized into a manifold $\mathcal{Q}$, its identity is determined as

$$\hat{n} = \arg \min_{n=1,2,...,N} d(\mathcal{Q}, \mathcal{P}^{[n]}), \tag{12}$$

where d calibrates the distance between two manifolds.

In the *Video-to-sStill* setting, for the probe still image $\mathbf{y}$, its identity is determined as

$$\hat{n} = \arg \min_{n=1,2,...,N} d(\mathbf{y}, \mathcal{P}^{[n]}), \tag{13}$$

where d calibrates the distance from a data point to a manifold.

Fitzgibbon and Zisserman [16] proposed to compute a joint manifold distance to cluster appearances. Li *et al.* [24] proposed identity surface that depicts face appearances presented in multiple poses. A video sequence corresponds to a trajectory traced out in the identity surface. Trajectory matching is used for recognition.

4.2   [P2: Temporal Continuity/Dynamics]

Property $P1$ strips the temporal dimension available in the video sequence. In this property $P2$, we bring back the temporal dimension. Clearly, the property $P2$ only holds for video sequence.

Successive frames in the video sequences are continuous in the temporal dimension. The continuity arising from dense temporal sampling is two-fold: the face movement is continuous and the change in appearance is continuous.

Temporal continuity provides an additional constraint for modeling face appearance. For example, smoothness of face movement is used in the face tracking.

As mentioned earlier, it is implicitly assumed that all face images are normalized before utilization of the property $P1$ of multiple observations. For the purpose of normalization, face detection is independently applied on each image. When temporal continuity is available, tracking can be applied instead of detection to perform normalization of each video frame.

Temporal continuity also plays an important role for recognition. Recently psychophysical evidence [20] reveals that moving faces are more recognizable. In addition to temporal continuity, face movement and face appearance follow certain dynamics, i.e., changes in movement and appearance are not random. Understanding dynamics is also important for face recognition.

Simultaneous tracking and recognition proposed by Zhou and Chellappa [43, 44] is the first approach that systematically studied how to incorporate temporal continuity in video-based recognition. Zhou and Chellappa modeled two tasks involved, namely tracking and recognition, in one probabilistic framework. They computer the posterior recognition probability $p(n_t, \theta_t | y_{0:t})$ where n_t is the identity variable, θ_t is the tracking parameter, and $y_{0:t} = \{y_0, y_2, \ldots, y_t\}$ is the video observation. Figure 1 illustrates the recognition results reported in [43, 44].

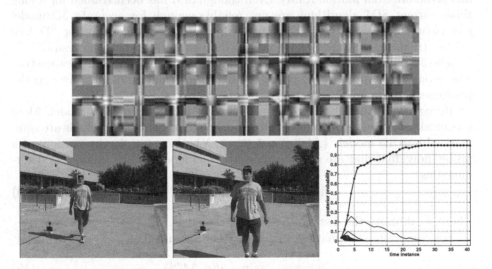

Fig. 1. Top row: the gallery images. Bottom row: The first (left) and the last (middle) frames of the video sequences with tracking results indicated by the box and the posterior probability $p(n_t | y_{0:t})$

Krueger and Zhou [21, 44] extended the approach in [43] to handle video sequence in the gallery set. Representative exemplars are learned from the gallery video sequences to depict individuals. Then simultaneous tracking and recognition [43] was invoked to handle video sequences in the probe set. Li and Chellappa [23] also proposed an approach somewhat similar to [43]. In [23], only tracking was implemented using SIS and recognition scores were subsequently derived based on tracking results.

Lee *et al.* [22] performed video-based face recognition using probabilistic appearance manifolds. The main motivation is to model appearances under pose variation, i.e., a generic appearance manifold consists of several pose manifolds. Liu and Chen [25] proposed to use adaptive HMM to depict the dynamics. Aggarwal *et al.* [4] proposed a system identification approach for video-based face recognition. The face sequence is treated as a first-order auto-regressive and moving averaging (ARMA) random process. Promising experimental results (over 90%) were reported when significant pose and expression variations are present in the video sequences.

Facial expression analysis is also related to temporal continuity/dynamics, but not directly related to face recognition. Approaches to expression analysis include [8, 36].

4.3   [P3: 3D Model]

This means that we are able to reconstruct 3D model from a group of still images and a video sequence. This leads to the literature of multiview geometry and structure from motion (SfM). Even though SfM has been studied for a long time, current SfM algorithms are not reliable enough for accurate 3D model reconstruction. Researchers therefore incorporate or solely use prior 3D face models (that are acquired beforehand) to derive the reconstruction result.

The 3D model usually possesses two components: geometric and photometric. The geometric component describes the depth information of the face and the photometric component depicts the texture map.

Recognition can then be performed directly based on the 3D model. More specifically, for any recognition setting, suppose that, galley individuals are summarized into 3D models $\{\mathcal{M}^{[n]}; n = 1, 2, \ldots, N\}$. For multiple observations of a probe individual that are summarized into a 3D model $\mathcal{N}$, its identity is determined as

$$\hat{n} = \arg \min_{n=1,2,\ldots,N} d(\mathcal{N}, \mathcal{M}^{[n]}), \tag{14}$$

where d calibrates the distance between two models.

For one probe still image y, its identity is determined as

$$\hat{n} = \arg \min_{n=1,2,\ldots,N} d(\mathbf{y}, \mathcal{M}^{[n]}), \tag{15}$$

where d calibrates the cost of generating a data point from a model.

It is interesting to note that Face Recognition Grand Challenge (FRGC) [1] also proposed the challenge of comparing 3D face models but obtained from a laser scan not from a 3D reconstruction algorithm.

Blanz and Vetter [9] fitted a 3D morphable model to a single still image. The 3D morphable model can be thought of an extension of 2D active appearance model [12] to 3D. However, the 3D morphable model uses a linear combination of dense 3D models. Xiao *et al.* [39] proposed to integrate a linear combination of 3D sparse model and a 2D appearance model. Examples of SfM for reconstructing the 3D model include [10, 29, 31]. Bundle adjustment [17, 34] is a combination of prior 3D model with SfM.

5   Conclusions

In this paper, we have studied three new properties present in the multiple still images and video sequences. We have also addressed the use of these properties in different recognition settings and briefly reviewed the proposed approaches in the literature.

Studying the recognition algorithms from the perspective of additional properties is very beneficial. In particular, we can forecast new approaches that can be developed to realize the full potentials of multiple still images or video sequences. For example, one can combine these properties [46] to arrive at possibly more accurate algorithms.

References

1. Face Recognition Grand Challenge. http://bbs.bee-biometrics.org.
2. The First IEEE Workshop on Face Processing in Video. http://www.visioninterface.net/fpiv04.
3. F. Fraser, "Exploring the use of face recognition technology for border control applications - Australia's experience," Biometric Consortium Conference, 2003.
4. G. Aggarwal, A. Roy-Chowdhury, and R. Chellappa, "A system identification approach for video-based face recognition," *Proceedings of International Conference on Pattern Recognition*, Cambridge, UK, August 2004.
5. O. Arandjelović and R. Cipolla, "Face recognition from face motion manifolds using robust kernel resistor-average distance," *IEEE Workshop on Face Processing in Video*, Washington D.C., USA, 2004.
6. M.S. Barlett, H.M. Ladesand, and T.J. Sejnowski, "Independent component representations for face recognition," *Proceedings of SPIE 3299*, pp. 528-539, 1998.
7. P. N. Belhumeur, J. P. Hespanha, and D. J. Kriegman, "Eigenfaces vs. fisherfaces: Recognition using class specific linear projection," *IEEE Trans. Pattern Analysis and Machine Intelligence*, vol. 19, pp. 711–720, 1997.
8. M.J. Black and Y. Yacoob, "Recognizing facial expressions in image sequences using local paramterized models of image motion," *International Journal of Computer Vision*, vol. 25, pp. 23-48, 1997.
9. V. Blanz and T. Vetter, "Face recognition based on fitting a 3D morphable model," *IEEE Transaction on Pattern Analysis and Machine Intelligence*, vol. 25, pp. 1063–1074, 2003.
10. M.E. Brand, "Morphable 3D Models from Video," *Proceedings of IEEE Conference on Computer Vision and Pattern Recognition*, Hawaii, 2001.
11. R. Chellappa, C. L. Wilson, and S. Sirohey, "Human and machine recognition of faces: A survey," *Proceedings of The IEEE*, vol. 83, pp. 705–740, 1995.
12. T.F. Cootes, G.J. Edwards, and C.J. Taylor, "Active appearance models," *IEEE Trans. on Pattern Analysis and Machine Intelligence*, vol. 23, no. 6, pp. 681-685, 2001.

13. R. O. Duda, P. E. Hart, and D. G. Stork, *Pattern Classification*. Wiley-Interscience, 2001.
14. G.J. Edwards, C.J. Taylor, and T.F. Taylor, "Improving idenfication performation by integrating evidence from sequences," *IEEE Intl. Conf. on Computer Vision and Pattern Recognition*, pp. 486-491, Fort Collins, Colorado, USA, 1999.
15. K. Etemad and R. Chellappa, "Discriminant analysis for recognition of human face images," *Journal of Optical Society of America A*, pp. 1724–1733, 1997.
16. A. Fitzgibbon and A. Zisserman, "Joint manifold distance: a new approach to appearance based clustering," *Proceedings of IEEE Computer Socienty Conference on Computer Vision and Pattern Recognition*, Madison, WI, 2003.
17. P. Fua, "Regularized bundle adjustment to model heads from image sequences without calibrated data," *Internationl Journal of Computer Vision*, vol. 38, pp. 153-157, 2000.
18. T. Jebara and R. Kondor, "Bhattacharyya and Expected Likelihood Kernels," *Conference on Learning Theory, COLT*, 2003.
19. R. Kondor and T. Jebara, "A Kernel Between Sets of Vectors," *International Conference on Machine Learning, ICML*, 2003.
20. B. Knight and A. Johnston, "The role of movement in face recognition," *Visual Cognition*, vol. 4, pp. 265-274, 1997.
21. V. Krueger and S. Zhou, "Exemplar-based face recgnition from video," *European Conference on Computer Vision*, Copenhagen, Denmark, 2002.
22. K. Lee, M. Yang, and D. Kriegman, "Video-based face recognition using probabilistic appearance manifolds," *IEEE Computer Society Conference on Computer Vision and Pattern Recognition*, Madison, WI, 2003.
23. B. Li and R. Chellappa, "A generic approach to simultaneous tracking and verification in video," *IEEE Trans. on Image Processing*, vol. 11, no. 5, pp. 530–554, 2002.
24. Y. Li, S. Gong, and H. Liddell, "Constructing face identity surface for recognition," *Internationl Journal of Computer Vision*, vol. 53, no. 1, pp. 71-92, 2003.
25. X. Liu and T. Chen, "Video-based face recognition using adaptive hidden markov models," *Proceedings of IEEE Computer Society Conference on Computer Vision and Pattern Recognition*, Madison, WI, 2003.
26. B. Moghaddam, "Principal manifolds and probabilistic subspaces for visual recognition," *IEEE Trans. Pattern Analysis and Machine Intelligence*, vol. 24, pp. 780–788, 2002.
27. P. Penev and J. Atick, "Local feature analysis: A general statistical theory for object representation," *Networks: Computations in Neural Systems*, vol. 7, pp. 477-500, 1996.
28. P.J. Phillips, H. Moon, S. Rizvi, and P.J. Rauss, "The FERET evaluation methodology for face-recognition algorithms," *IEEE Trans. Pattern Analysis and Machine Intelligence*, vol. 22, pp. 1090–1104, 2000.
29. G. Qian and R. Chellappa, "Structure from motion using sequential monte carlo methods," *Proceedings of International Conference on Computer Vision*, pp. 614 –621, Vancouver, BC, 2001.
30. S.T. Roweis and L.K. Saul, "Nonlinear Dimensionality Reduction by Locally Linear Embedding," *Science*, vol. 290, pp. 2323–2326, 2000.
31. A. Roy-Chowdhury and R. Chellappa, "Face reconstruction from video using uncertainty analysis and a generic model," *Computer Vision and Image Understanding*, vol. 91, pp. 188-213, 2003.
32. B. Schölkopf and A. Smola, *Support Vector Learning*. Press, 2002.

33. G. Shakhnarovich, J. Fisher, and T. Darrell, "Face recognition from long-term observations," *European Conference on Computer Vision*, Copenhagen, Denmark, 2002.

34. Y. Shan, Z. Liu, and Z. Zhang "Model-based bundle adjustment with applicaiton to face modeling," *Proceedings of Internationl Conference on Computer Vision*, pp. 645–651, Vancouver, BC, 2001.

35. J.B. Tenenbaum, V. de Silva and J.C. Langford. "A global geometric framework for nonlinear dimensionality reduction," *Science*, vol. 290, pp. 2319–2323, 2000

36. Y. Tian, T. Kanade, and J. Cohn, "Recognizing action units of facial expression analysis," *IEEE Trans. Pattern Analysis and Machine Intelligence*, vol. 23, pp. 1-19, 2001.

37. M. Turk and A. Pentland, "Eigenfaces for recognition," *Journal of Cognitive Neuroscience*, vol. 3, pp. 72–86, 1991.

38. L. Wolf and A. Shashua, "Kernel principal angles for classification machines with applications to image sequence interpretation," *IEEE Computer Society Conference on Computer Vision and Pattern Recognition*, Madison, WI, 2003.

39. J. Xiao, S. Baker, I. Matthews, and T. Kanade, "Real-time combined 2D+3D active appearance models," *IEEE Computer Society Conference on Computer Vision and Pattern Recognition*, Washington, DC, 2004.

40. O. Yamaguchi, K. Fukui and K. Maeda, "Face recognition using temporal image sequence," *Proceedings of International Conference on Automatic Face and Gesture Recognition*, Nara, Japan, 1998.

41. W. Zhao, R. Chellappa, and A. Krishnaswamy, "Discriminant analysis of principal components for face recognition," *Proceedings of International Conference on Automatic Face and Gesture Recognition*, pp. 361-341, Nara, Japan, 1998.

42. W. Zhao, R. Chellappa, A. Rosenfeld, and P.J. Phillips, "Face recognition: A literature survey," *ACM Computing Surveys*, vol. 12, 2003.

43. S. Zhou and R. Chellappa, "Probabilistic human Recognition from video," *European Conference on Computer Vision*, vol. 3, pp. 681-697, Copenhagen, Denmark, May 2002.

44. S. Zhou, V. Krueger, and R. Chellappa, "Probabilistic recognition of human faces from video," *Computer Vision and Image Understanding*, vol. 91, pp. 214–245, 2003.

45. S. Zhou, R. Chellappa, and B. Moghaddam "Intra-personal kernel subspace for face recognition ," *Proceedings of International Conference on Automatic Face and Gesture Recognition*, Seoul, Korea, May 2004.

46. S. Zhou and R. Chellappa, "Probabilistic identity characterization for face recognition," *Proceedings of IEEE Computer Society Conference on Computer Vision and Pattern Recognition*, Washington D.C., USA, June 2004.

47. S. Zhou and R. Chellappa, "Probabilistic distance measures in reproducing kernel Hilbert space," *SCR Technical Report*, 2004.

48. S. Zhou, "Trace and determinant kernels between matrices," *SCR Technical Report*, 2004.

Video-Based Face Recognition Using a Metric of Average Euclidean Distance

Jiangwei Li, Yunhong Wang, and Tieniu Tan

National Laboratory of Pattern Recognition, Institute of Automation,
Chinese Academy of Sciences, Beijing, 100080 P.R. China
{jwli, wangyh, tnt}@nlpr.ia.ac.cn

Abstract. This paper presents a novel approach for video-based face recognition. We define a metric based on an average L_2 Euclidean distance between two videos as the classifier. This metric makes use of Earth Mover's Distance (EMD) as the underlying similarity measurement between videos. Earth Mover's Distance is a recently proposed metric for geometric pattern matching and it reflects the average ground distance between two distributions. Under the framework of EMD, each video is modeled as a video signature and Euclidean distance is selected as the ground distance of EMD. Since clustering algorithm is employed, video signature can well represent the overall data distribution of faces in video. Experimental results demonstrate the superior performance of our algorithm.

1 Introduction

Face recognition based on video has been a focus recently [1-6]. It is very useful in the application of video surveillance and access control. Compared to still-based face recognition technology, multiple frames and temporal information facilitate face recognition. The discriminative information can be integrated across the video sequences. However, poor video quality, large illumination and pose variations, partial occlusion and small size images are the disadvantages of video-based face recognition. To overcome the above problems, many approaches, which attempt to utilize multiple frames and temporal information in video, are proposed. Based on whether the temporal information is utilized or not, these schemes can be divided into sequential approach and batch approach.

Sequential approach assumes temporal continuity between two adjacent samples. The continuity property propagates face position and identity frame by frame. The previous tracking and recognition result can be utilized for current face tasks. Zhou [2] proposes a tracking-and-recognition approach, which utilizes a very powerful unified probabilistic framework to resolve uncertainties in tracking and recognition simultaneously. Lee [3] represents each person with an appearance manifolds expressed as a collection of pose manifolds. In recognition, the probability of the test image from a particular pose manifold and the transition probability from the previous frame to the current pose manifold are integrated. Liu [4] applies adaptive HMM to perform video-based face recognition task.

S.Z. Li et al. (Eds.): Sinobiometrics 2004, LNCS 3338, pp. 224–232, 2004.

The other is batch approach, which assumes independence between any two samples, thus the dynamics of image sequences is ignored. It is particularly useful to recognize a person from sparse observations. The main idea of batch approach is to compute the similarity function $f(A,B)$, where A and B are training and testing video, respectively. The greater value of $f(A,B)$ indicates A and B are more likely sampled from the same individual. The way to define $f(A,B)$ differentiates various batch methods [5,6].

In this paper, we propose a novel model to identify the querying video. It is based on the measurement of average Euclidean distance between two videos so it is one of batch approaches. Instead of modeling set of video images as subspace [5] or Gaussian distribution [6], we represent the distribution of each set with a video signature. Video signature reflects the complex distribution of video data in image space. Earth Mover's Distance (EMD) is the proposed metric for average distribution distance measurement between two signatures. For simpleness and effectiveness, Euclidean distance is suggested to be the underlying ground distance of EMD. A new similarity function based on the average Euclidean distance metric is established and we verify its performance on a combined database.

This paper is organized as follows. Section 2 gives a brief review of some related work. In Section 3, the metric of average Euclidean distance is introduced. Section 4 discusses experimental results. At last, we conclude the paper and prospect future work.

2   Related Work

As mentioned above, for batch approach of video-based face recognition, the purpose is to define the similarity function $f(A,B)$, where A and B are training and testing video, respectively. MSM [5] defines similarity function as follows:

$$f(A,B) = \cos(\theta) = \max \frac{u_A{}^T u_B}{\|u_A\| \cdot \|u_B\|} \tag{1}$$

u_A and u_B are eigenvectors of A and B, respectively. MSM is thought that some discriminative statistical characteristics, e.g., eigenvalues or means of the data, are not considered. For K-L divergence [6] method, it is defined as.

$$f(A,B) = -\frac{1}{2} \cdot (\log \frac{|\Sigma_A|}{|\Sigma_B|}) + tr(\Sigma_B \Sigma_A^{-1} + \Sigma_A^{-1}(m_A - m_B)(m_A - m_B)^T) - d) \tag{2}$$

In this formula, Σ is the covariance matrix, while m is the mean vector. d corresponds to the dimensionality. It assumes each set of video images can be modeled as a multivariate Gaussian distribution, which is not precise enough to be the underlying distribution due to multiple poses and expressions in video. In addition, the computation of Equation (2) is very time-consuming since Σ is always a singular matrix [8].

3 The Proposed Metric

In this paper, to define the similarity function $f(A,B)$ between two videos, we introduce the notion of Earth Mover's Distance (EMD). EMD is a recently proposed metric for geometric pattern matching. It compares two distributions that have the same weights and it is proved much better than some well-known metrics (e.g., Euclidean distance between two vectors). It is based on an optimization method for the transportation problem [7] and is applied to image retrieval [9,14] and graph matching [11,12]. The name is suggested for road design [13].

3.1 Video Signatures

Given a set of points in image space, we represent the set with a signature. The signature is composed of numbers of clusters of similar features in a L_2 space. Each cluster is attached to a weight, which reflects the ratio of the number of images in this cluster to the total number of images. For video-based face recognition, each video corresponds to a distribution of points in image space and can be modeled as a *video signature*. We employ the technology of vector quantization [10] for clustering since it performs efficiently. Each cluster contributes a pair (u , p_u), where u is the prototype vector of the cluster and p_u is its weight which is the fraction of face images in the cluster.

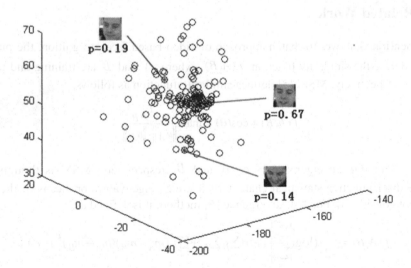

Fig. 1. A signature for video-based face recognition

For videos, poses and expressions change constantly. The images in a video form a complex distribution in high dimensional image space. It can not be simply expressed by a single subspace or a single multivariate Gaussian model. Since clustering algorithm is used, signature can well represent the overall data distribution of video data. Each cluster corresponds to a pose manifold. In addition, with clustering, some degree of variations, e.g., illumination, poses and expressions, can be tolerated. Moreover, changing the number of clusters, it provides a compact and flexible method to represent data distribution. More clusters are used, more precise the model is. Fig. 1 is an example of a signature in a reduced dimensionality space. Each signature contains a set of prototype vectors and their corresponding weights. In Fig. 1, the prototype is labeled with a red " $*$ " and the weight is denoted under the corresponding image.

3.2 Average Euclidean Distance Between Video Signatures

Assume two videos A and B are modeled as video signatures. We can imagine A is a mass of earth, and B is a collection of holes. EMD is a measurement of the minimal work needed to fill the holes with earth. This is the reason why it is named "Earth Mover's Distance". Fig. 2 shows an example with three piles of earth and two holes.

EMD can be formalized as the following linear programming problem: Let $A = \{(u_1, p_{u_1}), \ ,(u_m, p_{u_m})\}$ and $B = \{(v_1, p_{v_1}), \ ,(v_m, p_{v_n})\}$, where u_i, v_j are the

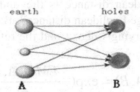

Fig. 2. An example of EMD

prototype vectors of clusters of A and B, respectively, and p_{u_i} and p_{v_j} are their corresponding weights. The cost to move an element u_i, to a new position v_j is the cost coefficient c_{ij}, multiplied by d_{ij}, where c_{ij} corresponds to the portion of the weight to be moved, and d_{ij} is the ground distance between u_i and v_j. EMD is the sum of cost of moving the weights of the elements of A to those of B. Thus the solution to EMD is to find a set of cost coefficients c_{ij} to minimize the following function:

$$\sum_{i=1}^{m}\sum_{j=1}^{n} c_{ij}d_{ij} \tag{3}$$

subject to: (i) $c_{ij} \geq 0$, (ii) $\sum_{i=1}^{m} c_{ij} \leq p_{v_j}$, (iii) $\sum_{j=1}^{n} c_{ij} \leq p_{u_i}$, and (iv)

$\sum_{i=1}^{m}\sum_{j=1}^{n} c_{ij} = \min(\sum_{i=1}^{m} p_{u_i}, \sum_{j=1}^{n} p_{v_j})$. Constraint (i) indicates only positive quantity of "earth" is allowed to move. Constraint (ii) limits the quantity of earth filled to a "hole". Each hole is at most filled up all the capacity. Constraint (iii) limits the quantity of earth provided to holes. Each pile of earth provides at most its capacity. Constraint (iv) prescribes that at least one signature contributes all its weights. If the optimization is successful, then EMD can be normalized as:

$$EMD\ (A,B) = \frac{\min(\sum_{i=1}^{m} \sum_{j=1}^{n} c_{ij} d_{ij})}{\min(\sum_{i=1}^{m} P_{u_i}, \sum_{j=1}^{n} P_{v_j})} \quad (4)$$

EMD extends the distance between single points to the distance between sets of points and it reflects the average ground distance that weights travels according to an optimal flow. In general, the ground distance d_{ij} can be any distance and it will be chosen according to the problem we encounter. For the simpleness and effectiveness, Euclidean distance is proposed to be the underlying ground distance of EMD. Since EMD is the basic distance framework to represent the average ground distance between signatures and Euclidean distance is the underlying ground distance, it is named as "a metric of average Euclidean distance". Based on this metric, the similarity function between the querying video A and the reference video B can be defined as:

$$f(A,B) = \exp(-\frac{EMD(A,B)}{\sigma^2}) \quad (5)$$

where σ is a constant for normalization. The value of the function shows the degree of similarity between A and B.

Particularly, if some weights of clusters are smaller than a threshold, we discard these clusters since it contributes a little for matching. For videos, these clusters generally consist of faces on bad condition, which deviate far away from normal face clusters. EMD provides a natural solution to this kind of partial matching. However, EMD with partial matching is not a metric for the distance measure of two distributions.

4   Experimental Results

4.1   Experimental Database

We use a combined database to evaluate the performance of our algorithm. The database can be divided into two parts: (i) Mobo (Motion of Body) database. Mobo database was collected at the Carnegie Mellon University for human identification. There are 25 individuals in the database. (ii) Our collected database. This part is collected from advertisements, MTV and personal videos. There are 15 subjects in the database. Totally, our combined database contains 40 subjects, and each subject has 300 face images. Fig. 3 shows some faces cropped from sequences in the database. Using the very coarse positions of eyes, we normalize it to 30×30 pixels and use it for experiments. Some location errors, various poses and expressions can be observed in the database.

4.2 Experimental Scheme

In order to verify the performance of our proposed algorithm, the scheme of data partition is illuminated as follows: given a video in database, we select the first 100 frames for training. In the remaining 200 frames, we randomly select a starting frame K and a length M. Then frames $\{I_{K+1}, I_{K+1}, \cdots, I_{K+M}\}$ form a sequence for testing.

This is similar to the practical situation where anyone can come to the recognition system at any time with any duration [4].

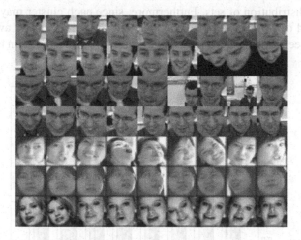

Fig. 3. Some cropped faces from sequences

Two experiments are performed. The first experiment changes the number of clusters of video signature. It wants to disclose how many clusters in signature are most beneficial to face recognition. The second experiment compares the algorithm with other general batch methods to demonstrate its performance.

4.3 Recognition Rate Versus Number of Clusters

For video-based face recognition, each video forms a video signature in image space by clustering algorithm. We think since clustering algorithm is used, signature can well represent the overall data distribution of videos. We further deduce that the number of clusters in a signature may affect the recognition rate. Based on above data partition scheme, testing video is obtained with a random starting frame and a random length. This experiment is performed four times with different length of testing video. The purpose of the experiment is to disclose the relationship between recognition rate and the number of clusters in a signature and the length of testing video. Fig. 4 illustrates the experimental results.

In Fig. 4, the horizontal axis represents the number of clusters used in a video signature. The vertical axis denotes the recognition rate. The legend on left top corner represents how many frames are used for testing. The length of testing video is 51, 92, 120 and 160, respectively. The number of clusters changes from one to eight. When only a cluster is used, EMD is actually the Euclidean distance between centers of videos. Directly using center vector to represent a video is very coarse so that the recognition rate is only about 55%. With the increment of the number of clusters, the model of video signature becomes more and more precise. When more than four clusters are used, the recognition rate is nearly 100%. From this figure, we can note that no matter how long the testing video is, five clusters is a preferable choice for recognition. This experiment demonstrates that video signature can well represent the overall data distribution of sets. Furthermore, since each cluster may correspond to a pose manifold of complex distributed video and EMD reflects the average Euclidean distance between videos, it is a reasonable result of high recognition rate.

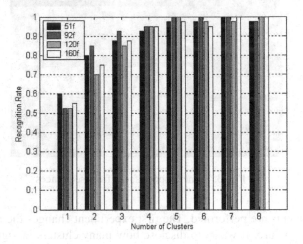

Fig. 4. Recognition rate Versus Number of clusters

4.4   Comparison with Other Algorithms

In this experiment, three batch algorithms are assembled together to compare their performance. They are MSM (Mutual Subspace Method), KLD (K-L Divergence) and EMD (Earth Mover's Distance). The underlying data distribution model of MSM is a single subspace, while that of KLD is a single Gaussian model and EMD is a video signature. The experiment is done ten times to obtain the recognition rate curve as shown in Fig. 5.

In Fig. 5, the horizontal axis shows the length of testing video. It ranges from 19 to 189 frames. The vertical axis shows the recognition rate. For MSM, we use all eigenvectors to compute the similarity function. For EMD, five clusters are contained in a video signature based on the former experiment. From this figure, we can observe that when less than 20 frames are for test, the performance of KLD is very weak. It is because that a representative Gaussian model needs more training samples. Its performance becomes better with the increasing of testing frames. However, the performance of KLD is still the worst one. This phenomenon demonstrates that K-L divergence between probabilistic models is not an effective classifier and a single Gaussian model is not robust for expressing complex data distribution of video. We also note that the performance of MSM and EMD is similar. Their difference is that when the length of testing video is short, EMD is much better than MSM, especially in the case that only 19 frames are used for testing. It proves that a single subspace can not reflect the distribution of small quantity of data. Video signature is a much more reasonable model of data distribution and EMD is a robust metric for classification since it reflects the average Euclidean distance between video signatures.

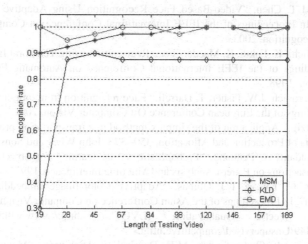

Fig. 5. Comparison of MSM, KLD And EMD

5 Conclusion

For video-based face recognition, conventional batch approaches supply two classical methods to estimate the similarity between testing video and training video. The one is to compute the angle between subspaces [5], and the other is to find K-L divergence [6] between probabilistic models. In this paper, we consider a most straight-forward method of using distance for matching. We propose a metric based on an average L_2 Euclidean distance between two videos as the classifier. This metric is established based on Earth Mover's distance and Euclidean distance is suggested to be the underlying ground distance metric. Signatures are built for modeling data distribution of image sets. This model is much better than subspace model [5] and single probabilistic model [6] since it divides a video into several clusters corresponding to different poses. In future, we will consider the update method to improve the representative capability of signatures. Moreover, as in [4], time information and transformation probability will be considered to build a more reasonable model to represent a video.

References

1. W. Zhao, R. Chellappa, A. Rosenfeld and P.J Phillips, "Face Recognition: A Literature Survey", Technical Reports of Computer Vision Laboratory of University of Maryland, 2000.
2. S. Zhou and R. Chellappa, "Probabilistic Human Recognition from Video", In Proceedings of the European Conference On Computer Vision, 2002.
3. K.C. Lee, J. Ho, M.H. Yang, D. Kriegman, "Video-Based Face Recognition Using Probabilistic Appearance Manifolds", In Proceedings of the IEEE International Conference on Computer Vision and Pattern Recognition, 2003.
4. X. Liu and T. Chen, "Video-Based Face Recognition Using Adaptive Hidden Markov Models", In Proceedings of the IEEE International Conference on Computer Vision and Pattern Recognition, 2003.
5. O. Yamaguchi, K. Fukui, K. Maeda, "Face Recognition using Temporal Image Sequence," In Proceedings of the IEEE International Conference on Automatic Face and Gesture Recognition, 1998.
6. G. Shakhnarovich, J.W. Fisher, T. Darrell, "Face recognition from long-term observations", In Proceedings of the European Conference On Computer Vision, 2002.
7. G. B. Dantzig, "Application of the simplex method to a transportation problem", In Activity Analysis of Production and Allocation, 359–373, John Wiley and Sons, 1951.
8. B. Moghaddam, A. Pentland, "Probabilistic visual learning for object representation", IEEE Transactions on Pattern Analysis and Machine Intelligence, 1997.
9. Y. Rubner, C. Tomasi, L.J. Guibas, "Adaptive Color-Image Embedding for Database Navigation", In Proceedings of the Asian Conference on Computer Vision, 1998.
10. "Learning Vector Quantization (LVQ)", <http://www.willamette.edu/~gorr/classes/cs449/Unsupervised/competitive.html>.
11. Y. Keselman, A. Shokoufandeh, M.F. Demirci, S. Dickinson, "Many-to-Many Graph Matching via Metric Embedding", In Proceedings of the IEEE Conference on Computer Vision and Pattern Recognition, 2003.
12. M.F. Demirci, A. Shokoufandeh, Y. Keselman, S. Dickinson, L. Bretzner, "Many-to-Many Feature Matching Using Spherical Coding of Directed Graphs", In Proceedings of the 8th European Conference on Computer Vision, 2004.
13. J. Stolfi, "Personal Communication", 1994.
14. S. Cohen, L. Guibas, "The Earth Mover's Distance under Transformation Sets", In Proceedings of the 7th IEEE International Conference On Computer Vision, 1999.

3D Face Recognition Based on G-H Shape Variation

Chenghua Xu[1], Yunhong Wang[1], Tieniu Tan[1], and Long Quan[2]

[1]National Laboratory of Pattern Recognition, Institute of Automation, CAS,
P. O. Box 2728, Beijing, P. R. China, 100080
[2]Department of Computer Science, Hong Kong University of Science and Technology,
Kowloon, Hong Kong
{chxu, wangyh, tnt}@nlpr.ia.ac.cn, quan@cs.ust.hk

Abstract. Face recognition has been an interesting issue in pattern recognition over the past few decades. In this paper, we propose a new method for face recognition using 3D information. During preprocessing, the scanned 3D point clouds are first registered together, and at the same time, the regular meshes are generated. Then the novel shape variation representation based on Gaussian-Hermite moments (GH-SVI) is proposed to characterize an individual. Experimental results on the 3D face database 3DPEF, with complex pose and expression variations, and 3D_RMA, likely the largest 3D face database currently available, demonstrate that the proposed features are very important to characterize an individual.

1 Introduction

Nowadays biometric identification has received much attention due to the social requirement of reliably characterizing individuals. Of all the biometrics features, the face is among the most common and most accessible so that face recognition remains one of the most active research issues in pattern recognition. Over the past few decades, most work has focused on the source of 2D intensity or color images [1]. Since the accuracy of 2D face recognition is influenced by variations of poses, expressions, illumination and subordinates, it is still difficult to develop a robust automatic 2D face recognition system.

With the rapid development of 3D acquisition equipment, 3D capture is becoming easier and faster, and face recognition based on 3D information is attracting more and more attention. 3D face recognition usually explores depth information and surface features to characterize an individual, which provides a promising way to understand human facial features in 3D space and has the potential possibility to improve the performance of a recognition system. The advantages of using 3D facial data: sufficient information, invariance of measured features relative to geometric transformation and capture process by laser scanners being immune to illumination variation, are attracting more and more attention. This makes 3D face recognition a promising solution to overcome difficulties faced with 2D face recognition.

S.Z. Li et al. (Eds.): Sinobiometrics 2004, LNCS 3338, pp. 233–243, 2004.

Using 3D features to characterize an individual is the most common method of 3D face recognition. This category mainly focuses on how to extract and represent 3D features. Some earlier researches on curvature analysis [2,3,4] have been proposed for face recognition based on high-quality range data from laser scanners. In addition, based on 3D surface features, some recognition schemes have been developed. Chua et al. [5] represent the facial rigid parts by point signatures to identify an individual. Beumier et al. [6,7] propose two methods of surface matching and central/lateral profiles to compare two instances. Both of these methods construct some central and lateral profiles to represent an individual. Tanaka et al. [8] treat the face recognition problem as a 3D shape recognition problem of rigid free-form surfaces. Each face is represented as an Extended Gaussian Image, constructed by mapping principal curvatures and their directions. In more recent work, Hesher et al. [9] use a 3D scanner for generating range images and registering them by aligning salient facial features. PCA approaches are explored to reduce the dimensionality of feature vector. Lee et al. [10] perform 3D face recognition by locating the nose tip, and then forming a feature vector based on contours along the face at a sequence of depth values.

In this paper, a novel local surface representation, GH-SVI (Shape Variation Information based on Gaussian-Hermite Moments) is extracted to represent the facial features. We first define a metric to quantify the shape information with a 1-D signal, and G-H moments [11,12] are then applied to describe the shape variation. This representation of shape variation is novel and shows its excellent performance in our experiments.

The remainder of this paper is organized as follows. Section 2 describes the methods of preprocessing: nose tip detection and registration. The process of feature extraction is described in Section 3. Section 4 reports the experimental results and gives some comparisons with existing methods. Finally, Section 5 summarizes this paper.

2 Preprocessing

Usually, the point clouds from laser scanners have different poses. It is essential to exactly align the point clouds prior to feature extraction. In this section, we finely register point clouds using the facial rigid area.

2.1 Nose Tip Detection

In the facial range data, the nose is the most distinct feature. Most existing methods [7,9,10] for nose detection is usually based on the assumption that the nose tip is the highest point in the range data. However, due to the noise and rotation of the subject, the assumption does not hold. Gordon [3] used curvature information to detect the nose. Her methods are suitable for clean 3D data and would not work in the case that there are holes around the nose.

Here, we locate the nose using local statistic features [13]. This method is immune to the rotation and translation, holes and outliers, and suitable for multi-resolution data. Of all the instances in our 3D database, 3DPEF, only two samples fail. We mark the nose tip manually in the wrongly detected point clouds to ensure the following processing.

2.2 Coarse Alignment

It is assumed that Ω is the point set of the cloud. Thus, its covariance matrix can be obtained:

$$Q = \sum_{x \in \Omega} (x - \bar{x}) \otimes (x - \bar{x}) \tag{1}$$

where $\otimes$ denotes the outer product vector operator, Q is 3×3 positive semi-definite matrix and $\bar{x}$ is the mean value of all the points. If $\lambda_1 \geq \lambda_2 \geq \lambda_3$ denote the eigenvalues of Q with unit eigenvectors v_1, v_2, v_3, respectively, we consider the orthogonal vectors, v_1, v_2, v_3, as the three main axis of the point cloud.

Then we rotate the point cloud so that v_1, v_2, v_3 are parallel to Y-, X- and Z- axis of the reference coordinate system, respectively. Finally, the point cloud is translated so that its nose tip overlaps the origin of the reference coordinate system. Thus, all the point clouds are coarsely registered together according to the above transformation.

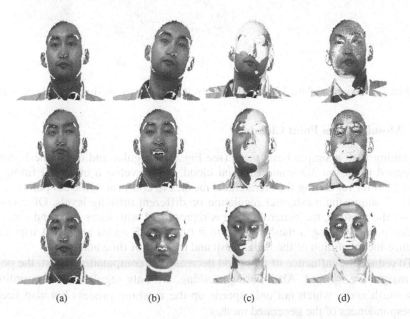

(a)   (b)   (c)   (d)

Fig. 1. Registration results. (a)(b)The original point clouds to register. (c) The results of coarse registration. (d) The final registration results. For clear display, we show the first model in shading mode in (c,d). The top row: point clouds with different poses; The middle row: point clouds with expressions of angry and laugh; The bottom row: point clouds of different persons with the same pose and expression

2.3 Fine Alignment

This process aims to register two point clouds finely. It can be formulated as follows: given two meshes, the individual mesh, P, and the ground mesh, Q, find the best rigid transformation, T, so that the error function, $d = \Gamma(T(P),Q)$, is minimized, where Γ is the distance metric.

Here we explore the classic algorithm of the Iterative Closest Point (ICP) [14]. ICP is an efficient, accurate and reliable method for the registration of free form surfaces, and it converges monotonically to a local minimum. At each iteration, the algorithm computes correspondences by finding the closest triangle for each vertex, and then minimizes the mean square error between the correspondences.

The facial point cloud contains expression variations. Strictly, the registration among different scans is non-rigid transformation. During registration, we only consider the points above the nose tip. Thus, the registration result can be avoided the unwanted influence of mouth and jaw, which is most prone to expressions. Fig.1 shows some results.

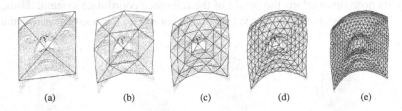

(a)   (b)   (c)   (d)   (e)

Fig. 2. The regulated meshes in different levels. (a)Basic mesh. (b)-(e)Level one to four

2.4 Meshing from Point Clouds

Beginning with a simple basic mesh (see Fig.2), a regular and dense mesh model is generated to fit the 3D scattered point cloud. We develop a universal fitting algorithm [15] for regulating the hierarchical meshes to conform to the 3D points.

Fig.2 shows the mesh after regulation on different refining levels. Of course, the denser the mesh is, the better the face is represented with more time and space cost. In this paper, we use a mesh refined four times (545 nodes and 1024 triangles) to balance the resolution of the facial mesh and the cost of time and space.

To reduce the influence of noise and decrease the computational cost, the points in the margin are ignored. Also, during meshing, we only regulate the Z coordinate of each mesh node, which not only speeds up the meshing process but also keeps the correspondences of the generated meshes.

3 Feature Extraction

So far, all the point clouds have been registered together, and also each is described with a regular mesh, which has corresponding nodes and assists in extracting features to characterize an individual. We extract shape variation information (GH-SVI) to characterize an individual.

We first define a metric to describe the local shape of each mesh node with a 1-D vector. To transfer the 3D shape onto a 1-D vector, we first define a metric to describe the local shape of one mesh node as shown in Fig.3. Since the mesh well approximates the point cloud, we can obtain the following local information of each mesh node, p_e, that is, its spatial direct neighboring triangles, $\{T_1, T_2, \cdots T_n\}$, its normal, N_{pe} and neighboring points in the point cloud within a small sphere. Due to the regularity of our mesh, the number of neighboring triangles of the common node (not the edge node) is always six. Its normal, N_{pe}, can be estimated according to its neighboring triangles. The radius of the sphere to decide the neighboring points is set as half of the length of one mesh edge in our work.

Further, the neighboring points can be classified into n categories, $\{C_1, C_2, \cdots C_n\}$. Which class one point belongs to depends on which triangle the point's projection falls in the same direction to the normal, N_{pe}. For each class C_k, we can define its surface signal as the following:

$$d_{ek} = \frac{1}{2} + \frac{1}{2m} \sum_{i=1}^{m} \cos(q_{ki} - p_e, N_{pe})$$ (2)

with

$$\cos(q_{ki} - p_e, N_{pe}) = \frac{(q_{ki} - p_e) \bullet N_{pe}}{\|q_{ki} - p_e\| \bullet \|N_{pe}\|}$$ (3)

where q_{ki} is the neighboring point belonging to the class, C_k, m is the number of the point in C_k, and $d_{ek} \in [0,1]$.

Then we can describe the local shape of each mesh node using the following vector:

$$s_e = \{d_{e1}, d_{e2}, \cdots, d_{en}\}$$ (4)

where d_{ek} is the surface signal. This vector describes the shape near this vertex. It is noted that if one class, C_k, does not contain any points, its surface signal can be replaced with the mean value of neighboring classes. If one mesh node lies in one hole in the point cloud so that it has no any neighboring points within the preset sphere, we can enlarge the radius until neighboring points are included. In addition, the order and the beginning position of the shape vectors, s_e, of all nodes, should be identical.

According to this metric, we can describe the shape of each row in the mesh with a combination of shape vectors of all nodes in this row respectively.

$$S_i = \{s_{i1}, s_{i2}, \cdots, s_{ir}\}$$ (5)

where S_i is the shape vector of i th row and s_{ij} is the shape vector of j th vertex in i th row. Further, from S_1 to S_n, we connect them in turn to form a long shape vector, S, in the alternate way of head and tail connection. The 1-D vector, S, is used to describe the shape of one mesh.

It is well-known that moments have been widely used in pattern recognition and image processing, especially in various shape-based applications. Here, Gaussian-Hermite moments are used for feature representation due to their mathematical orthogonality and effectiveness for characterizing local details of the signal [12]. They provide an effective way to quantify the signal variation. The n th order 1-D G-H moment $M_n(x, S(x))$ of a signal $S(x)$ is defined as:

$$M_n(x) = \int_{-\infty}^{\infty} B_n(t) S(x+t)\, dt \qquad n = 0,1,2,\ldots\ldots \tag{6}$$

with

$$B_n(t) = g(t,\sigma) H_n(t/\sigma)$$

$$H_n(t) = (-1)^n \exp(t^2) \frac{d^n \exp(-t^2)}{dt^n} \tag{7}$$

$$g(t,\sigma) = (2\pi\sigma^2)^{-1/2} \exp(-x^2/2\sigma^2)$$

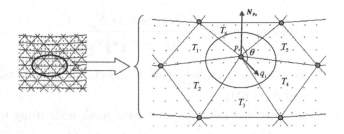

Fig. 3. Shape representation of one mesh node

where $g(t,\sigma)$ is a Gaussian function and $H_n(t)$ is a scaled Hermite polynomial function of order n. G-H moments have many excellent qualities, especially being insensitive to noise generated during differential operations. The parameter σ and the order of G-H moments need to be determined through experiments. Here we use 0 th to 4 th order G-H moments to analyze the shape variation when $\sigma = 2.0$. The top row in Fig.4 shows the spatial responses of the Gaussian-Hermite moments from order 0 to 4.

To shape vector, S, we calculate its n th order G-H moments, thus obtaining 1-D moment vectors, SM_n, which are called n th G-H shape variation information (GH-SVI). They describe the shape variation of the facial surface. The bottom row in Fig.4 shows a segment of SM_n using different orders of G-H moments.

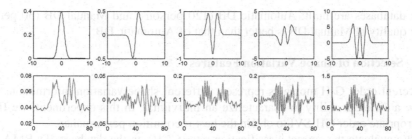

Fig. 4. Gaussian-Hermite moments. The top row: the spatial responses of the Gaussian-Hermite moments, order 0 to 4; the bottom row: the corresponding G-H moments of a segment of 1-D shape signal

4 Experiments

To test the proposed algorithm, we implement it with different databases. All the experiments are executed in the PC with a PIV 1.3GHz processor, 128M RAM and the display card Nvidia Getforce2 MX 100/200.

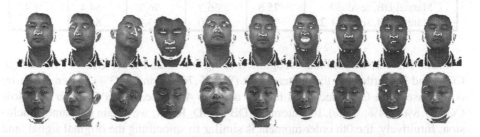

Fig. 5. Instances of two persons in 3DPEF. The variations from left to right are: normal, left, right, up, down, smile, laugh, sad, surprise, eye closed

4.1 Database

Unlike 2D face images, there is no common 3D face database of a feasible size for testing recognition algorithms. Here, we use two different databases to test our proposed algorithm. The first database (3D Pose and Expression Face Database, 3DPEF) is sampled in our lab using the Minolta VIVID 900 working on Fast Mode. This data set contains 30 persons (6 women), and each person includes five poses (normal, left, right, up, down) and five expressions (smile, laugh, sad, surprise, eye closed). The instances of two people are shown in Fig.5.

The second 3D face database is 3D_RMA [6,7], likely the biggest database in the public domain, where each face is described with a 3D scattered point cloud, obtained by the technique of structured light. The database includes 120 persons and two sessions. In each session, each person is sampled with three shots. From these sessions, two databases are built: Automatic DB (120 persons) and Manual DB (30 persons). The quality of Manual DB is better than that of Automatic DB.

4.2 Selection of Shape Variation Features

Different order G-H moments represent different shape variation information, which have a different ability to characterize an individual. In this experiment, we find an appropriate order GH-SVI to obtain the best recognition performance.

We evaluate the correct classification rate (CCR) on the database 3D_RMA under different order GH-SVI as shown in Table 1. Considering that the number of instances of each person is small, we use the leave-one-out scheme. In each test, one is the test sample, all the others are for training. The nearest neighbor method is adopted as the classifier. `Session1-2' means that the samples in session1 and session2 are blended together.

Table 1. CCR(%) in different sets in Manual DB of 3D_RMA using different order GH-SVI

Data sets	0th	1st	2nd	3rd	4th
Manual DB, session1	84.4	74.4	86.7	65.5	7.8
Manual DB, session2	75.6	66.7	76.7	64.4	4.4
Manual DB, session1-2	90.0	90.0	93.3	86.1	7.2

From Table 1, we find that recognition using 0th to 2nd order GH-SVI has a high CCR, and 2nd order has the highest CCR (86.7%,76.7% and 93.3%). When the order is increased, the CCR decreases largely and the 4th order GH-SVI has a very low CCR (7.8%, 4.4%, 7.2%). In Automatic DB of 3D_RMA, we obtain the same conclusion. Intuitively, the 0th order moment is similar to smoothing the original signal, and in fact, it does not describe shape variation. The face surface is smooth on the whole and high order moments usually describe the intense variation. So it is not necessary to calculate the higher order moments. In the following experiments, we use the 2nd order G-H moment to represent the shape variation information.

4.3 Recognition Performance Evaluation

Identification accuracy is evaluated with the different sets. Table 2 summarizes the Correct Classification Rate (CCR) using features, GH-SVI. As to 3DPEF, we use three samples (`normal', `right' and `left') as the gallery set and other samples as the test set. As to Manual DB and Automatic DB in 3D_RMA, we use the samples in session1 (three instances for each person) as the gallery set and the samples in session2 as the test set, which agrees with the regulation that there is an interval between the gallery set and the test set. After computing the similarity differences using the Euclidean distance in single classifiers, and the nearest neighbor (NN) is then applied to the classification.

From an overall view, we can draw the following conclusions:

- Shape variation contains important information to characterize an individual. Our proposed method for extracting shape variation feature is very effective.
- The highest recognition we obtain is 93.3% (30 persons) and 73.4% (120 persons). Although the testing database is not big enough, this result is obtained in the fully automatic way, which is fairly encouraging.

Table 2. CCR(%) in different databases

Databases	2nd GH-SVI
3DPEF (30 persons)	82.4
Manual DB in 3D_RMA (30 persons)	93.3
Automatic DB in 3D_RMA (120 persons)	73.4

- Noise and volume of the test database affect the CCR strongly. Automatic DB has more people and contains much noise, and its recognition performance is distinctly worse than Manual DB.

4.4 Comparisons with Existing Methods

Surface curvature is the classic property used in 3D face recognition [2,3,4]. Point signature is another important technique of representing free-form surfaces, and has obtained a good result in 3D face recognition [5] under a small database (6 persons). Here, we compare them with our proposed GH-SVI features in the way of CCR. Unfortunately, we cannot obtain the source codes and databases used in their publication. We only make a comparison in current databases and with our own codes.

We calculate the point signature for each mesh node and use them to characterize an individual. Twelve signed distances are calculated to describe the point signature of each mesh node. The detailed algorithm can be found in [16]. The curvature of each node is calculated using numerical estimation, surface normal change [17]. There are several representations for curvature and we use the mean curvature as features. Table 3 shows the CCR respectively using point signature (PS), surface curvature (SC) and shape variation information (GH-SVI, using 2nd order G-H moments) on Manual DB of 3D_RMA. In this test, we still use the leave-one-out scheme.

From this table, we can see that GH-SVI outperforms PS and SC on the whole. Compared with table 1, we find that the CCR obtained from point signature are similar to the results from GH-SVI using 0th order G-H moments.

Table 3. CCR (%) using point signature (PS), surface curvature (SC) and shape variation information (GH-SVI) in Manual DB of 3D_RMA

Algorithm	Session1	Session2	Session3
PS	83.3	76.7	88.3
SC	71.1	75.5	76.1
GH-SVI	86.7	76.7	93.3

5 Conclusions

Recently, personal identification based on 3D information has been gaining more and more interest. In this paper, we have proposed a new method for 3D face recognition. Based on the generated regular meshes, GH_SVI is extracted to characterize an individual. We test the proposed algorithm on 3DPEF and 3D_RMA, and the encouraging results have showed the effectiveness of the proposed method for 3D face recognition. Compared with previous work, our algorithm demonstrates an outstanding performance.

Acknowledgements

This work is supported by research funds from the Natural Science Foundation of China (Grant No. 60121302 and 60332010) and the Outstanding Overseas Chinese Scholars Fund of CAS (No.2001-2-8).

References

1. W. Zhao, R. Chellappa, P.J. Phillips, and A. Rosenfeld. : Face Recognition: A Literature Survey. ACM Computing Surveys (CSUR) archive. Vol. 35(4) (2003) 399-458
2. J.C. Lee, and E. Milios. : Matching Range Images of Human Faces. Proc. ICCV'90 (1990) 722-726
3. G.G. Gordon. : Face Recognition Based on Depth and Curvature Features. Proc. CVPR'92 (1992) 108-110
4. Y. Yacoob and L.S. Davis. : Labeling of Human Face Components from Range Data. CVGIP: Image Understanding Vol. 60(2) (1994) 168-178
5. C.S. Chua, F. Han, and Y.K. Ho. : 3D Human Face Recognition Using Point Signature. Proc. FG'00 (2000) 233-239
6. C. Beumier and M. Acheroy. : Automatic Face Authentication from 3D Surface. Proc. BMVC'98 (1998) 449-458
7. C. Beumier and M. Acheroy. : Automatic 3D Face Authentication. Image and Vision Computing Vol.18(4) (2000) 315-321
8. H.T. Tanaka, M. Ikeda and H. Chiaki. : Curvature-based Face Surface Recognition Using Spherical Correlation. Proc. FG'98 (1998) 372-377
9. C. Hesher, A. Srivastava, and G. Erlebacher. : A Novel Technique for Face Recognition Using Range Imaging. Inter. Multiconference in Computer Science (2002)
10. 10.Y. Lee, K. Park, J. Shim, and T. Yi. : 3D Face Recognition Using Statistical Multiple Features for the Local Depth Information. Proc. 16th Inter. Conf. on Vision Interface (2003)
11. 11.S. Liao, M. Pawlak. : On Image Analysis by Moments. IEEE Trans. on PAMI, Vol.18(3) (1996) 254-266
12. 12.J. Shen, W. Shen and D. Shen. : On Geometric and Orthogonal Moments. Inter. Journal of Pattern Recognition and Artificial Intelligence. Vol. 14 (7) (2000) 875-894
13. 13.C. Xu, Y. Wang, T. Tan, and L. Quan. A Robust Method for Detecting Nose on 3D Point Cloud. Proc. ICIP'04 (2004) (to appear).
14. 14.P.J. Besl, and N.D. Mckay. : A Method for Registration of 3-D shapes. IEEE Trans. PAMI. Vol.14(2) (1992) 239-256

15. 15.C. Xu, L. Quan, Y. Wang, T. Tan, M. Lhuillier. Adaptive Multi-resolution Fitting and its Application to Realistic Head Modeling. IEEE Geometric Modeling and Processing.(2004) 345-348
16. 16.C.S. Chua and R. Jarvis. : Point Signatures: A New Representation for 3-D Object Recognition. IJCV. Vol. 25(1) (1997) 63-85
17. 17.R.L. Hoffman, and A.K. Jain.: Segmentation and Classification of Range Images. IEEE Trans. on PAMI. Vol. 9(5) (1987) 608-620

3D Face Recognition Based on Geometrical Measurement

Mingquan Zhou, Xiaoning Liu, and Guohua Geng

Northwest University, Dept. of Computer Science, 229 Tai Bai Bei Road, Xi'an, P.R.China
mqzhou@nwu.edu.cn

Abstract. 2D face recognition is held back because the face is three-dimensional. The 3D facial data can provide a promising way to understand the feature of the human face in 3D space and has potential possibility to improve the performance of the system. There are some distinct advantages in using 3D information: sufficient geometrical information, invariance of measured features relative to transformation and capture process by laser scanners being immune to illumination variation. A 3D face recognition method based on geometrical measurement is proposed. By two ways, the 3D face data can be obtained, then their facial feature points are extracted and the measurement is done. A feature vector is composed of eleven features. Self-Recognition and Mutual-Recognition are tested. The results show that the presented method is feasible.

1 Introduction

Nowadays biometric identification has obtained much attention due to the urgent need for more reliable personal identification. Of all the biometrics features, face is among the most common and most reachable so that face recognition remains one of the most active research issues in pattern recognition.

In the past decades, most work focuses on the source of 2D intensity or color images. Since the accuracy of 2D face recognition is influenced by variations of poses, expressions, illumination and subordinates, it is still difficult to develop a robust automatic 2D face recognition system. Because the human face is a three-dimensional object whose 2D projection is sensitive to the above changes, utilizing 3D face information can improve the face recognition performance [1].

In 3D domain, many researchers have handled the 3D-face recognition problem. Dating back to 1989, the first 3D face recognition method is based on contour lines which presented by Cartoux and Lapreste[2]: Construct the 3D model through serial images and analyze the curvature of face, then extract the feature point on the contour lines and do recognition. Lee and Milios[3] introduced another way: the features convene is composed by the protuberant regions, compute their Gauss maps and matching the Gauss map to recognize face. Bernard[4] expanded the Eigenface and Hidden Markov Model(HMM) methods in 2D to 3D.

Point Signature and geometrical feature are simple yet effective, so we will use it to describe the facial shape in this paper. A person can be recognized even when the

S.Z. Li et al. (Eds.): Sinobiometrics 2004, LNCS 3338, pp. 244–249, 2004.

detail facial features are illegible. A 3D face recognition method, which based on geometrical measurement, is proposed in this paper.

In the following, section 2 describes the way to detect facial feature points. Section 3 describes which features are measured and the detail method. Section 4 gives the two ways to establish the 3D face Database and the recognition steps. Section 5 gives the experiment results. Section 6 concludes the paper and specifies the prospect.

2 Feature Points Detection

The feature points of face are converged at eye, nose and mouth. The vector of features is composed with distances and angles. To make the features be independent from scale, all the features need to be unified by the distance of two exocanthions. Their ratio is the final features.

Zhou Ming-quan [7] gives the detail steps of detection the facial features. For the lim-ited space, it is omitted here.

3 Feature Measurement

3.1 Features of Nose

The feature points of nose are pronasale (Nt), left-nosewing (Nl), right-nosewing (Nr), nasion (Nb) and subnasale (Nu).

Figure1 (a) is the projection of 3D face on the YOZ plane. A triangle is formed with pronasale, nasion and subnasale. Suppose that their coordinates are $(x1, y1, z1)$, $(x2, y2, z2)$ and $(x3, y3, z3)$ respectively, according to the plane geometry, the line equation from nasion to subnasale is:

$$Ay + Bz + C = 0 \tag{1}$$

Where

$$A = z_2 - z_3, \ B = y_3 - y_2, \ C = y_2(z_3 - z_2) - z_2(y_3 - y_2)$$

The distance (F1) from pronasale to the line is:

$$F1 = \frac{|Ay_1 + Bz_1 + C|}{\sqrt{A^2 + B^2}} \tag{2}$$

Then, the area (F2) of the triangle is:

$$F2 = \frac{1}{2} \times D \times F1 \tag{3}$$

Where D is the distance from nasion to subnasale.

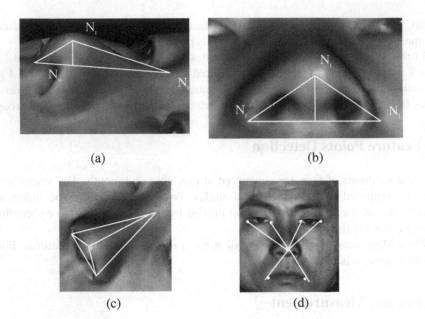

Fig. 1. Feature measurement (a) Feature of Nose YOZ (b) Feature of Nose XOZ (c) Volume of Nose (d) Global Angle

The angle (F3) of $\angle N_u N_t N_b$ is:

$$F3 = \sin^{-1}\left(\frac{2 \times F2}{T1 \times T2}\right) \tag{4}$$

Where T1 is the distance from Nu to Nt. T2 is the distance from Nu to Nb.

Figure1 (b) is the projection of 3D face on the XOZ plane. Another triangle is formed with pronasale, left-nosewing and right-nosewing. In the same way, the distance (F4) from pronasale to the line of left-nosewing and right-nosewing is got, the triangle area (F5) and the angle (F6) $\angle N_l N_t N_r$ are also calculated.

3.2 Features of Eye

The Feature points of eye are left-endocanthion (Eli), left-exocanthion (Elo), right-endocanthion (Eri) and right-exdocanthion (Ero)

The width (F8) of eye is an average value:

$$F8 = \frac{\left|E_{li} - E_{lo}\right| + \left|E_{ri} - E_{ro}\right|}{2} \tag{5}$$

The distance (F9) from left-endocanthion to right-endocanthion is:

$$F9 = \left|E_{li} - E_{ri}\right| \tag{6}$$

The distance (F10) from left-exocanthion to right-exocanthion is:

$$F10 = \left| E_{lo} - E_{ro} \right| \qquad (7)$$

3.3 Features of Mouth

The Feature points of mouth are left-cheilion(Ml) and right-cheilion(Mr).
The width (F11) of mouth is:

$$F11 = \left| M_l - M_r \right| \qquad (8)$$

3.4 Global Features

The Global features are showed in figure 1(d). The angle (F12) of left-exocanthion, pronasale and right-exdocanthion. The angle(F13) of left-endocanthion, pronasale and right-endocanthion. The angle(F14)of   left-cheilion,nasion and right-cheilion. They can be caculated according to equation (4).

4   3D Face Recognition

Now the recognition can be started. But firstly, the Database should be built up.

4.1 Features of Mouth

The 3D face data are obtained by two ways, the first is to directly scan the head with 3D laser scanner-FastSCAN. In this way, the head need to be fixed and a reference object is required, figure 2 (a) is an example, it is close to the real 3D face. Another way is to construct 3D face from the CT slices, such as figure 2(b). The constructed head is not vividly, but we human can recognize who he is, so it is also essential to be investigated.

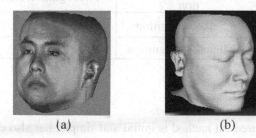

(a)   (b)

Fig. 2. The two ways to obtain the 3D faces. (a) From Scanner (b) From CT Slices

4.2 Features of Mouth

This paper is mainly research the recognition of 3D face, that's to say, 3D sample faces are stored in the Database, and the wanted face also is three-dimensional. The steps is as followings:

(1) Obtain the wanted 3D face
(2) Extract the Feature points
(3) Measure the mentioned features above
(4) Compare the feature vector of wanted 3D face and the sample feature vector. The formula is:

$$S = \sqrt{\sum_{i=1}^{14}(F_i - F_i')^2 w_i} \qquad (9)$$

Where, F_i and F_i' are respectively the ith feature of wanted 3D face and the sample 3D face, w_i is the weight of ith feature, it is determined according to experience and anthropology, ϕ is the liminal value, if $S < \phi$, then the two face is from the same person, or the different.

5 Experimental Results

Because of the difficulty of getting the 3D face data, we just scanned eight faces. To test the efficient of the proposed method, Self-Recognition and Mutual-Recognition are used. Self-Recognition is matching the same 3D face; Mutual-Recognition is matching the different ones. Table 1 is the results.

The rate of Self-Recognition is low mainly because of the small quantity of samples. Another reason is that the feature points are not accurate.

Table 1. The Result of 3D Face recognition

Types of Recognition	Recognition Rate
Self-Recognition	87.5%
Mutual-Recognition	3.57%

6 Conclusion

Geometrical Measurement method is initial and simple, but also efficient. Aim at the bottleneck of 2D face recognition field, this paper does some pilot study on 3D face recognition. A method, which based on 3D geometrical measurement, is proposed. Eight 3D faces are measured and tested mutually, the results show that the presented method is feasible.

This paper only measure the features of distance and angle, the recognition is only based on the two features. If more features, such as the curve and surface of face, are considered, the recognition rate can be improved greatly. But too many features are not helpful, it is necessary to confirm the essential features and their weights.

References

1. V. Blanz and T. Vetter.:Face Recognition Based on Fitting a 3D Morphable Model. IEEE Trans. PAMI. 25(9)(2003)1063-1074
2. R.Chellappa, C.L.Wilson, S.Sirohey.:Human and Machine Recognition of Faces: A Survey. Proceedings of the IEEE.83(5)(1995)705-740
3. D. Valentin, H. Abdi, Betty Edelman.:What Represents a Face: A Computational Approach for the Integration of Physiological and Psychological Data.Perception.26(1997) 1271-1288
4. J. Alice, O. Toole, T. Vetter, V. Blanz.:Three-dimensional shape and two-dimensional surface reflectance contributions to face recognition: an application of three-dimensional morphing. Vision Researc.39(1999)3145-3155
5. Gang Pan,Zhaohui Wu.:Automatic 3D Face Verification from Range Data. Advances in Biometrics(一). Tsinghua Publish House.129-134
6. Zhou Ming-quan, Geng Guo-hua, Wang Xue-song et.:Detection and mark of 3D face. Advances in Biometrics(一).Tsinghua Publish House.115-119
7. Geng guo-hua, Shu Xing-feng, Liu Zhi-ping.:Face Recognition based on 3D geometrical features.Advances in Biometrics(一).Tsinghua Publish House.125-128
8. C.S.Chua,F.Han,Y.K.Ho.:3D Human Face Recognition Using Point Signature. Proc.FG'00. Mar(2000)233-238
9. C.Beumier,M.Acherou.:Automatic 3D Face Authentication. Image and Vision Computing.18(4)(2000):315-321
10. W.Zhao, R.Chellappa, A.Rosenfeld and .J.Phillips.:Face Recognition:A Literature Survey. CVL Technical Report,University of Maryland,Oct.2000
11. H.Tanaka,M.Ikeda and H.Chiaki. Curvature-based face surface recognition using spherical correlation. Proc.Third Int.Conf.on FG(1998) 372-377
12. Y.H.Lee,K.W.Park,J.C.Shim and T.H.Yi.:3D Face Recognition using Projection Vectors. Preceeding of *IVCNZ*2002.151-156
13. V.Blanz and T.Vetter.:Face recognition based on fitting a 3D morphable model.IEEE Transactions on Pattern analysis and Machine Intelligence.,25(2003) 1063-1074
14. K. Chang, K. Bowyer, and P. Flynn.:Face recognition using 2D and 3D facial data. 2003 Multimodal User Authentication Workshop. December(2003)25–32
15. Y. Lee, K. Park, J. Shim, and T. Yi.:3D face recognition using statistical multiple features for the local depth information. 16th International Conference on Vision Interface, available at www.visioninterface.org/vi2003. June 2003
16. Y.Wang, C. Chua, and Y. Ho.:Facial feature detection and face recognition from 2D and 3D images. Pattern Recognition Letters, 23(2002)1191–1202
17. C. Hesher, A. Srivastava, and G. Erlebacher.:A novel technique for face recognition using range images.Seventh Int'l Symposium on Signal Processing and Its Applications(2003)
18. Γ. Tsalakanidou, D. Tzocaras, and M. Strintzis.:Use of depth and colour eigenfaces for face recognition.Pattern Recognition Letters, 24(2003)1427–1435

3D Face Recognition Using Eigen-Spectrum on the Flattened Facial Surface

Lei Zheng, Gang Pan, and Zhaohui Wu

Dept. of Computer Science, Zhejiang University, Hangzhou, China
{Leizheng, gpan, wzh}@zju.edu.cn

Abstract. This paper presents a novel 3D face recognition approach. The discrete facial surface firstly is mapped into an isomorphic 2D planar triangulation, attempting to preserve the intrinsic geometric properties. Then power spectrum image of the flattened surface is employed for the followed eigenface, instead of the flattened surface image, in order to achieve the invariance in planar rotation. Our method does not need 3D facial model registration during the whole recognition procedure. The experiment using 3D_RMA demonstrates its comparable performance.

1 Introduction

State-of-the-art face recognition systems are based on a 40-year heritage of 2D algorithms since 1960s [1]. However, traditional 2D face recognition methods appear to be sensitive to pose, illumination and expression. This paper focuses on face recognition using 3D facial surface to handle the problems. The 3D face data have the following advantages compared with 2D face data: firstly, the illuminating has no effect on the depth information of 3D face data. Secondly, the variation of facial pose doesn't lose any 3D face information. Thirdly, the 3D data have more clues to handle expression change than 2D image.

The current techniques in 3D acquiring system make it practical to quickly and accurately build the 3D face model. But the activities to exploit the additional information in 3D data to improve the accuracy and robustness of face recognition system are still weakly addressed. Only a little work on the 3D face recognition has been reported.

1.1 Previous Work

Curvature Based. Curvature is the intrinsic local property of curved surface. The local shape could be determined by its primary curvature and direction [2]. Therefore, most of the early studies used curvature to analyze the 3D facial data [3, 4, 5, 8].

Gordon [4, 5] presented a template-based recognition system involving descriptors based on curvature calculations from range image data. The sensed surface regions are classified as convex, concave and saddle by calculating the minimum and maximum normal curvatures. Then locations of nose, eyes, mouth and other features are determined, which are used for depth template comparison. An approach to label the components of human faces is proposed by Yacoob [8]. Qualitative reasoning about possible interpretations of the components is performed, followed by consistency of hypothesized interpretations.

Recover-and-Synthesis Based. For this kind of methods, their probe still is 2D image but not 3D data. The partial 3D information is recovered from the 2D image, then the facial image in virtual view is synthesized for recognition [10] or the recognition task is accomplished with the recovered parameters [9].

Spatial Matching Based. Recognizing is performed via matching facial surface or profile directly in 3D Euclidean space [6, 12, 21].

Shape Descriptor Based. Chua [11] describes a technique based on point signature - a representation for free-form surfaces. The rigid parts of the face of one person are extracted to deal with different facial expressions. Wang [19] used a new shape representation called Local Shape Map for 3D face recognition.

1.2   Overview

The 3D data have more clues for recognition than 2D image. However processing of 3D data generally requires expensive computational cost. A practical tradeoff is to convert the useful 3D information onto an 2D plane before recognition[20]. This paper presents a novel 3D face recognition approach. The discrete facial surface firstly is mapped into an isomorphic planar triangulation. In order to achieve the invariance in planar rotation, power spectrum image of the flattened surface is employed for the followed eigenface, instead of the flattened surface image. Our method does not need 3D model registration during the whole recognition procedure.

The rest of the paper is organized as follows. The next section introduces how to map the 3D facial surface into an isomorphic planar triangulation. In Section 3 describes how to achieve the recognition task using the planar triangulation, where DFT and eigenface is applied [17]. Section 4 presents some experimental results. Conclusions are drawn in Section 5.

2   Flattening of the Facial Surface

The ideal mapping from a discrete curved surface into an isomorphic planar circle is expected to be isometric, i.e. distance-preserving (both area-preserving and angle-preserving). However, there exists no such mapping for the most geometries. We want to preserve the geometric properties of a surface as much as possible. In other word, we should define a reasonable criterion to minimize the distortion when constructing the isomorphic mapping between 3D and 2D.

2.1   The Minimal Distortion Criterion

Since our matched region is non-closed manifolds, we focus on the flattening of non-closed triangulated surface. In reference [14], Desbrun introduces the desirable distortion measures that satisfy some properties such as rotation and translation invariance, continuity and additives. Here we give the two distortion measures for area-preserving and angle-preserving respectively.

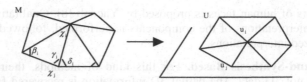

Fig. 1. 3D 1-ring and its flattened version

Angle-Preserving (Conformal). When working on the area problem minimization, Gray [15] shows that the minimum of Dirichlet energy is attained for conformal mappings. Here,

$$E_A = \sum_{neighbour\ edges(i,j)} \cot\alpha_{ij}\left|u_i - u_j\right|^2 \tag{1}$$

Where $\left|u_i - u_j\right|$ is the length of the edge (i, j) in the parameter plane, and α_{ij} is the opposite left angle in original triangle, shown in Fig.1.

Conformality of the map equivalently means angle preservation since any angle on the parameter plane will be keep through the mapping. Since the energy is continuous and quadratic, we conclude the linear equation for central node i:

$$\frac{\partial E_A}{\partial u_i} = \sum_{j\in N(i)}\left(\cot\alpha_{ij} + \cot\beta_{ij}\right)\left(u_i - u_j\right) = 0 \tag{2}$$

Area-Preserving. Similarly to E_A, we now discuss the property of area-persevering. The quadratic energy E_X is the integral of Gaussian curvature. From [14, 16], the following quadratic energy is defined:

$$E_X = \sum_{j\in N(i)}\frac{\left(\cot\gamma_{ij} + \cot\delta_{ij}\right)}{\left|x_i - x_j\right|^2}\left(u_i - u_j\right)^2 \tag{3}$$

Where the angles γ_{ij} and δ_{ij} are defined in Fig. 1. For the center node u_i, however u_j move in 1-ring region, the total 1-ring area won't change, so:

$$\frac{\partial E_X}{\partial u_i} = \sum_{j\in N(i)}\frac{\left(\cot\gamma_{ij} + \cot\delta_{ij}\right)}{\left|x_i - x_j\right|^2}\left(u_i - u_j\right) = 0 \tag{4}$$

The Combination of Criterions. The two generative parameterizations, discrete conformal mapping and discrete authalic mapping, use the linear combination of area-persevering and angle-persevering. A general distortion measure E can be defined as:

$$E = \alpha E_A + (1 - \alpha) E_X \quad 0 \le \alpha \le 1 \tag{5}$$

Thus the flattening procedure is equivalent to minimize the combined distortion measure E.

2.2 The Selection of Matched Region

To map the surface into a regular planar region, we need to crop each facial surface to obtain the consistent boundary, meanwhile, keep enough discriminative information for recognition.

Fig. 2. Using a sphere to crop the 3D facial surface

Since the accurate pose of each facial surface could not be available, we would better use a method to select the region independent of the face model's pose. Based on the observation that the most facial features cluster around the nose region, a sphere is employed to crop the facial surface to get the matched region shown in Fig.2. Since nose tip is the most significant key point in facial surface, it is comparably easy to detect. Considering the symmetry, the sphere is used to intersect the facial surface, with setting the nose tip as the sphere center, and with appropriate radius, so that the intersected surface contains the key characteristics. Because the sphere is isotropic, no matter how the face surface changes its pose, the sphere will always intersect the same region on the face surface (in Fig. 2).

2.3 Parameterizing the 3D Facial Surface

The non-closed manifolds here are topologically equivalent to a planar circle; hence this is the natural parameter domain for them. Here, parameterizing a triangular mesh onto the plane is just assigning a 3D position on the unit circle to each of the mesh vertices. Since we predefine the mapped boundary as a circle, there is only angle's variable on the mapped plane. It will be easier to match. We set the convex point of original surface as the boundary and mapped the boundary into a circle.

Given the mapped circle boundary U, the sparse linear system for parameterization induces the following equation:

$$MU = \begin{bmatrix} \lambda M^A + \mu M^X & \\ 0 & 1 \end{bmatrix} \begin{bmatrix} U_{inetrnal} \\ U_{boundary} \end{bmatrix} = \begin{bmatrix} 0 \\ C_{boundry} \end{bmatrix} = C \tag{6}$$

$$M_{ij}^{A} = \begin{cases} \cot(\alpha_{ij}) + \cot(\beta_{ij}) & if \quad j \in N(i) \\ -\sum_{k \in N(i)} M_{ik}^{A} & if \quad i = j \\ 0 & Otherwise \end{cases} \quad (7)$$

$$M_{ij}^{X} = \begin{cases} \left(\cot(\gamma_{ij}) + \cot(\beta_{ij})\right) / \left|x_i - x_j\right|^2 & if \quad j \in N(i) \\ -\sum_{k \in N(i)} M_{ik}^{X} & if \quad i = j \\ 0 & otherwise \end{cases} \quad (8)$$

Since the boundary has been defined, the sparse system is efficiently solved using generalized minimal residual algorithm [15, 16]. Some mapped results are shown with Fig. 3.

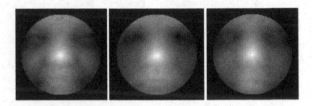

Fig. 3. The corresponding unfolded surfaces where the border has fixed on circle

3   Face Recognition Using Eigen-Spectrum

So far we have been processing images by mapping the 3D model to planar circle. The variability of original direction results in that the 2D image rotates around the mapped center. Some optimization algorithm used to minimizing the discrimination between images and aligned them with optimized result. But the process needs great computational cost.

Here, we give a new method using 2D DFT to compare images. Firstly the power spectrum image of the flattened image, in polar coordinates, is generated by 2D DFT, then eigenface of the spectrum image is exploited to perform the final recognition task, called Eigen-Spectrum.

The output of the transformation represents the image in the time or frequency domain, while the input image is the spatial domain equivalent. For a square image of size N×N, the two-dimensional DFT is given by:

$$F(k,l) = \frac{1}{N^2} \sum_{u=0}^{N-1} \sum_{v=0}^{N-1} f(u,v) e^{-i2\pi(\frac{ki}{N} + \frac{lj}{N})} \qquad k = 0,1,...K \quad l = 0,1,...,L \quad (9)$$

Since the rotation $\Delta\sigma$ in Cartesian coordinates is described with $p(r, \sigma + \Delta\sigma)$ by polar coordinates and the Fourier Transform is independent with coordinate translation transformation, we convert the mapped image from Cartesian coordinates $f(x,y)$ to polar coordinates $p(r,\sigma)$. This means that whatever it rotated around the center; the results transformed by 2D DFT must be same.

Because the result is independent of the mutation of angle, we can match the face image directly without aligning the face any more.

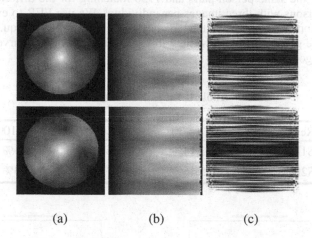

(a)   (b)   (c)

Fig. 4. DFT process where k=50, l=50 (a) the same person with planar rotation (b) Polar coordinates: Axis X: θ Axis Y: ρ (c) Spectrum image

As shown by Fig.4, each original image will generate the images that represent its power spectrum in 2-dimension. Thus the resulted spectrum images have the same size and don't need alignment any more. And it is easy to impose eigenface [17] on these images to do the recognition.

4   Experimental Results

Our experiments use the facial range data from 3D RMA database session 1 and session 2 [12]. Each session has 30 individuals with exactly three shots of range data per individual. The range data in this database were acquired by a 3D acquisition system based on structured light, represented in *xyz* form, i.e. in point cloud. Each model has only about 3000 points. For each person, the orientation of head in the three shots is different: straight forward, left or right, upward or downward. Some samples from the data set are shown in Fig. 5.

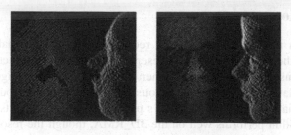

Fig. 5. The samples of 3D_RMA

We set the radius of sphere mentioned in Sec. 2.2 to 600 and make linear combination parameter $\alpha = 0.3$ for distortion criteria. For the S1M and S2M, there are 180 matching for the same person pairs and 7730 matching for the different person pairs due to 30 persons with three images per individual. We use EER to evaluate the recognition performance and make the parameters K,L mentioned in Equ.9 as 30, 50 and 100. Then we get the result shown in Table 1 and the EER ROC curve shown in Fig. 6 with our algorithm.

Table 1. The EER on 3D_RMA

Result	K,L=30	K,L=50	K,L=100
S1M	12.14%	**8.66%**	13.53%
S2M	15.46%	**10.73%**	14.93%

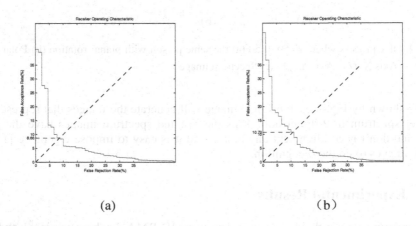

(a)   (b)

Fig. 6. The ROC on 3D_RMA. (a) EER on S1M =8.66% (b) EER on S2M=10.73% ($K,L = 50$)

Here, our operations including the matched-region's selection, the mapping from 3d face to 2D face and the eigenface building from the spectrum images of the mapped images at polar coordinates make it unnecessary to align either 3D facial surface or the flattened 2D image.

5   Conclusion

We proposed a novel approach to face recognition from 3D facial surface, which firstly flattens the 3D curved surface preserving the intrinsic geometric properties of facial surfaces using parameterization, then applies 2D DFT and eigenface to the resulted representation. Unlike many previously proposed solutions, our approach is insensitive to variation of the facial model's pose. Experimental results showed that the proposed algorithm performs well on the 3D_RMA, though the resolution of models in 3D_RMA is considerably low.

References

1. Bledsoe, W.W.: The Model Method in Facial Recognition. Technical report PRI15, Panoramic Research Inc., Palo Alto (1966).
2. Emanuele Trucco, Alessandro Verri: Introductory Techniques for 3-D Computer Vision. In: Prentice Hall Inc., 1998.
3. John Chun Lee, E Milios: Matching Range Images of Human Faces. In: Proceedings of IEEE International Conference on Computer Vision, pages 722–726, 1990.
4. Gaile G Gordon: Face Recognition based on Depth Maps and Surface Curvature. In: Geometric Methods in Computer Vision, SPIE Proceedings, volume 1570, pages 234–247, 1991.
5. Gaile G Gordon: Face Recognition from Depth and Curvature. In: PhD thesis, Harvard University, Division of Applied Sciences, 1991.
6. Gang Pan, Zhaohui Wu: 3D Face Recognition from Range Data. International Journal of Image and Graphics, 2004. Accepted.
7. Hiromi T. Tanaka, Masaki Ikeda, Hisako Chiaki: Curvature-based Face Surface Recognition using Spherical Correlation. In: Proceedings of IEEE International Conference on Automatic Face and Pose Recognition, pages 372–377, 1998.
8. Yacoob, Y., Davis, L.S.: Labeling of Human Face Components from Range Data. In: CVGIP: Image Understanding, 60(2):168-178, Sep. 1994
9. Volker Blanz, Sami Romdhani, Thomas Vetter: Face Identification across Different Poses and Illumination with a 3d Morphable Model. In: Proc. IEEE International Conference on Automatic Face and Pose Recognition, pp. 202–207, 2002.
10. Wenyi Zhao: Robust Image-based 3D Face Recognition. In: Ph.D. Thesis, Department of Electrical and Computer Engineering, University of Maryland, College Park, 1999.
11. Chin-Seng Chua, F Han, and Y K Ho.: 3D human face recognition using point signature. In: Proceedings of IEEE International Conference on Automatic Face and Pose Recognition, pages 233–238, 2000.
12. C. Beumier, M. Acheroy, Automatic 3D Face Authentication. Image and Vision Computing, vol. 18,no. 4, pp. 315–321, 2000.
13. Saad, Youcef, Martin H. Schultz, GMRES: A Generalized Minimal Residual Algorithm for Solving Nonsymmetric Linear Systems. SIAM J. Sci. Stat. Compute, Vol. 7, No. 3, pp. 856-869, July 1986.
14. Desbrun, M., Meyer, M., Alliez, P.: Intrinsic Parametrizations of Surface Meshes. In: Proceedings of Eurographics, 2002.
15. Gray, A.: Modern Differential Geometry of Curves and Surfaces. Second edition. In: CRC Press, 1998.
16. 16..Meyer, M., Desbrun, M., Schröder, P., Barr, A.H.: Discrete Differential-Geometry Operators for Triangulated 2-Manifolds, 2002.
17. Turk, M.A., Pentland, A.P.: Face Recognition using Eigenface. In: Proc. of Computer Vision and Pattern Recognition, pages 586-591, June 1991.
18. Barrett, R., Berry, M., Chan, T.F.: Templates for the Solution of Linear Systems: Building Blocks for Iterative Methods. In: SIAM, Philadelphia, 1994.
19. Y. Wang, Gang Pan, Zhaohui Wu: 3D Face Recognition using Local Shape Map. IEEE ICIP'04, 2004, to Appear.
20. Bronstein, A.M., Bronstein, M. M., Kimmel, R.: Expression-invariant 3D face recognition. In: AVBPA'03, LNCS-2688, pp. 62–70, 2003.
21. Yijun Wu, Gang Pan, Zhaohui Wu: Face Authentication based on Multiple Profiles Extracted from Range Data. In: AVBPA'03, LNCS-2688, pp515-522, 2003.

Building a 3D Morphable Face Model by Using Thin Plate Splines for Face Reconstruction*

Hui Guo, Jiayan Jiang, and Liming Zhang

Fudan University, Dept. of Electronic Engineering,
Laboratory of Image and Intelligence, 220 Handan Road, Shanghai, China
guohui@fudan.edu.cn
jiangjiayan@citiz.net

Abstract. In this paper, we introduce a semi-automatic deformation alignment method, Thin Plate Spline, to generate a 3D morphable face model from 3D face data. This model includes an average 3D face on both shape and texture, and a set of morphable coefficients for individual sample faces. A primary 3D morphable face model based on Chinese people is then set up. Simulation results show the feasibility of this 3D morphable model for 2D face recognition on with different PIE in future research.

1 Introduction

In the past decades, the mainstream of face recognition is based on 2D method, such as Eigenface, Fisherface, and ASM & AAM 3, etc. Previous studies on face recognition have shown that the main challenge is to separate intrinsic characteristic, such as shape and texture of a facial surface, from extrinsic ones, such as pose, illumination and expression (PIE). Traditional 2D methods can get satisfying results, provided that pose and illumination are under standard condition (for example, front view and normal illumination), but the performance drops dramatically when the extrinsic factors' variation presents in the input image 2. In principle, it attributes to the limitation of 2D representation of 3D structure like real human faces.

To tackle the aforementioned problem, a 3D model is therefore proposed 1. This morphable model is derived from 3D face data sampled from real human faces. If the 3D sample data are sufficient enough, the morphable model can represent any faces in real world. Then the face recognition is based on comparison between the input 2D picture and the 2D projection of 3D morphable face model, which is robust to pose and illumination. Thus, the key point of face recognition method is the construction of morphable 3D face model.

Unfortunately, open database of 3D faces is unavailable up to now. For the sake of 3D face recognition researches, some foreign universities, such as University of Tübingen, German 1 and the University of South Florida, USA 7, have set up their

---

* This research is supported by the NSF(60171036) and the significant technology project(03DZ14015), Shanghai.

own 3D face databases separately. But there are only few oriental people faces, especially Chinese faces, in these foreign 3D face databases.

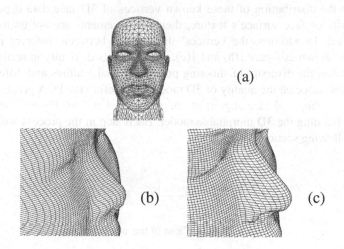

Fig. 1. 3D Vertices and meshes

The original 3D face data in this paper was derived from some 2D pictures taken by two cameras at the same time based on the principles of optics. A primary morphable 3D model was constructed based on these data, which are the foundation for building a 3D Chinese face model on more precise 3D data. The original data were a quadrangle mesh with about 100,000 vertices. The shape information S (x,y,z) and texture information T(R,G,B) are known on each vertex.

We replace the optical flow algorithm in 1 with the method of Thin Plate Spline (TPS) to perform the alignment for 3D data, based on which the morphable 3D model was obtained. Testing results show that the construction of model through this method is quite acceptable.

This paper is arranged as follows: Section 2 introduces 3D face modeling using Thin Plate Spline; Utilizing 3D morphable model for face reconstruction from 2D image is described in Section 3; Section 4 gives some experimental results; and conclusion is drawn in Section 5.

2   A Morphable Model of 3D Faces

The morphable model of 3D faces was generated from 60 Chinese individuals' 3D face data, including 33 males and 27 females, whose hair part was removed by cap. When taking the photos, the lighting was controlled to reduce the effect of illumination. These 3D data for one face have about 100,000 vertices. For each vertex the position (x,y,z) and texture information are already known.

To construct a 3D morphable model is to set up a unified mathematical expression with a few parameters, through which any 3D face can be reconstructed. Once these vertices for each 3D face data are put in order and all the faces in training data are aligned, we can use principle component analysis (PCA) to generate the 3D morphable model.

Since the distribution of these known vertices of 3D face data depends upon the complexity of face surface's texture, their displacements are not uniform, shown as figure 1(a). In addition, the vertices' distribution between different people is also different, shown as figure 1(b) and 1(c), which brings difficulty in sorting these vertices. Besides, the diversity of shooting position, facial features and different height of people also affected the quality of 3D model. So, before the PCA process, preprocessing, re-sampling and face alignment are considered at first. Figure 2 shows the flow chart of building the 3D morphable model. Each step in the process will be explained in the following sections.

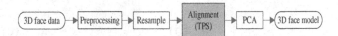

Fig. 2. Flow Chart of the whole process

2.1 Preprocessing of 3D Data

Since the diversity of size and pose of original data, preprocessing is introduced to manually adjust the 3D sample data into an approximate uniformity for eliminating the extrinsic characteristic in the morphable model.

2.2 Resampling of 3D Data

To homogenize the unequally distributed vertices, the progress of resampling is then employed. The Cartesian coordinates can not perfectly express the 3D information of human face since it is distributed on the surface of an ellipsoid. So we introduce the cylindrical coordinates (h,ϕ,r) to resample the 3D faces. The conversion of these two coordinates is shown as follows.

$$\gamma=\sqrt{x^2+y^2+z^2}; h=z; \phi=tg^{-1}(y/x) \tag{1}$$

Ignoring the depth information r, the 2D representation in cylindrical coordinates can be resampled from the facial surface by parameters h and ϕ. Where the variable ϕ covers 0- 360^0 in 360 angular steps and the variable h covers the height from neck to hair in 360 vertical steps. (h,ϕ) $h,\phi\in\{1,...360\}$.

The shape variable r and three texture variable R, G and B, indicating the red, green and blue components of the surface separately, are reorganized a texture vector at resampled position, shown as follows

$$I(h,\phi)=(r(h,\phi),R(h,\phi),G(h,\phi),B(h,\phi))^T \tag{2}$$
$$h,\phi\in\{1,...360\}$$

Thus, the vertices can be sorted by h and ϕ, and each vertex has its own texture value.

2.3 Thin Plate Spline (TPS)

As we mentioned above, one of the core process to generate a 3D morphable model is face alignment, that is, to find out the dense point-to-point correspondence between any sample face, I, in training data and a reference face I_0, an assigned 3D face in the 3D database. They are aligned by means of their semantic positions. Correspondence of vertices between I and I_0 is then obtained by the correspondent displacement of point to point as $(\Delta h_i(h,\phi), \Delta \phi_i(h,\phi)); i = 1,2,....M$, where M is the number of vertices.

The correspondent displacement can be worked out by optical flow algorithm 5 automatically. Our implementation, however, could not give a satisfying result using optical flow for our 3D face data. It's due to the large variance between each pair of different faces, so that the brightness conservation assumption doesn't work. Moreover, although there are varies optimizing algorithms, the essence of the optical flow algorithm is to deal with global optimization for all vertices displacements. So it is very time consuming to calculate the whole data of about $360 \times 360 = 129,600$ points after resampling. Thus, we replace the optical flow algorithm with Thin Plate Spline to do the face alignment.

Thin Plate Spline 4 is one of the conventional tools for interpolating surfaces over scattered data, which was popularized by Bookstein for statistical shape analysis and is widely used in computer graphics. It leads to smooth deformation upon the two sets of landmarks, which are decided manually. However, what we concern here is to calculate the displacement of each vertex, not the deformation result.

The TPS process is based on the 2D projection representation in cylindrical coordinates of the 3D face data. Ignoring the depth information r, we expand all the parameters in the plane of (h,ϕ) and then manually label 41 control points on all the sample faces. Using the method of TPS, we align all the vertices of each sample face to those of the reference face. We will introduce the TPS algorithm in the following part.

Suppose a to be warped face image I be labeled a set of control points $Q\{q_i\}$ $i = 1,...,N$, normally on the feature points like eyes, nose or mouth, on the reference face I_0, and then label the same parts of the novel face as another set of control points $P\{p_i\}$ $i = 1,...,N$, where q_i and p_i are the position vector (h,ϕ) of ith control point. We require a continuous vector mapping function f from P to Q, such that

$$f(p_i) = q_i \qquad \forall i = 1,...,N \qquad (3)$$

Given such a mapping function, we can project each vertex of face I into that of the reference face I_0.

We define the function **f** as a weighted sum of function U, called TPS function, shown as follows:

$$\mathbf{f}(o) = \sum_{i=1}^{N} \omega_i U(\|o - \mathbf{p}_i\|) + \mathbf{a}_1 + \mathbf{a}_h o(h) + \mathbf{a}_\phi o(\phi) \tag{4}$$

where $\omega_i, \mathbf{a}_1, \mathbf{a}_h, \mathbf{a}_\phi$ are the weight vectors, and o denotes the position vector (h, ϕ) of any vertex in novel face **I**. The special function U is defined as follows:

$$U(\|o - \mathbf{p}_i\|) = \begin{cases} \|o - \mathbf{p}_i\|^2 \log(\|o - \mathbf{p}_i\|)^2 & o \neq \mathbf{p}_i \\ 0 & o = \mathbf{p}_i \end{cases} \tag{5}$$

since $\|o - \mathbf{p}_i\|$ is the distance between two integral vertex, there always be $\log(\|o - \mathbf{p}_i\|)^2 > 0$.

And the constraints of the weights are:

$$\sum_{i=1}^{N} \omega_i = 0, \ \sum_{i=1}^{N} \omega_i \mathbf{p}_i(h) = 0, \ \sum_{i=1}^{N} \omega_i \mathbf{p}_i(\phi) = 0 \tag{6}$$

Formula (6) ensures that when o is at infinity, the first part in the right side of (4) sums to zero. Commonly, the right side of (4) is divided into two parts: a sum of function U which can be shown to be bounded and asymptotically flat, and an affine part representing the behavior of **f** when o is at infinity.

We can get N equations from (3) using the control points P and Q, and three equations from constraint function (6). Calculate the (N+3) linear vector equations, then we get the (N+3) unknown weight vectors $\omega_i, \mathbf{a}_1, \mathbf{a}_h, \mathbf{a}_\phi$.

Thus, the dense point-to-point correspondence between each face and a reference face can be easily decided by using the TPS function. And the difference of vertices' position on faces **I**, before and after TPS, is the required displacement $(\Delta h_j(h, \phi), \Delta \phi_j(h, \phi)); j = 1, 2, \ldots M$.

2.4 Principle Component Analysis

Since the original face data are represented in Cartesian coordinates and also our future work of face recognition will be based on it too, we replace the face data into Cartesian coordinate after alignment with TPS in cylindrical coordinates, to keep constancy. The shape and texture vector for a face data can be written as

$$\begin{aligned} \mathbf{S} &= (x_1, y_1, z_1, x_2, \ldots, x_M, y_M, z_M)^T, \\ \mathbf{T} &= (R_1, G_1, B_1, R_2 \ldots, R_M, G_M, B_M)^T \end{aligned} \tag{7}$$

We perform a Principle Component Analysis (PCA) 6 on the set of vectors. Ignoring the correlation of shape and texture, we perform the PCA separately on shape **S** and texture **T**.

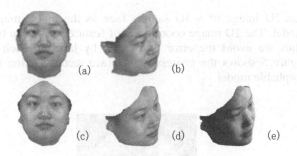

(a)   (b)   (c)   (d)   (e)

Fig. 3. The reconstruction of 3D models

For shape S, we calculate the average shape model by $\bar{S} = \frac{1}{m}\sum_{i=1}^{m} S_i$, where m is the number of the sample faces, m=60 in this paper. We define the covariance matrix as $C = \frac{1}{m}\sum_{i=1}^{m}(S_i - \bar{S})(S_i - \bar{S})^{T}$. After calculating the eigenvalue and eigenvector of C, 98% of total energy is selected to reduce the dimension of shape space from 60 to 27 by projecting the shape vectors to corresponding shape eigenvectors. By the same procedure, we reduce the dimension of texture space from 60 to 49.

Thus, we get the morphable 3D face model as following:

$$S = \bar{S} + \sum_{i=1}^{27} \alpha_i S_i, \quad T = \bar{T} + \sum_{i=1}^{49} \beta_i T_i \qquad (8)$$

where α_i and β_i are the shape and texture coefficients of PCA, and S_i and T_i present the basis vectors of shape and texture respectively.

Given the coefficient α_i and β_i, figure 3 shows the reconstruction of 3D face through the projection upon S_i and T_i. 3(a) and 3(b) shows the original face data, the reconstructed data using 98% energy in PCA is shown in 3(c) and 3(d), and 3(e) shows the illumination cast on 3(d) from orientation 50^0 in right side of frontal face.

3 Face Reconstruction with 3D Morphable Model

To testify the effectiveness of the acquired morphable model, we adopted a synthesis-by-analysis strategy to reconstruct the 3D shape and texture from a 2D face image with this model. We could get a rough evaluation by comparing the original input face image and the 2D projection of its 3D reconstruction.

For initialization of the algorithm, several feature points are labeled on the 3D average face. We manually define seven feature points, which are four eye-corners, one nose tip and two mouth corners as shown in figure 4. Because the correspondence of each point between every two 3D faces is already created, these feature points are applied to all 3D faces accordingly.

We use the 2D image of a 3D sample face as the input image to test our 3D morphable model. The 2D image coordinates of feature points can be acquired during projection, thus we avoid the error introduced by labeling such points on image manually. Figure 5 shows the process of 3D face reconstruction from input image with a 3D morphable model.

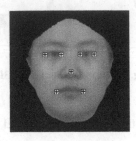

Fig. 4. The feature points defined on average face. They are eye corners, nose tip and mouth corners

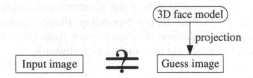

Fig. 5. Matching of input 2D image and 2D projection of 3D morphable model

According to (8), a novel 3D face can be generated from the coefficients α_i and β_i, which control the 3D shape and texture respectively. This novel 3D face is projected to 2D image plane, so that we get a "guess image" and the image coordinates of feature points.

The goal of face reconstruction is to minimize the difference between the "input image" and the "guess image", and the difference between the coordinates of feature points on these two images as well. If we can achieve this goal by adjusting the coefficients α_i and β_i, we accomplish a reliable 3D face reconstruction. The energy function is defined as follows:

$$E_I = \sum_{x,y} \left\| \mathbf{I}_{\text{input}}(x,y) - \mathbf{I}_{\text{guess}}(x,y) \right\|^2 \tag{9}$$

$$E_F = \sum_j \left\| \begin{pmatrix} q_{x,j} \\ q_{y,j} \end{pmatrix} - \begin{pmatrix} p_{x,j} \\ p_{y,j} \end{pmatrix} \right\|^2 \tag{10}$$

$$E = E_I + \sigma E_F \tag{11}$$

I_{input} is the 2D input image, I_{guess} is the guess image obtained from 3D morphable model, which is related to α_i and β_i. $(q_{x,j}, q_{y,j})^T$ is the 2D image coordinate of the jth feature point on input image, while $(p_{x,j}, p_{y,j})^T$ is the correspondent one on guess image, which is related to α_i. σ controls the relative weight of image's difference (9) and coordinate difference on feature points (10). We employ the classical Levenberg-Marquardt method to optimize our energy function (11). When the iteration finishes, the coefficients α_i and β_i are the most fitting ones for the 2D face image, and then we can get the correspondent 3D face according to (8). At first, σ is quite large to get feature points aligned, and in the following iterations, the function relies more on E_I.

4 Experimental Results and Discussion

The goal of model-based image analysis is to represent a novel 2D face image by model coefficients α_i and β_i and then provide the reconstruction of its 3D shape and texture.

To testify the effectiveness of our proposed method, we built a morphable model from a 3D face database of 60 individuals, which includes 33 males and 27 females.

In this section, we give some face reconstruction results using the method outlined before. The input images I_{input} are 2D projection images of 3D sample faces. We labeled seven feature points on 3D average face as Figure 4 shows, they are four eye corners, one nose tip and two mouth corners. The feature points coordinates $(q_{x,j}, q_{y,j})^T$ on input images can be acquired during projection. The algorithm starts from the average face (average shape and average texture), which means $\alpha_i = 0$ and $\beta_i = 0$.

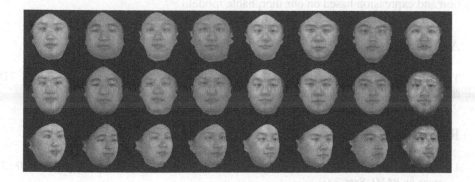

Fig. 6. The experimental results. The first row shows 2D projected exemplar faces, and the second and third rows are the 3D faces reconstructed with out algorithm

The experimental results revealed that the algorithm eventually gave a quite similar face with the input one. Most reconstructions of face images in database are satisfying. Figure 6 shows eight Chinese faces, the upper row are 2D input images projected from 3D sample faces, the middle row shows the reconstruction results through (9) (10) and (11), and the bottom row shows the same reconstructed faces with a different pose. However, there are some cases that the reconstructions are not very reliable, for example, the second and eighth column of figure 6. It may due to the fact that we do not include the face contour information when labeling the feature points, so that although the seven feature points are aligned well, the difference of chin contour is still large. In addition, the local minima problem of the optimization algorithm is inclined to give an unsatisfying texture reconstruction.

5 Conclusion

In this paper, we make an attempt to construct a morphable 3D face model based on Chinese faces utilizing the original face data from optics imaging. In this progress, we present a Thin Plate Splines method for establishing dense point-to-point correspondence needed by generating a 3D morphable model. This method needs to define several control points manually on each sample face, then it can find out all of the non-control points' displacement on every two faces. By this means, all of the points are aligned semantically, thus PCA is performed to derive a 3D morphable model.

Although our original data are not as precise as the foreign ones, which are recorded with a laser scanner, the reconstruction of faces in the database shows the feasibility of using the 3D morphable model for face recognition in future work and the possibility of 3D reconstruction on 2D input image.

Compared with the results given in [8], there are much work should be done to deal with our optimizing process to get a more precise result.

A laser scanner will be used in the near future. So, more works will be done to better our 3D morphable model based on a more comprehensive Chinese faces database. Besides, we will focus on performing face recognition with different pose, illumination and expression based on our morphable model.

Acknowledgement

The authors thank Shanghai Jiao Tong University for providing all the sample 3D face data.

References

1. V. Blanz and T. Vetter, "Face Recognition Based on Fitting a 3D Morphable Model", *IEEE trans on PAMI*, Sept 2003
2. P. Phillips, P. Grother, R. Micheals, D. Blackburn, E.Tabassi, M. Bone, "Face Recognition Vender Test 2002: Evaluation Report", *FRVT*, 2002
3. T.F.Cootes & C.J.Taylor "Statistical Models of Appearane for Computer Vision", October,2001

4. Fred L. Bookstein "Priniple Warps: Thin-Plate Spline and the Decomposition of Deformation", *IEEE trans on PAMI* VOL11,No 6,June:567-585,1989
5. B.K.P. Horn and B.G. Schunck, "Determining Optical Flow", *Artificial Intelligence*, vol.17, pp.185-203, 1981
6. Kenneth R. Castleman, "Digital Image Processing"
7. Yuxiao Hu, Dalong Jiang, Shuicheng Yan, Lei Zhang, Hongjiang Zhang, "Automatic 3D Reconstruction for Face Recognition", *FGR'04*
8. V. Blanz, T. Vetter, "A Morphable Model For the Synthesis Of 3D Faces", in SIGGRAPH'99 Conference Proceedings. ACM SIGGRAPH, 1999.

3D Surface Reconstruction Based on One Non-symmetric Face Image

Li Feng, Jianhuang Lai, and Lei Zhang

Center of Computer Vision, Sun Yat-sen University
fengli802@163.com, {stsljh, mcszl}@zsu.edu.cn

Abstract. Shape from shading (SFS) is an important research domain in the Computer Vision, in which the technology making use of the change in image brightness of an object to determine the relative surface depth receives a lot of attention. Now many algorithms have been developed to perform the goal, especially the model-based symmetric Shape-from-Shading approach presented by Zhao works well, but the symmetry supposition limits the application of the approach. In order to get rid of the limit, we have improved the traditional Jacobi's iterative method by making use of the brightness constraint and the smoothness constraint to implement the face 3D surface reconstruct, and we have gave the synthesis of the prototype image under the single frontal light source to verify the validity of the algorithm.

1 Introduction

In recent years, three –dimensional (3D) face reconstruction is receiving a lot of attention in the Computer Vision and Computer Graphics communities. It is a fast growing research field with many applications such as virtual reality, animation, face recognition. In all these cases, the recovered model must be compact and accurate, especially around significant areas like the nose, the mouth, the orbits. From the earliest work in facial modeling to more recent studies [1], [2], generating realistic faces has been a central goal. However, this remains as a challenging task due to the complex and individual shape of face and the subtle and spatially varying reflectance properties of skin. At present a common method for solving the difficulty is Shape from Shading.

The Shape from Shading was presented by Horn at first [4]. It is a basic problem in Computer Vision, and a key technology in Image Understanding and 3D Object Recognition. The goal of Shape from Shading is recovering the 3D surface of an object from its 2D intensity image. This is a map from 2D space to 3D space, so it is an ill-posed problem. In order to solve the ill-posed problem and find the unique solution, it requires additional constraints. According to the difference of the constraints, SFS techniques can be divided into four groups: minimization methods [3], propagation methods [4], local methods [5] and linear methods [6]. Minimization methods obtain the solution by minimizing an energy function. Propagation methods propagate the shape information from a set of surface points (e.g., singular points) to the whole

S.Z. Li et al. (Eds.): Sinobiometrics 2004, LNCS 3338, pp. 268–274, 2004.

image. Local methods derive shape based on the assumption of surface type. Linear methods compute the solution based on the linearization of the reflectance map.

Zhao and chellappa [11], [12], presented a model-based symmetric Shape-from-Shading algorithm on the assumption of Lambertian reflectance model. But in the practical application, the symmetry limits the extensive application of this approach. In order to get rid of the limit, we improved the Horn's iterative method to make better result.

Horn [4] made use of the brightness constraint and the smoothness constraint of the smooth surface object to construct a functional extremum problem and set up the iterative algorithm for computing the surface gradient. The algorithm's advantage is feasible and effective, but disadvantage is that the convergent speed is slow, and the computing time is long. Therefore, we properly improved on the algorithm to get a satisfying converge speed and compute time.

2 3D Reconstruction Based on the Smoothness Constrain

In the ideal condition of image formation, we have the image irradiance equation:

$$I(x, y) = R(p(x, y), q(x, y)) = \rho \frac{(\cos \tau \sin \alpha \cdot p + \sin \tau \sin \alpha \cdot q + \cos \alpha)}{\sqrt{p^2 + q^2 + 1}} \tag{1}$$

where $(p, q) = (\frac{\partial z}{\partial x}, \frac{\partial z}{\partial y})$ is surface gradient, $L = (\cos \tau \sin \alpha, \sin \tau \sin \alpha, \cos \alpha)$ is light source direction(slant α is the angle between the negative direction of light source and the positive z-axis, and tilt τ is the angle between the negative direction of light source and the $x - z$ plane), ρ is the albedo, $I(x, y)$ is the image intensity of the scene.

Shape from shading refers to the process of computing the surface gradient (p, q) of the object from its image intensity $I(x, y)$. To solve the ill-posed reflectance map equation, we introduced the constraints as follows. Considering the possibly existent error between the reconstructed image brightness and the input image intensity, we introduce the brightness constraint at first:

$$\varepsilon_1 = \iint_{\Omega} (I(x, y) - R(p(x, y), q(x, y)))^2 dxdy \tag{2}$$

where Ω is the domain of (x, y), brightness constraint indicates that the reconstructed shape produce the same brightness as the input image at each surface point. Then considering that the research object (human face) has a smooth surface, hence the adjacent surface points should have the similar surface gradient, so introduce the smoothness constraint:

$$\varepsilon_2 = \iint_{\Omega} (p_x^2 + p_y^2 + q_x^2 + q_{xy}^2)dxdy \tag{3}$$

where $p_x = \dfrac{\partial p}{\partial x}$, $p_y = \dfrac{\partial p}{\partial y}$, $q_x = \dfrac{\partial q}{\partial x}$, $q_y = \dfrac{\partial q}{\partial y}$.

The smoothness constraint ensures that the change of the surface gradient is smooth. Combining the smoothness constraint and the brightness constraint via the Lagrange constant, we obtain the whole error expression:

$$\varepsilon = \varepsilon_1 + \lambda\varepsilon_2$$
$$= \iint_{\Omega} [(I(x,y) - R(p(x,y),q(x,y)))^2 + \lambda(p_x^2 + p_y^2 + q_x^2 + q_y^2)]dxdy \tag{4}$$

Then solving the surface normal becomes minimizing the whole error expression. Derivating ε about p and q, and let the derivatives equal zeros, we get:

$$\begin{cases} \nabla p = \dfrac{1}{\lambda}[I(x,y) - R(p,q)]\dfrac{\partial R}{\partial p} \\[3mm] \nabla q = \dfrac{1}{\lambda}[I(x,y) - R(p,q)]\dfrac{\partial R}{\partial q} \end{cases} \tag{5}$$

Let $\overline{p}$ and $\overline{q}$ indicate the mean of p's neighbor and q's neighbor, respectively. Then using $\nabla p = p - \overline{p}$, and $\nabla q = q - \overline{q}$ in the equation (5), we clearly have:

$$\begin{cases} p(x,y) = \overline{p}(x,y) + \dfrac{1}{\lambda}[I(x,y) - R(p,q)]\dfrac{\partial R}{\partial p} \\[3mm] q(x,y) = \overline{q}(x,y) + \dfrac{1}{\lambda}[I(x,y) - R(p,q)]\dfrac{\partial R}{\partial q} \end{cases} \tag{6}$$

The iterative formulation for solving the above equation is given as follows (the iterative initialization can be the occluded boundary values):

$$\begin{cases} p^{(n+1)} = \overline{p}^{(n)} + \dfrac{1}{\lambda}[I(x,y) - R(p^{(n)},q^{(n)})]\dfrac{\partial R^{(n)}}{\partial p} \\[3mm] q^{(n+1)} = \overline{q}^{(n)} + \dfrac{1}{\lambda}[I(x,y) - R(p^{(n)},q^{(n)})]\dfrac{\partial R^{(n)}}{\partial q} \end{cases} \tag{7}$$

3 Convergence Problem

Using discrete grid form, the neighbors of p and q can be written as:

$$\overline{p}(i,j) = \frac{1}{4}[p(i-1,j)+p(i+1,j)+q(i,j-1)+q(i,j+1)]$$

$$\overline{q}(i,j) = \frac{1}{4}[q(i-1,j)+q(i+1,j)+q(i,j-1)+q(i,j+1)]$$

$$(8)$$

At the same time the partial derivatives of the surface gradients can be approximated by backward differences:

$$p_x = p(i+1,j)-p(i,j), \quad p_y = p(i,j+1)-p(i,j)$$

$$q_x = q(i+1,j)-q(i,j), \quad q_y = q(i,j+1)-q(i,j)$$

$$(9)$$

Because the surface gradients of the boundary points can not be predicted, we need introduce the nature boundary conditions, that is, the partial derivatives of the surface gradients are zeros. The surface gradients of the four vertexes of the image can be substituted by the surface gradient of the adjoining diagonal pixels. The surface gradient of the four boundaries of the image can be calculated by the extrapolation of the surface gradient of the inner pixels.

Since the synthetic image has no real surface, so the error computation can be done by using the common Horn's method, that is, regarding the energy function as the converge judgment criterion of the iterative process. With the increase of iterative number, the energy function will decrease gradually. When the calculate result closes the real value, the energy function will automatically go to the infinite minimum.

The implementation of the algorithm is given as followed:

Step1: Given the initialization to the weight factor and initial conditions

Step2: Compute the mean $\overline{p}, \overline{q}$ of the (p,q)

Step3: Compute $(p^{(n+1)}, q^{(n+1)})$ using the iterative formulae

Step4: If satisfy the convergence judgment criterion then stop; otherwise go to the step2

4 Experimental Results

According to the Lambertian reflectance law generating the synthetic image which represents the change of the object shape is the simple and effective way of verifying the 3D surface reconstruct. The experimental images come from the Yale Face Database B. The face surface reflectance characteristic accords with the Lambertian reflectance law. The light source direction is

$$(\cos \tau \sin \alpha, \sin \tau \sin \alpha, \cos \alpha) = (0.5662, 0.6919, -0.4481)$$

The size of the images is 112×92.

At first we select experientially the initial weight factor $\lambda = 0.1$ (Since for the smooth Lambertian surface, the change of the intensity is very slow, so in the error function, the brightness constraint is still dominant). Let all the arrays of the surface gradient (p, q) be zeros. Let the iterative boundary condition be that boundary height is zero. And then we use the energy function as the judgment criterion of the iterative convergence. In order to get reasonable results for the prototype images with light source $(0,0,1)$, we used $(0.001, 0.001, 1)$ instead as the light source direction. The synthetic results are shown in Fig. 1(a) (the input image is the frontal image) and Fig.2 (a) (the input image is the non-frontal image), and 3D surface reconstruction maps are shown in Fig. 1(b) and Fig. 2(b).

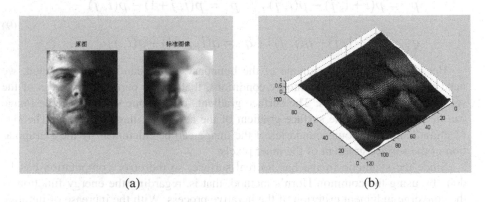

(a)   (b)

Fig. 1. (a) frontal input image and recovered prototype image. (b) 3D surface reconstruction

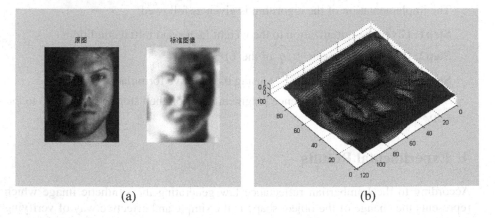

(a)   (b)

Fig. 2. (a) non-frontal input image and recovered prototype image. (b) 3D surface reconstruction

From Fig. 1 and Fig. 3 we can see that our algorithm is effective for not only the frontal symmetric face but also the non-frontal non-symmetric face. And in this example, the nose, eyes and lips are recovered reasonably, as shown in the 3D surface reconstruction in Fig. 1(b) and Fig. 2(b).

In Fig. 3, the error-iteration curve of the frontal input image and the non-frontal input image are shown.

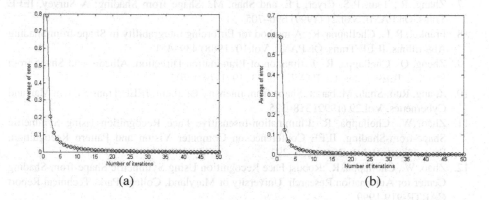

(a)   (b)

Fig. 3. (a) error-iteration curve of frontal input image. (b) error-iteration curve of non-frontal input image

5 Conclusion

We improve the iterative algorithm of recovering the shape of the object using a single image, and give the flow chart of the algorithm, and synthesis image under the ideal light source and reflectance material. The experimental result shows that our algorithm can reconstruct reasonably the 3D face surface, and fast converge, so verify the validity of the algorithm.

Acknowledgement

This project was supported by NSFC (No. 60144001), NSF of GuangDong, P.R. China(No. 021766).

References

1. Atick, J.J., Griffin, P.A., Redlich, A.N. :Statistical Approach to Shape From Shading: Reconstruction of Three-Dimensional Face Surfaces from Single Two-Dimensional Images. Neural Computation. Vol.8(6) (1996)
2. Lengagne, R., Fua, P., Monga, O. :3D stereo reconstruction of human face driven by differential constraints. Image and Computing. Vol. 18 (2000) 337–343
3. Ikeuchi, K. and Horn, B.K.P. :Numerical shape from shading and occluding boundaries. Artificial Intelligence. 17(1-3) (1981) 141–184

4. Horn, B.K.P. :Shape from Shading: A Method for Obtaining the Shape of a Smooth Opaque Object from One View. PhD thesis, MIT, 1970
5. Pentland, A.P. :Local shading analysis. IEEE Trans. On PAMI. Vol.6 (1984) 170–187
6. Pentland, A. :Shape information from shading: a theory about human perception. In Proceedings of International Conference on Computer Vision. (1988) 404–413
7. Zhang, R., Tsai, P-S, Cryer, J.E. and Shah, M. :Shape from Shading: A Survey. IEEE Trans. On PAMI. Vol.21 (1999) 690–705
8. Frankot, R.T., Chellappa, R. :A method for Enforcing integrability in Shape from Shading Algorithms. IEEE Trans. On PAMI. Vol.10 (1988) 439–451
9. Zheng, Q., Chellappa, R. :Estimation of Illumination Direction, Albedo, and Shape from Shading. IEEE Trans. On PAMI. Vol.13 (1991) 680–702
10. Zhang, Ruo, Shah, Mubarak :Shape from Intensity Gradient. IEEE Trans System Man and Cybernetics. Vol.29 (1999) 318–325,
11. Zhao, W., Chellappa, R. :Illumination-Insensitive Face Recognition Using Symmetric Shape-from-Shading. IEEE Conference on Computer Vision and Pattern Recognition, Proceedings. Vol. 1 (2000) 286–293
12. Zhao, W., Chellappa, R. :Robust Face Recognition Using Symmetric Shape-from-Shading. Center for Automation Research ,University of Maryland, College Park, Technical Report CARTR-919,1999
13. Zhao, W., Chellappa, R., Rosenfeld, A. and Phillips, P.J. :Face Recognition: A Literature Survey. ACM Computing Surveys. Vol. 35(4) (2003) 399–458
14. Fanany, M.I., Kumazawa, I. :Analysis of Shape from Shading Algorithms for Fast and Realistic 3D Face Reconstruction APCCAS2002., Circuits and Systems. APCCAS '02. 2002 Asia-Pacific Conference on, Vol.2 (2002.) 181–185

Recent Advances in Subspace Analysis
for Face Recognition

Qiong Yang[1] and Xiaoou Tang[2]

[1] Microsoft Research Asia, Beijing
t-qiyang@microsoft.com
[2] Chinese University of Hong Kong, Department of Information Engineering,
Shatin, Hong Kong
xtang@ie.cuhk.edu.hk

Abstract. Given the unprecedented demand on face recognition technology, it is not surprising to see an overwhelming amount of research publications on this topic in recent years. In this paper we conduct a survey on subspace analysis, which is one of the fastest growing areas in face recognition research. We first categorize the existing techniques in subspace analysis into four categories, and present descriptions of recent representative methods within each category. Then we discuss three main directions in recent research and point out some challenging issues that remain to be solved.

1 Introduction

In the past decade, face recognition has grown into one of the hottest research areas of image analysis and understanding. It is such a challenging yet interesting problem that it has attracted researchers from many different backgrounds, including psychology, pattern recognition, neural networks, computer vision, and computer graphics. A large number of algorithms have been developed in this field, such as pure geometry methods [1], subspace analysis [2~22], elastic graph matching [23,24], neural network [25,26], hidden Markov model [27], active appearance model [28], deformable intensity surface [29], and morphable model [30]. Among them, subspace analysis is one of the most important and successful branches since it outperforms other algorithms in a variety of famous international competitions such as FERET, FRVT2000, FRVT2002, XM2VTS, and BANCA.

The earliest work on subspace analysis may be traced to Oja [31], and it was introduced into face recognition by Kirby et al. [2,3] and Turk et al. [4] around 1990. The algorithm they used is well-known as Principal Component Analysis (PCA) or Eigenface. After that, many algorithms have been proposed for further improvements, including View-based Modular Eigenspace [5], Probabilistic Visual Learning [6], Bayesian Matching [7], Fisherface [8,9], Direct LDA (D-LDA) [10], Nullspace LDA (N-LDA) [11], Pair-wise LDA [12], Regularized Discriminant Analysis (RDA) [13], Kernel PCA/LDA [14], Local Feature Analysis (LFA) [15], Independent Component Analysis (ICA) [16], Independent Subspace Analysis (ISA) [17], Topological ICA

S.Z. Li et al. (Eds.): Sinobiometrics 2004, LNCS 3338, pp. 275–287, 2004.

[18], Principal Manifold [19], Isometric Feature Mapping (ISOMAP) [20], Locally Linear Embedding (LLE) [21], and Local Non-negative Matrix Factorization [22].

This paper will provide a critical survey of new advances in subspace analysis for face recognition in the past two years. The reasons are as follows. Firstly, subspace analysis is one of the fastest growing fields in face recognition. It attracts much attention of the research community and many new algorithms have emerged recently. It also leads the state-of-the-art research directions in recognizing faces. Secondly, subspace analysis covers some intrinsic problems in face recognition such as dimensionality, discrimination, and parameter estimation. Studying this field could help us better understand the nature of face recognition. Thirdly, it has wide applications in other research areas such as web search, data mining, signal processing and analysis, in addition to face recognition. Advances in subspace analysis will accelerate the progress in these fields beyond face related applications.

The paper will be organized as follows: In Sect. 2, we first categorize the existing techniques in subspace analysis into four categories, and present descriptions of recent representative methods within each category. Then we point out three main directions in recent research and some challenging issues in Sect. 3. Finally, a summary will be given in Sect. 4.

2   Subspace Analysis for Face Recognition

In subspace analysis, we generally compact the original data from a high-dimensional space into a considerably low dimensional subspace, and then design classifiers in the subspace. Therefore, it will naturally face a big challenge, that is, "Will the subspace be good enough to replace the original space?" This has two implications. On the one hand, by reducing the dimensionality of data space, it alleviates the risk of bad estimation and improves the generalization capability. However it may cause the loss of discriminative information. How to balance these two sides is not trivial. In addition, when the distribution is non-Gaussian, learning the manifold becomes necessary. Accordingly, we categorize the existing techniques in subspace analysis into the following four categories:

(1) *Reconstruction-Based Methods.* These methods generally try to construct a subspace which has least reconstruction error. Representative works include PCA [2~4], LFA [15], Kernel PCA [14], and View-based Modular Eigenspace [5].
(2) *Discrimination-Based Methods.* Typically, in these methods, best discrimination instead of best reconstruction is pursued as the objective function, e.g. Fisherface [8,9], direct LDA [10], null space LDA [11], and pair-wise LDA [12].
(3) *Factor-Based Methods.* This can be traced to factor analysis. The aim is to find a solution which best removes the statistical dependence between factors. ICA [16], ISA [17], and Topological ICA [18] are some typical algorithms in this category.
(4) *Manifold-Based Methods.* These methods seek to best detect the essential manifold structure, and various algorithms have been developed such as Principal Manifold [19], ISOMAP [20], and LLE [21].

2.1 Reconstruction-Based Approaches

In this field, recent advances in the past two years are multi-linear subspace analysis [32], symmetrical PCA [33], two-dimensional PCA [34], and eigenbands [35].

Multi-linear subspace analysis was proposed by Vasilescu and Terzopoulos [32]. It addressed subspace analysis within multi-linear framework via dimensionality reduction over the multiple affiliated vector spaces. It is based on a tensor decomposition known as the N-mode SVD, which is a natural extension to higher-order tensors of the conventional matrix SVD in PCA. The ensemble is represented as a higher-order tensor, which is decomposed into the product of a core tensor and several factor-specific mode matrices. The core tensor characterizes the interaction between the various factors, each of which is represented explicitly by a mode matrix whose orthonormal column vectors are factor-specific basis vectors. Its superior facial recognition rate relative to standard PCA was demonstrated by experiments on Weizmann.

Symmetrical Principal Component Analysis (SPCA) was proposed by Yang and Ding [33]. It provides a unique way to apply facial symmetry in face recognition by combining PCA with the even-odd decomposition principle. In the beginning, each image in the training set is decomposed into the sum of an even symmetrical image and an odd symmetrical one, forming an even symmetrical image set and an odd counterpart. Next, PCA analysis is implemented on these two sets respectively, and both even symmetrical PCA features and odd symmetrical ones are extracted. Then, all the features are selected altogether according to their energy ratios in faces and sensitivities to pattern variations. Finally, the classifier is designed on the selected features. This algorithm is valuable in at least four aspects. Firstly, it utilizes facial symmetry to increase available information, and thus performs better than the conventional PCA. Secondly, it naturally translates both the original image set and the mirror image set to be zero-mean, and thereby describes the largest statistical variation directions of samples more accurately than methods in [3] and [36]. Thirdly, it separates the even symmetrical components from the odd ones in order to select more even symmetrical features which are more stable than the odd symmetric ones. Finally, by even-odd decomposition, it exploits the symmetry in computation and memory allocation, and thus saves computational cost and the storage space.

Yang and Zhang [34] addressed the face representation in 2-D image matrices rather than 1-D vectors. Different from PCA, it constructed the image covariance matrix directly using the original image matrices, and extracted the features using the principal eigenvectors of this image covariance matrix. Another approach called Eigenbands was introduced by Cavalcanti et al. [35]. It divided the faces into vertical and horizontal bands, and extracted features using standard PCA for each band.

In general, reconstruction-based approaches are far less effective for face recognition than the discrimination-based approaches which we will discuss next. However, it may be used as a preprocessing step to reduce the high dimensions.

2.2 Discrimination-Based Approaches

Most approaches in this category were proposed to improve the conventional Linear Discriminant Analysis (LDA). In [37], Wang and Tang proposed a method using random subspace and bagging to improve Fisherface and N-LDA respectively. By random sampling on feature vector and training samples, multiple stabilized Fisherface and N-LDA classifiers were constructed. The two kinds of complementary classifiers were integrated using a fusion rule, so nearly all the discriminative information was preserved. This approach was also applied to the integration of multiple features to build a robust face recognition system integrating shape, texture, and Gabor responses. On the XM2VTS face database, it achieved 99.83% rank-1 accuracy, much better than Eigenface, Fisherface, Bayesian Matching and Elastic Bunch Graph Matching [24].

Another work by Wang and Tang is the dual-space LDA [38]. It addresses the small-sample-size problem of LDA to take full advantage of the discriminative information in the face space. Based on a probabilistic visual model, the eigenvalue spectrum in the null space of the within-class scatter matrix is estimated, and discriminant analysis is simultaneously applied in both the principal subspace and the null subspace of the within-class scatter matrix. The two sets of discriminative features are finally combined for recognition. In the experiments on FERET FA/FB dataset, it outperforms Fisherface, direct LDA, and null space LDA.

Using entirely different methods, the random sampling LDA and the dual-space LDA preserve discriminative information in both the principal subspace and the null space. It remains interesting to investigate the difference and possible integration of these two approaches. In addition, it may also be possible to integrate them with the unified framework [39] we will discuss next.

The unified framework was developed by Wang and Tang [39]. Based on a face difference model that decomposes face difference into three components, intrinsic difference, transformation difference, and noise, the inherent relationship among three subspace methods, PCA, Bayesian Matching, and LDA, and their unique contributions to the extraction of discriminative information were analyzed. This eventually led to the construction of a 3D parameter space that used three subspace dimensions as axis. Better recognition performance than the standard subspace methods were achieved on the FERET dataset.

Generalized Singular Value Decomposition (GSVD) was used in [40] and [41] to overcome the limitation of the conventional LDA when the scatter matrices are singular. In [40], GSVD was proposed as a generalization of discriminant analysis, and it can be applied even when the sample size is smaller than the dimension of the sample data. In addition, it provides a mathematical framework for better understanding of the singular case of the conventional linear discriminant analysis. In [41], the approximation algorithm for GSVD was presented. It reduces the computational complexity by finding sub-clusters of each cluster and using their centroids to capture the structure of each cluster. Experiments showed that the approximation algorithm produced results rather close to the exact GSVD algorithm.

On kernel-based discriminant analysis, Lu et al. [42] presented a kernel version of the D-LDA algorithm. It deals with both the nonlinearity of the face pattern distribution and the small-sample-size problem in most face recognition tasks. The new algorithm was tested on the multi-view UMIST face dataset. Results indicate that the error rate is approximately 34% of that of Kernel PCA and 48% of that of Generalized Discriminant Analysis (GDA) respectively. Lu et al. [43] also applied regularization on Direct LDA to further combat the small-sample-size problem in very high dimensional face image space. Direct Fractional-Step LDA [44] is another LDA related method by Lu et al. It utilizes a variant of D-LDA to safely remove the null space of the between-class scatter matrix and applies a fractional step LDA scheme to enhance the discriminatory power of the obtained D-LDA feature space. The effectiveness is reported by experiments on the UMIST and ORL datasets. Boosting LDA [45] was also developed by Lu et al. It utilizes a boosting algorithm to form a mixture of LDA models. With the introduction of the Pair-wise Class Discriminant Distribution (PCDD), a strong connection between the boosting algorithm and the LDA-based learners is built. By manipulating PCDD, a set of LDA sub-models can be produced in a manner of automatic gain control. Experiments on the FERET dataset report that it is effective on both boosting power and robustness against overfitting.

An improved LDA approach of Jing et al. [46] improves the discrimination technique in three areas. Firstly, it discards those discrimination vectors whose Fisher discrimination values are less than 0.5. Secondly, it combines Uncorrelated Optimal Discrimination Vector (UODV) and Fisherface to satisfy the statistical uncorrelation between discrimination vectors. Thirdly, it computes the Fisher discriminability of each principal component, and selects them from large to small until a threshold is met. Experimental results on different image databases showed the advantage of the method over LDA.

In [47], Yang and Ding proposed an algorithm called Discriminant Local Feature Analysis to provide a new solution for the small-sample-size problem in LDA. It applies LFA instead of PCA before LDA. On the one hand, LFA captures local characteristics with little loss of global information. On the other hand, it presents an effective low-dimensional representation of signals, and thus reduces the dimensionality for LDA.

The work in [48] by Liu et al. is a continuation and extension of Kernel Fisher Discriminant Analysis (KFDA). They not only proposed Cosine kernel to increase the discriminating capability of the original polynomial kernel function, but also adopted a geometry-based feature vector selection scheme to reduce the computational complexity of KFDA. Experiments were carried out on a database with 125 persons and 970 images, and they demonstrated the effectiveness of the new algorithm.

About selection of kernel parameters, Huang et al. [49] designed a new criterion and derived a new formation in optimizing the parameters in RBF kernel based on the gradient descent algorithm. Instead of setting the same parameters for all kernels, it individually optimizes the kernel parameters of RBF functions. The proposed formulation was further integrated into a subspace LDA algorithm for better face recognition. They also employed a component-based linear discriminant analysis method in [50] to solve the one training sample problem. The local facial feature component bunches were constructed by moving each local feature region in four directions, and subspace LDA was applied on each local component bunches.

Liu et al. [51] incorporated the kernel technique into the null space LDA which utilizes Cosine kernel instead of polynomial kernel; Marcel [52] added the even symmetric virtual samples into the training set to deal with the small-sample-size problem in LDA; Wu et al. [53] utilized a variant of discriminant analysis criterion to exploit the strength of the direct LDA algorithm; Liu et al. [54] developed a kernel scatter-difference based discriminant analysis to not only describe complex nonlinear variations but also avoid the singularity problem of the within-class scatter matrix.

2.3 Factor-Based Approaches

These methods can be traced to factor analysis. The aim is to find a solution which best removes the statistical dependence between factors. ICA is their typical algorithm, and most new advances lie in its improvements and applications.

In [55], Kim et al. applied ICA in the facial local residue space. They separated a face image into several facial components, and each facial component is represented by the ICA bases of its corresponding residual space. Experimental results show that the accuracy of face recognition is improved for large illumination and pose variations.

In [56], Liu and Wechsler combined Gabor, PCA, ICA, and PRM together to achieve 98.5% accuracy rate for the FERET dataset and 100% accuracy rate for the ORL dataset. Liu and Wechsler [57] also performed ICA in a subspace reduced by principal component analysis (PCA). The dimensionality of the PCA space is determined by balancing two competing criteria: the representation criterion for adequate data representation, and the magnitude criterion for enhanced performance.

Other works are from Huang et al. [58], Fortuna et al. [59], and Sengupta et al. [60] Huang et al. [58] adopted genetic algorithm to select ICA features. Fortuna et al. [59] treated ICA as the pre-filter of PCA subspace representation for illumination invariant face recognition. Sengupta et al. [60] presented a non-parametric approach to the ICA problem that is robust towards outlier effects. The algorithm starts from the very definition of independence itself, and it employs a kernel density estimation to provide a good approximation of the distributions.

2.4 Manifold-Based Approaches

In this area, new works include Locality Preserving Projection (LPP) [61], Embedded Manifold [62], Nearest Manifold Approach [63], and Discriminant Manifold Learning [64].

LPP [61] is a new method which finds an embedding that preserves local information, and it obtains a face space that best detects the essential manifold structure. In the beginning, an adjacency graph was constructed to model the local structure of the face manifold. Then, a locality preserving subspace for face representation was learned by using Locality Preserving Projections (LPP). The face subspace preserves local structure, and thus has more discriminating power than eigenfaces. Moreover, the locality preserving property makes the algorithm insensitive to the unwanted variations due to changes in pose, illumination, and expression. Better performance than Eigenface and Fisherface were shown on Yale, CMUPIE, and MSRA datasets.

Embedded Manifold [62] was proposed by Yan et al. to conduct discriminant analysis in term of the embedded manifold structure. They first proposed the Intra-Cluster Balanced K-Means (ICBKM) clustering to ensure that there are balanced samples for the classes in a cluster. Then, the local discriminative features for all clusters were simultaneously calculated by following the global Fisher criterion. It has the following three characteristics: 1) it is approximately a locally linear yet globally nonlinear discriminant analyzer; 2) it can be considered a special case of kernel discriminant analysis (KDA) with geometry-adaptive-kernel; and 3) its computation and memory cost are reduced significantly compared to traditional KDA. Experiments on YALE and PIE datasets show that it outperforms LDA, Mixture LDA, and Kernel LDA with Gaussian kernel.

Zhang et al. [63] presented a nearest manifold approach for face recognition. It adopts a manifold learning algorithm (MLA) for learning a mapping from high-dimensional manifold into the intrinsic low-dimensional linear manifold, and the nearest manifold (NM) criterion for the classification. Wu et al. [64] developed a discriminative manifold learning method which achieved the discriminative embedding from the high dimensional face data into a low dimensional hidden manifold. Unlike LLE, ISOMAP, and Eigenmap, this algorithm used the Relevance Component Analysis (RCA) to achieve nonlinear embedding and data discrimination instead of reconstruction. Also, a CK-nearest neighborhood rule was proposed to achieve better neighborhood construction.

2.5 Other Approaches

In the above discussion, most of the latest works have been covered. However, there are still some papers which are difficult to be categorized into any of the above four categories. Here we give a brief review.

One work is from Li and Tang [65]. They developed a direct Bayesian-based support vector machine in which SVM was trained to classify the face difference between intra personal variation and extra-personal variation. The improved performance over traditional subspace methods was reported by experiments on the FERET and XM2VTS datasets. Tang et al. also developed several new algorithms to apply subspace analysis to video-based face recognition [66], and sketch-based face recognition [67] with interesting results.

In [68], a method named nearest intra-class space (NICS) was presented. In the method, an intra-class subspace is constructed, and the classification is based on the nearest weighted distance between the query face and each intra-class subspace.

A comparison of subspace analysis for face recognition was provided by Li et al. [69] In particular, they studied four subspace representations, PCA, ICA, Fisher discriminant analysis (FDA), and probabilistic PCA (PPCA), and their 'kernelized' versions if available. Comparisons are conducted on two databases with three typical variations of face images, i.e. poses, illuminations and expressions.

3 Discussions and Challenges

It is interesting to point out that there are mainly three directions in subspace analysis for face recognition in the past two years. They are dimensionality reduction, discrimination preservation, and nonlinear learning.

(1) *Dimensionality Reduction.* The keynote of dimensionality reduction is to alleviate the conflict between the small sample size and high feature dimension. To achieve this, there are generally three approaches:

(a) *Partial Image.* This method divides the facial image into several parts. These parts sometimes are facial components, such as in component-based LDA [50] and Eigenbands [35], and sometimes are columns or rows, such as in 2D-PCA [34]. Kim et al. [55] also used partial image to improve ICA.

(b) *Feature Projection.* This method usually finds an optimal projection according to some objective function, and thereby projects the data from the original high-dimensional space into a lower-dimensional subspace. Liu [57] applied PCA before ICA; Yang and Ding [33] developed a new method for dimensionality reduction by combining PCA with the even-odd decomposition principle. In [47], LFA was applied to reduce the dimensionality for LDA.

(c) *Feature Selection.* Different from feature projection, feature selection pays more attention on how to form an optimal subset of features instead of finding an optimal projection, e.g. Huang and Luo [58] adopted genetic algorithm to select ICA features.

(2) *Discrimination Preservation.* The emphasis of these approaches is how to preserve discrimination. Wang and Tang [37] seek to fully exploit the discriminative information by firstly sampling a small subset of PCA features and secondly combining multiple stable LDA classifiers with each constructed on a feature subset. They further integrate this random subspace scheme with bagged N-LDA to preserve more discriminative information since Fisherface and N-LDA are complementary. With similar purpose yet a different approach, they [38] separate the total space of within-class matrix into principal subspace and null subspace, and then combine them to take full advantage of the discriminative information in the whole face space. Jing et al. [46] regard that only discriminative principal components should be selected to reduce the discrepancy between the training set size and the feature vector length. Howland et al. [40] and Ye et al. [41] both seek the solution for discrimination preservation from a mathematical framework. They applied the generalized singular value decomposition to circumvent the non-singularity requirement.

(3) *Nonlinear Learning*. The distribution of face images, under a perceivable variation in viewpoint, illumination or facial expression etc, is highly nonlinear and complex. Nonlinear learning methods try to deal with this nonlinearity of the face pattern
distribution. Some methods [42][51] work on kernelizing N-LDA or D-LDA. Some
[48,49] focus on choosing kernel functions or optimal parameters of kernel function.
Others try to find the essential manifold structure [61~64].

From above, we can see that there is much improvement in subspace analysis in
recent two years. However, there are still many challenging problems to be solved.
We list a few here.

(1) *How to determine the dimensionality of the subspace? Or what's the intrinsic
dimensionality of the face space?*
Currently, many approaches use empirical methods to set the dimensionality.
Could we get a theoretical solution?
(2) *How to define face-specific discrimination criteria?*
Most current works are constrained in a framework similar to LDA. However,
LDA is a general-purpose subspace method that has been developed long before face
recognition was even a research topic. Could we find better discrimination strategy?
(3) *How to describe the nonlinearity of face patterns?*
This means, how does the variation such as pose, illumination or expression influence the feature space of human faces?
(4) *What is the upper bound of face recognition?*
This is apparently application and dataset dependent. Given a database, when can
we confidently give an upper bound?
(5) *Larger databases are needed.*

Without larger and more difficult database, we cannot move forward, or at least it
is difficult to show that we are moving forward without new database.

4   Summary and Future Work

In this paper, we have presented a critical survey of new advances in subspace analysis for face recognition in the past two years. By categorizing them into four categories: reconstruction-based approaches, discrimination-based approaches, factor-based
approaches, and manifold-based approaches, we reviewed recent representative methods within each category.
To conclude, we give a brief summary of our discussions:

(1) Although significant improvements have been achieved in this field, subspace
analysis is still one of the hottest topics in face recognition.
(2) Most of the new advances focus on dimensionality reduction, discrimination
preservation, and nonlinear learning.
(3) Many difficult problems remain to be solved such as the intrinsic dimensionality,
the nonlinearity, and the new discrimination criteria of face space.
(4) Face recognition is such a complex problem that it cannot be completely solved
by subspace analysis alone. It is interesting to design fusion system to integrate mul-

tiple features or classifiers. Better features and adaptive learning may be another two promising topics in research on face recognition.

References

1. Bledsoe, W.: The Model Method in Facial Recognition. Panoramic Research Inc., Palo Alto (1964)
2. Sirovich, L., Kirby, M.: Low-dimensional Procedure for the Characterization of Human Faces. Journal of the Optical Society of America A 4 (1987) 519–524
3. Kirby, M., Sirovich, L.: Application of the Karhunen-Loéve Procedure for the Characterization of Human Faces. IEEE Trans. On Pattern Analysis and Machine Intelligence 12 (1990) 103–108
4. Turk, M., Pentland, A.: Eigenface for Recognition. Journal of Cognitive Neuroscience 3 (1991) 72–86
5. Pentland, A., Moghaddam, B., Starner, T.: View-based and Modular Eigenspaces for Face Recognition. Proc. IEEE Int'l Conf. on Computer Vision and Pattern Recognition (1994) 84–91
6. Moghaddam, B., Pentland, A.: Probabilistic Visual Learning for Object Representation. IEEE Trans. On Pattern Analysis and Machine Intelligence 19 (1997) 696–710
7. Moghaddam, B., Jebara, T., Pentland, A.: Bayesian Face Recognition. Pattern Recognition 33 (2000) 1771–1782
8. Swets, D. L., Weng, J.: Using Discriminant Eigenfeatures for Image Retrieval. IEEE Trans. On Pattern Analysis and Machine Intelligence 18 (1996) 831–836
9. Belhumeur, P. N., Hespanha, J. P., Kriegman, D. J.: Eigenfaces vs. Fisherfaces: Recognition Using Class Specific Linear Projection. IEEE Trans. On Pattern Analysis and Machine Intelligence 19 (1997) 711–720
10. Yu, H., Yang, J.: A Direct LDA Algorithm for High-dimensional Data with Application to Face Recognition. Pattern Recognition 34 (2001) 2067–2070
11. Chen, L., Liao, H., Ko, M., Lin J., Yu, G.: A New Lda-based Face Recognition System Which Can Solve the Small Samples Size Problem. Journal of Pattern Recognition 33 (2000) 1713–1726
12. Loog, M., Duin, R. P. W., Haeb-Umbach, R. Multiclass Linear Dimension Reduction by Weighted Pairwise Fisher Criteria. IEEE Trans. On Pattern Analysis and Machine Intelligence 23 (2001) 762–766
13. Friedman, J. H.: Regularized Discriminant Analysis. Journal of the American Statistical Association 84 (1989) 165–175
14. Schölkopf, B. Nonlinear Component Analysis as a Kernel Eigenvalue Problem. Neural Computation 10 (1998) 1299–1319
15. Penev, P. S., Atick, J. J.: Local Feature Analysis: A General Statistical Theory for Object Representation. Network Computation in Neural Systems 7 (1996) 477–500
16. Bartlett, M. S., Movellan J. R., Sejnowski, T. J.: Face Recognition by Independent Component Analysis. IEEE Trans. On Neural Networks 13 (2002)1450–1464
17. Hyvärinen, A., Hoyer, P. O.: Emergence of Phase and Shift Invariant Features by Decomposition of Natural Images into Independent Feature Subspaces. Neural Computation 12 (2000) 1705–1720
18. Hyvärinen, A., Hoyer P. O., Inki, M.: Topographic Independent Component Analysis. Neural Computation 13 (2001) 1525–1558

19. Moghaddam, B.: Principal Manifolds and Bayesian Subspaces for Visual Recognition. Proc. 7th IEEE Int'l Conf. On Computer Vision (1999) 1131–1136
20. Tenenbaum, J. B., Silva V., Langford, J. C.: A Global Geometric Framework for Nonlinear Dimensionality Reduction. Science 290 (2000) 2319–2323
21. Roweis, S. T., Saul, L. K.: Nonlinear Dimensionality Reduction by Locally Linear Embedding. Science 290 (2000) 2323–2326
22. Li, S. Z., Hou, X. W., Zhang, H. J., Cheng, Q. S.: Learning Spatially Localized Parts-Based Representation. Proc. Int'l Conf. Computer Vision and Pattern Recognition(2001) 207–212
23. Lades, M., Vorbrüggen, J. C., Buhmann, J., Lange, J., Malsburg, C., Würtz, R. P., Konen, W.: Distortion Invariant Object Recognition in the Dynamic Link Architecture. IEEE Trans. On Computers 42 (1993) 300–311
24. Wiskott, L., Fellous, J. M., Krüger, N., Malsburg, C.: Face Recognition by Elastic Bunch Graph Matching. IEEE Trans. Pattern Analysis and Machine Intelligence 19(1997)775–779
25. Kohonen, T.: Associative Memory: A System Theoretic Approach. Springer-Verlag, Berlin (1977)
26. Kung, S. Y., Taur, J. S.: Decision-based Neural Networks with Signal Image Classification Applications. IEEE Trans. On Neural Networks 6 (1995) 170–181
27. Samaria, F., Young, S.: HMM Based Architecture for Face Identification. Image and Computer Vision 12 (1994) 537–583
28. Cootes, T. F., Edwards, G. J., Taylor, C. J.: Active Appearance Models. IEEE Trans. On Pattern Analysis and Machine Intelligence 23 (2001) 681–685
29. Moghaddam, B., Nastar, C., Pentland, A.: Bayesian Face Recognition Using Deformable Intensity Surfaces. Proc. IEEE Int'l Conf. on Computer Vision and Pattern Recognition (1996) 638–645
30. Blanz, V., Vetter, T.: A Morphable Model for the Synthesis of 3D Faces. Proc. SIGGRAPH (1999) 187–194
31. Oja, E.: Subspace Methods of Pattern Recognition. Research Studies Press, Letchworth (1983)
32. Vasilescu, M. A. O., Terzopoulos, D.: Multilinear Subspace Analysis of Image Ensembles. Proc. IEEE Int'l Conf. on Computer Vision and Pattern Recognition (2003) 93–99
33. Yang, Q., Ding, X. Q.: Symmetrical Principal Component Analysis and Its Application in Face Recognition. Chinese Journal of Computers 26 (2003) 1146–1151
34. Yang, J., Zhang, D.: Two-Dimensional PCA: A New Approach to Appearance-Based Face Representation and Recognition. IEEE Trans. Pattern Analysis and Machine Intelligence 28 (2004) 131–137
35. Cavalcanti, G. D. C., Filho, E. C. B. C.: Eigenbands Fusion for Frontal Face Recognition. Proc. IEEE Int'l Conf. on Image Processing (2003) 665–668
36. Etemad, K., Chellappa, R.: Face Recognition Using Discriminant Eigenvector. Proc. IEEE Int'l Conf. On Acoustics, Speech, and Signal Processing (1996) 2148–2151
37. Wang, X., Tang, X.: Random Sampling LDA for Face Recognition. Proc. IEEE Int'l Conf. on Computer Vision and Pattern Recognition (2004) 259–265
38. Wang, X., Tang, X.: Dual-space Linear Discriminant Analysis for Face Recognition. Proc. IEEE Int'l Conf. on Computer Vision and Pattern Recognition (2004) 564–569
39. Wang, X., Tang, X.: Unified Subspace Analysis for Face Recognition. Proc. IEEE Int'l Conf. on Computer Vision (2003) 679–686
40. Howland, P., Park, H.: Generalized Discriminant Analysis Using the Generalized Singular Value Decomposition. IEEE Trans. On Pattern Analysis and Machine Intelligence 26 (2004) 995–1006

41. Ye, J. P., Janardan, R., Park, C. H., Park, H.: An Optimization Criterion for Generalized Discriminant Analysis on Undersampled Problems. IEEE Trans. On Pattern Analysis and Machine Intelligence 26 (2004) 982–994
42. Lu, J. W., Plataniotis, K. N., Venetsanopoulos, A. N.: Face Recognition Using Kernel Direct Discriminant Analysis Algorithms. IEEE Trans. Neural Networks 14(2003) 117–126
43. Lu, J. W., Plataniotis, K. N., Venetsanopoulos, A. N.: Regularized D-LDA for Face Recognition. Proc. IEEE Int'l Conf. on Acoustics, Speech, and Signal Processing (2003) 125–128
44. Lu, J. W., Plataniotis, K. N., Venetsanopoulos, A. N.: Face Recognition Using LDA-based Algorithms. IEEE Trans. On Neural Networks 14 (2003) 195–200
45. Lu, J. W., Plataniotis, K. N., Venetsanopoulos, A. N.: Boosting Linear Discriminant Analysis for Face Recognition. Proc. IEEE Int'l Conf. on Image Processing (2003) 657–660
46. Jing, X. J., Zhang, D., Tang, Y.-Y., An Improved LDA Approach. IEEE Trans. On Systems, Man, and Cybernetics 34 (2004) 1942–1951
47. Yang, Q., Ding, X. Q.: Discriminant Local Feature Analysis of Facial Images. IEEE Int'l Conf. on Image Processing (2003) 863–866
48. Liu, Q., Lu, H., Ma, S.: Improving Kernel Fisher Discriminant Analysis for Face Recognition. IEEE Trans. On Circuits and Systems for Video Technology 14 (2004) 42–49
49. Huang, J., Yuen, P. C., Chen, W. S., Lai, J. H.: Kernel Subspace LDA with Optimized Kernel Parameters on Face Recognition. IEEE Proc. Int'l Conf. on Automatic Face and Gesture Recognition (2004)
50. Huang, J., Yuen, P. C., Chen, W. S., Lai, J. H.: Component-based LDA Method for Face Recognition with One Training Sample. IEEE Int'l Workshop on Analysis and Modeling of Faces and Gestures (2003) 120–126
51. Liu, W., Wang, Y., Li, S. Z., Tan, T.: Null Space-based Kernel Fisher Discriminant Analysis for Face Recognition. IEEE Proc. Int'l Conf. on Automatic Face and Gesture Recognition (2004)
52. Marcel, S.: A Symmetric Transformation for LDA-based Face Verification. IEEE Proc. Int'l Conf. on Automatic Face and Gesture Recognition (2004)
53. Wu, X. J., Kittler, J., Yang, J. Y., Messer, K., Wang, S.: A New Direct LDA Algorithm for Feature Extraction in Face Recognition. IEEE Proc. Int'l Conf. on Pattern Recognition (2004) 545–548
54. Liu, Q., Tang, X., Lu, H., Ma, S.: Kernel Scatter-Difference Based Discriminant Analysis for Face Recognition. Proc. IEEE Int'l Conf. on Pattern Recognition (2004) 419–422
55. Kim, T. K., Kim, H., Hwang, W., Kee, S.-C., Kittler, J.: Independent Component Analysis in a Facial Local Residue Space. IEEE Proc. Int'l Conf. on Computer Vision and Pattern Recognition (2003) 579–586
56. Liu, C., Wechsler, H.: Independent Component Analysis of Gabor Features for Face Recognition. IEEE Trans. on Neural Networks 14 (2003) 919–928
57. Liu, C.: Enhanced Independent Component Analysis and Its Application to Content Based Face Image Retrieval. IEEE Trans. on Systems, Man and Cybernetics 34 (2004) 1117–1127
58. Huang, Y., Luo, S.: Genetic Algorithm Applied to ICA Feature Selection. Proc. Int'l Joint Conf. on Neural Networks (2003) 704–707
59. Fortuna, J., Capson, D.: ICA Filters for Lighting Invariant Face Recognition. Proc. IEEE Int'l Conf. on Pattern Recognition (2004) 334–337
60. Sengupta, K., Burman, P.: Non-parametric Approach to ICA Using Kernel Density Estimation. Proc. IEEE Int'l Conf. on Multimedia and Expo (2003) 749–752
61. He, X., Yan, S. C., Hu, Y. X., Zhang, H. J.: Learning a Locality Preserving Subspace for Visual Recognition. IEEE Proc. Int'l Conf. on Computer Vision (2003) 178–185

62. Yan, S. C., Zhang, H. J., Hu, Y. X., Zhang, B. Y., Cheng, Q. S.: Discriminant Analysis on Embedded Manifold. European Conf. on Computer Vision (2004) 121–132
63. Zhang, J., Li, S. Z., Wang, J.: Nearest Manifold Approach for Face Recognition. Proc. IEEE Int'l Conf. on Automatic Face and Gesture Recognition (2004) 223–228
64. Wu, Y., Chan, K. L., Wang, L.: Face Recognition based on Discriminative Manifold Learning. Proc. IEEE Int'l Conf. on Pattern Recognition (2004) 171–174
65. Li, Z., Tang, X.: Bayesian Face Recognition Using Support Vector Machine and Face Clustering. Proc. Int'l Conf. Computer Vision and Pattern Recognition (2004) 374–380
66. Tang, X., Li, Z.: Frame Synchronization and Multi-level Subspace Analysis for Video based Face Recognition. Proc. IEEE Int'l Conf. on Computer Vision and Pattern Recognition (2004) 902–907
67. Tang, X., Wang, X.: Face Sketch Synthesis and Recognition. Proc. IEEE Int'l Conf. on Computer Vision (2003) 687–694
68. Liu, W., Wang, Y., Li, S. Z., Tan, T.: Nearest Intra-Class Space Classifier for Face Recognition. IEEE Proc. Int'l Conf. on Pattern Recognition (2004)
69. Li, J., Zhou, S., Shekhar, C.: A Comparison of Subspace Analysis for Face Recognition. Proc. IEEE Int'l Conf. on Acoustics, Speech, and Signal Processing (2003) 121–124

Component-Based Cascade Linear Discriminant Analysis for Face Recognition

Wenchao Zhang[1], Shiguang Shan[2], Wen Gao[1], Yizheng Chang[1], and Bo Cao[2]

[1] School of Computer Science and Technology, Harbin Institute of Technology,
150001 Harbin, P.R. China
{wczhang, yzchang}@jdl.ac.cn
[2] ICT-ISVISION Joint R&D Laboratory for Face Recognition, CAS,
100080 Beijing, P.R. China
{sgshan, wgao, bcao}@ict.ac.cn

Abstract. This paper presents a novel face recognition method based on cascade Linear Discriminant Analysis (LDA) of the component-based face representation. In the proposed method, a face image is represented as four components with overlap at the neighboring area rather than a whole face patch. Firstly, LDA is conducted on the principal components of each component individually to extract component discriminant features. Then, these features are further concatenated to undergo another LDA to extract the final face descriptor, which actually have assigned different weights to different component features. Our experiments on the FERET face database have illustrated the effectiveness of the proposed method compared with the traditional Fisherface method both for face recognition and verification.

1 Introduction

Over the past 20 years, numerous algorithms have been proposed for face recognition. See detailed surveys [1][2][3]. In the following we will give a brief overview of face recognition methods.

In the early researches, methods based on geometric feature and template matching used to be popular technologies, which were compared in 1992 by Brunelli and Poggio. Their conclusion showed that template matching based algorithms outperformed the geometric feature based ones [4]. Therefore, since the 1990s, methods based on appearance have been dominant researches. In these methods, each pixel in a face image is considered as a coordinate in a high-dimensional space and the classification is carried out in a low-dimensional feature space projected from the image space.

In this paper, we outline a new approach for face recognition named by component-based cascade LDA. Thus, we divide face recognition techniques into the global approach and the component-based approach as [5].

S.Z. Li et al. (Eds.): Sinobiometrics 2004, LNCS 3338, pp. 288–295, 2004.

In the global approach, a feature vector that represents the whole face image is used as the input of a classifier. Several classifiers have been proposed in the literature: minimal distance classification in the eigenspace [6][7], Fisher's discriminant analysis [8], and the neural network [9]. However, they are not robust against pose changes since global features are highly sensitive to translation and rotation of the face [5]. To avoid this problem, an alignment should be added before classifying the face [10][11].

In contrast with the global approaches, another way is classifying local facial components. [12] performs face recognition in independently matching templates of three facial regions. Elastic Bunch Graph Matching (EBGM)[13][14] is another typical instance, which is based on Gabor wavelet coefficients computed on the nodes of the elastic graph.

In this paper, we present a component-based face descriptor with cascade LDA for face recognition. First, we split a face image into four components and reduce the dimension of each of the four components by PCA plus LDA. Next, the four feature vectors obtained from PCA plus LDA are combined into one feature vector. At last, the new vector enters LDA as an input.

Following is the outline of the paper: Section 2 gives a brief overview of PCA and LDA algorithms. Section 3 describes the component-based approach. Section 4 explains the component-based Cascade LDA approach. Experimental results and conclusions are presented in Section 5 and 6, respectively.

2 PCA Plus LDA

2.1 PCA

Nowadays, a technique commonly used for dimensionality reduction in computer vision-particularly in face recognition-is principal components analysis (PCA) [7]. Let a set of N face images $\{\mathbf{x}_1, \mathbf{x}_2 ..., \mathbf{x}_N\}$ take values in an n-dimensional image space and let W represent the linear transformation that maps the original n-dimensional space onto a m-dimensional feature subspace where $m \ll n$. The new feature vectors $\mathbf{y}_i \in \mathfrak{R}^m$ are defined by the following linear transformation:

$$\mathbf{y}_i = W^T \mathbf{x}_i \quad i = 1, 2, ..., N \tag{1}$$

where $W \in \mathfrak{R}^{n \times m}$ is a matrix with orthonormal columns. The columns of W are the eigenvectors $\mathbf{e}_i$ obtained by solving the eigenstructure decomposition

$$\lambda_i \mathbf{e}_i = U \mathbf{e}_i \tag{2}$$

Where

$$U = \sum_{i=1}^{N} (\mathbf{x}_i - \boldsymbol{\mu})(\mathbf{x}_i - \boldsymbol{\mu})^T \tag{3}$$

is the covariance matrix and λ_i is the eigenvalue associated with the eigenvector $\mathbf{e}_i$. In PCA, the projection matrix W_{opt} is chosen to maximize the determinant of the total scatter matrix of the projected samples, i.e.,

$$W_{opt} = \arg\max \left| W^T U W \right| = \left[\mathbf{e}_1 \; \mathbf{e}_2 \ldots \mathbf{e}_m \right] \tag{4}$$

where $\left\{ \mathbf{e}_i \mid i = 1, 2, \ldots, m \right\}$ is the set of n-dimensional eigenvectors of U corresponding to the m largest eigenvalues.

2.2 LDA

Linear Discriminant Analysis (LDA) [15] is a class specific method in the sense that it can represent data in form which is more useful for classification. Given a set of N images $\{\mathbf{x}_1, \mathbf{x}_2, \ldots, \mathbf{x}_N\}$, assume each image belongs to one of the c classes $\{X_1, X_2, \ldots, X_c\}$, and LDA selects a linear transformation matrix $\mathbf{W}$ in such a way that the ratio of the between-class scatter and the within-class scatter is maximized.

Mathematically, the between-class scatter matrix and the within-class scatter matrix are defined by

$$\mathbf{S}_B = \sum_{i=1}^{c} N_i (\boldsymbol{\mu}_i - \boldsymbol{\mu})(\boldsymbol{\mu}_i - \boldsymbol{\mu})^T \tag{5}$$

and

$$\mathbf{S}_W = \sum_{i=1}^{c} \sum_{\mathbf{x}_k \in X_i} (\mathbf{x}_k - \boldsymbol{\mu}_i)(\mathbf{x}_k - \boldsymbol{\mu}_i)^T \tag{6}$$

respectively, where $\boldsymbol{\mu}_i$ denotes the mean image of class X_i and N_i denotes the number of images in class X_i. If $\mathbf{S}_W$ is nonsingular, LDA will find an orthonormal matrix $\mathbf{W}_{opt}$ maximizing the ratio of the determinant of the between-class scatter matrix to the determinant of the within-class scatter matrix. That is, the LDA projection matrix is represented by

$$\mathbf{W}_{opt} = \arg\max_{\mathbf{W}} \frac{\left| \mathbf{W}^T \mathbf{S}_B \mathbf{W} \right|}{\left| \mathbf{W}^T \mathbf{S}_W \mathbf{W} \right|} = \left[\mathbf{w}_1 \quad \mathbf{w}_2 \quad \cdots \quad \mathbf{w}_m \right] \tag{7}$$

The set of the solution $\{\mathbf{w}_i \mid i = 1, 2, \ldots, m\}$ is that of the generalized eigenvectors of $\mathbf{S}_B$ and $\mathbf{S}_W$ corresponding to the m largest eigenvalues $\{\lambda_i \mid i = 1, 2, \ldots, m\}$, i.e.,

$$\mathbf{S}_B \mathbf{w}_i = \lambda_i \mathbf{S}_W \mathbf{w}_i, i = 1, 2, \ldots, m \tag{8}$$

In order to overcome the singularity of $\mathbf{S}_W$, PCA reduces the vector dimension before applying LDA. Each LDA feature vector is represented by the vector projections

$$\mathbf{y}_k = \mathbf{W}_{opt}^{\;\;T} \mathbf{x}_k, \; k = 1, 2, \ldots, N. \tag{9}$$

3 Component-Based Cascade LDA Face

Component-based face descriptors are less statistically complex than global image descriptors. The linear transformation like PCA/LDA in a component region becomes more suitable than that in the global image region. In addition, separated facial components overlap with neighboring components and the relationship is important to describe personal characteristics for face recognition [16].

Our method uses a component-based representation and we divide a face image into four overlapped components. An example of facial component division is shown in Figure.1.

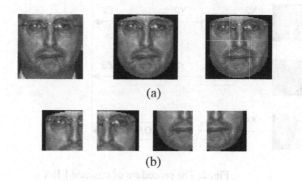

(a)

(b)

Fig. 1. An example of facial component separation

LDA is applied to the facial components separately to learn the most class-distinguishable basis vectors in each local region and the feature vectors of these components are combined into a new vector, then LDA is applied to the new combined vector. The procedure of the component-based cascade LDA is shown in figure 2.

3.1 Face Description

Firstly, the PCA transformation matrices are extracted. Given a set of N images $\{\mathbf{x}_1, \mathbf{x}_2, ..., \mathbf{x}_N\}$, each of the images is divided into four facial components according to the facial component separation definition. Each component patches are grouped and represented in a vector form; to the f th component, $\{\mathbf{x}_1^f, ..., \mathbf{x}_N^f\}$ $f = 1,2,...,4$, the corresponding PCA matrix is U^f. The reduced vector of each component for the N face images is

$$\mathbf{y}_n^f = (U^f)^T \mathbf{x}_n^f, f = 1,2,...,4; n = 1,2,...,N \qquad (10)$$

Secondly, LDA is applied to the set of the reduced vector of each component. For the f th facial component, the corresponding LDA matrix W^f is computed. Thus, the feature vectors obtained are computed by

$$\mathbf{z}_n^f = \left(W^f\right)^T \mathbf{y}_n^f, f = 1,2,\ldots,4; n = 1,2,\ldots,N. \tag{11}$$

At last, we combine the $\mathbf{z}_n^f$ s into a new vector $\mathbf{z}$, and LDA is applied to the new vector. The cascade LDA matrix is V, thus, the feature vector is computed by

$$\mathbf{s} = V^T \mathbf{z} \tag{12}$$

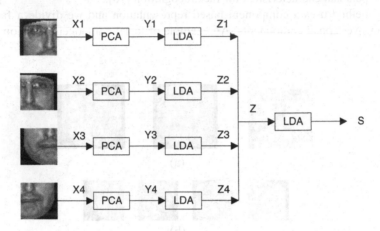

Fig. 2. The procedure of cascade LDA

4   Experimental Result

Identification and verification of a person's identity are two potential areas in application of face recognition systems. In identification, a system identifies an unknown face in an image. In verification, a system confirms the claimed identity of a face presented to it [17].

Thus, we have tested our face recognition algorithm in identification and verification respectively on the FERET test set which has been widely used to evaluate face recognition algorithms [18].

4.1   Experiments on FERET Face Database

There are 1002 images in the training set and all of the images come from parts of fa (regular facial expression) and fb (alternative facial expression) sets. The gallery consisted of images of 1,196 people with one image per person. In the probe category, there are 1195 images of FB.

All images are cropped and rectified according to the manually located eye positions supplied with the FERET data. We scale the images to 32 pixels height by 32 pixels width. To reduce the influence caused by different hairstyles and backgrounds, a mask is put on the face image. Figure 1(a) shows the cropped face image that is put on mask. Figure 1(b) shows an example of a face image in FERET set that is divided into four components.

The experimental results are presented in figure 3 and figure 4. The former shows the algorithm performance of the identification, and the latter shows the algorithm performance of the verification. In the figures, ➤ denotes our algorithm and ■ denotes the conventional LDA algorithm.

In the verification problem, we achieve a 1.6% equal error rate while that of the conventional LDA is 2.0%. The equal error rate is the point at which the percentage of correct verifications equals one minus the percentage of false alarms [19]. In the recognition problem, where there are 1196 gallery images and 1195 probe images, we achieve a rank-1 recognition rate of 93.47% while that of the conventional LDA is 91.8%. The verification and the identification experimental results are shown in figure 3 and figure 4 respectively.

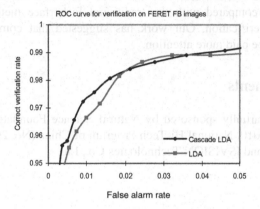

Fig. 3. ROC curve for verification task on FERET FB probe sets. The equal error rates are about 1.6% in Cascade LDA and 2% in LDA

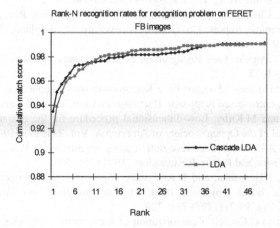

Fig. 4. Rank-N recognition rates for FERET FB images

5 Conclusion

In this paper, we have presented a novel face recognition method based on cascade Linear Discriminant Analysis (LDA) of the component-based face representation. In our method, a face image is divided into four components with overlap at the neighboring area according to the facial organs. This is quite different from the traditional method such as Eigenface or Fisherface that process the whole face patch in one time. We first perform LDA on each component individually to extract component discriminant features. Then, these features are further concatenated to undergo another LDA to extract the final face descriptor. Actually, the final LDA procedure has assigned different weights to different component features. Our experiments on the FERET face database have illustrated the effectiveness of the proposed method compared with the traditional Fisherface method both for face recognition and verification. Our work has suggested that component-based face descriptor should be paid more attention.

Acknowledgements

This research is partially sponsored by Natural Science Foundation of China under contract No.60332010, National Hi-Tech Program of China (No. 2001AA114190 and 2002AA118010), and ISVISION Technologies Co., Ltd.

References

1. Samal, P.A.IyenGar.: Automatic Recognition and Analysis of Human Faces and Facial Expressions: A Survey. Pattern Recognition. Vol. 25(1) (1992) 65–77
2. R.Chellappa, C.L.Wilson, S. Sirohey.: Human and Machine Recognition of faces: A survey. Proc. of the IEEE. Vol. 83(5) (1995.5) 705–740
3. W. Zhao, R. Chellappa, A. Rosenfeld and P. J. Phillips: Face Recognition: A Literature Survey, Technical Report, CS-TR4167, University of Maryland, 2000. Revised 2002, CS-TR4167R
4. R.Brunelli, T.Poggio: Face Recognition. Features versus Template, TPAMI. Vol. 15(10) (1993) 1042–1052
5. B.Heisele, P.Ho and T.Poggio: Face Recognition with Support Vector Machine: Global versus Component-based Approach. International Conference on Computer Vision. (2001)
6. L.Sirovitch and M.Kirby: Low-dimensional procedure for the characterization of human faces. Journal of the Optical Society of America A. Vol. 2 (1987) 519–524
7. M.Turk and A.Pentland: Face recognition using eigenfaces. In Proc. IEEE Conference on Computer Vision and Pattern Recognition. (1991) 586–591
8. P.Belhumer, P.Hespanha, and D.Kriegman: Eigenfaecs vs fisherfaces: recognition using class specific linear projection. IEEE Transactions on Pattern Analysis and Machine Intelligence. Vol. 19(7) (1997) 711–720
9. M.Fleming and G.Cottrell: Categorization of faces using unsupervised feature extraction. In Proc. IEEE IJCNN International Joint Conference on Neural Networks. (1990) 65–70

10. B.Moghaddam, W.Wahid, and A.Pentland: Beyond eigenfaces: probabilistic matching for face recognition. In Proc. IEEE International Conference on Automatic Face and Gesture Recognition. (1998) 30–35
11. A.Lanitis, C.Taylor, and T.Cootes: Automatic interpretation and coding of face images using flexible models. IEEE Transactions on Pattern Analysis and Machine Intelligence. Vol. 19(7) (1997) 743–756
12. P.Penev and J.Atick: Local Feature Analysis: A General Statistical Theory for Object Representation. Network: Computation in Neural Systems. Vol.7 (1996) 477–500
13. J.Zhang, Y.Yan, M.Lades: Face Recognition: Eigenface, Elastic Matching and Neural Nets. Proceedings of the IEEE. Vol.85(9) (1997) 1422–1435
14. L.Wiskott, J.M.Fellous, N.Kruger and C.V.D.Malsburg: Face Recognition by Elastic Bunch Graph Matching. IEEE Trans. On PAMI. Vol. 19(7) (1997) 775–779
15. R.Duda, P.Hart and D.Stork: Pattern Classification. Wiley Interscience, USA, Second Edition
16. T.-K. Kim, H. Kim, W. Hwang, S.C. Kee and J.H. Lee: Component-based LDA Face Descriptor for Image Retrieval. BMVC (2002)
17. S. Rizvi, P.J. Phillips, and H. Moon: The FERET Verification Testing Protocol for Face Recognition Algorithm, Image and Vision Computing J. to appear
18. P.Jonathon Phillips, Hyeonjoon Moon, Syed A. Rizvi, and Patrick J. Rauss: The FERET Evaluation Methodology for Face-Recognition Algorithms. IEEE Transactions on Pattern Analysis and Machine Intelligence. Vol. 22(10) (2000) 1090–1104
19. M.J.Jones, P.Viola: Face Recognition Using Boosted Local Features, Technical Report, MITSUBISHI ELECTRIC RESEARCH LABORATORIES, (2003) TR2003–25 April

Unified Locally Linear Embedding and Linear Discriminant Analysis Algorithm (ULLELDA) for Face Recognition

Junping Zhang[1], Huanxing Shen[2], and Zhi-Hua Zhou[3]

[1] Intelligent Information Processing Laboratory,
Fudan University, Shanghai 200433, China
[2] School of Software, Fudan University, Shanghai 200433, China
{jpzhang, 0158088}@fudan.edu.cn
[3] National Laboratory for Novel Software Technology,
Nanjing University, Nanjing 210093, China
zhouzh@nju.edu.cn

Abstract. Manifold learning approaches such as locally linear embedding algorithm (LLE) and isometric mapping (Isomap) algorithm are aimed to discover the intrinsical low dimensional variables from high-dimensional nonlinear data. While, in order to achieve effective recognition tasks based on manifold learning, many problems remain to be solved. In this paper, we propose unified algorithm based on LLE and linear discriminant analysis (ULLELDA) for those remained problems. First, training samples are mapped into low-dimensional embedding space and then LDA algorithm is used to project samples into discriminant space for enlarging between-class distances and decreasing within-class distance. Second, the unknown samples are directly mapped into discriminant space without the computation of the corresponding one in the low-dimensional embedding space. Experiments on several face databases show the advantages of the proposed algorithm.

1 Introduction

Faces with varying intrinsic features such as illumination, pose, expression, are thought of to constitute highly nonlinear manifolds in the high-dimensional observation space [1]. Visualization and exploration of high-dimensional nonlinear manifolds, therefore, become the focus of much of the current machine learning research. However, most recognition systems using linear method are bound to ignore subtleties of manifolds such as concavities and protrusions, which is a bottleneck for achieving highly accurate recognition. This problem has to be solved before we can build up a high performance recognition system.

During these years progresses have been made in modelling nonlinear subspaces or manifolds. Rich literature exists on manifold learning. On the basis of different representations of manifold learning, they can be roughly divided into four major classes: projection methods, generative methods, embedding methods, and mutual information methods.

S.Z. Li et al. (Eds.): Sinobiometrics 2004, LNCS 3338, pp. 296–304, 2004.

1. The first one is to find principal surfaces passing through the middle of data, such as the principal curves [2][3]. Although geometrically intuitive, this one has difficulty in how to generalize the global variable–arc-length parameter– into higher-dimensional surface.
2. The second one adopts generative topology models [4] [5], and hypothesizes that observed data are generated from the evenly spaced low-dimensional latent nodes. Then the mapping relationship between the observation space and the latent space can be modelled. Resulting from the inherent insufficiency of the adopted EM (Expectation and Maximization) algorithms, nevertheless, the generative models fall into local minimum easily and also have slow convergence rates.
3. The third one is generally divided into global and local embedding algorithms. ISOMAP [6], as a global algorithm, presumes that isometric properties should be preserved in both the observation space and the intrinsic embedding space in the affine sense. On the other hand, Locally Linear Embedding (LLE) [7] and Laplacian Eigenamp [8] focus on the preservation of local neighbor structure.
4. In the fourth category, it is assumed that the mutual information is a measurement of the differences of probability distribution between the observed space and the embedded space, as in stochastic nearest neighborhood (henceforth SNE) [9] and manifold charting [10].

While there are many impressive results about how to discover the intrinsical features of the manifold,few reports are published on the practical applications on manifold learning, especially on face recognition. A possible explanation is that the practical data includes a large number of intrinsic features and has high curvature both in the observation space and in the embedded space, whereas present manifold learning methods strongly depends on the selection of parameters.

Assuming that data are drawn independently and identically distributed from the underlying unknown distribution, we propose unified locally linear embedding and linear discriminant analysis algorithm for face recognition. Training samples are projected into the intrinsic low-dimensional space. To improve classification ability, LDA is introduced for enhancing between-class distances and decreasing within-class distances through mapping sample into the discriminant space. Based on the assumption that the neighborhood of unknown sample in the high-dimensional space is the same as that of sample in the low-dimensional discriminant space, finally, the unknown sample is directly mapped into discriminant space with the proposed algorithm. Experiments on several face databases show the advantages of the proposed recognition approaches. In the final section we discuss potential problems and further researches.

2 Unified Locally Linear Embedding and Linear Discriminant Analysis Algorithm (ULLELDA)

2.1 Locally Linear Embedding

To establish the mapping relationship between the observed data and the corresponding low-dimensional one, the locally linear embedding (LLE) algorithm [7] is used to obtain the corresponding low-dimensional data Y ($Y \subset \mathbb{R}^d$) of the training set X ($X \subset$

$\mathbb{R}^N, N \gg d$). Then the data set (X, Y) is used for modelling the subsequently mapping relationship.

The main principle of LLE algorithm is to preserve local neighborhood relation of data in both the embedding space and the intrinsic one. Each sample in the observation space is a linearly weighted average of its neighbors. The basic LLE algorithm is described as follows:

Step 1: Define

$$\psi(W) = \| x_i - \sum_{j-1}^{K} W_{ij} x_{ij} \|^2 \tag{1}$$

Where samples x_{ij} are the neighbors of x_i. Considering the constraint term $\sum_{j=1} W_{ij} = 1$, and if x_i and x_{ij} are not in the same neighbor, $W_{ij} = 0$, compute the weighted matrix W according to the least square.

Step 2: Define

$$\varphi(Y) = \| y_i - \sum_{j=1}^{K} W_{ij}^* y_{ij} \|^2 \tag{2}$$

where $W^* = arg\ \min_w \psi(W)$. Considering the constraint $\sum_i y_i = 0$ and $\sum_i y_i y_i^T / n = I$, where n is the number of local covering set. Calculate $Y^* = arg\ \min_Y \varphi(Y)$.

Step 2 of the algorithm is to approximate the nonlinear manifold around sample x_i with the linear hyperplane that passes through its neighbors $\{x_{i1}, \ldots, x_{ik}\}$. Considering that the objective $\varphi(Y)$ is invariant to translation in Y, constraint term $\sum_i y_i = 0$ is added in the step 2. Moreover, the other term $\sum_i y_i y_i^T / n = I$ is to avoid the degenerate solution of $Y = 0$. Hence, the step 2 is transformed to the solution of eigenvector decomposition which can be seen as follows:

$$
\begin{aligned}
Y^* &= arg\ \min_Y \phi(Y) \\
&= \| y_i - \sum_{j=1}^{K} W_{ij}^* y_{ij} \|^2 \\
&= arg\ \min_Y \| (I - W)Y \|^2 \\
&= arg\ \min_Y Y^T (I - W)^T (I - W)Y
\end{aligned}
\tag{3}
$$

The optimal solution of Y^* in Formula (3) is the smallest eigenvectors of matrix $(I - W)^T (I - W)$. With respect to the constraint conditions, the eigenvalue which is zero need to be removed. So we need to compute the bottom $(d + 1)$ eigenvectors of the matrix and discard the smallest eigenvector considering constraint term.

2.2   Linear Discriminant Analysis

Assuming the data of different classes have the same or similar categories, for instance, facial images sampled from difference persons are generally thought of owning the same cognitive concept. So data of different classes can be reduced into the same subspace with manifold learning approaches. While manifold learning is capable of recovering the intrinsic low-dimensional space, it may not be optimal for recognition. When the two highly nonlinear manifolds are mapped into the same low-dimensional subspace, there is no reason to believe that the optimal classification hyperplane also exists between the two unravelled manifolds. If the principal axes of the two low-dimensional mapping classes of manifolds have an acute angle, for example, the classification ability may be impaired [11]. Therefore, linear Discriminant analysis (LDA) is introduced to maximize the separability of data among different classes.

Suppose that each class is the equal probability of event, Within-class scatter matrix is therefore defined as: $S_w = \sum_{i=1}^{L} \sum_{j=1}^{n_i} (y_j - m_i)(y_j - m_i)^T$ for n_i samples from class i with class means m_i, $i = 1, 2, \ldots, L$. For the overall mean m for all samples from all classes, meanwhile, the between-class scatter matrix is defined as $S_b = \sum_{i=1}^{L} (m_i - m)(m_i - m)^T$ [11].

To maximize the between-class distances while minimizing the within-class distances of manifolds, the column vectors of discriminant matrix W are the eigenvectors of $S_b^{-1} S_w$ associated with the largest eigenvalues. Then Projection matrix W play a role that projects a vector in the low-dimensional face subspace into discriminatory feature space which can be formulated as follows:

$$Z = YW \quad Z \in R^{d'}, Y \in R^d, W \in R^{d' \times d} \tag{4}$$

2.3 The Proposed ULLELDA Algorithm

It is not difficult to see that the mentioned procedure comprises two steps. Data are first mapped into the intrinsic low-dimensional space based on LLE and then are mapped into the discriminant space based on LDA. In the paper, we expect to unify the two algorithm with one step only so that the computational effectiveness is improved.

Considering the nearest neighbor of unknown sample, the weighted values among unknown data and training data are first calculated based on the idea of LLE idea. The basis formula can be written as follows:

$$\phi(W') = \|x_i' - \sum_{j=1}^{K} w_{i'j} x_{i'j}\| \quad x_{i'j} \in X \in R^N \tag{5}$$

Where x_i' means the ith unknown sample, and $x_{i'j}$ the corresponding training samples according to the K values.

As soon as the weighted values of each neighbor samples of the unknown sample are obtained, we presume that the data in the high-dimensional space have the same neighborhood relationship as in the low-dimensional discriminant space. Therefore, the unified mapping formulate can be seen as follows:

$$z_i' = \sum_{i=1}^{K} W_{ij} z_{i'j} \quad z_{i'j} \in Z \in R^{d'} \tag{6}$$

Where z' is the corresponding one of the unknown samples in the discriminant space, $z_{i'j}$ are the closely training samples which have been obtained through the mentioned two steps and the neighbor indices are the same as that of sample in the original high-dimensional space.

Finally, recognition is carried out on the discriminant spaces. The proposed approach has several advantages: 1) Data are directly mapped into the discriminant space without the computation of the intrinsic low-dimensional space. 2) For classification, the neighbor relationship of the unknown sample implicitly embodies the capacity of discriminant analysis.

3   Experiments

To verify the proposed ULLELDA approach, three face databases (ORL database [12], UMIST database [13] and JAFFE database [14]) are investigated. Some examples can be seen in Figure 1 to Figure 3. The training samples and test samples are randomly separated without overlapping, the detail can be seen in Table 1. In the paper, the intensity of each pixel is regarded as one dimension. For example, 112*92 pixel is equal to 10304

Fig. 1. Examples of ORL Face Database

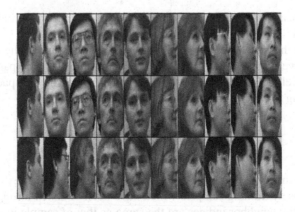

Fig. 2. Examples of UMIST Face Database

neutral happiness sadness surprise anger disgust   fear

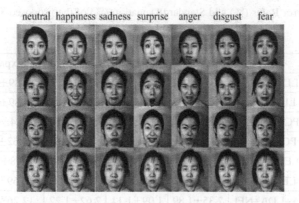

Fig. 3. Examples of JAFFE Face Database

Table 1. The number of training samples (TR) and test samples (TE) of each classes

	TR	TE	classes	Dimensions
ORL	200	200	40	$112 * 92$
UMIST	200	375	20	$112 * 92$
JAFFE	60	153	10	$146 * 111$
Expression	168	45	7	$146 * 111$

dimensions. All the samples are standardized to the range [0,1]. The results are the average of 100 runs.

For comparing the effectiveness of dimensionality reduction of the proposed approach, experiments are also performed on LLE and PCA [15], respectively. When using LLE for dimensionality reduction, for instance, test samples are first mapped into the intrinsic low-dimensional space based on the same mapping approaches as ULLELDA.

The dimensions of LLE-reduced data are set to be 150 except for JAFFE (where the dimension is 50). For the 2nd mapping (LDA-based reduction), the reduced dimension is generally no more than $L - 1$. otherwise eigenvalues and eigenvectors will have complex values. Actually, we remain the real-value part of complex values when the 2th reduced dimensions are higher than $L - 1$. In addition, neighbor factor K of LLE algorithm need to be predefined. Through broad experiments, we found that the selection of neighbor factor has little impact on result of the final recognition. Without loss of generality, we set K be 40 for ORL , UMIST and JAFFE expression database, 20 for JAFFE Face database.

Finally, two classification algorithms (1-nearest neighbor algorithm and nearest feature line (NFL) [16]) is adopted for final recognition. The corresponding combinational algorithm, for example, the combination of ULLELDA and NFL, is abbreviated with ULLELDA+NFL. Due to the adopted dimensionality reduction approaches are different, the experimental result of each algorithm listed in Table 2 is the lowest error rate under

Table 2. The Error Rates (%) and Standard Deviation (%) of the proposed algorithm and other algorithms

	ORL	UMIST	JAFFE	Express
LLE+NFL	4.35± 1.42	3.79±2.14	4.50±1.76	11.89± 5.14
LLE+NN	7.01±1.83	5.78±2.49	5.955±1.97	13.489± 5.212
PCA+NFL	8.27±2.41	9.65±2.7	5.435±1.74	17.4±6.16
PCA+NN	10.12±2.06	11.29±2.85	8.38±1.88	32.62±6.85
ULLELDA+NFL	4.06±1.4	2.144±1.45	2.40±1.18	10.8±5.14
ULLELDA+NN	4.13±1.33	2.18±1.38	2.20±1.22	10.69±5.26
PCA+LDA+NFL	7.35±1.89	1.09±1.11	2.62±1.22	12.26±4.95
PCA+LDA+NN	7.45±1.92	0.93±1.05	2.59±1.21	10.82±5.28

corresponding reduced dimensions. For example, the error rate of ULLE+NFL for ORL is obtained with 19 dimensions.

For better analysis, one of the recognition tasks is conducted in Figure 4. From the figure we can see that the proposed algorithm has better performance with either NFL or NN approaches. More experimental results will be presented in a longer version of this paper.

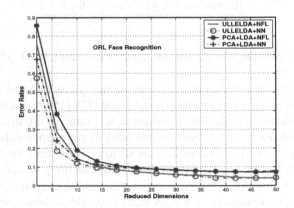

Fig. 4. ORL Face Recognition

It is clear to see that the proposed approach obtains improvements compared with LLE algorithm isolated or PCA. When LDA is introduced for both LLE and PCA, the recognition performances of the two approaches are comparable. Based on our observation, we can summarize it into two parts: 1) The proposed algorithm combine LLE and LDA with one step, some structure information may loss and therefore lead the decrease of recognition rate. Actually, we have implement different mapping approach (manifold learning algorithm) for face recognition, and some experimental results are better than that of the proposed ULLELDA algorithm. The detail can be seen in [17]. 2) For some high-dimensional data, the nonlinearity are inherent on the intrinsic variables other than generated by the nonlinear mapping of intrinsic variables. On this condition, LDA may be unsuitable for further recognition.

4   Conclusions

In this paper, we propose ULLELDA algorithm for face recognition. First, training set is projected into the intrinsic low-dimensional space and then LDA is adopted to enhance between-class distances and decrease within-class distances. Second, the unknown samples are projected into the discriminant space directly without the computation of corresponding counterpart in the low-dimensional space. Experiments show that the proposed algorithm is better than the LLE algorithm and PCA algorithm for recognition, and is comparable to the PCA+LDA approach.

However, several problems are worthy making further researches. First, we observe that the selection of neighbor factor K is relate to the error rates of recognition. We will study the feasibility of using ensemble approach to solve the problems[18]. Second, the proposed ULLELDA algorithm has lower recognition rate in some databases compared with the proposed MLA approach with LDA. [17]. The possible reason may be that the projection procedure of test sample based on the neighbor factor does not consider the distribution of data set and therefore the global structure information can not be embodied effectively. Finally, we will compare our proposed dimensionality reduction approach with the state-of-the-art approaches in the future.

Acknowledgements

This work was supported by 2003-HT-FD05 and the National Outstanding Youth Foundation of China under the Grant No. 60325207.

References

1. Haw-Minn Lu, Yeshaiahu Fainman, and Robert Hecht-Nieslen, "Image Manifolds", *in Proc. SPIE*, vol. 3307, pp.52-63, 1998.
2. T. Hastie, and W. Stuetzle, "Principla Curves," *Journal of the American Statistical Association*, 1988, 84(406), pp. 502-516.
3. B. Kégl, A. Krzyzak, T. Linder, and K. Zeger, (2000),"Learning and design of principal curves",*IEEE Transactions on Pattern Analysis and Machine Intelligence*, vol. 22, no. 3, pp. 281-297.
4. C.M. Bishop, M. Sevensen, and C.K.I. Williams, "GTM:The generative topographic mapping," *Neural Computation*, 1998,10, pp. 215-234.
5. K. Chang and J. Ghosh, (2001),"A unified model for probabilistic principal surfaces," *IEEE transactions on Pattern Analysis and Machine Intelligence*, 23(1), pp. 22-41.
6. J. B. Tenenbaum, de Silva, V.& Langford, J.C, "A global geometric framework for nonlinear dimensionality reduction,"*Science*, 2000, 290, pp. 2319-2323.
7. S. T. Roweis, and K. S. Lawrance, "Nonlinear Dimensionality reduction by locally linear embedding", *Science*, 2000, 290, pp. 2323-2326.

8. Mikhail Belkin, and Partha Niyogi, "Laplacian Eigenmaps for Dimensionality Reduction and Data Representation",2001.
9. G. Hinton and S. Roweis, "Stochastic Neighbor Embedding," *Neural Information Proceeding Systems: Natural and Synthetic*, Vancouver, Canada, December 9-14, 2002.
10. M. Brand, MERL, "Charting a manifold," *Neural Information Proceeding Systems: Natural and Synthetic*, Vancouver, Canada, December 9-14, 2002.
11. Daniel L. Swets and John (Juyang) Weng, (1996), "Using Discriminant Eigenfeatures for Image Retrieval", *IEEE Transactions on Pattern Analysis and Machine Intelligences*, Vol. 18, No. 8, pp.831-836.
12. F. S. Samaria, *"Face Recognition Using Hidden Markov Models"*,PhD thesis, University of Cambridge, 1994.
13. H. Wechsler, P. J. Phillips, V. Bruce, F. Fogelman-Soulie and T. S. Huang (eds), "em Characterizing virtual Eigensignatures for General Purpose Face Recognition", Daniel B Graham and Nigel M Allinson. In *Face Recognition: From Theory to Applications*; NATO ASI Series F, Computer and Systems Sciences, Vol. 163, pp. 446-456, 1998.
14. Michael J. Lyons, Julien Budynek, and Shigeru Akamatsu, "Automatic classification of Single Facial Images", *IEEE Transactions on Pattern Analysis and Machine Intelligence*, vol.21, no. 12, pp. 1357-1362, 1999.
15. M. Turk, and A. Pentland, "Eigenfaces for Recognition", *Journal of Cognitive Neuroscience*, vol 3, no.1, 1991, pp.71-86.
16. Stan Z. Li, K.L. Chan and C.L. Wang. "Performance Evaluation of the Nearest Feature Line Method in Image Classification and Retrieval". *IEEE Transactions on Pattern Analysis and Machine Intelligence*, 22(11):1335-1339. November, 2000.
17. Junping Zhang, Stan Z. Li, and Jue Wang, "Manifold Learning and Applications in Recognition". in *Intelligent Multimedia Processing with Soft Computing*. Yap Peng Tan, Kim Hui Yap, Lipo Wang (Ed.), Springer-Verlag, Heidelberg, 2004.
18. Opitz, D. and Maclin, R. "Popular ensemble methods : an empirical study". *J. Art. Intell. Research*, 11, 169-198,1999.

On Dimensionality Reduction for Client Specific Discriminant Analysis with Application to Face Verification

Xiaojun Wu[1,2,3], Kittler Josef[2], Jingyu Yang[4], Messer Kieron[2],
Shitong Wang[5], and Jieping Lu[1]

[1] Jiangsu University of Science and Technology, Zhenjiang, P. R. China 212003
[2] CVSSP, University of Surrey, GU2 7XH, Surrey, UK
[3] Robotics Laboratory, Chinese Academy of Sciences, Shenyang, P. R. China 110015
[4] School of Information, Nanjing University of Science & Technology,
Nanjing, P. R. China 210094
[5] School of Information and Control, Southern Yangtze University,
Wuxi, P. R. China 214036

Abstract. In this paper we propose a study on dimensionality reduction for client specific discriminant analysis with application to face verification. A new algorithm of face verification based on client specific discriminant analysis is developed. Two aspects of improvement are made in the new algorithm. First, a dimensionality reduction based on the between-class scatter matrix is introduced which is more efficient than that based on the population scatter matrix. The second improvement lies in the use of a new Fisher criterion function which is introduced in order to reduce the computational complexity of the client specific discriminant analysis problem. The experimental results obtained on the internationally recognized facial database XM2VTS using the Lausanne protocol show the effectiveness of the proposed method.

1 Introduction

The problem of the biometric verification has received a considerable attention over the past decades, resulting in a large number of approaches proposed in the literature [1]-[6]. Though the early strategies for face identification were based on geometrical features, holistic features which represent the intrinsic attributes of an image have become more popular since the publication of the work of Sirovich and Kirby [7]. Because of its emphasis on the discriminatory information content, the Foley-Sammon transform (FST) has been used extensively as one of the methods of dimensionality reduction in pattern recognition [9]-[12]. Various methods for determining FST under different conditions have been developed for human facial image recognition [13]-[16]. Liu proposed a modified class separability criterion, leading to a generalized optimal set of discriminant vectors [13]. Several algorithms for determining the generalized optimal set of discriminant vectors were developed

S.Z. Li et al. (Eds.): Sinobiometrics 2004, LNCS 3338, pp. 305–312, 2004.

[14]-[16]. The so called direct linear discriminant analysis (DLDA) algorithms advocated recently ensure that no loss of information is incurred [17]-[20].

All the above approaches are based on a shared framework for representing the input data, irrespective of its class identity. Departing from this paradigm, Kittler [1] proposed a client specific Fisher face representation in which there is only one Fisher face per client. Many attractive properties make the method ideally suited for both representation and authentication in personal identity verification systems.

In this paper an improved algorithm for client specific LDA for the verification is proposed. The results of experiments in face verification conducted on the XM2VTS database show the effectiveness of the proposed algorithm.

The rest of the paper is organized as follows. An efficient dimensionality reduction method based on the between-class scatter matrix for client specific LDA is introduced in Section 2. A new algorithm for client specific LDA is proposed in Section 3. Experimental results are presented in Section 4 and conclusions are drawn in Section 5.

2 An Efficient Dimensionality Reduction for Client Specific LDA

In small sample cases where the dimensionality of the data exceeds the cardinality of the training set, LDA has to be preceded by a dimensionality reduction in order to avoid the problem of rank deficiency of the population scatter matrix. In Ref.[2], PCA was introduced for this purpose. The method is effective but involves the choice of a meta parameter, i.e. the number of eigenvectors to be retained, that can affect the performance of LDA quite significantly. More over, the resulting subspace is influenced by within class scatter matrix, although it contributes no first order discriminatory information.

Motivated by these observations, we propose a more efficient dimensionality reduction method which is based on the between-class scatter matrix. The advantage of this method is that the subspace of reduced dimensionality is determined by the relevant information only. Moreover, the required dimensionality is uniquely defined as well. The between-class scatter matrix S_b is defined as $S_b = \Phi_b \Phi_b^T$, wher $\Phi_b = \left[\sqrt{N_1}(u_1 - u), \cdots \sqrt{N_C}(u_C - u) \right]$, N_i is the number of samples of i-th class, ω_i, u_i is the mean vector of i-th class, u is the total mean vector of all samples and C is the number of classes. The matrix is of size $M \times M$, where M is the dimensionality of the samples. Turk and Pentland [8] suggested an indirect method to solve for the eigenvectors of $S_b = \Phi_b \Phi_b^T$ which can be derived from the eigenvectors of the matrix $\Phi_b^T \Phi_b$ with size $C \times C$. Let λ_i and e_i be the i-th eigenvalue and its corresponding eigenvector of $\Phi_b^T \Phi_b$, where $i = 1, 2, \cdots, C$, sorted in a decreasing order of eigenvalues.

Since $\left(\Phi_b^T \Phi_b\right)\left(\Phi_b e_i\right) = \lambda_i \Phi_b e_i$, $y_i = \Phi_b e_i$ is the eigenvector of S_b. As the rank of S_b is determined by $m = rank(S_b) \leq min(M,C\text{-}1)$, there is no discriminative information in the null space of S_b. The first m eigenvectors, $Y = [y_1, y_2, \cdots, y_m] = \Phi_b E_m$, whose corresponding eigenvalues are greater than 0, are used, where $E_m = [e_1, e_2, \cdots, e_m]$.

3 An Improved Algorithm for Client Specific LDA

Let $D_b = diag[\lambda_1, \lambda_2, \cdots, \lambda_m]$, and further let $U = YD_b^{-\frac{1}{2}}$. Projecting all the training samples into the subspace spanned by U, we have

$$x_i = U^T (z_i - u) \quad i = 1, \cdots, N \tag{1}$$

Therefore, the population scatter matrix in the space spanned by X is:

$$\Phi = \frac{1}{N} \sum_{i=1}^{N} x_i x_i^T \tag{2}$$

Let us now consider the problem of discriminating class ω_i from all the other classes. In the context of the face verification problem this corresponds to discriminating between $i\text{-}th$ client and imposters modeled by all the other clients in the training data set. In this two class scenario, LDA involves finding one dimensional feature space. Given the mean vector of $i\text{-}th$ class as

$$\mu_i = \frac{1}{N_i} \sum_{j=1}^{N_i} x_j \quad x_j \in \omega_i \tag{3}$$

and assuming the population mean to be zero, it can be shown that the mean vector of impostors of $i\text{-}th$ class is

$$\mu_\Omega = -\frac{N_i}{N - N_i} \mu_i \tag{4}$$

and the between-class scatter matrix is

$$M_i = \frac{N_i}{N - N_i} \mu_i \mu_i^T \tag{5}$$

Then the within-class scatter matrix is

$$\Sigma_i = \Phi - M_i \tag{6}$$

The Fisher discriminant function can be defined as

$$J(v) = \frac{v^T M_i v}{v^T \Sigma_i v} \tag{7}$$

The solution to the problem can be found easily as

$$v_i = \Sigma_i^{-1} \mu_i \tag{8}$$

Thus the overall client i specific discriminant transformation a_i, which defines the client specific fisher face of the claimed identity, is given as

$$a_i = U v_i \tag{9}$$

However, we can see from equation (8) that the inverse of the within-class scatter matrix should be calculated for each client. In the rest of the section, we propose to utilize an equivalent Fisher criterion function defined in [10].

$$J(v) = \frac{v^T M_i v}{v^T \Phi v} \tag{10}$$

Similar to the above analysis, the optimal solution to the client specific discriminant problem can be found as

$$\tilde{v}_i = \Phi^{-1} \mu_i \tag{11}$$

Similarly, the new client specific fisher face of the claimed identity, can be given as

$$\tilde{a}_i = U \tilde{v}_i \tag{12}$$

We can find from Eq.(11) that the inverse of population scatter matrix is common to all clients which implies that less computation time is required.

4   Experimental Results and Analysis

In order to test the performance of the proposed algorithm, face verification experiments have been conducted on the XM2VTS database, which is a multi-modal database consisting of video sequences of talking faces recorded for 295 subjects at one month intervals. The data has been recorded in 4 sessions with 2 shots taken per session [6]. From each session two facial images have been extracted to create an experimental face database of size 55×51. Figure 1 shows examples of images in XM2VTS.

The experimental protocol (known as Lausanne evaluation protocol) divides the data set into 200 clients and 95 impostors. Within the protocol, the verification performance is measured using false acceptance and false rejection rates. The operating point where these two error rates equal each other is typically referred to as the equal error rate (EER) point. Details of the protocol can be found in [5]. The CS-LDA method in [1] provides two measures for authentication: a distance to the mean of clients which is called client model, and a distance to the mean of impostors which is called impostor model. The detailed description of the two models can be obtained in [1]. All the results were obtained using histogram equalization (HEQ) in conjunction with a global threshold determined by the EER point.

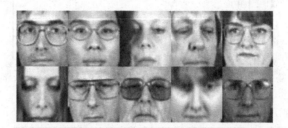

Fig. 1. Part of the extracted images in XM2VTS

Table 1. Performance comparison of several methods based on impostor model

Methods	Evaluation			Testing		
	FRR	FAR	TER	FRR	FAR	TER
Method 1	2.50	2.50	5.0	3.5	2.5	6.0
Method 2	1.75	2.00	3.75	2.25	2.68	4.93
Method 3	1.00	1.00	2.00	2.00	1.25	3.25

Table 1 shows the performance comparison of several methods based on the impostor model. In table 1, method 1 refers to the CS-LDA algorithm in [1], the only difference between method 1 and method 2 is that a more efficient dimensionality reduction method is used by the latter, while method 3 refers to the proposed algorithm which integrates the efficient dimensionality reduction strategy and the new Fisher discriminant criterion function. Comparing the performance of method 1 with that of method 2, the results verify that the dimensionality reduction strategy based on the between-class scatter matrix is more efficient than that on the conventional PCA. We find that method 3 improves the performance of face verification significantly. Figure 2 shows the ROC curve of method 1 and method 3 on XM2VTS for both client model and impostor model. Comparing the curves of Figure 2, we find that the difference in performance between the client model and impostor model based on method 1 is much greater than that on method 3, which implies that method 3 is more robust than method 1.

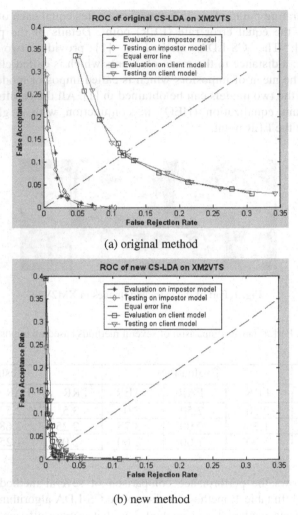

(a) original method

(b) new method

Fig. 2. Performance comparison of the two CS-LDA Methods

5 Conclusions

In this paper an improved algorithm for client specific LDA is proposed and applied
to face verification. The method has been tested on the XM2VTS database according
to the internationally agreed protocols and shown to deliver better performance as
compared with the original client specific LDA method. The experimental results also
indicate that the new method is more robust than the old method. Although
experiments were conducted only in face verification, we believe that the proposed
method is applicable to other biometric modalities. Our future work will focus on the
development of nonlinear methods for face verification.

Acknowledgements

This work was supported in part by the following sources: EU Project Banca, EU Project Vampire, National Natural Science Foundation of P. R. China (Grant No. 60072034), Robotics Laboratory, Chinese Academy of Sciences foundation (Grant No.RL200108), Natural Science Foundation of Jiangsu Province, P. R. China (Grant No. BK2002001 and BK2004058), and University Natural Science research program of Jiangsu Province, P. R. China (Grant No. 01KJB520002), Open foundation of Image Processing and Image Communication Lab (Grant No. KJS03038).

References

1. J.Kittler: Face authentication using client specific fisherfaces (patented in the UK). CVSSP, University of Surrey. (2001)
2. K Jonsson, G Matas, and J Kittler: Learning Salient Features for Real-Time Face Verification. In Proc. of AVBPA99. (1999) 60–65
3. K Jonsson, J Kittler, Y P Li and J Matas: Support Vector Machine for Face Authentication, In Proceeding of BMVC99. (1999) 543–553
4. J Matas, K Jonsson and J Kittler: Fast Face Localisation and Verification. In Proceeding of BMVC97. (1997) 152–161
5. K Messer, J Matas, J Kittler, J Luettin and G Maitre: XM2VTSDB: The Extended M2VTS Database. In Proc. of AVBPA99. (1999) 72–77
6. J.Kitter, and Mark S.Nixon: Audio-and Video-Based Biometric Person Authentication. AVBPA2003. Guildford, UK. (2003)
7. L.Sirovich and M.Kirby: Low-dimensional procedure for the characterization of human face. J.Opt.Soc.Am. A 4(3) (1987) 519–529
8. Turk M and Pentland A: Eigenfaces for recognition. J. Cognitive Neuroscience. Vol. 3(1) (1991) 71–86
9. D.H.Foley, J.W.Sammon: An optimal set of discriminant vectors. IEEE Trans. Computer. Vol. 24(3) (1975) 281–289
10. P.Devijver and J.Kittler: Pattern recognition: A statistical approach. Prentice-Hall, London, (1982)
11. J. Kittler: On the discriminant vector method of feature selection. IEEE Trans. Computers. Vol. 26(6) (1977) 604–606
12. P.N.Belhumeur, J.P.Hespanha, and D.J.Kriegman: Eigenfaces vs. fisherfaces: Recognition using class specific linear projection. IEEE Trans. on PAMI. Vol. 19(7) (1997) 711–720
13. K.Liu, Y.Q.Cheng, J.Y.Yang: A generalized optimal set of discriminant vectors. Pattern Recognition. Vol. 25(1) (1992) 731–739
14. Guo Yuefei, Yang Jingyu: An Iterative Algorithm for the Generalized Optimal Set of Discriminant Vectors and Its Application to Face Recognition. Chinese J. Computers. Vol. 23(11) (2000) 1189–1195
15. Wu Xiaojun, Yang Jingyu, Wang Shitong, et al.: A new algorithm for solving optimal discriminant vectors. Journal of Computer Science and Technology. Vol.19(3) (2002) 324–330
16. Xiaojun Wu, Josef Kittler, Jingyu Yang, etc: An analytical algorithm for determining the generalized optimal set of discriminant vectors. Pattern Recognition. Vol. 37(9) (2004) 1949–1952

17. Li-Fen Chen, Hong-Yuan Mark Liao, Ming-Tat Ko, etc: A new LDA-based face recognition system which can solve the small sample size problem. Pattern Recognition. Vol. 33(9) (2000) 1713–1726
18. Hua Yu, Jie Yang: A direct LDA algorithm for high-dimensional data-with application to face recognition. Pattern Recognition. Vol. 34 (2001) 2067–2070
19. Xiaojun Wu, Josef Kittler, Jingyu Yang, etc: A new direct LDA (DLDA) algorithm for face recognition. ICPR 2004. Cambridge, UK. (2004)
20. Juewei Lu, K.N.Plataniotis, and A.N. Venetsanopoulos: Face recognition using LDA based algorithms. IEEE Trans. NN. Vol. 14(1) (2003) 195–200

The Solution Space for Fisher Discriminant Analysis and the Uniqueness Under Constraints

Weishi Zheng[1], Jianhuang Lai[1], and P.C. Yuen[2]

[1] Department of Mathematics, Sun Yat-sen University
SunnyWeiShi@163.com, stsljh@zsu.edu.cn
[2] Department of Computer Science, Hong Kong Baptist University
pcyuen@comp.hkbu.edu.hk

Abstract. This paper studies the solution space of Fisher Criteria. The space is large and it is impossible to find the best solution generally. This paper intends to construct an optimal projection, which solves the Fisher criteria and is the unique solution under nonsingular linear transformation if some constraints are0020given. Therefore a theorem is proposed which shows the feasible for constructing the projection, with a simple way to process the construction from the traditional LDA. Experiment result shows the ability and feasible of the proposed solution.

1 Introduction and Problem

The Linear Discriminant Analysis (LDA) is popular in the pattern recognition field. It's basic idea is to maximize the between-class scatter matrix S_b meanwhile minimize within-class scatter matrix S_w, i.e. it is sufficient to find an optimal projection W_{opt} to optimize the following Fisher Criteria [1][4][5][6][7]:

$$W_{opt} = \arg\max_W F(W), \quad F(W) = \frac{|W^T S_b W|}{|W^T S_w W|}. \tag{1}$$

Where, $W \in R^{n \times l}$, which can be solved by the eigenvalue problem: $S_w^{-1} S_b W = W \Lambda$.

Let $T(W_{opt}) = \{W \mid F(W) = F(W_{opt}), W \in R^{n \times l}\}$ be the solution space of Fisher Criteria. Suppose $A \in R^{l \times l}$, $\det(A) \neq 0$, and then it is obvious that $F(W_{opt} A) = F(W_{opt})$, i.e. $W_{opt} A \in T(W_{opt})$, which is another optimal projection, which solves the criteria (1). Furthermore, a lot of optimal projections can be constructed similarly. Theoretically, the solutions are infinite; it is hard to distinguish which is the best. But from another point of view, can we set up a frame to make the solution space of the Fisher criteria (1) to be smaller or even make the solution to be

S.Z. Li et al. (Eds.): Sinobiometrics 2004, LNCS 3338, pp. 313–319, 2004.

unique under some conditions? It seems to refer to the problem of constraints on the optimal feature vectors. Foley, Sammon[3] and Z. Jin[2] have done some work on the constraints on the optimal feature vectors. Then a question may arise that can we utilize those two constraints meanwhile?

This paper intends to propose a theorem that tells us the solution of Fisher Criteria is unique under nonsingular linear transformation if involved constraints are considered. For application, a simple construction of this solution is presented from the traditional LDA.

For convenient, the most common use notations are described as follows: n be dimensional of the sample; l be number of optimal feature vectors, we always assume $l << n$; S_t be total-class scatter matrix; S_w be within-class scatter matrix; S_b be between-class scatter matrix; W_{opt} be the optimal solution for Fisher criteria, which belongs to $R^{n \times l}$.

The outline of the rest part of this paper is as follows: Section 2 gives some definition. Section 3 proposes a theorem. Section 4 gives a simple construction of the proposed solution from the traditional LDA method. Experiment results are reported in section 5, which show the ability and feasible of the proposed method. Finally we have a conclusion in section 6.

2   Definition of Nonsingular Linear Transformation

We firstly give some other definitions.

Define *Nonsingular linear transformation* of a matrix $M \in R^{\tilde{n} \times \tilde{m}}$ as $M' = M\,L$, where L is nonsingular $\tilde{m} \times \tilde{m}$ matrix.

Define $\Theta(W_{opt}) = \{ L | L$ is Nonsingular linear transformation of $W_{opt} \}$.

Define notation Δ be any set of constraint qualification. For some object L, let $\Delta(L)$ represent a set of constraint qualification on L, if $\Delta = \Phi$, where Φ means empty, then it means there is no constraint qualification on L.

Given constraints Δ, define $\Omega_{\Delta}(W_{opt}) = \{W | W = W_{opt}L$, $L \in \Theta(W_{opt})$ and W satisfies $\Delta(W)\}$, for a special case $\Omega_{\Phi}(W_{opt}) = \{W | W = W_{opt}L,\ L \in \Theta(W_{opt})\}$.

It is obvious that $W_{opt} \in \Omega_{\Phi}(W_{opt})$ and $\forall W \in \Omega_{\Phi}(W_{opt})$, we get $W \in T(W_{opt})$, and $\Omega_{\Delta}(W_{opt})$ is a subset of $T(W_{opt})$.

3   Unique Solution of the Fisher Criteria Under Constraints

As the problem mentioned in the introduction, the Fisher Criteria (1) has multiple solutions, and a puzzle problem happens that when we find an optimal features set and the feature space projection W_{opt}, $\Omega_{\Delta}(W_{opt})$ is infinite. Then we may have a question:

Which projection should be used, W_{opt} or $W_{opt} L$, where $L \in \Theta(W_{opt})$ and obviously they all satisfy the Fisher Criteria (1), but they may have different measurements on vectors. For example, a dialog matrix $\Lambda = diag(\frac{1}{2}, \frac{1}{3}, ..., \frac{1}{l+1})$, then $\Lambda \in \Theta(W_{opt})$, it is easy to get that $\| (W_{opt} \Lambda)^T a \| \neq \| W_{opt}^T a \|$.

The sub solution space $\Omega_\Lambda (W_{opt})$ is large that it may be not possible to search the best one under no constraint. From this point of view constraints may be needed for shrink the size of solution space.

Let's say the solution W_{opt} of the Fisher Criteria is *unique under nonsingular linear transformation* if and only if we can find specific constraint Δ_{opt} such that $\Omega_{\Delta_{opt}} (W_{opt}) = \{ W_{opt} \}$.

Following Theorem tells us that it is possible to find a solution of Fisher Criteria that is unique under nonsingular linear transformation.

Theorem 1: Suppose W_{opt} is the solution of Fisher Criterion (1). If W_{opt} satisfies constraint $\Delta_{opt} (W_{opt})$ as follows:

1. $W_{opt}^T W_{opt} = I$

2. $W_{opt}^T S_t W_{opt} = diag(\lambda_{W_{opt}}^1, \lambda_{W_{opt}}^2, ..., \lambda_{W_{opt}}^l), \lambda_{W_{opt}}^1 > \lambda_{W_{opt}}^2 > ... > \lambda_{W_{opt}}^l > 0$.

   Then $\Omega_{\Delta_{opt}} (W_{opt}) = \{ W_{opt} \}$.

Proof: Generally let the constraint defined as following relation:

$$\Delta_{opt} (W) = \begin{cases} W^T W = I \\ W^T S_t W = diag(\lambda_W^1, \lambda_W^2, ..., \lambda_W^l), \lambda_W^1 > ... > \lambda_W^l > 0 \end{cases} \quad (2)$$

Where $\Delta_{opt} (W)$ can be seen as a set of constraint qualification on W.

We begin the proof as follows.

Because any $\hat{W} \in \Omega_{\Delta_{opt}} (W_{opt})$, $\hat{W} = W_{opt} Q$, $Q \in \Theta(W_{opt})$, then $\hat{W}^T \hat{W} = I \Rightarrow Q^T W_{opt}^T W_{opt} Q = I \Rightarrow Q^T Q = I$. Thus Q is orthogonal matrix.

On the other hand, $\hat{W}^T S_t \hat{W} = diag(\lambda_{\hat{W}}^1, \lambda_{\hat{W}}^2, ..., \lambda_{\hat{W}}^l)$, $\lambda_{\hat{W}}^1 > ... > \lambda_{\hat{W}}^l > 0$, we have:

$$Q^T W_{opt}^T S_t W_{opt} Q = diag(\lambda_{\hat{W}}^1, \lambda_{\hat{W}}^2, ..., \lambda_{\hat{W}}^l) .$$

Then

$$Q^T diag(\lambda^1_{W_{opt}}, \lambda^2_{W_{opt}}, ..., \lambda^l_{W_{opt}})Q = diag(\lambda^1_{\hat{W}}, \lambda^2_{\hat{W}}, ..., \lambda^l_{\hat{W}}) .$$

Let $\Lambda_{W_{opt}} = diag(\lambda^1_{W_{opt}}, \lambda^2_{W_{opt}}, ..., \lambda^l_{W_{opt}})$, $\Lambda_W = diag(\lambda^1_{\hat{W}}, \lambda^2_{\hat{W}}, ..., \lambda^l_{\hat{W}})$, also let $Q = (q_1, q_2, ..., q_l)$, $q_i = (q_i^1, q_i^2, ..., q_i^l)^T$, $i = 1, 2, ..., l$.

Therefore

$$Q^T \Lambda_{W_{opt}} Q = \Lambda_W \Rightarrow \Lambda_{W_{opt}} Q = Q \Lambda_W .$$

It implies that $\lambda^i_{\hat{W}}$ is the eigenvalue of $\Lambda_{W_{opt}}$ corresponds to the eigenvector q_i, $i = 1, 2, ..., l$.

However, it is obvious that $\lambda^i_{W_{opt}}$ are the eigenvalues of $\Lambda_{W_{opt}}$, $i = 1, 2, ..., l$.

Since $\lambda^1_{\hat{W}} > \lambda^2_{\hat{W}} > ... > \lambda^l_{\hat{W}}$ and $\lambda^1_{W_{opt}} > \lambda^2_{W_{opt}} > ... > \lambda^l_{W_{opt}}$, so $\lambda^i_{\hat{W}} = \lambda^i_{W_{opt}}$, $i = 1, 2, ..., l$.

We have: $\Lambda_{W_{opt}} q_i = \lambda^i_{W_{opt}} q_i$, $i = 1, 2, ..., l$

Hence $\lambda^j_{W_{opt}} q_i^j = \lambda^i_{W_{opt}} q_i^j$, $j = 1, 2, ..., l, i = 1, 2, ..., l$,

Then we obtain:

$$(\lambda^j_{W_{opt}} - \lambda^i_{W_{opt}})q_i^j = 0, \quad j = 1, 2, ..., l, i = 1, 2, ..., l$$

Since $Q^T Q = I$, so $q_i^j = \delta_{ij}$.

Hence $Q = I$, $\hat{W} = W_{opt} Q = W_{opt}$

We get the conclusion $\Omega_{\Delta_{opt}}(W_{opt}) = \{W_{opt}\}$.

This finishes the proof.

Remark. The intuitive meaning of theorem 1 tells us that one can feasibly combine two constraints together. That is one can develop a set of optimal vectors subject to being orthogonal and statistical uncorrelated each other, where these two constrains have been reported to improve the pattern recognition.

4   Simple Construction from Theorem 1

The features projection derived from traditional LDA can be solved by the following equality:

$$S_b W_{opt} = S_w W_{opt} \Lambda_{opt} \, .$$

It is obvious that $W_{opt} \in \Omega_\Phi(W_{opt})$.

By theorem 1, a simple way to construction a linear stable projection is to find $\widetilde{W}_{opt} \in \Omega_\Phi(W_{opt})$ such that $\widetilde{W}_{opt}$ satisfies $\Delta_{opt}(\widetilde{W}_{opt})$. It is possible by the following steps:

There exists nonsingular matrix O such that $M_1 = W_{opt} \, O$ and $M_1^T M_1 = I$.

Since $M_1^T S_t M_1$ is semi-definition matrix, then an orthogonal matrix $\widetilde{Q}$ can be found and we have:

$$\widetilde{Q}^T M_1^T S_t M_1 \widetilde{Q} = \widetilde{\Lambda}_t \, .$$

Where $\widetilde{\Lambda}_t = diag(\widetilde{\lambda}_t^1, \widetilde{\lambda}_t^2, ..., \widetilde{\lambda}_t^l)$, $\widetilde{\lambda}_t^1 > \widetilde{\lambda}_t^2 > ... > \widetilde{\lambda}_t^l > 0$. Because of the randomicity of the sample, $\widetilde{\lambda}_t^1 > \widetilde{\lambda}_t^2 > ... > \widetilde{\lambda}_t^l > 0$ can be valid in practice.

Let $\widetilde{W}_{opt} = W_{opt} \, O \, \widetilde{Q} \in \Omega_\Phi(W_{opt})$, then:

$$\widetilde{W}_{opt}^T S_t \widetilde{W}_{opt} = \widetilde{\Lambda}_t \quad \text{and} \quad \widetilde{W}_{opt}^T \widetilde{W}_{opt} = \widetilde{Q}^T M_1^T M_1 \widetilde{Q} = \widetilde{Q}^T I \widetilde{Q} = I \, .$$

Hence $\widetilde{W}_{opt}$ satisfies $\Delta_{opt}(\widetilde{W}_{opt})$ and $\Omega_{\Delta_{opt}}(\widetilde{W}_{opt}) = \{ \widetilde{W}_{opt} \}$.

5   Experiment Result

In this section the evaluation result of proposed method (solution) from theorem 1 is reported.

We test the feasibility of proposed method on ORL database, YALE database and compare it with traditional LDA. The ORL database consists of 40 person that has 10 face images with resolution 92×112 for each. The faces have variations in pose, illumination and facial expression. The YALE database has 15 persons with 11 images for each. The images of one person have different facial expression or illumination. For each run of the test on ORL, we randomly select 5 images of each person for training and the others for testing. The test on YALE is similar. The results are report from the Table 1.

Followings are two figures describe the Cumulative Match Score that is a plot of rank 5 scores versus probability of average correct identification for ORL and Yale database respectively. One can see that the proposed algorithm is superior.

Table 1. Feasibility test of proposed method on ORL and YALE database

Database		ORL	YALE
Number of Training sample per person		5	5
Number of Testing sample for each		5	6
Times of run		30	30
Average Accuracy (%)	Proposed Method	95.25%	94.889%
	Traditonal LDA	91.82%	93.26%

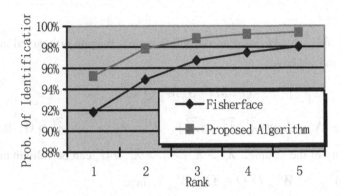

Fig. 1. Identification performance reported on a CMC of ORL database. 40 individuals are used, 200 images are used to train, and the other 200 images are used to test

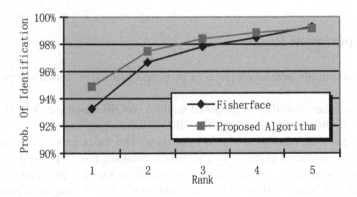

Fig. 2. Identification performance reported on a CMC of YALE database. 15 individuals are used, 75 images are used to train, and the other 90 images are used to test

6   Conclusion

We do some researches on the solution space of Fisher Criteria (1). We have ana-lyzed that the solutions for Fisher criteria are not unique. This paper sets up a frame to study the solution space and has found that the solution of Fisher Criteria is unique under nonsingular linear transformation if some restrictions are included. To evaluate the proposed solution, we have a simple way to construct it from the traditional LDA method. The experiment has shown the feasibility and superiority of the proposed solution.

Acknowledgement

This project was supported by NSFC (No. 60144001), NSF of GuangDong, P.R. China(No. 021766) and RGC Earmarked Research Grant HKBU-2119/03E. We would like to thank the Research Laboratory for providing the ORL and YALE databases. The author would also like to thank the reviewers for their valuable advice.

References

1. Belhumeur, P. N., Hespanha, J.P., Kriegman, and D.J.: Eigenfaces vs. Fisherfaces: recognition using class specific linear projection. IEEE Trans. Pattern Anal. Mach. Intell. . Vol.19 (7) (1997) 711–720
2. Jin, Z., Yang, J. Y., Hu, Z. S., and Lou, Z.: Face recognition based on the uncorrelated discriminant transformation. Pattern Recognition. Vol. 34 (2001) 1405–1416
3. Duchene, J., Leclercq, S.: An optimal transformation for discriminant and principal component analysis. IEEE Trans. Pattern Anal. Mach. Intell. . Vol.10 (6) (1988) 978 – 983
4. Martinez, A. M., Kak, A. C.: PCA Versus LDA. IEEE Trans. Pattern Anal. Mach. Intell. . Vol. 23 (2) (2001) 228–233
5. Fisher, R.A.: The Use of Multiple Measures in Taxonomic Problems. Ann. Eugenics. Vol.7 (1936) 179–188
6. Ye, J.P., Janardan, R., Park, C.H., and Park H.: An Optimization Criterion for Generalized Discriminant Analysis on Undersampled Problems. IEEE Trans. Pattern Anal. Mach. Intell. . Vol. 26(8) (2004) 982–994
7. Zhao, W., Chellappa, R., Phillips, J., and Rosenfeld, A.: Face Recognition: A Literature Survey. ACM Computing Surveys. Vol.35 (4) (2003) 399–458

A Novel One-Parameter Regularized Linear Discriminant Analysis for Solving Small Sample Size Problem in Face Recognition

Wensheng Chen [1,2], Pong C Yuen [2], Jian Huang [2], and Daoqing Dai [3]

[1] Department of Mathematics, Shenzhen University, P.R. China, 518060
chenws@szu.edu.cn
[2] Department of Computer Science, Hong Kong Baptist University Hong Kong
{wschen,pcyuen,jhuang}@comp.HKBU.edu.HK
[3] Department of Mathematics, Zhongshan University, P.R. China, 510275
stsddq@zsu.edu.cn

Abstract. In this paper, a new 1-parameter regularized discriminant analysis (1PRDA) algorithm is developed to deal with the small sample size (S3) problem. The main limitation in regularization is that the computational complexity of determining the optimal parameters is very high. In view of this limitation, we derive a single parameter (t) explicit expression formula for determining the 3 parameters. A simple and efficient method is proposed to determine the value of t. The proposed 1PRLDA method for face recognition has been evaluated with two public available databases, namely ORL and FERET databases. The average recognition accuracy of 50 runs for ORL and FERET database are 96.65% and 94.00% respectively. Comparing with existing LDA-based methods in solving the S3 problem, the proposed 1PRLDA method gives the best performance.

1 Introduction

Principle Component Analysis (PCA) and Linear Discriminant Analysis (LDA) are the two popular statistic methods in appearance-based approach. Based on the PCA and LDA methods, the well known Eigenface [1] and Fisherface [2] methods were developed in 1991 and 1997 respectively. After that, a large number of PCA-based and LDA-based algorithms/systems have been proposed. In general, LDA-based algorithms give better performance.

The goal of Fisher linear discriminant analysis is to find an optimal projection matrix $W^* : R^d \to R^m, d > m$,

$$W^* = \arg\max_w tr(W^T S_b W) tr(W^T S_w W)^{-1}$$

where $tr(A)$ denotes the trace of matrix A.

This problem is equivalent to solve the following eigenvalue problem:

$$S_w^{-1} S_b W = W\Lambda$$

where Λ is a $m \times m$ diagonal eigenvalue matrix.

S.Z. Li et al. (Eds.): Sinobiometrics 2004, LNCS 3338, pp. 320–329, 2004.

LDA is theoretically sound and a number of LDA-based face recognition algorithms/systems have been developed in the last decade. Encouraging results have been reported in many literatures [1-14, 16-19]. However, LDA suffers from a small sample size (S3) problem. Under this situation, the within-class scatter matrix S_w becomes singular and direct solving the eigenvalue problem is not possible. Some algorithms, such as PCA+LDA [2], Direct LDA [4] and RDA [16,17] etc, are developed to solve S3 problem. However, PCA+LDA and Direct LDA are implemented in the sub-feature-space, not in the full feature space. So it maybe lost some useful discriminant information in subspace for PR. The paper [16] proposed three parameters regularized method to solve S3 problem. Although this method is executed in the full sample space, it's very difficulty to determine three optimal parameters. Also, the computational complexity of this RDA algorithm is very high.

To overcome the existing problems, this paper proposes a new method in regularization approach. We re-define the 3-parameter regularization on the within-class scatter matrix $S_w^{\alpha\beta\gamma}$, which is suitable for parameter reduction. Based on the new definition of $S_w^{\alpha\beta\gamma}$, we obtain a single parameter explicit expression formula for determining the 3 parameters and develop a 1-parameter regularization on the within-class scatter matrix. A novel 1-parameter regularization discriminant analysis (1PRDA) algorithm is then developed. The proposed method for face recognition has been evaluated with two public available databases, namely ORL and FERET databases. Comparing with the existing LDA-based methods, the results are encouraging.

The rest of this paper is organized as follows. Our proposed 1PRDA method is given in Section 2. The experimental results are reported in Section 3. Finally, Section 4 draws the conclusion.

2 Proposed Regularization Method

This paper proposes and develops a novel one parameter regularization discriminant analysis method for face recognition. Details are discussed as follows.

2.1 Some Definitions

Assume the dimensionality of original sample feature space be d and the number of sample classes be k, the total original sample $C = \{C_1, C_2, \cdots, C_k\}$, the j-th class C_j contains N_j samples, $j = 1, 2, \cdots, k$. Let N be the total number of original training samples, i.e. $N = \sum_{j=1}^{k} N_j$, $\bar{x}_j = \frac{1}{N_j} \sum_{x \in C_j} x$ be the mean of the sample class C_j and $\bar{x} = \frac{1}{N} \sum_{j=1}^{k} \sum_{x \in C_j} x$ be the global mean of the total original sample C. The within-class scatter matrix S_w, between-class scatter matrix S_b are defined respectively as:

$$S_w = \frac{1}{N} \sum_{j=1}^{k} \sum_{x \in C_j} (x - \bar{x}_j)(x - \bar{x}_j)^T = \Phi_w \Phi_w^T$$

322 W. Chen et al.

$$S_b = \frac{1}{N}\sum_{j=1}^{k} N_j(\overline{x}_j - \overline{x})(\overline{x}_j - \overline{x})^T = \Phi_b \Phi_b^T$$

The Fisher's criterion function $J(W)$ is defined by

$$J(W) = tr(W^T S_b W) tr(W^T S_w W)^{-1}, \ W \in R^{d\times(k-1)}.$$

2.2 Regularization of S_w

In case of S3 problem occurs, LDA method can not be used since S_w is singular. In designing the regularized matrix S_w^τ for the singular matrix S_w, the criteria as suggested by Krzanowski etc [15] are used in this paper.

Assume $S_w = U_w \Lambda_w U_w^T$ is the eigenvalue decomposition of matrix S_w. We define the three-parameter family regularization $S_w^{\alpha\beta\gamma}$ for S_w^τ as $S_w^{\alpha\beta\gamma} = U_w \hat{\Lambda}_w U_w^T$, where $\hat{\Lambda}_w$ is a diagonal matrix with its diagonal elements ξ_i $(i=1,2,...d)$ given by,

$$\xi_i = \begin{cases} (\alpha\lambda_i + \beta)/M, & i=1,2,\cdots,\tau \\ \gamma, & i=\tau+1,\cdots,d \end{cases} \tag{1}$$

where M is a normalization constant and is given by

$$M = \frac{\alpha tr(S_w) + \tau\beta}{tr(S_w) - (d-\tau)\gamma}$$

where $\alpha \geq 1, \beta \geq 0, \gamma > 0$ and $(\alpha\lambda_\tau + \beta)/M - \gamma \geq 0$ \hfill (2)

It is easily verified that the regularized matrix $S_w^{\alpha\beta\gamma}$ satisfies all the criteria in [15].

2.3 Formulating One Parameter Regularization

In this section, we derive the one parameter formulation from the above defined three parameters regularization.

Denote $Q = diag(I_\tau,0) \in R^{d\times d}$, $\overline{Q} = I_d - Q$, $a = w^T S_w w$, $b = w^T U_w Q U_w^T w$, $c = w^T U_w \overline{Q} U_w^T w$ and $e = b + c = w^T w$. Then the regularized Fisher criterion function:

$$J^{\alpha\beta\gamma}(w) = \frac{w^T S_b w}{w^T S_w^{\alpha\beta\gamma} w}, \ w \in R^d$$

can be written as

$$J^{\alpha\beta\gamma}(w) = \frac{(\alpha tr(S_w) + \tau\beta) w^T S_b w}{(tr(S_w) - (d-\tau)\gamma)(a\alpha + b\beta) + c\gamma(\alpha tr(S_w) + \tau\beta)}, \ w \in R^d. \tag{3}$$

We determine α, β, γ from equation $\nabla_{\alpha\beta\gamma} J^{\alpha\beta\gamma}(w) = 0$, where ∇ is a gradient operator, as follows, $(1 \geq t > 0)$

$$\alpha = t+1, \quad \beta = \frac{tr(S_w)c - (d-\tau)a}{bd - e\tau} \cdot (t+1) \quad \text{and} \quad \gamma = \frac{tr(S_w)}{d-\tau}.$$

However, it is inconvenient to use these formula directly because β is a function of vector w. On the other hand, we hope that when t tends to zero, the regularized matrix tends to the original matrix, i.e. $\alpha \to 1$, β and $\gamma \to 0$ as $t \to 0$. So we slightly modify the above formula as

$$\alpha = t+1, \quad \beta = \frac{tr(S_w)}{\tau(d-\tau)} \cdot t, \quad \gamma = \frac{tr(S_w)}{d-\tau} \cdot t, \quad (0 < t \le 1). \tag{4}$$

From formula (4), the following theorem can be derived.

Theorem 1: If α, β, γ are given by (4), then $\left\| S_w^{\alpha\beta\gamma} - S_w \right\|_F \le o(t)$, where $\| \cdot \|_F$ denotes Frobenius norm of a matrix.

2.4 Determine the Value of t

The computational complexity has been greatly reduced when number of parameters is reduced from 3 to 1. This section further develops a method to determine the value of t to be employed by given a set of training data.

We want to find a t such that the inequality (2) is satisfied. However, there are a number of t in $(0,1]$ which satisfy (2). In order to determine a better t which satisfies (2), we propose a simple method as follows (given a set of labeled training images).

1. First, we find the largest t, say t_1, which satisfies the inequality (2), and determine the corresponding accuracy A_1.
2. Determining three smaller t by dividing it by 2 and find the corresponding accuracy, i.e. $t_2 = t_1/2$ with A_2, $t_3 = t_2/2$ with A_3, $t_4 = t_3/2$ with A_4.
3. Given a predefined threshold $\varepsilon > 0$, if $|A_{i+1} - A_i| \le \varepsilon$ (i=1,2,3), that can be considered as the stable range and the value of t_4 will be used. Otherwise, set $t_2 = t_1$ and goto step 2.

2.5 The Proposed 1PRDA Algorithm

Based on above sections, the 1PRDA algorithm is designed as follows.

Step 1: Calculate within-class scatter matrix S_w and between-class scatter matrix S_b.

Step 2: Do eigenvalue decomposition $S_w = U_w \Lambda_w U_w^T$, where U_w is an orthonormal matrix, $\Lambda_w = diag(\lambda_1, \cdots, \lambda_\tau, 0, \cdots, 0) \in R^{d \times d}$, $\lambda_1 > \lambda_2 > \cdots > \lambda_\tau > 0$. Let the initial value $t = 1$.

Step 3: Calculate α, β, γ in (4) and ξ_i defined in (1)($i = 1, 2, \cdots, N$) and set $t = t/2$.

Step 4: If $(\alpha\lambda_\tau + \beta)/M - \gamma < 0$, then goto step 3. Otherwise goto step 5.

Step 5: Let $Y = \hat{\Lambda}_w^{-1/2} U_w^T$ and $\hat{S}_b = Y S_b Y^T$, where $\hat{\Lambda}_w = diag(\xi_1, \cdots, \xi_d)$, then do eigenvalue decomposition $\hat{S}_b = V \Lambda_b V^T$, where Λ_b is a diagonal eigenvalue matrix of $\hat{S}_b$ with its diagonal elements in decreasing order and V is an eigenvector matrix. Rewrite $V = (v_1, \cdots, v_{k-1}, \cdots, v_d)$ and let $V_{k-1} = (v_1, v_2, \cdots, v_{k-1})$

Step 6: The optimal projection matrix $W_{1PRDA} = U_w \hat{\Lambda}_w^{-1/2} V_{k-1}$.

3 Experimental Results

The ORL database and FERET database are selected for the evaluation. In ORL database, there are 40 persons and each person consists of 10 images with different facial expressions, small variations in scales and orientations. The resolution of each image is 92x112. Image variations of one person in the database are shown in Figure 1.

Fig. 1. Images of one person from Olivetti database

For FERET database, we select 72 people, 6 images for each individual. All images are aligned by the centers of eyes and mouth and then normalized with resolution 92x112. This resolution is the same as that in ORL database. Images from one individual are shown in Figure 2.

Fig. 2. Images of one person from FERET database

3.1 Using ORL Database

The experimental setting on ORL database is as follows. We randomly selected n images from each individual for training while the rest (10-n) images are for testing. The experiments are repeated 50 times and the average accuracy is then calculated. The average accuracy are recorded and tabulated in the last column in Table 1. The first column shows the number of training images. It can be seen that the recognition accuracy of the proposed method increases from 84.79% with 2 training images to 96.65% with 9 training images. The results are encouraging.

Table 1. Performance of the proposed method with other LDA-based methods on ORL database. NT=Number of training samples

NT	Fisherface [2]	Direct LDA [4]	Huang's method [12]	Our method
2	37.38%	77.66%	79.63%	84.79%
3	60.81%	82.80%	87.84%	89.84%
4	67.22%	85.71%	91.62%	93.33%
5	70.74%	86.71%	92.78%	94.28%
6	73.88%	88.41%	94.27%	95.63%
7	76.88%	89.82%	94.18%	95.97%
8	79.93%	90.40%	94.50%	95.98%
9	82.45%	91.55%	95.40%	96.65%

In order to compare the performance of the proposed method with existing methods, the same experiments are conducted using Fisherface method [2], Direct LDA method [4] and Huang et al. method [12]. The results are recorded and tabulated in Table 1. It can be seen that when 2 images are used for training, the accuracy for Fisherface, Direct LDA and Huang et al methods are 37.38%, 77.66% and 79.63% respectively. The performance for each method is improved when the number of training images increases. When the number of training images is equal to 9, the accuracy for Fisherface is increased to 82.45% while Direct LDA and Huang et al methods are 91.55% and 95.40% respectively. The results show that our proposed 1PRLDA method gives the best performance for all cases in ORL database.

The recognition accuracy against the rank is recorded and plotted in Figures 3(a) to 3(b) with the number of training images from 2 to 8. It can be seen that for all cases, the proposed method is outperformed.

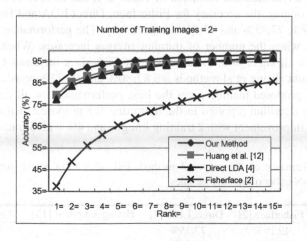

Fig. 3(a). The recognition accuracy against the rank with the training number is equals to 2

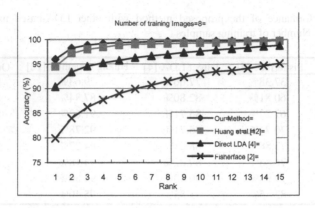

Fig. 3(b). The recognition accuracy against the rank with the training number is equals to 8

3.2 FERET Database

The experimental setting for the FERET database is similar with that of ORL database. As the number of images for each individual is 6, the number of training images is ranged from 2 to 5. The experiments are also repeated 50 times and the average accuracy are recorded and tabulated in the last column in Table 2. When comparing with other methods, same list will also be used. The first column shows the number of training images. It can be seen that the recognition accuracy of proposed method increases from 84.63% with 2 training images to 94.00% with 5 training images. The results are encouraging.

The same experiments are implemented by using Fisherface method, Direct LDA method and Huang et al. method with the same lists of training and testing images. The results are recorded and tabulated in Table 2. It can be seen that when 2 images are used for training, the accuracy for Fisherface, Direct LDA and Huang et al methods are 49.19%, 77.35% and 73.04% respectively. The performance is improved for each method when the number of training images increases. When the number of training images is equal to 5, the accuracy for Fisherface increases to 78.49% while Direct LDA and Huang et al methods are 87.80% and 90.71% respectively. It can be seen that the proposed method gives the best performance for all cases. Comparing with the best algorithm reported in the literature, the proposed method gives around 7% accuracy improvement with 2 training images and 4% with 5 training images.

Table 2. Performance of the proposed method and other LDA-based methods on REFET database. NT =Number of training samples

NT	Fisherface [2]	Direct LDA [4]	Huang's method [12]	Our method
2	49.19%	77.35%	73.04%	84.63%
3	64.29%	82.64%	84.28%	90.83%
4	73.24%	84.96%	88.64%	93.49%
5	78.49%	87.80%	90.71%	94.00%

The recognition accuracy against the rank is recorded and plotted in Figures 4(a) to 4(b) with the number of training images from 2 to 4. It can be seen that the proposed method gives better performance for all cases.

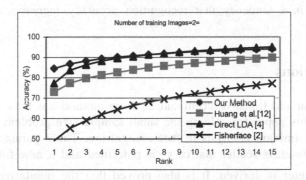

Fig. 4(a). The recognition accuracy against the rank with the training number is equals to 2

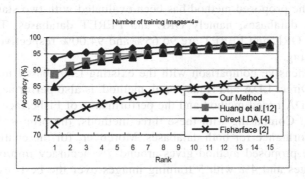

Fig. 4(b). The recognition accuracy against the rank with the training number is equals to 4

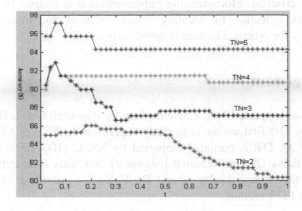

Fig. 5. Recognition accuracy vs parameter t with different number of training images on FERET database (one run only)

Finally, we randomly select an experiment out of 50 runs. For that particular experiment, we change the value of t in the interval $(0,1]$, step 0.01. For each value of t, we determine the corresponding accuracy. The results are plotted in Figure 5 with 2, 3, 4 and 5 training number (TN) images. It can be seen that for most of the cases, there is a tendency that recognition accuracy increases as parameter t decreases.

4 Conclusions

A new regularized linear discriminant analysis method has been developed and reported in this paper for solving the small sample size problem (S3) in Linear (Fisher) Discriminant Analysis in face recognition. The 3-parameter regularization on within-class scatter matrix S_w is redefined and a new formulation with single parameter is derived. It is also proved that the regularized within-class scatter matrix $S_w^{\alpha\beta\gamma}$ will approach to within-class scatter matrix S_w as parameter t tends to zero. A simple and efficient method is also developed in determining the value of t. The proposed method has been evaluated with two standard and public available databases, namely ORL and FERET databases. The recognition accuracy for ORL and FERET are 96.65% and 94.00% respectively. The results are encouraging.

A comprehensive comparison with the existing LDA-based methods, namely Fisherface, Direct LDA and Huang et al. method, is also performed. Fisherface is the classic LDA based method and the performance of Fisherface can be used as a benchmark. Comparing with these three methods, the proposed method gives the best performance for both databases. Moreover, for the challenging FERET database, the proposed method gives around 7% accuracy improvement with 2 training images and 4% with 5 training images over the best result reported in the literature.

In summary, the proposed method not only give the best performance, but also computational efficient. Moreover, the implementation is simple. By integrating the facial landmark detection for locating centers of eyes and mouth, the proposed method is ready for practical biometric applications.

Acknowledgement

This project was supported by the Science Faculty Research Grant, Hong Kong Baptist University. The first author is partially supported by NSF of China (60144001, 10101013). D. Q. Dai is partially supported by NSFC (10071096, 60175031). We would like to thank Olivetti Research Laboratory and Amy Research Laboratory for providing the face image databases, and Dr. H Yu for providing the Matlab source code on Direct LDA method.

References

1. Turk, M. and Pentland, A.: Eigenfaces for recognition. Journal of Cognitive Neuroscience, Vol. 3, No.1 (1991) 71–86
2. Belhumeur, P.N, Hespanha, J.P, Kriegman, D.J.: Eigenfaces vs. Fisherfaces: recognition using class specific linear projection. IEEE Trans. Pattern Anal. Mach. Intell., Vol. 19, No. 7 (1997) 711–720
3. Swets, D., Weng, J.: Using discriminant eigenfeatures for image retrieval. IEEE Trans. Pattern Anal. Mach. Intell., Vol. 18, No.8 (1996) 831–836
4. Yu, H. and Yang, J.: A direct LDA algorithm for high-dimensional data --- with application to face recognition. Pattern Recognition, Vol. 34 (2001) 2067–2070
5. Chen, L., Liao, H., Ko, M., Lin, J. and Yu, G.: A new LDA-based face recognition system, which can solve the small sample size problem. Pattern Recognition, Vol. 33, No. 10 (2000) 1713–1726
6. Liu, K., Cheng, Y., Yang, J.: Algebraic feature extraction for image recognition based on an optimal discriminant criterion. Pattern Recognition, Vol. 26, No.6 (1993) 903–911
7. Liu, K., Cheng, Y., Yang, J. and Liu, J.: An efficient algorithm for Foley-Sammon optimal set of discriminant vectors by algebraic method. International Journal of Pattern Analysis and Artificial Intelligence. Vol. 6, No. 5, pp. 817–829, 1992.
8. Jin, Z., Yang, J.Y., Hu, Z.S. and Lou, Z.: Face recognition based on the uncorrelated discriminant transform, Pattern Recognition. Vol. 34 (2001) 1405–1416
9. Martinez, A.M. and Kak, A.C.: PCA versus LDA. IEEE Trans. Pattern Anal. Mach. Intell., Vol. 23 (2001) 228–233
10. Martinez, A.M.: Recognizing imprecisely localized partially occluded and expression variant faces from a single sample per class. IEEE Trans. Pattern Anal. Mach. Intell., Vol. 24, No. 6 (2002) 748–763
11. Zhao, W., Chellappa, R. and Phillips, P. J.: Subspace linear discriminant analysis for face recognition. Technical Report CAR-TR-914, CS-TR-4009, University of Maryland at College Park, USA (1999)
12. Huang, R., Liu, Q., Lu H. and Ma, S.: Solving small sample size problem in LDA. Proceeding of International Conference in Pattern Recognition (ICPR 2002), Vol. 3 (2002) 29–32
13. Goudail, F., Lange, E., Iwamoto, T., Kyuma, K., Otsu, N.: Face recognition system using local autocorrelations and multiscale integration. IEEE Trans. Pattern Anal. Mach. Intell., Vol. 18, No.10 (1996) 1024–1028
14. Tian, Q., Barbero, M., Gu, Z.H., Lee, S.H.,: Image classification by the Foley-Sammon transform. Opt. Eng., Vol. 25, No. 7 (1986) 834–840
15. Krzanowski, W. J., Jonathan, P., McCarthy, W. V. andThomas, M. R., Discriminant analysis with singular covariance matrices: methods and applications to spectroscopic data. Appl. Statist., Vol.44 (1995) 101–115
16. Dai, D.Q. and Yuen, P.C.: Regularized discriminant analysis and its application on face recognition. Pattern Recognition, Vol. 36 (2003) 845–847
17. Dai, D.Q. and Yuen, P.C.: A wavelet-based 2-parameter regularization discriminant analysis for face recognition. Proceeding of The 4th International Conference on Audio and Video Based Personal Authentication, Accepted for publication (2003)
18. Lu, J., Plataniotis, K.N. and Venetsanopoulos, A.N.: Face Recognition Using Kernel Direct Discriminant Analysis Algorithms. IEEE Transactions on Neural Networks, Vol. 14, No. 1 (2003) 117–126
19. Lu, J., Plataniotis, K.N. and Venetsanopoulos, A.N.: Face Recognition Using LDA Based Algorithms. IEEE Transactions on Neural Networks, Vol. 14, No. 1 (2003) 195–200

Fast Calculation for Fisher Criteria in Small Sample Size Problem

WeiShi Zheng[1], JianHuang Lai[1], and P.C. Yuen[2]

[1] Department of Mathematics, Sun Yat-sen University
{SunnyWeiShi@163.com, stsljh@zsu.edu.cn}
[2] Department of Computer Science, Hong Kong Baptist University
{pcyuen@comp.hkbu.edu.hk}

Abstract. LDA is popularly used in the pattern recognition field. Unfortunately LDA always confronts the small sample size problem (S3), which leads the within-class scatter matrix to be singular. In this case, PCA is always used for dimensional reduction to solve the problem in practice. This paper analyzes that when the small sample size problem happens, the PCA processing is not only to play the role of solving the S3 problem but also can be used to induce a fast calculation algorithm for solving the fisher criteria. This paper will show that calculating the eigenvectors of within-class scatter matrix after dimensional reduction can solve the optimal projection for fisher criteria.

1 Introduction

Linear Discriminant Analysis (LDA) or Fisher Discriminant Analysis (FDA)[1][4][12] is popularly used in the pattern recognition field. It was proposed by R.A.Fisher[6] in 1936. In 1962, Wilks proposed the multiple classes LDA method [2]. One of the goals of LDA is to find an optimal projection W, such that the original samples are projected from high dimensional space to lower one, meanwhile making the ratio between between-class scatter matrix and within-class scatter matrix to be the maximum value. A lot of tests [5] have indicated that LDA performs well in Face Recognition field.

To get better recognition, there are mainly two constraints on the optimal projection suggested. In 1975, Foley and Sammon [2][3] suggested that the optimal vectors should be orthogonal each other, and in 2001 Z.Jin [2] showed that the constraint uncorrelated statistical was better. But the time of their algorithm's calculation costs much.

However LDA confronts the small sample size problem (S3 problem). There are three major approaches to solve this problem. A popular approach is PCA+LDA. It was proposed by P. N. Belhumeur[1]. The idea is that a PCA process is utilized to reduce the dimensional before the process of LDA. But the selection of the principle components for dimensional reduction is still a problem needed to study. The second approach is to adding a small perturbation to the within-class scatter matrix [10], so that it becomes non-singular. The idea is nice, but physical meaning and further analysis have not been given. Using pseudoinverse of the within-scatter matrix to solve the S3 problem is another interesting approach [7]. The computation of this approach can be processed by QR decomposition [9] and it has been proved that it is equivalence to this approach, which leads to a fast calculation.

The contribution to this paper is that we would reveal that the PCA is not only a step for dimensional reduction, but also be used for fast calculation of LDA in the small sample size case. We would do a further analysis on the PCA processing, and propose a fast algorithm to calculate the optimal projection for Fisher Criteria in the case of S3 problem. As a whole, this paper gives us a novel new point of view to PCA.

The outline of this paper is as follows: Section 2 will give some definitions on the notations and a simple introduction to LDA. Our major work will be presented in section 3, and then experiment results are showed in section 4. Finally we will obtain a conclusion.

2   Definition and Introduction of LDA

2.1   Definition of Notations

The following notations are commonly used in this paper. Assume the image can be presented as n dimensional vector and χ to be samples space. Given the samples, they can be separated into K classes, let $C = \{ C_1, C_2 \ldots C_K \}$, where C_j represents the jth class. Assume that the jth class C_j contains N_j samples, then $N = \sum_{j=1}^{K} N_j$ is the amount of the total samples. Let $m_j = \dfrac{1}{N_j} \sum_{x \in C_j} x$ be the mean image of the jth class, $m = \dfrac{1}{N} \sum_{j=1}^{K} \sum_{x \in C_j} x$ be the mean image of all samples. Let us define S_w be within-class scatter matrix, S_b be between-class scatter matrix, $S_t (= S_w + S_b)$ be total-class scatter matrix. In practice, S_w, S_b and S_t can be approximated as follows:

$$S_w = \tfrac{1}{N} \sum_{j=1}^{K} \sum_{x \in C_j} (x - m_j)(x - m_j)^T .$$

$$S_b = \tfrac{1}{N} \sum_{j=1}^{K} N_j (m_j - m)(m_j - m)^T .$$

$$S_t = \tfrac{1}{N} \sum_{j=1}^{K} \sum_{x \in C_j} (x - m)(x - m)^T .$$

2.2 Introduction to LDA

LDA aims to find the projection matrix $W = (w_1, w_2 \dots w_L)$, such that Fisher Criteria $J(W) = \frac{|W^T S_b W|}{|W^T S_w W|}$ is maximized, where $W \in R^{n \times L}$. If S_w is nonsingular, $w_1, w_2 \dots w_L$ are the eigenvectors of $S_w^{-1} S_b$ corresponding to the largest $L (\leq K - 1)$ eigenvalues[1][4]. If S_w is singular, i.e. the S3 problem exists, we have 3 major approaches to solve this problem as mentioned in section 1. One of these approaches is PCA pretreatment. This approach basically can make the within-scatter matrix to be nonsingular after PCA step in practice.

Unlike some other papers that like to find another methodology to reduce the dimensionality, the major work of this paper is to give a new point of view to the performance of PCA for LDA. One can find that PCA can also be used to make a faster computation for LDA in the small sample size problem. The next section will have a further analysis.

3   Fast Computation for LDA in S3 Problem

In this section we have a further analysis on the use of PCA in LDA processing under the small sample size case. The arrangement of this section is as follows: a preparation for the variables notations is developed in the section 3.1; then two lemmas are given before the main analysis for further analysis; finally section 3.3 gives our main work.

3.1 Preparation

It is easy for us to decompose S_t into (by svd):

$$S_t = W_t \, \Lambda_t \, W_t^T .$$

Where $W_t = (w_{t_1} \dots w_{t_m})$, $\Lambda_t = diag(\lambda_{t_1} \dots \lambda_{t_m})$, $\lambda_{t_1} \geq \dots \geq \lambda_{t_m} > 0$, $m \leq N - 1$. Let $W_{pca} = (w_{t_1} \dots w_{t_l})$, $\Lambda_{pca} = diag(\lambda_{t_1} \dots \lambda_{t_l})$, where $l = rank(S_w)$. Use PCA step to reduce the dimensional, and then we have the relations:

$$S_w^* = \Lambda_{pca}^{-\frac{1}{2}} W_{pca}^T \, S_w \, W_{pca} \, \Lambda_{pca}^{-\frac{1}{2}}, \quad S_b^* = \Lambda_{pca}^{-\frac{1}{2}} W_{pca}^T \, S_b \, W_{pca} \, \Lambda_{pca}^{-\frac{1}{2}} . \tag{1}$$

Where $\Lambda_{pca}^{-\frac{1}{2}}$ is added, a little different from the traditional PCA processing. Basically S_w^* will be nonsingular.

In this sense, in order to extract the optimal feature vectors of LDA, section 3.3 has declared that it is only sufficient to calculate the eigenvectors of S_w^* corresponding to the eigenvalues taking values in (0,1). Before we are going to analyze this proposition, we firstly need some lemmas and they are given in section 3.2.

3.2   Lemmas

Lemma 1: If λ is an arbitrary eigenvalue of $S_w^{*-1} S_b^*$, then $\lambda \geq 0$.

Proof: Since S_w^* is a positive definite and symmetrical matrix, then an orthogonal matrix U_w^* and dialog matrix Λ_w^* can be found so that

$$S_w^* = U_w^* \Lambda_w^* U_w^{*\,T}, \quad S_w^{*-1} = U_w^* \Lambda_w^{*-1} U_w^{*\,T}. \tag{2}$$

Let w be the eigenvector of $S_w^{*-1} S_b^*$ corresponding to λ, i.e

$$S_w^{*-1} S_b^* w = \lambda\, w$$

We write the equality in another way:

$$U_w^* \Lambda_w^{*-1} U_w^{*\,T} S_b^* w = \lambda\, w \tag{3}$$

Multiple ($\Lambda_w^{*\frac{1}{2}} U_w^{*\,T}$) on two sides of equality (3), then we obtain:

$$(\Lambda_w^{*-\frac{1}{2}} U_w^{*\,T}) S_b^* (\Lambda_w^{*-\frac{1}{2}} U_w^{*\,T})^T (\Lambda_w^{*\frac{1}{2}} U_w^{*\,T}) w = \lambda (\Lambda_w^{*\frac{1}{2}} U_w^{*\,T}) w$$

Let $G = \Lambda_w^{*-\frac{1}{2}} U_w^{*\,T}$, $S_{bg} = G\, S_b^*\, G^T$, $w_{bg} = (\Lambda_w^{*\frac{1}{2}} U_w^{*\,T}) w$.

Therefore $S_{bg}\, w_{bg} = \lambda\, w_{bg}$, it is obvious that λ is the eigenvalue of S_{bg}. Furthermore,

$$S_{bg} = G\, S_b^*\, G^T = (G\, \Lambda_{pca}^{\frac{1}{2}} W_{pca}^T\, \Phi_b)(G\, \Lambda_{pca}^{\frac{1}{2}} W_{pca}^T\, \Phi_b)^T.$$

It indicates S_{bg} is a semi definite matrix, then $\lambda \geq 0$ is valid.
This finishes the proof.

Lemma 2: Suppose w is the eigenvector of $S_w^{*-1} S_b^*$ corresponding to the eigenvalue $\lambda > 0$, then it is sufficient and necessary that w is the eigenvector of S_w^{*-1} corresponding to the eigenvalue $\lambda' = \lambda + 1 > 1$.

Proof: Since $S_t = S_w + S_b$ and $\Lambda_{pca}^{-\frac{1}{2}} W_{pca}^T S_t W_{pca} \Lambda_{pca}^{-\frac{1}{2}} = I_{l \times l}$, then we obtain the following easily:

$$I_{l \times l} = S_w^* + S_b^* .$$

Therefore

$$S_w^{*-1} S_b^* = S_w^{*-1}(I_{l \times l} - S_w^*) = S_w^{*-1} - I_{l \times l} .$$

Suppose w is an eigenvector of $S_w^{*-1} S_b^*$ corresponding to the eigenvalue $\lambda > 0$. So following is valid:

$$S_w^{*-1} S_b^* w = (S_w^{*-1} - I_{l \times l}) w = \lambda w .$$

$$S_w^{*-1} w = \lambda w + w = (\lambda + 1) w = \lambda' w .$$

It is obvious that w is the eigenvector of S_w^{*-1} corresponding to the eigenvalue $\lambda + 1$. Contrarily, it is also easy to prove if w is eigenvector of S_w^{*-1} corresponding to the eigenvalue $\lambda' > 1$, then w is the eigenvector of $S_w^{*-1} S_b^*$ corresponding to the eigenvalue $\lambda' - 1$.

This finishes the proof.

3.3   Fast Computation

By means of the above Lemma 1 and Lemma 2, we easily get our main theorem follows.

3.3.1   Main Theorem

Theorem 1: To calculate the eigenvectors of $S_w^{*-1} S_b^*$ corresponding to the nonzero eigenvalues, it is sufficient and necessary to calculate the eigenvectors of S_w^* corresponding to the eigenvalues that take values in the field $(0,1)$.

Proof: Recall the equality (2), from another point of view we have:

$$S_w^* U_w^* = U_w^* \Lambda_w^* . \qquad (4)$$

$$S_w^{*-1} U_w^* = U_w^* \Lambda_w^{*-1} . \qquad (5)$$

Comparing equalities (4) and (5), we have the following conclusion: If w is the eigenvector of S_w^{*-1} corresponding to the eigenvalue λ, then it is sufficient and necessary that w is the eigenvector of S_w^* corresponding to the eigenvalue $\frac{1}{\lambda}$.

By virtue of Lemma 1 and Lemma 2, the theorem is obvious. This finishes the proof.

3.3.2 The Intuitive Meaning of the Theorem 1 and Our Work

To solve the Fisher criteria after dimensionality reduction, it is sufficient to solve the following problem:

$$W_{lda} = \arg \max_{W} \frac{|W^T S_b^* W|}{|W^T S_w^* W|} . \tag{6}$$

In a traditional way to solve the equality is to solve the eigenvalue problem:

$$S_w^{*\,-1} S_b^* W_{lda} = W_{lda} \Lambda_{lda} . \tag{7}$$

Unlike the traditional way, according to our work in section 3.3.1, the theorem tells us another more efficient method can also solve the problem, which calculates some eigenvectors by solving the eigenvalue problem:

$$S_w^* W_{lda} = W_{lda} \Lambda_{lda}^* \tag{8}$$

As a result we only need to calculate equality (8), which we do not need to calculate the inverse of S_w^* and the step for matrix multiply operation $S_w^{*\,-1} S_b^*$ at least. In this sense solving the equality (8) is faster than solving the equality (7). This leads a faster computation for Fisher Criteria in Small Sample Size Problem.

4 Experiment

Section 3 has analyzed the theorem of the proposed algorithm; the analysis indicates its fast property. This section will show its feasibility for practice.

We test the algorithm on a subset of FERET Database. For FERET database, we select 72 people, 6 images for each individual. The six images are extracted from 4 different sets, namely Fa, Fb, Fc and duplicate [5]. The resolution of each image is cropped to size 75×80 where locates at the face area. All images are aligned by the centers of eyes and mouth. Images of one person in FERET database are show in Figure 1.

Fig. 1. Images of one person from FERET database that consists of 72 individuals and 6 images per person

In our experiment, if there are k images of each person for training and the others for testing, then we will run C_6^k times, e.g. if $k=3$, then we run 20 $(=C_6^3)$ times. For each running, the accuracy value is record, and finally we get the average value.

Following we compare the proposed algorithm in this paper with Fisherface[1]. All algorithms have the same order of images for training. Table 1 records the accuracy results.

Table 1. Classification accuracy (%) and comparison between proposed algorithm and Fisherface on FERET database

Method Number of Images training per person	Proposed Algorithm	Fisherface
2	72.94%	74.352%
3	89.352%	87.593%
4	93.009%	91.111%
5	94.907%	92.824%

Table 1 shows that the proposed algorithm performs well in the face recognition on FERET database, it performs better than Fisherface when the number of training sample per person is larger than 2.

If we have 3 images of each person for training, and the others are used to test, then Figure 2 is a Cumulative Match Score [11] that is a plot of rank 5 scores versus probability of average correct identification.

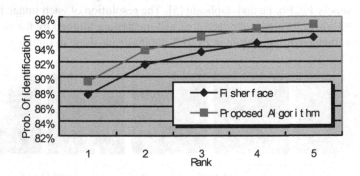

Fig. 2. Identification performance reported on a CMC. 72 individuals are used, 216 images are used to train, and the other 216 images are used to test

The accuracy of our proposed algorithm increases from 89.35% with rank 1 to 97.04% with rank 5. By virtue of table 1 and Figure 2, the proposed algorithm performs better than Fisherface. So the proposed algorithm is reasonable and moreover it has a faster computation for Fisher Criteria that analyzes in section 3.

5 Conclusion

This paper has revealed that in the case of the small sample size problem, the processing PCA can play 2 roles: one is to reduce the dimensional as we have known before; the other is to induce an algorithm which can solve the fisher criteria faster by equality (8). But one should point out that the selection of principle components for dimensionality reduction is still a problem. Because some principle components are not selected so that there is information lost during the step of dimensionality reduction. In conclusion, the new point of view to PCA has been given in this paper.

Acknowledgement

This project was supported by NSFC (No. 60144001), NSF of GuangDong, P.R. China(No. 021766) and RGC Earmarked Research Grant HKBU-2119/03E. We would like to thank the Amy Research Laboratory for providing the face image databases. The author would also like to thank the reviewers for their valuable advice.

References

1. Belhumeur, P. N., Hespanha, J.P., Kriegman, and D.J.: Eigenfaces vs. Fisherfaces: recognition using class specific linear projection. IEEE Trans. Pattern Anal. Mach. Intell. . Vol. 19(7) (1997) 711–720
2. Jin, Z., Yang, J.Y., Tang, Z.M., and Hu, Z.S.: A theorem on the uncorrelated optimal discriminant vectors. Pattern Recognition. Vol. 34 (2001) 2041–2047
3. Duchene, J., Leclercq, S.: An optimal transformation for discriminant and principal component analysis. IEEE Trans. Pattern Anal. Mach. Intell. . Vol 10(6) (1988) 978–983
4. Martinez, A. M., Kak, A. C.: PCA Versus LDA. IEEE Trans. Pattern Anal. Mach. Intell. . Vol. 23(2) (2001) 228–233
5. Phillips, P. J., Moon, H., Rizvi, S. A. and Rauss. P. J.: The FERET evaluation methodology for face recognition algorithms. IEEE Trans. Pattern Anal. Mach. Intell. . Vol. 22(10) (2000) 1090–1103
6. Fisher, R.A.: The Use of Multiple Measures in Taxonomic Problems. Ann. Eugenics. Vol. 7 (1936) 179–188
7. Ye, J.P., Janardan, R., Park, C.H., and Park H.: An Optimization Criterion for Generalized Discriminant Analysis on Undersampled Problems. IEEE Trans. Pattern Anal. Mach. Intell.. Vol. 26(8) (2004) 982–994
8. Zhao, W., Chellappa, R., Phillips, J., and Rosenfeld, A.: Face Recognition: A Literature Survey. ACM Computing Surveys. Vol.35 (4) (2003) 399–458

338   W. Zheng, J. Lai, and P.C. Yuen

9. Ye, J.P., Li, Q.: LDA/QR: an efficient and effective dimension reduction algorithm and its theoretical foundation. Pattern Recognition. Vol.37 (4) (2004) 851 – 854
10. Zhao, W., Chellappa, R., and Phillips, P.J.: Subspace linear discriminant analysis for face recognition. Technical Report CAR-TR-914, CS-TR-4009, University of Maryland at College Park, USA
11. Phillips, P.J., Grother, P., Micheals, R., Blackburn, D.M., Tabassi, E., and Bone, J.M.: Face Recognition Vendor Test 2002: Evaluation Results. Available at [http://www.frvt.org/DLs/FRVT_2002_Evaluation_Report.pdf]
12. Wang, X.G., Tang X.O.: A Unified Framework for Subspace Face Recognition. IEEE Trans. PAMI. Vol.26 (9) 2004 1222–1228

Vision-Based Face Understanding Technologies and Their Applications

Shihong Lao and Masato Kawade

Sensing Technology Laboratory, OMRON Corporation,
9-1, Kizugawadai, Kizu-cho, Soraku-Gun, Kyoto 619-0283, Japan
{lao, kawade}@ari.ncl.omron.co.jp

Abstract. We have developed a group of vision-based face understanding technologies called OKAO Vision (OKAO means face in Japanese) including face detection, facial feature point detection, face recognition and facial attribute estimation. Our face detection technology can detect both frontal and profile faces rotated to any angles. Facial feature point detection, face recognition and facial attribute estimation arc based on a common architecture: using Gabor wavelet transform coefficients as feature values and use SVM as classifier. Our experiments show that this architecture is very powerful. In this paper, we explain the key technologies of OKAO Vision and how these technologies are used in applications for entertainment, communication, security and intelligent interfaces.

1 Introduction

When a person directly meets other people and communicates, the information obtained from vision plays a large role in the communication. People acquire various sorts of information by looking at other people's faces: How many people are there? Who are they?Are they young?Are they male or female?Are they angry?Are they sleepy?Are they saying something?In re sponse to such information, people may consciously or unconsciously respond, for example, by speaking gently but in a loud voice to an elderly person, or changing our words when speaking to a foreigner. In the same way, we believe that if machines can sense and understand the human face with vision, this will revolutionize the conventional interfaces. We have been conducting R&D on vision-based face understanding technology with the aim of creating this sort of interfaces where the machine adapts to the human.

The rest of this paper is organized as follows: Section 2 introduces the key technologies and the structure of OKAO Vision; section 3 the omni-directional face detection; section 4 face detection implemented on LSI; section 5 facial feature point detection; section 6 face recognition; section 7 gender, age and ethnicity estimation; section 8 example applications; section 9 future deployments.

S.Z. Li et al. (Eds.): Sinobiometrics 2004, LNCS 3338, pp. 339–348, 2004.

2 The Key Technologies of Vision-Based Face Understanding

The process of vision-based face understanding key technologies is shown in Fig. 1.
First the system detects the position and angle of the face from an image. Then it
detects the feature points on the facial organs (like the center and end points of the
eyes and mouth), extracts feature values, does face recognition and estimates
attributes such as gender and age.

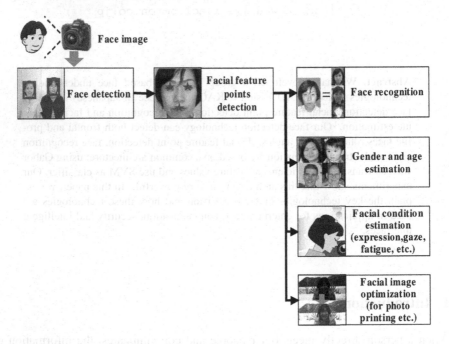

Fig. 1. Key technologies of OKAO Vision

3 Omni-Directional Face Detection

In order to understand a face, it is necessary to first find the position of the face in the
image. Viola and Jones proposed an algorithm for face detection based on integral
image and simple features together with a cascad structured classifier trained with
AdaBoost [1]. We propose a rotation invariant multi-view face detection method [2].
Human faces are divided into several categories according to the variant appearance
from different view points. For each view category, weak classifiers are configured as
confidence-rated look-up-table (LUT) of Haar feature. Real AdaBoost algorithm is
used to boost these weak classifiers and construct a nested cascade structured face
detector. To make it rotation invariant, we divide the whole 360-degree range into 12
sub-ranges and construct their corresponding view based detectors separately. To
improve the speed, a pose estimation method is introduced.

Our main contributions are:

1. Instead of the threshold type weak classifier as used in [1], the Look-Up-Table (LUT) type weak classifier is proposed. We also proposed a method to boost these LUT type weak classifiers, based on Schapire and Singer's improved boosting algorithms [3] that use real-valued confidence-rated weak classifiers. We call it Real AdaBoost in order to distinguish it from what we call Discrete AdaBoost, that is the original AdaBoost algorithm adopted in [1] using Boolean weak classifier.
2. A novel nested cascade detector is proposed and a corresponding pose estimation method for improving overall performance is developed (see Fig.2).
3. A fast multi-view face detection system which can deal with both frontal and profile faces rotated to any angles, based on the above structure is implemented.

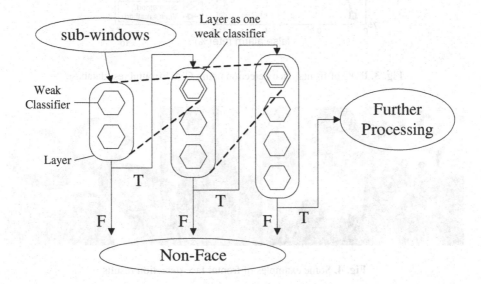

Fig. 2. Face detector with nested cascade structure

The test results of our face detection system are very encouraging. Fig. 3 shows the ROC of frontal face detection results comparing our method and Viola's method, our method are much better. The speed of our system is very fast, to processing a 320x240 image takes only about 250 msec. For multi-view faces which can be as small as 20x20 pixels.

Experiments on faces with 360-degree in-plane rotation and 90-degree out-of-plane rotation are reported, of which the frontal face detector subsystem retrieves 94.5%of the faces with 57 false alarms on   the CMU+MIT frontal face test set and the multi-view face detector subsystem retrieves 89.8%of the faces with 221 false alarms on the CMU profile face test set.

In Fig. 4 and 5 some samples of face detection results are shown.

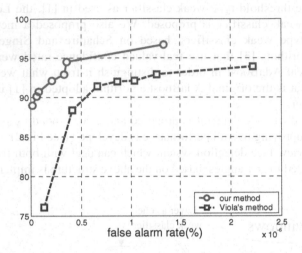

Fig. 3. ROC of frontal face detection using CMU frontal test database

Fig. 4. Some examples of frontal face detection results

Fig. 5. Some samples of the multi-view face detection results

For detail about this face detection algorithm see [2].

4   Face Detection Implemented on LSI

We have also implemented a face detection system on a FPGA chip [6]. The face detection engine has about 350,000 gates that can be embedded in various electronic devices such as camera, video camera and web camera etc. On a 27MHz Xilinx Vertex-II FGPA chip, the processing time is about 0.1 seconds for frontal faces which can be as small as 40x40 in a QGA sized image. From a data set of 17,000 portrait photos, the detection rate is 90% On average, less than 3 false detections can be found per 100 QGA sized images w ith complicated backgrounds.

Fig. 6. Face detection FPGA chip

5   Facial Feature Point Detection

Once the position of a face has been found, it is necessary to accurately detect the position of feature points which serve as the basis for extracting features, like the end and center points of the eyes and mouth. For this face feature point detection and face alignment, we use Gabor wavelet transform coefficients as feature values and use SVM as a classifier. The SVM classifier is trained using a database to output 1 at the predefined feature point and output 0 otherwise. While detecting the feature point, the SVM is used to search around the eye or mouth area, the position with the highest confidence is considered as the facial feature point.

6   Face Recognition

Face recognition is also implemented using the same framework as facial feature points detection. An overview of our face recognition algorithm is shown in Fig. 7.

The feature values for recognition are extracted from the face image using a Gabor wavelet transform and retinal sampling method [8]. SVM is used as classifier both for verification and identification.

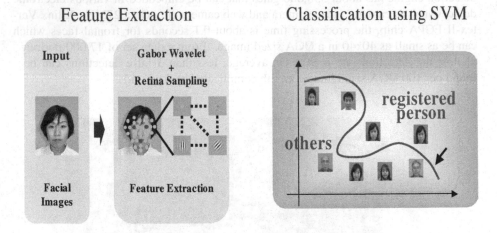

Fig. 7. Over view of face recognition algorithm

Our face recognition technology is implemented into the following 3 types:

1. Standing type: user should stand in front of the camera;
2. Walking through type: users are not required to stop in front of the camera;
3. Photo verification type: users are verified using the photo.

For the standing type, the top1 recognition rate is 99.5%while the FAR is set to 1%the FRR is below 1%On a Pentium III 700MHz PC, the processing time is 0.6 seconds.

7 Gender, Age and Ethnicity Estimation

Fig. 8 gives an overview of gender, age and ethnicity estimation. The feature values necessary for estimation are extracted from the face image using a Gabor wavelet transform and retina sampling too. Those feature values are given to a SVM, and gender and age are estimated. For gender estimation, performance is 91.6%with a Database of 1240 people. For age estimation, the percentages are 99.4%for child-hood (up to 10 years old), 90.5%for adolescence (10–19 years old), 82.6%for young adulthood (20–39), 81.4%for middle age (40–59), and 86.6%for old age (60 years or over). Processing speed was approx. 0.5 sec per image on PentiumIII-1GHz CPU.

We also developed a system for estimate ethnicity using the same framework [7]. The accuracy is as follows: Asian 96.3%, European 93.1%African 94.3% The processing time is 0.034 seconds per image.

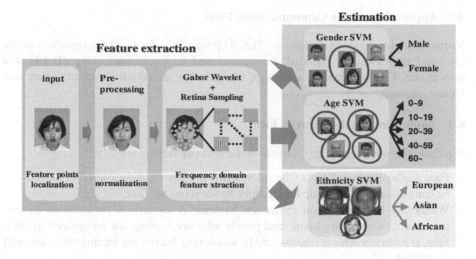

Fig. 8. Overview of algorithm of gender, age and ethnicity estimation

8 Example Applications

Vision-based face understanding technology can be used in applications in the following 4 fields.

    (1) Entertainment: Playing with faces
    (2) Communication: Talking with faces
    (3) Security: Easy identity authentication
    (4) Intelligent Interfaces: Universal design, human interfaces, automatic marketing

8.1 Applications in the Entertainment Field

We have developed the following systems in the entertainment field:

1. Automatic Caricature Generation: This system automatically draws caricature, by extracting facial features from an input face image, and exaggerating features which deviate greatly from the average.
2. Photo Sticker Vending Machine: This system is an application of face detection. Based on the face detection results, the system can provide user such functions such as automatic skin beautifying where smoothing processing is performed to conceal things like rough skin, freckles or pimples. Another function is hair color simulation, where the hair region is automatically extracted and its color changed.
3. "Okao-Net" (Face Net), a Face Image Entertainment Service for Mobile Phones with Cameras: This system can be used in applications like sending a face image taken with a camera-equipped mobile phone, and accessing services like fortune telling by features of the face, searching for the closest match with a celebrity, providing cosmetic advice to suit the person's facial type, automatic doodling on the face, or ranking in competitions of the features values of facial organs.

8.2 Applications in the Communication Field

Virtual Face Image Communication: The 3D pose of the face and the openness of the eyes and mouth can be encoded, transmitted and then recreated using 3D CG at a remote site. This will enable face image transmission in real time even on a very low bit rate network.

8.3 Applications in the Security Field

We have also made many applications in the security field:

1. Face Authentication Access Control System: If a person is registered in the system, he can unlock an electronic lock simply by showing his face.
2. Wandering Elderly Person Protection System: A camera is provided at the entrance/exit of a nursing home, and people who are leaving are recognized by their face. If a person who is unconsciously wandering leaves the facility, the care staff is notified.
3. Photo Matching System: When a person must be matched against a face photograph (driver's license or passport) in areas like consumer finance, the system can automatically match the photo against the actual person.
4. Automatic Face Feature Classification and Search System: The facial feature quantities (spacing between eyes, turn up of the eyes, thickness of mouth etc.) are classified. The system can search for faces with a certain feature, if the degree of the feature quantity is designated.
5. Monitoring/Face Authentication System: At entrances and exits, this system performs face authentication using video from a surveillance camera, and thereby provides support in detecting criminals and other specific persons, as well as persons who do not have permission to enter.
6. PC Login Security System: When logging into a PC, one can login simply by showing his face, instead of entering a login name and password. The system will also make it possible to lock the screen of one's PC if someone else looks at it.
7. Internet Security as Part of a Multi-biometrics System Combined with Fingerprint Authentication: One can access personal data on the internet with greater security by authenticating both his face and fingerprints at a biometric authentication site on the internet.

8.4 Applications in the Universal Design, Human Interface and Automatic Marketing Fields

1. Age Optimized Interfaces: These interfaces are optimized to suit the abilities of the user, for example, using large characters and loud audio for the elderly, and displaying text in Japanese phonetic script so children can read it.
2. Age Discrimination Interfaces: Interfaces which disable operation if the user is not above a certain age (cigarette and alcohol vending machines, TV programs with adult content or violent scenes etc.)

3. Interfaces Which Provide Information According to Gender and Age: These interfaces automatically display information and services to suit the gender and age of the user.
4. Automatic Customer Analysis: These systems collect marketing information, like what kind of customers buy what sort of things, by automatically estimating the age and gender of the customers.

9 Future Deployments

We have conducted R&D on vision-based face understanding technology, and made progress toward applications like those indicated above. In order to continue further toward improving these applications, we will address the following technical issues:

- ■ Improving robustness
  - Handling large variations in face direction
  - Handling large variations in lighting
  - Handling large variations in expression,
  - Handling variation in things like cosmetics, beards, eyebrows and hair on the cheeks
  - Improving robustness for glasses
- ■ Further improvement of accuracy
- ■ Handling change due to the passage of time
- ■ Developing more compact dedicated chips
- ■ Measures to protect privacy
- ■ Integration with other biometrics
- ■ Improving the speed, and achieving real-time processing

While dealing with the above issues, we will also study new applications and new related technologies.

References

1. P. Viola, M. Jones, "Rapid Object Detection using a Boosted Cascade of Simple Features", IEEE Conf. on Computer Vision and Pattern Recognition, pp. 511-518, 2001.
2. B. Wu, H. Ai, C. Huang and S. Lao, "Fast Rotation Invariant Multi-View Face Detection Based on Real Adaboost", IEEE Conf. on Automatic Face and Gesture Recognition, pp. 79-84, 2004 .
3. R. E. Schapire and Y. Singer, "Improved Boosting Algorithms Using Confidence-rated Predictions", Machine Learning, 37, pp.297-336, 1999.
4. H. Schneiderman and T. Kanade, "A Statistical Method for 3D Object Detection Applied to Faces and Cars", Proc. IEEE Conf. on Computer Vision and Pattern Recognition, 2000.
5. S. Z. Li, L. Zhu, Z. QZhang, et al., "S tatistical Learning of Multi-View Face Detection". Proceedings of the 7th European Conference on Computer Vision, 2002.
6. F. Imae et al., "Face detection system implemented on LSI", CVPR2004 demo program, 2004.

7. S. Hosoi, E. Takikawa and M. Kawade, "Ethnicity Estimation with Facial Images", IEEE Conf. on Automatic Face and Gesture Recognition, pp. 195-200, 2004.
8. F. Smeraldi, N. Capdevielle and J. Bigun, "Face Authentication by retinotopic sampling of the Gabor decomposition and Support Vector Machines", proc. of the 2nd International Conference on Audio and Video Based Biometric Person Authentication (AVBPA99), Washington DC (USA), pp. 125-129, 1999.

International Standardization on Face Recognition Technology

Technology

Wonjun Hwang and Seok Cheol Kee

Wonjun Hwang and Seok Cheol Kee

Computing Lab., Samsung Advanced Institute of Technology
Mt. 14-1, Noengseo-Ri, Giheung-Eup, Yonging-Si, Gyeonggi-Do, Korea 449–712
{wj.hwang, sckee}@samsung.com
http://www.sait.samsung.co.kr

Abstract. This paper details the international standard works on biometrics, especially face recognition, for example, which groups have an interest, what kind of works has been done, and why the standard works are needed. Moreover, the history of MPEG-7 Advanced Face Recognition descriptor and current situations are described.

1 Introduction

Biometrics is automatic person recognition method using physiological characteristics. The features in biometrics, for example, are face, iris, fingerprints, voice, retinal, vein, voice and etc. The main reason why the biometric technology is becoming apparent is because the need for the high security is increased these days. Commercially speaking, the recent biometrics is leaded by governments and military which have an ability to make a big market on each purpose. The driver's license with fingerprint is a good example. As the corresponding law is amended, all licenses will be replaced. In biometric technology, face is the most important feature because the face image is remarkably familiar to human beings. When you meet another man in real life, firstly you look at his face and know who he is. The face picture is already in most of identification cards, ex. passport, driving license, and national ID card, which is used to verify user's identity. To give another example, the face image has been a mandatory part in MRTD [1] (Machine Readable Travel Documents), a document containing eye- and machine-readable data and developed by ICAO (International Civil Aviation Organization).

Face recognition technology [2] is still developing and many papers are being published. Utilizing face recognition for personal authentication is convenient and more accurate than current method. This is because it is not necessary for user to carry or remember something. In case of old method such as PIN (Personal Identification Number), it is possible that a password can be used by unauthorized person for criminal purpose. Face recognition is no touch biometric technology and does not need expensive equipments. The good example using face recognition is the passport based on encrypted face templates which have an owner's personal characteristic.

S.Z. Li et al. (Eds.): Sinobiometrics 2004, LNCS 3338, pp. 349–357, 2004.
© Springer-Verlag Berlin Heidelberg 2004

In a point of view on the performance of face recognition, it is not easy problem which method are the best and which experimental scenarios should be used to measure. FERET [3] and FRVT [4] are useful samples to aim at independent and blind testing the performance of system, but in case of standard work, the one of important things is the interoperability. For this reason the standard works should be opened to the public, but we can not clearly know the operating principles from the result of such blind tests, even though the performance was assured.

In this paper we detail foreign organizations which have taking an interest in biometrics as standard works in Section 2. MPEG-7 Advanced Face Recognition descriptor contributed by us and the brief state of affairs is explained in Section 3.

2 Standardization Organizations on Biometrics

2.1 Korean Standardization Organizations

In Korea, the representative organizations related to biometrics are TTA (Telecommunications Technology Association) and KATS (Korean Agency for Technology and Standards), the purpose of TTA is to contribute to the advancement of technology and the promotion of information and telecommunications services by effectively establishing and providing technical standards, especially ITU-T and ITU-R, which reflect the latest domestic and international technological advances. Sub Groups 3 (SG3) which focuses on network and system security has a lot of interests in Biometrics. On the other hand, KATS establishes and distributes Korean Industrial Standards (KS) for the provision of industrial technology infrastructure and the protection of consumers. KATS explores and develops standards for new technologies and products according to market demands. They have been supporting a Korean expert group for ISO/IEC JTC1 SC27, SC37 and ISO TC68, relating to Biometrics. Korean standard works already established are K-X9.84, specifying the minimum requirements of security for management of biometric information, and K-BioAPI.

2.2 American Standardization Organization

After the tragic events of September 11, demands of biometrics standards are increased in America. NIST (National Institute of Standards and Technology) has played a leading role in biometrics standards and each group supported by NIST has been going to achieve the standard works organically for own purpose. For example, the work of M1-Biometrics Technical Committee in INCITS (InterNational Committee for Information Technology Standards) is to accelerate the deployment of standards-based security solutions for homeland defense and the prevention of identity theft. ANSI/X9F4 Working Group (WG) deals with standardization to reduce financial data security risk and vulnerability and they is developing ANSI X9.84-2000 Biometrics Management and Security for the Financial Services Industry which specifies the minimum security requirements for effective management of biometrics data for the financial services industry. BioAPI Consortium, non-governmental group, was formed to develop a widely available and widely accepted API that will serve for various biometric technologies. The remarked standard works are CBEFF (Common Biometric Exchange File Format) defines a common set of data elements necessary to support multiple biometric technologies and BioAPI V1.1, developed by BioAPI Consortium, defines an open system standard API that allows software applications to communicate with a broad range of biometric technologies in a common way.

2.3 International Standardization Organization

ISO (International Organization for Standardization) and IEC (International Electrotechnical Commission) form the specialized system for worldwide standardization. National Bodies that are members of ISO or IEC participate in the development of International Standards through technical committees established by the respective organization to deal with particular fields of technical activity. ISO and IEC technical committees collaborate in fields of mutual interest. For standardization in the field of Information Technology, ISO and IEC have established a Joint Technical Committee 1: ISO/IEC JTC 1 on Information Technology whose missions are develop, maintain, promote and facilitate IT standards required by global markets meeting business and user requirements concerning. In this time, there are total 17 subcommittees and SC17, SC27 and SC37 are a close relationship with biometrics. Moreover, SC29-WG11, described in detail afterward, is the only group that has been achieved the standard template on face recognition.

(1) **ISO/IEC JTC1/SC17** has responsibility for developing standards for identification cards and personal identification. WG (Working Group) 10, motor vehicle driver license and related documents, has been arguing on standards based on biometric information and recently WG11 is organized for biometric standard work in cards.

(2) **ISO/IEC JTC1/SC27** has been related to standardization of generic methods and techniques for IT Security. The works are biometric data protections techniques, biometric security testing, evaluations, and evaluations methodologies. They has been standardizing on Protection Profile (PP) with Biometrics and Biometrics Evaluation Methodology (BEM).

(3) **ISO/IEC JTC1/SC37** In June 2002, JTC 1 established a new Subcommittee 37 on Biometrics. The goal of this new JTC 1 SC is to ensure a high priority, focused, and comprehensive approach worldwide for the rapid development and approval of formal international biometric standards. These standards are necessary to support the rapid deployment of significantly better, open systems standard-based security solutions for purposes such as homeland defense and the prevention of ID theft.

The scope of SC37 is the standardization of generic biometric technologies pertaining to human beings to support interoperability and data interchange among applications and systems. Generic human biometric standards include: common file frameworks; biometric application programming interfaces; biometric data interchange formats; related biometric profiles; application of evaluation

352   W. Hwang and S.C. Kee

criteria to biometric technologies; methodologies for performance testing and
reporting and cross jurisdictional and societal aspects. Several fields of SC17,
SC27, and SC37 overlap each other in some places and so they have been briskly
collaborating in the biometric standard works. SC37 consists of total 6 Working
Groups and each mission is as follows; WG1 - Harmonized Biometric Vocabu-
lary, WG2 - Biometric Technical Interfaces, WG3 - Biometric Data Interchange
Formats, WG4 - Biometric Functional Architecture and Related Profiles, WG5 -
Biometric Testing and Reporting, and WG6 - Cross-Jurisdictional and Societal
Aspects.

WG3 especially considers the standardization of the content, meaning and
representation of biometric data formats which are specific to a particular biometric technology and has been working to ensure a common look and feel for
Biometric Data Structure standards, with notation and transfer formats that provide platform independence and separation of transfer syntax from content definition. Such being the case, we are interest in the standard work of WG3 as a
scope of face recognition technology. In this time the common format of face
picture is a raw image by itself but we can add more the standard format such as
the template extracted by face recognition algorithm with a compact size and
high performance. In this point, the MPEG-7 Advanced Face Recognition descriptor has been considering now.

3   ISO/IEC JTC1/SC29 WG11 - The Moving Picture Experts Group (MPEG)

3.1 Outline of MPEG

The Moving Picture Experts Group (MPEG) [5] is a Working Group (WG11) of
ISO/IEC JTC1/SC29 in charge of the development of standards for coded representation of digital audio and video. MPEG-7, the Committee Draft (CD) of the Multimedia Content Description Interface, was issued at the October meeting in 2000.
This MPEG-7 CD provides a rich source of core technologies which allow the
description of audio-visual data content in multimedia environments. During the
development of MPEG-7 it was realized that face recognition would be a vital part
of the MPEG-7 standard and provide many important functionalities. For this reason it was decided to investigate the extension of the existing face recognition
technology in the MPEG-7 CD.

3.2 Objectives of MPEG-7 Face Descriptor

There are many applications in which it is desirable to automatically identify a
person with MPEG-7 Face Descriptor (FD). Some example applications are:
(1)automatic login control by matching an image taken from a built-in camera

with a database of users who have authorized access to a computer, (2) using an image taken from a surveillance camera to find any possible matches in a database of known criminals, (3) automatic generation of metadata for creation of personal media libraries, and (4) automatic summarization of video clips based on the identity of the people in the scene. There are also many applications of search and retrieval by face; for example using a frame of a movie which contains a particular actor to locate all other scenes in the movie which contain this same actor. These applications usually involve three stages: location of the face region in the query image, extraction of the face descriptor from the located region and matching the descriptor extracted from the query image with face descriptors present in a database.

To determine which method coincides with objectives of face descriptor, participants should submit the document of Core Experiments (CE) at each MPEG meeting. The objectives of CE are (1) to evaluate the retrieval performance of the proposed face descriptors, (2) to evaluate the identification performance of the proposed face descriptors, (3) to evaluate size and computational complexity of the proposed technology (both extraction and matching), (4) to provide cross verification of all results. Thus we should develop a face descriptor with a balance of performance and complexity.

3.3 MPEG-7 Face Descriptor Versions 1.0

In the beginning, the 2nd-order eigenfaces [6] is standardized as MPEG-7 FD version 1.0 in 2001. The effective features are extracted by 2nd-order eigenface. Selecting different eigen sets made from a residual image, the method can be used for view-angle-invariant and lighting-invariant face description. The 2nd-order eigenfeatures are effective in describing high-passed face image and the 1st-order eigenfeatures are useful in describing the low-passed image. Considering the computing order, the method has the same computational complexity compared with the regular eigenface method [7].

The database is the important fact in face recognition because the performance of face recognition depends on the constitution of the database. In experiments of the 2nd-order eigenface, 1,355 face images of 271 persons are used to examine the performance of lighting-invariant and view-angle-invariant face description. The images are selected from AR (Purdue), AT&T, Yale, UMIST, University of Berne, and some face images obtained from the MPEG-7 news videos. The database is divided into two sections in conformity with CE conditions: One section is to be used for training and the other section is to be used for evaluating the retrieval performance of the algorithms. As a measure of retrieval performance and identification performance, we use ANMRR [8] (Average Normalized Modified Retrieval Rate) and ASR [9] (Average Success Rate), respectively. ANMRR is 0 when all ground truth images are ranked on top, and it is 1 when all ground images are ranked out of the first m images.

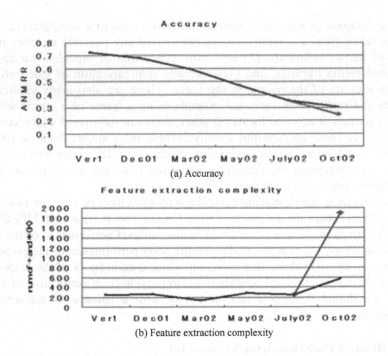

A c c u r a c y

(a) Accuracy

Feature extraction complexity

(b) Feature extraction complexity

Fig. 1. Increasing ratios (a) of recognition accuracy and (b) of feature extraction complexity for one year

3.4   MPEG-7 Advanced Face Recognition Descriptor

After promotion of MPEG-7 FD version 1.0, MPEG-7 visual group held new CE competition to set up the new FD because the 2nd-order eigenface has not shown the good performance in the extended database. MPEG-7 visual group enlarged the number of face images from 1,355 to 11,845 - it consists of five databases: the extended version 1 MPEG-7 face database, Altkom database, MPEG-7 test set in XM2VTS database, FERET database, and MPEG-7 test set in the BANCA database and also made 8 experimental scenarios - one for Face retrieval, seven for Person Identification. In total, 32 experiments should be performed, which means 8 scenarios (1 Face Image Retrieval+7 Person Identification)*2 training and testing definitions (1:1 and 1:4)*2 clipping sets (manual/automatic eyes detection). Therefore, the condition of new CE is more strict and complex than that of old CE.

For one year, 14 or more face recognition algorithms, ex., PCA, ICA, LDA, GDA, NDA and HMM[1], were competed with the extended database and experiments. The performances of new FDs were increased by stages at each MPEG meeting as shown in Fig. 1.

---

[1] The reference book on the basic descriptions of recognition algorithms is "Pattern Classification" written by Duda and etc (John Wiley&Sons).

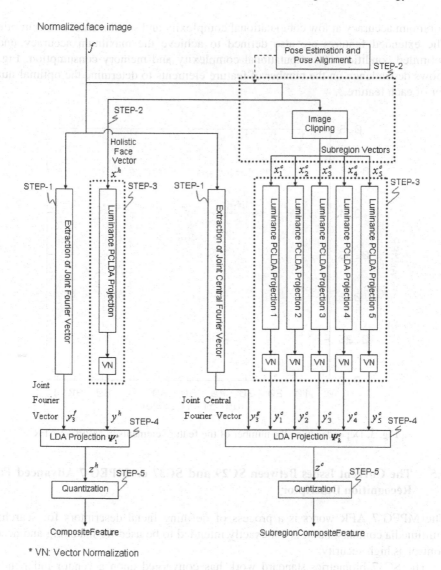

Fig. 2. Extraction of CompositeFeature and CentralCompositeFeature in MPEG-7 AFR

In 2004 we successfully promoted our face recognition algorithm to International Standardization [13] and the recursive matching scheme [10] were also achieved as informative part [11]. The new standardized MPEG-7 Advanced Face Recognition descriptor (AFR) [12] is using Fourier and Intensity LDA features. The descriptor consists of two major parts as shown in Fig. 2; (a) Fourier features of a facial image, (b) extended component features which are enhanced by merging the Fourier features with pose-compensated image intensity features. Twenty four elements of each Fourier feature are mandatory to extract for keeping interoperability in guaranteeing the minimum accuracy at low computational complexity and small memory consumption. The extended features are also defined to achieve the maximum accuracy under unlimited condition of computational complexity and memory consumption. Fig. 3 shows dependency on the number of feature elements to determine the optimal number of each feature.

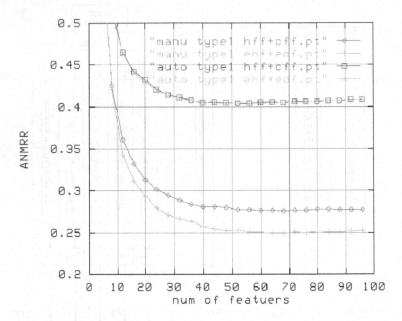

Fig. 3. Dependency on the number of the feature elements in MPEG-7 AFR

3.5   The Current Issues Between SC29 and SC37 on MPEG-7 Advanced Face Recognition Descriptor

The MPEG-7 AFR works is a process of defining facial descriptors for searching multimedia contents, but it is not exactly intended to be used for matching and access control as high security.

The SC37 biometrics standard work has converged upon a vendor independent face image representation. Because the SC37 group agreed that there does not exist a mature template representation that can be used, in a globally interoperable manner, with the security/access application profiles being developed by ISO and IEC. As a result, the face image format allows for virtually any photo of a face to be captured and stored. And furthermore, the photo image is specific to the frontal face with high quality and under restricted environments [14].

SC37 was not in existence when SC29 began its face recognition work. However, the face recognition work performed by SC29 does clearly fall into the mandate of SC37 as a facial template defined for the purposes of biometric identification. After exchanging the liaison statements between SC29 and SC37, the cooperation has been achieved in July 2004 and we will hope to achieve fruitful results.

4   Conclusions

This paper presents an introduction of international standardization organization related to biometrics and standard works for facial template, especially MPEG-7 Advanced Face Recognition. An indication of the current substantial growth and interest in biometrics is the emergence of biometrics industry standards and related activities. Standards, especially on face recognition, have become strategic business issues. For any given technology, industry standards assure the availability of multiple sources for comparable products and of competitive products in the marketplace. Standards will support the expansion of the marketplace for biometrics and it will awake many customers' interesting in standard works on biometrics.

References

1. "Biometrics Deployment of Machine Readable Travel Documents," ICAO TAG MRTD/NTWG, May, 2004.
2. W. Zhao, R. Chellapa, A. Rosenfeld, and P. Phillips, "Face recognition: A literature survey," UMD CfAR Technical Report CAR-TR-948, 2000.
3. P. J. Phillips, H. Moon, P. J. Rauss, and S. Rizvi, "The FERET evaluation methodology for face recognition algo-rithms", IEEE Transactions on Pattern Analysis and Ma-chine Intelligence, Vol. 22, No. 10, Oct., 2000.
4. "Face Recognition Vendor Test," http://www.frvt.org.
5. R. Koenen, "From MPEG-1 to MPEG-21: Creating an Interoperable Multimedia Infrastructure," ISO/IEC JTC1/SC29/WG11 N4518, Dec., 2001.
6. L. Wang and T. K. Tan, "Experimental results of face description based on the 2nd-order eigenface method," ISO/IEC JTC1/SC29/WG11 M6001, May, 2000.
7. M. A. Turk and A. P. Pentland, "Eigenfaces for recogni-tion," Journal of Cognitive Neuroscience, Vol. 3, No. 1, pp. 71–86, 1991.
8. B.S. Manjunath, P. Salembier, and T. Sikora, "Introduc-tion to MPEG-7: Multimedia Content Description Inter-face", John Wiley & Sons Ltd., 2002.
9. M. Bober, "Description of MPEG-7 Visual Core Experi-ments," ISO/IEC JTC1/SC29/WG11 N5166, Oct., 2002.
10. H. Kim, T. Kim, W. Hwang, S. Kee, "A Recursive Match-ing Method for Content-based Image Retrieval," WIAMIS2004, Portugal, Apr, 2004.
11. A. Yamada and L. Cieplinski, "MPEG-7 Visual part of eXperimentation Model Version 18.0," ISO/IEC JTC1/SC29/WG11 N5552, Mar., 2003.
12. T. Kamei, A. Yamada, H. Kim, T. Kim, W. Hwang, S. Kee, "Advanced Face Descriptor Using Fourier and Inten-sity LDA Features," ISO/IEC JTC1/SC29/WG11 M8998, Oct., 2002.
13. L. Cieplinski and A. Yamada, "Text of ISO/IEC 15938-3/FPDAM1," ISO/IEC JTC1/SC29/WG11 N5695, Jul., 2003.
14. "Biometrics Data Interchange Formats – Part 5: Face Image Data," ISO/IEC JTC1/SC37 N506, Mar., 2004.

System Design and Assessment Methodology for Face Recognition Algorithms

Hyeonjoon Moon

Center for Emotion Recognition and Robot Vision (CERRV),
School of Computer Engineering,
Sejong University, Seoul, 143-747, Korea
hmoon@sejong.ac.kr

Abstract. For biometric person authentication, system design and assessment methodology form essential part of the entire process. We design a performance evaluation methodology for face recognition system based on identification and verification model. To validate our model, we designed a projection-based face recognition system which requires numerous design decisions. We explicitly state the design decisions by introducing a generic modular face recognition system. We explore various implementations for preprocessing, representation and recognition modules. Our experiment includes major factors for system design and assessment: (1) changing the illumination normalization preprocessing; (2) varying the number of features in the representation; and (3) changing the similarity measure in recognition process. We perform experiments and present results for identification and verification scenarios.

1 Introduction

Over the last several years, numerous projection-based biometric algorithms have been developed including principal component analysis (PCA) [8] and independent component analysis (ICA) [6]. The main idea of projection-based approach is to reduce the dimensionality of a data set while retaining most of the variation present in the data set. There is an accepted basic design for the biometric recognition system, however, the details of the basic algorithm require a number of design decisions.

These design decisions include preprocessing of acquired biometric information, coefficients selected for representation, and similarity measure for comparing these feature vectors. Each of these system design decisions has an impact on the overall performance of the algorithm. Some of these design decisions have been explicitly stated in the literature; for example, the similarity measure for comparing two biometric feature vectors.

There are two main categories of research to advance the state of the art in face recognition [10]. The first category is the design of a system that can provide reliable solutions to face recognition problems. In algorithm development, a number of techniques have been proposed for preprocessing and enhancement [7],

S.Z. Li et al. (Eds.): Sinobiometrics 2004, LNCS 3338, pp. 358–369, 2004.

detection of face and facial components in a scene [2, 15], feature extraction algorithms [1], and classification techniques [9, 13]. Not one of these procedures should be neglected, since each component is critical and performs as a part of the face recognition system.

The second category is the development of an assessment methodology based on different scenarios and categories of images. Recently, empirical evaluation techniques have emerged as a serious research field in pattern recognition and computer vision. An empirical evaluation is defined as the assessment methodology for measuring the ability of algorithms to meet requirements for system level implementation.

In this paper, we designed a generic modular projection-based face recognition system and performance evaluation methodology to present the importance of system design and assessment methodology. Our face recognition system consists of preprocessing, representation, and recognition modules. Each module consists of a series of basic steps, where the purpose of each step is fixed. However, we systematically vary the algorithm in each step. Based on modular face recognition system model, we evaluate different implementations. Since we use a generic model, we can change the implementation in an orderly manner and assess the impact on performance of each modification.

We report identification and verification performance which is critical for person authentication scenario [11]. In identification model, the input to an algorithm is an unknown face, and the algorithm reports back the estimated identity of an unknown face from a database of known individuals. In verification model, The algorithm either accepts or rejects the claimed identity [14]. We report performance results using top rank score for identification and equal error rate (EER) for verification. We performed a detailed evaluation of variations in the implementation. By testing on standard galleries and probe sets, the reader can compare the performance of our implementations with the algorithms tested under the FERET program [12]. In this experiment, we vary the illumination normalization procedure, the number of feature vectors for representation, and the similarity measure.

2   Projection-Based Biometric Recognition System

2.1   Face Space

Projection-based approach is statistical dimensionality reduction method, which produces the optimal linear least squared decomposition of a training set [4, 8]. In our projection-based face recognition algorithm, the input is a training set $t_1, ..., t_W$ of N images such that the ensemble mean is zero ($\sum_i t_i = 0$). Each image is interpreted as a point in $\Re^{n \times m}$, where the image is n by m pixels. Projection finds a representation in a $(W-1)$ dimensional space that preserves variance. We utilize PCA which generates a set of $N-1$ feature vectors $(e_1, ..., e_{N-1})$. We normalize these feature vectors so that they are orthonormal. The low order feature vectors encode the larger variations in the training set. The face is

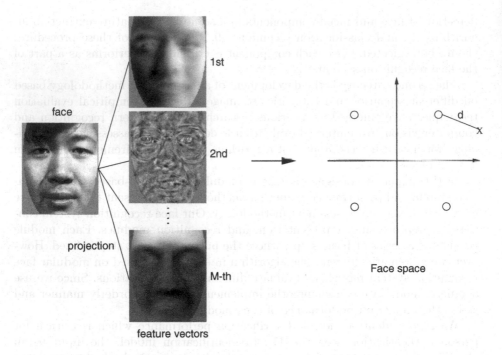

Fig. 1. Representation of face as a point in face space. A face is represented by its projection onto a subset of M feature vectors. PCA and ICA are most popular in face recognition system

represented by its projection onto a subset of M feature vectors, which we will call *face space* (see Figure 1). Thus the normalized face is represented as a point in a M dimensional face space. We have explored principal component analysis (PCA) and independent component analysis (ICA) which is most popular in face recognition literature.

2.2   System Design

Our face recognition system consists of three modules and each module is composed of a sequence of steps (see Figure 2). The first module normalizes the input image. The goal of preprocessing is to transform facial images into a standard format that removes variations that can affect recognition performance. This module consists of four steps. The first step filters or compresses the original image. The image is filtered to remove high frequency noise in the image. An image is compressed to save storage space and reduce transmission time. The second step places the face in a standard geometric position by rotating, scaling, and translating the center of eyes to standard locations. The goal of this step is to remove variations in size, orientation, and location of the face. The third step masks out background pixels, hair, and clothes to remove unnecessary variations. The fourth module removes some of the variations in illumination between images. Changes in illumination are critical factors in algorithm performance.

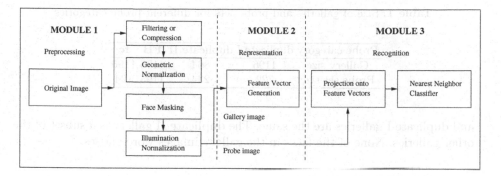

Fig. 2. Block Diagram of Projection-based Face Recognition System

The second module performs representation by the decomposition on the training set which produces the feature vectors (PCA or ICA coefficients).

The third module performs the recognition of the face from a normalized image, and consists of two steps. The first step projects the image onto the feature vectors for representation. The critical parameter in this step is the subset of feature vectors that represent the face. The second step recognizes faces using a nearest neighbor classifier. The critical design decision in this step is the similarity measure in the classifier. We presented performance results using L1 distance, L2 distance, angle between feature vectors, Mahalanobis distance. Additionally, Mahalanobis distance was combined with L1, L2, and angle between feature vectors mentioned above.

3   Test Design

3.1   Facial Database

We have used the FERET database for our experiment. We define *gallery* as a set of known images used for training data for the system and *probe* as a set of testing images which is unknown to our system. To allow for a robust and detailed analysis, we report identification and verification scores for four categories of probes. The first probe category was the **FB** probes. For each set of images, there were two frontal images. One of the images was randomly placed in the gallery, and the other image was placed in the **FB** probe set. (This category is denoted by **FB** to differentiate it from the **fb** images in the database.) The second probe category contained all duplicate frontal images in the database for the gallery images. We refer to this category as the duplicate I probes. The third category was the **fc** (images taken the same day, but with a different camera and lighting). The fourth consisted of duplicates where there is at least one year between the acquisition of the probe image and corresponding gallery image. We refer to this category as the duplicate II probes. The size of the galleries and probe sets for the four probe categories are presented in Table 1. The **FB**, **fc**,

Table 1. Size of galleries and probe sets for different probe categories

Probe category	duplicate I	duplicate II	**FB**	fc
Gallery size	1196	864	1196	1196
Probe set size	722	234	1195	194

and duplicate I galleries are the same. The duplicate II gallery is a subset of the other galleries. None of the faces in the gallery images wore glasses.

3.2   Identification Model

Our evaluation protocol is designed to assess the state of the art, advance the state of the art, and point to future directions of research. To succeed at this, the test design must solve the selection of images in the test set and the testing protocol. Tests are administered using a testing protocol, which states the mechanics of the tests and the manner in which the test will be scored. In face recognition, for example, the protocol states the number of images of each person in the test, how the output from the algorithm is recorded, and how the performance results are reported. The characteristics and quality of the images are major factors in determining the difficulty of the problem being evaluated.

The testing protocol is based on a set of design principles. Stating the design principle allows one to assess how appropriate the test is for a particular face recognition algorithm. Also, the design principles help in determining if an evaluation methodology for testing algorithm(s) for a particular application is appropriate. Before discussing the design principles, we state the evaluation protocol.

The second design principle is that training is completed prior to the start of the test. This forces each algorithm to have a general representation for faces, not a representation tuned to a specific gallery. Without this condition, virtual galleries would not be possible. For algorithms to have a general representation for faces, they must be gallery (class) insensitive. An algorithm is class sensitive if the representation is tuned to a specific gallery.

The third design rule is that all algorithms tested compute a similarity measure between two facial images; this similarity measure was computed for all pairs of images in the test set. Knowing the similarity score between all pairs of images from the target and query sets allows for the construction of virtual galleries and probe sets.

3.3   Verification Model

In our verification model, a person in image p claims to be the person in image g. The system either accepts or rejects the claim. (If p and g are images of the same person then we write $p \sim g$, otherwise, $p \nsim g$.) Performance of the system is characterized by two performance statistics. The first is the probability of accepting a correct identity; formally, the probability of the algorithm reporting

$p \sim g$ when $p \sim g$ is correct. This is referred to as the verification probability, denoted by P_V (also referred to as the hit rate in the signal detection literature). The second is the probability of incorrectly verifying a claim formally, the probability of the algorithm reporting $p \sim g$ when $p \not\sim g$. This is called the false-alarm rate and is denoted by P_F.

Verifying the identity of a single person is equivalent to a detection problem where the gallery $G = \{g\}$. The detection problem consists of finding the probes in $p \in P$ such that $p \sim g$.

For a given gallery image g_i and probe p_k, the decision of whether an identity was confirmed or denied was generated from $s_i(k)$. The decisions were made by a *Neyman-Pearson* observer. A Neyman-Pearson observer confirms a claim if $s_i(k) \leq c$ and rejects it if $s_i(k) > c$. By the Neyman-Pearson theorem [5], this decision rule maximized the verification rate for a given false alarm rate α. Changing c generated a new P_V and P_F.

By varying c from it's minimum to maximum value, we obtained all combinations of P_V and P_F. A plot of all combinations of P_V and P_F is a receiver operating characteristic (ROC) (also known as the relative operating characteristic) [3, 5]. The input to the scoring algorithm was $s_i(k)$; thresholding similarity scores, and computing P_V, P_F, and the ROC was performed by the scoring algorithm.

The above method computed a ROC for an individual. However, we need performance over a population of people. To calculate a ROC over a population, we performed a round robin evaluation procedure for a gallery G. The gallery contained one image per person.

The first step generated a set of partitions of the probe set. For a given $g_i \in G$, the probe set P is divided into two disjoint sets D_i and F_i. The set D_i consisted of all probes p such that $p \sim g_i$ and F_i consisted of all probes such that $p \not\sim g_i$.

The second step computed the verification and false alarm rates for each gallery image g_i for a given cut-off value c, denoted by $P_V^{c,i}$ and $P_F^{c,i}$, respectively. The verification rate was computed by

$$P_V^{c,i} = \begin{cases} 0 & \text{if } |D_i| = 0 \\ \frac{|s_i(k) \leq c \text{ given } p_k \in D_i|}{|D_i|} & \text{otherwise,} \end{cases}$$

where $|s_i(k) \leq c$ given $p \in D_i|$ was the number of probes in D_i such that $s_i(k) < c$. The false alarm rate is computed by

$$P_F^{c,i} = \begin{cases} 0 & \text{if } |F_i| = 0 \\ \frac{|s_i(k) \leq c \text{ given } p_k \in F_i|}{|F_i|} & \text{otherwise.} \end{cases}$$

The third step computed the overall verification and false alarm rates, which was a weighted average of $P_V^{c,i}$ and $P_F^{c,i}$. The overall verification and false-alarm rates are denoted by P_V^c and P_F^c, and was computed by

$$P_V^c = \frac{1}{|G|} \sum_{i=1}^{|G|} \frac{|D_i|}{\frac{1}{|G|} \sum_i |D_i|} P_V^{c,i} = \frac{1}{\sum_i |D_i|} \sum_{i=1}^{|G|} |s_i(k) \le c \text{ given } p_k \in D_i| \cdot P_V^{c,i}$$

and

$$P_F^c = \frac{1}{|G|} \sum_{i=1}^{|G|} \frac{|F_i|}{\frac{1}{|G|} \sum_i |F_i|} P_F^{c,i} = \frac{1}{\sum_i |F_i|} \sum_{i=1}^{|G|} |s_i(k) \le c \text{ given } p_k \in F_i| \cdot P_F^{c,i}.$$

The verification ROC was computed by varying c from $-\infty$ to $+\infty$.

In reporting verification scores, we state the size of the gallery G which was the number of images in the gallery set G and the number of images in the probe set P. All galleries contained one image per person, and probe sets could contain more than one image per person. Probe sets did not necessarily contain an image of everyone in the associated gallery. For each probe p, there existed a gallery image g such that $p \sim g$.

For a given algorithm, the choice of a suitable hit and false alarm rate pair depends on a particular application. However, for performance evaluation and comparison among algorithms, the *equal error rate* (EER) is often quoted. The equal error rate occurs at the threshold c where the incorrect rejection and false alarm rates are equal; that is $1 - P_V^c = P_F^c$ (incorrect rejection rate is one minus the verification rate.) In verification scenario, the lower EER value means better performance result.

4   System Assessment

The purpose of our experiment is to assess the effects of changing the algorithms in our projection-based face recognition system. We do this by establishing a baseline algorithm and then varying the implementation of selected steps one at a time. Ideally, we would test all possible combination of variations. However, because of the number of combinations, this is not practical and we vary the steps individually.

The baseline algorithm has the following configuration: The images are not filtered or compressed. Geometric normalization consists of rotating, translating, and scaling the images so the center of the eyes are on standard pixels. This is followed by masking the hair and background from the images. In the illumination normalization step, the non-masked facial pixels were normalized by a histogram equalization algorithm. Then, the non-masked facial pixels were transformed so that the mean is equal to 0.0 and standard deviation is equal to 1.0. The geometric normalization and masking steps are not varied in the experiments.

The training set for the PCA and ICA consists of 501 images (one image per person), which produces 500 feature vectors. We show results based on PCA coefficients but ICA coefficients shows reasonably better performance with proper projection method. In the recognition module, faces are represented by their projection onto the first 200 feature vectors and the classifier uses the L_1 norm.

Table 2. Identification performance results for illumination normalization methods. Performance score are the top rank match

Illumination normalization	Probe category			
	duplicate I	duplicate II	**FB** probe	**fc** probe
Baseline	0.35	0.13	0.77	0.26
Original image	0.32	0.11	0.75	0.21
Histogram Eq. only	0.34	0.12	0.77	0.24
$\mu = 0.0$, $\sigma = 1.0$ only	0.33	0.14	0.76	0.25

Table 3. Verification performance results for illumination normalization methods. Performance score are equal error rate (EER)

Illumination normalization	Probe category			
	duplicate I	duplicate II	**FB** probe	**fc** probe
Baseline	0.24	0.30	0.07	0.13
Original image	0.25	0.31	0.07	0.14
Histogram Eq. only	0.25	0.30	0.07	0.13
$\mu = 0.0$, $\sigma = 1.0$ only	0.25	0.29	0.07	0.14

4.1 Variation in Preprocessing: Illumination Normalization

We explored three variations to the illumination normalization step. For the baseline algorithm, the non-masked facial pixels were transformed so that the mean was equal to 0.0 and standard deviation was equal to 1.0 followed by a histogram equalization algorithm. First variation,the non-masked pixels were not normalized (original image). Second variation, the non-masked facial pixels were normalized with a histogram equalization algorithm. Third variation, the non-masked facial pixels were transformed so that the mean was equal to 0.0 and variance equal to 1.0. The identification and verification performance results from the illumination normalization methods are presented in Table 2 and 3.

4.2 Variation in Representation: Number of Low Order Bases

The higher order feature vectors encode small variations and noise among the images in the training set. One would expect that the higher order feature vectors would not contribute to recognition since those information generally represent lighting variations among the training set. We examined this hypothesis by computing performance as a function of the number of low order feature vectors in the representation. Figure 3 shows top rank score for **FB** and duplicate I probes as the function of the number of low order feature vectors included in the representation in face space. The representation consisted of $e_1, \ldots, e_n$, $n = 50, 100, \ldots, 500$, where e_is are the feature vectors.

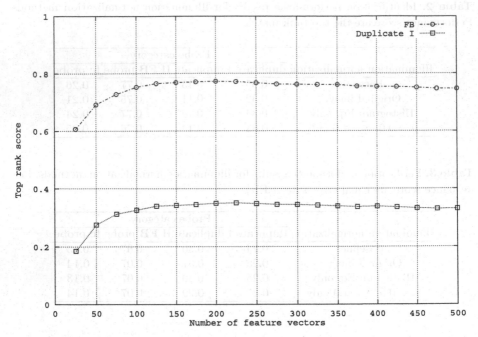

Fig. 3. Identification performance on duplicate I and FB probes based on number of low order feature vectors used

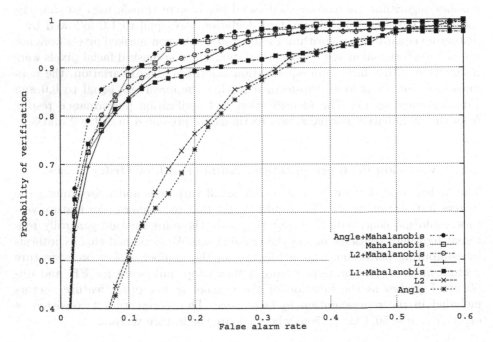

Fig. 4. Effects of nearest neighbor classifier on verification performances for **fc** probes

Table 4. Identification performance scores based on different nearest neighbor classifier. Performance scores are the top rank match

	Probe category			
Nearest neighbor classifier	duplicate I	duplicate II	**FB** probe	**fc** probe
Baseline (L_1)	0.35	0.13	0.77	0.26
Euclidean (L_2)	0.33	0.14	0.72	0.04
Angle	0.34	0.12	0.70	0.07
Mahalanobis	0.42	0.17	0.74	0.23
L_1 + Mahalanobis	0.31	0.13	0.73	0.39
L_2 + Mahalanobis	0.35	0.13	0.77	0.31
Angle + Mahalanobis	0.45	0.21	0.77	0.24

Table 5. Verification performance scores based on different nearest neighbor classifier. Performance scores are equal error rate (EER)

	Probe category			
Nearest neighbor classifier	duplicate I	duplicate II	**FB** probe	**fc** probe
Baseline (L_1)	0.24	0.30	0.07	0.13
Euclidean (L_2)	0.21	0.26	0.05	0.22
Angle	0.19	0.22	0.05	0.22
Mahalanobis	0.11	0.12	0.04	0.11
L_1 + Mahalanobis	0.34	0.39	0.12	0.13
L_2 + Mahalanobis	0.25	0.30	0.07	0.12
Angle + Mahalanobis	0.11	0.12	0.03	0.10

4.3   Variation in Recognition: Nearest Neighbor Classifier

We experimented with seven similarity measures for the classifier [10]. Their identification and verification performance results are listed in Tables 4 and 5. The performance score for **fc** probes shows most variation among different category of probes. In Figure 4, we reported detailed verification performance results for **fc** probes.

5   Discussion

In the preprocessing module, we varied the illumination normalization and compression steps. The results show that performing an illumination normalization step improves identification performance (see Table 2) but which implementation that is selected is not critical (see Table 3).

In the representation module, we explored the number of low order eigenvectors in the representation from 50 to 500 by steps of 50. Figure 3 shows that performance increases until approximately 150–200 eigenvectors are in the representation and then performance decreases slightly. Representing faces by the first 30–40% of the eigenvectors is consistent with results on other facial image sets that the authors have seen.

In the recognition module, the similarity measure in the nearest neighbor classifier was changed. This variation showed the largest range of identification and verification performance. In Table 4, identification performance of duplicate I probes performance ranged from 0.31 to 0.45, and **fc** probes the ranged from 0.07 to 0.39. In Table 5, verification performance of duplicate I probes performance ranged from 0.11 to 0.34, and **fc** probes the ranged from 0.10 to 0.22. For duplicate I, duplicate II and **FB** probes, the angle+Mahalanobis distance performed the best. For the **fc** probes, the L_1+Mahalanobis distance performed the best for identification and the angle+Mahalanobis distance performed the best for verification (see Figure 4).

Because of the range of performance, it is clear that selecting the similarity measure for the classifier is the critical decision in designing a projection-based face recognition system. However, decision of selecting similarity measure is dependent on the type of images in the galleries and probe sets that the system will process.

6   Conclusion

In this paper, we introduced a modular face recognition system which allowed us to systematically vary the components and measure the impact of these variations on performance. We assess the algorithms in each module based on a generic modular projection-based face recognition system. The goal of our experiments belongs to understand the effects of variations in system design by assessment of performance results and to point out the directions for designing a optimized face recognition system in each module.

From the series of experiments with modular configuration of PCA-based face recognition system, we have come to three major conclusions.

First, selection of the nearest neighbor classifier is the critical design decision in designing a projection-based algorithm. The proper selection of nearest neighbor classifier is essential to improve performance scores. Furthermore, our experiments shows similarity measures that achieve the best performance are not generally considered in the literature.

Second, the performance scores vary among the probe categories, and that the design of an algorithm need to consider the type of images that the algorithm will process. The **FB** and duplicate I probes are least sensitive to system design decisions, while **fc** and duplicate II probes are the most sensitive.

Third, the performance within a category of probes can vary greatly. This recommends that when comparing algorithms, performance scores from a set of galleries and probe sets need to be examined.

By following the performance assessment procedure presented in this paper, system designers can determine the optimal configuration of their applications based on identification and verification scenarios.

Acknowledgement

This research (paper) was performed for the Intelligent Robotics Development Program, one of the 21st Century Frontier R&D Programs funded by the Ministry of Science and Technology of Korea.

References

1. J. Atick, P. Griffin, and A. N. Redlich. Statistical approach to shape from shading: reconstruction of three-dimensional surfaces from single two-dimensional images. *Neural Computation*, 8:1321–1340, 1996.
2. T. Darrell, G. Gordon, J. Woodfill, and M. Harville. A virtual mirror using real-time robust face tracking. In *3rd International Conference on Automatic Face and Gesture Recognition*, pages 616–621, 1998.
3. J. P. Egan. *Signal Detection Theory and ROC Analysis*. Academic Press, 1975.
4. K. Fukunaga. *Introduction to statistical pattern recongition*. Academic Press, Inc., San Diego, CA, 1990.
5. D. Green and J. Swets. *Signal Detection Theory and Psychophysics*. John Wiley & Sons Ltd., 1966.
6. A. Hyvarinen, J. Karhunen, and E. Oja. *Independent Component Analysis*. John Wiley & Sons, 2001.
7. A. Johnston and P. J. Passmore. Shape from shading 1: Surface curvature and orientation. *Perception*, 23:169–189, 1994.
8. I. T. Jolliffe. *Principal Component Analysis*. Springer-Verlag, 1986.
9. B. Moghaddam, W. Wahid, and A. Pentland. Beyond eigenfaces: probablistic matching for face recognition. In *3rd International Conference on Automatic Face and Gesture Recognition*, pages 30–35, 1998.
10. H. Moon. *Performance Evaluation Methodology for Face Recognition Algorithms*. PhD thesis, Dept. of Computer Science and Engineering, SUNY Buffalo, 1999.
11. H. Moon. Biometric person authentication using projection-based face recognition system in verification scenario. In *Proceedings of the First International Conference on Biometric Authentication 2004*, volume LNCS 3072. Springer, 2004.
12. P. J. Phillips, P. Rauss, and S. Der. FERET (face recognition technology) recognition algorithm development and test report. Technical Report ARL-TR-995, U.S. Army Research Laboratory, 1996.
13. T. Randen and J.H. Husoy. Filtering for texture classification: A comparative study. *IEEE Trans. PAMI*, 21(4):291–310, 1999.
14. S. Rizvi, P. J. Phillips, and H. Moon. A verification protocol and statistical performance analyis for face recognition algorithms. In *Computer Vision and Pattern Recognition 98*, 1998.
15. K-K Sung and T. Poggio. Example-based learning for view-based human face detection. *IEEE Trans. PAMI*, 20(1):39–51, 1998.

Baseline Evaluations on the CAS-PEAL-R1 Face Database

Bo Cao[1,2], Shiguang Shan[1], Xiaohua Zhang[1], and Wen Gao[1,2]

[1]ICT-ISVISION Joint Research & Development Laboratory for Face Recognition,
Chinese Academy of Sciences, P.O. Box 2704, Beijing, China 100080
{bcao, sgshan, wgao}@ict.ac.cn
[2]Graduate School of the Chinese Academy of Sciences

Abstract. In this paper, three baseline face recognition algorithms are evaluated on the CAS-PEAL-R1 face database which is publicly released from a large-scale Chinese face database: CAS-PEAL. The main objectives of the baseline evaluations are to 1) elementarily assess the difficulty of the database for face recognition algorithms, 2) provide an example evaluation protocol on the database, and 3) identify the strengths and weakness of some popular algorithms. Particular description of the datasets used in the evaluations and the underlying philosophy are given. The three baseline algorithms evaluated are Principle Components Analysis (PCA), a combined Principle Component Analysis and Linear Discriminant Analysis (PCA+LDA), and PCA+LDA algorithm based on Gabor features (G PCA+LDA). Four face image preprocessing methods are also tested to emphasize the influences of the preprocessing methods on the performances of face recognition algorithms.

1 Introduction

Automatic Face Recognition (AFR) has become one of the most active research areas in pattern recognition, computer vision and psychology and much progress has been made in the past few years [1], [2]. However, AFR remains a research area far from mature and its application is still limited in controllable environments. Therefore, evaluating and comparing the potential AFR technologies exhaustively and objectively to discover the real choke points and the valuable future research topics, and developing algorithms robust to variations in pose, expression, accessories, lighting, etc. are becoming more and more significant.

Aiming at these goals, large-scale and diverse face databases are obviously one of the basic requirements. Internationally, FERET [3] and FRVT [4] have pioneered both evaluation protocols and database construction. Especially, the FERET database is widely used in the research field. Besides the significant FERET tests, its success can also be contributed to 1) the public availability of the database, 2) the large number of subjects and diverse images, and 3) the explicit and categorized partition of the gallery sets and probe sets. Actually, these sets are used by many different researchers to compare their algorithms and test the performances under different image variations, such as illumination, facial expression and aging variations.

S.Z. Li et al. (Eds.): Sinobiometrics 2004, LNCS 3338, pp. 370–378, 2004.

Despite its success in the evaluations of face recognition algorithms, the FERET database has limitations in the relatively simple and unsystematically controlled variations of face images for research purposes. Considering these limitations, we design and construct a large-scale Chinese face database (the CAS-PEAL face database), which is now partly made available as a released subset named by CAS-PEAL-R1.

In the paper, the recommended partition of the images in the CAS-PEAL-R1 database is proposed to compose the training set, the gallery set and the probe sets which can be used to evaluate a specific face recognition algorithm. Also, the evaluation results of three baseline face recognition algorithms combining different preprocessing methods are provided. This paper can be an informative complement to the documents on the database itself.

2   Contents of the Released CAS-PEAL Face Database: CAS-PEAL-R1

Currently, the CAS-PEAL face database contains 99,594 images of 1040 individuals (595 males and 445 females) with controlled Pose, Expression, Accessory, and Lighting variations. The details of the database can be referred to [5], [6].

The CAS-PEAL face database has been cut, arranged and labeled to form the first distribution: CAS-PEAL-R1. This distribution contains 30,863 images of 1,040 subjects. These images belong to two main subsets: frontal subset and pose subset.

1. In the frontal subset, all images are captured with the subject looking right into the camera. Among them, 377 subjects have images with 6 different expressions. 438 subjects have images wearing 6 different accessories. 233 subjects have images under at least 9 lighting changes. 297 subjects have images against 2 to 4 different backgrounds. 296 subjects have images with different distances from the camera. Furthermore, 66 subjects have images recorded in two sessions at a 6-month interval.
2. In the pose subset, images of 1040 subjects across 21 different poses without any other variations are included.

The content of CAS-PEAL-R1 is summarized in Table 1.

Table 1. The contents of CAS-PEAL-R1

Subset		# Variations	# Subjects	# Images
Frontal	Normal	1	1040	1,040
	Expression	5*	377	1,884
	Lighting	>= 9	233	2,450
	Accessory	6	438	2,616
	Background	2-4	297	651
	Distance	1-2	296	324
	Aging	1	66	66
	Total:			9,031
Pose		21 (3*7)	1040	21,832
Total:				30,863

5*: Neutral expression is not counted in.

3 Datasets Used in the Evaluations

To compare different algorithms convincingly, two additional aspects should be considered: 1) the scale of the datasets which are used in the training and testing of a specific algorithm, 2) the statistical significance of the differences between different algorithms.

These two aspects are closely related. If the scale of the test sets is very small, the performance scores may be highly stochastic and become incomparable. Though some methods do exist to tackle this problem, such as the permutation methodology proposed in [7], a large-scale test set is still helpful. Also, the scale of the training set can influence the comparison of two algorithms. Martinez et al. [8] demonstrates that PCA can outperform LDA when the training data set is small, while LDA is normally considered superior than PCA in face recognition. Considering these problems, we compose the test sets and the training set from the CAS-PEAL-R1 database as large as possible. And the test sets are categorized to restrict the images in one probe set to undergo one main variation, which can be used to identify the strengths and weakness of a specific algorithm and to address the variations associated with changes in the probe sets.

In the evaluation, three kinds of datasets are composed from the CAS-PEAL-R1 database: a training set, a gallery set and several probe sets. Their definition and descriptions are as follows:

1. **Training Set**. A training set is a collection of images which are used to generate a generic representation of faces and/or to tune parameters of the classifier. In the evaluation, the training set contains 1,200 images (300 subjects randomly selected from the 1,040 subjects in the CAS-PEAL-R1 database and each subject contains four images randomly selected from the frontal subset of the CAS-PEAL-R1 database).
2. **Gallery Set**. A gallery set is a collection of images of known individuals against which testing images are matched. In the evaluation, the gallery set contains 1,040 images of 1,040 subjects (each subject has one image under normal condition). Actually, the gallery set consists of all the normal images mentioned in Table 1.
3. **Probe Set**. A probe set is a collection of probe images of unknown individuals to be recognized. In the evaluation, nine probe sets are composed from the CAS-PEAL-R1 database. Among them, six probe sets correspond to the six subsets in the frontal subset: expression, lighting, accessory, background, distance and aging, as described in Table 1. The other three probe sets correspond to the images of subjects in the pose subset: looking upwards, looking right into the camera, and looking downwards. All the images that appear in the training set are excluded from these probe sets.

The datasets used in the evaluation are summarized in Table 2.

Table 2. The datasets used in the evaluation protocols

Datasets	Training set	Gallery set	Probe sets (frontal)					
			expression	lighting	accessory	background	distance	Aging
Num. of images	1,200	1,040	1,570	2,243	2,285	553	275	66
	Probe sets (pose)							
	looking upwards (PU)		looking right into the camera (PM)			looking downwards (PD)		
Num. of images	4,998		4,993			4,998		

4 Baseline Face Recognition Algorithms

The three baseline algorithms evaluated are Principle Components Analysis (PCA) [9], (also known as Eigenfaces), a combined Principle Component Analysis and Linear Discriminant Analysis (PCA+LDA, a variant of Fisherfaces) [10], and PCA+LDA algorithm based on Gabor features (G PCA+LDA). PCA and PCA+LDA based face recognition algorithms are both fundamental and well studied. Recently, 2D Gabor wavelets are extensively used for local feature representation and extraction, and demonstrate their success in face recognition [11], [12]. So, the PCA+LDA algorithm based on Gabor features is also used as a baseline algorithm to reflect this trend.

Instead of using the grey-scale images as the original features in the PCA and PCA+LDA algorithms, the representation of the original features in the third algorithm is based on the Gabor wavelet transform of the original images. Gabor wavelets are biologically motivated convolution kernels which are plane waves restricted by a Gaussian envelope function, and those kernels demonstrate spatial locality and orientation selectivity. In face recognition, Gabor wavelets exhibit robustness to moderate lighting changes, small deformations [11].

A family of Gabor wavelets (kernels, filters) can be defined as follows:

$$\psi_{u,v}(z) = \frac{\| k_{u,v} \|^2}{\sigma^2} e^{(-\| k_{u,v} \|^2 \| z \|^2 / 2\sigma^2)} \left[e^{i \vec{k}_{u,v} z} - e^{-\sigma^2/2} \right] \tag{1}$$

where $k_{u,v} = k_v e^{i\phi_u}$; $k_v = \frac{k_{max}}{f^v}$ gives the frequency, and $\phi_u = \frac{u\pi}{8}, \phi_u \in [0,\pi)$ gives the orientation, and $z = (x, y)$.

$$k_{u,v} = k_v e^{i\phi_u} \tag{2}$$

where $e^{i \vec{k}_{u,v} z}$ is the oscillatory wave function, whose real part and imaginary part are cosine function and sinusoid function respectively.

In this algorithm, we use the Gabor wavelets with the following parameters: five scales $v \in \{0,1,2,3,4\}$, eight orientations $u \in \{0,1,2,3,4,5,6,7\}$, $\sigma = 2\pi$, $k_{max} = \pi$, and $f = \sqrt{2}$. These parameters can be adjusted according to the size of the normalized faces.

At each image pixel, a set of convolution coefficients can be calculated using a family of Gabor kernels as defined by equation (1). The Gabor wavelet transform of an image is the collection of the coefficients of all the pixels. To reduce the dimensionality, the pixels are sampled and their convolution coefficients are concatenated to form the original features of the PCA+LDA algorithm. These concatenated coefficients are also called the augmented Gabor feature vector in [12]. In the experiments, the size of the normalized faces is 64×64 and the pixels are sampled every four pixel both in row and in column, so the dimensionality of the features is 9000 ($15 \times 15 \times 40$). It should be noted that each feature is normalized to zero mean and unit variance to compensate for the scale variance of different Gabor kernels.

5 Preprocessing

In the evaluation, the preprocessing of the face images is divided into three steps: geometric normalization, masking, and illumination normalization. The first two steps are to provide features that are invariant to geometric transformations of the face images, such as the location, the rotation and the scale of the face in an image, and remove irrelevant information for the purpose of face recognition, such as the background and the hair of a subject. Illumination normalization is to decrease the variations of images of one face induced by lighting changes while still keeping distinguishing features, which is generally much more difficult than the first two steps. The details of the three steps are described as follows:

In geometric normalization step, each face image is scaled and rotated so that the eyes are positioned in line and the distance between them equals a predefined length. Then, the face image is cropped to include only the face region with little hair and background as Fig. 1(a) shows (the size of the cropped face image is 64×64). In masking step, a predefined mask is put on each cropped face image to further reduce the effect of different hair styles and backgrounds which are not the intrinsic characteristics, as Fig. 1(b) shows. Typically, the hair style of a specific subject and the background are constant in a face database, so better performance can be obtained with larger face regions. However, this bias should be avoided as much as possible by restricting the above cropping and masking procedures.

In illumination normalization step, four illumination normalization methods are evaluated: Histogram Equalization (HE), Gamma Intensity Correction (GIC), Region-based Histogram Equalization (RHE) and Region-based Gamma Intensity Correction (RGIC) [13], [14]. Fig. 2(b) illustrates the effect of these four methods on an example face image.

(a)　　　　　　　　　　　(b)

Fig. 1. Example normalized face images in Step 1 and Step 2. (a) Geometrically normalized face images. (b) Masked face images

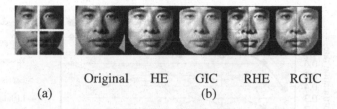

	Original	HE	GIC	RHE	RGIC
(a)			(b)		

Fig. 2. Partition of face region and example images processed by different illumination normalization methods. (a) Partition of face region for region-based illumination normalization methods. (b) Images processed by different illumination normalization methods

6   Evaluation Results

6.1   Frontal Face Images

The three baseline face recognition algorithms (PCA, PCA+LDA and G PCA+LDA) are trained on the training set, and evaluated on the six frontal probe sets as described in Section 3. Before training and testing, all the images are preprocessed as described in Section 5, using the four illumination normalization methods or no illumination normalization respectively. Table 3 and Fig. 3 show the performance of these algorithms on the frontal probe sets.

Table 3. Identification performance of the three baseline algorithms on the six frontal probe sets and the union (Total) set of these sets

Probe sets / Algorithms	Accessory	Background	Distance	Expression	Lighting	Aging	Total
PCA	0.371	0.805	0.742	0.537	0.082	0.500	0.282
PCA+LDA	0.610	0.944	0.935	0.713	0.218	0.727	0.422
PCA+LDA(HE)	0.710	0.975	0.975	0.802	0.288	0.773	0.484
PCA+LDA(GIC)	0.670	0.964	0.949	0.780	0.230	0.788	0.454
PCA+LDA(RHE)	0.698	0.955	0.949	0.785	0.296	0.788	0.478
PCA+LDA(RGIC)	0.675	0.949	0.953	0.762	0.247	0.712	0.455
G PCA+LDA	0.828	0.980	1.00	0.906	0.448	0.985	0.574
G PCA+LDA(HE)	0.851	0.989	1.00	0.929	0.443	0.939	0.583
G PCA+LDA(GIC)	0.821	0.984	0.993	0.911	0.469	0.955	0.578
G PCA+LDA(RHE)	0.785	0.955	0.982	0.904	0.352	0.909	0.537
G PCA+LDA(RGIC)	0.827	0.984	0.996	0.916	0.490	0.955	0.586

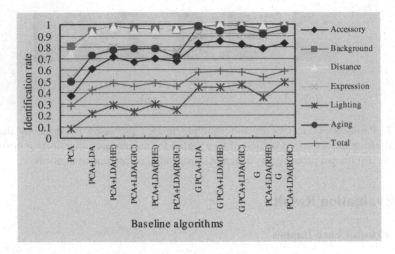

Fig. 3. Identification performance on frontal images

6.2   Face Images Under Different Poses

Two baseline face recognition algorithms (PCA+LDA and G PCA+LDA) are trained on the training set, and evaluated on the three pose probe sets as described in Section 3. Before training and testing, all the images are preprocessed as described in Section 5, using the RGIC illumination normalization method or no illumination normalization respectively. Table 4 and Fig. 4 show the performance of these algorithms on the pose probe sets.

Table 4. Identification performance of two baseline algorithms on the three pose probe sets and the union (Total) set of these sets

Probe sets Algorithms	PD	PM	PU	Total
PCA+LDA	0.061	0.380	0.128	0.190
PCA+LDA(RGIC)	0.092	0.432	0.174	0.233
G PCA+LDA	0.104	0.515	0.241	0.287
G PCA+LDA(RGIC)	0.149	0.556	0.28	0.328

7   Conclusion

In this paper, the evaluation results of three baseline algorithms with different preprocessing methods on the CAS-PEAL-R1 database are presented. Also, we describe the contents of the CAS-PEAL-R1 database which is a released version of the CAS-PEAL database, and the partition of the datasets used in the evaluation. From these results, the difficulty of the database, and the strengths and weakness of commonly used algorithms can be inferred, which may be some good references for the potential users of the database.

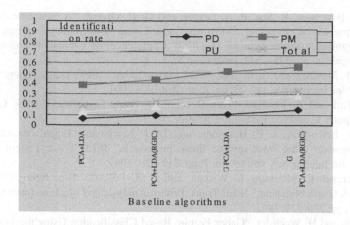

Fig. 4. Identification performance on images under poses

We believe that not only the characteristics of a face database itself, such as the scale, the diversity of the variations, the detailed ground-truth information and well organized structure, but also a standard evaluation protocol including the partition of training sets, gallery sets and probe sets, performance measures, etc. contributes to the success of the database. The paper sets an example of the evaluations on the CAS-PEAL-R1 database and provides baseline evaluation results to the research community.

Acknowledgements

This research is partially sponsored by Natural Science Foundation of China under contract No.60332010, National Hi-Tech Program of China (No. 2001AA114190 and 2002AA118010), and ISVISION Technologies Co., Ltd.

References

1. W. Zhao, R. Chellappa, A. Rosenfeld and P. J. Phillips, "Face Recognition: A Literature Survey," Technical Report, CS-TR4167, University of Maryland, 2000. Revised 2002, CS-TR4167R.
2. R. Chellappa, C. Wilson, and S. Sirohey, "Human and Machine Recognition of Faces: A Survey," Proc. IEEE, vol. 83, no. 5, pp. 705-740, 1995.
3. P. J. Phillips, H. Moon, S. Rizvi, and P. Rauss, "The FERET Evaluation Methodology for Face-Recognition Algorithms," IEEE Transactions on Pattern Analysis and Machine Intelligence, Vol. 22, No. 10, pp. 1090-1104, 2000.
4. P. J. Phillips, P. Grother, J. Ross, D. Blackburn, E. Tabassi, and M. Bone, "Face Recognition Vendor Test 2002: Evaluation Report," March 2003.
5. D. Zhou, X. Zhang, B. Liu, and W. Gao, "Introduction of the JDL Large-scale Facial Database," The 4th Chinese Conference on Biometrics Recognition (Sinobiometrics'03), pp. 118-121, 2003.
6. http://www.jdl.ac.cn/peal/index.html

7. J. R. Beveridge, K. She, B. A. Draper, and G. H. Givens, "A Nonparametric Statistical Comparison of Principal Component and Linear Discriminant Subspaces for Face Recognition," Proceedings of the IEEE Conference on Computer Vision and Pattern Recognition, pp. 535 – 542, December 2001.
8. A. M. Martinez and A. C. Kak, "PCA versus LDA," IEEE Trans. Pattern Analysis and Machine Intelligence, vol. 23, no. 2, pp. 228-233, 2001.
9. M. Turk and A. Pentland, "Face Recognition Using Eigenfaces," IEEE Conference on Computer Vision and Pattern Recognition, 1991.
10. P. N. Belhumeur, J. P. Hespanha, and D. J. Kriegman, "Eigenfaces vs. Fisherfaces: Recognition using class specific linear projection," IEEE Trans. Pattern Analysis and Machine Intelligence, vol. 19, no. 7, pp. 711-720, 1997.
11. N. Kruger, C. Malsburg, L. Wiskott, and J. M. Fellous, "Face Recognition by Elastic Bunch Graph Matching," IEEE Trans. Pattern Analysis and Machine Intelligence, vol. 19, no. 7, pp. 775-779, 1997.
12. C. Liu and H. Wechsler, "Gabor Feature Based Classification Using the Enhanced Fisher Linear Dsicriminant Model for Face Recognition," IEEE Trans. Image Processing, vol. 11, no. 4, pp. 467-476, 2002.
13. S. Shan, W. Gao, B. Cao, and D. Zhao, "Illumination Normalization for Robust Face Recognition against Varying Lighting Conditions," IEEE International Workshop on Analysis and Modeling of Faces and Gestures, pp. 157-164, Nice, France, 2003.
14. S. Shan, W. Gao, and L. Qing, "Generating Canonical Form Face Images for Illumination Insensitive Face Recognition," The 4th Chinese Conference on Biometrics Recognition (Sinobiometrics'03), pp. 29-35, 2003.

An Efficient Compression and Reconstruction Method of Face Image for Low Rate Net

Xing Li, JianHuang Lai, and ZhiBin Zhang

Center of Computer Vision, Sun Yat-sen University, Guangzhou, China 510275
mcp021x@student.zsu.edu.cn

Abstract. A generic 2D face image coding method used for face recognition or expression reconstruction in the low rate net is introduced in this article. By this method the author reconstructs facial texture images with partial areas of reference face pictures by least-square minimization (LSM) with a high compression ratio and a good PSNR value. Our experimental results show that reconstructed faces are very natural and plausible like real photos. This technique has improved outline shape control ability of PCA method, and at the same time, it can maintain details adjust ability of PCA method.

1   Introduction

Image and video coding is one of the most important topics in recent thirty years. And as the most important character of human, the face image has applied in image processing and digital communications. If the face compress rate could be promoted each frame, the whole code rate in transmission could be compensated for.

For many years, the Discrete Cosine Transform (DCT) has been applied in still image coding. Many important standards have incorporated this technology as the main method like JPEG, H.263 and MPEG4.   JPEG2000 [1] represents the state of the art with respect to still image coding standards. This is mainly due to the 20% improvement in coding efficiency with respect to the DCT as well as the new set of functionalities incorporated. Non-linear wavelet decomposition may bring further improvement [2]. Combining natural and synthetic content, MPEG-4 has become an international standard in 1999 [3]. Although other techniques, such as fractal coding or vector quantization have also being studied, they have not found their way into the standards. Other alternate approaches such as "second generation techniques" [4] raised a lot of interest for the potential of high compression ratios. However, they have not been able to provide very high quality. Second generation techniques and, in particular, segmentation based image coding schemes, have produced a coding approach more suitable for content access and manipulation than for strictly coding applications [5]. This will be too expensive to do with traditional waveform coders. Moghaddam and Pentland have used the KL transform to create a set of basic functions that depend on the input class [6]. A KL transform is performed to generate a set of basis functions called eigen- faces, which are combined linearly to approximate the image to encode.

S.Z. Li et al. (Eds.): Sinobiometrics 2004, LNCS 3338, pp. 379–385, 2004.

For the reconstruction aspect, Turk and Pentland proposed a method for reconstructing missing parts of a partially occluded face using eigenfaces based on Principal Component Analysis (PCA) [7]. Jones and Poggio proposed a method for recovering the missing parts in an input face and for establishing the correspondence of the input face with the iteration of the stochastic gradient procedure based on a morphable model [8]. But the algorithm of this method was slow led by iterative procedure. Hwang et al. proposed a method for reconstructing the face using a small set of feature points by least-square minimization (LSM) method based on pseudoinverse without iteration procedure [9]. And then Bon-Woo Hwang and Seong-Whan Lee gave a way to reconstruct the damaged face through Morphable Face Model [10]. Although it must satisfy two prior conditions, comparing to other studies on reconstruction, this method does not require iterative processes and is suitable for obtaining an optimal reconstruction image from a partially damaged one by simple projection for LSM. It gave us a good idea to decrease the pixel numbers to reconstruct and apply this method in the low rate net

The following section provides the schematic process of our method to encode and reconstruct the face images including the details of every step. In section three we present the preliminary result of our experiment. In the last section we give the next step forward of our research work.

2   The Schematic Process

In this paper, we propose an efficient encoding method for obtaining higher compress ratio and more effective transmission of face images mainly aiming at the dispatchers and the receivers of the low rate net like phone net and others. The frame in practice shows in the following diagram:

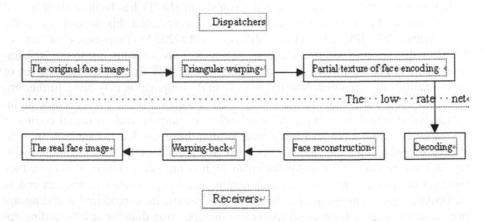

Fig. 1. The schematic process diagram in the low rate net

On the assumption that there is a same reference face model with frontal orientation on both net-sides, a given unknown face image which could different with training set can be justified through warping and be reversed through warping-back.

2.1   The Part of Dispatchers

First of all, we must choose feature points of fiducial face and every given face. The choice of these points refers to the points defined in MPEG4.

FDPs (Facial Definition Parameters) are a set of complex parameters defined by MPEG-4, containing a series data about facial feature points coordinates, texture co-ordinates, face scene graph (optional) and face animation table (FAT) (optional). It also defines 84 feature points of human face. The Feature Points are characteristic points on the face allowing of locating salient facial features. They are illustrated in Figure 2.

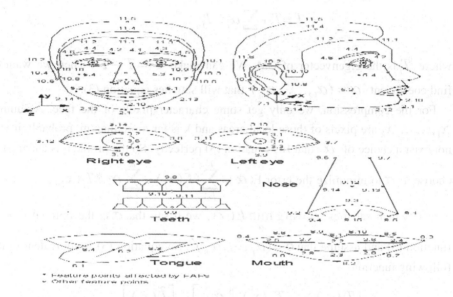

Fig. 2. Feature points defined in MPEG4

After warping we choose the interest local texture vector of the given face, which has the main characters of the face like eye, mouth and some other parts and we can differentiate people by these characters. These texture data and the vector of 58 points will be sent to the receivers. Because our primary idea is only to validate the feasibility of this method, we only use DCT to deal with the texture vector and then the Huffman is used to encode to assure the low bitrate in transmission.

2.2   The Part of Receivers

When the receivers get the compressed code, they must decode it firstly. The information needed in the reconstruction can be got in this step.

Next, we must use this information to revert the face we want by least-square minimization (LSM). If we define Texture(1), Texture(2)······Texture(m) as texture vectors of trained images, where m is the number of images to be trained. Then we can find the even texture vector $\overline{T}$ and the covariance matrix CM.

$$\overline{T} = \frac{1}{m}\sum_{i=1}^{m}Texture(i)$$
(1)

$$CM = \frac{1}{m}\sum_{i=1}^{m}(Texture(i) - \overline{T}) * (Texture(i) - \overline{T})'$$
(2)

Refering to the PCA method, we know that the whole face texture vector can be got by

$$T = \overline{T} + \sum_{i=1}^{m}\alpha_i * T_i$$
(3)

where T_i is the eigenvector of CM. We can make $\tilde{T} = T - \overline{T}$. Then we want to find coefficient $\alpha = (\alpha_1, \ldots \ldots \alpha_m)'$ that will satisfies equation (3).

For the compression, we only get some character pixels of the face. Assuming $x_1, \ldots \ldots, x_k$ are pixels of those local areas and k is far more than m, probably it will not exist a choice of α that fits equation (3) perfectly. So the problem is changed to choose a σ to minimize the error $E(\alpha) = \sum_{j=1}^{k}(\tilde{T}(x_j) - \sum_{i=1}^{m}\alpha_i * T_i(x_j))^2$. If there is a σ which satisfies $\sigma = \arg\min_{\alpha} E(\alpha)$, we'll say that σ is the optimal root of function (3) and assume that $\sigma = (\alpha_1^*, \cdots, \alpha_m^*)'$. So equation (3) is equivalent to the following function:

$$\begin{bmatrix} T_1(x_1)\ldots\ldots T_m(x_1) \\ \vdots \\ T_1(x_k)\ldots\ldots T_m(x_k) \end{bmatrix}\begin{bmatrix} \alpha_1^* \\ \vdots \\ \alpha_m^* \end{bmatrix} = \begin{bmatrix} \tilde{T}(x_1) \\ \vdots \\ \tilde{T}(x_k) \end{bmatrix}$$
(4)

let $S = \begin{bmatrix} T_1(x_1)\ldots\ldots T_m(x_1) \\ \vdots \\ T_1(x_k)\ldots\ldots T_m(x_k) \end{bmatrix}$ and $\tilde{S} = \begin{bmatrix} \tilde{T}(x_1) \\ \vdots \\ \tilde{T}(x_k) \end{bmatrix}$, we rewrite equation(4) as:

$S\sigma = \tilde{S}$.

The least-square solution to the equation $S\sigma = \tilde{S}$ of k equation in m unknowns satisfies $S'S\sigma = S'\tilde{S}$. If columns of matrix S are linearly independent, then the inverse of $S'S$ must exist and

$$\sigma = (S'S)^{-1} S'\tilde{S} \tag{5}$$

By using (3) and (5), we can obtain

$$T(x_j) = \overline{T}(x_j) + \sum_{i=1}^{m} \alpha^*_i * T_i(x_j) \qquad (j=1, \cdots\cdots, \ n) \tag{6}$$

where n is the pixel number of the whole human face.

Then using the coordinates of 58 feature points to warp-back the texture information, we can reconstruct the face image, which is sent by dispatchers.

3 Experiment and Results

In the experiment, we used 126 images of size 112*92 (10304) pixels from FERET, including 105 images as training images and 21 images as testing ones. A head-on face with even light was chosen as a fiducial model (Figure 3 (a)).

Referencing the facial feature points of MPEG-4, we choose 58 points from the model, including 6 of eyebrows, 10 of eyes, 11 of nose, 18 of mouth, 11 of face contour and 4 of cheeks and leading to a gird with 103 triangles. Using these points we can warp the given face image to the model and warp-back to the reconstructed face.

The textures of eyes and mouth from the test face were taken to encode (see in figure3 (b)). The real number of pixels to encode was only 1784 pixels.

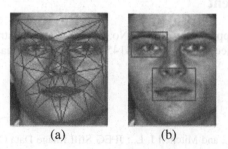

(a)   (b)

Fig. 3. The model face with warp grid (a) and the interest areas in the training sets (b)

Then we used DCT and Huffman coding to these textures and can get a smaller vector relative to the original face image. Transferring this vector to the receiver, we can use it to reconstruct the whole face image with a high compress ratio and a satisfying result. In our experiment, the compress ratio is reached 0.0918 and PSNR is resulted in 21.634 dB (PSNR values are the average over all components). It is also see that reconstructed images look so successful (see in figure 4). Ones on the first line are the original faces and ones on the second line are the reconstructed face images (Figure 4).

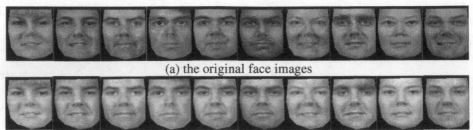

(a) the original face images

(b) the reconstructed face images with PSNR 21.634 dB

Fig. 4. the original face after wrapping in dispatchers (a) and the reconstructed face after decoding in receivers (b)

4   Conclusions

Although the main objective of this research work has been for the still face coding and reconstruction, it can be easily extended to video face coding. The presented results are of very high quality, but we think that face coding using recognition and reconstruction in video image sequence may be the next step forward in our research and maybe through the choice of feature points we can expand this method to the profile and 3D face images. And good object models with feature points will be needed, though, to encode any kind of object following this approach.

Acknowledgement

This project was supported by NSFC (No. 60373082), Ministry of Education in China under the key project grant No. 104145 and NSF of GuangDong in China (No. 021766).

References

1. Pennebaker W. B., and Mitchell J. L.,: JPEG Still Image Data Compression Standard. Van Nostrand Reihold, New York, 1992.
2. Wajcer D., Stanhill D., and Zeevi Y.,: Representation And Coding of Images With Non-separable Two-dimensional Wavelet," Proceedings of the IEEE International Conference on Image Processing, Chicago, USA, October 1998.
3. ISO/IEC ISO/IEC 14496-2: 1999: Information technology – Coding of audio visual objects –Part 2: Visual, December 1999.
4. Torres L. and Kunt M., Editors,: Video Coding: the second generation approach, Kluwer Academic Publishers, Boston, USA, ISBN: 0792396804, January 1996.
5. Luis Torres and Edward J. Delp,: New Trends In Image And Video Compression. Proceedings of the European Signal Processing Conference (EUSIPCO), Tampere, Finland, September,2000 5-8.
6. Baback Moghaddam and Alex Pentland,: An Automatic System for Model-Based Coding of Faces. M.I.T. Media Laboratory Perceptual Computing Section Technical Report No. 317.

7. Turk M. and Pentland A.,: Eigenfaces for Recognition. J. Cognitive Neuroscience, Vol. 3(1), 1991 71-86,.
8. Jones M.J. and Poggio T.: Multidimensional Morphable Models: A Framework for Representing and Matching Object Classes. Int'l J. Computer Vision, Vol.29, 1998, 107-131.
9. Hwang B.W., Blanz V., Vetter T., and Lee S.-W.,: Face Reconstruction From a Small Number of Feature Points. Proc. Int'l Conf. Pattern Recognition, Vol. 2, Sept. 2000 842-845.
10. Hwang Bon-Woo, Lee Seong-Whan,: Reconstruction of Partially Damaged Face Images Based on a Morphable Face Model. IEEE Transactions on Pattern Analysis And Machine Intelligence, VOL. 25(3), MARCH 2003 365-372.

How Can We Reconstruct Facial Image from Partially Occluded or Low-Resolution One?*

Seong-Whan Lee, Jeong-Seon Park, and Bon-Woo Hwang

Center for Artificial Vision Research,
Department of Computer Science and Engineering, Korea University
Anam-dong, Seongbuk-ku, Seoul 136-701, Korea
{swlee, jspark, bwhwang}@image.korea.ac.kr

Abstract. This paper presents our method for reconstructing facial image from a partially occluded facial image or a low-resolution one using example-based learning. Faces are modeled by linear combinations of prototypes of shape and texture. With the shape and texture information from an input facial image, we can estimate optimal coefficients for linear combinations of prototypes of shape and texture by simple projection for least square minimization. The encouraging results of the proposed method show that our method can be used to improve the performance of the face recognition by reconstructing facial image from a partially occluded facial image or a low-resolution one.

1   Introduction

There is a growing interest in visual surveillance systems for security areas such as international airports, borders, sports grounds, and safety areas. And various researches on face recognition have been carried out for a long time. But there still exist a number of difficult problems such as estimating facial pose, facial expression variations, resolving object occlusion, changes of lighting conditions, and the low-resolution images.

Handling occluded images or low-resolution images is one of the most difficult and commonly occurring problems in various image processing applications such as analysis of scientific, medical, astronomical, and weather images, archiving, retrieval and transmission of those images as well as video surveillance or monitoring[11].

In many studies, modeling the properties of noise, which contrast with those of an image, has been used for removing noise[8, 14]. However, those methods cannot remove the noise that is distributed in a wide region, because they use only local properties. In addition, the region in the image which has similar properties with noise gets degraded in the process of removing noise. Also, these methods cannot recover the occluded region by objects or cast-shadow. That not only is commonly discovered in many natural images but also generates problems in many practical applications such as face detection or object recognition.

---

* This research was supported by the Intelligent Robotics Development Program, one of the 21st Century Frontier R&D Programs funded by the Ministry of Science and Technology of Korea.

S.Z. Li et al. (Eds.): Sinobiometrics 2004, LNCS 3338, pp. 386–399, 2004.

Numerous methods have been reported in the area of reconstructing high-resolution images from a series of low-resolution images or single low-resolution image. Super-resolution is a typical example of techniques reconstructing a high-resolution image from a series of low-resolution images[1, 4], whereas interpolation produces a large image from only one low-resolution image.

We are concerned with reconstructing a facial image from a partially occluded facial image or a low-resolution one. Our reconstruction method is example-based, object-class-specific or top-down approach. It is highly tolerant to sensor noise[14], incompleteness of input images and occlusion by other objects. The example-based approach to interpreting images of deformable objects are now attracting considerable interest among many researchers[5, 6]. The motivation for example-based learning lies in its potential of deriving high-level knowledge from a set of prototypical examples.

This paper is organized as follows. Section 2 describes a morphable face model and an extended morphable face model where shape and texture are treated separately. In Section 3, we explain the overview of our reconstruction method based on extended morphable face model and describe the procedure of high-resolution shape estimation using example-based learning, the problem of high-resolution reconstruction and solution to solve the least square minimization of reconstruction error. In Section 4, experimental results with occluded facial images and low-resolution facial images are provided along with an analysis of these results. Finally, conclusions and future works will be discussed in Section 5.

2   Definition of Face Model

In this section, we define an extended morphable face model where shape and texture are treated separately and present mathematical representation of the extended face model which will be used to described the procedure of our reconstruction method.

2.1   Morphable Face Model

Our reconstruction method is based on the morphable face model introduced by Poggio *et al.*[2] and developed further by Vetter *et al.*[3, 13]. Assuming that the pixelwise correspondence between facial images has already been established[13], the 2D shape of a face is coded as the displacement fields from a reference face. The shape of a facial image is represented by a vector $S = (d_1^x, d_1^y, \cdots, d_N^x, d_N^y)^T \epsilon \Re^{2N}$, where N is the number of pixels in facial image, (d_k^x, d_k^y) the x, y displacement of a pixel that corresponds to a pixel x_k in the reference face and can be denoted by $S(x_k)$. The texture is coded as the intensity map of the image which results from mapping the input face onto the reference face. Thus, the shape normalized(or shape free) texture is represented as a vector $T = (i_1, \cdots, i_N)^T \epsilon \Re^N$, where i_k is the intensity or color of a pixel that corresponds to a pixel x_k among N pixels in the reference face and can be denoted by $T(x_k)$.

Next, we transform the orthogonal coordinate system by principal component analysis(PCA) into a system defined by eigenvectors s_p and t_p of the covariance matrices C_S and C_T computed over the differences of the shape and texture, $\tilde{S} = S - \bar{S}$ and

$\tilde{T} = T - \bar{T}$. Where $\bar{S}$ and $\bar{T}$ represent the mean of shape and that of texture, respectively. Then, a facial image can be represented by the following equation.

$$S = \bar{S} + \sum_{p=1}^{M-1} \alpha_p s_p, \quad T = \bar{T} + \sum_{p=1}^{M-1} \beta_p t_p \tag{1}$$

where α, $\beta \in \Re^{M-1}$.

2.2 Extended Morphable Face Model

In order to reconstruct a high-resolution facial image from a low-resolution one, we would like to define an extended morphable face model as an extended face is composed of a pair of low-resolution face and high-resolution one. Then, an extended face is separated by an extended shape and an extended texture according to the definition of morphable face model as shown in Fig. 1.

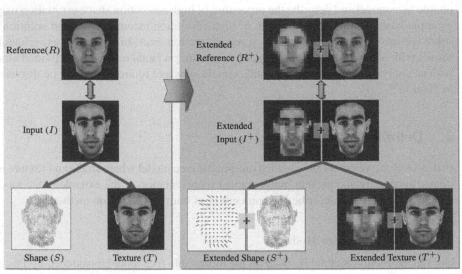

(a) Morphable face model   (b) Extended morphable face model

Fig. 1. Examples of face representations based on extended morphable face model

Then we can define $S^+ = (d_1^x, d_1^y, \cdots, d_L^x, d_L^y, d_{L+1}^x, d_{L+1}^y \cdots, d_{L+H}^x, d_{L+H}^y)^T$ to be an extended shape vector by simply concatenating low-resolution shape and high-resolution shape, where L is the number of pixels in low-resolution facial image and H is the number of pixels in high-resolution one. Similarly, let us define $T^+ = (i_1, \cdots, i_L, i_{L+1}, \cdots, i_{L+H})^T$ to be an extended texture vector.

Then, by applying PCA to both the extended shape S^+ and the extended texture T^+, the facial image in Eq. (1) can be expressed as follows.

$$S^+ = \bar{S}^+ + \sum_{p=1}^{M-1} \alpha_p s_p{}^+, \quad T^+ = \bar{T}^+ + \sum_{p=1}^{M-1} \beta_p t_p{}^+ \qquad (2)$$

where α, $\beta \in \Re^{M-1}$ and $\bar{S}^+$, $\bar{T}^+$ represent the mean of extended shape and that of extended texture, respectively.

2.3   Forward Warping and Backward Warping

Before explaining our example-based reconstruction procedure, we define two types of warping processes, forward and backward warping(see Fig. 2).

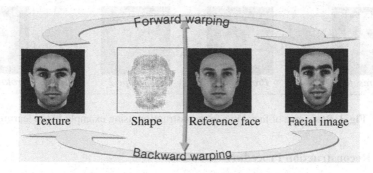

Fig. 2. Examples of forward warping and backward warping

Forward warping warps a texture expressed in reference face onto each input face by using its shape information. This process results in an input facial image. Backward warping warps an input facial image onto the reference face by using its shape information. This process results in a texture information expressed in reference shape. The mathematical definition and more details about the forward and backward warping can be found in reference [13].

3   Facial Image Reconstruction Using Example-Based Learning

Suppose that sufficiently large amount of facial images are available for off-line training, then we can represent any input facial image by a linear combination of a number of facial prototypes[13]. Moreover, if we know the information of partially occluded regions or resolution of input facial image, then we can obtained the deformed prototype faces using those information. Then, we can approximate the given occluded or low-resolution facial image by using the coefficients of deformed prototypes, and we can obtain a reconstructed facial image by applying the estimated coefficients to the corresponding high-quality example faces(see Fig. 3). Consequently, our goal is to find an optimal parameter set α which best estimates the high-quality facial image from a given facial image.

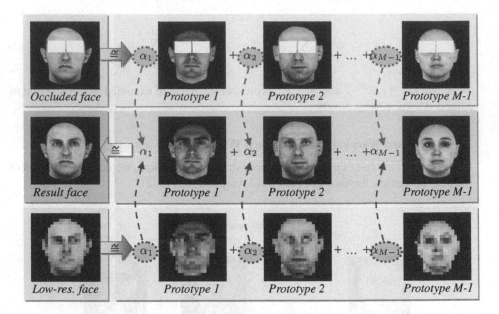

Fig. 3. Basic idea of facial image reconstruction using example-based learning

3.1   Reconstruction Procedure

Before describing a specific algorithm for reconstructing facial image, we explain two prior conditions and give an overview of the procedure for obtaining a reconstructed facial image from a partially occluded or low-resolution one.

Prior Conditions:

- Displacement among pixels in an input face which correspond to those in the reference face is known.
- Positions of pixels in occluded region by virtual objects on an input face are known for reconstructing partially occluded facial image.

Our reconstruction procedure consists of 4 steps, starting from a partially occluded facial image or a low-resolution one. Reconstructing partially occluded facial image or estimating high-resolution facial image have same procedure except that the types of input facial image are different as shown in Fig. 4. Therefore, we will mainly describe the procedure of reconstructing high-resolution facial image from an input low-resolution one using example-based learning of extended morphable face model.

Step 1.   *Obtain the texture of an input facial image by backward warping.*

Step 2.   *Estimate a high-resolution shape(or whole shape) from a given low-resolution shape(or partially occluded one).*

Step 3.   *Estimate a high-resolution texture(or whole texture) from the obtained texture at Step 1.*

Step 4.   *Synthesize a facial image by forward warping the estimated texture with the estimated shape.*

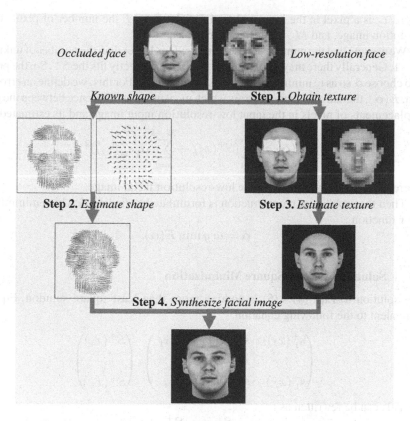

Occluded face   *Low-resolution face*

Known shape   **Step 1.** *Obtain texture*

Step 2. *Estimate shape*   **Step 3.** *Estimate texture*

Step 4. *Synthesize facial image*

Fig. 4. Reconstruction procedure based on 2D morphable face model

Step 1 and Step 4 are explained from the previous studies of morphable face models in many studies[6, 13]. Step 2 and Step 3 are carried out by similar mathematical procedure except that the shape about a pixel is 2D vector and the texture is 1D(or 3D for RGB color image) vector. Therefore, we will describe only the Step 2 of estimating a high-resolution shape from input low-resolution shape.

In addition, for obtaining better results of reconstructing facial image from partially occluded one, we can replace the pixels in the occluded regions by the reconstructed ones and combine the original and the reconstructed image in the border regions outside of the occluded region using a weight mask according to the distance from the border.

3.2   Problem Definition for Shape Reconstruction

Since there is a shape information about only low-resolution facial image, we need an approximation to the deformation required for the low-resolution shape by using coefficients of the bases(see Fig. 3). The goal is to find an optimal set α_p that satisfies

$$\tilde{S}^+(x_j) = \sum_{p=1}^{M-1} \alpha_p s_p^+(x_j), \ \ j = 1, \cdots, L, \tag{3}$$

where x_j is a pixel in the low-resolution facial image, L the number of pixels in low-resolution image, and $M - 1$ the number of bases.

We assume that the number of observations, L, is larger than the number of unknowns, $M-1$. Generally there may not exist a set of α_p that perfectly fits the $\tilde{S}^+$. So, the problem is to choose $\hat{\alpha}$ so as to minimize the reconstruction error. For this, we define an error function, $E(\alpha)$, the sum of square of errors which measures the difference between the known displacements of pixels in the input low-resolution input image and its estimated ones.

$$E(\alpha) = \sum_{j=1}^{L} (\tilde{S}^+(x_j) - \sum_{p=1}^{M-1} \alpha_p s_p^+(x_j))^2 \tag{4}$$

where $x_1, \cdots, x_L$ are pixels in the low-resolution facial image.

Then the problem of reconstruction is formulated as finding $\hat{\alpha}$ which minimizes the error function :

$$\hat{\alpha} = arg \min_{\alpha} E(\alpha). \tag{5}$$

3.3   Solution by Least Square Minimization

The solution to Eqs. (4) - (5) is nothing more than least square solution. Eq. (3) is equivalent to the following equation.

$$\begin{pmatrix} s_1^+(x_1) \cdots s_{M-1}^+(x_1) \\ \vdots \quad \ddots \quad \vdots \\ s_1^+(x_L) \cdots s_{M-1}^+(x_L) \end{pmatrix} \begin{pmatrix} \alpha_1 \\ \vdots \\ \alpha_{M-1} \end{pmatrix} = \begin{pmatrix} \tilde{S}^+(x_1) \\ \vdots \\ \tilde{S}^+(x_L) \end{pmatrix} \tag{6}$$

This can be rewritten as :

$$\mathbf{S}^+ \, \alpha = \tilde{\mathbf{S}}^+, \tag{7}$$

where

$$\mathbf{S}^+ = \begin{pmatrix} s_1^+(x_1) \cdots s_{M-1}^+(x_1) \\ \vdots \quad \ddots \quad \vdots \\ s_1^+(x_L) \cdots s_{M-1}^+(x_L) \end{pmatrix},$$

$$\alpha = (\alpha_1, \cdots, \alpha_{M-1})^T,$$

$$\tilde{\mathbf{S}}^+ = (\tilde{S}^+(x_1), \cdots, \tilde{S}^+(x_L))^T. \tag{8}$$

The least square solution to an inconsistent $\mathbf{S}^+\alpha = \tilde{\mathbf{S}}^+$ of L equation in $M - 1$ unknowns satisfies $\mathbf{S}^{+T}\mathbf{S}^+\alpha^* = \mathbf{S}^{+T}\tilde{\mathbf{S}}^+$. If the columns of $\mathbf{S}^+$ are linearly independent, then $(\mathbf{S}^{+T}\mathbf{S}^+)$ is non-singular and has an inverse

$$\alpha^* = (\mathbf{S}^{+T}\mathbf{S}^+)^{-1}\mathbf{S}^{+T}\tilde{\mathbf{S}}^+. \tag{9}$$

The projection of $\tilde{\mathbf{S}}^+$ onto the column space is therefore $\hat{\mathbf{S}}^+ = \mathbf{S}^+\alpha^*$. By using Eq. (9), we can obtain a high-resolution shape

$$S(x_{L+j}) = \tilde{S}^+(x_{L+j}) + \sum_{p=1}^{M-1} \alpha_p^* s_p^+(x_{L+j}), \; j = 1, \ldots, H, \tag{10}$$

where $x_{L+1}, \cdots, x_{L+H}$ are pixels in the high-resolution facial image, L and H is the number of pixels in the low-resolution facial image and that of high-resolution facial image, respectively.

By using Eq. (10), we can get the correspondence of high-resolution shape. Previously we made the assumption that the columns of $\mathbf{S}^+$ are linearly independent. Otherwise, Equation (9) may not be satisfied. If $\mathbf{S}^+$ has dependent columns, the solution $\boldsymbol{\alpha}^*$ will not be unique. The optimal solution in this case can be solved by pseudoinverse of $\mathbf{S}^+$[5]. But, for our purpose of effectively reconstructing a high-resolution shape(or texture) from a low-resolution one, this is unlikely to happen.

4   Experimental Results and Analysis

4.1   Face Database

For testing the proposed method, we used 200 2D facial images of Caucasian faces that were rendered from a database of 3D head models recorded with a laser scanner $(Cyberware^{TM})$[3, 13]. The resolution of the images was 256 by 256 pixels and the color images were converted to 8-bit gray level images. The hair of heads was removed completely from the images. PCA was performed on a random subset of 100 facial images. The other 100 images were used for testing our algorithm. In our face database, we use a hierarchical, gradient-based optical flow algorithm to obtain a pixel-wise correspondence[13]. The correspondence is defined between a reference facial image and an individual image in the database.

Partially Occluded Facial Images

Specifically, test data is a set of facial images, which have components such as a left eye, both eyes, a nose and a mouth occluded by virtual objects. The shape and size of the virtual objects are identical to every face, but each position of those is dependent on that of components for every face. The position of components is extracted automatically from correspondence to the reference face. Fig. 5(a) shows that virtual objects are inserted, according to the position of components in the reference face.

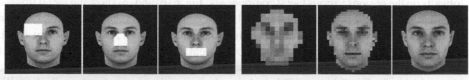

(a) Occluded reference face   (b) Resized reference face

Fig. 5. Examples of experimental facial images, (a) Virtual objects are inserted according to the position of components in the reference face : left eye, nose, and mouth, (b) various kinds of resolution of reference face : $16 \times 16, 32 \times 32$, and 256×256

Low-Resolution Facial Images

As described before, the original images were color image set of size 256×256 pixels.

They were converted to 8-bit gray level and resized to 16×16 and 32×32 for low-resolution facial images as shown in Fig. 5(b). PCA was applied to a random subset of 100 facial images for constructing bases of the defined face model. The other 100 images were used for testing our algorithm.

4.2 Results from Partially Occluded Facial Images

As mentioned before, 2D-shape and texture of facial images are treated separately. Therefore, a facial image is synthesized by combining the estimated shape and the estimated texture using example-based learning.

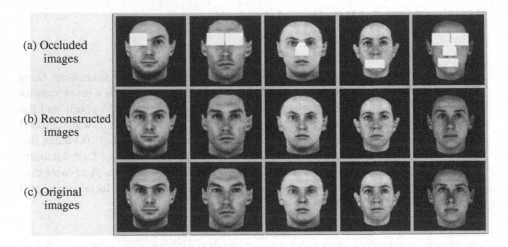

(a) Occluded images

(b) Reconstructed images

(c) Original images

Fig. 6. Examples of facial images reconstructed from shape and texture information occluded by virtual objects

Fig. 6 shows the examples of the facial image reconstructed from the facial images occluded by virtual objects. In this figure, (a) shows the occluded facial images by virtual objects on the regions various facial components. Fig. 6 (b) and (c) show the facial images reconstructed by the proposed method and the original facial images, respectively. Most of the reconstructed faces are similar to the original ones and a few are not. But in all, not only the shape information of each component, but also the texture information of that is very naturally reconstructed. Although we do not apply heuristic algorithms like symmetry in the first column of Fig. 6, the occluded eye is reconstructed similarly to the non-occluded opposite eye.

Fig. 7 (a) and (b) show the mean reconstruction errors for shapes, textures and synthesized images. Horizontal axes of Fig. 7 (a) and (b) represent the occluded components by virtual objects. Vertical axes of them represent the mean displacement error per pixel and the mean intensity error per pixel(for an image using 256 gray level), respectively. Standard deviations of errors are represented with mean errors, too. Err_S_x and Err_S_y

in Fig. 7 (a) imply the x-directional mean displacement error and the y-directional one for shape, respectively. And Err_T and Err_I in Fig. 7 (b) imply the mean intensity error for texture and that for image, respectively. In Fig. 7, the more virtual objects occlude a face, the more errors occur. But the errors do not increase as much as occlusion area does.(the ratio of occlusion area: the area of all occluded components/the area of a occluded nose=4.87, the ratio of the mean displacement error(S_x) : the Err_S_x for all components/the Err_S_x for nose= 1.22). Notice that the mean errors of texture and image in the case that both eyes are occluded are greater than those in the case that all components are occluded. We guess that flat gray values in a nose and a mouth reduce the mean intensity errors per pixel for texture and image in the case that all components are occluded.

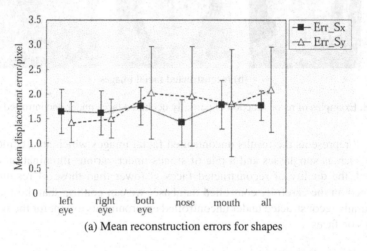

(a) Mean reconstruction errors for shapes

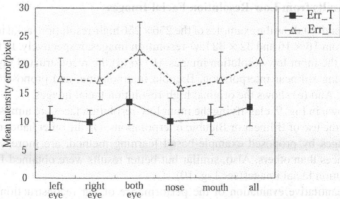

(b) Mean reconstruction errors for textures and reconstructed images

Fig. 7. Mean reconstruction errors for shapes, textures and synthesized images. Horizontal axes of (a) and (b) represent the occluded components by virtual objects

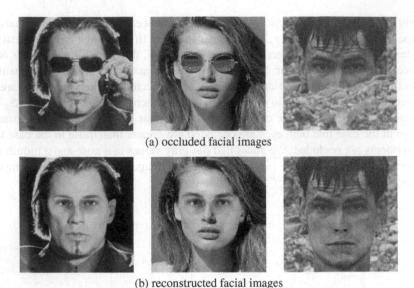

(a) occluded facial images

(b) reconstructed facial images

Fig. 8. Examples of reconstruction of partially occluded faces under uncontrolled condition

Fig. 8 represents the results uncontrolled facial images which are occluded by real objects such as sunglasses and a pile of stones under various illumination conditions. Although the quality of reconstructed faces is lower than those of results of Fig. 6 performed on the carefully controlled database, we can confirm that the facial images are naturally reconstructed under uncontrolled environments except for the wrinkles and shadows on faces.

4.3   Results from Low-Resolution Facial Images

Figures 9 and 10 show the examples of the 256×256 high-resolution facial images reconstructed from 16×16 and 32×32 low-resolution images, respectively. In these figures, (a) shows the input low-resolution images, (b) to (d) the reconstructed high-resolution images using Bilinear interpolation, Bicubic interpolation, and proposed method, respectively. And (e) shows the original high-resolution facial images.

As shown in Fig. 9, classifying the input low-resolution faces are almost impossible, even with the use of Bilinear or Bicubic interpolations. On the other hand, reconstructed facial images by proposed example-based learning method, are more similar to the original faces than others. Also, similar but better results were obtained from 32×32 low-resolution facial images(see Fig. 10).

For quantitative evaluation of the performance of our reconstruction method, we measured the mean reconstruction errors in shape, texture and facial image from the original high-resolution data, respectively. The horizontal axes of Fig. 11 represent the input low-resolution, two interpolation methods and the proposed reconstruction method. Vertical axes of them represent the mean displacement error per pixel of shape vectors and the mean intensity error per pixel(for an image using 256 gray level) of texture vector and that of image vector, respectively. Err_S_x and Err_S_y in Fig. 11 are the x-

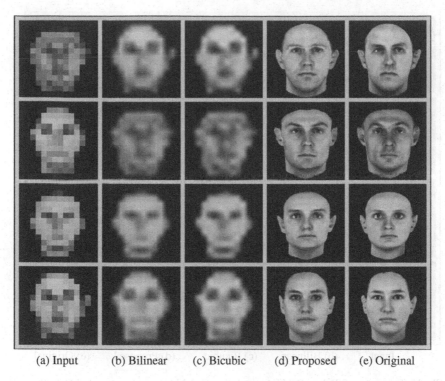

(a) Input   (b) Bilinear   (c) Bicubic   (d) Proposed   (e) Original

Fig. 9. Examples of 256×256 high-resolution facial images reconstructed from 16×16 low-resolution facial images

directional mean displacement errors along the $x-$ and $y-$ axes for shape, respectively. And Err_T and Err_I implies the mean intensity error of texture and that of facial image, respectively. As shown in Fig. 11, the reconstruction errors of the proposed method are smaller than others.

5   Conclusions and Further Researches

In this paper, we provided efficient methods of reconstructing facial image from an occluded facial image or a low-resolution one using example-based learning method of extended morphable face model. Our reconstruction method consists of the following steps : computing linear coefficients minimizing the error or difference between the given shape or texture and the linear combination of the shape or texture prototypes in the input occluded or low-resolution facial image, and applying the coefficient estimates to the shape and texture prototypes in the original facial image, respectively.

The experimental results are very natural and plausible like original facial images. From the encouraging results of the proposed method we can expect that our reconstruction method can be used to improve the performance of face recognition systems by reconstructing a high-resolution facial image from a low-resolution facial images captured in visual surveillance systems.

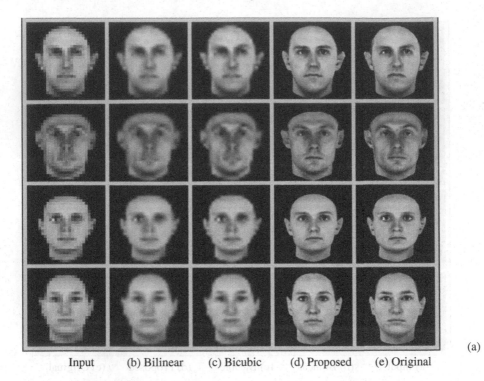

(a)

Input   (b) Bilinear   (c) Bicubic   (d) Proposed   (e) Original

Fig. 10. Examples of 256×256 high-resolution facial images reconstructed from 32×32 low-resolution facial images

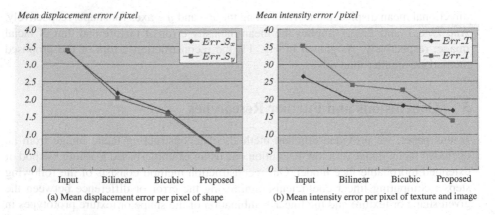

Mean displacement error / pixel

Mean intensity error / pixel

(a) Mean displacement error per pixel of shape   (b) Mean intensity error per pixel of texture and image

Fig. 11. Comparisons of mean reconstruction errors

In order to apply our example-based reconstruction methods to real-environment visual surveillance systems, we must develop an automatic algorithm to overcome restrictions of prior conditions that the displacement among pixels in an input face which correspond to those in the reference face is known.

Acknowledgments

We would like to thank the Max-Planck-Institute for providing the MPI Face Database.

References

1. S. Baker and T. Kanade, "Limit on Super-Resolution and How to Break Them," *IEEE Transactions on Pattern Analysis and Machine Intelligence*, Vol. 24 No. 9, pp. 1167-1183, Sep. 2002.
2. D. Beymer and T. Poggio, "Image Representation for Visual Learning," *Science*, vol. 272, pp. 1905-1909, 1996.
3. V. Blanz, S. Romdhani, and T. Vetter, "Face Identification Across Different Poses and Illuminations with a 3D Morphable Model," In *Proceedings of the 5th Internatioal Conference on Automatic Face and Gesture Recognition*, Washington, D.C., pp. 202-207, 2002.
4. F. Dekeyser, P. Perez, and P. Bouthemy, "Restoration of Noisy, Blurred, Undersampled Image Sequences Using Parametric Motion Model," In *Proceedings of the International Symposium on Image/Video Communications over Fixed and Mobile Networks, ISIVC 2000*, Rabat, Morocco, April 2000.
5. B.-W. Hwang, S.-W. Lee, "Reconstruction of Partially Damaged Face Images Based on a Morphable Face Model," *IEEE Transactions on Pattern Analysis and Machine Intelligence*, Vol. 25, No. 3, pp. 365-372, 2003.
6. M. J. Jones, P. Sinha, T. Vetter, and T. Poggio, "Top-down Learning of Low-level Vision Tasks[Brief Communication]," *Current Biology*, Vol. 7, pp. 991-994, 1997.
7. M. G. Kang and S. Chaudhuri, "Super-Resolution Image Reconstruction," *IEEE Signal Processing Magazine*, Vol. 23 No. 3, pp. 19-36, May 2003.
8. P. M. Narendra, "A Separable Median Filter for Image Noise Smoothing," *IEEE Trans. on Pattern Analysis and Machine Intelligence*, vol. 3, no. 1, pp. 20-29, 1981.
9. T. Poggio, and T. Vetter, "Recognition and Structure from One 2D Model View: Observations on Prototypes, Object Classes and Symmetries," *AI Memo 1347/CBIP Paper 69*, Massachusetts Institute of Technology, Feb. 1992.
10. G. Strang, "*Linear Algebra and Its Applications*," Harcourt Brace Jovanovich College publishers, pp. 442-451, 1988.
11. B. Tom and A. K. Katsaggelos, "Resolution Enhancement of Monochrome and Color Video Using Motion Compensation," *IEEE Transactions on Image Processing*, Vol. 10, No. 2, pp. 278-287, Feb. 2001.
12. M. Turk and A. Pentland, "Eigenfaces for Recognition," *Journal of Cognitive Neuroscience*. vol. 3, no. 1, pp. 71-86, 1991.
13. T. Vetter and N. E. Troje, "Separation of Texture and Shape in Images of Faces for Image Coding and Synthesis," *Journal of the Optical Society of America A*. Vol. 14, No. 9, pp. 2152-2161, 1997.
14. P. S. Windyga, "Fast Impulsive Noise Removal," *IEEE Transactions on Image Processing*, Vol. 10, No. 1, pp. 173-178, 2001.

A Matrix-Oriented Method for Appearance-Based Data Compression – An Idea from Group Representation Theory

Deli Zhao[1], Chongqing Liu[1], and Yuehui Zhang[2]

[1] Institute of Image Processing and Pattern Recognition,
Shanghai Jiao Tong University, Shanghai, 200030, China
zhaodeli@sjtu.edu.cn
[2] Department of Mathematics,
Shanghai Jiao Tong University, Shanghai, 200030, China

Abstract. Motivated by ideas of group representation theory, we propose a matrix-oriented method to dimension reduction for image data. By virtue of the action of Stiefel manifold, the original image representations can be directly contracted into a rather low-dimensional space. Experimental results show that the performance of PCA and LDA is significantly enhanced in the transformed space. In addition, the reconstructed images by proposed algorithm are better than those by 2DPCA.

1 Introduction

As is known, the complexity in the very nature of two dimensional image data gives rise to a host of problems in image processing. To avoid this difficulty, one frequently resorts to principal component analysis (PCA) for dimension reduction [1],[2]. PCA is a type of vector-oriented method, which results in the huge size of covariance matrix when employed to reduce dimension for 2D image data. Then comes two well-known limitations of PCA. One is the poor estimation of covariance matrix in case where the small sample size problem occurs, the other is the complexity of eigenanalysis. So it is natural for one to pursue much easier tool for dimension reduction. More recently, Yang et al. [3] presented a matrix-oriented approach coined two-dimensional PCA (2DPCA) for appearance-based face representation and recognition. Compared to conventional PCA, 2DPCA does not extend the size of covariance matrix significantly. As a consequence, it is more straightforward to proceed eigenanalysis. Additionally, Yang argued that 2DPCA is more suited to small sample size problem. However, much more coefficients needed to represent the original image is the critical weakness of 2DPCA. As a result, LDA is still inapplicable for the subsequent feature extraction.

Motivated by the way of seeking the equivalent representation of matrix group, we propose a novel method to dimension reduction for matrix data. In light of the action generated by a semi-orthogonal matrix, we can obtain rather small size representation

S.Z. Li et al. (Eds.): Sinobiometrics 2004, LNCS 3338, pp. 400–404, 2004.

of original data. Experimental results show that the performance of the traditional PCA and LDA can be significantly enhanced in the transformed space.

2 The Proposed Algorithm

2.1 Motivation of Idea

Groups and their representations play an essential role in quantum mechanical study of physical systems, the central task of which is to find the efficient equivalent representations. Particularly, in the situation of finite groups or compact Lie groups, advantages may be taken of the considerable simplifications that result from using representations that are unitary. The following theorem shows the existence of unitary representations for such groups.

Theorem[4]. If G is a finite group or a compact Lie group then every representation of G is equivalent to a unitary representation.

More formally, suppose that the order of G is g and $\Gamma(T_i)$ denotes the $n \times n$ representation of element T_i in G. Define the $n \times n$ matrix H by

$$H = \frac{1}{g}\sum_{i=1}^{g}\Gamma(T_i)\Gamma^\dagger(T_i)$$ (1)

It is easy to verify that H is Hermitian, say $H^\dagger = H$, so there exits an $n \times n$ unitary matrix U (i.e. $U^\dagger = U^{-1}$) that carries H diagonal, namely that

$$U^\dagger HU = d$$ (2)

Generally, H is positive definite, leading to that all the diagonal elements of d are real and positive. This property of d allows us to form the following matrix

$$S = Ud^{\frac{1}{2}}$$ (3)

We define the following similarity transformation via S

$$\tilde{\Gamma}(T_i) = S^{-1}\Gamma(T_i)S$$ (4)

It has been proven that

$$\tilde{\Gamma}(T_i)\tilde{\Gamma}^\dagger(T_i) = I_n$$ (5)

Thus, the collection of $\tilde{\Gamma}(T_i)$ forms a $n \times n$ unitary representation of G. For detailed survey, [4],[5] can be consulted.

2.2 Derivation of Algorithm

Let the set of face representations be $M(n) = \{A_1,...,A_c\}$. By convention, A_i is a nonnegative matrix whose entries vary from 0 to 225. It is apparent that $M(n)$ cannot form a well-defined group. Naturally, $M(n)$ does not possess the properties that a real group does. Nevertheless, the collection of human faces is so analogous to a finite group that it is hard for us not to bridge both together. To this end, we form the strategy that follows.

As shown above, matrix S reshape the structure of each element in group G, in the sense that the new representation possesses a list of better properties for a variety of subsequent operations. Hence, it is reasonable to assert that S carries power of system. To go one step further, diagonal matrix $d^{\frac{1}{2}}$ is , in effect, a weight matrix that gives less contribution to carrier in the transformation. It makes sense therefore to investigate the action of U on system for the involved tasks in image fields.

Let $S(n, p)$ denote the Stiefel manifold, showing that

$$S(n, p) = \left\{ V \in R^{n \times p} \middle| V^t V = I_p \right\} \tag{6}$$

Considering the action of $S(n, p)$ on $M(n)$ as follows

$$M(n) \times S(n, p) \to M(p)$$
$$A_i \mapsto V^t A_i V \tag{7}$$

The action carries matrices in $R^{n \times n}$ into $R^{p \times p}$. Sequentially, the size of original matrices is reduced to be a smaller one, by which the purpose of dimension reduction is accomplished.

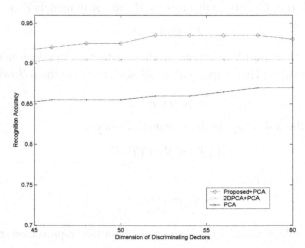

Fig. 1. Recognition accuracy of PCA-related methods. For the proposed method, $p = q = 14$ in the first phase for dimension compresion and for 2DPCA, 10 projection axes are facilitated

For the derivation of matrix V , we impose the relationship between G and $M(n)$ by $g = c$ and $\Gamma(T_i) = A_i$. We call the obtained H the group scatter matrix. Assume that the columns of U are arranged by the correspondence that the eigenvalues of H are ordered non-increasing. Then, we form V by

$$V = U(:,1:p) \tag{8}$$

In the real-world application, however, we prefer the following manner to achieve the representation B_i of face A_i

$$B_i = U'(:,1:p)A_iU(:,1:q) \tag{9}$$

where p and q are the readily determined parameters. Obviously, A_i can be approximately reconstructed by means of transformation $\tilde{A}_i = U(:,1:p)B_iU'(:,1:q)$.

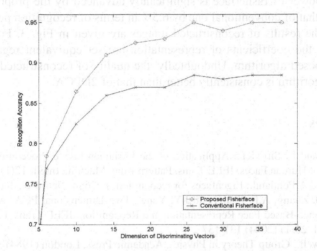

Fig. 2. Recognition accuracy of LDA-related methods. For the proposed method, $p = 8, q = 5$ in the first phase for dimension compression. 50 principal components are utilized in PCA phase for conventional Fisherface

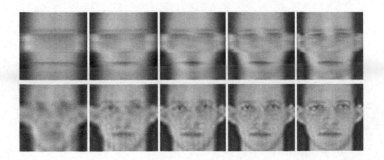

Fig. 3. Reconstructed images. The upper row shows the 2DPCA-reconstructed images. The remainders are the results of the proposed methods

3 Experiment

The experiments are conducted on ORL face database (http://www.cam-orl.co.uk). Here, it suffices to clarify that the size of each face in this database is re-normalized to be 92×92 , due to that square matrices guarantee the successful proceeding of the proposed algorithm. The nearest neighbor classifier is used.

Firstly, we compare the discriminating performance of considered algorithms. We first adopt the proposed method to reduce the dimension of original face data, then performing the traditional Eigenface method. 2DPCA is also executed in the parallel way. Fig.1 demonstrates that the proposed PCA appears to be the best in the transformed space. Secondly, the proposed algorithm and PCA are, respectively, utilized for data compression, following the implementation of Fisherface. As evident by Fig. 2, the power of Fisherface is significantly advanced by the proposed algorithm, higher than that of conventional one by 6.5% in terms of recognition performance.

Finally, the results of reconstructed images are given in Fig. 3. For a reasonable comparison, the coefficients of representation are set equivalent regarding 2DPCA and the proposed algorithm. Undoubtedly, the quality of reconstructed images by the proposed algorithm is consistently better than that of 2DPCA.

References

1. M. Kirby and L. Sirovich.: Application of the Karhunen-Loeve Procedure for the Characterization of Human Faces. IEEE Trans. Pattern Anal. Machine Intell. 12(1) (1990) 103-108
2. M.Turk and A.Pentland.: Eigenfaces for recognition. J. Cogn. Neurosci. 3(1) (1991) 71-86
3. J. Yang, D. Zhang, A.F. Frangi and J.Y. Yang.: Two-Dimensional PCA: A New Approach to Appearance-Based Face Representation and Recognition. IEEE Trans. Pattern Anal. Machine Intell. 26(1) (2004) 131-137
4. J. F. Cornwell.: Group Theory in Physics. Academic Press, London (1984)
5. A. W. Joshi.: Elements of Group Theory for Physicists. 3rd edn. Wiley, New Delhi (1982)

An Adaptive Fingerprint Post-processing Algorithm Based on Mathematical Morphology

Fei Su and Anni Cai

Beijing University of Posts and Telecommunications,
Box 113, 100876
{Sufei, annicai}@bupt.edu.cn

Abstract. In this paper, an adaptive post-processing method using mathematical morphology combined with analyzing the properties of each candidate minutia based on the gray-level image, binary image, local ridge spacing and local orientation is presented to decide whether the minutia is false or true and to eliminate the false one. The experiment results demonstrate the effectiveness to reduce the number of false minutiae encountered and improve the thinning fingerprint images at the same time.

1 Introduction

Fingerprints are the pattern of ridges and valleys on the surface of human fingers. Lifetime "immutability" and "uniqueness" are fingerprint's distinctive characteristics that have determined the use of fingerprints as one of the most reliable techniques for personal identification [1]. Fingerprint identification systems are now widely used in many commercial and security applications. Most automatic fingerprint identification systems are based on minutiae pattern matching or the hybrid matching that combines the minutiae with textures [2]-[4]. In fingerprint images, minutiae are the local discontinuities which represent terminations and bifurcations in the flow pattern (Fig.1).

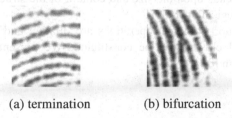

(a) termination   (b) bifurcation

Fig. 1. Examples of minutiae

Operationally, fingerprint identification can be decomposed into two steps: fingerprint preprocessing and matching. Fingerprint preprocessing includes filtering, binarizing, thinning and post-processing, and minutiae are extracted from the thinning image. Accurate minutiae extraction in the fingerprint image is critical to the

S.Z. Li et al. (Eds.): Sinobiometrics 2004, LNCS 3338, pp. 405–413, 2004.
© Springer-Verlag Berlin Heidelberg 2004

performance of an automatic identification system. Therefore, a post-processing stage of minutiae purifying is required before fingerprint matching. Some researchers have proposed the fingerprint post-processing methods to eliminate false minutiae [4]-[7].

In this paper, an adaptive post-processing method using mathematical morphology combined with the analysis of some local gray-level image properties, local ridge spacing and local orientation is presented to eliminate the false minutiae which represent as small holes, spikes, bridges, spurs and ladder structures based on the binary and thinning fingerprint images. According to the analysis results of each candidate minutia based on the properties of gray-level image, local ridge spacing and local orientation, the algorithm decides how to use mathematical morphology structure elements to eliminate those false minutiae. The experimental results demonstrate the effectiveness to reduce the number of false minutiae encountered in the fingerprint images and improve the thinning fingerprint image at the same time.

In the following sections, the basic definitions of mathematical morphology are defined in section 2. In section 3, the adaptive approach based on mathematical morphology is described. In section 4 presents the results obtained. Finally, some conclusions are drawn.

2 Mathematical Morphology

Mathematical morphology is a theory for analysis of spatial structures, which aims at analyzing the shape and the forms of the objects. The analysis is based on set theory, topology, random function, etc. [7]. Mathematical morphology is considered as a powerful tool to extract information from images.

In the general case, morphological image processing operates by passing a structuring element over the image in an activity similar to convolution. Like the convolution kernel, the structuring element can be of any size, and it can contain any complement of 1's and 0's. At each pixel position, a specified logical operation is performed between the structuring element and the underlying binary image. The effect created depends upon the size and content of the structuring element and upon the nature of the logical operation.

The primary morphological operations are dilation and erosion, and from these two, opening and closing can be constituted. We present them here using Minkowski's formalism [8].

2.1 Dilation

The morphological transformation dilation $\oplus$ combines two sets using vector addition. The dilation is the point set of all possible vector additions of elements, one from each of the sets X and B.

$$X \oplus B = \left\{ p \in \varepsilon^2 : p = x + b, x \in X \text{ and } b \in B \right\}. \tag{1}$$

2.2 Erosion

Erosion Θ combines two sets using vector subtraction of set elements and is the dual operator of dilation.

$$X\Theta B = \left\{p \in \varepsilon^2 : p + b \in X \text{ and } b \in B\right\}. \tag{2}$$

2.3 Opening

The process if erosion followed by dilation is called opening. It has the effect of eliminating small and thin objects, breaking objects at thin points, and generally smoothing the boundaries of larger objects without significantly changing their area. Open is defined by

$$X \circ B = (X\Theta B) \oplus B. \tag{3}$$

2.4 Closing

Dilation followed by erosion is called closing. It has the effect of filling small and thin holes in objects, connecting near objects. Closing is defined by

$$X \bullet B = (X \oplus B)\Theta B. \tag{4}$$

3 Adaptive Post-processing Algorithm

In order to extract minutia points from fingerprint images, some preprocessing needs to be done. Generally the procedures include filtering, binarizing, thinning, minutiae extraction and post-processing.

Due to the case of different noises (e.g. blurred prints smeared with under-inking or over-inking, uneven pressure, worm prints, etc.), the thinned image contains a large number of false minutiae which may highly decrease the matching performance of the system. Those false minutiae include small holes, spikes, breaks, bridges, creases, and spurs and so on. As we know, holes will produce false loops, and spurs will form false bifurcation minutia points in the thinned images. There are some false minutiae structures examples in Fig. 2. The original images are showed in Fig. 2 (a) and (c), and the thinned images are in Fig. 2 (b) and (d).

From the Fig. 2, it is clear that a post-processing stage is necessary to purify minutiae before matching. Unfortunately, in some cases, the false and true minutiae have similar ridge structures in the thinning image. In this paper, we explore their difference in the binary image and the original image in order to eliminate the false ones by using the proposed adaptive post-processing algorithm based on mathematical morphology.

Of course, in some cases, it is difficult to decide whether a minutia is true or false, since the binary image and the thinning image can not keep the original information (such as width, gray-level, etc.). An example is shown in Fig.3. It can be seen that the upper loop is the true one, whereas, the lower one is false in Fig.3 (a). But both of these two loops have the similar structures in the thinned image, even in the binary image.

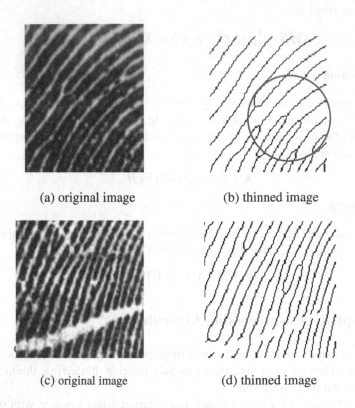

(a) original image   (b) thinned image

(c) original image   (d) thinned image

Fig. 2. False minutiae structures

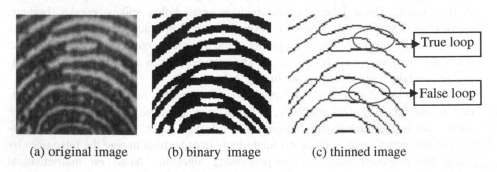

(a) original image   (b) binary image   (c) thinned image

Fig. 3. Examples of false and true minutiae

Under the properties of each candidate minutia both on the binary and original image, the algorithm analyzes whether the minutia is true or false firstly, and an adaptive filtering method based on mathematical morphology is used to smooth the binary fingerprint image for eliminating the false minutiae. According to the width of the ridges, local direction in around the candidate minutia, the fingerprint image, the different templates (i.e. structure elements) are chosen for mathematical morphology.

Firstly, divide the original image into the blocks of size W×W, then estimate the local orientation[1] and local ridge spacing. Here, Local ridge spacing is estimated using the projection of the local image along a line segment perpendicular to the orientation vector and passing through the center point of the block. The projection is smoothed and the distances between consecutive peaks are calculated, then the maximum distance gives the ridge spacing. We assume the ridge spacing is assumed to be constant inside the block. We choose all 1s structure template for mathematical morphology to filter the binary fingerprint image. The templates are created based on the width of ridges and the local direction. For avoiding the distortion of the original binary image after the mathematical morphology, in the process of moving the structure template, it is necessary to rotate the template based on the local fingerprint direction and to modify the size of the template based on the local ridge spacing.

Here we only list two basic groups of the templates for the demonstration in Fig.4. As for group a, it is used in the narrow ridge areas for avoiding the breakage of the ridges in the process of using mathematical morphology, whereas the group b is used in the wide ridge areas for avoiding the conglutination of the ridges.

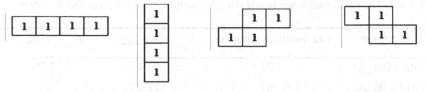

(a) Structure templates used in narrow ridge areas

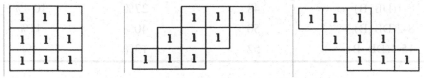

(b) Structure templates used in wide ridge areas

Fig. 4. Examples of structure templates

In some cases, such as the loop, it is difficult to decide the minutia is true or false in the binary or thinning image. It is better to trace those kinds of minutiae by using not only the thinning and binary images, but also the surrounded gray-level images. In these cases, some distinctive features (such as the mean and variance in the hole areas, etc.) of the surrounded gray-level image are computed firstly, and then using the above adaptive post-processing method to smooth the binary image and thinning image.

4 Experimental Results

A statistical analysis of the performance achieved by this proposed method has been carried out using two kinds of data collections, labeled DB_A and DB_B. DB_A includes 800 fingerprints taken by inked paper with scanner, and the image size is 512*512 pixels. DB_B is from fvc2002 fingerprint database, includes 800 fingerprints taken by live scanner, and the image size is 296*560. Some examples are shown in Fig.5 and Fig.6.

In order to study the effect of the proposed algorithm, one hundred processed images with different quality have been selected individually from those two databases.

The main performance criterion is given by how many false minutiae are cancelled. That is equal to the percent of the false minutiae included in the whole minutiae set. Here, a parameter F_{error} is defined as follows to measure the error rate of the extracted minutiae.

$$F_{error} = \frac{\text{the total number of false minutiae}}{\text{the total number of true minutiae}} \times 100\% \ . \tag{5}$$

Some experimental results before and after the post-processing for some images are listed in Table 1.

Table 1. The performance before and after the application of the proposed algorithm

fingerprint	true minutiae numbers	F_{error} (before)	F_{error} (after)
306-0(DB_A)	91	23%	7.7%
110-8(DB_A)	87	21%	9%
190-1(DB_A)	95	19%	10%
8-1(DB_B)	48	27%	10.4%
8-2(DB_B)	50	40%	11%
15-1(DB_B)	52	13%	4%

The statistical results show that the false minutiae made up 23% of the total minutiae before processing and only about 14% after processing in DB_A. As for DB_B, it was 15% before and 9% after using the application of the proposed method. The results reveal that the proposed algorithm is able to eliminate some false minutiae in the fingerprint images. For clearly showing the results, we zoom some typical areas before and after the post-processing in Fig. 5 (f) and (g), and the same in Fig. 6 (f) and (g).

In Fig. 6 (f), it would generate more than 20 false bifurcations, and in Fig. 6 (g), it is clear to see that the proposed algorithm can validate all these false minutiae, and the breaks and discontinuities of the ridges are improved throughout the fingerprint images at the same time.

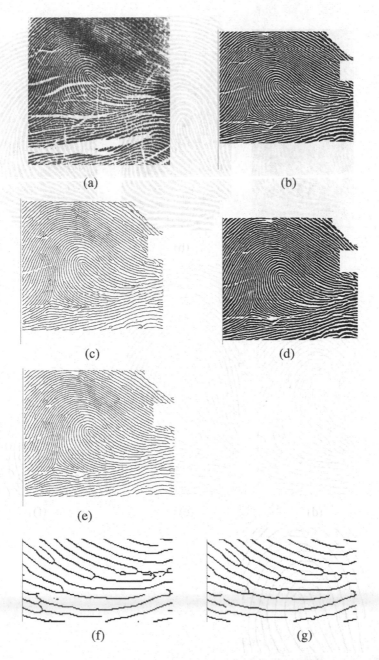

Fig. 5. Experimental results for the rolled fingerprints (a) the original image (b) the original binary image after segmentation (c) the original thinning image after segmentation (d) the binary image after post-processing (e) the thinning image after post-processing (f) zoom in the typical area in the original thinning image (g) the area in (f) after post-processing

Fig. 6. Experimental results for the fingerprints taken by optical scanner (a) the original image (b) the original binary image (c) the original thinning image (d) the binary image after post-processing (e) the thinning image after post-processing (f) zoom in the typical area in the original thinning image (g) the area in (f) after post-processing

5 Conclusion

Combined with the consideration of gray-level properties, ridge spacing and local orientations of the fingerprint images, a new adaptive fingerprint post-processing algorithm based on mathematic morphology has been proposed in this paper. The experimental results show that the proposed algorithm succeeds to eliminate some false minutiae associated with holes, spikes, bridges, breaks, and spurs in better performance, and to improve the thinning and binary images at the same time.

References

1. A. K.Jain and et al., "On-Line Fingerprint Verification," IEEE Trans. On Pattern Analysis and Machine Intelligence, Vol. 19,No. 4 (1997)
2. A.Ross and et al, "Fingerprint Matching Using Feature Space Correlation," Proc. of Post-ECCV Workshop on Biometric Authentication, LNCS 2359, Denmark, June 1, (2002) 48-57
3. A. K. Jain and et al, "Fingerprint Matching Using Minutiae and Texture Features," in Proc. International Conference on Image Processing (ICIP), (2001) 282-285
4. N.K.Ratha and et al, "Adaptive Flow Orientation-based Feature Extraction in Fingerprint Images," Pattern Recognition, Vol.28, NO.11, (1995) 1657-1672
5. ZhaoQi Bian and et al, "Knowledge-based Fingerprint Post-processing," Pattern Recognition and Artificial Intelligence, Vol.16, NO.1, (2002) 53-67
6. Q.Xiao and H.Raafat, "Fingerprint Image Postprocessing: A combined Statistical and Structure Approach," Pattern Recognition, Vol.24, NO.10, (1991) 985-992
7. SERRA J. Image Analysis and Mathematical Morphology: Theoretical Advances. Academic Press, London (1989)
8. Milan Sonka and et al., Image Processing, Analysis, and Machine Vision, Thomson (2001)

Fingerprint Image Segmentation by Energy of Gaussian-Hermite Moments

Lin Wang[1], Mo Dai[1], and Guohua Geng[2]

[1] Institute EGID-Bordeaux 3, University of Michel de Montaigne - Bordeaux 3,
1 Allée Daguin 33607 Pessac cedex, France
{wang, dai}@egid.u-bordeaux.fr
[2] Visualization Technology Institute, Northwest University,
229 North Taibai Street, Xi'an 710069, China
mqzhou@nwu.edu.cn

Abstract. An important step in automatic fingerprint recognition systems is the segmentation of fingerprint images. In this paper, we present an adaptive algorithm based on Gaussian-Hermite moments for non-uniform background removing in fingerprint image segmentation. Gaussian-Hermite moments can better separate image features based on different modes. We use Gaussian-Hermite moments of different orders to separate background and foreground of fingerprint image. In order to further improve the segmentation result, morphology is applied as postprocessing to removing small areas and filling small interior holes. Experimental results show that the use of Gaussian-Hermite moments makes a significant improvement in fingerprint image segmentation performance.

1 Introduction

An important step in automatic fingerprint recognition systems is the segmentation of fingerprint image. A fingerprint image usually consists of a region of interest (ridges and valleys of fingerprint impression) in the printed rectangular bounding box, smudgy patches, blurred areas of the pattern and the background. We need to segment the fingerprint area (foreground) to avoid false feature extraction due to the background areas. Accurate segmentation is especially important for the reliable extraction of features like minutiae and singular points.

Several approaches to fingerprint image segmentation are known in the literatures. In [1], the fingerprint image is partitioned in blocks of 16×16 pixels. Then each block is classified according to the distribution of the gray value gradients in the block. In [2], this method is extended by excluding blocks with a gray-scale variance lower than a threshold. In [3], the gray-scale variance in the direction orthogonal to the orientation of the ridges is used to classify each 16×16 block. In [4], the output of a set of Gabor filters is used as input to a clustering algorithm that constructs spatially compact clusters. In [5], fingerprint images are segmented based on the coherence, while morphology is used to obtain smooth regions. In [6], this method is extended by use of the coherence, the mean and the variance, and an optimal linear classifier is trained for the classification of each pixel.

S.Z. Li et al. (Eds.): Sinobiometrics 2004, LNCS 3338, pp. 414–423, 2004.

In many segmentation algorithms, features extracted cannot completely represent the characteristics of pixels, so they are not adaptive. Threshold for segmentation is difficult to determine in these algorithms. In this paper, we present an adaptive algorithm based on Gaussian-Hermite moments for non-uniform background removing in fingerprint image segmentation.

Our paper is organized as follows. First, Section II introduces the Gaussian-Hermite moments and analyzes their behavior. Then, Section III presents the algorithm based on Gaussian-Hermite moments for fingerprint image segmentation, Section IV presents the postprocessing based on morphology. And Section V presents some experimental results. Finally, Section VI concludes this paper.

2   Gaussian-Hermite Moments (GHM)

2.1   Gaussian-Hermite Moments

Moments, such as geometric moments and orthogonal moments, are widely used in pattern recognition, image processing, computer vision and multiresolution analysis. In order to better represent local characteristics in noisy images smoothed orthogonal GHM were proposed [7][8]. Unlike commonly used geometric moments, orthogonal moments use orthogonal polynomes or more complicated orthogonal functions as transform kernels, which produces minimal information redundancy. A detailed study on the different moments and their behavior evaluation can be found in [7][8].

Given a Gaussian smoothing function $g(x,\sigma)$ with

$$g(x,\sigma) = (2\pi\sigma^2)^{-1/2} \exp(-x^2 / 2\sigma^2) \tag{1}$$

the nth order smoothed GHM $M_n(x, S(x))$ of the signal $S(x)$ is defined as

$$M_n(x, S(x)) = \int_{-\infty}^{\infty} B_n(t)S(x+t)dt \qquad n = 0,1,... \tag{2}$$

with

$$B_n(t) = g(t,\sigma)P_n(t/\sigma) \tag{3}$$

where $P_n(t/\sigma)$ is a scaled Hermite polynomial function of order n, defined by

$$P_n(t) = (-1)^n \exp(t^2)(d^n / dt^n)\exp(-t^2) \tag{4}$$

Fast recursive algorithms have been developed for the calculation of GHM [8].

2D orthogonal GHM of order (p, q) of an input image $I(x, y)$ can be defined similarly

$$M_{p,q}(x, y, I(x, y)) = \int\int_{-\infty}^{\infty} G(t,v,\sigma)H_{p,q}(t/\sigma,v/\sigma)S(x+t, y+v)dtdv \tag{5}$$

where $G(t,v,\sigma)$ is the 2D Gaussian function, and $H_{p,q}(t/\sigma,v/\sigma)$, the scaled 2D Hermite polynomial of order (p, q), with

$$H_{p,q}(t/\sigma, v/\sigma) = H_p(t/\sigma)H_q(v/\sigma) \tag{6}$$

Obviously, 2D orthogonal GHM are separable, so the recursive algorithm in 1D cases can be applied for their calculation.

2.2 Behavior of GHM

In [8], J. Shen et al. analyzed carefully the behavior of GHM. Because the nth order Hermite polynomial $H_n(x)$ has n different real roots, the Gaussian-Hermite base function $g(x,\sigma)H_n(x/\sigma)$ will also have n different real roots. Therefore the Gaussian-Hermite base function of order n will consist of n oscillations. The use of GHM of different orders can thus decompose image features based on different modes more efficiently. Fig.1 shows the spatial behavior of 1D Gaussian-Hermite base functions of different orders. Fig. 2 shows the spatial responses of the bidimensional GHM kernels of different orders.

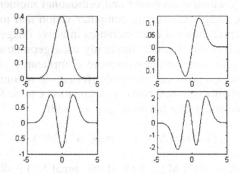

Fig. 1. Spatial behavior of 1D Gaussian-Hermite base functions (order 0 to 3)

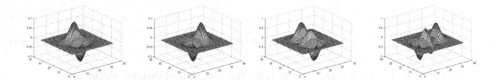

Fig. 2. 2D Gaussian-Hermite base functions (orders: (0,1), (1, 0), (0, 3) and (3, 0))

From Fig. 1, we can see that with the increase of the order of the moment base functions, oscillations of the moment base function also increase. This implies that the GHM kernels of different orders characterize different spatial modes.

It has been shown that GHM are, in fact, linear combinations of different order derivatives of the signal filtered by a Gaussian filter. Moreover, GHM provide an approach to construct orthogonal features from different Gaussian-filtered derivatives. The Gaussian-Hermite base functions are much more smoothed than other moment base functions and do not exhibit a discontinuity even at the window boundary. So

GHM are much less sensitive to noise and avoid the artifacts introduced by window function discontinuity.

As is well known, the derivatives have been extensively used for image representation in pattern recognition. Fingerprint images can be considered as oriented texture patterns. The segmentation algorithm aims at separating the foreground and the background in a fingerprint image. The foreground is the region of interest containing the fingerprint pattern, and the background, the area where no significant fingerprint pattern is presented. The foreground and the background can thus be regarded as different modes. That is why we use GHM to better separate the foreground and the background of fingerprint images.

3 Segmentation Based on GHM

3.1 Energy of Gaussian-Hermite Moments (GHM Energy) of a Fingerprint Image

The local intensity surface in fingerprint images is comprised of ridges and valleys whose directions vary smoothly, which constitutes an oriented texture. The gray level in the fingerprint foreground region alternates between black and white. So the GHM in the foreground would vary much more than in the background (see Fig. 3).

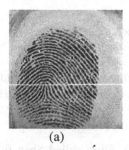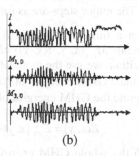

(a)   (b)

Fig. 3. Gaussian-Hermite moments of fingerprint image: (a) fingerprint image, (b) Gray level I and GHM $M_{1,0}, M_{3,0}$ of fingerprint of the white line in (a)

In order to characterize the image by the GHM, the GHM energies of fingerprint image are defined as

$$E_{p,q}(x, y) = (M_{p,q}(x, y, I(x, y)))^2 \tag{7}$$

where $I(x, y)$ is input fingerprint image and $M_{p,q}$, GHM of order (p, q) of $I(x, y)$. When p or q is odd, the foreground (fingerprint area) exhibits a very high GHM energy and the background, a very low one. In Fig. 3, we show the GHM energies of a fingerprint image, where $E_{p,q}=0$ is visualized as black, while the maximum GHM Energy, as white.

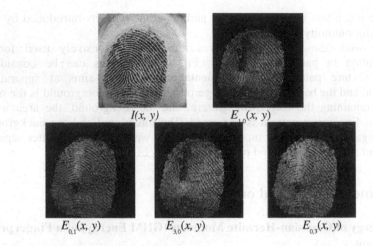

$I(x, y)$ $E_{1,0}(x, y)$

$E_{0,1}(x, y)$ $E_{3,0}(x, y)$ $E_{0,3}(x, y)$

Fig. 4. GHM energy images $E_{p,q}(x, y)$ for the fingerprint image $I(x,y)$

3.2   Segmentation by GHM Energy

Using the orthogonality of the Gaussian-Hermite moments, we take the GHM energy of the Gaussian-Hermite moments $M_{0,1}$, $M_{1,0}$, $M_{0,3}$ and $M_{3,0}$ to represent the fingerprint image. The major steps are as follows:

- Given a fingerprint image $I(x, y)$ of size $M \times N$, calculate the Gaussian-Hermite moments $M_{p,q}(x, y, I(x, y))$ of order (p, q) of the fingerprint image by (5). In our algorithm, we use the moments $M_{0,1}$, $M_{1,0}$, $M_{0,3}$ and $M_{3,0}$.
- Calculate GHM energies of $I(x, y)$ by (7), which gives $E_{0,1}$, $E_{1,0}$, $E_{0,3}$ and $E_{3,0}$.
- Integrate the GHM energies of different orders to obtain the whole GHM energy:

$$E(x, y) = E_{0,1}(x, y) + E_{1,0}(x, y) + E_{0,3}(x, y) + E_{3,0}(x, y) \qquad (8)$$

- With the whole GHM energy, a fast low-pass filter, called Shen filtering [9], is applied as follows:

$\mathbf{F_{R1}}$:

$$E_R^1(0,0) = E(0,0);$$
$$E_R^1(i, j) = a \times E(i, j) + (1-a) \times E_R^1(i-1, j) \qquad (i = 1, 2, ..., M-1; \ 0 \le j < N)$$

$\mathbf{F_{R2}}$:

$$E_R^2(M-1, 0) = E_R^1(M-1, 0);$$
$$E_R^2(i, j) = a \times E_R^1(i, j) + (1-a) \times E_R^2(i+1, j) \qquad (i = M-2, \ M-3, ..., 0; \ 0 \le j < N)$$

$\mathbf{F_{C1}}$:

$$E_C^1(0,0) = E_R^2(0,0);$$
$$E_C^1(i, j) = a \times E_R^2(i, j) + (1-a) \times E_C^1(i, j-1) \qquad (j = 1, 2, ..., N-1; \ 0 \le i < M)$$

$\mathbf{F_{C2}}$:

$$E_C^2(0, N-1) = E_C^1(0, N-1);$$
$$E_C^2(i, j) = a \times E_R^2(i, j) + (1-a) \times E_C^2(i, j+1) \qquad (j = N-2, \ N-3, ..., 0; \ 0 \le i < M)$$

where $0<a<1$, and M, N are the width and height of the fingerprint image respectively. The diagram of the filtering is shown in Fig.5.

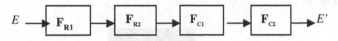

Fig. 5. Low-pass filtering of the GHM energy image

In Fig. 6(a), we show some results of the GHM energy, where black represents $E=0$, while white, the maximum of E'. We see that in general, E' is very high in the foreground. The histogram of E' is bimodal (Fig. 4(b)), so the foreground and the background can be easily segmented.

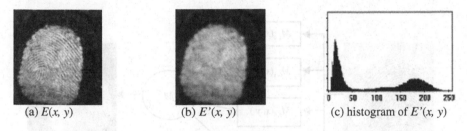

(a) $E(x, y)$ (b) $E'(x, y)$ (c) histogram of $E'(x, y)$

Fig. 6. $E'(x, y)$ and its histogram for the fingerprint image in Fig. 3 (shown as grayscale image)

Calculate the threshold from the histogram of $E(x,y)$ for segmentation. In Fig. 6(c), the two peaks correspond to the relatively the foreground and the background. The dip between the peaks corresponds to the relatively few points around the edge of the foreground. In cases like this, the valley point between the peaks is commonly used to establish the threshold gray level. This threshold is adaptive. Fig. 5 shows thresholding of E'.

Fig. 7. Thresholding of E'

4 Postprocessing

In Fig. 7, in blank area corresponding to the background, there still exist some patches and small interior holes due to the noise. Obviously, this segmentation result is not satisfactory. In order to further improve the segmentation result, and get a smooth closed fingerprint area, morphological operations are applied to the segmentation by

GHM energy. As illustrated in Fig. 7, first the mask is *opened* [10]. This operation has the effect that small foreground areas are removed. Then, the mask is *closed*, which causes holes in the foreground to be filled. The final result of the segmentation is shown in Fig. 8.

Fig. 8. Morphology applied to GHM energy estimate of Fig. 5

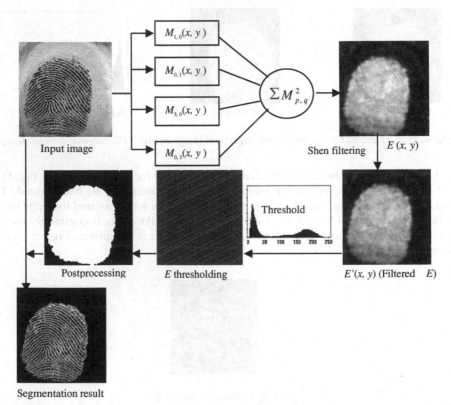

Fig. 9. Segmentation result by GHM energy

In Fig. 9 we show the overall flow diagram of our segmentation algorithm. This result show that the use of GHM energy can effectively distinguish fingerprint signal area from background.

5   Experimental Results

In this section, we present some experimental results of our fingerprint image segmentation algorithm and a comparison with other fingerprint image segmentation algorithms. First, in order to validate the performance of our algorithm, it is tested with Database 3 of the Fingerprint Verification Competition (FVC2000) [11], FVC2002 database 3 and NIST 4 database. In Fig. 10 are shown the segmentation results for two fingerprint images from these Databases. Human inspection can confirm that our algorithm provides satisfactory results.

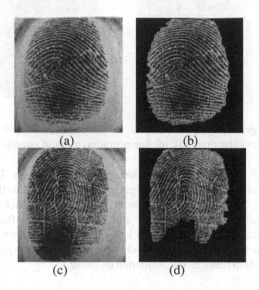

(a)   (b)

(c)   (d)

Fig. 10. Segmentation results of some fingerprint images: (a)(c) is input image and (b)(d) is segmentation results

Now we present the comparison of our algorithm with the segmentation algorithm based on gray-scale variance in the direction orthogonal to the ridge orientation [3] and the segmentation algorithm based on coherence [5]. We randomly selected 500 fingerprint images in the FVC2000 and NIST 4 databases respectively and used the three algorithms to detect the foreground and the background. The experimental results showed that our algorithm is better than the other two algorithms and is robust in fingerprint image segmentation. Fig. 11 shows the resultants for a fingerprint image.

6   Conclusion

In this paper, a new method based on Gaussian-Hermite moments (GHM) is presented for fingerprint image segmentation. First, the GHM energy is used to distinguish fingerprint areas from the background, allowing to well separate the fingerprint regions and the blank background regions. Second, morphological oper-

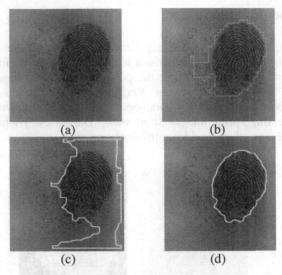

(a)   (b)

(c)   (d)

Fig. 11. (a) Original fingerprint images, (b) Segmentation result of algorithm [3], (c) Segmentation result of algorithm [5], (d) Segmentation result of our algorithm

ations are applied to further improve the segmentation result. Human inspection on experimental results for real fingerprint images shows that the method proposed provides accurate high-resolution segmentation results, which would facilitate the fingerprint image feature extraction and classification afterwards. Comparison between our method and some methods known in the literatures for fingerprint image segmentation shows that our method not only has a good performance of segmentation but also reduces the influence of noise.

References

1. B.M. Mehtre, N.N. Murthy, S. Kapoor, and B. Chatterjee: Segmentation fingerprint images using the directional image. Pattern Recognition, 20 (4) (1987) 429 – 435.
2. B.M. Mehtre and B. Chatterjee: Segmentation of fingerprint images - a composite method, Pattern Recognition. 22 (4) (1989) 381 – 385.
3. N. Ratha, S. Chen, and A. Jain: Adaptive flow orientation based feature extraction in fingerprint images, Pattern Recognition, 28 (11) (1995) 1657 – 1672.
4. A.K. Jain and N.K. Ratha: Object detection using Gabor filters. Pattern Recognition, 30 (2) (1997) 295 – 309.
5. A.M. Bazen and S.H. Gerez: Directional field computation for fingerprints based on the principal component analysis of local gradients. in: Proceedings of ProRISC2000, 11th Annual Workshop on Circuits, Systems and Signal Processing, Veldhoven, Netherlands, 2000.
6. A.M. Bazen and Sabih H. Gerez: Segmentation of Fingerprint Images. in: Proc. RISC 2001 Workshop on Circuits, Systems and Signal Processing, Veldhoven, Netherlands, 2001.

7. J. Shen: Orthogonal Gaussian-Hermite Moments for Image Characterization. in: Proc. SPIE, Intelligent Robots and Computer Vision XVI: Algorithms Techniques, Active Vision, and Materials Handling, Pittsburgh, USA, 1997.
8. J. Shen, W. Shen and D.F. Shen: On geometric and orthogonal moments. International Journal of Pattern Recognition and Artificial Intelligence, 14 (7) (2000) 875-894.
9. J. Shen and Serge Castan: An Optimal linear operator for step edge detection. CVGIP : Graphical Model and Image Processing, 54 (2) (1992) 121-124.
10. F.V.D. Heijden: Image Based Measurement Systems. John Wiley & Sons Ltd., Chichester, 1994.
11. D. Maio, D. Maltoni, R. Cappelli, J.L. Wayman, and A.K. Jain: FVC2000: Fingerprint verification competition. IEEE Trans. Pattern Anal. Mach. Intell. 24 (3) (2002) 402-412.

Robust Ridge Following in Fingerprints

Jianjiang Feng[1], Fei Su[2], and Anni Cai[2]

[1,2] Beijing University of Posts and Telecommunications, 100876 Beijing, P.R. China
fjianjiang@263.net, {sufei, annicai}@bupt.edu.cn

Abstract. In this paper, we presented an improved approach of minutiae detection by following the ridges. Our algorithm is based on the two characteristics of the ridge points on the same ridge: connectivity and randomicity. Because our algorithm takes full advantage of the characteristics of the ridge points, it is robust to noise. Using our algorithm, good quality ridge images can be obtained which can be used to assist minutiae-based fingerprint matching, or directly used for fingerprint matching. Experimental results are included.

1 Introduction

Fingerprints have been used in the identification of individuals because of the famous fact that each person has a unique fingerprint. Most fingerprint verification and identification systems are based on minutiae matching. As the first step of the whole system, minutiae extraction is very important. However, robust extraction of minutiae in low quality fingerprint images is still a challenge, although lots of algorithms have been proposed in the literature [1-4].

The classical approach uses a series of image processing steps to extract the minutiae from a fingerprint image [1]. First, the image is filtered to suppress noise. Then, the ridges are extracted using a locally adaptive thresholding method. Then, a thinning operation is used to obtain a skeleton image. Finally, minutiae are extracted by computing the connection number. However, this method is sensitive to noise and image quality. The image enhancement step is generally time-consuming. The ridge extraction step will lose lots of information.

Maio and Maltoni [3] presented a novel approach to extract minutiae directly from gray-level fingerprint images. Their algorithm extracts ridges by following the ridges until they terminate or intersect other ridges. Meanwhile, minutiae are detected. As fingerprint image need not be filtered at every pixel, the computational complexity of the algorithm is low. However, this method is also sensitive to noise and image quality. Jiang et al. [4] improved Maio's algorithm by using variable step size and directional filtering. Although this improved the robustness of original algorithm more or less, there is still much space for improvement.

In this paper, we improved Maio's method in terms of robustness to noise. Based on analysis of the ridge following procedure and characteristics of ridges, we proposed three improvements:

S.Z. Li et al. (Eds.): Sinobiometrics 2004, LNCS 3338, pp. 424–431, 2004.

1. Stricter stop criterion is used.
2. Multiple paths are explored.
3. A criterion is used to choose the best path among all explored paths.

For low quality fingerprint, our method is robust. And for high quality fingerprint, the computation complexity of our method is comparable with that of Maio's.

The rest of the paper is organized as follows. In section 2, the overview of minutiae detection algorithm by following ridges is presented. In section 3, we describe the basic idea of ridge following algorithm in [3]. The details of our ridge following algorithm are presented in section 4. The result and evaluation is given in section 5. Finally in section 6, our conclusions and plans for future work are presented.

2 Overview

Let I be a gray fingerprint image. A ridge can be seen as a set of local maximums along a local direction. A minutia is the end of a ridge or the intersection of two ridges. Our algorithm extracts all the ridges in fingerprints and the minutiae are found as byproducts of this procedure.

First, the directional field is estimated. We used the gradient-based approach introduced by Jain et al. in [6].

After the directional field has been estimated, there are two problems left. This first problem is, given an initial position, how to extract a ridge. The basic idea is to locate local maximums and to connect them. This step is the most important step of the whole algorithm.

The second problem is how to extract all the ridges in a fingerprint image. This can be done by starting a ridge following procedure on pixels spaced in image. When a new ridge is extracted, a line labeled as the count of current ridges is recorded in the ridge image T.

Finally, spurious minutiae are inevitable, so post-processing will be necessary. Some heuristics can be used to eliminate the spurious minutiae like [5].

Our method differs from the method in [3] mainly on the first problem. As a result, in section 3 and 4, we will describe the ridge following algorithm in [3] and ours respectively.

3 Ridge Following in [3]

The ridge following algorithm works in a predict-correct manner. Given a local maximum of a ridge as start point, the next point is predicted. Then measurement is taken around the predicted point and the predicted point is corrected. This process repeats until the stop criteria are met. The three main steps involved are described briefly in the following. More details can be found in [3].

The first step is to predict the next point P_n. Given the current point P_c, the predicted next point P_t is obtained by moving μ pixels along the local ridge direction from P_c.

The second step is to take measurement and correct. Centered in P_l, the profile which is $2\sigma+1$ pixel long and along the direction normal to the local ridge direction is obtained. The local maximum of the profile is P_n. Regularization process is executed on the profile in order to control noise.

The third step is to check the following stop criteria:

1. Exit from interesting area.
2. Termination. No local maximum can be found in the profile.
3. Intersect with another already extracted ridge.
4. Excessive blending.

If any criterion above is satisfied, the ridge following procedure stops.

4   Robust Ridge Following

When the quality of fingerprint images is high, the ridges are well defined and flow in a locally constant direction. In this case, the ridge following algorithm in [3] works well. However, the quality of fingerprint images is often low, in which ridges include many breaks and parallel ridges are not separated well. In this case, the algorithm in [3] will generate lots of spurious minutiae and bad quality ridge images. Because amount of information is lost, it is hard to distinguish spurious minutiae from genuine minutiae using heuristics. So we use a complex method to extract ridges, rather than use a complex post-processing method.

Our algorithm is based the two characteristics of the ridge points on the same ridge: connectivity and randomicity. Connectivity means that two ridge points on the same ridge are reachable each other. This is an obvious characteristic, but it is only partly used in [3]. Randomicity means that the position of reliable ridge points on the same ridge is random. It's especially correct for poor quality fingerprint images, but this characteristic is neglected in [3]. These two characteristics are illustrated in Fig. 1.

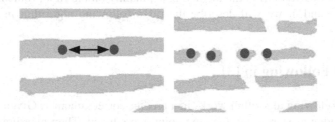

Fig. 1. Two characteristics of ridge points: connectivity and randomicity

Based on these two characteristics, we present three improvements to the algorithm in [3], which increase the robustness to noise greatly. In the following subsections, we will discuss the details of these improvements.

4.1 Stricter Stop Criterion

Errors that can arise during ridge following include false terminations and intersections, in which false intersections are even worse than false terminations, because false intersections can cause more errors later. So we introduce a new stop criterion to avoid it. Our experimental results show the new criterion is very important.

Given A and B are two points in a fingerprint image, connectivity means A can reach B, and B can reach A. But in [3], only the first constraint is considered. In our algorithm, both constraints are considered. The new criterion is: only if the new point B can trace back into the current point A the new point is accepted. The positive and negative examples are illustrated in Fig. 2. In Fig. 2, A and B are reachable each other. A can reach C, but C cannot reach A. So B is the next point of A, but C is not the next point of A.

When such a strict criterion is used, the number of false terminations will increase greatly. In the following two sections, two approaches based on the second feature of ridges are presented, which can be used to avoid this.

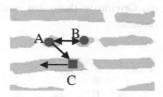

Fig. 2. Positive and negative samples of connectivity. B is the next point of A, and C is not

4.2 Multiple Predictions

In low quality fingerprint images, ridges include many breaks and parallel ridges are not separated well. In this case, reliable ridge points are not always available, as a result, if tracing in fix-length step like [3], many spurious minutiae will be generated.

To solve this problem, there are two ways: enhancing the image around the predicted pixel or making more predictions. Considering fingerprint image enhancement is a time-consuming process, we choose to make more predictions. Like [3], we assume the directional field is accurate. So we make m predictions with different step size along the same direction. For each prediction, we find the local maximum (if have) and check the stop criteria. The possible value of next points can be intersection point, none or intermediate point.

Then we have to select the ridge point from the candidates. We leave this problem to the next section.

4.3 Ridge Point Selection

To decide which one is the next ridge point, we need a criterion that can stably distinguish between genuine and spurious ridge points. Our criterion is to keep on following if possible. According to this criterion, intermediate point is the first choice. In some sense, this criterion can make the current ridge as long as possible and the ridge image as simple as possible. Although not always true, in most case this will also decrease the number of spurious minutiae. It should be mentioned that the directional field, curvature and grayscale are not directly used to make decisions, but used as constraint conditions to decrease the number of candidates.

According to our criterion, the intermediate point is the first choice. However, if there are multiple intermediate points, which one should be selected as the ridge point? In our algorithm, the selection is delayed to the next loop. If one point is selected as current ridge point, there are intermediate points in the next loop, then this point is selected. If multiple points satisfy this condition, the first one is selected.

Two reasons cause us to do so. The first reason is the ridge following algorithm works in a predict-correct manner, so there is a danger of error propagation. This is illustrated in Fig. 3. A is the current point. B and B' are the possible next points of A. If B' is selected as the next point of A, C' will be the next point of B' and that will generate two false minutiae. By delaying the selection to next loop, this type of error can be avoided. The second reason is trying more combinations can decrease the possibility that the following procedure stops. If there are 3 candidates in each loop, there will be 9 combinations. Obviously there are more opportunities to make the ridge following procedure continue.

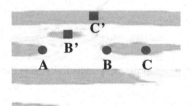

Fig. 3. Error propagation. *ABC* is the correct path, *AB'C'* is the false path caused by error propagation

The pseudo code of our ridge following algorithm is given below:

Note: The following algorithm is just for illustration and it is not very efficient in speed. The more efficient one should not try all possible paths and select the best, but explore possible paths until the first path that satisfies the constraint conditions is found.
P_c is a local maximum of a ridge line of *I*.
theta is the local ridge direction at P_c.
The algorithm uses three lists: *CurrentPointList*, *NextPointList* and *RidgePointList*. The purpose of these lists can be seen from their names.

```
Ridge Following(Pc, theta)
{
    Clear RidgePointList, CurrentPointList;
    Add Pc to CurrentPointList;
    while(continue)
    {
```

```
      continue = false;
      for each current ridge point
      {
        Clear NextPointList;
        Make m predictions;
        for each predicted position
        {
          Measure the actual position;
          if(Do not satisfy stop criteria)
          {
            Add the actual position to NextPointList;
            continue = true;
          }
        }
        if(continue)
        {
          Store current ridge point in RidgePointList;
          Replace CurrentPointList with NextPointList;
          break;
        }
      }
    }
    Select the best path;
    return RidgePointList;
}
```

5 Experimental Results

To evaluate the performance of our algorithm, we have implemented our algorithm
and the algorithm in [3] using Matlab (so the speed of our algorithm is not reported).
Fingerprints are taken from FVC2002's database [7]. One hundred fingerprint images
with different quality have been selected.

The first experiment is to evaluate the quality of minutiae detected using our algorithm. The minutiae of fingerprints have been labeled by a human expert. Table
1 reports the results in terms of dropped minutiae and spurious minutiae. From
table 1, we see the performance of our algorithm is slightly better than that of the
algorithm in [3].

The second experiment is to evaluate the quality of ridges extract by the ridge following algorithm. Except that post-processing is not included, the second experiment
is the same as the first one. Unlike minutiae, a ridge can be broken or connected to
other ridges. So it is hard to compare ridges from two fingerprint images directly.
Here we just compare the number of ridges extracted by our algorithm with algorithm
in [3]. Although it is not always true, in most cases less ridges means better result.
The fingerprint images have been manually classified into three classes according
their quality: good, average and poor. The numbers of ridges of each fingerprint images are counted manually. Table 2 shows the average ratio of the number of ridges
extracted by two algorithms to the actual ridge count. Two samples are given in Fig. 4.

From table 2, we see the algorithm in [3] extracted more ridges than ours. And the difference is especially apparent for poor quality fingerprint images. This shows our algorithm is more robust than [3].

Fig. 4. The first fingerprint is from an optical sensor; the second one is from a capacitive sensor. The left are original images, the middle are the results of Maio's, and the right are that of ours

Table 1. Average result for minutiae detection

	dropped	spurious
Maio's	7.2%	15.2%
ours	6.1%	12.6%

Table 2. Average result for ridge extraction

	good	average	poor
Maio's	1.2	2.8	4.1
ours	1.05	1.7	2.0

6 Conclusions and Future Work

We have proposed a method for feature extraction from fingerprint images based on following ridges. The basic idea is to use stronger constraint conditions, make more attempts, and make decisions that can lead to longer ridges. Since our algorithm has been designed according to the characteristics of fingerprint images (especially low quality fingerprint images), it performs well even on low quality fingerprint images.

As we see, in some sense, our algorithm is like a greedy algorithm that makes the current ridge as long as possible while satisfying the given constraint conditions. In some case, it will fail to extract the correct ridge. But it is comparatively simple and works well in most cases.

Developing more complex algorithm that considers the relation between adjacent ridges is our future work. Though the number of ridges has been used to evaluate the performance of our algorithm, we still need a better evaluation method that will evaluate each curve itself.

References

1. B. M. Mehtre, "Fingerprint Image Analysis For Automatic Identification," Machine Vision and Applications, 6:124- 139, 1993
2. N. Ratha, S. Chen, and A. K. Jain, "Adaptive Flow Orientation Based Feature Extraction In Fingerprint Images," Pattern Recognition, 28(11): 1657-1672, 1995
3. D. Maio and D. Maltoni, "Direct Gray-Scale Minutiae Detection in Fingerprints," IEEE Trans. PAMI 19(1): 27-40, 1997
4. X. Jiang, W. Y. Yau, and W. Ser, "Minutiae Extraction by Adaptively Tracing the Gray Level Ridge of the Fingerprint Image," IEEE Sixth Int. Conf. On Image Processing, pp. 852-856, 1999
5. Q. Xiao and H. Raafat, "Fingerprint image postprocessing: A combined statistical and structural approach," Pattern Recognition 24(10): 985-992, 1991
6. A. K. Jain, L. Hong and R. Bolle, "On-line fingerprint verification," IEEE Trans. PAMI 19(4): 302-314, 1997
7. D. Miao and et al., "FVC2002: Second Fingerprint Verification Competition," 16th Proceedings of Pattern Recognition, Canada, 2003

A New Approach for Fingerprint Minutiae Extraction

Qingshi Tang, Duoqian Miao, and Wenjie Fu

Department of Computer Science and Engineering,
Tongji University, Shanghai 200092,
P.R. China
tangqingshi@yahoo.com.cn

Abstract. Minutiae extraction is a critical step in fingerprint identification, so it is important to find a proper approach to extract minutiae. In this paper, we propose a new method which extracts minutiae via principal curves. At first, we get a group of principal curves which reflect the structural features of the fingerprint; then we extract minutiae of fingerprint from these principal curves. From the result of experiment, we conclude that this new approach is feasible.

1 Introduction

Fingerprint minutiae include ridge bifurcation, ridge ending, short ridge and enclosure etc, these four sorts of fingerprint minutiae are shown in figure 1. Each individual has unique fingerprint, The uniqueness of a fingerprint is exclusive determined by the local ridge characteristics and their relationships [3]. Among various minutiae, ridge bifurcations and ridge endings are commonly used in fingerprint recognition. So far, there is much research for minutiae extractions, and most of algorithms for minutiae extraction are implemented based on thinning fingerprint images which compose of a set of pixels. However, when we look at the image of a fingerprint, we regard it as a collection of curves instead of a set of pixels. So, in this paper, we use principal curves to represent the skeletons of a fingerprint, and propose an approach to extract minutiae of fingerprints based on principal curves.

Principal curves were defined by Hastie and Stuetzle[1,2](thereafter HS) as "self consistent" smooth curves which pass through the "middle" of a d-dimensional probability distribution or data cloud. However, HS principal curves are not fit for represent fingerprint skeletons, so we choose the principal graph algorithm[2] to get skeletons.

Section 2 introduces the definition of principal curves and principal graph algorithm. Section 3 introduces our approach of minutiae extraction in details. Section 4 gives the experimental results. At the end of this paper, we give our conclusion in Section 5.

S.Z. Li et al. (Eds.): Sinobiometrics 2004, LNCS 3338, pp. 432–438, 2004.

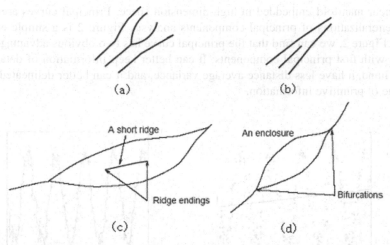

(a)   (b)

A short ridge   An enclosure

Ridge endings   Bifurcations

(c)   (d)

Fig. 1. Examples of minutiae. (a) ridge bifurcation (b) ridge ending (c) short ridge (d) enclosure

2 Definition of Principal Curves and Principal Graph Algorithm

In this section, we introduce the definition of principal curves [1, 2] and principal graph algorithm [2] proposed by Balazs Kegl.

2.1 Definition of Principal

Definition 1. Given a random vector $Y = (Y_1, Y_2, ..., Y_p)$ whose probability density is $g_y(y)$. If a smooth curve $f(s)$ which pass through the "middle" of the Y distribution satisfy:

$$f(s) = E(Y \mid s_f(y) = s) \tag{1}$$

$f(s)$ is a principal curve. $s_f(y)$ is the projection point of Y to $f(s)$, ie.

$$s_f(y) = \sup\{s : \|y - f(s)\| = \inf_{\tau} \|y - f(\tau)\|\} \tag{2}$$

Definition 2. The smooth curve $f(t)$ is a principal curve if the following hold: 1) $f(t)$ does not intersect itself, 2) $f(t)$ has finite length inside any bounded subset of Rd 3) $f(t)$ is self-consistent, i.e.

$$f(t) = E[X \mid t_f(X) = t] \tag{3}$$

By definition of the principal curve, we know that any point of the principal curve is the condition expectation of those points that project to this point, and it satisfies "self-consistent property". Theory foundation of principal curve is low-dimensional nonlinear manifold embedded in high-dimension space. Principal curves are nonlinear generalizations of principal components analysis. Figure 2 is a simple example. From Figure 2, we can find that the principal curve has two obvious advantages compared with first principal components: It can better keep information of data, on the other hand, it have less distance average variance, and it can better delineated out the outline of primitive information.

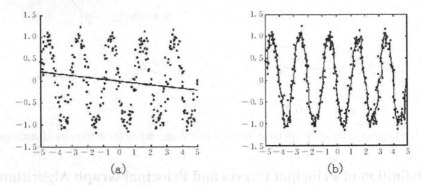

(a)   (b)

Fig. 2. (a) first principal components, (b) principal curve

2.2 Principal Graph Algorithm

In this paper, we adopt generalized principal graph algorithm which is proposed by Balazs Kegl to extract the skeleton of fingerprints. This algorithm is made up of the following several steps mainly:

The Initialization Step: A thinning algorithm is adopted to obtain the approximate skeletons of a graph. The skeleton is denoted by G_{vs}. G_{vs} consist of two sets V and S: $V = \{v_1, v_2,...,v_n\} \subset R^d$ is   a   set   of   vertices,   and $S = \{(v_{i1}, v_{j1}),...,(v_{ik}, v_{jk})\} = \{s_{i1ji},...,s_{ikjk}\}$ is a set of edges.

Fitting-Smoothing Step: The objective of this step is adjusting smoothness of G_{vs} and making G_{vs} better fit for the graph. Given a dataset $X_n = \{x_1, x_2,...,x_n\}$, it minimizes a penalized distance function $E(G) = \Delta(G) + \lambda P(G)$ to optimize G_{vs}. The first component $\Delta(G)$ is the excepted squared distance between points in X_n and G_{vs}. The second component $P(G)$ is a penalty on the average curvature of the graph. The smaller the value of $\Delta(G)$ is, the better the graph fits these data. The smaller the value of $P(G)$ is, the better smoothness of the graph is. In this step, projection step is done firstly. After projection step, the data points are partitioned into "nearest neighbor region" according to which segment or vertex they project. Then the vertex optimization step is performed to adjust the positions of vertexes and segments for finding a local minimum of $E(G)$.

The Restructuring Step: The step complements and perfects the fitting-smoothing step. It uses geometric properties of the skeleton graph to modify the configuration of vertices and edges. Goal of the step is to eliminate or rectify imperfections of the initial skeleton graph. For example removing short branches, removing short loops etc.

3   Approach for Minutiae Extraction Based on Principal Curves

In this section, we propose an approach to extract fingerprint minutiae based on principal curves which are generalized by principal graph algorithm. The steps as follow: At first, given a fingerprint image that has been enhanced by Gabor algorithm [3], all ridges are extracted from it. In this section, we choose two ridges as samples. Figure 3 shows a fingerprint image, and two ridge samples.

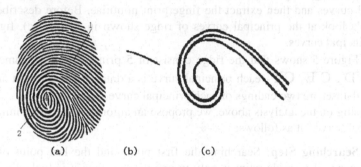

(a)   (b)   (c)

Fig. 3. (a)A enhanced fingerprint image. (b) A simple fingerprint ridge, (c) A complex fingerprint ridge

Then principal graph algorithm described in section 2.2 is used to get principal curves of ridges. We analyze a simple ridge shown in figure 3(b) firstly. Figure 4 is the principal curve of ridge shown in figure 3(b).

A

B

Fig. 4. A principal curved of a simple ridge

From figure 4, we find that the principal curve is fit to fingerprint ridge. The ridge consist of a single principal curve which is named A⌒B (Note: A and B are two endings of this principal curve). The data of the principal curve A⌒B are shown in table 1.

Table 1. The data of principal curve shown in figure 5

	Rectangular coordinate of Data points
A⌒B	51.7608, 76.7328
	54.6401, 76.1603
	59.2785, 75.0582
	......
	79.3904, 65.3305
	82.2814, 63.6042
	84.2326, 62.4981

In fact, the principal curve A⌒B is a data set, and the first point and last point are two endings of principal curve. So our algorithm is just to analyze endings of principal curves and then extract the fingerprint minutiae. Before describe our algorithm, let's look at the principal curves of ridge shown in figure 3(c), figure 5 shows its principal curves.

Figure 5 shows that the ridge consist of 5 principal curves named A⌒B, B⌒C, B⌒D, C⌒E, C⌒F, each principal curve is a dataset, and the first and the last point of dataset are two endings of each principal curve.

Basing on the analysis above, we propose an algorithm to extract minutiae from principal curves, it as follows:

1. **Searching Step:** Searching the first point and the last point of each principal curve: if a single point is only in one dataset, then it is looked as a ridge ending; else if a point is found in 3 dataset, then it is looked as a ridge bifurcation.
2. **Filtering Step:** Filtering the ridge endings and ridge bifurcation obtained in Searching Step, deleting the border points and pseudo minutiae.

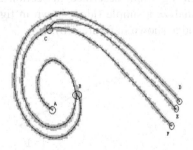

Fig. 5. Principal curved of a complex ridge

So we will obtain results via our algorithm that the point A and point B in figure 4 and point A in figure 5 is ridge endings, and that point B and point C in figure 5 is ridge bifurcation.

4 Experimental Results

In our experiment, we chose 320 pieces of fingerprint images with various qualities from FVC2002 fingerprint database (note: we use Gabor Filter to enhance the fingerprint image [3].). One result of our experiments is shown in figure 6. In this section, we define an accuracy rate as follows:

$$A = 1 - \frac{p+l}{m-p+l} \tag{4}$$

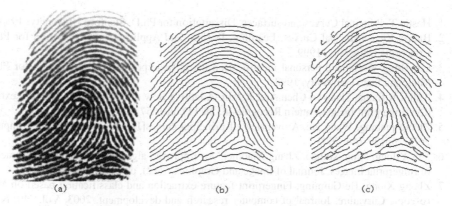

(a)   (b)   (c)

Fig. 6. (a) Original fingerprint; (b) Skeleton obtained by principal graph algorithm; (c) Minutiae obtained by algorithm described in section 3

In formula 4, p is the number of pseudo minutiae, l is the number of lost minutiae, and m is the number of minutiae obtained by our algorithm.

In our experiments, the average number of pseudo minutiae is 2.3, that of lost minutiae is 2.7, and that of obtained minutiae is 42.7. So the average accuracy rate is

$A = 1 - \dfrac{p+l}{m-p+l} = 88.4\%$, which is similar to the rate described in reference [6].

So we conclude that this algorithm is compatible with the requirement of fingerprint matching.

5 Conclusion

In this paper, principal curves are used to extract fingerprint minutiae. It is a new approach to minutiae extraction. From the results of the experiment, the accuracy of the approach suffices the requirement of fingerprint matching. For that using a collection of principal curves represent fingerprint skeletons, so we can get other information of minutiae more easily, such as minutiae's orientation and relationship which are used in fingerprint matching. From the result of experiments, we can conclude that minutiae extraction based on principal curves is feasible. Our future investigation is whether using minutiae which are extracted based on principal to fingerprint matching has more efficiency.

Acknowledgement

This work is supported by National Natural Science Foundation (No.60175016).

References

1. Hastie T. Principal Curves and surfaces. Dissertation for Ph.D. Stanford University, 1984.
2. Balazs Kegl. Principal Curves: Learning, Design, and Applications. Dissertation for Ph.D. Concordia University, 1999.
3. Lin Hong. Automatic personal identification using fingerprints [D]. Dissertation for Ph.D. Michigan State University. 1998.
4. Nalini K.Ratha, Shaoyun Chen,Anil K.Jain. Adaptive flow orientation based feature extraction fingerprint images.Pattern Recognition, 28(11), pp1657 – 1672, 1995.
5. Zhang junping, Wang jue. A overview of principal curves[J]. Chinese journal of computer, 26(2), pp129-146, 2003.
6. Yin Yilong, Ning Xinbao, Zhang Xiaomei. An improved algorithm for minutiae extraction in fingerprint images. Journal of Image and Graphics, 7(12), pp1302-1306, 2002.
7. Zhang Xiong, He Guiming. Fingerprint feature extraction and classification based on Macroscopic Curvature. Journal of computer research and development, 2003, Vol. 40, No 3, pp453-458.
8. Xiping Luo, Jie Tian and Yan Wu. A Minutia Matching algorithm in Fingerprint Verification, 15th ICPR, Vol.4, pp833-836, Barcelona, 2000.

A Top-Down Fingerprint Image Enhancement Method Based on Fourier Analysis

Guocai Zhu and Chao Zhang

National Laboratory on Machine Perception, Peking University,
Beijing, 100871, China
chzhang@cis.pku.edu.cn

Abstract. We present a top-down fingerprint image enhancement method which is based on Fourier analysis. Our method takes advantage of two filtering methods in Fourier domain proposed previously and employs a top-down iteration filtering technique, which enables the enhancement procedure not to rely severely on an accurate estimation of ridge frequency and orientation and also enables us to make use of more than the local information in local fingerprint filtering. Consequently, our method is robust to handle low quality fingerprint images. Results of enhancement are presented for some representative fingerprint images.

1   Introduction

Fingerprint matching has long been used in criminal applications and recently also used in some social security applications for verifying a person's identity [7], for the reason that its ridge-valley structures and the presence of certain ridge anomalies termed as minutiae points make every fingerprint unique, and ultimately make every person unique. Thus the ridge-valley structures and minutiae points of a fingerprint are the main source for the information to be extracted from the fingerprint when we use fingerprints for personal authentication. So the performance of a fingerprint recognition algorithm inevitably relies heavily on the quality of an input fingerprint image from which the fingerprint features – distinguishing information of fingerprint ridge-valley structures and minutiae – are extracted. In an ideal fingerprint image where ridges and valleys alternate and flow clearly in a locally constant direction and minutiae are anomalies of ridges, the fingerprint ridges and minutiae can be easily and accurately detected, located and analyzed. While in a low quality fingerprint image where those distinguishing fingerprint patterns are unclear, some real fingerprint features may be mistakenly extracted or even be ignored and furthermore some spurious features may be created. This will lead to form incorrect or false fingerprint features, consequently reduce the performance of a fingerprint recognition system. Unfortunately, there are a lot of low quality fingerprint images in practice as a result of various reasons, such as fingerprint definition diminishing along with aging, calluses on the fingertip due to manual working, limitations of image acquisition methods and so on. In order to ensure the performance of

S.Z. Li et al. (Eds.): Sinobiometrics 2004, LNCS 3338, pp. 439–448, 2004.

a fingerprint recognition system dealing with low quality fingerprint images, an enhancement algorithm which can improve the quality of a fingerprint image becomes necessary for a recognition system.

Actually many sophisticated enhancement algorithms have been proposed since the enhancement algorithm plays an important role in a fingerprint recognition system after which drew a substantial amount of attention. Those enhancement algorithms usually make use of fingerprint ridge properties which consist of ridge frequencies and ridge directions. They can be broadly classified as being spatial domain based [2, 3, 5] and Fourier domain based [1, 4, 6, 8, 9] according to their concrete implementation methods. [2] introduced a representative spatial domain based method that employs a Gabor filter, which has frequency-selective and orientation-selective properties. Fourier domain based methods mean those methods that handle the filtering procedure by directly modifying the frequency spectrum of the original image. The directional filtering method proposed by [8] is a sort of Fourier domain based methods that at first filter a raw image by a few directional filters, which can transmit the spectrum of a certain direction and attenuate the spectra of other directions, then, form the enhanced image by appropriately combining these filtered images. [9] proposed a Fourier domain based method different to [8] that boosts up a low quality fingerprint image by multiplying its frequency spectrum by the magnitude of it.

This paper proposes a Fourier domain based method too which is based on but different from the methods in [8, 9]. We explore the enhancement procedure not in spatial domain but in Fourier domain because spatial domain based methods such as the Gabor filtering are considered to be complicated and computation consuming as compared to Fourier enhancement. Our method combines the two types of Fourier domain based methods mentioned above by multiplying their each filter vectors with well designed weights, which are relevant to local image qualities everywhere, to form a new filter vector that is ultimately used to filter the raw image. Especially, our method employs a top-down iteration technique in addition which can make our method robust enough to handle very low quality fingerprint images.

We describe our fingerprint enhancement method in detail in the following sections. At first the Fourier analysis for fingerprint images is addressed in Sect. 2. Section 3 describes the implementation steps of our method particularly. Some representative samples of low quality fingerprint images and their enhanced versions done by our method are shown in Sect. 4. In Sect. 5, we give the conclusion and the ways of our future work.

2   Fourier Analysis for Fingerprint Images

We can consider a gray level fingerprint image as an oriented texture pattern that consists of narrow ridges separated by narrow valleys. So the local ridge orientation and ridge frequency are two intrinsic features of a fingerprint image. They can be revealed clearly by the frequency domain representative of a fingerprint image derived from the Fourier transformation, which converts an image from its spatial-domain form of bright intensities into a frequency-domain form of frequency components. Figure 1(a) shows an example fingerprint and its corresponding Fourier spectrum. We can see an annular region with higher values in the spectrum image. In fact, the location of the annular region characterizes the two ridge features: the radius of the annulus indicates the main frequency of ridges and the angles of those dots inside the annulus indicate the directions of the component ridges. This can be apprehended better by Fig. 1(b).

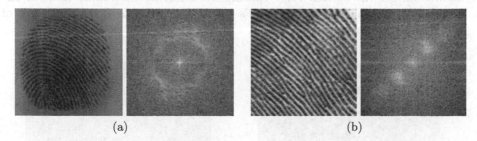

(a)   (b)

Fig. 1. Fingerprint images with their respective Fourier spectra

By representing the Fourier spectrum of a fingerprint image in polar form as $F(r, \theta)$, we can define the probability density function, the angular marginal density function and the radial marginal density function of the spectrum as following:

$$f(r, \theta) = \frac{|F(r, \theta)|^2}{\iint_{r, \theta} |F(r, \theta)|^2 \, dr d\theta} \tag{1}$$

$$f(\theta) = \int_r f(r, \theta) \, dr \tag{2}$$

$$f(r) = \int_\theta f(r, \theta) \, d\theta \tag{3}$$

2.1   Ridge Frequency Normalization

Although the local ridge frequency varies everywhere in a fingerprint image due to various causes, we can consider the whole fingerprint has a central frequency and other frequencies do exist but are minority and constrained within a small range of values just as a Gaussian distribution depicted by following:

$$G_{radial}(r|r_o, \sigma_r) = e^{-(r-r_o)^2/2\sigma_r} \tag{4}$$

The r_o indicates the central frequency and the σ_r indicates the width of the annulus in the spectrum of a fingerprint image. The central frequency of a fingerprint image is mainly decided by the resolution of the image acquisition device though its own central ridge frequency varies from an individual to another individual. In order to eliminate the potential scaling variance of fingerprint images caused by different image acquisition device resolutions, we can normalize the central ridge frequency of a fingerprint image to a fixed and appropriate value, which is the half of Nyquist frequency in this paper.

Since the Nyquist frequency is the minimum theoretical sampling rate that fully describes a given signal, the normalization proceeding is generally to scale down the original fingerprint image with a scale factor derived from the current ridge spacing. As discussed above, the central frequency of a fingerprint image is indicated by the radius of the annulus in the corresponding spectrum image. So we can get the current ridge spacing by detecting the radius value of the annulus in original fingerprint image's spectrum. Figure 2 shows the result of ridge frequency normalization.

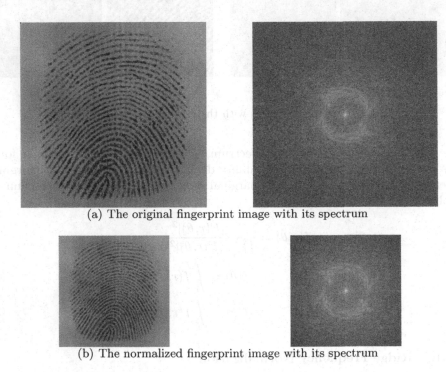

(a) The original fingerprint image with its spectrum

(b) The normalized fingerprint image with its spectrum

Fig. 2. The ridge frequency normalization of a fingerprint image

The resolution of a fingerprint image acquisition device is generally "overqualified" according to Nyquist Theorem for discretizing the fingerprint. So the ridge frequency normalization not only eliminate the images' scaling variance but also greatly reduces the amount of image data to be processed in all later stages of the enhancement procedure. Typically it can scale down the original fingerprint image to a half size.

2.2   Local Image Quality Measurement

A measurement of local image quality is defined by us with respect to the ridge frequency characteristic of a fingerprint. Regarding a fingerprint image as a signal corrupted by noises, we define a signal band and a noise band in frequency domain. After applying the bandpass filtering for signals and noises respectively to the fingerprint image, we can get a signal field image $S(i,j)$ and a noise field image $N(i,j)$ correspondingly. We define the measurement of local image quality as following:

$$Q(i,j) = \frac{|S(i,j)|^2}{|S(i,j)|^2 + |N(i,j)|^2} \tag{5}$$

An example quality image is shown in Fig. 3.

(a) The original   (b) $S(i,j)$ (c) $N(i,j)$ (d) $Q(i,j)$
fingerprint image

Fig. 3. The local image quality measurement

The quality measurement of a fingerprint image also can be used to segment the fingerprint region from the background. In fact, it has been done in our enhancement proceeding and the results can be viewed in Fig. 6.

2.3   Ridge Orientation Determination

The ridge orientation estimation usually has been done in spatial domain, for example the projection method in [8] and the gradient method in [2] both are spatial domain based. Here we present a method that estimates the ridge orientation in Fourier domain.

Based on the angular marginal density function (2), we have a ridge orientation determination procedure described by the following pseudocode:

```
maxValue = 0;
sumWidth = 0;
sumVector(theta) = angularDensity(theta);
while(maxValue < threshold),
```

```
        sumWidth = sumWidth + 1;
        sumVector(theta) = sumVector(theta) +
                          angularDensity(theta - sumWidth) +
                          angularDensity(theta + sumWidth);
        [ maxValue, thetaIndex ] = max(sumVector(theta));
        theTheta(sumWidth)= thetaIndex;
    endWhile
    orientation = mean(theTheta);
    reliability = -std(theTheta);
    sharpness = sumVector(orientation) - mean(sumVector);
    orientation = orientation + 90;
```

The reliability of the orientation estimation measurement and the sharpness of the orientation measurement are also proposed together with detected orientation in the pseudocode above. The ridge orientation determination results are shown in Fig. 4.

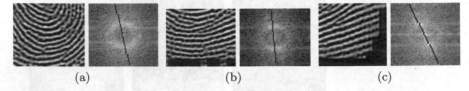

(a)   (b)   (c)

Fig. 4. Results of the ridge orientation determination. The line in the spectrum is normal to the determined orientation

For the orientation filtering in later stages, we present a following Gaussian model for ridges' orientation by assuming fingerprints have the spatial smoothness.

$$G_{direction}(\theta|\theta_o, \sigma_\theta) = e^{-(\theta-\theta_o)^2/2\sigma_\theta} \tag{6}$$

where θ_o is the determined "orientation" and σ_θ is the determined "sumWidth" multiplied by a factor which is relevant to the value of "threshold" and Gaussian distribution.

3   Implementation of Image Enhancement

3.1   Fourier Domain Filter Design

[9] proposed a Fourier domain based method noted "bootstrap" method here that enhances a low quality fingerprint image by multiplying its frequency spectrum by the magnitude of it and gets a well result. This method is simple, fast and adapt to all kinds of ridges regardless of their curvature. But it is not effective to

restore the real ridges from a fingerprint image corrupted heavily by some types of noises such as cuts. Whereas the directional filtering method in [8] can easily recover the ridge flows from a fingerprint image degraded by cuts, calluses or other similar noises. But it is disabled in those fingerprint regions that consist of ridges with high curvature. Figure 5 shows the two methods' enhancement results where the advantages and the disadvantages of each method appear obviously.

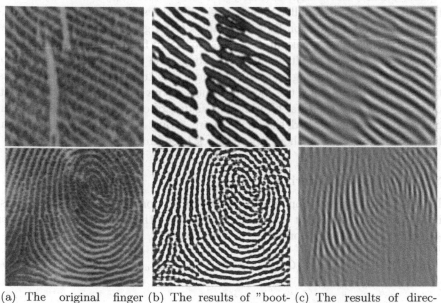

(a) The original finger print image

(b) The results of "bootstrap" filtering

(c) The results of directional filtering

Fig. 5. Results of the "bootstrap" enhancement method and the directional filtering for ridges with low and high curvature

The two methods each have their own virtues and shortcomings simultaneously, but they can be considered to be complementary to some extent. We can employ them together to implement the filtering procedure. For those ridges with low curvature, we can apply the directional filtering. While for those ridges with high curvature, we apply the "bootstrap" method. Developed from the same considering, we can apply the "bootstrap" method for a large fingerprint block but apply the directional filtering to a small fingerprint block. In this paper, the two methods are combined by a weighted multiplication technique which will be detailed in Sect. 3.3.

3.2   Top-Down Iteration

The directional filtering method relies severely on an estimation of the local ridge frequency and orientation. However, for a low quality fingerprint image, it is difficult to reliably estimate the ridge features, especially for a small low quality fingerprint region. We try to address this problem by utilizing a certain iteration technique – the top down iteration.

In our method, we accomplish the whole enhancement procedure by applying a series of top-down iterative filtering operations. First we filter the whole fingerprint image and then divide the filtered image to four sub-images. Then we continue to filter each sub-image and divide the corresponding filtered image to four smaller sub-images similarly. We do so iteratively until the size of the filtered sub-image is smaller than a presetting threshold.

The top-down iteration filtering enables us to get a strongly filtering result but just by applying weak filters in each iterative filtering step. In this way we can still get a good result finally even though the orientation is not estimated exactly in a weak filtering step. Furthermore, the top-down iteration enables us to make use of not only the local information but also the global information of a fingerprint in the local filtering just as described in Sect. 3.3. Consequently our enhancement method should be more robust to handle very low quality fingerprint images than those simply block based methods.

3.3   Weighted Filtering

In the top-down iteration filtering proceeding, for a current fingerprint sub-image, the final filter that is directly used to tune the original image's frequency spectrum has following forms:

$$H(r,\theta) = |F(r,\theta)| * W(G_{direction}(\theta), w_1) * W(G_{radial}(r), w_2) * W(f_T(\theta), w_3) \tag{7}$$

where

$$W(\Lambda(x), w) = \frac{\Lambda(x)}{\max(\Lambda(x))} * w + 1 - w \tag{8}$$

The r_o and σ_r in $G_{radial}(r)$ both can be set to fixed values in our method resulted from our ridge frequency normalization step. The $f_T(\theta)$ is the angular marginal density function of the "father" fingerprint image from which the current fingerprint sub-image is divided. The design of w_1, w_2 and w_3 plays an important role in our enhancement method and now they are influenced by following factors: the relevant image quality, the size of current sub-image, the reliability of determined ridge orientation and the sharpness of the peak of the current sub-image's angular marginal density function.

4   Experiments and Results

Our enhancement method was applied to some fingerprint images that come from the NIST database 4, the FVC2002 database and a database collected by

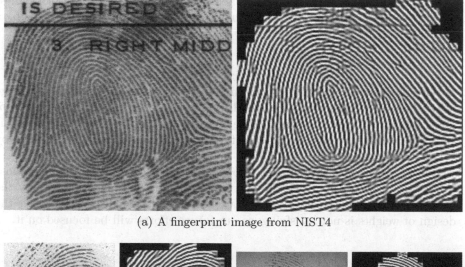

(a) A fingerprint image from NIST4

(b) A fingerprint image from capacitive   (c) A fingerprint image from FVC2002
scanners

Fig. 6. Three fingerprint image samples and the corresponding results enhanced by our method

using a capacitive scanner respectively. Some representative samples of these images and their enhanced versions are shown in Fig. 6.

From those experimental results, we can see our enhancement method does enhance input low quality fingerprint images. It can effectively remove overlapped printed letters and lines from fingerprint images, and it can recover those ridges interrupted by calluses, creases and cuts, also it can reconstruct the fingerprint ridge structure from faint and disconnected fingerprint images. But for those input fingerprint images that have snatchy ridges with high curvature, our current enhancement procedure still can not get smooth enough enhanced results. This is partially caused by our ridge frequency normalization that usually scales down a original fingerprint image. To ensure the accurateness of the Fourier domain filtering, the size of a fingerprint image block to be filtered should be larger than a certain value, e.g. 16x16. As a result of the ridge frequency normalization, a block with the least size will contain more ridges. So in regions with ridges of high curvature, the coherence of ridge directions in a smallest block decreases and it results in the enhanced ridges are not smooth enough.

5 Conclusions and Future Work

A new fingerprint image enhancement method is proposed which takes advantage of two Fourier domain filtering methods proposed previously and employs a top-down iteration filtering technique. The experimental results show our method is effective to enhance those low quality fingerprint images which are degraded by various reasons.

We think our method should be robust enough to effectively enhance those recoverable fingerprint images no matter how low their qualities is if only the weights in the weighted filtering step are perfectly designed. But nowadays the design of weights is not satisfying, so our future efforts will be focused on it.

Acknowledgement

This work was supported by the FANEDD China, under Grant 200038.

References

1. Chen, X.J., Tian, J., He, Y.L.: Low Quality Fingerprint Enhancement Algorithm Based on Filtering in Frequency Domain. The 4th Chinese Conference on Biometric Recognition (2003) 145–150
2. Hong, L., Wan, Y. Jain, A.K.: Fingerprint Image Enhancement: Algorithm and Performance Evaluation. IEEE Trans. PAMI **20(8)** (1998) 777–789
3. Jiang, X.D.: A Study of Fingerprint Image Filtering. Proc. Image Processing **3** (2001) 238–241
4. Kamei, T., Mizoguchi, M.: Image Filter Design for Fingerprint Enhancement. Proc. Computer Vision (1995) 109–114
5. Kim, B.G., Kim, H.J., Park, D.J.: New Enhancement Algorithm for Fingerprint Images. Proc. Pattern Recognition **3** (2002) 879–882
6. Ko, T.: Fingerprint Enhancement by Spectral Analysis Techniques. Proc. Applied Imagery Pattern Recognition (2002) 133–139
7. Maltoni, D., Maio, D., Jain, A.K., Prabhakar, S.: Handbook of Fingerprint Recognition. Springer-Verlag, New York (2003)
8. Sherlock, B., Monro, D., Millard, K.: Fingerprint Enhancement by Directional Fourier filtering. IEE Proc. Vision, Image and Signal Processing **141(2)** (1994) 87–94
9. Willis, A.J., Myers, L.: A Cost-effective Fingerprint Recognition System for Use with Low-quality Prints and Damaged Fingertips. Pattern Recognition **34(2)** (2001) 255–270

Fingerprint Templates Combination

Wei-Yun Yau, Kar-Ann Toh, and Tai-Pang Chen

Institute for Infocomm Research,
21 Heng Mui Keng Terrace,
Singapore 119613
{wyyau, katoh, tpchen}@i2r.a-star.edu.sg

Abstract. The commercially available touch type fingerprint sensor, especially the solid state sensor, usually has a small capture area that is not sufficient to cover the entire finger. This causes the false rejection experienced by the user to be higher if the region of the finger scanned by the sensor is not significantly similar to the region presented when the user is enrolled in the fingerprint recognition system. This paper introduces an approach to reduce the high false rejection rate of the small touch sensor. We propose a fingerprint template combination approach which combines the fingerprint template obtained from multiple independent image capture to form an image that would represent the template obtained using a large fingerprint sensor. The combination process takes into account the deformation of the finger. Main advantages of this approach over existing image mosaicing approach include low memory storage requirement and low computational complexity. Moreover, a new region of the finger can be registered into the template at any time without having to store the entire fingerprint image and the overhead needed to search for the matching fingerprint can be reduced due to the reduction in the data redundancy. Extensive experiments were conducted to determine the best transformation suitable for minutiae alignment. Among the three transformations studied, quasi-affine transformation is found to be most suitable. The proposed combination approach is experimentally shown to improve the false rejection rate due to the user using different fingerprint regions while touching the sensor for recognition.

Keywords: fingerprint template combination, minutiae data transformation, fingerprint recognition.

1 Introduction

Biometrics is recognized as a crucial technology for automatic identity authentication. Among the various biometric technologies available, fingerprint is getting popular in the consumer market [1]. A robust low cost, yet secure automatic fingerprint recognition system is thus an important development for automated identity authentication. There are various types of fingerprint sensors available that capture live fingerprint images. Traditionally law-enforcement type requires a sensor with a sensing area of at least 1" x 1". However, the consumer version

S.Z. Li et al. (Eds.): Sinobiometrics 2004, LNCS 3338, pp. 449–460, 2004.
© Springer-Verlag Berlin Heidelberg 2004

is usually much smaller, such as the newer solid state sensors, including the capacitive and electric field types. Although the imaging area is smaller, the fingerprint recognition system will work fine so long as the sensor is able to acquire a consistent portion of the fingerprint. However, it is not easy to acquire the same area consistently using such sensor with smaller sensing area. This means that if the user does not put the finger such that the contact portion of the skin is mostly similar to the portion used during registration, then the fingerprint will not match. The user will then not be positively recognized, resulting in false rejection that inconveniences the user. This paper attempts to solve such a problem.

There are several possible approaches to solving the problem of higher false rejection. The easiest is to acquire several separate fingerprint images of different portion of the same finger during registration. However, much of the acquired information is redundant (due to common regions) and hence takes up unnecessary storage space. Moreover, the processing time required by the matching process would increase significantly due to the increasing number of records available for matching. In [2], an image mosaicing technique is developed for constructing a rolled fingerprint from an image sequence of partial fingerprints while [3] proposes similar image mosaicking technique for individual images captured at different instances. An alignment approach using the RANSAC method was proposed in [4] for the mosaicking process. Although fingerprint mosaicing technique possesses the capability of acquiring an effectively larger area of the finger, it is at the expense of larger computational cost and larger working memory since the computation is done at the image level. In addition, as the final fingerprint image is not stored, the user is not able to add to the mosaic, new portion of the finger that is not included in the earlier mosaic. To do so will require the user to repeat the whole mosaicing process, which again may not fully cover all the portions of the finger.

Instead of working at the image level, we focus on the fingerprint template derived from the minutia of the fingerprint image. We proposed a fingerprint template combination or template synthesis technique for fingerprint recognition. The proposed methodology is able to combine the various templates derived from different portions of a finger captured at different instances to form a single template. In addition, the proposed technique possesses several desirable features:

1. small storage requirement since the combined data contains only the necessary minutiae information needed for matching. This is especially useful for fingerprint matching within a large database during identification process or in an embedded system with memory constraint;
2. low computational complexity for the combination algorithm;
3. a new portion of the finger can be added to the combined template at any time without having to repeat the entire combination process or to store the resultant fingerprint image.

2   Minutiae Extraction

Feature extraction is crucial for accurate identity authentication. The features selected must be unique enough to uniquely distinguish an individual and remain permanent or vary to only a limited extent throughout the lifespan of the individual. In general, there are two different approaches in fingerprint matching based on the features used, namely the pattern approach and minutia approach [5]. We use the minutia approach as it is accepted legally and used widely in the forensic applications[6, 5].

The fingerprint minutiae are mainly characterized by the ridge ending and ridge bifurcation. To detect these minutiae in the fingerprint image, we employ an adaptive ridge tracing algorithm [7, 8]. It adaptively traces the gray-level ridges of the fingerprint image and applies adaptive oriented filters to enhance only at those regions that require enhancement. Each tracing line represents the skeleton of a ridge. As the tracing line ends or forks out within the region of interest, the minutia is extracted. Minutiae outside the region of interest will not be considered. Post-processing is performed to eliminate false minutiae caused by scar and noise. More details can be found in [7].

Each minutia, F, is represented by a parameter vector

$$F = (x, y, \varphi, t)^T \qquad (1)$$

where (x, y) is the location, φ the local ridge direction and t the type of the minutia. The minutia template, $\mathbf{S}$, of a fingerprint image is then the set of all n valid minutia parameter vectors found in the fingerprint image given by:

$$\mathbf{S} = F_k = (x_k, y_k, \varphi_k, t_k), \ k = 1, 2, \ldots, n \qquad (2)$$

From (1), other than t, the parameters x, y and φ are subjected to geometrical transformation. To overcome this, local structures are formulated [9]. For each minutia F_k, the relative distance d_{ki}, radial angle θ_{ki} and minutia direction φ_{ki} between minutia F_k and its l-nearest neighbor minutia F_i are calculated using:

$$d_{ki} = \sqrt{(x_k - x_i)^2 + (y_k - y_i)^2} \qquad (3)$$

$$\theta_{ki} = d\phi \left(\arctan \left(\frac{y_k - y_i}{x_k - x_i} \right), \varphi_k \right) \qquad (4)$$

$$\varphi_{ki} = d\phi(\varphi_k, \varphi_i) \qquad (5)$$

where

$$d\phi(t_1, t_2) = \begin{cases} t_1 - t_2, & \text{if } -\pi < t_1 - t_2 \leq \pi \\ 2\pi + t_1 - t_2, & \text{if } t_1 - t_2 \leq -\pi \\ 2\pi - t_1 + t_2, & \text{if } t_1 - t_2 > \pi \end{cases} \qquad (6)$$

Fig. 1 shows a minutia local structure consisting of 2 nearest neighbors with the respective relative distance, radial angle and minutia direction definitions.

Therefore, the local structure feature vector, Fl_k of a minutia F_k with its l nearest neighbors is given by:

$$Fl_k = (\{d_{ki} \mid 1 \leq i \leq l\} \{\theta_{ki} \mid 1 \leq i \leq l\} \{\varphi_{ki} \mid 1 \leq i \leq l\} t_k \{t_i \mid 1 \leq i \leq l\})^T \qquad (7)$$

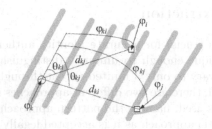

Fig. 1. A minutia local structure with 2 nearest neighbors

Fl_k is then invariance to rigid geometric transformation such as rotation and translation.

3   Template Combination

Assuming now that the minutia template $\mathbf{S}$ is obtained from a fingerprint image acquired using a small touch sensor which is not able to cover the entire finger. In order to reduce the false rejection caused by improper positioning of the finger, a total of m fingerprint images from different portions of the same finger are acquired during the registration process. As the registration is done only once, it will not cause inconvenience to the user. For each image, the corresponding minutia template is derived, giving $\mathbf{S}_m$ templates. Therefore, the task of template combination is to obtain a single template $\mathbf{S}_u$ from $\mathbf{S}_m$.

Each template in $\mathbf{S}_m$ is derived from a different coordinate space. Therefore, to obtain $\mathbf{S}_u$, a common reference coordinate space is required and the various coordinate spaces transformed to the reference coordinate space using the respective transformation function $f_k, k = 1, \ldots, m-1$. This will require computing the correspondences in the minutia for each $\mathbf{S}_k, k = 1, \ldots, m-1$ with respect to $\mathbf{S}_u$.

3.1   Computing Correspondence

Consider two minutia templates $\mathbf{S}_i$ and $\mathbf{S}_j$, $(\mathbf{S}_i, \mathbf{S}_j) \in \mathbf{S}_m$. Assuming that these templates have a common overlap region. Therefore, there exist some minutiae in $\mathbf{S}_i$ similar to those in $\mathbf{S}_j$. Since the two templates have different coordinate spaces related by a geometric transformation, the local structure feature vector, Fl in (7) is used to compute the minutiae correspondence, CS, as:

$$CS(p,q) = \mid Fl_p^i - Fl_q^j \mid, \ p = 1, 2, \ldots, g; q = 1, 2, \ldots, h \qquad (8)$$

where Fl_p^i is the local structure feature vector for minutia p in template i, g the total number of minutia in $\mathbf{S}_i$ and h the total number of minutia in $\mathbf{S}_j$. Exhaustive search is performed for all minutiae and the minutia pair with the lowest $CS(p,q)$ score below a predetermined threshold T_{CS} is taken as the correspondent minutia pair.

Upon completing the whole process, a list of correspondent minutia pairs is obtained. As there could be outlier minutia pairs, a new matching is required to remove them. The correspondent minutia pair with the lowest $(CS(p,q)$ score in the list is taken as the reference minutia pair, F_r^i, F_r^j. Then compute the feature vector, Fcs for each correspondent minutia pair with respect to the reference minutia pair in the respective template using equation (3) - (5) as:

$$Fcs_p^i = (d_{pr}^i, \ \theta_{pr}^i, \ \varphi_{pr}^i) \tag{9}$$

$$Fcs_q^j = (d_{qr}^j, \ \theta_{qr}^j, \ \varphi_{qr}^j) \tag{10}$$

The correspondent minutia pair is considered a valid pair if it satisfies:

$$\mid Fcs_k^i - Fcs_k^j \mid < T_v, \ k = 1, 2, \ldots, \min(g, h) - 1 \tag{11}$$

where T_v is the predetermined minimum similarity threshold. All the valid correspondent minutia pairs are the correspondent minutiae between template $\mathbf{S}_i$ and $\mathbf{S}_j$.

3.2   Computing Transformation Function

The purpose of the transformation function is to transform the various templates $\mathbf{S}_m$ into a reference template $\mathbf{S}_u$ so that all the parameters are aligned in the same coordinate space. Assuming that m fingerprint images are acquired as shown in Fig. 2. Then a reference image, I_0, with minutia template $\mathbf{S}_u$ is selected. Usually it is the image at the center, though not necessarily so. Then for a template $\mathbf{S}_k, k \in \{1, \ldots, m\} \wedge k \neq u$, a transformation function f_k which transforms $\mathbf{S}_k$ to $\mathbf{S}_u$ can be computed using the correspondent minutia pairs found in section(3.1) where:

$$f_k(\mathbf{S}_k) \cup \mathbf{S}_u \Rightarrow \mathbf{S}_u \tag{12}$$

The work in [10] proposed a fingerprint image deformation model which identified three regions in a fingerprint image - region a which is the close contact region, region b which is the transition region and region c, the external region. To incorporate such a deformation model, we assume that the user just

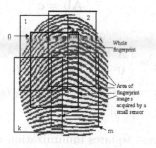

Fig. 2. Fingerprint images covered by a small fingerprint sensor

touches the sensor. Thus the traction and torsion forces are negligible and region c can be omitted. As in [10], region a is elliptical with size prefixed to a factor k ($0 \leq k \leq 1$) of the region bounded by all the minutiae in the template. Since the gradual transition in region b is given by the brake function [10], we linearize this region by taking the inverse of the brake function. This linearization is applied to all templates.

Our earlier work [11] proposed that affine transformation is suitable compared to projective and topological transformation. By incorporating the distortion model, we re-evaluate the possible transformation functions. Here, projective transformation is ruled out since it is unlikely that the transformation is invariant at only a finite point (i.e. the vanishing point) [12]. The respective transformation functions are as below:

Consider two sets of points in different coordinate space, $\mathbf{x} = (x, y)$ and $\mathbf{X} = (X, Y)$, related by a transformation f where $\mathbf{x} = f(\mathbf{X})$. For linear transformations, we have $\mathbf{x} = \mathbf{TX}$ where $\mathbf{T}$ denotes the transformation matrix.

1. Affine transform:
   This is a linear transform represented by a 2x3 matrix $\mathbf{T} = [t_{ij}]$ where $i = 1, 2$ and $j = 1, 2, 3$, $\mathbf{X} = [X, Y, 1]^T$. At least three pairs of non-collinear corresponding points are required to solve for $\mathbf{T}$.
2. Quadratic non-interactive topological transform:
   This is a non-linear transform that has no interaction between the orthogonal coordinates.

$$\hat{x} = t_1 X + t_2 Y + t_3 + t_7 X^2 + t_8 Y^2 \tag{13}$$
$$\hat{y} = t_4 X + t_5 Y + t_6 + t_9 X^2 + t_{10} Y^2 \tag{14}$$

The unknowns $t_i, i = 1, \ldots, 10$ are solved by least square minimization of the objective function f:

$$f = \sum_i \left[(x_i - \hat{x})^2 + (y_i - \hat{y})^2 \right], \tag{15}$$

where x_i and y_i are the measured image point coordinates. Packing (13) and (14) in matrix form gives:

$$\mathbf{Ab} = \mathbf{c} \tag{16}$$

where

$$\mathbf{A} = \begin{bmatrix} X & Y & 1 & 0 & 0 & 0 & X^2 & Y^2 & 0 & 0 \\ 0 & 0 & 0 & X & Y & 1 & 0 & 0 & X^2 & Y^2 \end{bmatrix}$$
$$\mathbf{b} = [t_1 \ t_2 \ t_3 \ t_4 \ t_5 \ t_6 \ t_7 \ t_8 \ t_9 \ t_{10}]^T$$
$$\mathbf{c} = [x \ y]^T \tag{17}$$

The solution to the least squares minimization objective (15) is the parameter vector $\mathbf{b}$ satisfying the normal equation:

$$\mathbf{A}^T \mathbf{Ab} = \mathbf{A}^T \mathbf{c} \tag{18}$$

where $\mathbf{A}$ and $\mathbf{c}$ are stacked according to multiple data points for over-determined systems.

3. Quadratic interactive topological transform:
This is similar to the above but with the orthogonal coordinates interacting:

$$\hat{x} = t_1 X + t_2 Y + t_3 + t_7 X^2 + t_8 Y^2 + t_9 XY \tag{19}$$
$$\hat{y} = t_4 X + t_5 Y + t_6 + t_{10} X^2 + t_{11} Y^2 + t_{12} XY \tag{20}$$

Similar to the pure quadratic topological transformation, the minimization objective (15) can be used to solve for the unknown transformation parameters.

4. Quasi-affine transformation:
This is a linear transform similar to affine but with additional restriction for certain parameters to behave like those in a rotational transformation as follows

$$\begin{bmatrix} x \\ y \end{bmatrix} = \begin{bmatrix} t_{11} & t_{12} & t_{13} \\ -t_{12} & t_{11} & t_{23} \end{bmatrix} \begin{bmatrix} X \\ Y \\ 1 \end{bmatrix}, \tag{21}$$

Here, the two equations can be packed into the following matrix form

$$\begin{bmatrix} X & Y & 1 & 0 \\ Y & -X & 0 & 1 \end{bmatrix} \begin{bmatrix} t_{11} \\ t_{12} \\ t_{13} \\ t_{23} \end{bmatrix} = \begin{bmatrix} x \\ y \end{bmatrix} \tag{22}$$

which can be easily solved as in (16).

Once the most suitable transformation function f_k is determined, then all the minutia parameter vectors, F, in the template $\mathbf{S}_k$ can be transformed to the reference minutia template $\mathbf{S}_u$. Transforming the minutiae coordinates (x, y) is straight forward. For the local ridge direction, φ, it will require a two-step approach. First convert the radial angle to Cartesian coordinate form, then convert back to the original angular form. Let (X', Y') be some point along the direction given by φ with respect to a minutiae at (X_o, Y_o). Both (X_o, Y_o) and (X', Y') are first transformed using $(x', y') = f(X', Y')$. Then the transformed minutiae orientation is computed using

$$\phi = \tan^{-1} \left(\frac{y' - y_o}{x' - x_o} \right), \quad -2\pi \leq \phi \leq 2\pi. \tag{23}$$

The combination process will be done iteratively, with the merged templates being used in the next iteration as in the pseudocode below:

For $k = 1$ to m And $k \neq u$
  Compute correspondence between $\mathbf{S}_k$ and $\mathbf{S}_u$
  Compute f_k
  $f_k(\mathbf{S}_k) \cup \mathbf{S}_u \Rightarrow \mathbf{S}_u$
End

In the combination process, those minutiae in the template $\mathbf{S}_k$ that correspond to the minutiae in the reference template $\mathbf{S}_u$ will be ignored as these are redundant. Essentially, the total number of minutia in the final combined template, n_u, is given by:

$$n_u = \sum_{k=1}^{m} n_k - \sum_{k=1}^{m-1} o_k, \qquad (24)$$

where m is the total number of templates available, n_k is the number of minutia in $\mathbf{S}_k$ and o_k is the number of overlapping minutiae between $\mathbf{S}_u$ and $\mathbf{S}_k$. Therefore, the final combined template will have a reduction in the number of minutia as compared to the total number of minutia in all the templates. If the overlap is significant, then the reduction will be significant.

4   Experiments

4.1   Transformation Study

In this section, we performed experimental study using physical fingerprint data to determine the most suitable transformation function for minutiae combination. In this experiment, we collected 5 images corresponding to 5 different areas (center, top-left, top-right, bottom-left and bottom-right) of each finger. A total of 200 images were thus captured using the *Veridicom Sensor* for 40 fingers.

Matching was first performed to obtain the corresponding minutia pair between two fingerprint templates which were to be combined. We used the template derived from the image at the center as the reference template to match with one of the other templates (top-left, top-right, bottom-left and bottom-right) of the same finger. The matched template pairs with 10 or more corresponding minutia pairs were then used for the following transformation study. As a result, only 50 matched pairs were found to have 10 or more matched minutiae among the 200 images.

To assess the accuracy of each transformation discussed in section 3.2, 75% of the matched minutiae were used to identify the transformation function (fitting) and the balance were used for extrapolation test (testing). The sum of squared errors (SSE) between the transformed and actual matched pairs were computed. The mean value and the standard deviation (STD) for these errors are tabulated in Table 1 for fitting and testing for all the 50 matched image pairs. From Table 1 the mean SSE and the standard deviation (STD) for the quadratic interactive topological transform is the smallest among the four transformations in the fitting test. However, for test data not included in the fitting process, the results show that affine transform gives the best result, in the sense of lowest mean SSE and lowest STD. The quasi-affine performance is very close. It is important to note that both the mean SSE and STD for the other two transformations (interactive and non-interactive topological transforms) are considerably large compared to those by affine transformation. This could mean that the coordinate warping according to the fit data may not necessary fit well the test data.

Table 1. Averaged Sum of Squared Errors: fitting and testing

	Affine	Non-int. Topology	Int. Topology	Q-Affine
Mean (fitting)	31.1304	21.1617	16.4531	37.5744
STD (fitting)	25.3905	21.8095	19.4167	27.5466
Mean (testing)	28.2344	117.7227	464.9472	28.9567
STD (testing)	29.7245	370.5094	1559.9000	31.1596

In the next experiment, we studied the extrapolation capability of each transformation. Here we used only 8 corresponding minutiae to solve for the transformation matrix. The computed transformation matrix was then used to align all the other minutiae. Detailed results for this study are tabulated in Table 2. From these results, we found that the Quasi-Affine transformation provide the best average extrapolation capability and is the most suitable for use in template combination.

Table 2. Averaged Sum of Squared Errors: fitting and testing

	Affine	Non-int. Topology	Int. Topology	Q-Affine
Mean (fitting)	30.7463	17.3667	10.4799	40.3084
STD (fitting)	27.2789	18.6171	13.1401	34.0138
Mean (testing)	57.4085	532.1907	1680.4000	43.7867
STD (testing)	72.2822	1344.7000	5150.4000	50.4781

4.2 A Minutiae Combination Example

In this part, we showed an example of combining three fingerprint images. As shown in Fig. 3(a)-(d), three fingerprint images were captured from three different portions of the same finger. Minutiae (shown in circles in Fig. 3(a)-(c)) were detected from these fingerprint images using the ridge tracing algorithm described earlier. A visual examination on these figures reveal that the minutiae information extracted in each image contains similar points (found in the overlap regions) and dissimilar points (found outside the overlap regions). It is also observed that even within the overlap region, some minutiae detected in one image may not be detected in another image due to different image qualities. As such, when any two of these three images are used for matching in a fingerprint identification or verification system, false rejection would occur when the threshold related to the total number of matched minutiae from the query image is set rather high.

Fig. 3(d) shows the combined minutiae from Fig. 3(a)-(c) using Fig. 3(a) as the reference image. The 'circles' in the figure indicates the original detected minutiae from Fig. 3(a), whereas the 'plus' and 'stars' indicate those additional minutiae transferred from Fig. 3(b) and Fig. 3(c) respectively. As seen from this figure, these additional minutiae have found correct correspondences on the reference fingerprint image which are not detectable in the original capture (Figures 3(a)).

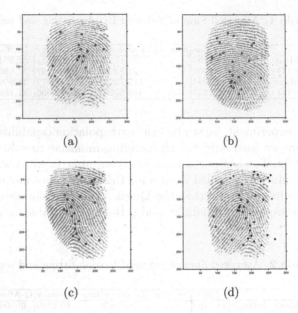

(a)   (b)

(c)   (d)

Fig. 3. (a) Fingerprint sample 1 with detected minutiae, (b) Fingerprint sample 2 with detected minutiae, (c) Fingerprint sample 3 with detected minutiae, (d) Fingerprint sample with combined minutiae (o: from sample 1; +: from sample 2; *: from sample 3)

4.3   Performance Evaluation

In this experiment, we show that the proposed fingerprint combination method can improve the recognition performance in terms of False Rejection caused by the use of different regions of the fingerprints for matching. A test sample database consisting of 600 query images and 2×60 template data sets (set(a) and set(b)) were used for this matching evaluation. The query images were randomly acquired from different partial regions (some of these are very much towards the edge) of each finger. The set(a) template data were obtained from the central region of each finger while the set(b) template data were obtained from combining five different regions of each finger.

Results in term of the match-score distribution plots and ROC plots are shown in Fig. 4 for 36000 matchings. The continuous curves and the dashed curves represent matching results using set(b) templates and set(a) templates respectively. Due to the use of different partial fingerprint regions for matching, results obtained from using set(a) templates are rather poor as seen from the figure. The situation has been significantly improved by using set(b) templates for matching. Notice that by using the combined templates, both matching curves for the same fingers (curves on the right) and those for different fingers (curves on the left) in the frequency plots show a shift of scores towards the higher region. However, this does not show deterioration of performance in terms of false acceptance rate. In fact it shows improvement of matching performance as seen from the ROC curves.

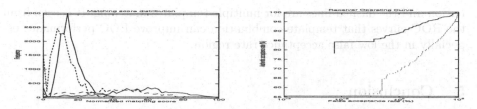

Fig. 4. Frequency and ROC curves (continuous-line: combination, dashed-line: single)

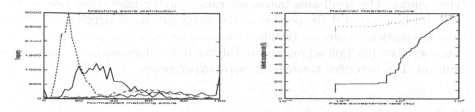

Fig. 5. Frequency and ROC curves (continuous-line: simple-merge, dashed-line: Combination)

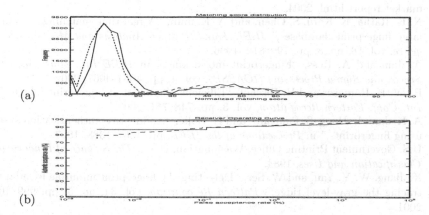

Fig. 6. (a) Score distributions (continuous-line: Combination, dashed-line: Best-of-5-single), (b) ROC plots (continuous-line: Combination, dashed-line: Best-of-5-single)

To further illustrate the effectiveness of the proposed combination approach, in Fig.5, we showed a case of simply collating those minutiae data from different regions of the same finger into a single file. The result shows that such a simple collection of minutiae data without establishing relevant reference (by transformation) can result in a poor matching performance.

We further evaluate the performance of the proposed combination method to the one that stored all the templates of the same finger (5 in this experiment) and select the best matched out of the 5 (Best-of-5-single) for verification. Matching results are shown in Figure 6(a)-(b) where the continuous lines are for combination and the dashed lines are for multiple templates matching. It is seen from the ROC curves that template combination can improve ROC performance especially in the low false acceptance rate region.

5   Conclusion

Fingerprint sensor suitable for mass consumer applications has to trade-off the large size of the sensing area with low sensor cost, especially the solid-state type sensors. The small area inevitably causes higher false reject rate as the user will be rejected if the portion of the finger presented significantly differs from the portion registered. Template combination algorithm using quasi-affine transformation function is proposed and shown to be effective in overcoming this problem. This is verified through extensive experiments.

References

1. IBG, "Biometrics market and industry report 2004-2008," tech. rep., International Biometric Group, http://www.biometricgroup.com/reports/public/market_report.html, 2004.
2. N. K. Ratha, K. Karu, S. Chen, and A. K. Jain, "A real-time matching system for large fingerprint databases," *IEEE Trans. Pattern Analysis and Machine Intelligence*, vol. 18, no. 8, pp. 799–812, 1996.
3. A. Jain and A. Ross, "Fingerprint mosaicking," in *IEEE Int. Conf. Acoustics, Speech and Signal Processing (ICASSP)*, vol. 4, pp. 4064–4067, 2002.
4. B. W. H. Ramoser and H. Bischof, "Efficient alignment of fingerprint images," in *Int. Conf. Pattern Recognition*, vol. 3, pp. 748–751, 2002.
5. A. K. Jain, L. Hong, S. Pankanti, and R. Bolle, "An identity-authentication system using fingerprints," in *Proceedings of the IEEE*, pp. 1365–1388, 1997.
6. U.S. Government Printing Office, Washingtion, D. C., *The Science of Fingerprints: Classification and Uses*, 1984.
7. X. Jiang, W. Y. Yau, and W. Ser, "Detecting the fingerprint minutiae by adaptive tracing the gray-level ridge," *Pattern Recognition*, vol. 34, no. 5, pp. 999–1013, 2001.
8. D. Maio and D. Maltoni, "Direct gray-scale minutiae detection in fingerprints," *IEEE Trans. Pattern Analysis and Machine Intelligence*, vol. 19, no. 1, pp. 27–40, 1997.
9. X. Jiang and W. Y. Yau, "Fingerprint minutiae matching based on the local and global structures," in *15th International Conference on Pattern Recognition*, vol. 2, pp. 1042–1045, 2000.
10. R. Cappelli, D. Maio, and D. Maltoni, "Modelling plastic distortion in fingerprint images," in *Int. Conference on Advances in Pattern Recognition (ICAPR2001)*, (Rio de Janeiro), March 2001.
11. K.-A. Toh, W.-Y. Yau, X. Jiang, T.-P. Chen, J. Lu, and E. Lim, "Minutiae data synthesis for fingerprint identification applications," in *Proceedings of the 2001 International Conference on Image Processing (ICIP)*, vol. 3, (Greece), pp. 262–265, October 2001.
12. K. Kanatani, *Geometric Computation for Machine Vision*. Clarendon Press, 1993.

Skeletonization of Fingerprint Based-on Modulus Minima of Wavelet Transform

Xinge You[1,2], Jianwei Yang[1], Yuan Yan Tang[1], Bin Fang[1], and Luoqing Li[2]

[1] Department of Computer Science, Hong Kong Baptist University, Hong Kong
{xyou, yjianw, yytang, fangb}@comp.hkbu.edu.hk
[2] Faculty of Mathematics and Computer Science, Hubei University, 430062, China
{xyou, lilq}@hubu.edu.cn

Abstract. This paper presents a direct and general algorithm based on the local minima of wavelet transform moduli for computing skeletons of fingerprint objects. The development of the method is inspired by some desirable characteristics of the local minimum of wavelet transform moduli. These significant properties are substantially investigated and corresponding results are mathematically proven with respect to a special wavelet function. A minima-modulus-theoretic algorithm is developed to extract skeletons of the fingerprint with a wide variety of width structures. We tested the algorithm on the natural fingerprint image with a variety of widths structures in gray image and binary image. Experimental results show that the skeletons of object obtained from the proposed algorithm overcome greatly some of the undesirable effects and limitations of previous methods, moreover, the proposed algorithm is insensitive to noise as well as efficient computability.

1 Introduction

Shape skeletonization description is the most active field of research and also an essential task in pattern recognition and computer vision. The skeletons are especially suitable for describing fingerprint object since they have natural axes and it is extensively applied to fingerprint analysis. Approaching skeletonization from a practical point of view, representing a shape by a set of thin curves rather than by a raster of pixels is useful for reducing the storage space and processing time of shape image. It was found that this representation is particularly effective in finding relevant salient features of the fingerprint for further optical recognition.

So far, more than 300 skeletonization algorithms have been proposed [8]. All these algorithms of skeletonization can be classified into direct and indirect computing methods [8, 18, 19]. However the following respects are needed to improve for the direct computing method. First, the generated skeletons are generally in discrete forms where skeleton points are discrete pixels. Such a skeleton is not helpful for recognizing the underlying shape unless skeleton pixels are linked by lines or curves implicitly or explicitly to form a graph. Second, even if skeleton pixels are linked, the resulting skeleton may not be centred inside the underlying shape due to the use of discrete data. Third, the computation complexity is high, since all foreground pixels

S.Z. Li et al. (Eds.): Sinobiometrics 2004, LNCS 3338, pp. 461–470, 2004.

are used for computation in a skeletonization process. It usually takes $O(n^3)$ [18,19] time to compute the skeleton of an $n \times n$ image by thinning.

Alternatively, skeletons can be computed indirectly [18, 14]. In an indirect skeletonization processing, a shape is first partitioned into simpler parts. Then, the skeleton of shape is obtained from the skeletons of those parts. Generally, the skeleton of shape is referred to as the locus of the symmetric points or symmetric axes of the local symmetries of the shape contour [2]. Different local symmetry analyses maybe result in different symmetric points, and hence different skeletons are produced. The *Symmetric Axis Transform* (SAT) introduced by Blum [2], *Smoothed Local Symmetry* (SLS) by Brady [3], *Process-Inferring Symmetry Analysis* (PISA) by Leyton [9] and the latest maximum modulus symmetry of wavelet transform (MMSWT)[14] are employed and contribute greatly to skeletonization of the shapes.

However, the major problem of the indirect computing technique is difficult to accurately identify local symmetries of the underlying shape. In fact, given a contour pixel of a digital shape, it may be impossible to find another pixel on the opposite contour such that they are exactly mathematically symmetrical in the discrete domain. And even if a pair of symmetric contour pixels can be exactly found, their corresponding symmetrical center may not exist.

Moreover, most existing methods are also sensitive to noise and shape variations, such as rotation and scaling, etc. Thus these methods are strictly limited within processing binary image rather than being more widely applicable to any gray levels images, especial fingerprint image. The recently proposed technique based on maximum modulus symmetry of wavelet transform [17, 14] improved greatly in these respects. Anyway, it has a poor performance with wide-structure objects. Because the computation cost depends fully on the width of the structure of the object. As mentioned in [14], the wider the structure of a shape is, the more time it takes to compute WT. Therefore, the MMSWT algorithm is not applicable for computing skeletons of object with a relatively wide structure. In addition, as we mentioned in our previous discussion [14], it is still puzzled how to choose proper scale for wavelet transform according to the width of shape in practice.

In this paper, we present a novel algorithm based on the local minima of wavelet transform moduli for computing the skeleton of the fingerprint objects. The proposed method is completely different from those known earlier. The skeleton computing is implemented directly over a conventional indirect process depending on edges and contours detected. We first investigate substantially the properties of the local minima of wavelet transform moduli from the viewpoint of mathematical analysis. It shows that these desirable properties are particularly suitable to be used to characterize and compute inherent skeletons of a ribbon-like shape, such as fingerprint objects. Furthermore, we propose a modulus-minimum-based algorithm, which provides simple and direct strategies for detecting and characterizing the skeletons of ribbon-like object with gray level and various kinds of width structure. The algorithm based on maximum modulus symmetry analysis in [14] fail to deal with them. Finally, experiment evaluation is performed on various conditions with reasonable comparisons.

2 Minima of Wavelet Transform Modulus

In computer vision, it is relatively important to detect the singularities point of signal such as edges that appear in images. Most of developed techniques are based on multiscale transforms [4, 11, 10, 13]. These multiscale transforms are equivalent to a wavelet transform but were studied before the development of the wavelet formalism. It is the key issue in the paper that the skeleton of the underlying shape is implemented by the minima of wavelet transform modulus.

Edge points of shape in the image plane are often located where the image intensity has sharp transition. The local maximum of the absolute value of the first derivative are sharp variation points of $f * \theta_s(x)$. Where a real smoothing function $\theta(x)$ satisfies $\theta(x) = O\left(\dfrac{1}{1+x^2}\right)$ and whose integral is nonzero. It can be viewed as the impulse response of a low-pass filter. Let $\theta_s(x) = \dfrac{1}{s}\theta(\dfrac{x}{s})$ and $f(x) \in L^2(R)$. Singular points (such as edges in images) at the scale s are defined as local sharp variation points of $f(x)$ smoothed by $\theta(x)$. Whereas the skeleton point of underlying shape should be midpoint between the two edge points along the gradient and where the image intensity of shape has the slowest transition. Hence the skeleton points of the underlying shape correspond to the local minima of the wavelet transform modulus $|\nabla Wf(s,x)|$. From a viewpoint of mathematical analysis, there should be a local minimum locating between the two consecutive local maxima of $|\nabla Wf(s,x)|$. Moreover, if the wavelet has a compact support, a value of $\nabla Wf(s,x_0)$ depends upon the values of $f(x)$ in a neighborhood of x_0, of size proportional to the scale s. At fine scales, it provides a localized information on $f(x)$. For details of mathematical discussion, one can be referred to [4, 11, 10, 12-14]. Where we suppose that the wavelet $\psi(x)$ is continuously differentiable, with real values and compact support, although the last two conditions are not necessary for a general wavelet theory.

As we known, the edge points are characterized by using the local maximum of WT modulus, as Canny mentioned in [4], in practice, The points marked as edges from the local maximum of WT modulus just be as close as possible to be the centre of the true edge but it is not the exact centre or the true edge, especially for step changes in intensity. Virtually, the ideal points marked as edge is an output, which is optimized the trade-off in localization and bandwidth.

Fortunately, the location of point correspond to the local minima of WT modulus is fixed at different scale although the bandwidth of the local minima may change along with the scale of WT. Therefore, the description for underlying shape by using the local minima of WT modulus also preserve most of the structural information in an image. Thus, by adjusting the transform scale, the minimum modulus point locates at the center between two consecutive modulus maxima points and is independent of the scale. In other words, the local minimum of $|\nabla Wf(s,x)|$ exists mathematically between the corresponding maximum points and may be unique for the fine fixed scale s. Moreover, for the fixed scale s and some "fine" wavelet, the two maxima modulus points are symmetric with the minimum one. Further all these minima points form the skeleton of the underlying shape. Hence, the skeleton of the underlying shape in an gray image can be measured from points where the modulus of the WT is locally minimum along the gradient.

2.1 Characteristics of Modulus Minima Based on B-Spline Wavelet Function

A typical multiscale analysis of image is implemented by smoothing the surface with a convolution kernel $\theta(x, y)$ that is dilated at dyadic scales s. Such an edge detector can be computed with two wavelets that are the partial derivative of $\theta(x, y)$

$$\psi^1(x, y) := \frac{\partial}{\partial x}\theta(x, y) \text{ and } \psi^2(x, y) := \frac{\partial}{\partial y}\theta(x, y)$$

Let us denote $\theta_s(x, y) = \frac{1}{s}\theta(\frac{x}{s}, \frac{y}{s})$. For wavelets $\psi^i(x, y)$, $i = 1, 2$, defined above, their scale wavelet transforms can be written as

$$W_s^1 f(x, y) = (f * \psi_s^1)(x, y) = s\frac{\partial}{\partial x}(f * \theta_s)(x, y), \tag{1}$$

$$W_s^2 f(x, y) = (f * \psi_s^2)(x, y) = s\frac{\partial}{\partial y}(f * \theta_s)(x, y). \tag{2}$$

This formula tells us that $W_s^1 f(x, y)$ is essentially the derivative of the smoothness function along the horizontal axis and then the local maxima of the derivative function correspond to the points of the smoothness image with sharp variation along the horizontal axis. A similar explanation for wavelet transform $W_s^2 f(x, y)$ defined above can also be made. However, the partial derivative is along the vertical direction instead of the horizontal one. Its corresponding the wavelet transform modulus and gradient can be written respectively as follow:

$$|\nabla W_s f(x, y)| := \sqrt{|W_s^1 f(x, y)|^2 + |W_s^2 f(x, y)|^2}, \tag{3}$$

And

$$Af(s, x, y) := \arg \tan\left(\frac{W^2 f(s, x, y)}{W^1 f(s, x, y)}\right) \tag{4}$$

We note that the most of multiscale shape representation or analysis methods are based on Gaussian kernel [1]. The traditional scale-space that is mainly based on the Gaussian kernel in that the Gaussian function is the unique kernel, which satisfies the causality property as guaranteed by the scaling theorem [1].

It has been shown [16] that B-spline wavelet perform better than other wavelets for singularities detection applications. As is well known, B-spline is a good approximation to Guassian kernel [16]. Besides inheriting almost all the good properties of Gaussian scale-space, B-spine derived scale-space exhibits many advantages. In fact, the orthogonal multiresolution pyramid originally proposed by S. Mallat [11] and the biorthogonal pyramid [6] in wavelet theory can all be derived from B-splines [16].

Other types of wavelets such as the wavelets on a interval [5], the periodic wavelets [7] and the cardinal spline wavelets [15] are all related to B-splines. In addition, the latest research result in [13] has shown that B-spline wavelet is particularly suitable to characterize Dirac-Structure edges in an image

We investigate substantially some desirable properties of the minima of WT modulus with B-spline function and develop a novel modulus-minimum-based algorithm for extracting skeletons of the ribbon-like shape as an improvement of the traditional skeletonization technique. We consider the quadratic B-spline function. The corresponding smoothing function $\theta(x)$ is given by

$$\theta(x) := \begin{cases} 8 \mid x \mid^3 - 8 \mid x \mid^2 + 4/3 & \text{if } \mid x \mid \leq 0.5, \\ -(8/3) \mid x \mid^3 + 8 \mid x \mid^2 - 8 \mid x \mid + 8/3 & \text{if } 0.5 \leq \mid x \mid \leq 1, \\ 0 & \text{if } \mid x \mid \geq 1. \end{cases} \tag{5}$$

Accordingly, for two-dimension case, it is easy to see that the smoothness function $\theta(x, y)$, which is defined by $\theta(x, y) := \phi(\sqrt{x^2 + y^2})$, is the reasonable choice.

We proved mathematically some desirable properties of the local minima of the B-spline WT modulus. These properties can be summarized the following theorem:

Theorems. Let l_d be a straight segment of ribbon-like shape with width d. If the scale of wavelet transform $s \geq d$, the local minima of WT modulus locates in the mid position of the ribbon-like shape and is fixed at different scales, especially, for some fine scale s, the point exists uniquely between the two consecutive local maximum then the local WT modulus minima corresponding to the wavelet function of Eq. (5) locate at the center line of l_d and the location of modulus minimum be independent of the scale of WT. Further, The two maxima of WT modulus are symmetric with respect to the corresponding minimum in the gradient direction.

Remark 1. This conclusion implies that the local minima of WT modulus are suitable to characterize the center line of fingerprint objects. Therefore the connective curve of all minimum points of WT modulus is defined as primary *Modulus-Minimum-Based Wavelet Skeleton* MMINBWS of the underlying shape.

Remark 2. A short segment of a shape can be approximated by a straight line with certain width. Accordingly, we may assume that l_d in the theorem is a straight segment without the loss of generality.

Remark 3. In fact, the theorem directly characterizes the relationship between the maxima and the minima of wavelet transform modulus of ribbon-like shapes as follows: If the transform scale s is bigger than or equals to the width of a shape, then the location of minimum of the wavelet transform moduli covers exactly the inherent central line of the shape. Meanwhile, the location of maxima of the wavelet transform moduli, which locate nearly at the points of the original boundary, form the two new lines and they are symmetrical with respect to the inherent central line of the shape which is produced by the local minima points.

A simple and direct strategy for characterizing and extracting the skeleton of the underlying ribbon-like shape is strongly motivated by the local minima analysis of the WT modulus. The primary skeleton of a fingerprint object is referred to as the sets which consist of all minimum points of the WT moduli of the underlying shapes in our approach and is called Modulus-Minimum-Based Wavelet Skeleton (MMINBWS). In other words, MMINBWS means the connective curve of all minima point of the WT moduli along the gradient direction of the underlying shapes. In practice, the detection of the local minimum point of the WT moduli in the discrete domain can be implemented analogously as the local maximum of the WT moduli in [14] is computed.

2.2 Implementation of Algorithms Based on Minimum Modulus of WT

Ideally, the skeletons of a shape are represented by a set of thin curves which consist of single pixels rather than by a bandwidth which consists of multiple pixels.

It is shown in the theorem that if and only if the scale of wavelet transform matches well with the width of the shape, namely, its value is much bigger than the width of the shape, the modulus minimum point between two homologous modulus maximum points exists uniquely. Otherwise, maybe there exists numerous modulus minimum points and all of these points form a continuous region or bandwidth, which is called skeleton ribbon or primary skeleton. Obviously, the skeleton ribbon contains multiple pixels and is distributed symmetrically along the central line of the underlying shape. However, it does not obviously conform to human perceptions of the underlying shape although it closely describes the underlying shapes, as the skeleton curve consisting of a single pixel does.

In practice, it is impossible to choose the suitable scale of the WT according to the width of shape structure so that the skeleton locus obtained from the modulus-minimum-based algorithm consists of the single pixels. For most of cases, the primary skeleton obtained from the modulus-minimum-based algorithm is generally the bandwidth skeleton consisting of multiple pixels than the thin skeleton line containing a single pixel. Even if the relatively big scale is favorable to processing on wide-structure shape and may result in a single-pixel skeleton, but it usually suffers from too heavy computational cost.

To solve this problem, the following multilevel-based skeletonization approach is proposed. And it is demonstrated that this is a simple and effective solution to extract the skeleton of a shape with various kinds of complicated structures. Our basic idea is as follows: For each input image, we randomly choose a scale of wavelet transform and extract its corresponding skeleton of the underlying shape by computing all local minimum points of WT moduli. Thus all of these local minimum points produce the primary skeleton ribbon of the underlying shape which consists of multiple pixels. Meanwhile, these primary skeleton ribbons also contains the inherent central curves of the underlying shape. These primary skeleton ribbons are apparently thinning from the original shapes with thinning down width structure and preserve exactly the topological properties of the original shape. Likewise, we choose a much smaller scale than the prior one to perform the second wavelet transform on the image which contains these primary skeleton ribbons, and compute the second level primary skeletons.

We will repeat the above computing procedure until the central curves which consist of single pixels are eventually extracted.

In practice, a set of scheme for computing the primary skeletons of the shapes based on the local minima of the WT moduli is designed below.

Multilevel-Threshold-Based Algorithm (MTBA). For most of the fingerprint objects, the widths of their structures usually appear as more or less variations even have sharp contrasts. Therefore, it is very difficult to choose a fairly appropriate scale which is suitable for various kinds of width structures. Even if the widths of the shape structures in the same image distribute uniformly and equidistantly but are too wide, it still suffers from high computational cost in that a large scale has to be selected to perform WT. On the other hand, the modulus value of the local minimum points is generally equal to zero or approximate it. Consequently, one relatively small modulus value may be set as threshold firstly. All points of the underlying shape, whose modulus values of wavelet transform are less than the given threshold, are selected as the candidates of skeleton points of the underlying shape. Thus all candidates form a thinning skeleton ribbon which consist of multiple pixels around the inherent central curve of the underlying shape as the first-level skeleton. The foregoing computation step is called the first level thinning. The primary skeleton ribbon produce next the image which contains these skeleton ribbons of the underlying shape will be regarded as a new input image for further processing. In other words, these skeleton ribbons obtained from the above modulus-minimum-based algorithm are certainly considered as the new underlying objects.

Repeating the previous thinning approach for the new input image containing the first-level skeleton ribbon, By iteratively computing minimum moduli of the second wavelet transform with much smaller scale than the prior one, we may obtain the second-level skeletons which are further thinning and gradually approximates the inherent central curves of the original shape. The above procedure is iterated until the skeleton curve which consist of single pixels is eventually extracted from the underlying shape. We call it multilevel threshold algorithm and it is described in detail below:

Algorithm 1. (Based on MTBA) Let $f(x, y)$ be a ribbon-like shape image.

Step 1. Evaluate a threshold T_g for the gray value of the original image processed for further partitioning the underlying shape from the background (if necessary);

Step 2. Select randomly a scale according to the width of ribbon-like shape to perform WT with the wavelets defined by Eq. (5) on the input image.

Step 3. Calculate the moduli of wavelet transforms $|\nabla W_s f(x, y)|$ and set an initial threshold T_m for the modulus of WT.

Step 4. Determine the primary skeleton points based on the comparison of the following parameters: the modulus $|\nabla W_s f(x, y)|$ and T_m, the gray value and T_g.

Step 5. Repeat Step 2, perform the second WT for the primary skeletons obtained from Step 1, 2, 3, and 4.

Step 6. Calculate the gradient direction $f_{gradient}$ and the local minima of the underlying shape $f_{loc\ min}$ of $|\nabla W_s f(x,y)|$ as the candidate skeleton;

Step 7. Determine the skeleton points from the all candidates by comparing the gray value of the candidates with the threshold T_g.

2.3 Experiments

The algorithm we designed has its own features and is suitable for extracting skeletons of shape with different structures. To evaluate the behavior of MTBA for various kinds of structures of the fingerprint objects, some experimental results are illustrated in this subsection.

The scale employed in MTBA can be chosen freely without any preconditions imposed but the previous technique in [14] fail to do as shown in fig: result-compare. As the algorithm of MTBA described, in practice, an initial scale is randomly chosen to perform wavelet transform on an image and detect its corresponding minimum modulus points as initial skeletons. If the skeletons obtained from the initial step consist of single-pixels curves or agree with human perceptions, then detection procedure end. Otherwise, the second wavelet transform need to be performed with re-given scale. the process do not be ended until final skeletons which satisfy with predefined criteria are obtained. Obviously, the scale selection in every wavelet transform step of MTBA is independent of the width structures. In other words, no any prerequisite width information of the shape have been estimated in advance for computing wavelet transform. Thus the developed MTBA is very well adapted to computing skeletons of ribbon-like shapes with not only uniform but also various width structures. Therefore MTBA also describes an almost fully automatic technique for computing skeletons of ribbon-like shape in a sense. To compare with the proposed algorithm in [14], An original image with Chinese character "rong" is shown in Fig. 1,

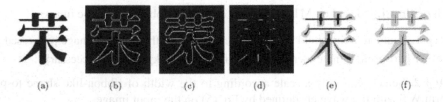

(a)   (b)   (c)   (d)   (e)   (f)

Fig. 1. (a) Pattern consisting of Chinese character; (b) The raw output of maximum modulus obtained from wavelet transform with scale s= 4; (c) The raw output of maximum modulus obtained from wavelet transform with scale s= 8; (d) Skeleton obtained from the proposed algorithm [14] with scale s= 8. (e) Primary Skeleton obtained from MTBA; (f) Skeleton obtained from MTBA with the second extraction

we applied MTBA to extracting its skeletons. Here, no any width information is provided beforehand. Moreover, the width of the character structures sharply changes in the global object. As expected, primary skeletons and final result, as shown in Fig.1(e) and (f) respectively, are extracted successfully and comply well with the geometrical structure of the underlying shape. But in [14], by using the algorithm based on maximum modulus symmetry analysis, we failed to find proper scale to implement it due to contrast change of width structures of the character object as shown in Fig. 1(d).

Finally, the raw fingerprint image with varying gray level distributed and noise is illustrated in Fig. 2.

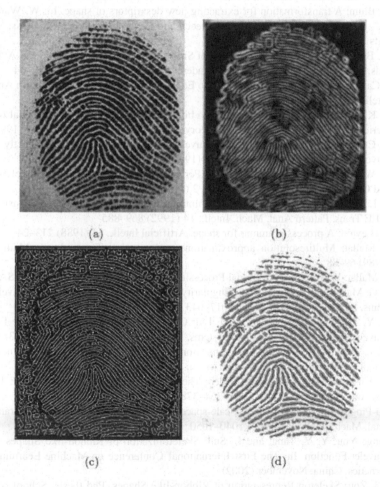

(a)   (b)

(c)   (d)

Fig. 2. (a) The original fingerprint image; (b) the raw output of modulus obtained from WT with scale s= 8; (c) the modulus maximum of the WT; (d) skeleton directly obtained from the proposed algorithm

Acknowledgements

This work was supported by Research Grant 2002A00009 from Depart of Education in Hubei Province and Research Grant 2003ABA012 from China Hubei Provincial Science and Technology Department.

References

1. V. Anh, J. Y. Shi, and H. T. Tsui: Scaling theorems for zero-crossings of band limited signals. IEEE Trans. Pattern Anal. Mach. Intell., 18 (1990) 309–320
2. H. Blum: A transformation for extracting new desxriptors of shape. In: W. Wathen-Dunn (eds.): Models for the Perception of Speech and Visual Form. The MIT Press, Massachusetts (1967) 362–380
3. M. Brady: Criteria for Representation of Shape. In: J. Beck and B. Hope and A. Rosenfeld (eds.): Human and Machine Vision. Academic Press, New York (1983) 39–84
4. J. Canny: A Computational Approach to Edge Detection. IEEE Trans. Pattern Anal. Mach. Intell., 8 (1986) 679–698
5. C. K. Chui and E. Quak: Wavelets on a bounded interval. In: D. Brasess et.al (eds.): Numerical Methods in Approximation Theory, Vol. 9. Birhauser Verlag, Basel (1992) 53–65
6. A. Cohen, I. Daubechies, and J. C. Feauveau: Biorthogonal bases of compactly supported wavelets. Comm. Pure Appl. Math., 45 (1992) 485–560
7. Y. W. Koh, S. L. Lee, and H. H. Tan: Periodic orthogonal splines and wavelets. Applied and Computational Harmonic Analysis, 2 (1995) 201–218
8. L. Lam, S. W. Lee, and C. Y. Suen: Thinning Methodologies - a Comprehensive Survey. IEEE Trans. Pattern Anal. Mach. Intell., 14 (1992) 869–885
9. M. Leyton: A process-grammar for shape. Artificial Intell., 34 (1988) 213–247
10. S. Mallat: Multiresolution approximations and wavelet. Trans. Amer. Math. Soc., 11 (1989) 69–88
11. S. Mallat: Wavelet Tour of Signal Processing. Academic Press, San Diego, USA, (1998)
12. S. G. Mallat and W. L. Hwang: Singularity detection and processing with wavelets. IEEE Trans. Inform. Theory, 38 (1992) 617–643
13. Y. Y. Tang, L. H. Yang, and J. M. Liu: Characterization of Dirac-Structure Edges with Wavelet Transform. IEEE Trans. Systems, Man, Cybernetics (B), 31 (2000) 93–109
14. Y. Y. Tang and X. G. You: Skeletonization of ribbon-like shapes based on a new wavelet function. IEEE Trans. Pattern Anal. Mach. Intell., 25 (2003) 1118–1133
15. M. Unser, A. Aldroubi, and M. Eden: The polynomial spline pyramid. IEEE Trans. Pattern Anal. Mach. Intell., 15 (1993) 364–378
16. Yu-Ping Wang and S. L. Lee: Scale-space derived from B-splines. IEEE Trans. Pattern Anal. Mach. Intell., 20 (1998) 1040–1050
17. Xinge You, Y. Y. Tang, and L. Sun: Skeletonization of Ribbon-like Shapes with New Wavelet Function. In: The First International Conference on Machine Learning and Cybernetics, China, November (2002)
18. J. J. Zou: Skeleton Represetation of Ribbon-like Shapes. Phd thesis, School of Electical and Information Engineering, University of Sydney, Sydney, March (2001)
19. J. J. Zou and Hong Yan: Skeletonization of Ribbon-Like shapes Based on Regularity and Singularity Analyses. IEEE Trans. Systems. Man. Cybernetics (B), 21 (2001) 401–407

Transformation-Variants Estimation Using Similarity Relative Histogram Grouping Model*

Yuliang He[1,2] and Jie Tian[1,2,**]

[1] Biometrics Research Group, Key Laboratory of Complex Systems and Intelligence Science, Institute of Automation, CAS, P.O.Box 2728, Beijing, 100080, China
[2] Graduate School of the Chinese Academy of Science Beijing, 100039, China
tian@doctor.com

Abstract. This paper proposes a novel method that estimates parameters of a geometric transformation by means of grouping and statistical inference in relative histogram grouping models borrowed from the law of large number. Since an image is divided into many local partial objects, each of which is represented by groups of transformation-invariant and transformation-variant (e.g., translation, rotation, and shearing) and whose deformations are considered to be linear, we construct minutiae-simplexes to represent partial objects in a fingerprint. A relative histogram grouping model describes the relationship between transformation-invariant and variant. Even if the image is transformed at random, partial objects still maintain their linear representation, from which the relative histogram techniques extract grouping centers that account for transformation-variations in partial objects for geometric alignment. Our promising experimental results show that our technique is efficient in alignment and match.

1 Introduction

In the last decade, fingerprint based biometric systems have attracted great interest of researchers to find new algorithms and techniques for fingerprint recognition. Supported by current technologies, fingerprint identification is in fact much more reliable than other possible personality identification methods based on signature, face, or speech alone [1]. Although fingerprint verification is usually associated with criminal identification and police work [1], it has become more popular in civilian applications, such as access control, financial security and verification of firearm purchasers [2], etc. In other words, a fingerprint is a sort of identity card that people carry with them continuously. Significant improvements have been achieved on the algorithmic side.

---

* This paper is supported by the Project of National Science Fund for Distinguished Young Scholars of China under Grant No. 60225008, the Key Project of National Natural Science Foundation of China under Grant No. 60332010, the Project for Young Scientists' Fund of National Natural Science Foundation of China under Grant No.60303022.
** Corresponding author: Jie Tian; Telephone: 8610-62532105; Fax: 8610-62527995.

Fingerprint is a pattern of ridges and valleys on the surface of the finger. The uniqueness of a fingerprint can be determined by an overall pattern of ridges and valleys as well as local ridge anomalies, ridge bifurcations or ridge endings, called minutia points. Many fingerprint experts have designed intuitive fingerprint representation schemes based on visual matching, under the very strong assumption that input image and template image have been acquired through the same sensor and thus present the same intensity range, allowing a certain amount of noise. In addition, fingerprint identification techniques [3-8] have been developed to recover geometric distortions and misalignments in fingerprints. However, the workload of one by one alignment of the fixed geometric transformation, which is derived from some certain local deformation, is overwhelming, and all the alignments as a whole occupy too much memory.

Thereby, taking both local and global deformations into account, we propose a novel method that estimates parameters of a geometric transformation to minimize the sum of the differences (or the squared sum of the differences) of their intensity values or feature similarity by means of grouping and statistical inference in relative histogram models borrowed from the law of large number. At the very beginning, an image is divided into many local partial objects, such as triangular feature structures [3, 8], each of which is represented by groups of transformation-invariant and transformation-variant (e.g., translation, rotation, and shearing) and whose deformations are considered to be linear. Rather than employing triangular feature structures as many researchers do, we construct minutiae-simplexes to represent partial objects in a fingerprint. Minutia-simplexes are more easily combined with their local texture information, contain enough local transformation-invariants and variants to analyze the relationship between global transformation-invariants and variants, and help alleviate workload and reduce memory cost as well. Then, a relative histogram grouping model, based on general histogram, which is a simple effective grouping way to derive useful representations of data, such as images and videos, describes the relationship between transformation-invariant and variant. Even if the image is transformed at random, partial objects still maintain their linear representation, from which the relative histogram techniques extract grouping centres that account for transformation-variations in partial objects. Barycentre of a confident interval of transformation-variant under a given confidence denotes the optimal transformation-variant, by which to align each partial object. The alignment verifies the local matching results of partial objects. We illustrate performance of our method over the fingerprint databases provided by Fingerprint Verification Competition in 2002 (FVC2002)[9].

This paper is organized as follows: Fingerprint features are described in Section2. Section 3 introduces our method to estimate the transformation-variant during matching using similarity-based relative histogram grouping model. Our experimental results are illustrated in Section 3. And we conclude our work in this paper in Section 4.

2 Fingerprint Features and Their Relational Structures

2.1 Fingerprint Features

The complementary features of a fingerprint include its minutiae and their local associated ridge information. A complementary feature M_i is represented by a feature vector $(x_i, y_i, \alpha_i, \beta_i, \varphi_{ij})^T$ $(i=1,...,m(F), j=1,...,L)$, where 1) x_i and y_i are its coordinates. 2) α_i is its tangent direction at M_i. 3) β_i is the local grey variance of an area whose centre is M_i (Since the type feature of M_i, ending or bifurcate, which brings out error matching, we replace type feature of the minutia by its local grey variation. 5) φ_{ij} is the direction from M_i to R_{ij}, one of sampled points on the ridge close to the minutia M_i. φ_{ij} ($j =1,...,L$) represents curvature of the ridge associated with M_i and the local texture information for matching. 6) $m(F)$ denotes the number of minutia points in fingerprint F and L the threshold of the number of sampled points.

Let $M^F = \{M^F_i = (x_i,\ y_i,\ \alpha_i,\ \beta_i,\ \varphi_{ij})^T;\ (i=1,...,\ m(F),\ \ j =1,...,\ L)\}$ denote the comprehensive minutiae set of fingerprint F. $M(F)$ determines the global minutia structure of this fingerprint. We choose the representation of the ith minutia point by M^F_i.

2.2 Relational Structure of Features

For each pair of minutia points M^F_i and M^F_j ($1\leq i<j\leq m(F)$) in M^F, if their Euclidean distance $d(M^F_i, M^F_j) =[(x_j -x_i)^2+(y_j -y_i)^2]^{1/2}$ satisfies $d_l \leq d(M^F_i, M^F_j) \leq d_h$, M^F_i and M^F_j are to be connected as a feature segment T^F_k (partial object in a fingerprint image) presented by a feature vector which is composed of index features (r^F_k, e^F_k), transformation-invariants (l^F_k, β^F_{k1}, β^F_{k2}, u^F_k, v^F_k), and transformation-variants (θ^F_k, φ^F_{k1p}, φ^F_{k2p}, α^F_{k1}, α^F_{k2})($p=1,...,L$) where:

1) Index features (r^F_k, e^F_k) denote the serial numbers of two minutiae in M^F associated with T^F_k, i.e. $r^F_k=i$ and $e^F_k=j$.
2) Transformation-invariants (l^F_k, β^F_{k1}, β^F_{k2}, u^F_k, v^F_k) describe the attributes of a minutiae simplex, which maintain unchanged with transformation, where $l^F_k=d(M^F_i, M^F_j)$, $\beta^F_{k1}=\beta^F_i$, $\beta^F_{k2}=\beta^F_j$, $u^F_k=\alpha^F_i - \theta^F_k$, $v^F_k=\alpha^F_j - \theta^F_k$.
3) Transformation-variants (θ^F_k, φ^F_{k1p}, φ^F_{k2p}, α^F_{k1}, α^F_{k2})($p=1,...,L$) represent the transformation attributes and rotation of the minutiae simplex where $\theta^F_k =\arctan((y^F_i - y^F_j)/(x^F_i - x^F_j))$; $\varphi^F_{k1p}= \varphi^F_{ip}$ and $\varphi^F_{k2p} = \varphi^F_{jp}$ ($p=1,...,L$) are directions of sampled points on texture curves of M^F_i and M^F_j respectively; $\alpha^F_{k1} =\alpha^F_i$ and $\alpha^F_{k2} =\alpha^F_j$.

All minutiae simplexes constitute a geometric graph of points, segments, and triangles, i.e. a simplex set $E^F = \{T^F_k;\ k=1, ..., t(F)\}$, where $t(F)$ is the size of set E^F. E^F represents the global characteristics of fingerprint more accurately than the minutia set M^F. $t(F)$ is much smaller than $m(F)(m(F)+1)/2$ because many minutiae simplex which are constructed by a pair of minutiae don't satisfy $d_l \leq d(M_i, M_j) \leq d_h$, M^F_i. It is very convenient to change the size of minutiae simplex E^F for matching by changing d_l and d_h.

3 Similarity-Based Transformation Variant Space Estimation

3.1 Similarity Measurement of Relational Structures

Let E^F and E^G denote the minutia simplex set of input fingerprint F and the template minutia simplex set respectively. For each minutia simplex vector T^F_m in E^F and U^G_n in E^G, there are two matching cases as follows:

1) If M^F_{rm} and M^F_{em} are matched with M^G_{rn} and M^G_{en} respectively, the transformation-invariant similarity and the transformation-variant difference between T^F_m and U^G_n are

denoted by feature vector $e^{(0)}_{mn} = (l^F_m - l^G_n, \beta^F_{m1} - \beta^G_{n1}, \beta^F_{m2} - \beta^G_{n2}, u^F_m - u^G_n, v^F_m - v^G_n)^T$ and $o^{(0)}_{mn} = (\theta^F_m - \theta^G_n, \varphi^F_{m1p} - \varphi^G_{n1p}, \varphi^F_{m2p} - \varphi^G_{n2p}, \alpha^F_{m1} - \alpha^G_{n1}, \alpha^F_{m2} - \alpha^G_{n2})^T$ respectively.

2) If M^F_{em} and M^F_{rm} are matched with M^G_{rn} and M^G_{en} respectively, the transformation-invariant similarity and the transformation-variant difference between T^F_m and U^G_n are denoted by feature vector $e^{(1)}_{mn} = (l^F_m - l^G_n, \beta^F_{m1} - \beta^G_{n1}, \beta^F_{m2} - \beta^G_{n2}, u^F_m - u^G_n - 180, v^F_m - v^G_n - 180)^T$ and $o^{(1)}_{mn} = (\theta^F_m - \theta^G_n - 180, \varphi^F_{m1p} - \varphi^G_{n2p}, \varphi^F_{m2p} - \varphi^G_{n1p}, \alpha^F_{m1} - \alpha^G_{n2}, \alpha^F_{m2} - \alpha^G_{n1})^T$ $(p=1,...,L)$ respectively.

If $\|e^{(0)}_{mn}\| > \varepsilon$ and $\|e^{(1)}_{mn}\| > \varepsilon$, T^F_m and U^G_n don't match each other, and select the next pair minutiae simplex; otherwise, the transformation-invariant similarity between T^F_m and U^G_n is denoted by $s_{mn} = 1 - \min(\|e^{(0)}_{mn}\|, \|e^{(1)}_{mn}\|)/\varepsilon$ $(0 \le s_{mn} \le 1)$, where ε is the error threshold of the transformation-invariant feature vector. The more similar T^F_m and U^G_n are, the greater s_{mn} is. All similarities s_{mn} constitute a $t(F) \times t(G)$ discrete similarity function $s(i,j) = \{s_{ij}; (1 \le i \le t(F), 1 \le j \le t(G))\}$, which represents the similarity between partial objects in fingerprint F and G. In addition, a $t(F) \times t(G)$ discrete directional error function $\theta(i,j) = \{\theta_{ij}; 1 \le i \le t(F), 1 \le j \le t(G)\}$ is also composed of all θ_{ij}, where θ_{ij} is the mean of all elements in the transformation-variant error vector o_{mn}.

Let e_{mn} index the matching case, if $\min(\|e^{(0)}_{mn}\|, \|e^{(1)}_{mn}\|) = \|e^{(0)}_{mn}\|$, $e_{mn} = 0$, $o_{mn} = o^{(0)}_{mn}$; otherwise, $o_{mn} = 1$, $o_{mn} = o^{(1)}_{mn}$, where o_{mn} denotes the right transformation difference between T^F_m and U^G_n. The transformation-variant difference vector o_{mn} describes the directional difference between partial objects T^F_m and U^G_n. By the same way, we can get the translation variants and analyze their distributions. Therefore, we won't discuss them in the next sections.

3.2 Transformation-Variant Analysis Using Relative Histogram Grouping Model

Histogram is an important measurement of the value or density in a digital image, representing the value distribution of the image. We adopt and expend this function to relative histogram in analyzing transformation variants (rotation, translation, and shearing) with transformation-invariant in images. The better the local transformation-invariants of a partial object perform in the global ones, the more important the local transformation-variants are in calculation of the values of global transformation-variants.)

For $s(x,y)(x \in I_x, y \in I_y, I_x$ and I_y are two continuous intervals of x and y respectively), a bounded and continuous function about transformation-invariant similarity, and $\theta(x,y)(x \in I_x, y \in I_y, \theta_1 \le h(x,y) \le \theta_2, \theta_1 < \theta_2)$, a bounded and continuous function about transformation-variant error, a relative histogram function of transformation invariant is built up as

$$h(\theta) = \iint_{x \in I_x, y \in I_y} \delta(\theta(x,y) - \theta) ds(x,y) \tag{1}$$

where transformation variant θ $(\theta_1 \le \theta \le \theta_2)$ is self-variant, and $\delta(x)$ is an impulsive function($\delta(x) = 1$ if $x = 0$; otherwise, $\delta(x) = 0$).

In real computation, $s(i,j)$ ($i \in I_i$, $j \in I_j$, I_i and I_j are two discrete and bounded intervals of x and y respectively) and $\theta(i, j)$ ($i \in I_i$, $j \in I_j$, $\theta_1 \leq h(i, j) \leq \theta_2$, $\theta_1 < \theta_2$), are discrete and bounded. The discrete relative histogram function is defined as:

$$h(\theta) = \sum_{i \in I_x} \sum_{j \in I_y} \delta(\theta(i, j) - \theta) \times s(i, j) \qquad (2)$$

which shows that for each pair of i and j ($i \in I_x$, $j \in I_y$) satisfying $\theta(i,j) = \theta$, $s(i,j)$ will sum up.

$h(\theta)$ shows the relationship of the transformation-invariant similarities and transformation-variant differences between partial object sets. If $h(x_1) > h(x_2)$, F is more similar to G under transformation-variant x_1 than under transformation-variant x_2, by which to align fingerprint G to fingerprint F. In theory, the maximum of the relative histogram function $h(\theta)$ denotes the optimal value of the transformation-variant. A filtering function $f(i)$ in Equality 3 is introduced to filter noises from those the histogram function.

$$\begin{cases} f(i) = \dfrac{1}{2}(1 - \cos(\dfrac{i\pi}{d})) \\ \sum_{i=1}^{2d+1} f(i) = 1 \end{cases} \qquad (3)$$

where $f(i) \geq 0$, $i = 1, \ldots, 2d+1$, and d is a natural integer. The filter function is a simplified Gaussian filter function. These filtered $h(\theta)$ looks smoother than before, and are of Gaussian distribution, which is deduced from the law of large number. The maximum of $h(\theta)$ is regarded as the optimal site that optimizes the transformation model and minimizes the differences between two partial objects sets of fingerprints F and G.

To accurately locate the site, we define a confident interval $[u - \lambda\sigma, u + \lambda\sigma]$, centred at the maximum of $h(\theta)$, with its confidence a, where u and σ are the mean and variance of $h(\theta)$. In theory, $\theta = u$ maximizes $h(\theta)$, but it is very difficult to obtain the variance σ of θ. Therefore, we first find the maximum of $h(\theta)$ and obtain u, and then select a threshold γ and find sites $\theta = u \pm \sigma(2\ln\gamma)^{-1/2}$ where $h(\theta) = \max\{h(\theta)\}/\gamma$ ($\gamma > 1$), $\lambda = (2\ln\gamma)^{-1/2}$, and the confidence of the confident interval $[u - \sigma(2\ln\gamma)^{-1/2}, u + \sigma(2\ln\gamma)^{-1/2}]$ is $2\phi((2\ln\gamma)^{-1/2}) - 1$. We align γ according to confidence a and its confident interval $[u - \lambda\sigma, u + \lambda\sigma]$. There are noises in $h(\theta)$ and it is more advisable to use the barycentre of θ, calculated by Equality 4, as the optimal transformation-variant in the transformation model rather than $\theta = u$, where $h(\theta) = \max\{h(\theta)\}$. Our experiments show that this scheme is efficient. If θ_0 and $\sigma(2\ln\gamma)^{-1/2}$ are beyond the areas, which we pre-set for the transformation-variant, two fingerprints are assumed to be from the different finger.

$$\theta_o = \int_{u-\lambda\sigma}^{u+\lambda\sigma} h(\theta)d\theta \Bigg/ \int_{u-\lambda\sigma}^{u+\lambda\sigma} dh(\theta) \qquad (4)$$

4 Experimental Results

We evaluate our algorithm based on the fingerprint databases provided by Fingerprint Verification Competition in 2002 (FVC2002 [9]), which is more suited for testing on online fingerprint systems than other fingerprint data sets, such as data sets provided by the US National Institute of Standards and Technology (NIST)[10-12].

4.1 Performance of Relative Histogram Grouping Model

We made three groups of experiments to analyze and present the attributes of $H(\theta)$, which is a periodical function about θ and extended by half a period both at the beginning point and at the ending point before being filtered. in our method, an angle is set within the interval [0, 255) rather than in the interval [0,360) to reduce the memory cost, without affecting the performance. In the first group of experiments (Figure 1), two fingerprints, acquired from the same finger, are used to build up their relative histogram grouping model. The distribution of the model is smooth, has only a peak in a period, and is of normal distribution. In the second group of experiments (Figure 2), two fingerprints, acquired from two different fingers and very similar to each other, are used to build up their relative histogram grouping model. The distribution of the model is peaky in a period. Obviously, it is not of normal distribution although the two fingerprints are very similar to each other. In the third group of experiments (Figure 3), two fingerprints, acquired from two different fingers and very dissimilar to each other, are used to build up their relative histogram. The distribution of the relative histogram grouping model is very peaky and out of order in a period.

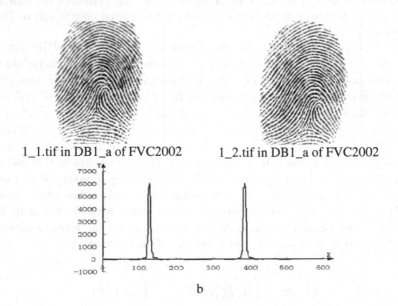

1_1.tif in DB1_a of FVC2002   1_2.tif in DB1_a of FVC2002

b

Fig. 1. Distribution of the relative histogram grouping model of two fingerprint, acquired from the same finger

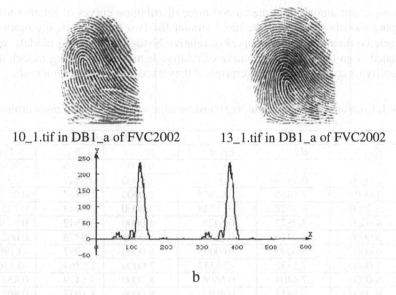

10_1.tif in DB1_a of FVC2002   13_1.tif in DB1_a of FVC2002

b

Fig. 2. Distribution of the relative histogram grouping model of two fingerprints from different fingers and very similar to each other

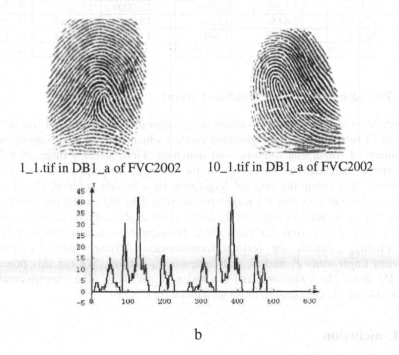

1_1.tif in DB1_a of FVC2002   10_1.tif in DB1_a of FVC2002

b

Fig. 3. Distribution of the relative histogram grouping model of two fingerprint from different fingers and very dissimilar to each other

Comparison among aforementioned three distribution curves of relative histogram grouping models shows that the more similar the two fingerprints, the more smooth and ordered their distribution curves of relative histogram grouping models. θ_0 and σ, estimated from the distribution curve of relative histogram grouping model, are used to identify its corresponding fingerprints if they exceed their preset intervals.

Table 1. Comparison between estimated transformation-variant and real transformation-variant

Clockwise			Anticlockwise		
θ_k	θ'_k	Error	θ_k	θ'_k	Error
0.0000	0.6666	-0.6666	0.0000	0.6666	-.6666
1.0000	0.7947	0.2053	1.0000	0.6447	0.3553
2.0000	2.1465	-0.1465	2.0000	1.9467	0.0533
3.0000	3.1748	-0.1748	3.0000	2.8743	0.1257
4.0000	3.3572	0.6428	4.0000	3.1542	0.8458
5.0000	4.7316	0.2684	5.0000	4.9378	0.0622
6.0000	6.0095	-0.0095	6.0000	6.1997	-0.1997
7.0000	7.1332	-0.1332	7.0000	7.3364	-0.3364
8.0000	7.4404	0.5596	8.0000	7.5479	0.4521
9.0000	8.5917	0.4083	9.0000	8.1973	0.8027
10.0000	9.7634	0.2366	10.0000	9.5637	0.4363
11.0000	10.0817	0.9183	11.0000	10.5413	0.4587
12.0000	11.1290	0.8710	12.0000	11.3211	0.6789
13.0000	12.4436	0.5564	13.0000	12.4537	0.5463
14.0000	13.5593	0.4407	14.0000	13.6584	0.3416
Average of Errors		0.331757	Average of Errors		0.2637

4.2 Precision of Estimated Rotation-Variant

Experiments are designed to evaluate the precision of the estimated transformation-variant in relative histogram grouping model, which plays a very important role in alignment of fingerprint minutiae and matching, First, select a fingerprint from the fingerprint databases of FVC2002 as the template fingerprint G and extract its features. Then, rotate the original fingerprint by a certain angle θ_k (k=-M, ..,0.., M, M>0), $k < 0$ indicates that the fingerprint is rotated by $|\theta_k|$ clockwise; otherwise, it is rotated by $|\theta_k|$ anticlockwise) with its centre point as the conferring point, and extract fingerprint features from the transformed fingerprint as input fingerprint F_k (k=1,.., M). Finally, calculate the optimal transformation-variant value, θ'_k (k=1,.., M), between fingerprints F_k and G, and compare θ'_k with θ_k. We ran this procedure M (M=15) times clockwise and anti-clockwise respectively. The experimental results clockwise are almost equal to those anticlockwise (Table1).

5 Conclusion

We propose a novel method for parameters estimation of a geometric transformation and fingerprint identification by means of grouping and statistical inference in relative histogram grouping models borrowed from the law of large number. At the very beginning, an image is divided into many local partial objects, such as triangular feature structures, each of which is represented by groups of transformation-invariant and transformation-variant (e.g., translation, rotation, and shearing) and whose deformations are considered to be linear. Rather than employing triangular feature structures as many researchers do, we construct minutiae-simplexes to represent partial objects in a fingerprint. Minutia-simplexes are more easily combined with their local texture information, contain enough local transformation-invariants and variants to analyze the relationship between global transformation-invariants and variants, and help alleviate workload and reduce memory cost as well. Then, a relative histogram grouping model describes the relationship between transformation-invariant and variant. Even if the image is transformed at random, partial objects still maintain their linear representation, from which the relative histogram techniques extract grouping centres that account for transformation-variations in partial objects. Barycentre of a confident interval of transformation-variant under a given confidence denotes the optimal transformation-variant, by which to align each partial object. The alignment verifies the local matching results of partial objects. Experimental results illustrate that our technique is efficient in alignment is of little memory cost.

Our method is based on the assumption that input fingerprint and template fingerprint are captured with the same sensor. However, if matching between two different modal fingerprints [14,15], transformation-invariants and variants of partial objects (minutiae-simplexes in this paper) become invalid. Therefore, we have to redefine them and should use other novel relationship between minutiae further to present the uniqueness of the fingerprint, which are challenging and should be realized in our future work. In addition, our method will fail for low-quality fingerprints, which is our further work. We are doing aforementioned works.

References

1. Jain, A.K., Lin, H., Pankanti, S. and Bolle, R.: An Identity Authentication System using Fingerprints. Proceedings of the IEEE, Vol. 85, No. 9 (1997), pp.1365-1388.
2. Jain, A. K. et al.: BIOMETRICS Personal Identification in Networked Society. Kluwer Academic Publishers (1999).
3. Jiang, X. and Yau, W.Y.: Fingerprint minutiae matching based on the local and Global Structures. Proceedings of the 15th international conference on Pattern Recognition (ICPR 2000) , Vol.2, pp.1042-1045.
4. Luo, X. and Tian J.: A Minutia Matching algorithm in Fingerprint Verification. Proceedings of the 15th International Conference on Pattern Recognition (ICPR2000), Vol.4, pp.833-836.
5. Jain A.K, Ross, A. and Prabhakar, S.: Fingerprint matching using minutiae and texture features. Proceedings of the fourth International Conference on Image Processing (ICIP2001), pp.282-285.
6. Gold, S. and Rangarajan, A.: A Graduated Assignment Algorithm for Graph Matching. IEEE Transactions on Pattern Analysis and Machine Intelligence, Vol. 18, No. 4 (1996) , pp. 377-388.
7. Hrechak, A.K. and McHugh, J.A.: Automated fingerprint recognition using structural matching", Pattern Recognition, Vol. 23 (1990), pp. 893-904.

8. Zsolt Mitlos Kovacs-Vajna: A Fingerprint Verification System Based on Triangular Matching and Dynamic Time Warping. IEEE Transactions on Pattern Analysis and Machine Intelligence, Vol. 22, No. 11 (2000), pp.1266-1276.
9. Maio, D., Maltoni, D., Cappelli, R., Wayman,J.L. and Jain, A.K.: FVC2002: Second Fingerprint Verification Competition. Proceedings of 16th International Conference on Pattern Recognition (ICPR 2002), Vol 3, pp.811-814.
10. Maio, D., Maltoni, D., Cappelli, R., Wayman,J.L. and Jain, A.K.: FVC2000: Fingerprint Verification Competition. IEEE Transactions On Pattern Analysis and Machine Intelligence, Vol.24, No.3 (2002), pp.402-412.
11. Watson, C. I. and Wilson, C. L.: NIST Special Database 4, Fingerprint Database. US National Institute of Standards or Technology (1992).
12. Watson, C. I.: NIST Special Database 14, Fingerprint Database. US National Institute of Standards or Technology (1992).
13. Watson, C. I.: NIST Special Standard Reference Database 24, NIST Digital Video of Live-Scan Fingerprint Database. US National Institute of Standards or Technology (1998).
14. He, Y., Tian, J., Ren, Q. and Yang, X.: Maximum-Likelihood Deformation Analysis of Different-Sized Fingerprints. Proceedings of the 4th International Conference on Audio and Video-based Biometric Person Authentication (AVBPA2003), pp.421-428.
15. Tico, M. and Kuosmanen, P.: Fingerprint matching using an orientation-based minutia descriptor. IEEE Transactions on Pattern Analysis and Machine Intelligence, Vol.25, No. 8 (2003), pp.1009 -1014.

A Study of Minutiae Matching Algorithm Based on Orientation Validation

Zhongchao Shi, Jin Qi, Xuying Zhao, and Yangsheng Wang

Institute of Automation, Chinese Academy of Sciences,
100080, Bei Jing, China,
{zcshi,jqi, xyzhao, wys}@mail.pattek.com.cn

Abstract. In this paper, we promote a new fingerprint minutia matching algorithm based on orientation validation. Firstly, we use 1 Nearest Neighbor of the minutiae local structure to find some corresponding point pairs and get the best one by clustering. Secondly, A structure matching algorithm is used to match the global minutiae, and a matching table is used to avoid multi-minutiae match to one minutia and vice versa. Moreover, we promote a new decision method based on orientation validation, and a new rule is proposed to make the final judgment. Finally, the experimental results conducted in DB3, from FVC2002, show that the performance of our algorithm is good.

1 Introduction

Fingerprint-based identification has been used for a very long time owning to their uniqueness and immutability. Today, fingerprints are the most widely used biometrics features in automatic verification and identification systems [1, 2].

The key issue of the fingerprint recognition is the matching algorithm. There already exist a lot of matching algorithms [1, 3-5, 7, 9]. In [3], Xudong Jiang has proposed a matching algorithm which based on local and global structure, where he first used local structure to find the corresponding points to align the feature vector, and then match the global feature vector. This method has some advantages in processing speed and robustness to rotation. However, the algorithm needs to extract the minutiae type and ridge line count between each minutiae and its k-nearest neighborhood exactly, therefore the performance of his algorithm will be greatly affected by noise. In [1], Jain has proposed an alignment-based elastic algorithm in which the ridge linking to the minutiae is used to alignment the feature vector. Luo in [4] improves Jain's algorithm by introducing a elastic bounding box. In [7], Z. Chen et al. have proposed a topology-based matching algorithm of fingerprint authentication. In their algorithm, they construct a structure for minutiae in a pre-specified neighborhood, then they use tree matching algorithm to match two fingerprint templates. This algorithm is invariant to translation and rotation, but is greatly affected by noise. Andrew K. Hrechak has presented a structural matching algorithm [9] which just uses the local structure.

There are also some other fingerprint matching algorithms based on minutiae [6, 8, 10]. But all of them just use the minutiae features, which ignore that the fingerprint has abundant texture information. So Jain et al., propose several algorithms combining minutiae and texture in [11-13]. But these algorithms need a set of 8 *Gabor filters* to extract texture features, which is time-consuming.

Therefore, in this paper, we propose a new matching algorithm which uses minutiae to get matching score and validates the score using orientation information. The paper is organized as follows: First, we use 1 Nearest Neighbor of the minutiae local structure to find some corresponding point pairs and get the best one by clustering in Section 2. Then global matching method is presented in Section 3, and in Section 4, orientation based matching validation is analyzed. The experimental results, presented in Section 5, show the performance of our algorithm on the public domain collection of fingerprint images, DB3 from FVC2002. At last, Conclusions are presented in Section 6.

2 Corresponding Minutiae Identification

When an expert recognizes fingerprints, usually, he first finds the correspondence of two features, and then compares the two fingerprints based on the correspondence. We usually let the computer do as the human expert does. That is, firstly we use the local structure of the fingerprint to find some corresponding point pairs, and then the two global feature vectors are matched using the corresponding point pairs.

2.1 Selection of Corresponding Minutiae

Researchers incline to select the corresponding minutiae by using the topology information of the minutiae directly, such as k-Nearest Neighbor (k-NN) [14], MAG [5], the lines between arbitrary minutiae, core-based K-NN, and other methods. In order to make the algorithm efficient, we use 1-NN in our algorithm. The selecting method is described as follows:

Suppose the transformation between two fingerprints is rigid, the transformation parameters can be denoted as: $G(t_x, t_y, \theta, s)$, where $(t_x, t_y)^T$ is the translation vector, θ is rotation angle and s is scaling parameter. Because the images we used are captured by the same sensor, the scaling parameter s can be omitted, and the new transformation can be denoted as: $G(t_x, t_y, \theta, 0)$. The translation and rotation parameters can be obtained by two methods. One is based on Hough transformation [1], and another is to eliminate the unknown quantities in the transformation formula. In [15], Chang et al. have proved that if 1-NN is adopted to construct the feature vector, the transformation formula $G(0,0,0,0)$ can be obtained, which means a precise matching.

In order to implement the selection of corresponding minutiae, we adopt the 1-NN method and compute the following features using Formula 1, which are shown in Fig.1:

$$D_{AB} = Dist(A, B)$$
$$Rc_{AB} = RidgeCount(A, B)$$
$$\alpha_1 = O_A - angle(A, B)$$ (1)
$$\alpha_2 = O_B - angle(A, B)$$
$$T_A, T_B$$

where $Dist()$ is the distance between minutiae A and B; $RidgeCount()$ is the number of lines between two minutiae; $angle()$ is the angle between the line and horizontal orientation; O_A, O_B are the orientations of the two minutiae; T_A, T_B are the types of two minutiae.

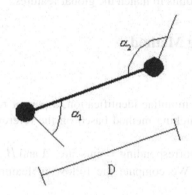

Fig. 1. Sketch map of selection of corresponding minutiae

We construct the local feature vector as: $\{D_{AB}, Rc_{AB}, \alpha_1, \alpha_2, T_A, T_B\}$. If there is no elastic deformation, the local features are invariable to translation and rotation. Otherwise, we can consider that the two nearest minutiae have the same deformation. So these features are also considered to be invariable to translation and rotation.

Now, we can compare the local feature vectors of two images and find the corresponding point pairs lower than a threshold. If a pair is corresponded to many pairs, the closest pair is selected as the corresponding pair.

2.2 Clustering of Corresponding Minutiae

After the above steps, we get some corresponding minutiae. In order to utilize these minutiae to match the fingerprint reliably and obtain high performance, we need to find the most possible corresponding pairs as the reference minutiae by use of the clustering algorithm.

The clustering algorithm adopted here is very simple and can be described as follows:

Let $\{i_1, i_2, \cdots, i_n\}$ and $\{j_1, j_2, \cdots, j_n\}$ represent the corresponding minutiae sets obtained by the above method. Every corresponding point is corresponded to a affine matrix denoted as $\{(R_1, b_1), (R_2, b_2), \cdots (R_n, b_n)\}$. All of the corresponding pairs are transformed according to the mth pair, whose affine matrix is R_m and b_m using the Formula 2.

$$|i_k - (R_m j_k + b_m)| < d .$$ (2)

where $|\ |$ is the norm distance between the two points, if the corresponding minutiae meet the affine transform, add 1 to the confidence of mth pair.

We iterate above processing for every corresponding pair, and can get different confidence for each corresponding pair. Several most believable pairs are chosen as the true corresponding points to match the global features.

3 Global Matching Method

3.1 Global Matching

After the corresponding minutiae identification, a pair of reliable reference points is obtained. The global matching method based on the reference points is described as follows:

Suppose the initial corresponding points are A and B, and the minutiae to be matched are C and D. We compute the following features, which are marked in Fig. 2:

1. The angle α_1 between line AC and horizontal direction;

2. The angle α_2 between line BC and the orientation of minutia C;

3. The angle α_3 between line AC and the orientation of minutia A;

4. The angle α_4 between line BC and the orientation of minutia B;

5. The angle α_5 between line AC and the line BC;

6. The length d_1 of line AC;

7. The length d_2 of line BC.

A feature vector $\lambda = \{\alpha_1, \alpha_2, \alpha_3, \alpha_4, \alpha_5, d_1, d_2\}$ is constructed using the above features. For every minutia, we first compute the feature vector corresponded to the reference point, and then compare the vectors of two images using weighted distance Formula 3:

$$D = W^T * (\lambda_1 - \lambda_2) .$$ (3)

where, $W = \{w_{\alpha 1}, w_{\alpha 2}, w_{\alpha 3}, w_{\alpha 4}, w_{\alpha 5}, w_{d1}, w_{d2}\}$, which is selected based on the experimental data and experience. If $|D| < T$, the two minutiae are considered matched.

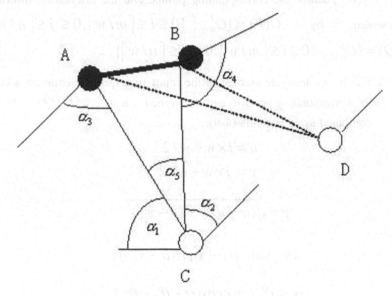

Fig. 2. Sketch map of global matching

In order to eliminate multi-minutiae match to one minutia and vice versa, we establish a matching table to register the matching cost of each minutia and avoid them by processing the table.

3.2 Amendment of Matching Result

We have obtained first matching pairs by the global matching. But influenced by the elastic deformation, some minutiae may be dropped and may mismatch the two images. So it is necessary to amend the matching result by the following method:

For each minutia not matched in first matching, we first find a nearest matched minutia in this image, and then search near the corresponding point in another image to see if there is a matched point for it using the method proposed in Sect. 3. We use this method to process all the minutiae not matched in first matching to decrease the influence on matching of the variant elastic deformation.

4 Orientation-Based Matching Validation

We have found that only use the matched minutiae to judge whether the two images matched is instable, so an orientation-based validation method is proposed to confirm the matching result. The orientation information used here has been computed in preprocessing using the algorithm presented in [16], therefore, the computational expense is not increased. The validation method can be described as follow:

Suppose T, Q as the template fingerprint and input fingerprint. Let $(x_{r1}^T, y_{r1}^T, \theta_{r1}^T)$, $(x_{r2}^Q, y_{r2}^Q, \theta_{r2}^Q)$ denote the corresponding points, and the orientation information is represented by $O(T) = \{O_{W(i,j)}^T \mid 0 \leq i \leq \lceil m/w \rceil, 0 \leq j \leq \lceil n/w \rceil\}$, $O(Q) = \{O_{W(i,j)}^Q \mid 0 \leq i \leq \lceil m/w \rceil, 0 \leq j \leq \lceil n/w \rceil\}$.

1. Firstly, we translate and rotate the input fingerprint orientation according to the corresponding point to get the aligned orientation $O^A(Q)$, which can be computed using Formula (4-9).

$$u = i \times w + w/2$$
$$v = j \times w + w/2 \quad . \tag{4}$$

$$\gamma = \sqrt{(u - x_{r1}^T)^2 + (v - y_{r1}^T)^2} . \tag{5}$$

$$\alpha = \tan^{-1}((v - y_{r1}^T)/(u - x_{r1}^T)) . \tag{6}$$

$$x = x_{r2}^Q + \gamma \times \cos(\alpha - \theta_{r1}^T + \theta_{r2}^Q) . \tag{7}$$

$$y = y_{r2}^Q + \gamma \times \sin(\alpha - \theta_{r1}^T + \theta_{r2}^Q) . \tag{8}$$

$$O_{W(i,j)}^A(Q) = \begin{cases} O_{W(x,y)}^Q & 0 \leq x \leq m, \ 0 \leq y \leq n \\ -1 & \text{else} \end{cases} \tag{9}$$

2. Then, the similarity S_{ori} between two orientation features in the overlapped region can be evaluated by formula Formula 10.

$$S_{ori} = \frac{\sum_{i,j} |O_{W(i,j)}(T) - O_{W(i,j)}^A(Q)|}{N_{OverB}} . \tag{10}$$

where, N_{OverB} is the number of the overlapped blocks.

When the matching is true, the S_{ori} is very small, or else, the S_{ori} is big.

4.1 Rule of Judgement

In order to design the rule, we first research the distributions of FMR and FNMR, which are shown in Fig. 3 and Fig.4. From the figures, we can see that the mismatch usually occur in interval [0.1, 0.4], while there is few mismatch out of the interval. So in order to improve the system efficiency, the orientation based validation should be focused on the match on this interval.

The final judgment rule can be described as:

1. When the matching score located at [0, 0.1], the match is false;
2. When the matching score located at [0.4, 1], the match is true;
3. When the matching score located at [0.1, 0.4], we compute the orientation similarity S_{ori}. If S_{ori} lower than a threshold, the match is true, otherwise, the match is false.

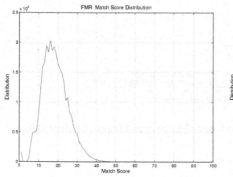

Fig. 3. Distribution of FMR   **Fig. 4.** Distribution of FNMR

5 Experimental Results and Analysis

To validate our algorithm, we choose the public domain collection of fingerprint images, DB3, from FVC2002. It comprises 800 fingerprint images of size 300×300 pixels captured at a resolution of 500 dpi, from 100 fingers (eight impressions per finger).

Each fingerprint in the set is matched with the other fingerprints in the set. So a total of (800×799)/2 matches have been performed. A Receiver Operating Characteristic (ROC) curve is used to show the match results in Fig. 5. In this figure, the dash-dot curve indicates the performance of the minutiae-based algorithm, while the solid curve indicates the performance after orientation validation. From this figure we can see that the performance is improved by the proposed algorithm. Moreover, the average processing time is 0.03 second on a PC PIII 550, so the algorithm is efficient.

6 Summary and Conclusions

In this paper, we present a new fingerprint matching algorithm which uses the orientation information to validate the match results. Firstly, we use 1-NN method and clustering to find the corresponding pairs. Then a global matching algorithm is proposed to compute the match score. Furthermore, orientation validation as well as a new judgment rule is proposed to process the match score. Finally, the experimental results show that the performance of the system is improved and the matching algorithm is very efficient.

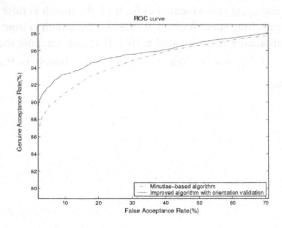

Fig. 5. ROC curves for minutiae-based algorithm and improved algorithm

References

1. Anil Jain, Lin Hong, and Ruud Boole: On-Line Fingerprint Verification. IEEE Trans. PAMI. Vol. 19(4) (1997) 302-314
2. Anil K. Jain, R. M. Bolle, S. Pankanti: Biometrics: Personal Identification in a Network Society. Kluwer Academic Publishers (1999)
3. Xudong Jiang: Fingerprint Verification Method Based on Local and Global Structure. Porceeding of 15th ICPR. (2000) 30-35
4. X.P. Luo, J. Tian, and Y. Wu: A Minutia Matching Algorithm in Fingerprint Verification. International Conference on Pattern recognition. Vol.4 (2000)
5. Nalini K. Ratha, Ruud M.Bolle, Vinayaka D.Pandit, and Vaibhav Vaish: Robust Fingerprint Authentication using Local Structural Similarity. Fifth IEEE Workshop on Applications of Computer Vision. (2000) 29-34
6. Zsolt Miklos Kovacs-Vajna: A Fingerprint Verification System Based on Triangular Matching and Dynamic Time Warping. IEEE Transactions on Pattern Analysis and Machine Intelligence. Vol.22(11) (2000)
7. Z.chen, CH. Kou: A Toplogy-Based Matching Algorithm for Fingerprint Authentication. Proc. of 25th Annual IEEE International Carnahan Conference on Security Technology. (1991) 84-87
8. D.K.Isenor, S.G.Zaky: Fingerprint Identification Using Graph Matching. Pattern Recognition. Vol.19(2) (1986)
9. Andrew K. Hrechak, James A.Mchugh: Automated Fingerprint Recognition Using Structural Matching. Pattern Recognition.Vol.23(8) (1990) 839-904
10. Andres Almansa, Laurent Cohen: Fingerprint Image Matching by Minimization of a Thinplate Energy Using a Two Step Algorithm With Auxiliay Variables. Proc. Fifth IEEE Workshop on Applications of Computer Vision. (2000) 35-40

11. A.K. Jain, Arun Ross, and Salil Prabhakar: Figerprint Matching using Minutiae and Texture Features. Proc. International Conference on Image Processing(ICIP). (2001)282-285
12. Anil K. Jain, Salil Prabhakar, Lin Hong, and Sharat Pankanti: Filterbank-based fingerprint matching. IEEE Transactions on Image Processing. Vol.9(5) (2000) 846-859
13. A. Ross, A.K. Jain. and J. Reisman: A Hybrid Fingerprint Matcher. Pattern Recognition. Vol. 36(7) (2003) 1661-1673
14. A. Wahab: Novel Approach to Automated fingerprint Recognition. IEE Proc.-Visual Image Signal Process. Vol. 145(3) (1998) 160-166
15. Shih-Hsu Chang, Fang-Hsuan Cheng: Fast Algorithm for Point Pattern Matching: Invariant to Translations, Rotations and Scale Changes. Pattern Recognition. Vol. 30(2) (1997) 311-320
16. Zhongchao Shi, Ke Xu and Yangsheng Wang: A New Fingerprint Image Segmentation Algorithm Based on ROI. Accepted by EGMM. (2004)

Cascading a Couple of Registration Methods for a High Accurate Fingerprint Verification System

Jin Qi, Zhongchao Shi, Xuying Zhao, and Yangsheng Wang

Institute of Automation, Chinese Academy of Sciences,
95 Zhongguancun Road East,
Beijing, 100080, P.R.C.
jqi@mail.pattek.com.cn, jqi7@yahoo.com.cn

Abstract. As far as we know, although various approaches of combining multiple fingerprint matchers have been proposed in the literature, no previous attempts to combine multiple fingerprint registration algorithms have been tried. In this paper, we have presented a novel registration algorithm by cascading a couple of different registration techniques to improve the accuracy of fingerprint matching system. A series of experiments conducted on the public data collection, FVC2002 DB3 set A (800 fingerprints), demonstrates the effectiveness of our method.

1 Introduction

Among all the biometric indicators [1], fingerprints have one of the highest levels of reliability [2] and have been extensively used by forensic experts in criminal investigations [3]. The accuracy of a fingerprint verification system is critical in a wide variety of forensic, civilian, and commercial applications such as criminal investigation, issuing driver's license, welfare disbursement, credit cards and cellular phone usage, and access control. Generally, a complete fingerprint recognition system consists of two components: feature extraction and matching. Fingerprint matching component has a critical impact on the accuracy of fingerprint recognition system. Hence, Many researchers focus their attentions on the development of fingerprint matching methods. These include methods based on optical correlation [4, 5], transform features [6, 7, 8], graph matching [9], structural matching [10, 11], and point pattern matching [12, 13, 14]. In alignment-based fingerprint matching techniques [15, 16], the accuracy of recognition systems relies heavily on the accuracy of registration methods. Different alignment algorithms use different information on fingerprints to reach their aims. Hence, Different registration algorithms have different advantages and disadvantages. A specific aligning algorithm can work well under some special circumstances. Such case can also be met in comparing the performance of different fingerprint classifiers which use different fingerprint information [17]. Inspired by the idea of combining multiple fingerprint classifiers for improving the accuracy of fingerprint verification systems [17, 18, 19, 20, 21], we propose a novel registration algorithm by cascading a couple of fingerprint registration methods proposed by Jiang [15] and Tico [16].

S.Z. Li et al. (Eds.): Sinobiometrics 2004, LNCS 3338, pp. 490–497, 2004.

As far as we known, no previous work on this aspect has been done. In [16], an orientation-based minutiae descriptor (OMD) is used to register two fingerprint images, which makes use of orientation fields estimated from fingerprint impressions. Because orientation fields capture the global appearance of fingerprints, the algorithm based on OMD makes the appearances of two fingerprints similar as soon as possible. But it has the weak power of discriminating the minutiae close to each other [16]. On the other hand, in [15], a minutia local structure (MLS) based registration algorithm is utilized to align two fingerprint images. Because the MLS captures the local information around each minutia, the algorithm based on MLS makes the local appearance around the reference minutiae similar as soon as possible. The advantage of the MLS based registration algorithm is capable of distinguishing several close minutiae. But it has the weak power of registering two fingerprint images in the global appearance sense. Therefore, we can see that the two registration algorithms are complemental mutually. The work of cascading the two alignment algorithms is natural, reasonable and can improve the accuracy of fingerprint recognition accuracy. The experimental results in the following also demonstrate this point. The rest of the paper is organized as follows: Section 2 gives a brief description of the two different fingerprint registration algorithms used in our case study. Section 3 presents the cascading strategy. The complete matching process is given in Section 4. The experimental results are reported in Section 5. Finally, Section 6 concludes the paper.

2   Fingerprint Registration Methods

In general, the registration algorithm often takes advantage of fingerprint minutiae and orientation fields. The features (minutiae) are extracted from a fingerprint image using a minutiae extraction algorithm [12]. The orientation fields are estimated from a fingerprint impression using the estimation algorithm in [12]. A brief description of the two registration approaches used in our cascading scenario is given below.

2.1   MLS-Based Fingerprint Registration Algorithm

Here we simply introduce the MLS-based registration algorithm proposed by Jiang [15]. The minutia local structure (MLS) is defined as the 2-nearest neighborhood of each minutia, as illustrated in Fig. 1. A feature vector for each minutia can be derived from its local structure and a similarity level can be defined between feature vectors. The main steps of the registration algorithm are: (1) define the 2-nearest neighborhood, i.e. MLS, for each minutia; (2) derive the feature vector from each MLS; (3) define a similarity level between the feature vectors from Step 2; (4) find the reference minutia pair which maximizes the value of the similarity function defined in Step 3; (5) estimate the transformation parameters of the rigid transform between the two images using the reference pair from Step 4; (5) align the two minutia sets using the estimated parameters from Step 4. Details of the algorithm can be found in [15].

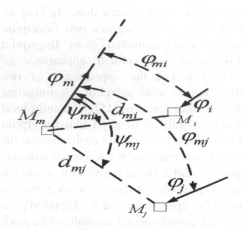
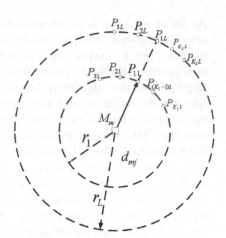

Fig. 1. A minutia local structure of
2-nearest neighborhood

Fig. 2. Sampling points organized in a
circular pattern around a minutia detail

2.2 OMD-Based Fingerprint Registration Algorithm

Different from the commonly used fingerprint minutia registration algorithms [10, 11, 15] which use a group of neighboring minutiae to define a local structure, the registration algorithm [16] using the orientation-based minutia descriptor (OMD) integrates the orientation field estimated from the fingerprint image with the minutiae and captures global appearance information of the fingerprint. The OMD consists of one central minutia and some sampling points around the central minutia in the fingerprint image, as shown in Fig. 2. This registration algorithm [16] is summarized as follows: (1) Define a OMD for each minutia extracted from the fingerprint image. (2) Derive a feature vector for each minutia from its OMD. (3) Define a similarity function between minutiae. (4) Find the reference pair which maximizes the value of the similarity function from Step 3. (5) Estimate the parameters of the rigid transformation between two fingerprint impressions. (6) Align two sets of minutiae with the estimated parameters. More information on this alignment algorithm can be available in [16].

3   Cascading Strategy

In this section, we are elaborating two problems: why the two registration algorithms are selected and how to cascade both of them.

3.1 Registration Algorithm Selection

There exists many registration algorithms proposed in the literature [5, 10, 11, 12, 13, 14, 15, 16]. It is necessary to analyze which registration algorithms are suitable for being cascaded. Different from those methods combing multiple fingerprint classifiers at decision level [17, 18, 19, 20, 21], our method in this paper combines different registration algorithms at representational level, i.e. minutiae level. Hence, the registration algorithms used in the cascading process are selected according to the following criteria: (1) output of one algorithm can be the input of another algorithm due to the cascading operation; (2) each of selected registration algorithms should use different kinds of fingerprint information. Especially, the complemental information is more preferred. According to the mentioned-above criteria, we choose the two registration algorithms, MLS-based and OMD-based, proposed by Jiang [6] and Tico [16], respectively. Both of them use fingerprint minutia point sets as their inputs, and their outputs are also minutia point sets aligned with respect to each other. So the two algorithms selected by us satisfy the Criterion 1. In addition, the MLS-based algorithm uses a group of neighboring minutiae which characterizes the local ridge structure in the neighborhood of each minutia. Contrast with the MLS-based algorithm, the OMD-based registration algorithm employs the orientation information in a broad region of each minutia which characterizes the global texture-oriented pattern in the fingerprint image. In the intuitive interpretation of the case, the OMD-based algorithm aligns two fingerprint images in the global pattern sense and the MLS-based algorithm registers two fingerprint impressions in the local fine pattern sense. Cascading the two registration algorithms means that two fingerprint images are first registered in a coarse level and then registered in a fine level. Therefore, the cascading operation simulates the behavior of fingerprint expert to register two fingerprint images. It is obvious that the two algorithms selected by us meet with the Criterion 2 and that the cascading operation can improve the accuracy of registering algorithm. The new alignment technique formed by the cascading operation owns the advantages of the two algorithms cascaded and overcomes the difficulties encountered by the two algorithms.

3.2 Cascading Strategy

In our cascading process, the output of the OMD-based algorithm is used as the input of the MLS-based registration algorithm. Because the interdependency of minutiae is used in the MLS-based method [15], the true corresponding points may be lost when using the similarity level defined in [15] to identify the corresponding minutia pairs. On the other hand, the OMD-based registration algorithm is independent from the relationship among minutiae [16], so the most majority of true corresponding minutiae points can be identified by the OMD-based algorithm even if under the presence of many spurious minutiae and absence of many genuine minutiae. Hence we first use the OMD-based registration algorithm to identify some corresponding minutia points which are ordered decreasingly according to the value of the similarity function defined in [16]. Then we select the top ten pairs of minutia points as the input of the MLS-based registration algorithm. The corresponding minutia pairs identified by the MLS-based algorithm are ordered decreasingly according to their similarity levels. Finally, The top first pair of minutiae is used as the reference point pair which is employed to estimate the parameters of the rigid transform between two fingerprint impressions [15]. The cascading algorithm is given below:

Cascading Strategy

1. Enter two lists of minutia points into the OMD-based registration algorithm and identify some corresponding minutia pairs

2. Order the corresponding minutia pairs decreasingly according to their similarity values

3. Select the top ten pairs of minutiae as the inputs of the MLS-based registration algorithm and identify the corresponding minutia pairs
4. Order the corresponding minutia pairs obtained decreasingly according to their similarity values
5. Select the top first pair as the reference pair and estimate the transformation parameters
6. Register the two fingerprint images using the estimated transformation

4   Fingerprint Matching

The complete process of fingerprint matching is composed of two stages, registration stag and matching stag. In registration stage, two fingerprint images are aligned using the estimated rigid transformation with respect to each other. After registration, mated minutiae can be counted. Unfortunately, the minutiae from the template fingerprint will not overlap exactly over their corresponding counterparts from the input fingerprint due to the presence of local nonlinear deformations and the errors induced by the minutiae extraction algorithm. Consequently, fingerprint matching algorithm must be elastic. The elastic matching algorithm uses geometric constraints and the similarity level of the minutiae pair. The details of the tolerant-distortion matching algorithm are available in [16].

5   Experimental Results

The experiments reported in this paper have been conducted on the public domain collection of fingerprint images, FVC2002 DB3 set A, which comprises 800 fingerprint images captured at a resolution of 500 dpi, from 100 fingers (eight impressions per finger). In Fig. 3, a few of pictures are given to illustrate the process of registration using our cascading algorithm. The leftmost two images in the first row of Fig. 3 are the original impressions of the same finger and the two minutia sets extracted from them are shown as the rightmost two images in the first row of Fig. 3. The leftmost two images in the second row of Fig. 3 show the top ten minutia pairs identified by the OMD-base algorithm. It should be noted that the one to many map or many to one map is allowed. Hence, there are only nine minutiae in the leftmost second image in the second row of Fig. 3. We also note that many minutiae without their corresponding counterparts in the two minutiae patterns have been discarded. The final reference point pair is marked by two blue circular regions in the middle image and the rightmost second image in the second row of Fig. 3. The registration result is shown in the rightmost image in the second row of Fig. 3. From the Fig. 3 we know that our registration algorithm is effective. A set of experiments has been conducted in order to compare our registration approach with the OMD-based and MLS-base registration algorithms in [15, 16]. Using the same minutiae pairing and matching score computation algorithms described in Section 4, the matching results obtained by the three algorithm (our algorithm, OMD algorithm and MLS algorithm)

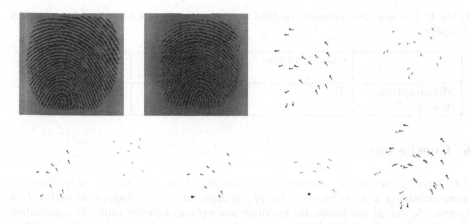

Fig. 3. Process of registration: leftmost two images in the top row: original images; rightmost two images in the top row: minutiae patterns: leftmost two images in the bottom row: ten pairs of corresponding minutiae identified by MLS algorithm; the middle image and the rightmost second image in the bottom row: reference point pair marked as blue circular patterns; rightmost image: result of registration

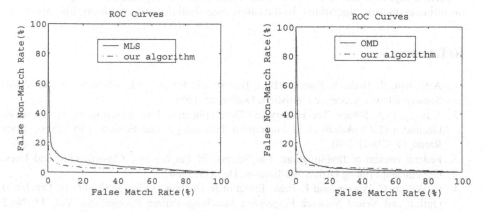

Fig. 4. ROC-curves obtained with our algorithm, MLSbased algorithm and OMD-based algorithm

are shown in Fig. 4, in terms of ROC curves. The comparison results of our algorithm and the MLS-based algorithm are shown in the top row image of Fig. 4. The bottom image of Fig. 4 shows the comparison results of our algorithm and the OMD-based algorithm. Table 1 presents the average execution time for a matching on a Pentium IV, 1.8 GHz. From the table we can see that our algorithm takes nearly the same amount of time as the OMD algorithm. This is because that the number of minutiae processed by the MLS registration algorithm is small (ten here) and the processing time is nearly negligible. We note that our algorithm outperforms the OMD algorithm and MLS algorithm.

Table 1. Matching time estimated on DB3 using our algorithm, OMD algorithm and MLS algorithm

	Our Algorithm	OMD Algorithm	MLS Algorithm
Matching time (msec)	23	22	15

6 Conclusions

We have presented a scheme for cascading two registration algorithms at representational level to improve the recognition rate of the fingerprint verification system. As far as we know, no previous attempts to cascade multiple registration algorithms have been tried. In this paper, we have proposed the strategy for cascading a couple of registration algorithms [15, 16]. The composite registration algorithm obtained by our cascading operation owns the advantages of both cascaded algorithms and overcomes the difficulties encountered in each of the two algorithms individually. Experimental results have shown the effectiveness of our proposed method in this paper. The idea of cascading operation can be applied to cascading other algorithms to form a higher accurate composite algorithm, such as segmentation algorithms and minutiae extraction algorithms. In the future, we shall do more work on this aspect.

References

1. A.K. Jain, R. Bolle, S. Pankanti(Ed.): Biometrics: Personal Identification in Networked Society. Kluwer Academic Publishers, Dordrecht, 1999
2. J. Berry, D.A. Stoney: The History and Development of Fingerprinting. in: H.C. Lee, R. Gaensslen (Ed.): Advances in Fingerprint Technology. 2nd Edition, CRC Press, Boca Raton, FL (2001) 1-40
3. Federal Bureau of Investigation: The Science of Fingerprints: Classification and Uses. Government Printing Office, Washington, DC, US, 1984
4. C. Wilson, C. Watson, and E. Paek: Effect of Resolution and Image Quality on Combined Optical and Neural Network Fingerprint Matching. Pattern Recognition, Vol. 33, No.2 (2000) 317-331
5. F. Gamble, L. Frye, and D. Grieser: Real-Time Fingerprint Verification System. *Applied Optics,* Vol. 31, No. 5 (1992) 652-655
6. A.K. Jain, S. Prabhakar, L. Hong, and S. Pankanti: Filterbank-Based Fingerprint Matching. IEEE Trans. Image Processing, Vol. 9, No. 5 (2000)846-859
7. C.J. Lee and S.D.Wang: Fingerprint Feature Extraction Using Gabor Filters. Electronics Letters, Vol. 35, No. 4 (1999) 288-290
8. M. Tico, P. Kuosmanen, and J. Saarinen: Wavelet Domain Features for Fingerprint Recognition. *Electronics Letters,* Vol. 37, No. 1 (2002) 21-22
9. D.K. Isenor and S.G. Zaky: Fingerprint Identification Using Graph Matching. Pattern Recognition, Vol. 19, No. 2 (1986) 113-122
10. A.K. Hrechak and J.A. McHugh: Automatic Fingerprint Recognition Using Structural Matching. *Pattern Recognition,* Vol. 23, No. 8 (1990) 893-904

11. A. Wahabk, S.H. Chin, and E.C. Tan: Novel Approach to Automated Fingerprint Recognition. IEE Proc. Visual Image Signal Processing, Vol. 145, No. 3 (1998) 160-166
12. A.K. Jain, L. Hong, S. Pankanti, and R. Bolie: An Identity- Authentication System Using Fingerprints. Proc. IEEE, Vol. 85, No. 9 (1997) 1365-1388
13. N.K. Ratha, K. Karu, S. Chen, and A.K. Jain: A Realtime Matching System for Large Fingerprint Databases. IEEE Trans. Pattern Analysis and Machine Intelligence, Vol. 18, No. 8 (1996) 799-813
14. A.K. Jain, L. Hong, and R. Bolle: On-Line Fingerprint Verification. IEEE Trans. Pattern Analysis and Machine Intelligence, Vol. 19, No. 4 (1997) 302-313
15. X. Jiang and W-Y. Yau: Fingerprint Minutiae Matching Based on the Local and Global Structures. Proc. 15th Int'l Conf. Pattern Recognition, Vol. 2 (2000) 1038-1041
16. M. Tico and P. Kuosmanen: Fingerprint Matching Using an Orientation-Based Minutia Descriptor. IEEE Trans. Pattern Analysis and Machine Intelligence, Vol. 25, No. 8 (2003) 1009- 1014
17. A. Ross, A.K. Jain, J. Reisman: A Hybrid Fingerprint Matcher. Pattern Recognition, Vol. 36 (2003)
18. R. Cappelli, D. Maio, D. Maltoni: Combining Fingerprint Classifiers. First International Workshop on Multiple Classifier Systems (MCS2000), Cagliari (2000) 351-361.
19. A.K. Jain, S. Prabhakar, S. Chen: Combining Multiple Matchers for a High Security Fingerprint Verification System. Pattern Recognition Lett., Vol. 20 (1999) 1371-1379
20. A.K. Jain, S. Prabhakar, L. Hong: A Multichannel Approach to Fingerprint Classification. IEEE Trans. Pattern Anal. Mach. Intell. Vol 21, No. 4 (1999) 348-359
21. S. Prabhakar, A.K. Jain: Decision-Level Fusion in Fingerprint Verification. Vol. 35 (2002) 861-874

A Hierarchical Fingerprint Matching Method
Based on Rotation Invariant Features

Dequn Zhao, Fei Su, and Anni Cai

Beijing University of Posts and Telecommunications,
School of Telecommunication Engineering, Beijing 100876, P.R. China
peacepigeon1225@163.com, {sufei, annicai}@bupt.edu.cn

Abstract. A hierarchical matching algorithm based on rotation invariant features to align two fingerprints is proposed in this paper. The translation and rotational offsets are extracted using the maximum overlapped fingerprint images. The proposed method can reduce the searching space in alignment, and what is more attractive is that it obviates the need for extracting minutiae points or the core point to align the fingerprint images. Experimental results show that the proposed method is more robust than using the reference point or using the minutiae to align the fingerprint images.

1 Introduction

As today's society becomes more complex, the security of information becomes more and more important [1, 2]. Various methods for biometric personal identification have been proposed nowadays. Among all the biometric indicators, fingerprints have one of the highest levels of reliability [3, 4].

A fingerprint is the pattern of ridges and valleys on the surface of the human's finger [5]. The ridge structure in a fingerprint image can be viewed as an oriented texture pattern having a dominant spatial frequency and orientation in a local neighborhood [6]. There are many algorithms in the open literature for texture feature extraction and Fingerprint Matching [6, 7, 8]. These algorithms all apply multi-channel Gabor filtering to a fingerprint image. In [7] and [8], the filtered images are then tessellated into cells, and the grayscale variance within a cell is used to quantify the underlying ridge structure. Matching two fingerprints features requires a suitable alignment of the template and query images. In [7], the core point is used for the alignment, and it uses the minutiae fields of the two fingerprint images for alignment in [8], while it captures optimal translation offsets using correlation at all possible translation offsets for alignment in [6]. However, these techniques have some drawbacks.

1. Detecting the core point is not an easy problem, and it will not work in such case due to the lack of a core point. In poor quality images, the alignment described in [8] may be erroneous [6].
2. The algorithm used in [6] makes an assumption that all fingerprint images are captured under the same orientation, that is to say, it does not account for the rota-

S.Z. Li et al. (Eds.): Sinobiometrics 2004, LNCS 3338, pp. 498–505, 2004.
© Springer-Verlag Berlin Heidelberg 2004

tional offset between the query and the template images. In many practical applications, such an assumption is difficult to realize.

In this paper, a novel hierarchical matching algorithm based on rotation invariant features to align two fingerprints is proposed. The translation and rotational offsets are extracted using the maximum overlapped fingerprint images. The proposed method can reduce the searching space in alignment, and what is more attractive is that it obviates the need for extracting minutiae points or the singular points to align the fingerprint images. The extracted rotation invariant features provided by the global image information can tolerate local nonlinear deformation. Experimental results show that the proposed method is more robust than using the reference point or using the minutiae to align the fingerprint images.

The paper is organized as follows. In section2, details attendant to the rotation invariant features extraction, transformation parameters estimation and the matching algorithm based on rotation invariant features are described. Section 3 gives the experimental results and some discussions are presented in section 4.

2 Fingerprint Hierarchical Matching Method Based on Rotation Invariant Features Preparation

In fingerprint matching, it is necessary to extract the translation and rotational offsets in order to align the query and template fingerprint images. The translation and rotational invariance could be established based on the characteristics of the fingerprint images. As we know, the ridge orientation in a local neighborhood of the fingerprint image has a dominant direction in a fingerprint image. Thus, features associated with the strength of the ridges in a local neighborhood, at various orientations, are used to represent a fingerprint image.

2.1 Printing Area Rotation Invariant Features Extraction

The rotation invariant features used here are similar to those in [9]. A 2DGabor filter can be thought of as a complex plane wave modulated by a 2D Gaussian envelope. By tuning a Gabor filter to a specific frequency and direction, the local frequency and orientation information can be obtained. Thus, they are suited for extracting texture information from images [10]. A pair of real Gabor filters $G_e(x,y;f,\theta)$ and $G_o(x,y;f,\theta)$ has the following general form in the spatial domain:

$$\begin{cases} G_e(x,y;f,\theta)=\exp\left\{\frac{-1}{2}\left[\frac{x'^2}{\delta_x^2}+\frac{y'^2}{\delta_y^2}\right]\right\}\cos(2\pi f x') \\ G_o(x,y;f,\theta)=\exp\left\{\frac{-1}{2}\left[\frac{x'^2}{\delta_x^2}+\frac{y'^2}{\delta_y^2}\right]\right\}\sin(2\pi f x') \\ x'=x\sin\theta+y\cos\theta, y'=x\cos\theta-y\sin\theta \end{cases} \tag{1}$$

where f and θ are the radial frequency and orientation which define the location of the filters in the frequency plane, and δ_x and δ_y are the standard deviation of the Gaussian envelope along the x and y axes, respectively.

The rotation invariant feature $R(f,\theta)$ can be defined as

$$R(f,\theta)=\frac{1}{\Omega}\iint_{\Omega} r(x, y; f,\theta)dxdy \tag{2}$$

where Ω is the area of $r(x, y)$ and $r(x, y; f,\theta)$ is computed as

$$\begin{cases} r(x, y; f,\theta) = \sqrt{r_e^2(x, y; f,\theta) + r_o^2(x, y; f,\theta)} \\ r_e(x, y; f,\theta) = G_e(x, y; f,\theta) * p(x, y) \\ r_o(x, y; f,\theta) = G_o(x, y; f,\theta) * p(x, y) \end{cases} \tag{3}$$

where $p(x, y)$ is the input image, and $*$ denotes 2D linear convolution. The rotation invariant feature $R(f,\theta)$ provides powerful and more noise resistant in the texture classification [11].

The rotation invariant feature $R(f,\theta)$ is described in [9] in terms of rotation invariance. That is, for a fixed radial frequency f, $R(f,\theta)$ or simply $R(\theta)$ is a periodic function of θ with a period of π. It can be expanded into a Fourier series:

$$R(\theta)=\sum a_k e^{j2k\theta}$$
$$a_k=\frac{1}{\pi}\int_{\pi} R(\theta)e^{-j2k\theta}d\theta \tag{4}$$

Since the rotation of the input image $p(x, y)$ corresponds to the translation of $R(\theta)$, and since the Fourier amplitude is invariant to translation, $|a_k|$ (note $|a_k|=|a_{-k}|$) thus provides a set of rotation invariant features for the input texture $p(x, y)$ [9].

In order to extract the rotation invariant features of the input image $p(x, y)$, the parameters $(f,\delta_x,\delta_y,\theta)$ should be set:

1. Based on empirical data [12], both standard deviation values are set to 4, i.e., $\delta_x=\delta_y=4$.
2. M different orientations are examined. These correspond to $\theta_i = i\pi / M, i = 0,1,\cdots M-1$ (M $=8$ in our implementation).
3. The frequency f, is set to correspond to reciprocal of the inter-ridge spacing in fingerprint images. Local ridge spacing is estimated using the projection of the local image along a line segment perpendicular to the orientation vector and passing through the center point of the local area. The maximum distance between consecutive peaks gives the ridge spacing. Unlike in [6]-[8], for consideration of the different pressure, the variant frequency is used in replace of the constant one.

2.2 Hierarchical Matching Based on Rotation Invariant Features

Firstly, the query image is segmented to get rid of the useless background areas, then 8 pairs of the Gabor filters is applied to this processed image, resulting in 8 images r_θ demonstrated in Fig.1 (a). Each r_θ here is used to construct a standard deviation image D_θ (Fig.1(b)), where $D_\theta(x,y)$ is computed as the standard deviation of the pixel intensities in a 16×16 neighborhood of (x, y) in r_θ .

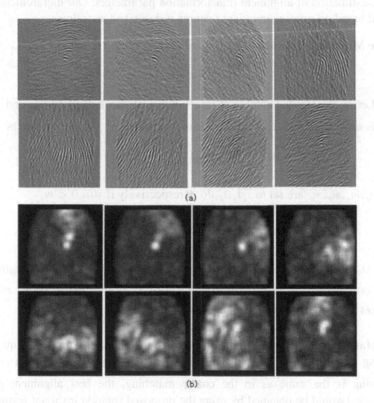

(a)

(b)

Fig. 1. (a) The filtered image by Gabor filter. (b) The standard deviation of the filtered image

It is not difficult to see that a_k in equation (4) corresponds to the number of pixels N_k in D_θ. In practice, the ratio of N_k / N_t is used as the rotation invariance feature to calculate the transformation parameters (t_x, t_y, t_ϕ). Here N_t is the total number of pixels in the foreground of the image. Suppose that $s = \{s_i\}$ and $S = \{S_j\}, i, j = 0,1,\cdots k$ $(k \Rightarrow M)$ are the largest rotation invariant features of the query and the template fingerprint images respectively.

We classify the matching procedure as two layers (coarse matching and fine matching) in order to get the reliable and precise estimation of translation and rotational offsets and reduce the searching space. In the phase of coarse matching, the translation and rotational offsets would be calculated by comparing our defined rotation invariant features in obtained $s = \{s_i\}$ and $S = \{S_j\}, i, j = 0,1, \cdots k$ $(k <= M)$. Let D_θ^Q and D_θ^T denote the standard deviation image of the query and that of the template fingerprint images respectively, and (m_x, m_y, m_ϕ, m_d) denotes the matched set. According to the extracted translation and rotational offsets, in fine matching phase, 10 Gabor filters by smaller angles around the m_ϕ is applied to the processed image to get the precise estimation of alignment transformation parameters. Our hierarchical matching method based on rotation invariant features is described as follows.

Coarse Matching. For each pair of s_i and S_j, t_ϕ is set to $\theta_j - \theta_i$ and D_{θ_i, t_ϕ}^Q is obtained as

$$D_{\theta_i, t_\phi}^Q = Rot_{t_\phi}(D_{\theta_i}^Q) \tag{5}$$

• Let N_o denotes the number of pixels in the overlap area of $D_{\theta_i, t_\phi, t_x', t_y'}^Q$ and $D_{\theta_j}^T \cdot (t_x, t_y)$ is set to (t_x', t_y') if N_o is the maximum one, where $D_{\theta_i, t_\phi, t_x', t_y'}^Q$ is obtained as

$$D_{\theta_i, t_\phi, t_x', t_y'}^Q = Translate_{t_x', t_y'}(D_{\theta_i, t_\phi}^Q) \tag{6}$$

• m_x, m_y, m_ϕ, m_d are set to $t_x, t_y, t_\phi, d(i, j)$ respectively if $d(i, j) < m_d$,

$$d(i, j) = \sum_{n=0}^{M-1} (Q_n - R_n)^2 \tag{7}$$

where Q_n is the nth rotation invariant feature extracted from the obtained image which is transformed from the query image by (t_x, t_y, t_ϕ), and R_n is the nth rotation invariant feature extracted from the template image.

Fine Matching. The set of 10 Gabor filters is applied to the processed query image, resulting in 8 images r_{θ_i}, where θ_i is set to $m_\phi \pm 2\pi i / 180, i = 0,1, \cdots 4$. Then the processing is the same as in the coarse matching, the best alignment parameters (m_x, m_y, m_ϕ) would be obtained by using the proposed rotation invariant feature through calculating the maximum overlapped areas in query image and the template one.

2.3 Fingerprint Matching

Once the important transformation parameters (m_x, m_y, m_ϕ) are obtained, the query image can be aligned with the template image. After the query image is transformed by (m_x, m_y, m_ϕ), the matching algorithm adopted here is similar to the Ross's [7] using ridge feature maps. The Euclidean distance between corresponding nonzero overlapped foreground elements in $\{D_\theta^Q\}$ and $\{D_\theta^T\}$ is computed. This distance is treated as the matching score between the query image and the template image. Based on the matching score, and the pre-specified threshold, the query image is said to have matched successfully or unsuccessfully with the template image.

3 Experimental Results

The Fingerprint database used in our experiments consists of 1080 fingerprint impressions (352×256) obtained from 120 fingers. Nine fingerprint impressions in different orientation and translation obtained from each finger.

The purpose of our experiments is to test the capability of the algorithm to extract the precise transformation parameters (m_x, m_y, m_ϕ). Fig.2 illustrates the matching result based on the proposed rotation invariant features, the calculated (m_x, m_y, m_ϕ) is (-29, -53, $\pi/9$) here. After the query image is transformed by (-29, -53, $\pi/9$), the high fingerprint matching score results in a true matching. The Euclidean distance, d, between s and S is computed as (7). The mean and deviation value of the d obtained from the same finger and those of different fingers are listed in Table 1. As expected, the discriminative power of d is quite high, and the d from the same finger is low and has small mean and deviation value at the same time. We compare the proposed algorithm with a texture fingerprint matching using feature space correlation [6] and our own minutiae-based matching method by plotting the False Acceptance Rate (FAR) and False Reject Rates (FRR) at different thresholds. The Equal Error Rate (EER) is about 9.1% in our experiment. Fig.3 illustrates the ROC Curve of our test. Though the performance of the proposed approach fingerprint is inferior to our minutiae-based matching, it has better performance than the texture fingerprint matching using feature space correlation. Minutiae-based fingerprint matching is a very mature technology while the proposed approach is being developed and refined. It has its own advantages, such as no limitations on the enough number of corresponding points or singular images of the two images. It performs well when the multiple impressions of the same finger have only a small region of overlap areas.

The performance of fingerprint matching is more sensitive to the reliability and precision of the global transformation parameters estimation. The coarse-fine technique based on rotation invariant features gives more reliably and precisely global transformation parameters than the fingerprint alignment method using feature space correlation does.

(a)   (b)   (c)

Fig. 2. (a) and (b) are two different impressions of the same finger. (c) Difference image after alignment

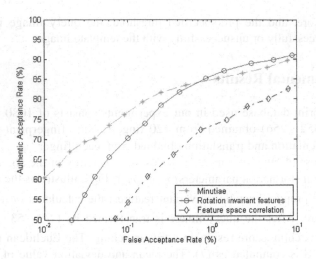

Fig. 3. ROC Curve

Table 1. Mean and Standard Deviation of the d value for the rotation invariant features from the same fingerprint and that from the different fingerprint

Mean (same)	0.12	Mean(different)	0.67
Standard Deviation(same)	0.27	Standard Deviation(different)	0.43

4 Conclusions

A novel hierarchical matching algorithm that makes use of rotation invariant features to align two fingerprints has been presented. The proposed rotation invariant feature provides discriminatory information and results in reliable and precise estimation of global transformation parameters between two fingerprint images. In the alignment phase, coarse matching is adopted firstly to determine the coarse transformation parameters, and then fine matching is applied to get the reliable and precise estimation of global transformation parameters in a greatly reduced searching space, and what is more attractive is that it obviates the need for extracting minutiae points or the core point to align the fingerprint images. The effectiveness of the proposed algorithm has been demonstrated in the fingerprint alignment. Although experiment results have clearly shown the potential of our approach, there are still some problems to be solved. We are working on the fast matching based on the rotation invariant features.

References

1. R. Clarke, Human identification in information system: Management challenges and public policy issues, Info. Technol. People, 7(4):6–37, 1994.

2. S. G. Davies, Touching Big Brother: How biometric technology will fuse flesh and machine, Info. Technol. People, 7(4):60–69, 1994.
3. John Berry and David A. Stoney, "The history and development of fingerprinting," in Advances in fingerprint Technology, Henry C. Lee and R.E. Gaensslen, Eds., pp. 1–40. CRC Press, Florida, 2nd edition, 2001.
4. Emma Newham, "The biometric report," SJB Services, 1995.
5. H. C. Lee and R. E. Gaensslen, Eds., Advances in Fingerprint Technology, New York: Elsevier, 1991.
6. Arun Ross, James Reisman and Anil Jain,Appeared, "Fingerprint Matching Using Feature Space Correlation," Proc. of Post-ECCV Workshop on Biometric Authentication, LNCS 2359, pp.48-57, Denmark, June 1, 2002.
7. A. K. Jain, S. Prabhakar, L. Hong, and S. Pankanti, "Filterbank-based fingerprint matching," IEEE transactions on Image Processing, vol. 9, pp. 846-859, May 2000.
8. A. K. Jain, A. Ross, and S. Prabhakar, "Fingerprint matching using minutiae and texture features,"in Proc. International Conference on Image Processing (ICIP), (Thessaloniki, Greece), pp. 282-285, Oct 2001.
9. T.N. Tan, "Rotation Invariant Texture Features and Their Use in Automatic Script Identification," Proc. Transactions on Pattern Analysis and Machine Intelligence, IEEE CS Press, VOL. 20, NO. 7, JULY 1998.
10. Arun Rossa, Anil Jaina, James Reismanb, "A hybrid fingerprint matcher," Pattern Recognition 36 1661-1673, 2003.
11. T.N. Tan, "Texture Feature Extraction Via Cortical Channel Modelling," Proc. 11th IAPR Int'l Conf. Pattern Recognition, IEEE CS Press, C607-C610, 1992.
12. L. Hong, Y. Wan, A.K. Jain, "Fingerprint image enhancement: Algorithms and performance evaluation," IEEE Trans. Pattern Anal. Mach. Intell., Vol. 20, NO. 8, 777 – 789, 1998.

Phase-Correlation Based Registration of Swipe Fingerprints

Yongliang Zhang[1], Jie Yang[1], Hongtao Wu[2], and Yunfeng Xue[1]

[1] Inst. of Image Processing & Pattern Recognition, Shanghai JiaoTong Univ.,
200030 Shanghai, China
yongliangzhang@sjtu.edu.cn
[2] School of Computer Science & Software, Hebei University of Technology,
300130 Tianjin, China

Abstract. Thermal swipe sensor is one of the technologies behind many of to-day's fingerprint sensors. This paper presents a new direct Fourier-based algorithm for performing swipe fingerprints registration to subpixel accuracy, where the fingerprint image differences are restricted to translations and uniform changes of illumination. The method is based on the extension of the well-known phase correlation technique and is able to estimate large translations of swipe fingerprints with pixel and subpixel accuracy. Excellent experimental results have been obtained for pixel and subpixel translation estimation of swipe fingerprints. And experimental data show that the algorithm has less time consumption and more robustness against noise and superior registration precision.

1   Introduction

The market for identification and authentication using biometric technologies is experiencing strong growth. Currently, the dominant technology is based on fingerprint identification, known to be one of the most reliable personal identification methods [7]. Today, fingerprint sensors have found an array of applications that improve the development of a number of new fingerprint sensor technologies.

Thermal swipe sensor is one of the technologies behind many of today's fingerprint sensors (Fig. 1 (a)). The sensor captures a fingerprint by swiping the finger past it. The data is then "stitched" together to form a fingerprint image. Thermal swipe sensor tends to be low cost and compact (It is smaller than a finger by nature of its swipe design), so it is suitable for mobile phones, PDAs, portable computers and security applications [1].

Swipe fingerprints (Fig. 1 (b)) are the continuous fingerprint frames captured by the thermal swipe sensor. We assume that two adjacent swipe fingerprint frames represent the same scene sampled on identical grids but offset from each other by an unknown translational shift, as well as differing by a uniform change of intensity, perhaps also disturbed by independent additive noise.

S.Z. Li et al. (Eds.): Sinobiometrics 2004, LNCS 3338, pp. 506–515, 2004.

(a)   (b)

Fig. 1. (a) FPC1031B swipe fingerprint sensor [1], (b) some frames of swipe fingerprints

In order to obtain the stitched fingerprint, the registration of swipe fingerprints is necessary. The basic idea of the registration is the "image-to-image" registration. In the image-to-image registration, it is the most important to estimate the translation between a pair of images sharing some mutual support. In recent years the applications of image registration increase hugely in remote sensing, medicine, cartography and computer vision [13]. So many methods have been developed to estimate the translational displacement between similar images [13]. A majority of image registration methods only have the pixel accuracy. However some important applications in remote sensing and biomedical imaging have requirement for subpixel registration [5]. To identify non-integer shifts, the phase correlation method is a popular choice due to its robust performance and computational simplicity. A important property of phase correlation methods is due to whitening of the signals by normalization, which makes the phase correlation notably robust to those types of noise that are correlated to the image function, e.g., uniform variations of illumination, offsets in average intensity, and fixed gain errors due to calibration [5]. The idea behind this method [2] [4] is quite simple and is based on the Fourier shift property [3][9], which states that a shift in the coordinate frames of two functions is transformed in the Fourier domain as linear phase differences. Shekarforoush et al [5] introduced extension of phase correlation to subpixel registration by means of the analytic expression of phase correlation on down sampled images. However, subpixel translations in [5] will cause the peak in certain coordinate to spread to neighboring pixels and the resolution of the peak can degrade due to the presence of aliasing and edge-effects [11][12]. So after obtaining an integer-precision alignment of the input images, Stone et al in [6] apply a Blackman or Blackman–Harris window in the pixel domain to eliminate image-boundary effects in the Fourier domain. And Stone et al in [10] say that windowing the image to eliminate boundary artifacts can reduce aliasing artifacts.

This paper presents a new direct Fourier-based algorithm for performing swipe fingerprints registration to subpixel accuracy, where the fingerprint image differences are restricted to translations and uniform changes of illumination. The paper is organized as follows. In the next section, we describe the phase correlation method and the subpixel registration method. Implementation issues and results are discussed in section 3. Finally in section 4 some concluding remarks are provided.

2 Strategy

In this section, we present the necessary theories to the registration of swipe finger-prints including the method of phase correlation and the theory of subpixel translation estimation.

2.1 The Pixel Level Phase Correlation

This method relies on the translation property of the Fourier transform. The purpose of the phase correlation algorithm is to estimate the translation between a pair of swipe fingerprints: Let $f_1(x, y)$ and $f_2(x, y)$ are two swipe fingerprints that differ only by a displacement (x_0, y_0), their mutual support satisfies the following equation

$$f_2(x, y) = f_1(x + x_0, y + y_0) \tag{1}$$

According to the Fourier shift property

$$\frac{\hat{f}_2(\omega_x, \omega_y)}{\hat{f}_1(\omega_x, \omega_y)} = e^{j(\omega_x x_0 + \omega_y y_0)} \tag{2}$$

The translation (x_0, y_0) can be estimated by taking the inverse FFT of Eq. 2:

$$Corr(x, y) = F^{-1}(e^{j(w_x x_0 + w_y y_0)}) = \delta(x - x_0, y - y_0) \tag{3}$$

In order to compensate for possible gain changes and since we are only interested in pure phase shifts, by normalizing the input images' magnitude, the *Normalized phase correlation* can be rewritten as:

$$\hat{Corr}(\omega_x, \omega_y) = \frac{\hat{f}_2(\omega_x, \omega_y)\hat{f}_1^*(\omega_x, \omega_y)}{\left|\hat{f}_1(\omega_x, \omega_y)\right|\left|\hat{f}_1^*(\omega_x, \omega_y)\right|} = e^{j(\omega_x x_0 + \omega_y y_0)} \tag{4}$$

where * denotes the complex conjugate and the middle part is referred to as the *cross power spectrum* to the two functions f_1 and f_2.

It is now a simple matter to determine x_0 and y_0, since the inverse FFT of the right hand side is a *Dirac* delta function centered at (x_0, y_0):

$$F^{-1}\left(\frac{\hat{f}_2(\omega_x, \omega_y)\hat{f}_1^*(\omega_x, \omega_y)}{\left|\hat{f}_1(\omega_x, \omega_y)\right|\left|\hat{f}_1^*(\omega_x, \omega_y)\right|}\right) = F^{-1}\{e^{j(\omega_x x_0 + \omega_y y_0)}\} = \delta(x_0, y_0) \tag{5}$$

The pixel level phase correlation can be seen in Fig. 2 and there is a distinct sharp peak at the point (x_0, y_0) of registration.

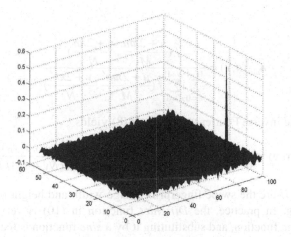

Fig. 2. The pixel level phase correlation

2.2 Subpixel Translation Estimation

The model in [5] presented by Shekarforoush et-al is based on the assumption that images with subpixel shifts are in fact on the assumption that images with subpixel shifts are in fact originally displaced by integer values, which subsequently have reduced to subpixel values due to downsampling.

Consider two discrete swipe fingerprint images given by $f_1(x, y) = f(x, y)$ and $f_2(x, y) = f_1(x + x_0, y + y_0)$, where (x_0, y_0) is an integer-valued vector. Let $\hat{f}_1(u, v) = \hat{f}(u, v)$ and $\hat{f}_2(u, v) = \hat{f}(u, v) \cdot e^{i(ux_0 + vy_0)}$ denote their Discrete Fourier Transforms (DFTs). Then the corresponding DFTs after downsampling the swipe fingerprint images by factors of M and N along x and y axes respectively, will be given by:

$$\hat{f}_{d1}(u, v) = \frac{1}{MN} \sum_{m'=0}^{M-1} \sum_{n'=0}^{N-1} \hat{f}\left(\frac{u + 2\pi m'}{M}, \frac{v + 2\pi n'}{N} \right) \qquad (6)$$

$$\hat{f}_{d2}(u, v) = \frac{1}{MN} \sum_{m=0}^{M-1} \sum_{n=0}^{N-1} \hat{f}\left(\frac{u + 2\pi m}{M}, \frac{v + 2\pi n}{N} \right)$$
$$\cdot \exp\left(i\left(\frac{u + 2\pi m}{M} x_0, \frac{v + 2\pi n}{N} y_0 \right) \right) \qquad (7)$$

Therefore, Eq. 8 gives the *cross-power spectrum* of the downsampled swipe fingerprint images:

$$\hat{Corr}(u, v) = \sum_{m=0}^{M-1} \sum_{n=0}^{N-1} \hat{h}_{mn}(u, v) \cdot \exp\left(i\left(\frac{u + 2\pi m}{M} x_0, \frac{v + 2\pi n}{N} y_0 \right) \right) \qquad (8)$$

where

$$\hat{h}_{mn}(u,v) = \frac{\hat{f}(\dfrac{u + 2\pi m}{M}, \dfrac{v + 2\pi m}{N})}{\displaystyle\sum_{m'=0}^{M-1}\sum_{n'=0}^{N-1}\hat{f}(\dfrac{u + 2\pi n'}{M}, \dfrac{v + 2\pi n'}{N})} \tag{9}$$

The discrete inverse Fourier transform of (8) yields

$$\hat{Corr}(x,y) = \frac{1}{W \cdot H} \cdot \frac{\sin(\pi(Mx + x_0)}{\sin(\pi(Mx + x_0)/W)} \cdot \frac{\sin(\pi(Ny + y_0))}{\sin(\pi(Ny + y_0)/H)} \tag{10}$$

where W and H are the swipe fingerprint image width and height respectively before downsampling. In practice, the *Dirichlet* function in (10) is very closely approximated by a *sinc* function, and substituting it by a *sinc* function is feasible. Therefore,

$$\hat{Corr}(x,y) \cong \frac{\sin(\pi(Mx + x_0))}{\pi(Mx + x_0)} \cdot \frac{\sin(\pi(Ny + y_0))}{\pi(Ny + y_0)} \tag{11}$$

For two images with subpixel displacements the signal power is largely concentrated in the vicinity of the main peak of the phase correlation (modulo periodicity). To be more precise, for subpixel displacements the signal power in the phase correlation is usually concentrated in a main peak at some coordinates (x_m, y_m) and two side-peaks at (x_s, y_m) and (x_m, y_s) where $x_s = x_m \pm 1$ (modulo X) and $y_s = y_m \pm 1$ (modulo Y). X and Y are image dimensions after downsampling. Using these three points one can then solve for the subpixel shift values. The subpixel level phase correlation can be seen in Fig.3 and the signal power is largely concentrated in the vicinity of the main peak of the phase correlation.

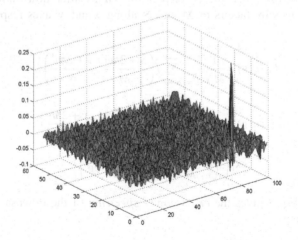

Fig. 3. The subpixel level phase correlation

3 Experiment Results and Analysis

The swipe fingerprint frames must be smoothed by *Gaussian kenerl* before registration in order to reduce the effect of noise. The windowing operation is well known and eliminates the spurious introduction of high-frequency spectral energy due to edge effects. Therefore in this paper we apply a separable Blackman window in our algorithm to eliminate image-boundary effects in the Fourier domain.

3.1 Simulation A: Subpixel Registration Without Noise

Fig. 4 (a) and (b) are two adjacent swipe fingerprint frames and they are downsampled before registration. Fig. 4 (c) is the image of the registration result with subpixel accuracy.

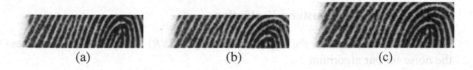

(a)   (b)   (c)

Fig. 4. (a) and (b) are two adjacent swipe fingerprint frames after downsample, (c) is the image of the registration result with subpixel accuracy

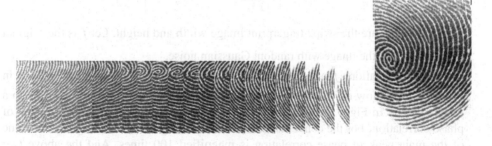

Fig. 5. Swipe fingerprints and the registration result

The swipe fingerprints and its registration result can be seen in Fig. 5.

The translational estimations of simulation fingerprint frames are tested in our experiments, and the experimental results can be seen in Table 1,where (x_0, y_0) is the actual shift vector of the fingerprint frames and $(\Delta x, \Delta y)$ is the estimation of (x_0, y_0) using the extension of phase correlation method. The experimental data indicate that the swipe fingerprint registration algorithm based on the extension of phase correlation has 0.05-pixel accuracy.

Table 1. Subpixel translation estimation

(x_0, y_0)	$(\Delta x, \Delta y)$
(0.0000,0.0000)	(0.0000,0.0000)
(0.0000,0.2500)	(0.0156,0.1642)
(0.0000,0.5000)	(0.0543,0.4766)
(0.2500,0.0000)	(0.2344,0.0036)
(0.2500,0.2500)	(0.2755,0.2487)
(0.2500,0.5000)	(0.2758,0.4977)
(0.5000,0.0000)	(0.4768,0.0069)
(0.5000,0.2500)	(0.4899,0.2233)
(0.5000,0.5000)	(0.4878,0.4766)

3.2 Simulation B: Robustness Evaluation

In this issue, we introduce the *Signal-Noise-Ratio* (*SNR*) to evaluate the robustness to the noise for our algorithm

$$SNR = 10 \cdot \log \left| \frac{\sum\limits_{i=1}^{W}\sum\limits_{j=1}^{H} f^2(i,j)}{\sum\limits_{i=1}^{W}\sum\limits_{j=1}^{H}(f'(i,j) - f(i,j))^2} \right| \tag{12}$$

where W and H are the swipe fingerprint image width and height. Let f is the original image and f' is the image with random Gaussian noise.

In this simulation, f_1 and f_2 are two adjacent swipe fingerprint frames (see in Fig. 6). Fig. 7 show the effect of the noise to the main peak of phase correlation to a certain extent. In Fig. 7, the bottom curve represents the variety of the main peak of phase correlation. For the convenience of demonstrating in the same figure, the value of the main peak of phase correlation is magnified 100 times. And the above two curves represent the varieties of the SNR of f_1 and f_2. A great deal of simulations (we have done 500 simulations in our experiments) present that the main peak of the phase correlation is degressive with the SNR decrease of f_1 and f_2; and the registration is good until the *SNR*s of f_1 and f_2 decrease to about 20.0.

Fig. 6. Two adjacent swipe fingerprint frames

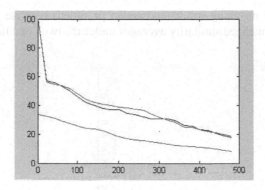

Fig. 7. Effect of the noise to main peak

3.3 Similarity of UrU4000 and Swipe Fingerprints

U.are.U 4000 [8] products utilize optical fingerprint scanning technology for superior image quality and product reliability. The user simply places his/her finger on the glowing sensor window, and the device quickly and automatically captures the fingerprint image. Fig. 8 are two fingerprints, (a) is captured by *U.are.U 4000* sensor, and (b) is the registration of swipe fingerprints for the same fingertip. The normalized similarity evaluated by the matching algorithm given in [7] is 50.

(a)   (b)

Fig. 8. (a) U.are.U 4000 fingerprint, (b) registration of swipe fingerprints

And then, we have random captured 1000 fingerprints of 20 persons (every fingertip is captured five times, two times are captured with U.are.U 4000 sensor, the others are the swipe fingerprints). Finally, we use the matching algorithm given in [7] to evaluate the normalized similarity between the U.are.U 4000 fingerprints and the swipe fingerprints. The results are shown in Fig. 9.

The average of normalized similarity is 39.000 and the standard deviation of the normalized similarity is 17.3502 if the two fingerprints are captured from the same fingertip; whereas the average is 0.23 and the standard deviation is 0.4230 if the two fingerprints are captured from two different fingertips. So it is easy to set a threshold to determine the matching result (succeeded or failed) because of the fact that the difference of normalized similarity averages under the two conditions is very high.

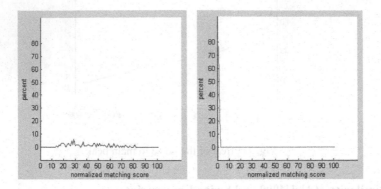

Fig. 9. The similarity between two fingerprint types

3.4 Complexity Analysis

For two adjacent swipe fingerprint frames, our registration algorithm requires computation of two FFT's (to compute Fourier spectra for both frames) and one IFFT (to find translation shift value). For example, if the swipe fingerprint which has 42 frames (every frame of size 32*152), our algorithm needs computation of 42 FFT's and 41 IFFT's. Because the thermal swipe sensor is compact (It is smaller than a finger by nature of its swipe design), the size of every frame is small. So the speed of our registration algorithm can satisfy the need for on-line applications.

4 Conclusions

In this paper, we propose a new approach to robust registration of swipe fingerprints. The algorithm uses the phase correlation method to obtain the registration of swipe fingerprints with pixel accuracy and utilizes the extension of phase correlation method to subpixel accuracy. Experimental results show that our algorithm possesses less time consumption, more robustness against noise and superior registration precision. Because we haven't found the literature about the phase-correlation based registration applied to swipe fingerprints, we can't compare our experimental results to others'. In the future work we will establish theory model to discuss the accuracy of registration and error analysis.

References

1. http://www.fingerprints.com
2. Kuglin C. D, Hines D. C.: The Phase Correlation Image Alignment Method. Proc. Int. Conf. Cybernetics Society (1975) 163–165

3. Papoulis A.: Signal Analysis. New York: McGraw-Hill (1977)
4. Pearson J. J., Hines D. C., Golosman S., Kuglin C. D.: Video Rate Image Correlation Processor. Proc. SPIE (1977) 197–205
5. Shekarforoush H., Zerubia J., Berthod M.: Extension of Phase Correlation to Subpixel Registration. IEEE Transactions on Image Processing, Vol. 11, (2002) 188–200
6. Stone Harold S., Orchard Michael T., Chang Ee-Chien, Martucci Stephen A.: A Fast Direct Fourier-Based Algorithm for Subpixel Registration of Images. IEEE Transactions on Geoscience and Remote Sensing, Vol. 39, (2001) 2235-2243
7. Jain, Anil K., Hong Lin, Pankanti Sharath, Bolle Ruud.: An Identity-Authentication System Using Fingerprints. Proceedings of the IEEE, Vol. 85, (1997) 1365-1388
8. http://www.europe.omron.com
9. Ronald N. Bracewell.: The Fourier Transform and Its Applications, McGraw-Hill, New York,1965.
10. Stone Harold S.: Fourier-based Image Registration Techniques, NEC research.
11. Hoge William Scott.: A Subspace Identification Extension Phase Correlation Method. IEEE Transactions on Medical Imaging, Vol. 22, (2003) 277–280
12. Hoge William Scott.: Identification of Translational Displacements between N-Dimensional Data Sets Using the High Order SVD and Phase Correlation. IEEE Transactions on Image Processing, (2004) 1-7
13. Zitova B., Flusser J.: Image Registration Methods: A Survey. Image and Vision Computing, Vol.21, (2003) 977–1000

An Improved Method for Singularity Detection of Fingerprint Images

Hongwei Zhang, Yilong Yin, and Guozhen Ren

School of Compute Science and Technology, Shandong Univercity, China
zhang_hng_wei@hotmail.com

Abstract. It is important for automatic fingerprint identification system to detect singularities of fingerprint images accurately and reliably. This paper proposes an improved method for singularity detection of fingerprint images. First, a fingerprint image is divided into non-overlapping blocks with the same size, the column which the core belongs to is acquired by detecting the horizontal part of the ridge, and then the row which the core belongs to is got. Also, the column and the row, which the delta belongs to, are acquired according to those acute variable ridge directions of left and right parts of the delta. Then, singularities are detected with Poincare index within the block image which the column and the row belong to. If no singularity is detected in the block image, search area is expanded to detect. At worst, the whole image is searched. Experimental results indicate that the improved method is effective and, even to low quality image, it still can detect the singularities reliably.

1 Introduction

Fingerprint identification is the most popular biometric technology and has drawn a substantial attention recently [1]. An automatic fingerprint identification system (AFIS) includes fingerprint acquisition, feature extraction, fingerprint matching and/or fingerprint classification [2-8]. Most AFISs use ridge ending and bifurcation to implement verification and identification. While the singularity is intrinsic global feature of fingerprints and it is invariant to the rotation and transformation. It has important use in the fingerprint classification and matching. So, it is necessary to detect the singularity of fingerprint images accurately and reliably.

The singularities are, namely, the core and the delta, as illustrated in Fig.1. Up to now, some articles have touched directly upon singularity detection of fingerprint images. Kawagoe and Tojo [3] have used Poincare index to detect singularities. Srinivasan and Murthy [9] have detected singularities with histogram of ridge directions. Bazen et al. [10] has brought out a method to detect singularities by tracking gradient directions of ridges. Tan et al. [14] has detected singularities based on block images through shifting position of the whole image many times at the same block size and the concentrative region of singularities has been detected and the centroid of the region is computed as the accurate position of singularities. ZHANG et al. [11] has brought out the corner detection method to find the region of singularities and gray level of ridge has been tracked to get the position of singularities.

S.Z. Li et al. (Eds.): Sinobiometrics 2004, LNCS 3338, pp. 516–524, 2004.
© Springer-Verlag Berlin Heidelberg 2004

The main differences of those methods are the cost of computation and the accuracy of singularities. When the quality of fingerprint image is good, most methods above perform well. As to the low quality fingerprint images, up to now, it is still hard to detect singularities accurately and reliably. The prevailing method for singularity detection is that based on the Poincare index, while this kind of method is time consuming. Furthermore, often many pseudo singularities are detected with this method when the quality of fingerprint images is poor. This paper studies an improved method based on Poincare index for singularity detection. The main concern of our method is to decrease computation and improve accuracy.

This paper is organized as follows. Traditional Poincare index theory and Jain's method are introduced in section 2. Our improved method is described in section 3. The last section is experiment and discussions.

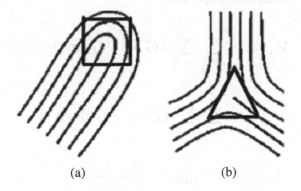

(a)   (b)

Fig. 1. Singularities of fingerprint image. core(a),delta(b)

2   Notations

2.1   Poincare Index

In an orientation field, Poincare index of a coreshaped singularity has a value of (1/2) and that of a delta-shaped singularity has a value of (-1/2). Let ψ_x and ψ_y represent the x and y coordinates of a closed digital curve with N_ψ pixels. Let o' be the interpolated orientation field. The Poincare index at pixel (i, j) which is enclosed by the digital curve can be computed as follows:

$$Poincare(i, j) = \frac{1}{2\pi} \sum_{k=0}^{N_\psi} \Delta(k) \tag{1}$$

where

$$\Delta(k) = \begin{cases} \delta(k), & if \ |\delta(k)| < \pi/2 \\ \pi + \delta(k), & if \ \delta(k) \le -\pi/2 \\ \pi - \delta(k), & otherwise \end{cases} \tag{2}$$

$$\delta(k) = o'(\psi_x(i'), \psi_y(i')) - o'(\psi_x(i), \psi_y(i))$$
$$i' = (i+1) \bmod N_\psi \tag{3}$$

2.2 Jain's [13] Method

(a) Divide the fingerprint image into blocks of size W × W.

(b) Compute the gradients G_x and G_y at each pixel in each block.

(c) Estimate the local orientation at each pixel (i, j) using the following formulae, Where W is the size of the local window; G_x and G_y are gradient magnitudes in x and y directions, respectively.

$$V_x(i, j) = \sum_{u=i-\frac{W}{2}}^{i+\frac{W}{2}} \sum_{v=j-\frac{W}{2}}^{j+\frac{W}{2}} 2G_x(u,v)G_y(u,v) \tag{4}$$

$$V_y(i, j) = \sum_{u=i-\frac{W}{2}}^{i+\frac{W}{2}} \sum_{v=j-\frac{W}{2}}^{j+\frac{W}{2}} (G_x^2(u,v) - G_y^2(u,v)) \tag{5}$$

$$\theta(i, j) = \frac{1}{2}\tan^{-1}(\frac{V_x(i, j)}{V_y(i, j)}) \tag{6}$$

(d) Compute the consistency level of orientation field in the local neighborhood of a block (i, j) with the following formulae:

$$C(i, j) = \frac{1}{N}\sqrt{\sum_{(i',j')\in D} |\theta(i', j') - \theta(i, j)|^2} \tag{7}$$

$$d' = (\theta' - \theta + 360) \bmod 360$$
$$|\theta' - \theta| = \begin{cases} d' & \text{if } d' < 180 \\ d' - 180 & \text{otherwise} \end{cases} \tag{8}$$

Where D represents the local neighborhood around the block (i, j) (the size of D is 5 ×5), N is the number of blocks within D, $\theta(i', j')$ and $\theta(i, j)$ are local ridge orientations of blocks (i', j') and (i, j), respectively.

(e) If the consistency level is above a certain threshold T_c, then local orientations around this region are re-estimated at a lower resolution level until $C(i, j)$ is below a certain level.

3   Our Improved Method

Our improved method mainly includes following steps: I. fingerprint segmentation, II. core detection, III. delta detection, IV the location of singularities.

3.1   Fingerprint Segmentation

It is the first step to acquire valid fingerprint region from a whole fingerprint image. This paper use Ratha's[12] method to implement image segmentation.

3.2   Core Detection

Compute the Orientation Field
Divide the input fingerprint image into blocks of size W×W. Compute the orientation field.

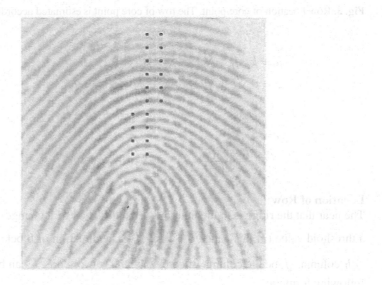

Fig. 2. Column Location of core point.The horizontal part of ridges in each row is dotted. The column of core point is estimated according to formula (9)

Location of Column
Henry's[15] definition of core is that the uppermost point of the innermost ridge. The uppermost point of ridge is in the area of the horizontal part of ridge. So we can record columns of horizontal part of the ridge in each row, and estimate the column of core from them. Let j be column of the core and C_i be the ith column we got,

N_i be the number of C_i, n be the total column number:

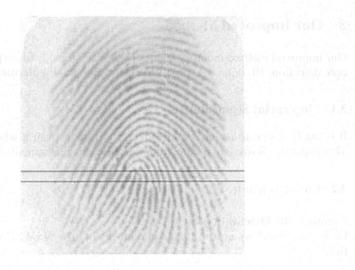

Fig. 3. Row Location of core point. The row of core point is estimated according to formula (10)

$$u = k, \ if \ \ N_k \geq N_i, k, i = 1,2,\dots n$$
$$v = t, \ if \ \ N_u \geq N_t \geq N_i, t, i = 1,2,\dots n$$

$$j = \begin{cases} C_i & if \quad \dfrac{N_i}{\sum\limits_{i=1}^{n} N_i} >= \dfrac{1}{2} \\[4ex] \dfrac{C_u + C_v}{2} & otherwise \end{cases} \qquad (9)$$

Location of Row

The near that the ridge is to the innermost, the direction of it changes acute. Let T_1 be a threshold value (in this paper, $T_1 = 2$), $d_{i,j}$ be direction of block in the *ith* row and *jth* column, j be the column of core, i be the row of core. i can be estimated by the following formula:

$$i = u + T_1$$
$$u = v, RC_v > RC_x, x = 1,2,\dots v-1$$
$$RC_v > RC_y, y = v+1, v+2,\dots v+5 \qquad (10)$$

$$RC_i = \sum_{k=j-4}^{j+4} d_{i,k}$$

3.3 Delta Detection

The property of ridge around the delta is very different from others. The direction of ridge between left side and left side has dramatic change, while the bottom of it is not so obvious. Let T_2, T_3 and T_4 be threshold value, n be number of rows, (u, v) be the block to which the delta belongs. The following shows the pseudocode in C:

```
for each row i
{
    for each column j
    {
        if d i,j  <  d i,j+2  +  T 2  &&  d i+1,j  <  d i+1,j+2  +  T 2
        {
            int u, number;
            for each u in i+1…i+5
                if d u,j  <  d u+1,j  +  T 3
            number++;
            if number  >=T 4  &&  i / n  >=1/2
            {
                (u , v) = (i , j+1)
                exit;
            }
        }
    }
}
```

3.4 Location of Singularities

Let (i, j) be the block we got, singularities are detected based on Poincare index within this block. If no singularity is found in this block, the neighboring block is searched. This can be done a variety of ways. The current implementation first searches the top three blocks, then the bottom three, followed by the left and the right blocks. It stops as soon as it finds singularities. If it still finds no singularities, it continues by searching the top five blocks, the bottom five, the left three, and the right three, and so on.

4 Experiment and Discussions

The performance of our method is evaluated with 50 typical low quality images of Nanjing University fingerprint database (1200 live-scan images; 10 per individual). The hardware we used was a legend Pentium® 4 CPU 2.80GHz/512M RAM under Windows XP.All pseudo singularities are not erased. Figure 4 shows the results of detection of typical images.

Table 1 shows timing examples in CPU seconds. Our method used only 0.093 seconds while Bazen's method and Kawagoe's method used six times more than ours. Table 2 shows the number of singularities detected with these methods. Our method has decreased the false rate dramatically from 71.78% to 17.03% compared with the

Kawagoe's method. Experimental results indicate that our method can detect the singularities reliably and also is timesaving.

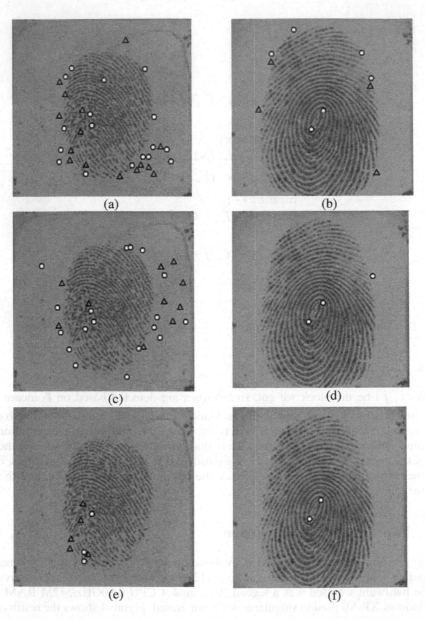

(a)

(b)

(c)

(d)

(e)

(f)

Fig. 4. Result of detection of singularities with three methods: (a),(b) and (c),(d) and (e),(f) are results of singularities detection with Kawagoe's method, Bazen's. method and our method, respectively. Delta (△), core (○)

Table 1. Average timing of three methods

Method	Timing (s)
Improved method	0.093309
Bazen's method	0.613002
Kawagoe's method	0.579985

Table 2. Results of singularities detection with three methods

Method	Total number	False points	False rate	Omitted rate
Improved method	135	23	17.03%	3.45%
Bazen's method	180	64	36.67%	0
Kawagoe's method	404	290	71.78%	1.72%

Our method can detect the approximately location of core points even with presence of Serious noise around core points. However, as for delta points, Serious noises around delta points may lead to: (i) inaccurate detection results of column and/or row. In such a case, a bigger area may be searched. (ii) omission of delta points.Tabel 2 indicate that 3.45 percent of singularities are omitted.

References

1. Yin Y. L., Ning XB, Zhang XM. Development and application of automatic fingerprint identification technology. Journal of Nanjing University (Natural Sciences Edition), 2002, 38(1):29~35 (in Chinese).
2. Jain A. K., Prabhakar S, Hong L. A multi-channel approach to fingerprint classification. In: Proceedings of the Indian Conference on Computer Vision, Graphics, and Images Processing (ICVGIP'98). New Delhi, 1998. 153~158.
3. Kawagoe M, Tojo A. Fingerprint pattern classification. Pattern Recognition, 1984,17(3):295~303.
4. Maio D. , Maltoni D. A structural approach to fingerprint classification. In: Proceedings of the 13th International Conference on Pattern Recognition (ICPR). Vienna, 1996. 578~585.
5. Karu K, Jain AK. Fingerprint classification. Pattern Recognition, 1996, 29(3):389~404.
6. Jain A. K., Prabhakar S, Pankanti S. Matching and classification: A case study in fingerprint domain. Proceedings of the INSA-A (Indian National Science Academy), 2001,67(2):67~85.
7. Lumini A, Maio D, Maltoni D. Continuous vs. exclusive classification for fingerprint retrieval. Pattern Recognition Letters, 1997, 18(10):1027~1034.
8. Cheng J. G., Tian J, Ren Q, Zhang TH. Singular point-based fingerprint classification. In: Proceedings of the 2nd Workshop on Biometrics in Conjunction with the 6th International Conference for Young Computer Scientists. Hang Zhou: 2001. S4-27~S4-34.
9. Srinivasan V. S., Murthy NN. Detection of singular points in fingerprint images, Pattern Recognition, 1992,25(2):139~153.

10. Bazen A. M. , Gerez SH. Extraction of singular points from directional fields of finger-prints. In: Annual CTIT Workshop. Enschede, 2001.
11. Zhang W. W., Wang S, Wang YS. Corner detection based singularity detection of finger-print image. In: Proceedings of the 2nd Workshop on Biometrics in Conjunction with the 6th International Conference for Young Computer Scientists. Hang Zhou: 2001.S4-51~S4-56.
12. Ratha N., Karu K, Chen S Jain AK. A real-time matching system for large fingerprint da-tabase. IEEE Transactions on Pattern Analysis and Machine Intelligence, 1996, 18(8): 799~813.
13. Jain A. K., Hong L, Bolle R. On-Line fingerprint verification. IEEE Transactions on Pat-tern Analysis and Machine Intelligence, 1997, 19(4):302~314.
14. TAN T. Z. 1+ , NING Xin-Bao 1 , YIN Yi-Long 2 , ZHAN Xiao-Si 1 , CHEN Yun 3. A Method for Singularity Detection in Fingerprint Images. Journal of Software, Vol.14, No.6, 2003, 1082~1088
15. Henry E. R., Classification and uses of fingerprints, George Routeledge and Sons, London, 1990.

Fingerprint Classifier Using Embedded Hidden Markov Models

Zongying Ou, Hao Guo, and Honglei Wei

CAD&CG Lab., School of Mech. Eng., Dalian Univ. of Technol.,
Dalian 116024, China
ouzyg@dlut.edu.cn

Abstract. Automatic fingerprint classification provides an important indexing scheme to facilitate efficient matching in large-scale fingerprint databases. Fingerprints are classified mainly based on their print textures. A fingerprint texture pattern across a predefined path on the finger surface can be viewed as a Markov chain. The orientation field of a fingerprint can be modeled with a pseudo 2D Hidden Markov Model (HMM), which can also be called embedded Hidden Markov Model. A novel method of fingerprint classification based on embedded HMM is described in this paper., Compared with conventional method, the novel fingerprint classification approach is simpler and more robust, since it is less sensitive to the noise and distortions in fingerprint images and the pretreatment processes such as image enhancement and thinning, minutiae and singular point extraction etc can be skipped.

1 Introduction

Fingerprint classification processing is frequently used in an Automatic Fingerprint Identification System (AFIS) in reducing the size of the search space of a fingerprint database. The reduction ratio can be up to a rate of 3.37~3.39[1], and hence the reduction will increase the matching speed significantly while processing with a large-scale fingerprint database.

Fingerprints are classified mainly based on their print textures. The most widely used system of fingerprint classification, Henry system and its variants [2], classified fingerprints into five classes (left loop, right loop, whorl, arch and tented arch), which are shown as Fig.1. There are also existed some other fingerprint classification systems, which use four classes by treating arch and tented arch as identical.

A fingerprint texture with specified details changing across a predefined path on the finger surface can be viewed as a Markov chain. HMM is expected to be an efficient approach in fingerprint classification and identification, since it has been successfully applied to speech recognition and other recognition systems [3],[4],[5].

Andrew Senior presented a HMM approach in fingerprint classification, and verified that the HMM approach is effective [1],[6]. Andrew Senior's approach uses a number of fingerprint parameters; some of them are related to ridge details, which will be extracted only after smoothing and thinning processes and that is time-consuming.

S.Z. Li et al. (Eds.): Sinobiometrics 2004, LNCS 3338, pp. 525–531, 2004.
© Springer-Verlag Berlin Heidelberg 2004

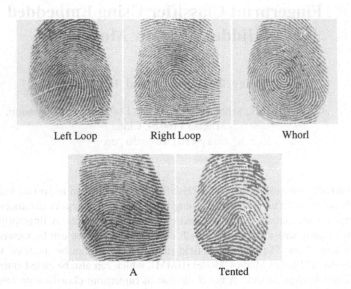

Left Loop   Right Loop   Whorl

A   Tented

Fig. 1. Five fingerprint categories

An orientation field composed of the orientations of fingerprint across whole finger surface can be used for well describing the print texture pattern, which can be expressed as a discrete orientation angle series along a predefined path region chain. In this paper a new HMM based classification approach using only orientation angle parameters is presented.

2 The Embedded HMM for a Fingerprint Image

A HMM provides a statistic model for a set of observation data sequences [3]. It includes two forms of stochastic finite process. One is a Markov chain of finite state, which describes the transfer from one state to another; the other describes the probabilities between states and observation data. What is necessary to statistically characterize a HMM is a state transition probability matrix, an initial state probability distribution, and a set of probability density functions associated with the observations for each state.

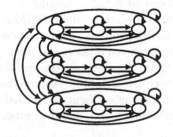

Fig. 2. Topology structure of an embedded HMM

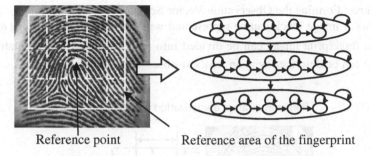

Reference point   Reference area of the fingerprint

Fig. 3. The embedded HMM of the fingerprint

Typically a HMM is a 1-D structure suitable for analyzing 1-D random signals, for example speech signals. A 1-D HMM can be developed to a pseudo 2-D structure (Fig.2) by extending each state in a 1-D HMM as a sub HMM. In this way the HMM consists of a set of super states, along with a set of embedded states. This pseudo 2-D HMM is also called embedded HMM. The super states were used to model 2-D data along one direction, with the embedded HMM modeling the data along the other direction.

In this paper the embedded HMM scheme of an input fingerprint image is shown as fig. 3. The embedded HMM includes three super states, which represent three parts of a fingerprint from the top to bottom. Each super state is composed of five sub states (embedded states) horizontally.

3   Feature Extraction and Observation Vector Formation

The feature extraction and observation vector formation include the following steps (Fig.4):

Step One: Fingerprint Image Discretization

A fingerprint image is scanned with a $W \times H$ sampling window (image block) left to right and top to bottom [4]. The overlap between adjacent windows is N pixels distance in the vertical direction and M pixels distance in the horizontal direction. In this way a fingerprint can be divided into an $Y \times X$ image blocks matrix, and the size of each block is $W \times H$. This technique can improve the ability of an embedded HMM to model the neighborhood relations between the sampling windows. The sampling scheme is shown in Fig.4. In this paper, $W \times H$ is taken as 16×16, M and N are equal to 8.

Step Two: Constructing the Observation Vectors

Each 16×16 image block includes four 8×8 sub image blocks. By estimating the local orientation θ of each sub block, we can get an observation vector (θ_1 θ_2 θ_3 θ_4), which can described the features of the 16×16 image block reasonably.

Step Three: Forming the Observation Vector Sequence

Each 16×16 image block can be represented with an observation vector (θ_1 θ_2 θ_3 θ_4), and a fingerprint image can be divided into an $Y \times X$ image blocks matrix, so a fingerprint can be described with an $4 \times Y \times X$ observation vector sequence.

Fingerprint image discretization by sampling

Sampling window

Forming a image blocks matrix

Feature extraction

Orientation

Forming a observation vector

$$O_{yx} = (\ \theta_1\ \ \theta_2\ \ \theta_3\ \ \theta_4)$$

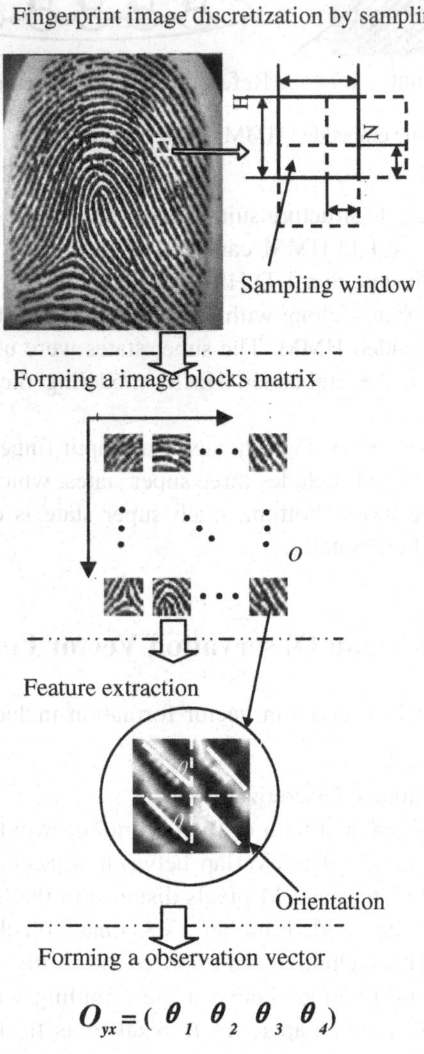

Fig. 4. Feature extraction and observation vector formation

4   Pretreatment

Since a captured fingerprint appears randomly in an image, a pretreatment is needed for adjusting the location of a fingerprint and setting the reference area, which includes the whole area for fingerprint feature extraction. The basic steps of a pre-treatment are (Fig. 5):

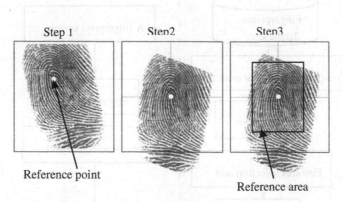

Fig. 5. The pretreatment of the location of a fingerprint

1) A reference point of a fingerprint is detected, and the location of the reference point is adjusted to the image center. The reference point detection algorithm based on the orientation field of fingerprint images has been described in reference [7] and is not detailed here;

2) The fingerprint is rotated based on the ridges structure around the reference point, which has been described in the M82[8];

3) After the location of a fingerprint is adjusted, a reference area can be set.

5   HMM Training and Fingerprint Classification

A category of the fingerprints can be commonly depicted and defined with a corresponding category embedded HMM. A category embedded HMM is built by collecting a set fingerprint images of the specified category and implementing a training processing, which is a process for estimating the corresponding embedded HMM parameters. Fingerprint classification processing of a test fingerprint is to find the maximum matching likelihood of the embedded HMM among different categories. The general training and classification process scheme is summarized shown in Fig. 6. The main procedures in training and classification process are re-segmentation and iterative re-estimations of model parameters. Traditional HMM technique solves those problems with Viterbi algorithm and Baum-Welch algorithm [8].

6   Experimental Results

A fingerprint classification system based on the above algorithm has been developed and tested on FVC2002-DB1, which includes 880 (110×8) fingerprint images with

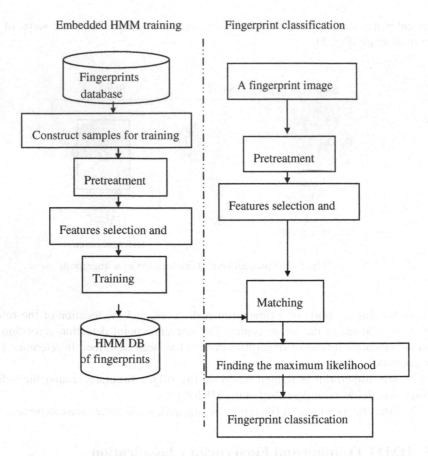

Fig. 6. Training and classification for fingerprints based on embedded HMM

374×388 pixels in 256 gray scale levels. The classifier was trained to distinguish four classes, treating arch and tented arch as identical. The training set selected from the FVC2002-DB1 including the following category images: Left Loop 119, Right Loop 110, Tented Arch 77 and Whorl 116. The test set was a random sample of 467 prints from the 880 available. Table 1 shows the classification results on FVC2002-DB1, the error rate was 5.7%. A comparison with other HMM approaches is provided in Table 2.

Table 1. The classification results of FVC2002-DB1

Fingerprints for test	Results	Error	
Left Loop: 131	Right: 23	Error: 8	
Right Loop: 132	Right:122	Error: 10	5.7%
Tented Arch: 77	Right: 73	Error: 4	
Whorl: 127	Right:122	Error: 5	

Table 2. Comparison with other HMM approaches

Classification System	Error (%)	Test set
References [6]	10.0~23.2	542 NIST-4
References [1]	5.1~20.8	2000 NIST-4
Classification system presented in this paper	5.7	467 FVC2002-DB1

7 Conclusions

Fingerprint classification is used in AFIS to reduce the size of the search space of a fingerprint database and accordingly increase the speed of fingerprint matching, which is very important while processing with a large-scale fingerprint database. The paper presents a fingerprint classification system based on the embedded HMM approach, the system has the following characteristics:

1) The performance is good and robust. The classification only depends on the orientation field of a fingerprint, so it is less sensitive to the noise and distortions of a fingerprint image than the conventional approaches in which the dependent parameters include more fingerprint details.
2) The pretreatment process is simple. The algorithm skipped the processes of thinning the ridge image, selecting minutiae and getting singular points. The enhancement of the fingerprint is also not necessary usually.

References

1. Andrew Senior. A Combination Fingerprint Classifier. IEEE Transactions on pattern analysis and machine intelligence, Vol. 10(23) (2001) 1165-1174.
2. Federal Bureau of Investigations. The Science of Fingerprints (Classification and Uses). 12-84 edition. US Department of Justice, Superintendent of Documents. Washington D.C.: US Government Printing Office, (1984).
3. Nefian A V, HayesIII M H. Face recognition using an Embedded-HMM. Proceedings of IEEE International Conference on Audio and Video-based Biometric Person Authentication. Washington D.C.USA, (1999) 19-21.
4. Rabiner L. A tutorial on HMM and selected applications in speech recognition. Proc. IEEE, Vol. 77(2) (1989) 257-286.
5. Ou Zongying, Xue Bindang. Face Recognition Using Hidden Markov Model and Artificial Neural Network Techniques. Lecture Notes Series on Computing Vol. 11, Geometric Computation (Chapter 14). Word Scientific Publishing Co., (2003).
6. Andrew Senior. A Hidden Markov Model Fingerprint Classifier. In proceedings of the 31st Asilomar conference on Signals, Systems and Computers, (1997) 306-310.
7. Chul-Hyun Park, Sang-Keun Oh, Dong-Min Kwak, Bum-Soo Kim, Young-Chul Song, Kil-Houm Park. A New Reference Point Detection Algorithm Based on Orientation Pattern Labeling in Fingerprint Images. IBPRIA, (2003)697-703.
8. D. Maltoni, D. Maio, Anil K. Jain, Salil Prabhakar. Handbook of Fingerprint Recognition. New York, USA: Springer-Verlag, (2003).

A Robust Pseudoridges Extraction Algorithm for Fingerprints

Taizhe Tan, Yongquan Yu, and Fangli Cui

Faculty of Computer, Guangdong University of Technology, 510090, Guangzhou, China
tantaizhe@263.net

Abstract. The global geometric framework of fingerprint ridges of pattern area represents an intrinsic property of a fingerprint image, which is one of the most important features of fingerprints, and is of the signification for fingerprint classification. In this paper, we presented a robust pseudoridges extraction algorithm for fingerprints to gain the global geometric shape of fingerprint ridges of pattern area. The algorithm adopts the skillful processing method for orientation field estimates, so that the pseudoridge traced remains constant under large variations of local ridge orientation. Hence it is more robust than the feature of the specific ridges .In the tracing process, we present a method with adaptive tracing and estimating the orientation only on the traced point, so that the operation time is reduced. The algorithm for pseudoridges extraction is simple and intuitive, and gets the good performance according to the experimental results.

1 Introduction

Fingerprints have long been used for identification in many social conditions such as access control, crime investigation, and personal trust, since they will remain almost constant during people's life time[1].

In the fingerprint images, there are mainly two types of features that are useful for fingerprint identification: (*i*) local ridge and furrow details (minute details) which have different characteristics for different fingerprints, and (*ii*) global pattern configurations. The global shape of ridges determines the global configuration of fingerprints. Ridges in fingerprints are highly structured. Generally, in the middle region, depending on the fingerprint class, ridges may be of special types. The presence of a particular type of ridges defines the class of a fingerprint. If the ridge type can be accurately determined, then fingerprint can be correctly classified. The extracted global ridge shape by pseudoridge tracing also provides important clues about the global pattern configuration of a fingerprint image [2]. Local fingerprint features essential to the classification process, such as cores and deltas, might be missing due to noise and as a result would most likely lead to erroneous classification. Instead of using local fingerprint features (e.g. core and delta points), an analysis of the global geometric shape of fingerprint ridges extracted by pseudoridges tracing may be utilized to discriminate between the different classes.

S.Z. Li et al. (Eds.): Sinobiometrics 2004, LNCS 3338, pp. 532–538, 2004.

Since fingerprints can be regarded as flow-like textures or oriented textures [3],[4], it is reasonable to use direction as the representation of fingerprint ridges or valleys. The orientation field of a fingerprint consists of the ridge orientation tendency in local neighborhoods and forms an abstraction of the local ridge structures. Therefore, in order to gain the global geometric shape feature, we present a robust pseudoridges extraction algorithm by directly tracing the orientation field (flow field) but not the ridges within the pattern area. This global geometric shape feature is gained by tracing the smoothing orientation field processed skillfully, and is a shape approximation of neighbouring ridges. Hence it is more robust than the feature of the specific ridges. And the traced pseudoridge embodies an intuitive and viable framework for fingerprint classification. Since the framework makes use of a global shape feature instead of local features such as core and delta points, it is less susceptible to fingerprint image noise as being faced by most other methods. This global shape feature is also robust against large variations of local ridge orientation within any particular fingerprint class.

Many literatures [2],[4],[5],[6],[7],[8] use the global geometric shape of fingerprint ridges and stress its importance in fingerprint classifications. However, to the best of the present author's knowledge, only several of them suggested the approaches for gaining the global geometric shape of fingerprint ridges. K. Rao and K. Black [6] proposed syntactic approach to extract the fingerprint ridges shape and make the fingerprint classification. In this approach, a grammar representation is in the form of a string of primitives, which would be parsed according to a set of production rules to determine the class of a particular fingerprint. However, the grammatical inference of these approaches has not been well understood and they tend to suffer from parsing complexities as the grammar becomes more general. A. K. Jain et al. [7] presented a method to get the global ridge shape of pattern area for fingerprint classification, which fits many kernels of a predefined shape and size constructed by using polynomial splines to a vector field. Furthermore, M. M. S. Chong et al. [5] proposed the utilization of a global geometric feature to describe uniquely the general shape of fingerprint ridges within a particular class for the purpose of classification. In this approach, it includes the preprocessing such as ridges thinning, geometric contour representations, postprocessing and geometric grouping and so on complicated processing stages.

In our approach, we start the pseudoridge tracing from core point, which only use the flow field, avoiding the complicated computation of thinned ridges, minutia and other trivial processing. Because the fingerprint is flow-modal, the flow field reflects the global tendency of fingerprint ridges, and the flow field is continuous except for in the individual singularity, not as the gray ridges are sometimes conjoint, disconnected and furcated now and then. And the ridge structures in poor quality fingerprint images are not robust. Hence, it is more reasonable to trace the flow field than to trace the ridges directly. In order to cause the traced pseudoridges to be more accurate, we suggest a skillful and effectual method for orientation field estimates, and only on the exact points traced but not in the whole fingerprint image, orientation field estimates are performed, so that the operation time will be reduced. We also adopt a method with adaptive tracing, in which if the variety of flow field is dull, the tracing step is large, whereas (such as on the core points), the tracing step is small. This characteristic may be useful for checking the singularities. Moreover, our algorithm operation is irrelative with a fixed state of orientation and position, so it is invariant under translation and rotation.

In the following sections, we will present the details or our pseudoridges extraction algorithm. In section 2, we present our method in detail; experimental results are given in section 3; finally, we conclude the paper in section 4.

2   Pseudoridges Extraction Algorithms

2.1   Algorithm Presentations

If there exists one core point, we will start the pseudoridge tracing. The detailed steps are as follows:

1. Image Segmentation. Image area is segmented for the sake of getting the valid fingerprint area. In our method, the blockwise average grayscale and standard deviation are used to segment the image. The block is considered as foreground if its grayscale mean and standard deviation satisfy some predefined standard, otherwise, the background.
2. Determining the Start Tracing Point and Tracing Wises. The some point that is the around of the reliable core point detected by the method mentioned in [9] is as the start tracing point, and the point direction $(0 \sim \pi)$ of the start tracing point is estimated. The tracing wises are determined by clockwise orientation or counter-clockwise orientation.
3. Initializing the Point *OriginPoint*. The *OriginPoint* is endued with the information of the position and the point direction of the above start tracing point, which should be plus with π and change the tracing wise if the tracing in reverse direction is performed.
4. According to the *OriginPoint*, determining the next tracing target point *TracePoint*. The method is as follows:

(1) The current tracing point *CurPoint* is endued with *OriginPoint*,
(2) According to *CurPoint*, selecting the predetermined tracing step (*Step*=5), and along with the direction angle *TrackDirection* adjusted by the direction of *OriginPoint* performing tracing, the next tracing point *NextPoint* is determined. With the difference between the clockwise tracing and the counter-clockwise tracing, the method of adjusting angle is:

$$TrackDirection = OriginPot.Angle \mp M \times Threshold \tag{1}$$

where, *OriginPot.Angle* is the direction of the start tracing point, *Treshold* is the threshold for adjusting the angle, M is a coefficient with a initial value 1, whose value is 0 or 1 by the tracing situation. The intention of adjusting angle is that the tracing direction must be adapted to the change tendency of the flow field. The coordinate of *NextPoint* can be computed as follows:

$$\begin{pmatrix} NextPot \cdot x \\ NextPot.y \end{pmatrix} = \begin{pmatrix} CurPot.x \\ CurPot.y \end{pmatrix} + \left\lfloor Step \times \begin{pmatrix} \cos(TrackDirection) \\ \sin(TrackDirection) \end{pmatrix} + n \times 0.5 \right\rfloor \tag{2}$$

where, *CurPot.x* and *CurPot.y* represent the X and Y coordinate of *CurPoint* respectively, and according to the plus sign or minus sign of the sine or cosine value, n is evaluated by 1 or 0.

(3) Judge whether *NextPoint* is in the valid image area. If it is in the valid area, the direction of *NextPoint* $(0\sim\pi)$ is computed and adjusted by the tracing wises, otherwise, the function of backwards-tracing will be transferred to determine the end point. In the case of the tracing direction angle being larger than π, in order to trace the pseudoridge in the accurate direction sequentially, the range of the direction angle of *NextPoint* must be adjusted to $0\sim2\pi$ by the tracing wises.

(4) The next tracing target point *TracePoint* is determined with the different conditions of different tracing wises. Judge whether the change between the adjusted direction angle of *NextPoint* and the point direction angle of the start tracing point *OriginPot.Angle* is consistent with the tracing tendency and the change value between them (in the case of acute angle) is less than a threshold. (i) If the conditions are meet, then *CurPoint* is endued with *NextPoint*, transfer the procedure (2) to trace the next step, and judge the tracing conditions sequentially. The repeating tracings in which the tracing step is increased are performed until the next tracing target point *TracePoint* is determined. In the repeating tracing, there are several cases such as the traced point being beyond the valid area, or the angle change being consistent with the tracing tendency but the change value being larger than a threshold, or the angle change being not consistent with the tracing tendency and $M=1$. We take the different measures to solve these situations respectively. (ii) If the conditions are not meet, ulteriorly, then we will consider whether the change between the adjusted direction angle of *NextPoint* and the point direction angle of the start tracing point *OriginPot.Angle* is reversed with the tracing tendency and $M=1$. If it is this case, then M is endued with 1, transfer procedure (2) and restart the tracing by returning the iteration and adjusting the tracing direction until the *TracePoint* point is determined. (iii) Otherwise, the function of backwards-tracing will be transferred to determine the *TracePoint* point. Judge the M value, if $M=0$, then let $M=1$, change the tracing wise, set the continuous tracing flag and exit the iteration synchronously. Last, the coordinate position and point direction of the *TracePoint* point is registered in the array S in order.

5. Finally, judge whether the *TracePoint* point meets the end conditions. If the conditions are met, then the tracing along with a direction (wise) is end, return the start tracing point and perform the other tracing in the opposite direction. When the tracing in the opposite wise is finished, a set of the tracing points for pseudoridges will be gained. If the conditions are not met, then the *OriginPoint* is endued with *TracePoint* as the start tracing point of the next tracing, transfer the procedure 4 and continue the tracing.

6. In the end the pseudoridges are smoothed.

2.2 Traced Point Direction Estimate

It is the basis of performing the accurate pseudoridges extraction that the traced point direction estimates are robust. In our method, we propose an effective point direction estimates approach. The approach utilizes the ridges orientations around the aim point to smooth the aim point direction skillfully, which reflects the general orientations of the neighbor ridges and alleviates the local noises accordingly. The detailed idea is as follows:

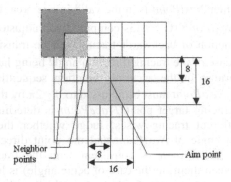

Neighbor points

Aim point

Fig. 1. Sketch map of computing point direction and smoothing processing

The point direction is usually specified for a region (block) that centered on this point. In this paper, the 16×16 pixels region is used to compute the point directions, the directions of the points that locate on the neighborhood of every 8 pixels along X and Y coordinates of aim point are used to smooth the aim point direction, and the mask size for smoothing point directions is 5×5. Thus, the smoothing area is more reasonable, the smoothing degree is stronger, and the result is better.

2.3 Function of Backwards-Tracing and Tracing End Conditions

The function of backwards-tracing is used to find a tracing target point *TracePoint* which meets some conditions backwards along the tracing direction. Its method is as follows:

1. Firstly, the tracing directions are adjusted by the direction angle of the start tracing point *OriginPot.Angle* and the tracing wises. This approach is as formula (1).
2. Secondly, according to the following step, every point is traced backwards from the last point in the tracing orientation and judge if the end conditions are met. The next traced point *NextPoint* is determined by the following formula:

$$\begin{pmatrix} NextPot \cdot x \\ NextPot.y \end{pmatrix} = \begin{pmatrix} CurPot.x \\ CurPot.y \end{pmatrix} + \left\lfloor (Step - i) \times \begin{pmatrix} \cos(TrackDrection) \\ \sin(TrackDrection) \end{pmatrix} + n \times 0.5 \right\rfloor \quad (3)$$

where, *i* denotes the *ith* point of count backwards, other parameters are same as in the formula (1). And consider if the traced point is in the valid fingerprint image area.

- If the condition is met, then this traced point direction is computed and adjusted by the approaches mentioned above, and the tracing target point *TracePoint* is determined by the situations such as if the angle change being consistent with the tracing tendency, if the change value being larger than a threshold, or if the last point being traced and so on.
- Otherwise, then judge if the last point has been traced. If it is the case, then the point *TracePoint* is endued with *CurPoint* and set the end flag. Otherwise, return the iteration to trace the next point backwards.

3. Lastly, the point *TracePoint* and the end flag are returned.

The Tracing End Conditions Are:

- The tracing stops whether it reaches the segmented boundary.
- Or the total tracing steps reach a predefined value (50 in our algorithm).

3 Experimental Results and Conclusion

A fingerprint pseudoridges extraction experiment based on the proposed algorithm is carried out on 500 typical fingerprint samples of NJU fingerprint database which contains 2500 images taken from 250 different fingers, 10 images per finger, and the quality of these fingerprint images is of varying quality in order to provide for a realistic situation. Figure 2 shows some examples of pseudoridges extraction for typical fingerprints. In the illustrations, the different color lines denote the results gained by the different tracing wises (the clockwise tracing or the counter-clockwise tracing). The global geometric shapes of fingerprint ridges extracted by pseudoridges tracing are compared with the true classes of these fingerprints observed by manual work, and table 1 summarizes the results of the experiment. Numbers shown in bold font are correct classification. According as the experimental results, the accuracy rises to 92.6%, and a lower error rate can be achieved by adding the reject option based on the quality of the images.

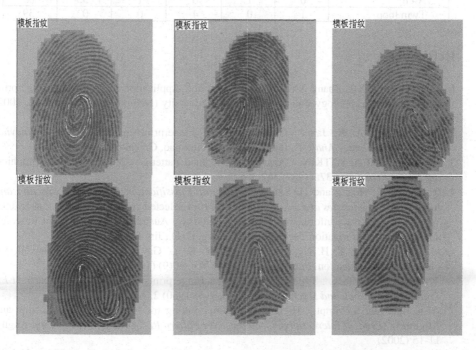

Fig. 2. Examples of pseudoridges extraction for typical fingerprints

In this paper, we have presented a robust pseudoridges extraction algorithm. With tracing the flow field directly but not the ridges, avoiding the complicated computation of thinned ridges, minutia and other trivial processing, the global geometric shape of fingerprint ridges is gained compactly for the purpose of fingerprint classification, this method is intuitive and viable. We have also suggested a skillful and effectual method for orientation field estimates, and adopted a method with adaptive tracing, thereby the algorithm for pseudoridges extraction is simple, reliable and robust. Experimental results demonstrate that our algorithm has better performance and may meet the need of fingerprint classification. In the future, we will focus on improving the algorithm and investigating a practical fingerprint classification scheme which is based on the global shape feature of fingerprint.

Table 1. Experiment results tested on NJU; As.-Assigned Class

True Class \ As	Left loop	Right loop	Whorl	Tended Arch	Arch	Twin loop
Left loop	122	1	2	1	5	0
Right loop	2	129	2	0	4	1
Whorl	1	1	90	0	0	3
Tended Arch	2	2	1	48	2	0
Arch	0	1	0	1	35	0
Twin loop	1	0	4	0	0	39

References

1. Yin YL, Ning XB, Zhang XM. : Development and Application of Automatic Fingerprint Identification Technology. Journal of Nanjing University (Natural Sciences Edition), 2002, 38(1)29~35
2. L. Hong and A. K. Jain. : Classification of Fingerprint Images. *11th Scandinavian Conference on Image Analysis*, June 7-11, Kangerlussuaq, Greenland (1999)
3. M. KASS, and A. WITKIN. : Analyzing Orientaed Patterns. Computer Vision, Graphics, *ans Image Processing* 37: (1987) 362-385
4. Q. Zhang, K. Huang and H. Yan. : *Fingerprint Classification Based on Extraction and Analysis of Singularities and Pseudoridges*. In Proc. Selected papers from 2001 Pan-Sydney Workshop on Visual Information Processing, Sydney, Australia. Conferences in Research and Practice in Information Technology, **11**. Feng, D. D., Jin, J., Eades (2002)
5. M. M. S. Chong, T. H. Ngee, L. Jun, and R. K. L. Gay. : Geometric framework for Fingerprint Classification. *Pattern Recognition*, Vol. 30(9) (1997)1475-1488
6. K. Rao and K. Black. : Type Classification of Fingerprints: A Syntactic Approach. *IEEE Trans. Pattern Anal. and Machine Intell.*, Vol. 2(3)(1980) 223-231
7. A. K. Jain and S. Minut. : Hierarchical Kernel Fitting for Fingerprint Classification and Alignment. *Proc. of International Conference on Pattern Recognition*, Quebec City, August 11-15 (2002)
8. M. Kawagoe and A. Tojo. : Fingerprint pattern classification. *Pattern Recognition*. Vol..17 (3)(1984) 295-303
9. Tan TZ, Ning XB, Yin YL. : A Improved New Method for Detection of the Fingerprint Singularities. *4th Chinese National Conference on Biometric Recognition,* Beijing, China(2003) 184-187

Iris Image Capture System Design
for Personal Identification

Yuqing He, Yangsheng Wang, and Tieniu Tan

Center for Biometric Research and Testing, National Laboratory of Pattern Recognition,
Institute of Automation, Chinese Academy of Sciences, Beijing, P.R. China 100080
yuqing.he@mail.ia.ac.cn, {wys, tnt}@nlpr.ia.ac.cn

Abstract. Iris image acquisition is a key issue in iris recognition, as the quality of the captured image greatly affects the performance of the overall system. This paper first discusses the current status of iris capture devices and then describes the design of a new iris sensor. Experimental results with the iris images captured using the new iris image acquisition device are also presented in this paper.

1 Introduction

Iris recognition is an emerging personal identification method in biometrics. It mainly uses pattern recognition and image processing methods to describe and match the iris feature of the eyes, and then realizes automatic personal authentication. Iris recognition has many advantages such as non-invasiveness, uniqueness, stability, non-impingement and low false recognition rate, so it has broad applications and good prospects. Iris recognition has recently attracted many researchers and enterprisers' attention, and is becoming a hot research topic.

The basic structure of an iris recognition system[1] is shown in Fig. 1.

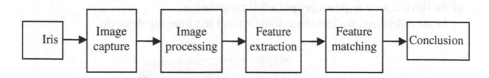

Fig. 1. Basic structure of an iris recognition system

First, we use an image capture device to obtain a proper iris image, and then perform some image pre-processing such as iris location and the removal of the eyelid, eyelash and some other noise. From the pre-processed image, we extract some iris features. By comparing the extracted features with those stored in the database, we obtain the recognition result.

Iris image capture is a key issue in an iris recognition system, and the image quality will greatly affect the performance of the recognition algorithm. Iris is a small

S.Z. Li et al. (Eds.): Sinobiometrics 2004, LNCS 3338, pp. 539–545, 2004.
© Springer-Verlag Berlin Heidelberg 2004

apparatus with a diameter of only about 10mm. The captured image should have high resolution and high contrast to show the texture in detail. In addition, iris has great color differences between different races. This character brings more difficulties to iris image acquisition. We cannot get proper image through normal capture device under normal condition, so we need to design special iris capture device according to the optical characteristics of the iris. This paper mainly discusses iris image capture, analyzes the current status and presents a new iris sensor.

2   Current State of Iris Imaging

Different from the image acquisition of other biometric features such as face, fingerprint and gait, an iris capture device involves the design of a proper optical system, necessary illumination and electronic control unit. In the past 10 years, there has been great and rapid development in iris imaging, from simple short-distance device to complicated long-distance device.

Early iris image capture devices have simple function and require good cooperation from the user. The distance between the device and the user's eye is very short, so it has low usability. Most of the devices in that period were designed by researchers in the computer vision field. With the huge application market and the potential commercial benefit, many companies join the efforts in designing iris capture device and recognition system, which makes the iris image capture system more practical.

A number of companies such as Iridian Technologies, British Telecommunications PLC, Matsushita Electric, OKI Electric and LG Electronics have developed several automatic iris capture devices with working distance from 10 to 60 cm. The cost of these devices tends to be high.

We began iris recognition research in 1998, and developed an automatic iris recognition system[2] in 2000. Our first home-made iris sensor uses CCD camera and image capture card together to capture the iris image. Fig. 2 shows this iris capture device. When capturing the iris image, people should put their eyes in the black patch of the device, so it requires people's full cooperation.

In the following, we introduce some typical iris imaging devices.

Fig. 2. The first iris sensor we developed for research purpose

2.1 Iris Image Capture Device of Panasonic

Panasonic Inc. has a series of capture devices, such as BM-ET100US Authenticam, BM-ET300 and BM-ET500. Fig. 3 shows BM-ET100. It is connected with computer through USB line, and does not need external power, so it must work with computer together. The working distance is 48-53 cm when capturing iris image. It also has normal video capture module used for video meeting. BM-ET300 and BM-ET500 are embedded iris capture system. They can work alone without connecting to the computer, but they need external power supply. The BM-ET300's working distance is 30-40cm and BM-ET500 is 30-60cm which can auto-focus a user's iris.

2.2 Iris Image Capture Device of LG Inc.

The main type of LG's recognition system is IrisAccess 3000, shown in Fig. 4. It has several parts: EOU (Enrolled Optical Unit), ROU (Remote Optical Unit), ICU (Identification Control Unit), FGB (Frame Grabber Board), DIB (Door Interface Board) and server PC.

It uses external power of 100-240VAC. Its working distance is 8-25cm, and the output signal is analog video. Through RS 232C port, it can work with frame grabber card together to get the digital iris image for computer, so its size is a little big.

Fig. 3. Panasonic BM-ET 100   **Fig. 4.** LG Iris Access 3000

2.3 Iris Image Capture Device of Iritech Inc.

Iritech inc. has developed a series of devices from handheld to automatic iris capture system. All its devices use special port to work with computer and relative software. Its automatic iris capture device[5] can search the face automatically, then locate the iris' position, adjust the camera's position and automatically focus the lens to get the clearest iris image. Besides the fundamental image capture function, it also can control the luminous source's intensity continuously, then capture the image sequence, and analyzes the changes between different iris images to determine whether the iris is alive and valid. Since it needs more time to analyze image sequence, the recognition time is a little longer, but in general, it reaches the advanced level in the world.

3   Design Method of Iris Imaging Device

When designing the iris image capture device, we should combine the hardware and software together, and should focus on optical and electronic control design. Particular attention should be paid to the following three issues:

1) Special optical imaging system. This includes optical lens, active light source and etc;
2) Imaging sensor and electronic control module. This module is to change optical signal to digital image, control the image capture, send the image to processing unit through special port and store it.
3) Iris distance location. We need to estimate the iris' special position precisely, which can be realized through changing the lens' focus or instructing the user to move to the correct position.

Iris capture system maybe divided into two categories. One is using auto-focus lens to capture iris image. This kind of device is easily to be used, but it has high cost, and adds complicated mechanical structure in the device, so its size is big. The other category is using fixed lens, which can reduce the complicated mechanical structure, and has great advantages such as small size, but it needs user's cooperation and moving to the proper imaging area.

According to the above analysis, the iris image capture system's basic structure can be shown in Fig. 5.

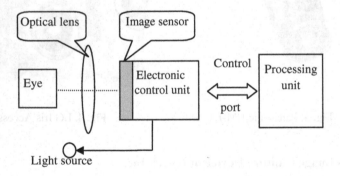

Fig. 5. Basic structure of iris image capture system

The iris first passes optical lens and is imaged on the sensor. With proper illumination, we can improve the image contrast. The image sensor transforms the optical signal into electric signal. Through the electronic control unit and special port, the image reaches the processing unit (such as computer or other embedded processor unit). By controlling the light source, the image sensor and the lens or indicators, we can obtain a proper image for subsequent processing.

In the following, we describe the modules of the system in more details.

3.1 Optical System

The optical system design is based on well-known techniques, but the parameters have to be changed according to the different situations. So designing proper optical system is also a hard task.

When designing the optical system, we should consider the device's working distance, and combine it with the image sensor and the light source to acquire high image resolution and high quality, so that the image preserves the iris texture information.

3.2 Illumination

The iris is very small. Without illumination, the captured image may be a little dark, so it will affect the recognition algorithm. The eye can only detect visible light (wavelength between 400-760nm), so we can choose the light source in near infrared band (700-900nm) to avoid the user's uncomfortable feeling. In addition, the illumination can also enhance the iris image texture. But too strong infrared light may hurt the eye tissue, so when designing the light source, we should abide to the international illumination safety standard IEC 60825-1 and other relevant standards.

3.3 Image Sensor and Electronic Control Unit

The commonly used image sensor is CCD (Charge Coupled Device) or CMOS (Complementary Metal-Oxide Semiconductor) image sensor[6]. CCD image sensor outputs analog signal, so an A/D converter or frame grabber card is needed to change the signal into digital image. CMOS image sensor can directly output digital signal, so the imaging and control circuit can be more compact, and the imaging unit can be easily connected to the computer through a USB line.

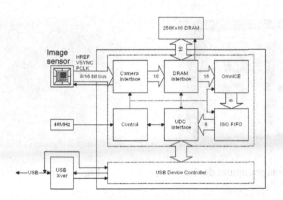

Fig. 6. Block diagram of electronic module

The sensor's resolution and spectrum response are important parameters, and will affect the image quality. They should be considered together when designing optical system to get proper image[7]. Besides imaging unit, electronic control unit is also needed to get the iris image. It can adjust the sensor's auto-exposure, brightness, contrast, auto-white balance and other registers. Electronic control unit can also communicate with processing unit to control image capture and send captured image to the recognition algorithm. The functional block diagram of the electronic module is shown in Fig. 6.

3.4 User's Distance Location

To acquire clear iris image, the user's eye should stay in specific area. This area is limited by the optical lens. We use two methods to realize the distance location: one is auto-focus technique which can automatically change the camera's direction and the lens' focus to get clear image; the other is user's self-location, where the user can move to the correct area according to instructions from the system.

Auto-focus system has complicated mechanical structure, so the device size is relatively large and the cost is high, but people can easily use the device; user's self-location system often uses fixed-focus so the device size is small and the cost is low, but it needs user's good cooperation. Image analysis algorithm or distance measurement is needed to realize this function.

4   Our Iris Image Capture Device

According to the design method, we developed an iris image capture device, which is shown in Fig. 7. This device can connect to the computer through USB. Combining with recognition algorithm, a personal identification system is realized. The device's working distance is about 30cm. An example iris image captured by this device can be seen in Fig. 8.

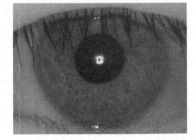

Fig. 7. Our iris image capture device   Fig. 8. Captured iris image

The iris image captured by our device conforms to the INCITS (InterNational Committee for Information Technology Standard) iris image quality standard. Through testing the 23 classes of iris images captured by this device with two different recognition algorithms[9,10], we get the results shown in Table 1. From the results, we can see that the FAR (False Acceptance Rate) and FRR (False Rejection Rate) are relatively low, demonstrating the high recognition rate of the overall system.

Table 1. Test result of captured iris images on different recognition algorithms

Item	Average Time	FAR	FRR	Remark
Algorithm 1	10.19 ms	0.013523	0.024922	Normal quality enroll images
Algorithm 2	12.38 ms	0.000000	0.015009	High quality enroll images
		0.000000	0.256410	Normal quality enroll images

5 Conclusion

The iris image capture system described in this paper integrates optical-electric imaging, electronic control, image pattern recognition and mechanical design. It is a key part in iris recognition system. More and more efforts have been made on this issue, leading to more and more products. However, much remains to be done in device and system design, such as live iris detection, eyeglass reflection light elimination, and user's self-location in fixed-focus systems. With the broad application of iris recognition systems, there have many demands on convenient, high efficiency, multifunctional and cheap products, and we should put more attention and more efforts on device and system design.

References

1. Y. Wang, Y. Zhu, T. Tan, "Biometrics personal identification based on iris pattern", *ACTA Automatica Sinica*, 28(1): 1-10, 2002.
2. T. Tan, Y. Zhu, Y. Wang , "Iris image capture device", *Chinese Patent*, No. CN_2392219U, 1999
3. L. Flom, A. Safir, "Iris Recognition System," *United States Patent*, No.4641349, 1987
4. J. McHugh, J. Lee, C. Kuhla, "Handheld iris imaging apparatus and method", *United States Patent*, No. 6289113, 1998
5. D. Kim, J. Ryoo, "Iris Identification system and method of identifying a person through iris recognition", *World Patent*, No. WO0062239, 2000
6. Y. Hou, Y. He, Y. Chen, "Image sensor of digital still camera", *Optical Technique*, 29(1): 59-62, 2003
7. Y. Hou, Y. He, "The specific parameters and selection of CMOS image sensor for DSC designing", *Optical Technique*, 29(2): 174-176, 2003
8. B. Lin, L. Wang, X. Cao, "Study of iris image capturing system for iris recognition", *Laser & Infrared*, 32(5): 347-349, 2002
9. Z. Sun, Y. Wang, T. Tan, "Improving Iris Recognition Accuracy via Cascaded Classifiers", *International Conference on Biometric Authentication*, 2004
10. J. Cui, Y. Wang, L. Ma, T. Tan, "An Iris Recognition Algorithm Using Local Extreme Points", *International Conference on Biometric Authentication*, 2004

An Iris Segmentation Procedure for Iris Recognition

Xiaoyan Yuan and Pengfei Shi

Institute of Image Processing and Pattern Recognition,
Shanghai Jiao Tong University, 200030, P.R. China
{yanr, pfsh}@sjtu.edu.cn

Abstract. Iris segmentation is a critical stage in the whole iris recognition process. In this paper, a procedure of iris segmentation is presented which was designed on the basis of the natural properties of the iris. The proposed procedure consists of two main steps: circles localization and non-iris region detection. In our method, we took into consideration of some typical problems most likely to appear in practice. And experiments show that our method can achieve good results and robust as well.

1 Introduction

Nowadays, biometric recognition is becoming one of the most promising and reliable way to authenticate the identity of a person. Biometric feature can serve as a kind of living passport or a living password that one need not remember but one always carried along. And iris-based identification has been receiving more and more attention since its emergence in 1992 [1].

A good biometric feature should be: (1) high uniquely – so the chance of two people with the same feature will be very small; (2) much stable – should not change over time; and (3) easily captured – should be convenient and should avoid intrusion to the users.

Iris as a biometric feature can fulfill all the requirements mentioned above. Iris is defined as the region between the pupil and the sclera where exits very complex texture. Among all kinds of human biometric features, such as face, fingerprint, speech etc, iris is thought to be the best. Because (1) It is distinctive and unique for each person including identical twins and each eye of one person. Moreover, its physiological response to light provides a natural test against fake irises[2][3]; (2) it is a protected internal organ. Its visual texture is developed during his embryonic stage and will never change since then [4]. Also, (3) people can accept the iris-based recognition technique for it is non-invasive and don't cause any damage to users. And nowadays only one glance at the iris capture instrument will be ok. It is very convenient.

In the following sections, we propose an integrated procedure that was designed especially for iris segmentation. Section 2 introduces SJTU-IDB we applied and our procedure of iris segmentation is described in detail. In section 3, experiment results are demonstrated. And in section 4, a conclusion is presented.

S.Z. Li et al. (Eds.): Sinobiometrics 2004, LNCS 3338, pp. 546–553, 2004.
© Springer-Verlag Berlin Heidelberg 2004

2   Iris Segmentation Procedure

Iris segmentation is the first step and also the key step of the whole iris recognition. Its objective is to separate the usable iris pattern from other parts of the eye and the noise as well. It is obvious that the accuracy of the iris segmentation will have great impact on the result of future processing.

In our research work, we utilized SJTU-IDB (Iris Database of Shanghai Jiao Tong University) which contains 400 grayscale eye images that collected from 100 persons. The age of the person we chose range from 22 to 70. And it includes the eye samples of both male and female. The eye images in this database were all set to the same size: 372×245, the iris pattern we are interested is well confined in this area. Some samples from the SJTU Iris Database are shown in Figure 1.

It can be noticed in Figure 1, that the iris can be explicit and integrated in some samples, as Figure 1.(a). But few are seriously occluded by the eyelashes, as (c), or by the eyelids, as (b) and (d). Those images are always excluded from some iris databases for their low quality. But some of these low-quality iris images are not caused by eye motion or unsuitable eye position. It is because of people's natural eye shape, or dense eyelashes, or because of the old age.

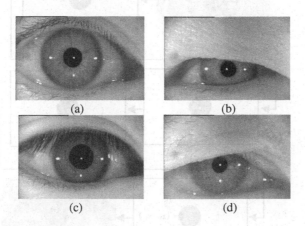

Fig. 1. Samples from SJTU-IDB (Scaled for the purpose of saving room)

The existence of those low-quality cases discussed above brings much difficulty to the segmentation of the iris, so the algorithm is required to be correct and much robust.

Our procedure is implemented in two major stages: first, the circles localization, and second, the non-iris region detection (include eyelids, eyelashes and reflection spots).

2.1   Circles Localization

It has been proved to be feasible to regard the inner boundary (between pupil and iris) and the outer boundary (between iris and sclera) of the iris both as the exact circles[4][5], thus our objective is to determine the parameters of inner circle and the outer circle of the iris in the eye image. The inner circle was localized first in our method.

Inner Circle. Mathematical morphology was applied to find the parameters of the inner circle. The whole process is illustrated in Figure 2. First the original 256 gray-scale eye image was converted to a binary image, as shown in (b). Then found the biggest connective area in (b) and erased all other parts, here we got (c) which had only one part left corresponded to the rough pupil area. Performed open operator on (c) to fill the pupil area, we got (d). The contour of the only connective part in (d) is nearly a circle, then fitted this contour to an exact circle, in this way the parameters (x_i, y_i) and r_i of this exact circle can be obtained, as shown in (e). By overlapping this circle on the original eye image, as shown in (f), the inner circle is seen to be well localized.

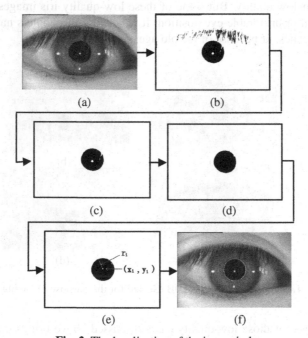

(a)   (b)

(c)   (d)

(e)   (f)

Fig. 2. The localization of the inner circle

Outer Circle. For the reason of the occlusion by the eyelids and the eyelashes, and the relatively low contrast between the iris and the sclera, the localization of the outer circle is more difficult.

First a rotationally symmetric Gaussian low pass filter was convoluted with the eye image to smooth the image. Then the derivatives are filtered to be selective for verti-cal edge information to reduce the influence of the eye-lids when next performing circular Hough transform. Next, a voting method was applied through circular Hough transform to find the parameters x_o, y_o and r_o of the outer circle. The circular Hough transform is defined as:

$$H(x_c, y_c, r) = \sum_{i=1}^{n} h(x_i, y_i, x_c, y_c, r) \tag{1}$$

in which:

$$h(x_i, y_i, x_c, y_c, r) = \begin{cases} 1 & |d(x_i, y_i, x_c, y_c, r)| < \varepsilon \\ 0 & otherswise \end{cases} \tag{2}$$

with:

$$d(x_i, y_i, x_c, y_c, r) = (x_i - x_c)^2 + (y_i - y_c)^2 - r^2 \tag{3}$$

For each edge point (x_i, y_i) in the edge map, $|d(x_i, y_i, x_c, y_c, r)| < \varepsilon$ for every parameter triple (x_c, y_c, r) that represents a circle through that point. The parameter triple (x_o, y_o, r_o) that can maximize H was chosen as our result.

A satisfactory result has been got by using the procedure proposed in this section. Figure 3 is an example to show its effectivity of locating the inner and outer circles.

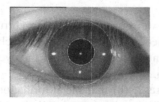

Fig. 3. The result of the circle finding

2.2 Non-iris Region Detection

There are always eyelids, eyelashes or reflections in the region that between the two circles. If they are not excluded from the real iris region, they will be considered as part of the iris pattern in the future matching stage. As a result, the percentage of the matched region will increase, so the accuracy of personal identification based on the corrupted iris pattern would be reduced seriously. In that sense, the non-iris region detection is indispensable.

Eyelid. According to the natural shape of the eyelids, the upper and lower eyelids were modeled as parabolic arcs. This model was first proposed by Wildes et al. [1].

The parabolic Hough transform was employed to detect parabolic arc, and it can be represented as:

$$\left(-(x-h_j)\sin\theta_j+(y-k_j)\cos\theta_j\right)^2 = a_j\left((x-h_j)\cos\theta_j+(y-k_j)\sin\theta_j\right) \quad (4)$$

where a_j controls the curvature of the parabola, (h_j, k_j) is the peak of the parabola and θ_j is the rotation angle.

First, performed horizontal Prewitt edge detector to get the edge map, then the parabolic Hough transform could help to set the parameters of the parabolic arcs by checking its 4-dimension accelerator.

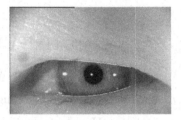

Fig. 4. Eyelids detected

Though the parabolic Hough transform can always get a good result, its time efficiency is relatively low.

Eyelash. Since the iris texture has already been corrupted by the occlusion of the eyelashes, it is not much necessary to detect every eyelash. So it is reasonable to find an easier method to minimum the influence of the eyelashes and make more use of the iris texture information.

We can see from Figure 2. (b) that the information of the eyelashes can be got from the binary image of the eye, by removing the pupil area after thresholding with a proper value, the rough information of the eyelashes can be obtained. But this method is very sensitive to this threshold value. So here we choose the method of hysteresis thresholding to detect eyelashes. Hysteresis thresholding was first proposed by John Canny to detect edges [9]. He applied two thresholds to avoid the streaking phenomenon and false edges.

Here, the eye image was thresholded with two different values T_1, T_2 and $T_2 > T_1$. We got those two values from the statistic property by checking the histogram of the eye image. Pixels with values lower than threshold T_1 were marked as eyelashes. Pixels adjacent to (we choose eight-connectivity) points that have been marked as eyelashes and with values lower than threshold T_2 were also marked as eyelashes.

Using hysteresis thresholding could avoid losing faint eyelashes and also could ignore the noises.

This process and result are illustrated in Figure 5.

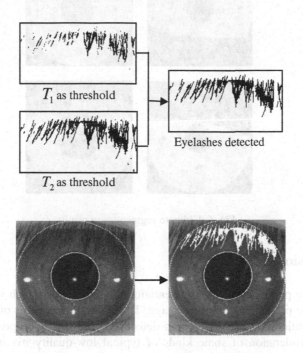

T_1 as threshold

T_2 as threshold

Eyelashes detected

Fig. 5. Hysteresis thresholding to detect eyelashes

Reflection. In some papers, reflection spot was modeled as normal distribution or Gaussian distribution [10]. While the reflection spots in most iris images are much lighter than other part of the iris, so it is an easier and also effective way to detect them just by thresholding. That's the way we did it.

3 Experiment Results

After the iris has been segmented following the procedure proposed in section 3, it is necessary to separate the iris pattern from the surrounding for further processing. Figure 6 provides the ultimate segmentation results of the four eye images showed in Figure 1.

Figure 6 shows that not only those eye images with a good quality can yield a good segmentation result. Even for those whose iris patterns are seriously occluded by upper or lower eyelid (or both) or by eyelashes, the iris pattern can still be segmented correctly by following the proposed procedure.

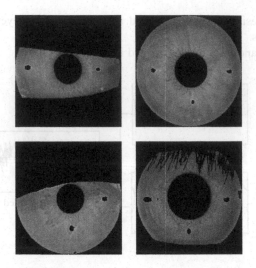

Fig. 6. Ultimate segmentation results

4   Conclusion

In this paper, a procedure of iris segmentation was presented which was designed on the basis of the properties of the iris image. This procedure consists of two main steps: circles localization and non-iris region detection. And in the proposed method, we took into consideration of some kinds of typical low-quality iris images likely to appear in practice. And experiments show that this procedure achieved good results and robust as well.

References

1. Wildes R.: Iris Recognition, An Emerging Biometric Technology. Proc. of the IEEE, Vol.85 (1997)
2. Gerald O.Williams.: Iris Recognition Technology. IEEE AES Systems Magazine (1997)
3. Daugman J.: How Iris Recognition Works. IEEE Transactions on Circuits and Systems for Video Technology. Vol.14 (2004) 21- 30
4. Daugman J.: How Iris Recognition Works. Proc. of International Conference on Image Processing (2002)
5. Li Ma, Tieniu Tan, Yunhong Wang, Dexin Zhang : Personal Identification Based on Iris Texture Analysis. IEEE Transaction on Pattern Analysis and Machine Intelligence, Vol.25, No.12 (2003)
6. N. Ritter: Location of the Pupil-Iris border in slit-lamp images of the cornea. Proc. of the International Conference on Image Analysis and Processing (1999)
7. Daugman J.: High confidence personal identification by rapid video analysis of iris texture. Proc. of the IEEE, International Carnahan conf. on security technology (1992)
8. Junzhou Huang, Li Ma, Yunhong Wang, Tieniu Tan : Iris Model Based on Local Orientation Description. Proc. of Asian Conference on Computer Vision, Korea (2004) 954-959

9. Canny, J.: A Computational Approach to Edge Detection. IEEE Transaction on Pattern Analysis and Machine Intelligence (1986) 679-714
10. W. K. Kong and D. Zhang: Accurate Iris Segmentation Based on Novel Reflection and Eyelash Detection Model. Proc. of International Symposium on Intelligent Multimedia, Video and Speech Processing (2001)
11. Ramy Zewail, Ahmed Seil, Nadder Hamdy, Magdy Saeb: Iris Identification Based on Log-Gabor Filtering. Proceedings of the IEEE Midwest Symposium on Circuits, Systems, & Computers (2003)
12. W.W. Boles and B. Boashash.: A Human Identification Technique Using Images of the Iris and Wavelet Transform. IEEE Transaction on Signal Processing, Vol.46,   No. 4 (1998)

Zernike Moment Invariants Based Iris Recognition

Chenhong Lu and Zhaoyang Lu

National Key Lab. of Integrated Services Networks, Xidian University, Xi'an, China
Lu_chenh@hotmail.com

Abstract. Iris recognition, a relatively new biometric technology, has great advantages, such as variability, stability and security, thus it is the most promising for high security environments. For iris recognition it is desirable to obtain an iris representation invariant to translation, scale and rotation. Translation invariance and approximate scale invariance usually can be easy achieved by preprocessing, but rotation invariance is still a problem. In this paper, a new iris recognition algorithm is proposed, which adopts Zernike's moment invariants to extract iris moment-based rotation invariant features without any iris rotation adjustment. These invariant features are selected automatically based on the discrimination measure defined for the invariant features. Experimental results show that the proposed method has an encouraging performance. In particular, it achieves a lower Equal Error Rate than which in [2] proposed by Daugman without rotation adjustment.

1 Introduction

Biometric identification technologies, including facial recognition, fingerprint recognition, speaker verification and so on, offer a new solution for personal identification due to natural manner and secure access. Among these biometric technologies, iris recognition is a new method for personal identification and becomes a hot topic in machine learning research area because of the following advantages: the iris recognition is non-invasive; the iris pattern does not change after its structures are largely complete; and it is almost impossible that irises are modified by surgical without risk.

The iris is complex enough to be used as a biometric signature with impostor odds ranging as high as 1 in 10^{35}[1]. This means that the probability of finding two people with identical iris patterns is almost zero. Therefore, in order to use the iris pattern for identification, it is important to define a representation that is well adapted for extracting the iris information from images of the human eyes.

In 1993, Daugman developed a successful system by using the 2-D Gabor wavelet transform [2]. In Daugman's approach, an iris image is first mapped into a representation invariant to differences in translation and scale, and then is filtered by the quadrature bandpass filter banks. The resulting representation is closely quantized for bitwise matching. In 1996, Wildes et al. developed a prototype system based on automated iris verification which uses a very computationally demanding image registration technique [5]. Boles and Boashash [6] proposed an iris identification system in which zero-crossing of the wavelet transform at various resolution levels is calculated over

S.Z. Li et al. (Eds.): Sinobiometrics 2004, LNCS 3338, pp. 554–561, 2004.

concentric circles on the iris, and the resulting 1-D signals are compared with the model features using different dissimilarity functions. Ma, Tan and Wang [7] proposed an algorithm for local iris texture feature extraction by characterizing key local variations.

In all these systems, it is desirable to obtain an iris representation invariant to translation, scale, and rotation. Translation invariance and approximate scale invariance can be achieved by easy normalizing the original image at the preprocessing step, but rotation invariance is still a difficult problem. Most existing schemes achieve approximate rotation invariance either by rotating the feature vector before matching [2], [3], [4], [6],[8], or by registering the input image with the model before feature extraction [5] [7]. In this paper, a new iris recognition algorithm is proposed, which Zernike's moment invariant is adopted to extract iris features without any compensating for iris rotation. The proposed algorithm takes advantage of the rotation invariant property of the Zernike moments and then can reduce the computational cost for iris recognition matching on a larger iris image database.

2   Rotation Invariant Feature Based on Zernike Moment

In this section, we will give a generalized expression for obtaining the rotation invariant features. In this paper, translation invariance and scaling invariance are achieved in the same way as the existing schemes by using a normalization based on circle detection.

2.1   Translation and Scaling Normalization

Irises from different people may be captured in different size, and even for irises from the same eye, the size may change due to illumination variations and changes of the camera-to-eye distance. This will affect the matching results. For the purpose of achieving more accurate recognition results, it is necessary to compensate for such elastic deformation. Daugman [2-4] solved this problem by establishing zones of analysis on the iris in a doubly dimensionless projected polar coordinate system. Regardless of size and pupillary dilation, this system assigns to each point in the iris a pair of dimensionless real coordinates (r, θ) where r lies on the unit interval [0,1] and θ is the usual angular quantity that is cyclic over $[0, 2\pi]$. The remapping of the iris image $f(x, y)$ from raw coordinates (x, y) to the doubly dimensionless non-concentric polar coordinate system (r, θ) can be represented as

$$f(x(r, \theta), y(r, \theta)) \rightarrow f(r, \theta), \tag{1}$$

where $x(r, \theta)$ and $y(r, \theta)$ are defined as linear combinations of both the set of pupillary boundary points $(x_p(\theta), y_p(\theta))$ around the circle that was found by integro-differential operators, and the set of limbus boundary points along the outer perimeter of the iris $(x_s(\theta), y_s(\theta))$ bordering the sclera, that was also found by integro-differential operators:

$$x(r,\theta) = (1-r)x_p(\theta) + rx_s(\theta),\qquad (2)$$

$$y(r,\theta) = (1-r)y_p(\theta) + ry_s(\theta).\qquad (3)$$

2.2 Zernike Rotation Invariant Moments

To get rotation invariant moments, typically the following generalized expression in polar coordinate is used

$$F_{pq} = \iint f(r,\theta)g_p(r)e^{jq\theta}rdrd\theta \qquad (4)$$

where F_{pq} is the pq-order moment, $g_p(r)$ is a function of radial variable r, p and q are integer parameters. It is easy to prove that the value of $\|F_{pq}\|$ is rotation invariant. The proof can be briefly given as follows. If an image object $f(r,\theta)$ is rotated by an angle of β, its corresponding moment will become $F_{pq}^{rotated} = F_{pq}e^{jq\beta}$. Since $\|F_{pq}^{rotated}\| = \sqrt{F_{pq}^{rotated}(F_{pq}^{rotated})^*} = \|F_{pq}\|$, hence, $\|F_{pq}\|$ has the rotation invariant property.

In order to reduce the problem of feature extraction from a 2-D image object to that from a 1-D sequence, expression (4) is rewritten as follows:

$$F_{pq} = \int S_q(r)g_p(r)rdr \qquad (5)$$

where $S_q(r) = \int f(r,\theta)e^{jq\theta}d\theta$.

When setting $g_p(r)$ to be the following orthogonal polynomials

$$g_p^{Zernike}(r) = \sum_{s=0}^{(p-|q|)/2}(-1)^s \times \frac{(p-s)!}{s!(\frac{p+|q|}{2}-s)!(\frac{p-|q|}{2})!}r^{p/2-s}, \qquad (6)$$

and some constraints on p and q ($p-|q|$ even and $|q| \le p$), we can obtain Zernike's moment invariants $\|F_{pq}^{Zernike}\|$, which are the magnitude of Zernike moments [8]. Since the higher-order moments are too sensitive to noise. They cannot be used as the discriminative features of an object. Here we constrain the orders p and q such that: $p \leq 12, 0 \leq q \leq p$, and $(p-q)$ even.

3 Discriminative Features Selection and Classification

It is well known that the selection of discriminative features is a crucial step in any pattern recognition system. Since the nest stage sees only these features and acts upon them. Thus it is important to design a rank order procedure of selecting discriminative features which have small intraclass variance and large interclass separation. Many feature selection methods have been developed [9]. In this paper, standard variance-based feature discrimination technique, such as between-to within-class variance ratio, are used for defining the discrimination measures of features. It should be pointed out that the feature selection criterion is dependent on the classification method. Thus, the choice of between-to within-class variance ratio would be better suited to the use of the minimum-distance classifier discussed in Section 3.2.

3.1 An Automatic Discrimination Feature Selection Algorithm

The mean of each invariant feature $\left\| F_{pq}^{Zernike} \right\|$ for iris I_i, $m(I_i, \left\| F_{pq}^{Zernike} \right\|)$, and the standard deviation $\sigma(I_i, \left\| F_{pq}^{Zernike} \right\|)$ can be estimated from the samples of the iris I_i. The between-to within-class variance ratio may be used to describe the discrimination degree of a certain feature for discriminating two class. We specifically use the following discrimination measure which evaluates the effectiveness of using the feature $\left\| F_{pq}^{Zernike} \right\|$ to differentiate between two irises I_i and I_j:

$$Q(\left\| F_{pq}^{Zernike} \right\|, I_i, I_j) = \frac{\eta(\sigma(I_i, \left\| F_{pq}^{Zernike} \right\|) + \sigma(I_j, \left\| F_{pq}^{Zernike} \right\|))}{\left| m(I_i, \left\| F_{pq}^{Zernike} \right\|) - m(I_j, \left\| F_{pq}^{Zernike} \right\|) \right|} \tag{7}$$

where $\eta = 3.0$. This is based on the property that the probability of a class conditional Gaussian variable distributed in the interval $[m - 3\sigma, m + 3\sigma]$ is about 99.8%. Thus, if $Q(\left\| F_{pq}^{Zernike} \right\|, I_i, I_j)$ is smaller than 1, then the feature $\left\| F_{pq}^{Zernike} \right\|$ is guaranteed to be able to differentiate between irises I_i and I_j.

In order to select discriminative features, we calculated the discrimination measures for each feature and select a set whose values are smaller than 1. The discrimination number is defined as:

$$NDD(\left\| F_{pq}^{Zernike} \right\|) = \sum_{i=1}^{N_{class}} \sum_{j=1, j \neq i}^{N_{class}} w(Q(\left\| F_{pq}^{Zernike} \right\|, I_i, I_j)) \tag{8}$$

where $w(x) = 1$ if $x < 1$, otherwise $w(x) = 0$. For each feature, we define the worst overall discriminative measure as:

$$Q^{worst}\left(\left\|F_{pq}^{Zernike}\right\|\right) = \max_{1 \le i, j \le N_{class}, i \ne j} \left\{Q(\left\|F_{pq}^{Zernike}\right\|, I_i, I_j)\right.$$
$$\left. \cdot w(Q(\left\|F_{pq}^{Zernike}\right\|, I_i, I_j)\right\}. \tag{9}$$

Using these measures, we can select the discriminative features as follows:

Rank All Zernike Invariant Moments. The feature with the largest discrimination number is ranked first. For features with the same discrimination number, we rank them in the ascending order according to their worst overall discriminative measures.

Select features. Select the top $N_{feature}$ features from the ordered feature list as discriminative features.

3.2 Minimum Distance Classification

An unknown testing iris with feature vector X is compared with those of a set of known irises. The distance between X and the ith class iris is measured using the square of the normalized Euclidean distance. The iris X is classified into class i^*, where i^* satisfies

$$d(i^*) = \underset{i}{Min}\, d(i) = \underset{i}{Min} \sum_k \frac{(X_k - m_k^i)^2}{\sigma_k^i}, \tag{10}$$

where m_k^i and σ_k^i denotes the mean and standard deviation of the kth feature of iris i.

4 Experimental Results

Research in this paper use the CASIA Iris Image Database collected by Institute of Automation, Chinese Academy of Sciences. CASIA Iris Image Database includes 756 iris images from 108 eyes (hence 108 classes) [10]. For each eye, 7 images are captured in two sessions, where three samples are collected in the first session and four in the second session. Several samples from CASIA iris database are shown in Figure 1.

We test the algorithm in two modes: classification and verification. For each iris pattern, we randomly choose 4 samples for training and the rest for testing. Based on our discriminative feature extraction method, the classification rates using various numbers of selected features are shown in Figure 2. The horizontal axis represents the number of selected features, and the vertical axis represents the percentage of correct classification. The classification rate obtained is 100% when 14 features are used. It is noted that these moment features in the experiment are unstable as the classification rate slightly oscillates when the number of features increases. This probably is due to insufficient number of training samples used in feature selection process, while the testing samples are relatively large.

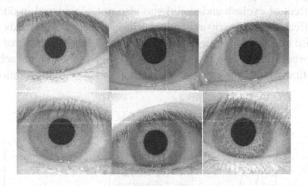

Fig. 1. Samples of iris image

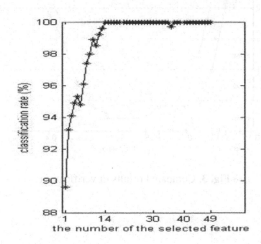

Fig. 2. Classification rate varies with the number of selected feature

In a verification system, the performance can be measured in terms of three different rates:

False Acceptance Rate (FAR): the probability of identifying an intruder as an enrolled user.

False Rejection Rate (FRR): the probability of rejecting an enrolled user, as if he were an intruder.

Equal Error Rate (EER): the value where the FAR and FRR rates are equal.

In Figure 3, the performance of the proposed scheme was compared with which proposed by Daugman in [2]. In order to show the rotation invariant of Zernike moments, Daugman's algorithm was imitated without any rotation compensate. Furthermore, the effect of eyelash and eyelid was also not considered in our experiments. This will not affect the comparison results because these two methods are compared in the same noise condition. It can be seen in Figure 3 that Equal Error Rate, i.e., the cross point between the FAR and the FRR curves of our scheme, achieves 0.24%, which is lower than that of the Daugman's method in [2] without rotation compensating.

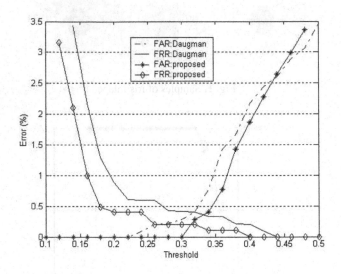

Fig. 3. Compared results in verification

5   Conclusion

In this paper, a new iris recognition scheme is proposed based on the Zernike invariant moments. In order to obtain an iris representation invariant to rotation, most existing schemes either rotate the feature vector before matching or register the input image with the model before feature extraction. Our proposed algorithm takes advantage of the rotation invariant property of the Zernike moments, so it can reduce the computational cost for iris recognition matching on a larger iris image database. On the CASIA Iris Database, the proposed method achieves encouraging results.

Now, we expect to improve the performance by using more effective moment features such as wavelet moment invariants, which can capture not only the rotation invariant global information but also the rotation invariant local information of the interest objects.

References

1. W. H. Peter: Recognising Human Eyes. SPIE Vol. 1570, Geometric Methods in Computer Vision, (1991) 214-226.
2. John G. Daugman: High Confidence Visual Recognition of Person by a Test of Statistical Independence. IEEE Trans. PAMI 15(11), (1993) 1148-1161.
3. John G. Daugman: The Importance of being Random: Statistic Principles of Iris Recognition. Pattern Recognition 36(2), (2003) 279-291.
4. John G. Daugman: How Iris Recognition Works. IEEE Trans. CSVT 14(1), (2004) 1-17.
5. R. Wildes et al.: A System for Automated Iris Recognition. Proc.2nd IEEE workshop Applications on Computer Vision (1994) 121-128.
6. W. W. Boles and B. Boashash: A Human Identification Technique Using Image of the Iris and Wavelet Transform. IEEE Trans. Signal Processing 46(4), (1998) 1185-1188.
7. Li Ma, Tieniu Tan and Yunhong Wang: Personal Identification Based on Iris Texture Analysis. IEEE Trans. Pattern Analysis and Machine Intelligence 25(12), (2003) 1519-1533.
8. Li Ma, Tieniu Tan and Yunhong Wang: Efficient Iris Recognition by Characterizing Key Local Variations. IEEE Trans. Image Processing 13(6), (2004) 739-750.
9. M. R. Teague: Image Analysis via the General Theory of Moments. J. Opt. Soc. Amer., Vol.70, (1980) 920-930.
10. P. A. Devijver and J. Kittler: Pattern Recognition: a Statistical Approach. Prentice-Hall Englewood Cliffs, NJ, (1982).
11. CASIA Iris Image Database, Chinese Academy of sciences, Institute of Automation, http://www.sinobiometrics.com/casiairis.htm.

Two-Dimensional Projection and Crossing
for Iris Optimal Localization

Xueyi Ye, Peng Yao, Liang Wu, and Zhenquan Zhuang

Department of Electronic Science & Technology,
University of Science and Technology of China, HeFei, Anhui 230026, P.R. China
xueyi_ye@ustc.edu

Abstract. This paper investigates some factors possibly disturbing iris localization in an iris image operated by the localizing pre-processing, and gives an optimal localization method from a new viewpoint different with the past. After establishing two-dimensional projection histograms and corresponding matrices of an image edge-rude-field, the method researches the relation between every dimensional projecting character and the tangled distributing traits in the edge-rude-field. Then it obtains an as good as possible rude-field of the iris edge using the way of scout and crossing which detect and get rid of the bad points in the edge-rude-field, finally calculates the exact iris boundary. After the comparing test and the analysis to an iris image database, the experiment result shows that the robust method can quickly and accurately completes iris localization and is not sensitive to different filters worked on the pre-processing of the localization.

1 Introduction

Recently, the increasing requirements of people to public safety and personal safety (privacy) propel the surge development of biometric authentication. It is widely acknowledged that iris recognition is one of the most reliable biometric identification methods. To the iris recognition, getting the iris part from an original import image apparently is the premise to accomplish the operation. Moreover, the true ratio of the recognition is directly dependent on the precision of the localization because both the increase of the iris part or not will bring an error, and the localizing process occupies considerable system time (the total calculating time). Therefore, a real-time iris recognition system does require an accurate, fast, and robust localization method.

Iris localization is generally divided into 2 parts, the edge detection and the segmentation [7]. By the parameters of the centers and boundaries of an iris through the localizing process, a recognition system can confirm the position of the iris part in an import image and attain the iris texture for the next process. Nevertheless, two important interferefering factors must be considered in the localization. One is eyelashes and eyelids in the image, and the other is faculae in the image because of all kinds of light sources. They, especially the former, not only decrease the precision of the localization, but also consume much more system time. Previous iris localization methods approximately regard the inner and outer boundary of a typical iris as circles. J. Daugman[2] used a circular detector to iteratively search an maximum contour integral derivative. Richard P. Wildes et al. [1][5] reported a similar method, but a differ-

S.Z. Li et al. (Eds.): Sinobiometrics 2004, LNCS 3338, pp. 562–568, 2004.

ent searching space, and finally calculated the exact parameters of these two circles using Hough transform. Ye et al. [6] localized an iris by polling the candidate edge-points. Li et al. [3] developed a certain region Hough transform to find better parameters of two circles, after using Canny operator to detect their edges. Wang et al. [8] used an improved Sobel operator to extract an iris edge, and then calculated two circles by radius histogram of Hough transform. Ye et al. [9] calculated both the inner and outer circles only by Hough transform of iris edged points.

However, most localizing methods need acquire the primitive iris edged points or the searching space of an iris image that exist lots of interferefering factors as shown in figure 2. What important is how can get as pure as possible edged points or as small as possible searching space. But these aforementioned methods have not particularly represented and qualitatively analyzed the above problem. At the same time, the experiment result has proved that the edge-rude-field (the primitive iris edged points or the searching space of an iris image) distinctly works on the precision and the calculating time of its localization [5][4]. This paper, with a view to this new idea, details a great deal of disturbing phenomena possibly appearing in the rude-field of an import iris image disposed the localizing pre-process, figures some typical examples, and then deals with them by two-dimensional projection and crossing.

The remainder of the paper is organized as follows: Section 2 describes the proposed method for iris localization. Experiments and results analysis are given in Section 3 followed by conclusion Section 4.

2   Two-Dimensional Projection and Crossing Method

Before an operation, almost all localization methods need to pre-process an original import iris image. Generally, they use some low-pass filters to deal with it for smoothing and eliminating noises. As the description in Section 1, main factors against the iris-localization are eyelids, eyelashes, and faculae of light sources. These filters can possibly compact but not entirely remove the acting region of them. Because of the time-restriction (To a practical equipment, one recognition operation can not expend much more time.), a real-time system hardly adopts excessively complex pre-processing algorithms as which use various grad-operators or other gauges to detect eyelids, eyelashes and faculae, get some perfect boundaries, and then mark them for segmenting the image. However, other common tools, such as inflation and erosion operators, only deal with some given cases in effect. Their robusticity is not good.

The two-dimensional projection and crossing method, using a 2-D projecting matrix and its histogram, accurately marking the distribution of the disturb area by scouting and crossing, and finding the relationship between distributing characters of disturbing areas and relevant projecting matrices, finally purifying the edge-rude-field by the relationship, can dispose this problem better.

2.1   Two-Dimensional Projection of an Edge-Rude-Field

The pupil boundary and the iris boundary are similarly regarded as circles in here, as well as the processing method. The localization of the inner circle (the pupil), for example, after pre-processing the original image $I(x, y)$, first can get a new image

$I_f(x,y)$ as shown in figure 3(a). All primitive possible boundary points are high-light in the figure. They constitute the edge-rude-field $A(x,y)$. It is evident that the edge-rude-field comprises many false boundary points (interferefering points) that affect seriously the localizing result and the calculating time. Secondly, $A(x,y)$ is respectively projected to build the projection matrix $P_x(X,M)$ and the $P_y(Y,N)$ (defined in Formula (1) and (2)) along the x dimension and the y dimension.

$$P_x(X,M) = \begin{bmatrix} X & M \end{bmatrix} \tag{1}$$

$$P_y(Y,N) = \begin{bmatrix} Y & N \end{bmatrix} \tag{2}$$

In the formula(1)and(2), $X = [x_0 \cdots x_k]^T$, $0 < k <= \max(x)$, $Y = [y_0 \cdots y_l]^T$, $0 < l <= \max(y)$, $M = [A_0^{crest}, A_0^{trough}, \cdots, A_m^{crest}, A_m^{trough}]^T$, $0 <= m <= k$, and $N = [B_0^{crest}, B_0^{trough}, \cdots, B_n^{crest}, B_n^{trough}]^T$, $0 <= n <= l$.

Both histograms of $P_x(X,M)$ and $P_y(Y,N)$ are shown in figure 3 (b) and 3(c). The *crest* and the *trough* constitute these histograms as marked on above figures. Where sub-matrix X in $P_x(X,M)$ is the set of x coordinate value of the edge-rude-field and similarly Y in $P_y(Y,N)$ the y's, $max(x)$ indicates the maximum of x, M and N (two matrices) comprise the *crest* or the *trough* of the histogram of $P_x(X,M)$ and $P_y(Y,N)$, respectively. Both A_m^{crest} and A_m^{trough} are the sub-matrix of the M, they are respectively composed of consecutive *crest*s and *trough*s as well as B_n^{crest} and B_n^{trough} in N.

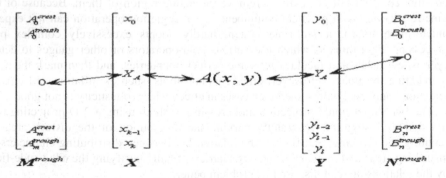

Fig. 1. The crossing principle

2.2 The Crossing Process

To begin with the *tough*, in M or N, the present A_m^{trough} or B_n^{trough} of the *trough* maximum length (the maximum of the size of A_m^{trough} or B_n^{trough}) set up 0, and

M or N turned into M^{trough} or N^{trough}. In the same way, to the *crest*, M^{crest} or N^{crest} is created (by the maximum crest in A_m^{crest} or B_n^{crest}). As shown in figure 2, 4 double-arrows mean 4 sorts of crossing. Moreover, the whole crossing is an iterative course. When the crossing of the first "0" (the first iteration) was completed, new M^{trough}, N^{trough}, M^{crest} and N^{crest} will be produced by setting up the maximum "0" in old M^{trough}, N^{trough}, M^{crest} and N^{crest}, respectively. And the same process will be done again and again until searching all sub-matrices in M and N. All 4 sorts of crossing defined in figure 2 are accomplished in a similar way.

The figure 1 shows particularly the first sort of crossing, for example. First, the operation searches 0 in the M^{trough}, and then can get a sub-matrix in M corresponding the same position. Second, the sub-matrix denotes a scope of x coordinate in X. Third, some pixel points in the edge-rude-field are marked by the x scope, therefore the operation can get hold of a scope of y coordinate in Y by these points. Finally, whether or not 0 is found in the N^{trough} corresponding the position of the scope in Y, the crossing is tenable or not. The operation is from M^{trough} to N^{trough}, because all sorts of crossing are reversible as double-arrow shown in figure 2, the result is same as from N^{trough} to M^{trough} in figure 1.

After having finished all sorts of crossing, clearing disturbing areas or points in the edge-rude-field is easy and reliable by the judge whether the result of the crossing to the pertinent sub-matrix is tenable. For instance, if a certain crossing 1 is tenable or crossing 2 and 4 tenable simultaneously, their relevant sub-matrix A_m^{trough} or B_n^{trough} corresponding area in the edge-rude-field is corrupt. As the former, it means that both its pertinent area projection *to x*-D and *y*-D are the *trough*, so the area and the outside are not the real edge-field. And the latter means not only that both projections of the area are the *crest*, but also that the sub-area of the *y*-D projection appears the *trough* as shown the ① field not belonging to the real edge-field in figure 3(a). It is apparent that above 2 ratiocinations are not indispensable but sufficient.

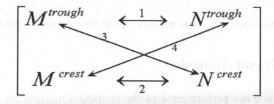

Fig. 2. 4 relationships of crossing

There is a pure edge-field after the process of the 2-D projection and the crossing. Therefore, the exact parameters of the inner circle or the pupil can be calculated by the polling algorithm [6] or searching the maximum and minimum of the x and y coordinate value of the edge-field. The step computation needs very short time because it only is a sample numerical calculation. As shown in figure 3 (d), the pupil area is filled with the black color and its boundary is highlight by the result of the localization. In the same way, the parameters of the outside circle will be done and its boundary is the big circle in the figure 3(d).

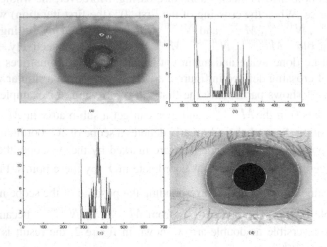

Fig. 3. The method of 2D projection

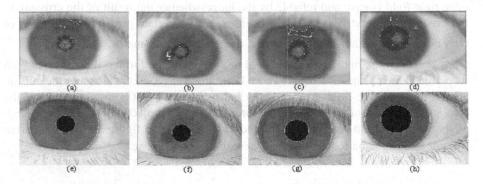

Fig. 4. The experiment result to some typical distributions of the interference

3   Test Result and Analysis

In order to evaluate the performance of the proposed method for iris optimal localization, the experiment collects 112 real-time iris images using the iris identification equipment designed the IIP Lab of USTC (the Intelligent Information Processing Laboratory in University of Science and Technology of China) at the occasion of a certain exhibition of electronic technology. Figure 4a, b, c, d show some typical rude-edge-field existing interference and respectively highlight their distributions. After the process of the method, Figure 4e, f, g, h show their pertinent localization result. The inner and outer circles of these irises are displayed in the way of highlight. This experiment result proves that the method can robustly disposes several trouble situations.

Moreover, other performances of the method including the time of localization and the localizing precision are tested in the database. It is well known that the time of accomplishing localization is, after ending the de-noising process to an original iris image, the time having calculated the parameters of the inner and outer circles of the iris. But there are not any common and quantitative gauges about how to estimate the localizing precision. Generally, it is evaluated by the visual effect or the possible maximum error of a kind of method itself by qualitative analysis. In this paper, the estimation is completed according to the comparing outcome between the localizing result of the proposed method and the calculating result of the formula (3). Where x, y, and r respectively is the x, y coordinate value of the center of a circle, and the radius. (x_1, y_1), (x_2, y_2) and (x_3, y_3) are the three points in the boundary of the circle, manually collected from the real boundary in the iris image.

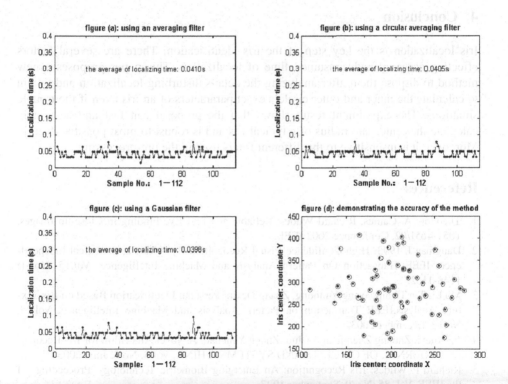

Fig. 5. The experiment result of localizing time and accuracy

$$\begin{cases} (x - x_1)^2 + (y - y_1)^2 = r^2 \\ (x - x_2)^2 + (y - y_2)^2 = r^2 \\ (x - x_3)^2 + (y - y_3)^2 = r^2 \end{cases} \qquad (3)$$

Figure 5a, b, and c respectively demonstrate the consumed time for localization using different filters (average filter, circle filter and Gaussian filter) to all samples of the iris database. The average localizing time is about 40ms using a personal computer (AMD2100⁺CPU) and compiling in Matlab, as the Daugman method's is 80ms according to the published paper [2] using a 300MHz working station. Furthermore, this method is insensitive to different filters. As shown in figure 5d, a black solid point denotes the iris center of a sample by the way of the formula (3), and a hollow circle is same meaning to the sample by the proposed method. Two observations can be made from this figure. First, the method can localize all irises of the database. Second, the compared result shows that the circle parameters of most samples are identical, and few have slim wrap but the black solid point still in the scope of the relevant hollow circle.

4   Conclusion

Iris localization is the key step of the iris identification. There are several factors effecting accuracy and consumed time of localization. This paper proposes a new method to dispose them after analyzing the details disturbing localization and to aim to calculate the inner and outer circle's exact parameters of an iris even if the trouble situations. The experiment result shows that the proposal can fast and accurately calculate the center and radius of a typical iris and is robust to most possible disturb. Moreover, it is insensitive to the different filters used in the pre-processing.

References

1. Theodore A. Camus, Richard Wildes: Reliable and Fast Eye Finding in Close-up Images. 1051-4651/02, Conference 2002 IEEE.
2. Daugman J. 1993: High Confidence Visual Recognition By A Test at Statistical Independence. IEEE Transaction On Pattern Analysis and Machine Intelligence, Vol.15, No.11: 1148-1162.
3. Ma Li, Tan Tieniu, Wang Yunhong, Zhang Dexin: Personal Identification Based on Iris Texture Analysis.IEEE Transaction on Pattern Analysis and Machine Intelligence, Vol.25, No.12, December 2003.
4. Ye Xueyi, Zhuang Zhenquan, Li Jun, Zhang Yunchao: A Novel Algorithm for Iris Recognition. JOURNAL OF CIRCUITS AND SYSTEMS, CHINA, Vol.8, No.3, June 2003.
5. Richard P. Wildes: Iris Recognition: An Emerging Biometric Technology. Proceedings of the IEEE, Vol. 85, No. 9, September 1997.
6. Ye Xueyi, Zhuang Zhenquan, Zhang Yunchao: A New and Fast Algorithm of Iris Localization. Computer Engineering and Application. China, Vol.39, July 2003
7. Zhang Yujing: Image Segmentation: Science Published, China, 2001.2.
8. Wang Chengru, Hu Zhengping: An Iris Location Algorithm. Journal of Computer-Aided Design and Computer Graphics. China, 2003,Vol.8, No.6
9. Ye Miaoyuan, Ye Hunian, He Jiafeng: An Improved method of Iris Location. Computer Engineering. China, 2002,Vol.28, No.12

Improvement of Speaker Identification by Combining Prosodic Features with Acoustic Features

Rong Zheng, Shuwu Zhang, and Bo Xu

High Technology and Innovation Center, National Laboratory of Pattern Recognition Institute
of Automation, Chinese Academy of Sciences, Beijing, China
{rzheng, swzhang, xubo}@hitic.ia.ac.cn

Abstract. In this paper, we study prosodic features derived from pitch parameters to improve the performance of speaker identification (SID) system. In order to deal with the problem of missing pitch in telephone speech, we use pitch estimation for each frame, even in unvoiced regions. After silence frames removal, we also improve prosodic modeling by a weighting form of logarithm of pitch. Then new prosodic features are combined with MFCC parameters. Based on our Gaussian Mixture Model-Universal Background Model (GMM-UBM) recognizer, SID experiments are conducted on the NIST 2001 cellular telephone corpus. Compared to MFCC features, combined features yield 7.0% relative error reduction for male and 2.5% for female. We also discuss the advanced pitch extraction and modeling approach for the improvement of SID systems.

1 Introduction

The dominant approach used to speaker identification is based on the use of Mel Frequency Cepstral Coefficients (MFCCs) as the parameters, and adopt Gaussian Mixture Models (GMMs) for speaker modeling and classification. MFCC coefficients are extracted from the power spectrum of the speech signal and are supposed to represent the vocal track contribution.

Although many experiments conducted on clean speech show high identification rates, results on adverse environments, such as telephone-quality speech and cellular speech, are usually too poor for practical identification tasks.

The main obstacles in speaker recognition can be classified into four broad categories: effect of the noise, channel distortions, handset variability and the number of speakers [1]. World-wide researchers have proposed various approaches to improve the performance of the speaker recognition systems. Current research has gone some way towards utilizing prosodic features, especially those related to F0 [2][3][4][5].

The vibration frequency of the vocal folds has proven to be an important feature to characterize speech and has been effectively used for automatic speech and speaker recognition [6][7]. Statistics of pitch have been presented as prosodic features in speaker recognition systems with good results. An important characteristic of pitch is its robustness to noise and channel distortions and have proven to be more robust than cepstra to acoustic environmental mismatches [2].

S.Z. Li et al. (Eds.): Sinobiometrics 2004, LNCS 3338, pp. 569–576, 2004.
© Springer-Verlag Berlin Heidelberg 2004

Different pitch detection algorithms have been developed in the past years [8][9][10]. Although some algorithms have very high accuracy for voiced pitch estimation, the error rate with respect to voicing decision is still high as the speech signal condition deteriorates. Our work focuses on applications which require high identification rates using short utterance from cellular telephone speech and robustness to degradations produced by low bit-rates codec effects and cellular transmission channel. Due to weak fundamental frequency and low signal to noise ratio (SNR), the performance of pitch extraction for telephone speech degrades significantly.

To deal with discontinuity of the F0 space and pitch halving/doubling errors for prosodic modeling, we use pitch fitting to estimate a pitch value for unvoiced frame, and then purpose pitch modeling to reflect the relative importance of prosodic features better. The consideration mentioned above bases on three aspects: first, voicing decision error is not showed as absent pitch values; second, the shape of pitch contour is more reliable as pitch detection; third, statistics of voicing probability is more applicable than a hard decision of voicing and unvoicing [10].

The paper is organized as follows. In section 2, we will discuss the method of pitch tracking and pitch modeling, which include pitch tracking algorithm, pitch fitting for unvoiced frames, pitch modeling and silence frames removal. The GMM-UBM based speaker identification system is described in section 3. Section 4 gives a brief description of database. The experimental results are reported in Section 5. Finally, we will show our discussions as well as conclusions.

2 Pitch Tracking and Pitch Modeling

2.1 Pitch Tracking Algorithm

A reliable pitch tracking algorithm is crucial in the field of speech processing and speech technologies. But most existing pitch determination algorithms (PDAs) are limited to clean speech or in modest noise.

Our pitch detection algorithm is similar to [8]. A pitch candidate is generated if each peak exceeds a threshold when searches for peaks in autocorrelation function. The pitch for frame is selected from the set of candidates generated for that particular frame. The pitches from adjacent frames are used to weight the candidates, due to a continuity considered between the candidates and the pitches of adjacent frames. If no candidate exceeds the preset threshold, the pitch is set to zero. Dynamic programming search is employed to pitch tracking. The search space for F0 is from 60Hz to 550Hz. However some errors will occur. These errors correspond to pitch halving and pitch doubling which are usual mistakes made in pitch estimation.

2.2 Pitch Fitting for Unvoiced Frames

The pitch extraction algorithm produces two outputs: an indicator whether the speech frame is voiced or unvoiced and, for voiced frame, an estimation value of pitch frequency. In very noise environments, the pitch estimation may fail.

In this paper, we address the problem of missing pitch for cellular speech, instead of measuring the effectiveness of the pitch extraction algorithm. One pitch period of speech signal is an impulse response of vocal tract [11]. We focus on the overall harmonic structure and continuity pitch analysis. We think it is more reliable and appropriate than a hard pitch decision because of error of pitch estimation caused by the noise and channel distortion.

This paper presents a brief approach to fit pitch for unvoiced frames. First, the pitch median over one speech utterance is calculated over voiced frames. Second, for voiced speech frames, the pitch estimation value is not changed; for unvoiced frames, we use the following procedure to fit a pitch value in unvoiced regions.

For an unvoiced frame vector $x(t)$,

$$p(t) = \alpha * p(t-1) + (1-\alpha) * p_{median} . \tag{1}$$

where, $p(t)$ stands for the probabilistic pitch estimation for unvoiced frame $x(t)$, $p(t-1)$ is the pitch value of $x(t-1)$, p_{median} is the pitch median, α is the smoothing parameter.

2.3 Pitch Modeling

Speech prosody and mechanisms of speech production are complex. Prosodic features contain glottis source information, whereas MFCC coefficients convey vocal tract information. The major problem is how to combine and model the source and vocal tract information.

Previous experiments on pitch for speaker identification supposed that pitch had a normal probability distribution [2]. Sonmez et al. [3] presented Lognormal Tied Mixture (LTM) filtered F0 for robustness against pitch halving and doubling errors. But modeling the pitch by a lognormal distribution can be considered unsuitable and inappropriate for the telephone-quality speech [1]. Ganchev et al. [4] only extracted voiced speech frames to represent the speaker's identity and propose $\ln(f0 - f0_{min})$ to replace the traditional $\ln(f0)$, which was found to be much more effective, due to the extended dynamic range that better corresponds to the relative importance of the F0.

Previous experiments showed that pitch frequencies mainly range between 150 and 220Hz for female speakers and 90 and 150Hz for male speakers [1]. In order to model the probability distribution and reflect relative importance of pitch more appropriately, we first detect the minimal pitch value over the whole utterance, and then set an empirical proportion of minimal pitch as the constant $f0_{min}$. This empirical proportion is dependent on speech corpus when male speech and female speech are considered. After that, a scaling factor, w, is used to weight the $\ln(f0 - f0_{min})$ to reflect the relative importance of pitch.

2.4 Silence Frames Removal

In any given sentence, silence frames often appear between words. These silence segments do not contain much speaker information. In order to improve the performance of the speaker recognition systems, state of the art systems usually remove silence utilizing a silence/speech detector. In this paper, we use a form of trade-off strategy to silence frames removal.

Speech utterance is divided into frames first and is pre-emphasized with parameter 0.97. The speech frames are of 192 samples, shifted by 96 samples. After Hamming-windowed, a frame is marked as a silent frame if $\sum_{i=1}^{192} (\omega_i s_i)^2 < 20000$, where s_i is the pre-emphasized signal, ω_i is Hamming window, 20000 is an empirical threshold. In addition, another removal proportion is set to ignore low energy frames (about 20%). These two aspects are combined in baseline system or when unvoiced regions are considered.

We believe this silence removal strategy mentioned above can effectively reduce the influence of non-discriminative information. It is also useful to discard some pitch halving/doubling error frames so as to model the feature vectors with GMM more appropriately.

3 GMM-UBM Based Speaker Identification System

Over the past ten years, Gaussian mixture models (GMM) for the modeling of speaker spectral characteristics has become the dominant approach for speaker identification systems which use unconstrained (text-independent) training data.

Reynolds et al. [12] presented GMM-based speaker verification system which used a universal background model (UBM) for alternative speaker representation, and a form of Bayesian adaptation to derive speaker models from UBM. We introduce the UBM technique into speaker identification (SID) system to setup our baseline system, which achieves a significant gain in performance for highly mismatched telephone speech. A detailed description of this SID system can be found in [13].

Fig. 1 shows a block diagram of the GMM-UBM speaker identification system. It can be mainly divided into three parts: UBM training, Bayesian adaptation of speaker models and speaker identification.

The Universal Background Model represents the characteristic of all different speakers. Instead of performing Maximum-Likelihood training, each speaker model can be created by employing Maximum a Posteriori (MAP) adaptation from the UBM using speaker-specific training speech. The training operation is illustrated at the upper part of Fig. 1.

From previous experiments conducted for speaker recognition, Reynolds et al. [12] has found that only a few of the mixtures of a GMM contributes significantly to the likelihood value for a speech feature vector. In addition, the mixtures components of the adapted model of each speaker model share a certain correspondence with the UBM, therefore log-likelihood score of the speaker model can be computed by scoring only the more significant mixtures. In our SID system, the top 5 mixtures are used. Because of the correspondence of mixtures between the UBM and the speaker models, these significant mixtures can be obtained by calculating the mixtures from the UBM that have the highest score. The computation requirement for recognition is reduced significantly by employing this mixture scoring strategy. The procedure is shown at the lower part of Fig. 1.

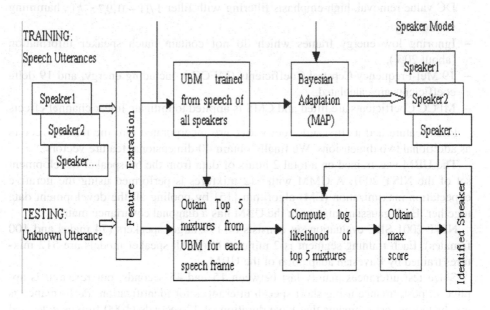

Fig. 1. Block diagram of the GMM-UBM speaker identification system

4 Database

In the following experiments, the 2001 NIST speaker recognition evaluation-one speaker detection database is used. The data in the 2001 SRE is part of the Switchboard-Cellular corpora, which had been processed to remove any pauses and transmission channel echoes. This corpus includes files from 60 development speakers (2 minutes of speech for each of 38 males and 22 females) and files from 174 target speakers (2 minutes of speech for each of 74 males and 100 females). The training data consists of spontaneous speech recorded in different environmental conditions: inside, outside, and vehicle. All of training data transmitted over the mobile cellular networks of USA. Test utterances range between few seconds and a minute. A detailed description of the speech corpus may be found in the 2001 NIST SRE Plan [14].

5 Experiments

The speaker identification experiments are conducted on cellular telephone conversational speech from the Switchboard corpus mention above.

The feature extraction process is performed using the following steps:

- Divided into 24ms frames, shifted by 12ms,
- DC value removal, high-emphasis filtering with filter $1/(1 - 0.97 z^{-1})$, hamming windowing
- Ignoring low energy frames which do not contain much speaker information (about 20%),
- 19 Mel-Frequency Cepstral Coefficients (MFCCs), including energy, and 19 delta coefficients are calculated,
- MFCC Coefficients are lifted and CMS is applied to mitigate linear channel effects.

Pitch feature and its first order derivative are incorporated into the feature vectors as additional two dimensions. We finally obtain 40-dimensional feature vectors.

The UBM was trained on a total 2 hours of data from the 60-speaker development set of the NIST 2001. A GMM with 512 mixtures is performed using the iterative expectation-maximization (EM) algorithm [15] by pooling all the development data together. Each gaussian mixture in the UBM has a diagonal covariance matrix.

NIST 2001 SRE evaluation set consists of 174 target speakers (74 males and 100 females). Each training segment is 2 minutes long. All speaker models are 512 mixtures trained by Bayesian adaptation of the UBM.

Since test utterances mainly last between 15 and 45 seconds, our research is applied in performance using short speech utterances for identification. Performance is conducted on test segments that have duration of 12 seconds (1000 frames extracted from the beginning of the test utterances, but some test utterances are shorter than 1000 frames). There are totally 850 test segments for male and 1188 test segments for female speakers.

Baseline system only contains MFCC coefficients. In order to compare the difference between female and male speakers, we perform the experiments respectively. The experiments are conducted on four strategies:

- MFCC: Baseline system,
- MFCC + Voiced + Pitch: Only the voiced speech regions are used to train a GMM and no pitch derivative used,
- MFCC + Voiced + Pitch + Pitch derivative: Only the voiced speech regions are used to train a GMM and pitch derivative used,
- MFCC + Voiced Unvoiced + Pitch + Pitch derivative: Voiced and Unvoiced regions are modeled after pitch fitting and purposed pitch modeling used.

The results of the experiments on cellular telephone speech are reported in Table 1.

Table 1. Speaker identification correction rates (%)

Experiment	Male (74 spks)	Female (100 spks)
MFCC	60.2	43.7
MFCC+V+P	60.7	44.0
MFCC+V+P+PD	61.9	44.4
MFCC+VU+P+PD	63.0	45.1

The results show that based on GMM-UBM recognizer, MFCCs achieve 60.2% identification rate for male and 43.7% for female respectively. When purposed prosodic features, pitch and pitch derivative in voiced and unvoiced regions, are incorporated into MFCC coefficients, the performance is increased to 63.0% for male and 45.1% for female, which achieve a modest improvement 7.0% and 2.5% relative error reductions over the baseline system. Better separation among target speakers is achieved in higher dimensional feature space when additional discriminative information is introduced into acoustic features. In addition, by employing fast-scoring strategy in GMM-UBM speaker identification system, the computation requirement for recognition is reduced significantly.

6 Conclusions and Discussions

This paper has presented a speaker identification system using the prosodic features derived from pitch parameters. Reliable pitch detection is very important to the statistical modeling of speech prosody. Due to acoustic noise and channel distortion, pitch halving and doubling errors are usual mistakes made in pitch estimation. In order to deal with the pitch detection error and model pitch probability distribution more appropriately for telephone speech, we utilized the following approach to incorporate prosodic features to MFCC coefficients: fitting a pitch value for unvoiced frame; a weighting form of logarithm of the pitch is used to model statistics of pitch; a tradeoff silence removal strategy to discard non-discriminative information.

Based on our GMM-UBM recognizer, experiments conducted on NIST 2001 cellular telephone corpus showed that combing prosodic features with MFCC can improve the performance of speaker identification. Due to additional discriminative information introduced into acoustic features, better separation among target speakers is obtained in higher dimensional feature space.

Although modest contribution of pitch is achieved for speaker identification, it is found that combing source information and vocal tract information is useful to speaker recognition. As future work, we suggest applying more robust pitch detection algorithm which is less affected by noise and channel distortion, for example, multipitch tracking [16] or auditory model [17]. Also more appropriate probability distribution model for statistics of pitch should be investigated [5][10].

References

1. Ezzaidi, H., Rouat, J.: Pitch and MFCC Dependent GMM Models for Speaker Identification Systems. IEEE CCECE (2004) 43–46
2. Carey, M.J., Parris, E.S., Lloyd-Thomas, H., Bennett, S., Bunnell, H.T., Idsardi, W.: Robust Prosodic Features for Speaker Identification. ICSLP, Vol. 3 (1996) 1800–1803
3. Sonmez, K., Heck, L., Weintraub, M., Shriberg, E.: A Lognormal Tied Mixture Model of Pitch for Prosody-based Speaker Recognition. EUROSPEECH (1997) 1391–1394
4. Ganchev, T., Fakotakis, N., Kokkinakis, G.: Toward 2003 NIST Speaker Recognition Evaluation: The WCL-1 System. Int. Workshop Speech and Computer (2003) 256–261

5. Adami, A., Mihaescu, R., Reynolds, D., Godfrey, J.: Modeling Prosodic Dynamics for Speaker Recognition. ICASSP (2003) 788–791
6. Atal, B.S.: Automatic Recognition of Speakers From Their Voices. Proceedings of the IEEE, Vol. 64 (1976) 460–475
7. O'Shaughnessy, D., Tolba, H.: Towards a Robust/Fast Continuous Speech Recognition System Using a Voiced-Unvoiced Decision. ICASSP (1999) 413–416
8. Rouat, J., Liu, Y.C., Morissette, D.: A Pitch Determination and Voiced/Unvoiced Decision Algorithm for Noisy Speech. Speech Communication, Vol. 21 (1997) 191–207
9. Droppo, J., Acero, A.: Maximum a Posteriori Pitch Tracking. ICSLP (1998) 943–946
10. Wang, C., Seneff, S.: Robust Pitch Tracking for Prosodic Modeling in Telephone Speech. ICASSP (2000) 887–890
11. Zicla, R.D., Navratil, J., Ramaswamy, G.N.: Depitch and the Role of Fundamental Frequency in Speaker Recognition. ICASSP (2003) 81–84
12. Reynolds, D.A., Quatieri, T.F., Dunn, R.B.: Speaker Verification Using Adapted Gaussian Mixture Models. Digital Signal Processing, Vol. 10 (2000) 19–41
13. Zheng, R., Zhang, S.W., Xu, B.: Text-independent Speaker Identification Using GMM-UBM and Frame Level Likelihood Normalization. Accepted by ISCSLP2004
14. http://www.nist.gov/speech/tests/spk/2001/doc/2001-spkrec-evalplan-v05.9.pdf [Online]
15. Bilmes, J.A.: A Gentle Tutorial of the EM Algorithm and Its Application to Parameter Estimation for Gaussian Mixture and Hidden Markov Models. Tech. Rep.TR-97-021, ICSI, U.C.Berkeley (1998) 1–13
16. Wu, M.Y., Wang, D.L., Brown, G.J.: A Multi-Pitch Tracking Algorithm for Noisy Speech. ICASSP, Vol.1 (2002) 369–372
17. Shao, X., Milner, B., Cox, S.: Integrated Pitch and MFCC Extraction for Speech Recognition and Speech Recognition Applications. EUROSPEECH (2003) 1725–1728

Bimodal Speaker Identification Using Dynamic Bayesian Network

Dongdong Li, LiFeng Sang, Yingchun Yang, and Zhaohui Wu

Department of Computer Science,
Zhejiang University, Hang Zhou, P.R. China
{lidd, slf, yyc, wzh}@zju.edu.cn

Abstract. The authentication of a person requires a consistently high recognition accuracy which is difficult to attain using a single recognition modality. This paper assesses the fusion of voiceprint and face feature for bimodal speaker identification using Dynamic Bayesian Network (DBN). Our contribution is to propose a general feature-level fusion framework in bimodal speaker identification. Within the framework, the voice and face feature are combined into a single DBN to obtain better performance than any single system alone. The tests were conducted on a multi-modal database of 54 users who provided voiceprint and face data of different speech type and content .We compare our approach with mono-modal system and other classic decision-level methods and show that feature-level fusion using dynamic Bayesian network improved performance by about 4-5%, much better than the others.

1 Introduction

The authentication of a person is a complex task with high performance and robustness. The system that combines different authentication modules is motivated by the fact that fusing multi-modals can increase correct identification rates over mono-modal biometrics. Also it has been suggested to fuse voiceprint and face these two easily accepted biometric traits could achieve an acceptable level of distinctiveness and user friendliness at the same time.

Most current Voiceprint-face speaker recognition systems are based on decision-level fusion [1-4]. According to the fusing rules, there are two different strategies for decision-level fusion [5]. One strategy is fixed fusion methods, such as Majority Vote and Sum. The second strategy is trained fusion methods, such as Dempster-Shafer and Behavior-knowledge space. However, the significant different pair-wise of each individual classifier affects the performance of the fixed rule methods [5, 6]. Otherwise, the bad quality and/ or the limited size of training sets quickly cancel the theoretical advantages of optimal trained rules methods [7].

Feature-level fusion [8] is based on the effective information extracted from the raw data. It operates as conveniently as mono-modal recognition once merging the separate features into a single data representation. It is also less sensitive to noise in raw data and has more advantages in real-time system. It forces the synchronous integration of audio and visual information.

S.Z. Li et al. (Eds.): Sinobiometrics 2004, LNCS 3338, pp. 577–585, 2004.

Dynamic Bayesian Network [9] is a new statistical approach from the perspective of Bayesian networks proposed for temporal data modeling. It is nonlinearity, interpretability, factorization and extensibility. We supposed that it would be a greatly useful tool for information fusion.

Our paper contributes a general framework to conduct feature-level fusion in bimodal speaker identification using dynamic Bayesian network. This paper is organized as follows: we give a brief introduction of the architecture of the fusion system in Section 2. In Section 3, we discuss dynamic Bayesian network briefly and propose details of feature-level fusion. The data set is presented in Section 4 with the experimental comparison and discussion between feature-level fusion using dynamic Bayesian network and other classical decision-level methods such as Majority Vote, Sum, BKS. Finally, we give a conclusion in Section 5.

2 Fusion Architecture

2.1 Identification Architecture

With the identification problem, we assume that only enrolled persons will access the system. So, identification is concerned with determining that person from a closed-set, whose features best match the features of the person to identify.

The DBNs combination incorporates two domain-specific features – one for the acoustic speaker another for the visual speaker domain. The final decision for closed-set person identification is implemented as high scores decision procedure applied to the DBN module outputs.

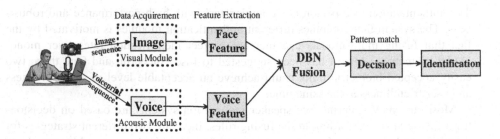

Fig. 1. The Voiceprint-face identification architecture

2.2 The Individual Biometric Feature Extraction

2.2.1 Voice Features
Mel-frequency cepstral coefficients (MFCCs) [10] are one type of acoustic feature that has proven to result in good performance. In the voiceprint feature extraction, the hamming window is 32 mm and the frame shift is 16mm. The silence and unvoiced

segments are discarded based on an energy threshold. The feature vectors are composed by 16 MFCC and their delta coefficients.

2.2.2 Face Features

The face feature extraction method is based on standard Principal Component Analysis (PCA) [11]. We have skipped the first step involving localization and registration of the face part in the input image by manually locating the eye coordinates. Given a face image X, the normalization can be gotten as

$$\Phi = X - \Psi \tag{1}$$

where Ψ is the average face vector. Here, we get 32 largest eigenvalues of Φ as the eigenvetors in the principal directions of Φ. Then project onto the eigenspace to obtain a feature vector Y:

$$Y = W^T X \tag{2}$$

The rows of the projection matrix W are the principal directions.

3   DBN Fusion

3.1   Dynamic Bayesian Network

Dynamic bayesian networks (DBNs) [9] are a general framework with a broad class of learning and inference algorithms and can characterize probability relationships among temporal data and perform exact or approximate inference. In this case, one assumes causal dependencies between events in time leading to a simplified network structure, such as the one depicted in Figure 2. The first two slices are unrolled here. We follow standard convention and use shading to mean a node that is observed; clear nodes are hidden.

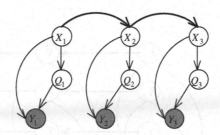

Fig. 2. A simple example of DBNs with 3slices

Namely, in its simplest form, the states of some system described as a DBN satisfy the following conditions [12]:

1. The structure is always the same at each time slice t. DBNs are time-invariant so that the topology of the network is a repeating structure, and its conditional probabilities do not change in each time-slice.
2. The state of a system at time t depends only on its immediate past: its state at time t-1. DBNs satisfy the Markov assumption: the future states of the domain are conditionally independent of the past states given the present states.

   Given a DBN, there are two important parts to operate it: inference and learning.

   Inference concerns with the estimation of the probability distribution function of hidden states given some known observations $P(X_i \mid parent(X_i), Y)$. The log-likelihood of the observation set $Y = \{Y_1, Y_2, ..., Y_M\}$ is calculated as

$$L = \log \prod_{m=1}^{M} Pr(Y_m \mid G)$$
$$= \sum_{i=1}^{N} \sum_{m=1}^{M} \log P(X_i \mid parent(X_i), Y_m) \tag{3}$$

Here G is a DBN model with N variables. We use the junction tree algorithm [13] to calculate the posteriori probability distributions. This algorithm is similar to the Baum-Welch algorithm used in HMM. Further details may be found in [12].

Learning involves estimation of the parameters of a DBN such that it "best" models the data when given a number of sequences of observations. The learning algorithm for dynamic Bayesian networks follows directly from the EM or GEM algorithm.

3.2 Feature-Level Fusion

Here we present a topology of feature-level fusion using DBNs. Each kind of feature is considered as separate information corresponding to an observation node, see figure 3.

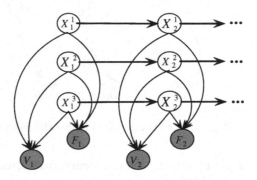

Fig. 3. Feature-level fusion topology

This topology shows that the same state set affects both voiceprint feature and face feature, but there is no relationship between these two kinds of features.

In this topology, every observation nodes V (represent the voiceprint feature) and F (represent the face feature) are conditionally dependent on state variable X. If an N slice data, $V = \{v_1, v_2,..., v_N\}$ and $F = \{f_1, f_2,..., f_N\}$, corresponds to a series of states, $X = \{x_1, x_2,..., x_N\}$. Then the joint probability is then defined as the product of all the local probability distributions: $P(v_n \mid x_n)P(f_n \mid x_n)$.

There are two cases for the local probability distribution of the observed nodes [14]:

- For a discrete node v_n or f_n with discrete parents, its local probability distributions are defined by a table of discrete probabilities (it is not allowed to have any continuous parents in this framework).

$$P(v_n \mid x_n = k) = \mathrm{H} \tag{4}$$

$$P(f_n \mid x_n = k) = I \tag{5}$$

Here H is a k*m matrix and I is a k*l matrix. m is the number of values that v_n can take. n is the number of values that f_n can take and k is the number of values that x_n can take.

- For a continuous node v_n or f_n, its local probability distributions are defined by a Gaussian if it has no continuous parents or by a conditional Gaussian if it has continuous parents; if there has discrete parents, there will be a (conditional) Gaussian for each possible instantiation of the discrete parents.

$$P(v_n \mid x_n = k) = \mathcal{N}\ (v; \mu_k, \sigma_k) \tag{6}$$

$$P(f_n \mid x_n = k) = \mathcal{N}\ (f; \mu_k, \sigma_k) \tag{7}$$

In our feature fusion case, the hidden nodes X_t, $t = 1,2,..., T$, have discrete values. The observed nodes V_t and F_t, $t = 1,2,..., T$, satisfy Gaussian distributions, and here T is the length of time slices.

4 Experiments

4.1 Database

There is now a lack of multi-modal database in china. We are building multi-modal corpus to meet the current needs. This work is taken at one month interval. We have collected 54 people to evaluate our system. Each visitor has two recordings made: a speech shot and face recording. In addition, all subjects are native Chinese-language speakers from many different regions of the country (from large cities to the small ones), belonging to a relatively narrow age bracket (20-39 years old). This gives us a large variability of speakers with different accents.

The speech content is rich and various, including Mandarin, Dialect and English in terms of language type, and prompted text and free talking in terms of speech type. The corpus contains 54 subjects with 216 images and 2916 sentences.

The experimental details are given below:

- Subjects: gender-balanced set of 54 persons including 17 females and 37males.
- Utterance set:
  - Personal information: the visitor's own information such as name, gender, birthday, mailing address, email address, telephone number, favorite sports, and pets is asked to read three times.
  - Mandarin digits: randomly select 8 digits to make a prompt, 10 prompts are asked to read.
  - Dialect digits: the context is the same with the mandarin session with 10 prompts. Each prompt consists of 8 random digits, but is asked to read in dialect.
  - English digits: the context is the same with the mandarin and the dialect session, but is asked to read in English.
  - Province phrase: 10 prompts are asked to read, each prompt has three Chinese province phrases.
  - Paragraph: a subsection from a famous Chinese essay which is a standard mandarin test material with lots of phones and tones.
  - Free talking: whatever you can say in this session, but 10 sentences are asked. For facility, 10 pictures are given. Visitors can describe what ever they see if they don't know what to say.
- Images set: the images data consists of frontal images and side profile images with 4 shots for every visitor, 2 frontal ones and 2 side ones.
- Data recording conditions: the recording environment is an office with low level of acoustic noise and sufficient lighting.

In this way, we obtain a corpus of 54 subjects, with 2 frontal face images and 54 voiceprint sentences per subjects.

The protocol of the corpus is that for voiceprint identification, we use the personal information and the paragraph sessions for training and the other sessions for testing. For face identification, we use one frontal face for training and the other for testing. We replaced the test image with the training image, and repeated this procedure.

4.2 Results and Discussion

In order to investigate if the method is robust under different speech content of different speech type, we made experiments on some subsets of our multi-modal data corpus: Mandarin, Dialect, English, Phrase, and Free talk. We also compare the feature-level DBN fusion method to mono-modal speaker identification expert and other classical decision-level fusion methods such as Sum, Weighted Sum, Majority Vote and Behavior-knowledge space method (BKS). The voiceprint-only speaker identification expert is based on Dynamic Bayesian Network approach. The face identification system is a standard Principal Component Analysis classifier (PCA).

The results are listed in table 1.

Table 1. Experimental results under different speech type and content of test sets. I means identification rate. Man means Mandarin type. Eng means English type. Dia means dialect type. Phr means phrase type. FTlk means free talk

Fusion Method	I for each speech content and type (%)				
	Man	Dia	Eng	Phr	FTlk
Voice Only	84.63	85.55	91.11	87.78	87.78
Face Only	85.18				
Feature fusion based DBN	90.21	91.11	94.81	92.03	92.96
Sum	85.37	85.18	86.11	85.18	85
Weighted Sum	85.37	85.18	86.67	85.18	85
Majority Vote	85.18	85.18	85.18	85.18	85.18
BKS	89.15	89.68	92.33	90.21	88.10

From the results in table 1, we can achieve the following conclusions:

- The bimodal speaker identification system based feature-level fusion using DBN outperforms than any mono-modal speaker system. The considerable performance achieved in the test shows that it is a promising way of using feature-level DBN fusion method in multi-modal problems.
- The performance of the feature-level DBN fusion method is the best in these experiments. Fusion based on feature-level overcomes the problems meet in decision-level fusion.
- The sum rule and the weighted sum rule do little in our system where the face expert always gives a significant high score to the class which it classifies to. This is because the equal weight and the error rate based weight can not remedy the score difference given by the wrong classification of the face expert.
- The Majority Vote rule does the worst here, because only two experts fused. The rule operates on the crisp decision profile. Once the two experts give the different answer, the rule chooses one of them randomly.
- The BKS rule indeed enhances the performance of the system. It is limited because the training data set is limited.

5   Conclusion

This paper presents an approach of fusing the voiceprint and face features for bimodal speaker identification. We discuss how to fuse two different features for speaker identification, and propose an effective feature-level fusion method using dynamic

Bayesian network. Encouraging results of experiments on multi-modal corpus including different speech type and content demonstrate that the performance of multi-biometric system can be further improved by feature fusion using DBN.

In future work we will investigate improvements on the fusion topology for combining features.

Acknowledgments

This work is supported by National Natural Science Foundation of P.R.China (60273059), Zhejiang Provincial Natural Science Foundation for Young Scientist of P.R.China (RC01058), Zhejiang Provincial Natural Science Foundation (M603229) and National Doctoral Subject Foundation (20020335025).

References

1. Benoit Duc.el.: Fusion of audio and video information for multimodal person authentication. Pattern Recognition Letters. Vol. 18 (1997) 835–843
2. P. Verlinde., G. Chollet.: Comparing decision fusion paradigms using k-NN based classifiers. decision trees and logistic regression in a multi-modal identity verification application. In: Proc. 2nd Int.l Conf. on Audio- and Video-Based Biometric Person Authentication. Washingtion D.C. (1999) 188–193
3. S. Ben-Yacoub. Y. Abdeljaoued. and E. Mayoraz.: Fusion of face and speech data for person identity verification. IEEE Transactions on Neural Networks. (1999) 1065–1074
4. J. Luettin and S. Ben-Yacoub.: Robust Person Verification based on Speech and Facial Images. in: Proceedings of the European Conference on Speech Communication and Technology. (1999)
5. Fabio Roli. Josef Kittler. Giorgio Fumera. Daniele Muntoni.: An Experimental Comparison of Classifier Fusion Rules for Multimodal Personal Identity Verification Systems. Multiple Classifier Systems. (2002) 325–336
6. Roli. F., Raudys. S., Marcialis. G.L.: An experimental comparison of fixed and trained fusion rules for crisp classifier outputs. 3rd Int. Workshop on Multiple Classifier Systems (MCS 2002). Cagliari. Italy. (2002)
7. Roli. F., Fumera. G.: Analysis of linear and order statistics combiners for fusion of imbalanced classifiers. 3rd Int. Workshop on Multiple Classifier Systems (MCS 2002). Cagliari. Italy. (2002)
8. Chibelushi. C.C., Mason. J.S.D., Deravi. F.: Feature-level data fusion for bimodal person recognition. 6th International Conference on Image Processing and its Applications. Vol. 1 (1997) 399–403
9. Murphy. K.: Dynamic Bayesian Networks: Representation. Inference and Learning. Ph.D. thesis. U.C. Berkeley. (2002)
10. Vergin. R. O'Shaughnessy. D. Gupta. V.: Compensated mel frequency cepstrum coefficients. Proceedings of the International Conference on Acoustics, Speech, and Signal Processing. Minneapolis, USA. Vol. 1 (1996) 323–326
11. Y. Wang. T. Tan and A. K. Jain.: Combining Face and Iris Biometrics for Identity Verification. Proc. of 4th Int'l Conf. on Audio- and Video-Based Biometric Person Authentication (AVBPA). Guildford. UK. (2003) 805–813

12. Lifeng Sang. Zhaohui Wu. Yingchun Yang. Wanfeng Zhang.: Automatic Speaker Recognition Using Dynamic Bayesian Network. IEEE ICASSP 2003. Vol. 1 (2003) 188–191
13. Cowell. R.: Introduction to inference for Bayesiannetworks. In Jordan. (1999) 9–26
14. Stephenson. T.A. Escofet. J. Magimai-Doss. M. Bourlard. H.: Dynamic Bayesian network based speech recognition with pitch and energy as auxiliary variables. In 2002 IEEE International Workshop on Neural Networks for for Signal Processing (NNSP 2002). Martigny, Switzerland. (2002) 637–646

A Novel Pitch Period Detection Algorithm Based on Hilbert-Huang Transform[*]

Zhihua Yang[1], Daren Huang[2], and Lihua Yang[2],[**]

[1] School of Information Science and Technology,
Sun Yat-sen University, Guangzhou city 510275, China
[2] School of Mathematics and Computing Science,
Sun Yat-sen University, Guangzhou city 510275, China

Abstract. In this paper, a novel event detection pitch detector is presented. Hilbert-Huang Transform is employed to locate the instant at which the glottal pulse takes place. Then, the pitch period is detected accurately by measuring the time interval between two glottal pulses. Experiments show encouraging detection results.

Keywords: pitch period detection, Hilbert-Huang transform.

1 Introduction

The detection of pitch period from speech signals has been studied by many researches in the past decades. As an important parameter in the analysis and synthesis of speech signals, pitch period information has been used in various applications such as 1) speaker identification and verification, 2) pitch synchronous speech analysis and synthesis, 3) linguistic and phonetic knowledge acquisition and 4) voice disease diagnostics [2, 3, 8]. However, reliable and accurate determination of the pitch period is difficult due to the complexity of the speech signal, which can be viewed as the output of a time-varying system excited by a quasi-periodic train of pulse for voiced speech, or by wideband random noise for unvoiced speech. Therefore, it is still a challenging task to develop algorithms for different applications. Roughly, the techniques that have been developed for automatic detection of the pitch period over the past several years can be classified two categories: (a) event detection pitch detectors, which estimate the pitch period by locating the instant at which the glottis close, and then measuring the time interval between two such events; (b) nonevent detection pitch detectors, which are mainly based on the short-term autocorrelation function and the average magnitude difference function [2, 3]. Generally, the nonevent based pitch

---

[*] This work was supported by GDSF (No. 036608), the foundation of scientific and technological planning project of Guangzhou city (No. 2003J1-C0201), NSFC(No. 60133020, 69873001) and the National 973 Program (No. G1998030607).
[**] Corresponding author. Email: mcsylh@zsu.edu.cn, Phone: (8620)84115508, Fax: (8620)84111696.

S.Z. Li et al. (Eds.): Sinobiometrics 2004, LNCS 3338, pp. 586–593, 2004.

detectors are computationally simple. However, they assume that the pitch period is stationary within each segment, so the draw-backs of these techniques are their insensitivity to non-stationary variations in the pitch period over the segment length and unsuitability for both low pitched and high pitched speakers. Comparing with nonevent detection pitch detectors, the event detection pitch detectors are immature. Only a few event based pitch detectors [4, 5, 6, 8, 9] have been developed. Despite the high accuracy, most of them are either applicable to only a part of vowels or of computationally complexity. In this paper, a novel event detection pitch detector is presented based on Hilbert-Huang transform (HHT), which was first introduced by N. E. Huang and et al. in 1998 [7]. Because of the high time-frequency local character and being applicable to nonlinear and non-stationary process, HHT is employed to locate the instant at which the glottal pulse takes place. Then, the pitch period is detected accurately by measuring the time interval between two glottal pulses. Experiments show encouraging detection results.

This paper is organized as follows: Section 2 is a brief summary on Hilbert-Huang Transform; A novel algorithm for automatic detection of the pitch period is proposed based on HHT in Section 3; In Section 4, experiments are conducted to support the algorithm. The experimental results are analyzed and used to compare our algorithm with other classical techniques; Finally, Section 5 is the conclusion of this paper.

2   Hilbert-Huang Transform

Hilbert-Huang Transform (HHT) was proposed by N. Huang et al in 1998 [7]. It consists of two parts: (1) Empirical Mode Decomposition (EMD), and (2) Hilbert Spectral Analysis. With EMD, any complicated data set can be decomposed into a finite and often less number of intrinsic mode functions (IMFs). An IMF is defined as a function satisfying the following conditions:

(a) The number of extrema and the number of zero-crossings must either equal or differ at most by one;
(b) At any point, the mean value of the envelope defined by the local maxima and the envelope defined by the local minima is zero.

An IMF defined as above admits well-behaved Hilbert transforms. EMD decomposes signals adaptively and is applicable to nonlinear and non-stationary data. In this section, a brief introduction is given to make this paper somewhat self-contained. The readers are referred to [7] for details.

For an arbitrary function, X(t), in Lp-class[1], its Hilbert transform, Y(t), is defined as

$$Y(t) = \frac{1}{\pi} P \int_{-\infty}^{\infty} \frac{X(t')}{t - t'} dt' \tag{1}$$

where P indicates the Cauchy principal value. Consequently an analytic signal, Z(t), can be produced by

$$Z(t) = X(t) + iY(t) = a(t)e^{i\theta(t)}, \tag{2}$$

where

$$a(t) = [X^2(t) + Y^2(t)]^{\frac{1}{2}}, \theta(t) = \arctan(\frac{Y(t)}{X(t)}) \tag{3}$$

are the instantaneous amplitude and phase of X(t).

Since Hilbert transform Y(t) is defined as the convolution of X(t) and $1/t$ by Eq. (1), it emphasizes the local properties of X(t) even though the transform is global. In Eq. (2), the polar coordinate expression further clarifies the local nature of this representation. With Eq. (2), the instantaneous frequency of X(t) is defined as

$$\omega(t) = \frac{d\theta}{dt}, \tag{4}$$

However, there is still considerable controversy on this definition. A detailed discussion and justification can be found in [7].

EMD is a necessary preprocessing of the data before the Hilbert transform is applied. It reduces the data into a collection of IMFs and each IMF, which represents a simple oscillatory mode, is a counterpart to a simple harmonic function, but is much more general. We will not describe EMD algorithm here due to the limitation of the length of the paper. The readers are referred to [7] for details.

By EMD, any signal X(t) can be decomposed into finite IMFs, $imf_j(t)$, $j = 1, \cdots, n$ and a residue $r(t)$, where n is nonnegative integer depending on $X(t)$, i.e.,

$$X(t) = \sum_{j=1}^{n} imf_j(t) + r(t). \tag{5}$$

For each $imf_j(t)$, its corresponding instantaneous amplitude, $a_j(t)$, and instantaneous frequency, $\omega_j(t)$, can be computed with Eqs.(3) and (4). By Eqs.(2) to (5), X(t) can be expressed as the real part, RP, in the following form:

$$X(t) = RP \sum_{j=1}^{n+1} a_j(t) e^{i \int \omega_j(t) dt}, \tag{6}$$

where the residue $r(t)$ is regarded as a special IMF and is included into Eqs. (6).

Equation (6) enables us to represent the amplitude and the instantaneous frequency as functions of time in a three-dimensional plot, in which the amplitude is contoured on the time-frequency plane. The time-frequency distribution of amplitude is designated as the Hilbert amplitude spectrum or simply Hilbert spectrum, denoted by $H(\omega, t)$.

Having obtain Hilbert spectrum, one will have no difficult to define the instantaneous energy as follows:

$$IE(t) = \int H(\omega, t) d\omega, \tag{7}$$

which offers a measure of total energy contribution from various frequency components at each time location.

3   Pitch Period Detection Algorithm Based on Hilbert-Huang Transform

It's well known that voiced can be viewed as the output of an attenuation system excited by a quasi-periodic train of pulse [2, 3]. Its instantaneous energy will sharply increase at the instant at which the pulse takes place, which is useful for the automatic detection of the pitch period. By exploiting this fact, a novel algorithm for pitch period detection is developed based on HHT as follows:

Algorithm 1. *Let x(t) be a segment of voiced speech signal,*

Step 1 *Decompose x(t) into IMFs by EMD algorithm;*
Step 2 *For each imf, Compute its Hilbert transform, instantaneous amplitude and instantaneous frequency by Eq. (1), (2) and (4) respectively;*
Step 3 *Compute H(ω, t) based on the results of Step 2;*
Step 4 *Compute instantaneous energy IE(t) by Eq. (7);*
Step 5 *Compute the derivative of IE(t) and denote it as DIE(t);*
Step 6 *Let TH be a given threshold, we process the DIE(t) as below:*

$$\tilde{DIE}(t) = \begin{cases} DIE(t) \ if & DIE(t) > TH \\ 0 & if & DIE(t) \leq TH \end{cases} \tag{8}$$

Step 7 *Search the local maxima of $\tilde{DIE}(t)$ and the instants at which the local maxima of $\tilde{DIE}(t)$ take place. They correspond to those instants at which the glottal pulse takes place. Finally, the pitch period is detected by measuring the time interval between two glottal pulses.*

It should be pointed out that each speech signal has been divided into some segments with a suitable length according to our former work [10] for the purpose of saving CPU time before the algorithm is carried out. Each signal x(t) contains 800 data in our experiments.

4   Experiment Results and Analyses

In this section, experiments are conducted to support the algorithm. The experimental results are analyzed and used to compare our algorithm with some classical techniques.

At first, to test the validity of our algorithm, a synthesized signal is generated as follows:

- Let the sampling frequency $fs=8000HZ$ and the length of signal be 800 data;
- The serial formant frequencies and bandwidths for three formants are (250HZ, 50HZ), (1300HZ, 70HZ) and (2100HZ, 120HZ);
- The glottal source signal is modeled by using Liljencrants-Fant (LF) model and the instants at which the pulses take place are set at 79, 165, 253, 337, 428, 523, 613, 705 and 789, which means the glottal source signal is a quasi-periodic train of pulse whose time intervals between two glottal pulses are 86, 88, 84, 91, 95, 90, 92 and 84 respectively.

The synthesized signal and its detected results are shown in Fig. 1, in which the synthesized signal and the glottal pulse train are plotted in solid line and dot line respectively in (a); (b) is $D\tilde{I}E(t)$; the synthesized signal is plotted again in (c) and the arrows are plotted to indicate the detected instants at which the glottal pulse take place; Finally, the detected pitch period are plotted in horizontal segments in (d) and the detected results and their true value are also marked above and below the horizontal segments respectively for convenience to compare.

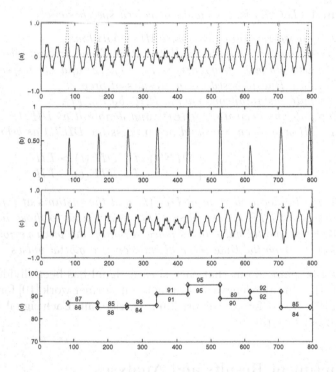

From this experiment, it is clear that our algorithm is of the high accuracy and is able to trace the variation of a pitch period during a segment of signal. To test our algorithm for real speech signals, we conduct it for two segments of practical speech signals. Both of them are recorded in common microphone with sampling frequency of 8000Hz under natural environment. One of them is the speech signal of vowel 'e' spoken by a male speaker. The speech signal, its $D\tilde{I}E(t)$, the detected instants at which the glottal pluses take place and the track of the pitch period are plotted in Fig. 2 from top to bottom as marked by (a), (b), (c) and (d). To compare our algorithm with classical algorithms, we also compute the autocorrelation function of the same speech signal and the detected result is plotted on the bottom of Fig.2 marked by (e). Another is the speech signal of vowel 'a:' spoken by a female speaker. Similarly, the speech signal and its detected result are plotted in Fig.3. From both Fig.2 and Fig. 3, it is clear that our algorithm exhibits superior performance and high accuracy.

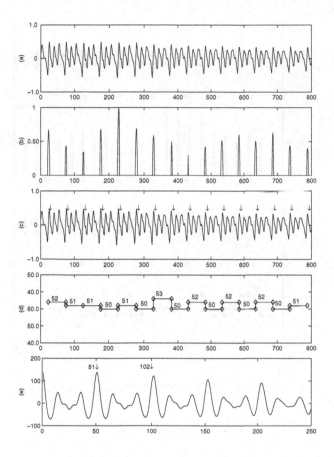

5   Conclusion and Discussion

In this paper, a novel event detection pitch detector is presented, in which HHT is employed to locate the instant at which the glottal pulse takes place. Then the pitch period is detected accurately by measuring the time interval between two glottal pulses. Experiments show encouraging detection results. The main advantages can be concluded as follows.

It is unnecessary to assume that the pitch period is stationary within each segment. Despite that we still segment the speech signal before the detection is carried out, it is just for the purpose of saving CPU time. Theoretically, our algorithm is applicable to the speech signal with any length.

High accuracy can be received, which is derived from the high local properties both in time and frequency domains of HHT.

It is able to trace the variation of a pitch period during a segment of the speech signal. Our technique breaks down the assumption that the speech signal processed should be stationary within each a frame, instead, in our algorithm it is treated as non-stationary signal as it is. Therefore the result is more reliable than those detected by most classical techniques.

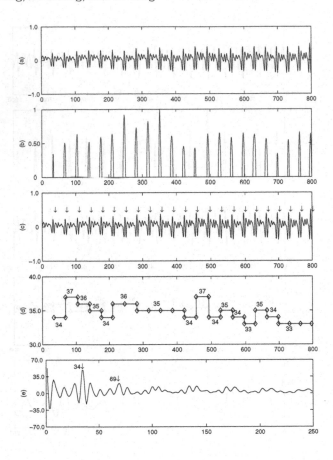

References

1. E. C. Titchmarsh: Introduction to the Theory of Fourier Integrals. Oxford University Press (1948)
2. Hang Hu: Speech Signal Processing, Harbin Institute of Technology Press. Harbin (2000)
3. Li Zhao: Speech Signal Processing. China Machine Press. China, Beijing (2003)
4. T. V. Ananthapadmanabha and B. Yegnanarayana: Epoch extraction of voiced speech. IEEE Transacions on Acoust, Speech, Signal Processing **23**(6) (1975) 562–570
5. T. V. Ananthapadmanabha and B. Yegnanarayana: Epoch extraction from linear prediction residual for identification of closed glottis interval. IEEE Transacions on Acoust, Speech, Signal Processing **ASSP-27**(4) (1979) 309–319
6. Y. M. Cheng and D. O'Shaughnessy: Automatic and reliable estimation of glottal closure instant and period. IEEE Transactions on Acoust, Speech, Signal Processing, **37**(12) (1989) 1805–1815
7. N. E. Huang, Z. Shen and S. R. Long et al: The empirical mode decomposition and the Hilbert spectrum for nonlinear and non-stationary time series analysis. Proceedings of the Royal Society of London **A**(454) (1998) 903–995

8. Shubha Kadambe and G. Faye Boudreaux-Bartels: Application of the wavelet transform for pitch detection of speech signals. IEEE Transactions on Information Theory **38**(2) (1992) 917–924
9. H. W. Strube: Determination of the instant of glottal closure from the speech wave. Journal of the Acoustical Society of America **56**(5) (1974) 1625–1629
10. Zhihua Yang, Dongxu Qi, and Lihua Yang: A novel automated detection of spindles from sleep EEGs based on Hilbert-Huang transform. Technical Report (2004) Sun Yat-sen University

Noisy Speech Pitch Detection Based on Mathematical Morphology and Weighted MACF

Xia Wang[1], Hongmei Tang[1], and Xiaoqun Zhao[2]

[1] School of Information Engineering, Hebei University of Technology,
Tianjin, 300130, China
huixia@eyou.com
[2] School of Electronic Information and Engineering, Tongji University,
Shanghai, 200092, China
Zhao_xiaoqun@mail.tongji.edu.cn

Abstract. In speech processing, pitch period is a very important characteristic parameter, but accurate pitch is not easy to be detected, especially in noisy environments, because speech signal is nonstationary and quasiperiodical. This paper describes a new method based upon mathematical morphology and weighted modified autocorrelation function(MACF). Morphology is a nonlinear method which is based on set-theoretical algebra, we can form kinds of morphology filters using different structuring elements. Weighted MACF modifies traditional autocorrelation method with reciprocal of AMDF. Experiments show that the combination of these algorithms provides robust performance and makes better result in noisy speech pitch detection.

1 Introduction

Pitch is a very important parameter in speech processing applications, such as speech analyzing, coding, recognition and speaker verification. Although there are many methods of pitch estimation, both in time and frequency domains, accurate and robust detection is still a difficult problem. Most of pitch detection methods are based on the assumption that speech signal is stationary in short time, but this is not accord with actuality that speech signal is nonstationary and quasiperiodical, it will sometimes induce detection error. Among these methods, autocorrelation-based method is comparatively robust against noises[1], but it may result in a half-pitch or double-pitch error, and if noise is high, this method can't detect pitch properly. In this paper we employ an algorithm based on mathematical morphology and modified autocorrelation function.

There are some nonlinear methods used in pitch detection, such as wavelet[2,3]. Mathematical morphology[4,5] is also nonlinear filtering method which is a process of set-theoretical algebra. It was firstly applied in processing binary image, called binary morphology, then extended to multilevel signal, called graylevel morphology. It can match signals using kinds of predefined structuring elements to maintain detail and reduce noise, and was used in pitch contrail smoothing[6]. Results show that it is very effective using this method.

S.Z. Li et al. (Eds.): Sinobiometrics 2004, LNCS 3338, pp. 594–601, 2004.

2 Mathematical Morphology

Mathematical morphology was proposed by J.Serra and G. Matheron in 1966, and was theorized in the mid-seventies, matured from the beginning of 80's. It is easy to process parallel and realize by hardware.

Mathematical morphology consists of two fundamental operators, dilation and erosion. It can process binary signal and graylevel signal. In both signal processing, structuring element is very important and essential,, it is a set in Euclidean space, which has various shape(circle, line, etc). Using different elements will achieve different results.

A binary signal is considered as a set, dilation and erosion are Minkowski addition and subtraction[7]with the structuring element. In graylevel signal processing, addition and subtraction operations in binary morphology are replaced by suprermum and infimum operations.

The definition of these operations[8] are expressed as follows

$$f(x) \oplus g(x) = \sup_{y \in G}\{f(x-y) + g(y)\} . \tag{1}$$

$$f(x) \ominus g(x) = \inf_{y \in G}\{f(x+y) - g(y)\} . \tag{2}$$

Where $f(x)$ is graylevel signal, $g(x)$ is structuring element.

In digital signal processing, supremum and infimum of function can be replaced by maximum and minimum, that is

$$f(x) \oplus g(x) = \max_{y \in G}\{f(x-y) + g(y)\} . \tag{3}$$

$$f(x) \ominus g(x) = \min_{y \in G}\{f(x+y) - g(y)\} . \tag{4}$$

Dilation use structuring element as template, searching the maximum of graylevel addition in structuring field, this operation increases vale value of signal, expand apex, erosion use structuring element as template, searching the minimum of graylevel subtraction in structuring field, this operation decreases apexes of signal, widen out vale field.

The combinations of dilation and erosion can form further morphology operations, open and close. The open definition is

$$f(x) \circ g(x) = [(f \ominus g) \oplus g](x) . \tag{5}$$

the close definition is

$$f(x) \bullet g(x) = [(f \oplus g) \ominus g](x) . \tag{6}$$

Open and close operations are basic morphology filters, and can form kinds of filters, close operation has filter function, filling up crack, open operation has smooth function for signal, clearing edge burr and isolate dot, we use level structuring element (Fig.1) to strengthen period of signal, the results of these operations are

596   X. Wang, H. Tang, and X. Zhao

shown in Fig.2, (a)shows a segment of speech signal, (b) close operation act on original signal, the result shows that close operation restrain negative impulse noise, (c)open operation act on original signal, the result shows that close operation restrain positive impulse noise, (d) open-close operation act on original signal, and we can also use close-open, these operations restrain bi-impulse noise . The length of element will influent result, close operation in different L shows in Fig.3, (a)shows result of L=20, (b) shows result of L=40, we can see the crack is full filled, pitch is more evident.

The graylevel operations have some important properties, such as increasingness, extensivity and dempotency.

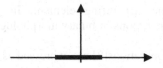

Fig. 1. Level structuring element

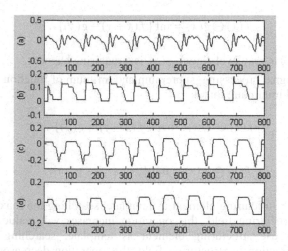

Fig. 2. (a) original signal   (b) close operation result   (c) open operation result   (d) open-close operation result

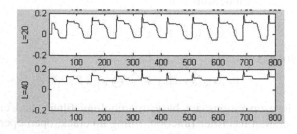

Fig. 3. Close operation result in different length of level structuring element

3 Weighted Modified Autocorrelation Function Method

Autocorrelation function is used to express the likeness of a signal with itself. It is generally calculated by

$$R_N(k) = \sum_{m=-\infty}^{\infty}[x(n+m)w^{'}(m)][x(n+m+k)w^{'}(m+k)] \ . \tag{7}$$

where $x(n)$ is speech signal, $w^{'}(n)$ is window function of length N, and $0 \le k \le N-1$.

When $k = 0$, $R_N(k)$ will obtain maximum value. If speech signal is periodic, autocorrelation has peaks at multi-period, and the peak values decrease as k increase. So autocorrelation function can demonstrate the periodicity of unvoiced signal. But if the length of window is not suitable, for example, too long or too short, the result will deviate from its true value. To solve the problem, modified autocorrelation function(MACF) should be adopted. MACF can be written as

$$\hat{R}_N(k) = \sum_{m=-\infty}^{\infty}[x(n+m)w_1^{'}(m)][x(n+m+k)w_2^{'}(m+k)] \ . \tag{8}$$

Compared with (7), in this formula, the length of $w_1^{'}(n)$ and $w_2^{'}(n)$ are different, this method ensures that peaks occurred at multi-period and peak values don't decrease as k increases. But speech signal is not accurately periodic and often polluted by noise, we need make more modification. Because in the autocorrelation function and in the average magnitude difference function(AMDF), additive noise behaves independently, the ACF can be weighted by the reciprocal of AMDF[9,10]. We use this idea to MACF. The weighted MACF can be expressed as

$$\tilde{R}_N(k) = \frac{1}{r_n(k)+1} \cdot \hat{R}_N(k) \ . \tag{9}$$

where $r_n(k)$ is the AMDF of speech, is defined as

$$r_n(k) = \sum_{m=-\infty}^{\infty}\left|x(n+m)w_1^{'}(m) - x(n+m+k)w_2^{'}(m+k)\right| \ . \tag{10}$$

4 Pitch Detection

Pitch detection system is shown in Fig. 4.

At first, use an ellipse bandpass to filter low and high frequency signal, and the passband is 60—900Hz, then adopt the combination form of basic operations as morphology filter unit which is shown in Fig. 5.

noisy speech

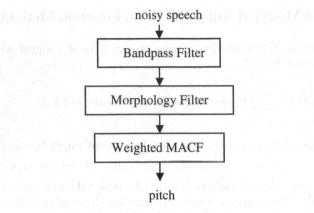

pitch

Fig. 4. Pitch detection diagram

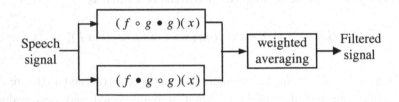

Fig. 5. Morphology filter unit

Units defined above link in series forming morphology filter, at last, weighted MACF is used to calculate pitch period.

5 Experimental Results

Tested speech are selected from CASIA Monosyllabic& Isolated Word Speech Corpus which was made by Institute of automation of Chinese academy of sciences. Speech signal is sampled by 16kbps(sampling rate) and quantized by 16bit, added white Gaussian noise in various SNR. In all experiment, speech is divided into frames, each frame contained 300 samples and 150 samples overlapped. And all programs are written in MATLAB language. Pitch detection error is calculated by pitch frequency difference between the actual pitch frequency $F_{APF}(n)$ and the estimated pitch frequency $F_{EPF}(n)$ [10]. The error is expressed as

$$Error(n) = \left| F_{APF}(n) - F_{EPF}(n) \right| . \tag{11}$$

If error is greater than 10Hz, the error was treated as a gross pitch error, and its proportion is denote as gross pitch error rate(GPER). In mandarin 'a' pitch detection using new method, GPER is less than 8% as 10db SNR, less than 15% as 0db SNR. Some waveform results are given below, include two monosyllabic word and pitch frequency using different method.

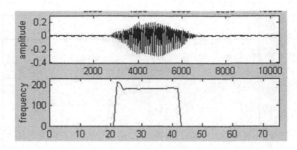

Fig. 6. Original waveform and pitch frequency of mandarin 'a'

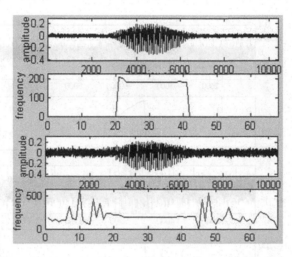

Fig. 7. Noisy speech and pitch frequency (using correlation method)

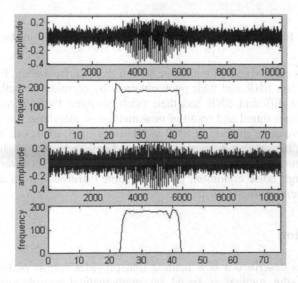

Fig. 8. Noisy speech and pitch frequency(using new method)

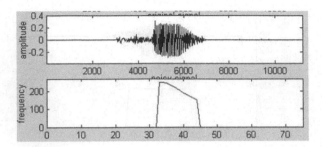

Fig. 9. Original waveform and pitch frequency of mandarin 'ku'

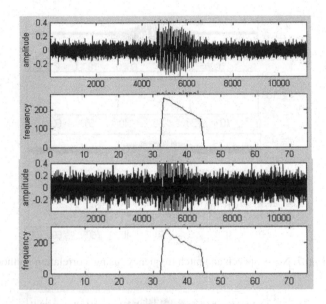

Fig. 10. Noisy speech and pitch frequency(using new method)

Fig.6 shows clean signal of mandarin 'a' and its pitch frequency, Fig.7 shows noisy signal of different SNR and their pitch obtained by correlation method, Fig.8 shows noisy signal of different SNR and their pitch obtained by new method, Fig.9 and Fig.10 show clean signal and result of new method of mandarin 'ku'. From Fig.7, we can see, in correlation method, if SNR is relatively high, the result is fine, if SNR is relatively low, the result gets worse. Fig.8 and Fig.9 show that pitch can be detected in noisy environments using new method. When noise is not very high, pitch is accurate. In high noise condition, pitch has some difference from accurate one, but can still represent character of speech.

6 Conclusion

This paper has described a new method that provides robust performance in noisy environments, the method is based on mathematical morphology and weighted

MACF. Experiments show that this method can detect pitch frequency effectively. And further studies might focus on algorithm analysis and practical use in speech processing.

References

1. OH, K.A, and UN, C.K.: A performance comparison of pitch extraction algorithm for noisy speech. Proc. IEEE Int. Conf. on ASSP, (1984) 18B4.1-18B4.4
2. CHEN Hai-hua, QU Tian-shu, WANG Shu-xun.: Speech Signal Fundamental Frequency Detection Based on Wavelet Transform. Journal of Jilin University Engineering and Technology Edition, 32(2) (2002) 68-72
3. Zhao Ruizhen, Song Guoxiang,: A Fast Algorithm for Pitch Detection with Wavelet Tansform. Electronic Science and Technology, No.1 (1998) 16-19
4. Petros Maragos and Ronald W. Schafer.: Morphological Filters—Part I and II : Their Relations to Median, Order-Statistic, and Stack Filters. IEEE Trans. ASSP 35(8) (1987) 1170-1184
5. J. Serra, Image Analysis and Mathematical Morphology. New York: Academic(1982)
6. Zhao Xiaoqun and Wang Guangyan.: A New Approach of the Morphology Filter for Pitch Contrail Smoothing of Chinese Tone. Signal Processing, 19(4) (2003) 354-357
7. Johm H. L. Hansen.: Morphology Constrained Feature Enhancement with Adaptive Cepstral Compensation(MCE-ACC) for Speech Recognition in Noise and Lombard Effect. IEEE Transaction on Speech and Audio Processing, 1.2(4)(1994)598-614
8. Joseph H.Boseorth..: Morphological local monotonicity for multiscale image segmentation. Ph.D Paper, University of Virginia, (2002)
9. W.Hung,: Use of fuzzy weighted autocorrelation function for pitch extraction from noisy speech. Electronics letters, .38(19) (2002) 1148-1150,
10. TETSUYA.S.,HAJIME.K.: Weighted autocorrelation for pitch extraction of noisy speech. IEEE Trans Speech Audio Process, 9(7) (2001) 727-730

Glottal Information Based Spectral Recuperation in Multi-channel Speaker Recognition

Pu Yang, Yingchun Yang, and Zhaohui Wu

College of Computer Science and Technology, Zhejiang University,
Hangzhou, 310027, P. R. China
{kuvun, yyc, wzh}@zju.edu.cn

Abstract. Recently, expansion of mobile communication arise lots of research interests in robust speaker recognition under multi-channel environments. Thus, building robust automatic speaker recognition (ASR) system becomes an urgent and necessary problem. Though glottal information was successfully used in many speaker recognition systems, the spectral variations caused by it were not taken into account under multi-channel environment. In this paper, a method that can utilize this influence, using both long-term and short-term glottal information, is proposed. Through this recuperation, spectral features will behave more robust in text-independent ASR system under channel influences. Our method was applied to the large multi-channel SRMC corpus. The experimental works show promising results.

1 Introduction

Nowadays, people may use various devices such as telephone, PDA, mobile phone to make communications. Note that mismatched channel during the enrollment and test phase have been shown to cause an order of magnitude degrade in performance of speaker recognition system, ever after standard channel compensation techniques are applied [1].

Meanwhile, glottis is one of the most important parts of human phonation system. Feature parameters based on it have been adopted in many speaker identification or verification systems because they could provide speaker dependent factors as well as the robustness against channel influences. These features, apart from the traditional short-term spectral information, include fundamental frequency, voicing rate, power, etc [2].

By utilizing the glottal features, various methods have been proposed to ASR systems [3] [4]. Although these systems produce better performance than those without the usage of glottal information, they only focus on the glottal features' varieties. They ignore the correlation information between spectral variations and glottal changes [5], which will affect ASR system much with channel effects.

In this paper, we present a robust approach by using this correlation information in text-independent speaker recognition system under multi-channel environments. It is supposed that, with the channel effects, the original spectral information is distorted by glottal distribution, which is more robust to channel. So we proposed a model to

S.Z. Li et al. (Eds.): Sinobiometrics 2004, LNCS 3338, pp. 602–609, 2004.

amend the distortion caused by glottal changes. And our work focuses on getting the assumed original unaffected spectral features holding more discriminative abilities. This text-independent recuperation simultaneously takes both short-term glottal information and long-term one into account. Especially, we novelly utilize multi-level long-term information.

We organized the paper as follows: the next section briefly describes spectral variations caused by glottal changes with channel distortion. It is followed by describing our proposed model and how to recuperate spectral features in section 3. Then, in section 4, we describe our experiments' setup. Results and discussions are given in section 5. And session 6 gives the conclusions.

2 Spectral Variations Caused by Glottal Changes

As well known, spectral representations, such as Linear Prediction Coefficient (LPC) [6], Mel Frequency Cepstral Coefficient (MFCC) [7], provides a good approximation to vocal tract spectral envelope. Because they present difference among speakers, they are wildly used in ASR task. Meanwhile, glottis is one of the most important parts of human vocal apparatus. Features based on this glottal sound source, fundamental frequency for example, have been used in speaker identification of verification system as complementary information, because such features also reflect many speaker dependent factors.

In most studies of these tasks, people did not associate these spectral features with glottal ones, whereas, people treated them as irrelevant. Although this simple-ness was competent for most ideal situations, problems occurred when environments became worse and channel variation existed. Nobuaki [8] has firstly analyzed these correlations in vowel space. But his theory was only provided to speech recognition task. Later in this part, we will list our observation in ASR task to show that spectral features do vary under such changes. And in following parts of this article, we adopt fundamental frequency as our primary glottal information.

It is easy to think that speed of glottis vibration would metamorphose the shape of vocal tract more or less. We now illustrate the variation of feature distribution caused by fundamental frequency changes. Our speech materials contain the daily used words and conversations. They were recorded from mobile phone. And the total length of materials is about 7 to 8 minutes. We chose one speaker for demonstrating and extracted out his MFCC vectors and his fundamental frequency vectors. According to its corresponding fundamental frequency value, every short-term MFCC vector was sorted to one of 20 bins with 25Hz width each. Then we select continuous three bins, into which more than 85% MFCC vectors fall, and so does the expectation of all fundamental frequency vectors. Because of the adequate data, each bin is enough for ASR modeling. And Figure 1 exhibits distribution of these coefficients from the view of the relationship of 2nd and 3rd MFCC coefficient in Euclidian space.

With the help of the grids on figure, we can observe that these spectral coefficients' distributions do vary in different fundamental frequency range bins. Difference includes shape, density and position. Familiar variations were also detected in other order spectral coefficients as well as those of other speakers. Though not very notable, they do exist among small fundamental frequency gaps and these could surely lead to alternations of sequent ASR model's parameter applying either statistic of template methods. Compared to the model built on features of only one fundamental frequency bin, if owns enough speaker dependent data, model built on features from all fundamental frequency range could be thought to have a less stable and less compact shape. In other words, fundamental frequency's influence on spectral features would increase intra-speaker distance, which is adverse to ASR task.

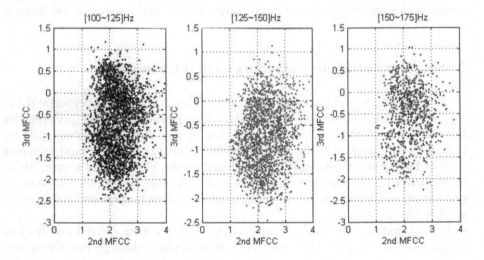

Fig. 1. One speaker's 2nd to 3rd MFCC distributions of the three prominent pitch frequency range bins. The expectation of this speaker's pitch frequency value -***Hz falls in middle bin which plotted in red asterisk

3   Recuperating Spectral Features

Usually, glottal changes themselves, especially fundamental frequency changes, were modeled as complementary information in ASR task. Either modeling short-term changes as speaker dependent features or modeling long-term changes as high-level features was introduced. However, we can also observe that different fundamental frequency bin holds different spectral features' distribution. So we can suppose that fundamental frequency changes around its expectation bring variations of spectral features. And without this influence, spectral features could represent speaker more exactly.

3.1   Proposed Model

Due to the influence described above, we can propose a spectral model in form of glottal information. Here we present our two suppositions:

1) Spectral feature vector is affected by the glottal feature vector, and the unaffected value could better characterize speaker.
2) Spectral feature vector, which corresponding glottal value is the average of this speaker's distribution, suffers least influence.

We denote $S(t)$, $G(t)$ as spectral and glottal features respectively. Then we write $\vec{s}(t)$ as the estimated spectral feature vector at time $t\Delta T$ and $\vec{g}(t)$ as the estimated glottal feature at $t\Delta T$. In practice, $\vec{s}(t)$ is MFCC vector estimated from a windowed signal centered at time $n\Delta T$, and $\vec{g}(t)$ is the fundamental frequency also estimated at time $t\Delta T$. For each estimated $\vec{s}(t)$, we assume that it corresponds to an original representation $\vec{s}_{opt}(t)$, which is considered to better characterize speaker.

According to supposition 1), we write their relationship as the function of fundamental frequency $\vec{g}(t)$. So the respective model is:

$$\vec{s}(t) = \Lambda\big(\vec{s}_{opt}(t), \Theta(\vec{g}(t))\big) \tag{1}$$

This holds true for every time $n\Delta T$. The operator $\Lambda(\ )$ describes a certain kind of relation of two variables at time $n\Delta T$. And operation $\Theta(\ )$ interprets transformation of fundamental frequency $\vec{g}(t)$ accordingly, which serves as the influence factor.

3.2 Multi-part Long Term Information

Usually, people think that distribution of all-frequency long-term fundamental frequency provides valuable speaker dependent information. But, illuminated by previous observations, we consider that different fundamental frequency bin should hold different information that can contribute differently to ASR task. So in order to utilize more speaker dependents, we can not treat them as a whole. We must get each bin's long-term feature separately. This is a novel concept of multi-level long-term glottal information.

Applying in our proposed model, we consider that:

3) Fundamental frequency, based on its value, has different effects on spectral features; but fundamental frequency falling in the same bin affects spectral features equally. It is just as what the long-term average of this bin acts.

Above is the third supposition of our proposed model. Then let us define I_k, $k = 1, \ldots, N$ as continuous bins of fundamental frequency. Here, N is the number of bins with $I_1 \cup \cdots \cup I_N = [50Hz, 550Hz]$, which is the ordinary range of person's fundamental frequency. And because fundamental frequency has only one dimension, we denote $E(\ )$ as the expectation and replace $\vec{g}(t)$ with $g(t)$. Referring to supposition 3), we define:

$$\Theta(\vec{g}(t)) = \Theta(g(t)) = \Theta\big(E\big(\hat{G}_{I_k}(t)\big)\big) \tag{2}$$

$$\text{where} \qquad \hat{G}_{I_k}(t) = \{g(t) | g(t) \in I_k\}$$

Now referring to supposition 2), we interpret $\Theta(x)$ as the distance measure $D(\ )$ of its variable x and variable's expectation. That is:

$$\Theta(\bar{g}(t)) = \Theta\left(E\left(\hat{G}_{I_k}(t)\right)\right) = D\left(E\left(\hat{G}_{I_k}(t)\right), E(\hat{G}(t))\right) \tag{3}$$

Combining with equation (1), we get:

$$\bar{s}(t) = \Lambda\left(\bar{s}_{opt}(t), \Theta(\bar{g}(t))\right) = \Lambda\left(\bar{s}_{opt}(t), D\left(E\left(\hat{G}_{I_k}\right), E(\hat{G}(t))\right)\right) \tag{4}$$

So we can get the assumed optimal spectral feature as:

$$\bar{s}_{opt}(t) = \Lambda^{-1}\left(\bar{s}(t), D\left(E\left(\hat{G}_{I_k}(t)\right), E(\hat{G}(t))\right)\right) \tag{5}$$

4   Experimental Setup

4.1 Speech Database

We used SRMC (Speaker Recognition for Mobile Communication) [9] speech corpuses to evaluate method in speaker recognition. It is a large multi-channel speech database, which contains two rounds speech data of 303 speakers. Its data was recorded from mobile phone, PDA, telephone and microphone simultaneously. Each speaker in our subset has Person-Information (PI) session of 3 sentences, Paragraph (PR) session of 1 sentence, and Mandarin Digit (MD), Dialect Digit (DD), English Digit (ED), Province Phase (PP), Free Talking (FT) session of 10 sentences each. The total length of speech material for one speaker in corpus is about 10 minutes. And we select the first round data for our experiments.

Speech was first pre-emphasized; then, a sliding Hamming window with a length of 32ms and a shift of 16ms was positioned on the signal. The silence and unvoiced segments were discarded based on an energy threshold. The spectral feature vectors were composed by 16 MFCC. And the fundamental frequency feature was extracted every segment using SHR methods provided by Sun [10]. We considered only the problem of text-independent speaker identification of closed set test.

4.2 Baseline Strategy

In the baseline strategy, spectral feature vectors, which were composed by 16-dimension MFCC and their delta coefficients, were directly delivered to classifiers as the input. The classifiers we adopted include VQ (code book size being 512), GMM (mixture number being 32), HMM (with 5 states, 10 Gaussian mixture density output). This is the convenience method applying in speaker identification task and we put no alternations on features or classifiers.

4.3 Solution to Model in Speaker Identification

Impregnating our proposed model, the 32-mixture GMM was also employed as the classifier. We set $\Lambda(\ )$ as the linear function and $D(\ )$ as the Euclidian distance. This is the rudimental settlement for our model. And in future work, we will investigate more proper and exact formation for these two operators.

With the normalization of Euclidian distance, we deduce equation (6) from equation (5):

$$\vec{s}_{opt}(t) = \vec{s}(t) - \vec{\lambda} \left| E(\hat{G}_{I_k}(t)) - E(\hat{G}(t)) \right| / \left| E(\hat{G}(t)) \right| \tag{6}$$

Here $\vec{\lambda}$ is the impact vector which has the same dimensions as spectral feature vector $\vec{s}(t)$. And we suppose that each dimension of $\vec{\lambda}$ is independent of others. So in order to get every dimension of $\vec{\lambda}$, we used local optimization solution. The properly recuperated spectral features could make system's performance maximum. And for each speaker's model, $\hat{G}(t)$ and $\hat{G}_{I_k}(t)$ were acquired in training.

5 Results and Discussions

In order to find out whether our method is robust under different number of speakers, we made experiments using first 50, first 100 and total 303 speakers of SRMC. And we select all sentences from PR and PI sessions for training. And the remaining 50 sentences of each speaker were all used for testing. Table 1, 2, 3, 4 shows the results of experiments on mobile phone channel, telephone channel, PDA channel and microphone channel respectively.

There are several important points to be noted. Firstly, our proposed model obtain higher identification rate than the baseline in all classifiers in each channel. It is obvious that the recuperated spectral features behave better than the unsettled ones. Though identification rate falls as the numbers of speakers increase, basedline method decreases more rapidly than ours. We can find in Table 1 that, when identification rate of GMM classifier descends from 84.7% to 73.4%, however, only 6.3 percents descend is fond in our model. The similar cases can also be found in almost all other sets of our experiments.

There are several important points to be noted. Firstly, our proposed model obtain higher identification rate than the baseline in all classifiers in each channel. It is obvious that the recuperated spectral features behave better than the unsettled ones. Though identification rate falls as the numbers of speakers increase, basedline method decreases more rapidly than ours. We can find in Table 1 that, when identification rate of GMM classifier descends from 84.7% to 73.4%, however, only 6.3 percents descend is fond in our model. The similar cases can also be found in almost all other sets of our experiments.

Secondly, our method outperforms the baseline method in all four channels. Here, 3.1%, 1.9%, 1.8% and 1.9% increases in first 100 speaker set using HMM classifier were found in Table 1, Table 2, Table 3 and Table 4 respectively. It is obviously that out method does increase the performance of ASR system in spite of the type of channel.

Thirdly, our model has only adopted simple operators of $\Lambda(\ )$ and $D(\ )$. Future work would be concentrated in looking for more proper and correct ones to better reflect this influence.

Table 1. Speaker Identification of Mobile Channel

Method	First 50 (%)		First 100 (%)		Total 303 (%)	
	Based	Ours	Based	Ours	Based	Ours
VQ	78.9	79.4	73.5	76.9	61.4	69.2
GMM	79.3	79.7	74.3	77.2	63.1	70.6
HMM	79.5	80.2	74.9	78.0	64.2	71.4

Table 2. Speaker Identification of Telephone Channel

Method	First 50 (%)		First 100 (%)		Total 303 (%)	
	Based	Ours	Based	Ours	Based	Ours
VQ	84.3	84.8	80.6	82.4	72.9	78.5
GMM	84.7	85.1	81.4	83.3	73.4	78.8
HMM	85.2	85.9	82.1	84.0	75.0	79.7

Table 3. Speaker Identification of PDA Channel

Method	First 50 (%)		First 100 (%)		Total 303 (%)	
	Based	Ours	Based	Ours	Based	Ours
VQ	88.3	88.7	84.8	86.9	78.3	82.0
GMM	88.9	89.2	85.8	87.5	79.6	82.8
HMM	89.0	89.3	86.2	88.0	80.6	83.9

Table 4. Speaker Identification of Microphone Channel

Method	First 50 (%)		First 100 (%)		Total 303 (%)	
	Based	Ours	Based	Ours	Based	Ours
VQ	86.9	87.3	83.6	85.4	77.0	81.5
GMM	87.2	87.7	84.3	86.2	78.2	82.4
HMM	87.4	87.8	84.9	86.8	79.5	83.0

6 Conclusion

In this paper, we present a robust approach by using correlation information of spectral and glottal features in text-independent speaker recognition system under multi-channel environments. Our utilizing both short-term and long-term information is quite different from other current methods. Here, we suppose the original spectral information is distorted by glottal distribution. And our work focuses on getting the assumed original unaffected spectral features holding more discriminative abilities. Promsing results of experiments on different channels of SRMC corpus are achieved.

Acknowlegement

This work is supported by National Natural Science Foundation of P.R.China (60273059), Zhejiang Provincial Natural Science Foundation for Young Scientist of P.R.China (RC01058), Zhejiang Provincial Natural Science Foundation (M603229) and National Doctoral Subject Foundation (20020335025).

References

1. Heck, L. et al.: Handset-dependent background models for robust text-independent speaker recognition, *ICASSP*, 1987
2. Farrell, K. R., Mammone, R. J. and Assaleh, K. T.: Speaker Recognition Using Neural Networks and Conventional Classifiers, *IEEE Trans. on Speech and Audio processing*. Vol. 2, No. 1, PART II, Jan. 1994
3. Kemal Sonmez, Elizabeth, Shriberg, Larry Heck and Mitchel Weintraub: Modeling Dynamic Prosodic Variation for Speaker Verification, *Proc. Intl. Conf. on Spoken Language Processing*, Vol. 7, pp. 3189-3192, 1998
4. Adami, A., Mihaescu, R., Reynolds, D. and Godfrey, J.: Modeling Prosodic Dynamics for speaker Recognition, *ICASSP'03*, Vol. 4, pp. 788-791, April 2003
5. Mizuno, H. et al.: Pitch dependent phone modeling for HMM-based speech recognition, *J. Acoust. Soc, Jpn. (E)*, Vol. 15, No. 2, pp. 77-86, 1994
6. Campbell J.P. Jr.: Speaker Recognition: A Tutorial, *Proceeding of the IEEE*, Vol. 85, No. 9, pp. 1436-1462, 1997
7. Dautrich, B. A., Rabiner, L. R. and Martin, T. B.: On the effects of varying filter bank parameters on isolated word recognition, *IEEE Trans. Acoust., Speech, Signal Processing*, Vol. 31, pp. 793-807, 1983
8. Nobuaki MINEMATSU and Seiichi NAKAGAWA: Modeling of Variations in Cepstral Coefficients Caused by F0 Changes and Its Application to Speech Processing, *Proc. Intl. Conf. Spoken Language Processing*, pp. 1063-1066, 1998
9. Lifeng Sang, Zhaohui Wu and Yingchun Yang: Speaker Recognition System in Multi-Channel Environment, *IEEE International Conference on System, Man & Cybernetics*, pp. 3116-3121, Oct. 5-8, 2003
10. Sun, X.: A pitch Determination Algorithm Based on Subharmonic-to-harmoic ratio, *The 6th International Conference of Spoken Language Processing*, Beijing, China, Vol. 4, pp. 676-679, 2000

Speaker Modeling Technique Based on Regression Class for Speaker Identification with Sparse Training

Zhonghua Fu and Rongchun Zhao

School of Computer Science, Northwestern,
Polytechnical University, Xi'an 710072, P.R. China
mailfzh@vip.sina.com

Abstract. Speaker modeling technique with sparse training data is an active branch of robust speaker recognition research. This paper presents a novel modeling approach named Multi-EigenSpace modeling technique based on Regression Class (RC-MES), which integrates the common eigenspace technique and the regression class (RC) idea of Maximum Likelihood Linear Regression (MLLR). RC-MES not only solves the problem of prior knowledge limitation of Gaussian Mixture Models (GMM) but also remedies the shortcoming of common eigenspace that confuses speaker differences and phoneme differences. The eigenvoice analysis in RC can provide better discrimination ability between different speakers. The experimental results on speaker identification of 75 males show that, when enrolment data is sparse, RC-MES provides significant improvement over GMM, and the number of eigenvoices in RC-MES is fewer than that in common eigenspace.

1 Introduction

Speaker recognition is one of the most flexible approaches in biometric recognition field. One key issue in speaker recognition is the speaker modeling technique. Gaussian Mixture Models (GMMs) [1] might be the most successful one, but this data-driven approach depends entirely on training data so that the recognition performance will deteriorate drastically when training data is sparse [2][3]. In practice, for some low-security tasks, clients might be impatient if the enrolment procedure extends 5 seconds. Therefore new modeling approach is needed for speaker recognition with sparse training data.

The shortcoming of GMMs consists in the limitation of prior knowledge. One possible way to solve this problem is adopting speaker adaptation techniques [4]. Thyes [2] proposed an eigenvoices approach that client and test speaker models are confined to a low-dimensional linear subspace obtained previously from a different set of training data. This approach ignores the phoneme differences that are integrated in speech data, which will possibly influence the discrimination ability of Eigenspace. In other words, the recognition performance will be further improved if every tester speaks the same utterances.

S.Z. Li et al. (Eds.): Sinobiometrics 2004, LNCS 3338, pp. 610–616, 2004.

This paper proposed a new approach named Multi-EigenSpace modeling based on Regression Class (RC-MES). We employ the concept of Regression Class (RC) from Maximum Likelihood Linear Regression (MLLR) approach used in speaker adaptation [5]. The traditional eigenspace is separated into several sub eigenspaces according to the phoneme differences. Then the Eigenvoices analysis is carried out in each subspace. In the experiments of speaker identification on 75 males, the new RC-MES technique is shown to provide significant performance improvements over GMMs when enrolment data is sparse, and the number of eigenvoices in RC-MES is fewer than that in common eigenspace.

In the next section we briefly review the eigenvoices approach and the regression class idea used in MLLR. We next describe the RC-MES approach and then deduce the parameters estimation formulas. This is followed by a description of the experiment data, design and results.

2 Eigenvoices and Regression Class

The eigenvoice approach [2] constrains the adapted model to be a linear combination of a small number of basis vectors obtained offline from a set of reference speakers. The modeling procedure contains two parts, offline part and online part.

In offline part, firstly a reference set of n well-trained speaker-dependent (SD) models and a speaker-independent (SI) model are built on a large speech database. From each of the SD models, a "supervector" that contains the means of the Gaussian components in GMMs is extracted, noting that the number D of extracted parameters and the order must be the same for all speakers. Then a dimen-sionality reduction technique (DRT) such as principle component analysis (PCA) is applied to the n supervectors to get R eigenvectors, namely "eigenvoices". Those Eigenvoices are orthogonal to span the eigenspace. The computationally intensive SD training and DRT steps are carried out offline before recognition begins.

In online part, each new speaker S is represented by a point in eigenspace, and his supervector is assume to be a linear combination of the eigenvoices:

$$P = e(0) + w(1) \cdot e(1) + \cdots + w(R) \cdot e(R) \tag{1}$$

where $e(0), e(1), \cdots, e(R)$ are the eigenvoices, $w(1), \cdots, w(R)$ are the corresponding weights. Thus the modeling problem for the new speaker is to estimate the weight vector.

The eigenvoices can be thought as the basis vectors that correspond to the maximum-variance directions in the original speaker space. However, in speaker recognition, the differences between two utterances relate to not only the differences between speakers, but also the corresponding phoneme differences. When enrolment time is limited and the training context is unrestricted, arbitrarily building a single eigenspace will confuse these two kinds of differences. In ideal situation, to comparing utterances from different speakers with the same context will emphasize the speaker differences. Therefore, we decide to restrict the eigenspace to certain phoneme level by using RC approach referred in MLLR [5].

Leggetter has introduced RC idea in the MLLR approach, which proposed a feasible way to adapt those models that no corresponding adaptation data is available.

MLLR adapts the mean vectors of continuous density HMM's by multiplying the mean vector for the initial model with a transformation matrix:

$$\hat{\mu} = W_s \cdot \bar{\xi}_s \tag{2}$$

where W_s is the transformation matrix for mixture component s, $\hat{\mu}$ is the adapted mean vector, ξ_s is the extended mean vector for mixture component s

$$\bar{\xi}_s = [w, \mu_{s1}, \cdots, \mu_{sn}]' = [w, \bar{\mu}_s]' \tag{3}$$

where $\bar{\mu}_s$ is the original mean vector, w is an offset term and n is the number of features. A RC is a set of mixture components for which it is assumed that the same transformation matrix may be used for all components in the RC.

By tying mixture components the main object is to tie components that are assumed to undertake a somewhat similar transformation. That is to say, inside the RC, the components are very similar. So to calculate the Eigen-voices in RC level might be a possible way to separate the speaker differences from phoneme differences.

The number of RCs and the clustering of Gaussian mixtures are the essential problems of MLLR. Theoretically speaking, the division of RCs can be a single globe RC that contains all components or a tiny RC that each component belongs to a different RC. In practical, the number of RCs should be defined according to the data quantity available during enrollment. The base rule is to make sure that each RC has enough adaptation data to estimate the transformation matrix. Commonly, a RC tree is built according to some distance measure between Gaussian components beforehand, where the root node corresponds to the globe RC and the leave node corresponds to the tiny RC.

3   RC-MES Approach

In RC-MES, the eigenvoices and the RC idea are integrated by adapting new speaker model in subeigenspace based on RC. The modeling steps are as follows:

Offline Steps:

(1) Building SI model (in terms of GMM) for each phoneme based on a large speech corpus such as TIMIT database [9]. Then a RC tree is built using the divergence measure [6] between all Gaussian components as the distance measure.

(2) Determining the division of the RC tree according to the adaptation material available during enrolment, while keeping sufficient adaptation data for each RC.

(3) Based on this division (assume all components are divided into S RCs), rebuilding a new GMM inside each class to get S SI models of RC level (SI_{RC}).

(4) For each of R reference speakers, training S SD models of RC level (SD_{RC}). For example, with S SI_{RC}, for speaker S_i, distributing his feature vectors into S classes based on the maximum likelihood rule. Then in each RC, we adapt the SI_{RC} to S_i dependent model via MAP using the adapting data belongs to that class. Now we have $R \times S$ SD_{RC}.

(5) In each RC, with the R SD models and one SI model, we can calculate $k+1$ eigenvoices $(e_i(0), e_i(1), \cdots, e_i(k)), i = 1, \cdots, S$.

Online Steps:

(1) Obtaining the enrolment data of a new speaker and executing feature extraction.

(2) With S SI_{RC}, separating the enrolment feature vectors into S RCs based on the maximum likelihood (ML) rule.

(3) Inside of each RC, e.g. class j, according to eigenvoices $(e_j(0), e_j(1), \cdots, e_j(k))$ and adaptation data of the class, the weight vector $(w_j(1), \cdots, w_j(k))$ is estimated. Then for all RCs, we have S groups of weight vectors $(w_i(1), \cdots, w_i(k)), i = 1, \cdots, S$.

(4) In each RC, iterating the estimation process of the weight vector until likelihood score reaches its maximum. Then constructing the supervector of the RC level for new speaker to build his or her SD_{RC}.

(5) Integrating all SD_{RC} of the new speaker to build the final SD GMM.

In the above procedure, we assume that the amount of enrolment data available is known in advance, and if it is not, all possible divisions of RC must be defined in offline steps and the final division is built in dynamic manner [5] according to the data available.

4 Parameters Estimation of RC-MES

In RC-MES, the model adaptation for a new speaker is actually the estimation of weights of eigenvoices $w_s(k), k = 0, \cdots, K; s = 1, \cdots, S$ (k is the index of eigenvoice, s is the index of RC, $w_s(0) = 1$) and the estimation of weights and covariance matrixes of GMMs. Since the eigenvoices of RC-MES are dispersed into RCs, the estimation is carried out in each regression class. The eigenvoice of RC s can be written as

$$e^s(j) = \left[e_0^s(j)^T, e_1^s(j)^T, e_2^s(j)^T, \cdots, e_m^s(j)^T, \cdots \right] j = 0, 1, \cdots, K \qquad (4)$$

where $e_m^s(j)$ is the means vector of m-th component in RC s.

Firstly, for each observation from the new speaker, one needs to calculate the likelihood score for each SI_{RC} well trained in offline steps and to deliver the observations to each RC. Then we obtain a group of observation sets, $O^{(1)}, O^{(2)}, \cdots, O^{(S)}$, each consisting of an individual number of observation vectors. That is

$$O = \bigcup_{s=1 \cdots S} O^{(s)}, o_t \in O^{(s)} \quad when \ s = \arg \max_{j=1 \cdots S} \left(p\left(o_t | SI_{RC}(j) \right) \right) \qquad (5)$$

where $p(\bullet)$ is the observation probability of GMM, o_t is the observation vector at time t.

The estimation of weight vectors of eigenvoices in each RC is as same as the method proposed in [7]. We also use a maximum-likelihood estimator called maximum likelihood Eigen-decomposition (MLED) to derive the estimation formula of $w(j)$ in RC-MES. In each RC, for $i = 0, \cdots, K$, the weights of eigenvoices are iterative re-estimated using

$$\sum_{t=1}^{T}\sum_{m=1}^{M}r^{(m)}(t)\cdot\left[e_m^s(i)\right]'\cdot C_m^{-1}\cdot o_t^{(s)} = \sum_{t=1}^{T}\sum_{m=1}^{M}r^{(m)}(t)\cdot\left\{\left[\sum_{k=0}^{K}w_s(k)\cdot e_m^s(k)\right]'\cdot C_m^{-1}\cdot e_m^s(i)\right\} \qquad (6)$$

where $o_t^{(s)}$ is observation vector at time t, which belongs to RC s, C_m^{-1} is the inverse of covariance matrix of m-th component in RC s, $r^{(m)}(t)$ is the occupation probability

$$r^{(m)}(t) = P\left(i_t = m \middle| o_t^{(s)}, \lambda_s\right) = p_m^s \cdot b_m^s\left(o_t^s\right) \middle/ \sum_{k=1}^{M} p_k^s \cdot b_k^s\left(o_t^s\right) \qquad (7)$$

where p_m^s and $b_m^s()$ are the weight and pdf of m-th component in RC s.

In eq. (5) there are $K+1$ equations to solve for the $K+1$ unknown weights ($w_s(i)$ values) of RC s. The new model thus obtained yields new values for the occupation probabilities $r^{(m)}(t)$; this estimation process can be iterated until converge. The same estimation procedures are executed in other RCs. Note that in each RC, the number of Gaussian components is rather small, therefore the computation cost is similar with the traditional eigenspace.

After the estimation of weights of eigenvoices, the supervector of the new speaker is obtained, so does the means of each Gaussian component in each RC. Then the components in each RC are bound together to build the GMM for the new speaker, the corresponding covariance matrixes come directly from SI$_{RC.}$ The component weights are normalized and then re-estimated once using EM algorithm.

5 Speaker Identification Experiments

The database used in the identification experiments consists utterances collected from 75 males. The reading contents are selected from TIMIT database and recorded with 8kHz sampling frequency and 8-bit quantification. Each speaker has about 27s speech data after silence removing, using adaptive energy thresholds. The feature extraction includes the pre-emphasis and short time analysis using hamming window, then Mel-Frequecy Cepstral Coefficients (MFCC), ΔMFCC and $\Delta\Delta$MFCC are calculated as feature vector. The corresponding parameters are list in Table1.

Table 1. Parameters used for feature extraction

Para.	Form
Pre-emphasis	$1 - 0.97z^{-1}$
Window type	Hamming
Frame length	25ms
Frame shift	10ms
Features	12MFCC+12ΔMFCC+12Δ^2MFCC (c_0 removed)

The building procedures of eigenvoices and RC are as follows:

(1) Selecting 100 males from TIMIT database and extracting feature vectors;

(2) Training GMM with 6 components for each phoneme using HTK toolbox [8].

(3) Because the adaptation data is already known, we don't build the whole regression class tree but divide the GMMs into 10 RCs instead.

(4) Re-normalized the Gaussian weights inside each RC to build SI_{RC}.

(5) With these SI_{RC}, separating the data from 100 males into each RC according to maximum likelihood rule. Then building SD GMM with 3 components in each RC for each of the 100 speakers, i.e. each speaker has a GMM with 30 components.

(6) Calculating eigenvoices in each RC.

During online steps, the speech features from experiment database are separated into each RCs. Then the MELD algorithm is used to estimate the weight vectors of Eigenvoices in each RC. Finally after the binding, each new speaker obtains his GMM.

Table 2 illustrates the comparison results of GMM, common eigenspace and RC-MES. It is clear that when training data is sparse, the performance of GMM is deteriorating drastically. The recognition rate of GMM with 30 components is only 47.2%, even lower than GMM with 10 components. On the other hand, eigenspace approaches all provide better performances, which proves that using prior knowledge can overcome the shortcoming of GMM. RC-MES provides the best performance and the result of 40 eigenvoices is close to that of 65 eigenvoices in common eigenspace, which indicates that by separating the speaker differences from phoneme differences, the discriminate ability of eigenspace is enhanced.

Table 2. Recognition Rate (RR) using GMM vs. Common EigenSpace (CES) vs. RC-MES

Train time	Test time	GMM(%)		CES(%)		RC-MES(%)	
		RR	Gaussians	RR	Eigenvoices	RR	Eigenvoices
20s	5s	85.2	30	93.2	65	96.1	65
		80.3	10	88.5	40	92.9	40
10s	5s	47.2	30	90.8	65	95.2	65
		79.0	10	86.7	40	90.5	40

6 Conclusions

This paper has presented a new speaker modeling technique called Multi-Eigen-Space technique based on Regression Class (RC-MES), which integrates the common eigenspace technique and the regression class idea of MLLR. This technique provides a better solution for speaker recognition application where the training and enrolment speech is limited. This technique employs the prior knowledge about speaker differences and remedies the shortcoming of common eigenspace that confuses speaker differences and phoneme differences. The experimental results on speaker identification show that RC-MES provides significant improvement over the GMM approach, and the number of eigenvoices in RC-MES is fewer than that in common eigenspace. Future work will focus on noise corrupted speech and microphone distortion situations.

Acknowledgements

This paper is supported by Doctoral innovation Foundation of Northwestern Polytechnical University.

References

1. D. A. Reynolds, "Speaker identification and verification using Gaussian mixture speaker models", Speech Communication, Vol. 17, Issues 1-2, pp. 91-108, August 1995.
2. O. Thyes, R. Kuhn, P. Nguyen, J. –C. Junqua, "Speaker identification and verification using eigenvoices", ICSLP2000, Beijing-China, Vol.2, pp. 242~246, Oct. 2000.
3. N. J. –C. Wang, W. –H. Tsai, L.–S. Lee, "Eigen-MLLR coefficients as new feature parameters for speaker identification", Eurospeech, Vol. 2, pp. 1385-1388, 2001.
4. C. Tadj, M. Gabrea et al, " Towards robustness in speaker verification: enhancement and adapataion", The 2002 45th Midwest Symposium on Circuits and Systems, Vol. 3, pp. 320-323, Aug. 2002.
5. C. J. Leggetter, P. C. Woodland, "Maximum likelihood linear regression for speaker adaptation of Continuous Density Hidden Markov Models", Computer Speech and Language, Vol. 9, pp. 171-185, 1995.
6. J P Campbell, JR. "Speaker recognition: a tutorial", Proceedings of the IEEE, Vol. 85(9), Sept. 1997.
7. R. Kuhn, J-C Junqua, P. Nguyen, N. Niedzielski, "Rapid speaker adaptation in Eigenvoice space. IEEE Trans", On Speech and Audio Processing. Vol.8 (6), pp. 695-706, Nov. 2000.
8. S. J. Young, D. Kershaw, J. Odell, and P. Woodland: The HTK Book (for HTK Version 3.0), Http://htk.eng.cam.ac.uk/docs.shtml, 2000.
9. J. Garofolo, et al. "DARPA TIMIT Acoustic-Phonetic Continuous Speech Corpus CD-ROM", National Institute of Standards and Technology, 1993.

Some Issues Pertaining to Adaptive Multimodal Biometric Authentication

Kar-Ann Toh, Quoc-Long Tran, and Wei-Yun Yau

Institute for Infocomm Research,
21 Heng Mui Keng Terrace, Singapore 119613
{katoh, qltran, wyyau}@i2r.a-star.edu.sg

Abstract. In this paper, we address some issues pertaining to adaptive multimodal biometric authentication. These issues include new user registration, sensor decay and small sample data size. A recursive formulation is introduced to track changes due to new user registration and possible sensor decay. The small sample size problem is handled using a feature scaling-space learning technique. Empirical experiments are conducted to observe the effects.

1 Introduction

Due to inherent properties in each biometric and external manufacturing constraints in sensing technologies, no single biometric method can warrant an authentication accuracy of hundred percent by itself to date. This problem can be alleviated by combining multiple biometric methods. The importance of multimodal biometrics is thus obvious.

In a typical biometric application scenario, new user registration is a frequent task. Adding a new user to the database and perform re-training may be a time-consuming process. In this paper, we introduce a Recursive Least Squares (RLS) formulation (see e.g. [1]) to adapt the parameters of a polynomial model to new registered patterns in multimodal biometric applications. Since the process is incremental, it does not require to re-train the model all over again when new training data arrives.

On top of the new user registration problem, we shall focus on two other issues pertaining to the above recursive formulation, namely the sensor decay problem and the small sample size problem. For sensor decay problem, it is known that the performance of sensors can deteriorate over time and usage (e.g. CMOS type of fingerprint sensors). Very often, these sensors become noisy upon heavy usage due to wear and tear. An adaptive algorithm to adapt to these changes could be beneficial. It is further noted that usually a small number of training samples are added for each new user. A stable learning methodology would thus be helpful for such a system.

2 Problem Statement

In single biometric verification system, the decision that the input pattern being accepted (genuine user) or rejected (impostor) is usually based on a comparison

S.Z. Li et al. (Eds.): Sinobiometrics 2004, LNCS 3338, pp. 617–628, 2004.

between the match scores (evaluated by matching the input and the templates) and a specified threshold. The biometric verification task can thus be treated as a pattern classification problem. In a measurement-output-level-based multiple biometric verification system [2], the match scores of all single biometric classifiers are passed through a decision fusion module and are combined adopting some fusion strategies to make the final decision. Combining different biometrics in this way results in a system that can outperform individual classifiers. This is especially true if the biometrics are not correlated [3].

The problem of combining different biometric match scores can be defined as follows: Suppose an object have all biometrics needed to present to the system using l single biometric classifiers. Let $\boldsymbol{x} = [x_1, x_2, \ldots, x_l]$ be the vector consisting of the outputs (match scores) of these classifiers. The object can be either a *genuine user* or an *impostor*. Let $y \in \{0, 1\}$ be the class label of the object (0 for impostor, 1 for genuine user), then $(\boldsymbol{x}, y)$ forms a training pair. Suppose we have N objects, the corresponding training pairs form a training set $\boldsymbol{D} = \{(\boldsymbol{x}_i, y_i)\}, i = 1, 2, \ldots, N$. The problem is to find a mapping from the match scores space into the class label space that best fits the training data. We shall adopt the least squares fitting in this work.

New User Registration. Given that, at time t, the training set $\boldsymbol{D}_t = \{(\boldsymbol{x}, y)\}_t$ (we omit the subscript i for simplicity) was presented to the system. The parameters of the model at time t, $\boldsymbol{\alpha}_t$ was calculated such that a learning model best fits the training data. At time $t + 1$, a new training sample $(\boldsymbol{x}, y)$ arrives and the new training set is $\boldsymbol{D}_{t+1} = \boldsymbol{D}_t \bigcup \{(\boldsymbol{x}, y)\}_{t+1}$. The problem is to calculate the new parameter $\boldsymbol{\alpha}_{t+1}$ incrementally using only the new training sample rather than using the entire new and old training sets.

Sensor Decay. Upon heavy usage, the biometric sensors may decay over time. This decaying process would cause noisy biometric measurement. Because of this, the distribution of genuine and impostor match scores could overlap more and more over time. As a result, the performance of a fixed classifier which is trained only once at the beginning may be affected badly. Under this circumstance, an adaptive learning algorithm would be a good solution.

Small Sample Size. In contrast to the usual decision fusion formulations (see. e.g. [2–7]), the adaptive formulation as per user and over time may not enjoy the luxury of having a large data size at each iteration. Under typical application scenario, a user may have only a few samples of biometric data enrolled. The size of genuine-user scores is thus limited to the intra-matchings among these few enrolled samples from the same person. As for the imposter scores, the data is obtained from inter-matching the selected user across all other users. These imposter scores constitute a much larger sample size then that of genuine-users. This unbalance of different classes may affect the density based training. Another yet more important problem is that the small number of genuine-user score samples may not be representative enough for possible large variations during query applications. A feature scaling-space learning technique proposed by [8] is applied to handle this problem.

3   A Reduced Multivariate Polynomial (RM)

Grounded on Weierstrass's approximation theorem, the multivariate polynomial (MP) possesses the universal approximation capability [1]. A general form of MP is a summation of all possible polynomial (product) terms $x_1^{n_1} x_2^{n_2} \cdots x_l^{n_l}$ with $n_1, n_2, \ldots n_l$ vary such that $\sum_{j=1}^{l} n_j \leqslant r$. The number r is the order of the polynomial and we denote K as the total number of parameters α_j. A full multivariate polynomial faces the problem of parameter explosion. The number of polynomial terms, K, grows exponentially with the order and the number of inputs [1]. In [9], a reduced multivariate polynomial model (RM), which has less parameters while still keeping the crucial polynomial terms, was proposed as follows:

$$f_{RM}(\boldsymbol{\alpha}, \boldsymbol{x}) = \boldsymbol{\alpha}^T p_{RM}(\boldsymbol{x})$$

$$= \alpha_0 + \sum_{k=1}^{r} \sum_{j=1}^{l} \alpha_{k,j} x_j^k + \sum_{k=1}^{r} \alpha_k \left(\sum_{j=1}^{l} x_j \right)^k$$

$$+ \sum_{k=2}^{r} \left(\sum_{i=1}^{l} \alpha_{k,i} x_i \right) \left(\sum_{j=1}^{l} x_j \right)^{k-1},$$

$$l, r \geqslant 2, \tag{1}$$

where $\{x_j\}, j = 1, \ldots, l$ are the polynomial inputs, $\alpha_0, \alpha_{k,j}, \alpha_k, \alpha_{k,i}, \cdots$ are the weighting coefficients to be estimated, and l, r correspond to input-dimension, order of system respectively. The number of terms in this model can be expressed as: $K = 1 + r + l(2r - 1)$.

To stabilize the solution for least square error, in [6, 10], a regularization was performed. The criterion function to be minimized is thus:

$$J = ||\boldsymbol{y} - \boldsymbol{F}^T \boldsymbol{\alpha}||^2 + b||\boldsymbol{\alpha}||^2, \tag{2}$$

where $\boldsymbol{y} = [y_1, y_2, \cdots, y_N]^T$ is the target output vector and $\boldsymbol{F} = [\boldsymbol{f}_1, \boldsymbol{f}_2, \cdots, \boldsymbol{f}_N]^T$ with $\boldsymbol{f}_i$ being the vector of all polynomial terms in (1) which is applied to the i-th training sample. The estimated outputs is $\hat{\boldsymbol{y}} = \boldsymbol{F}^T \boldsymbol{\alpha}$ and the solution for $\boldsymbol{\alpha}$ that minimize J is

$$\boldsymbol{\alpha} = (\boldsymbol{F}^T \boldsymbol{F} + b\boldsymbol{I})^{-1} \boldsymbol{F}^T \boldsymbol{y}, \tag{3}$$

where b is a regularization parameter (b is usually chosen to be a small value, say 10^{-4} [11], for stability).

4   Recursive Least Squares Algorithm (RLS)

The solution for $\boldsymbol{\alpha}$ in (3) is a single-step solution which is suitable when the training set is rich, the environment does not change with time, i.e. a static problem. For problems where the training set grows with time, re-training the system using (3) might be very costly. If that is the case, the RLS approach [1] can be applied to the RM model in order to find the new parameters [12]. Let $f_i \in \mathcal{R}^K$ be the vector of all polynomial terms in (1) which is applied to the i-th training sample. We can pack all training samples as

$$F_t = [f_1, f_2, \cdots, f_t]^T. \tag{4}$$

Let $M_t = F_t^T F_t + bI$, equation (3) becomes

$$\alpha_t = M_t^{-1} F_t^T y_t. \tag{5}$$

When all training samples are considered equally important, we can rewrite M_t and $F_t^T y_t$ in terms of their past and present instances as follows:

$$M_t = F_t^T F_t + bI = M_{t-1} + f_t f_t^T, \tag{6}$$

$$F_t^T y_t = F_{t-1}^T y_{t-1} + f_t y_t. \tag{7}$$

The above equations show that the matrices M_t and $F_t^T y_t$ can be calculated accumulatively using the new samples. Besides, from (5), if these matrices are averaged by the number of samples, we still get the same solution for α_t. By averaging M_t and $F_t^T y_t$, we have

$$M_t = \frac{t-1}{t} M_{t-1} + \frac{1}{t} f_t f_t^T, \tag{8}$$

$$F_t^T y_t = \frac{t-1}{t} F_{t-1}^T y_{t-1} + \frac{1}{t} f_t y_t. \tag{9}$$

If we want to make the system forget the old training samples, we can modify (8) and (9) as follows:

$$M_t = (1-\lambda)M_{t-1} + \lambda f_t f_t^T, \tag{10}$$

$$F_t^T y_t = (1-\lambda)F_{t-1}^T y_{t-1} + \lambda f_t y_t, \tag{11}$$

where λ ($0 \leqslant \lambda \leqslant 1$) is called the forgetting factor and (8) and (9) are special cases with $\lambda = \frac{1}{t}$. To derive the recursive formulation, we need the formula below.

Sherman-Morrison-Woodbury Matrix Inversion Formula. Let the matrices A, B, C, D satisfy

$$A = B + C^T DC, \tag{12}$$

then the inverse of A is

$$A^{-1} = B^{-1} - B^{-1}C^T(CB^{-1}C^T + D^{-1})^{-1}CB^{-1}.$$

Let $A = M_t, B = (1-\lambda)M_{t-1}, C = f_t^T, D = \lambda$ and apply the Sherman-Morrison-Woodbury matrix inversion formula to (10), we have (see [1])

$$M_t^{-1} = \frac{1}{1-\lambda}M_{t-1}^{-1} - \frac{\frac{1}{1-\lambda}M_{t-1}^{-1}f_tf_t^T\frac{1}{1-\lambda}M_{t-1}^{-1}}{f_t^T(\frac{1}{1-\lambda}M_{t-1}^{-1})f_t + \frac{1}{\lambda}}, \tag{13}$$

Substitute (13) and (11) into (5), we have

$$\alpha_t = \alpha_{t-1} + \frac{1}{1-\lambda}\frac{M_{t-1}^{-1}f_t(y_t - f_t^T\alpha_{t-1})}{f_t^T\frac{1}{1-\lambda}M_{t-1}^{-1}f_t + \frac{1}{\lambda}}. \tag{14}$$

Multiply both sides of (13) by f_t, we have

$$M_t^{-1}f_t = \frac{1}{\lambda(1-\lambda)}\frac{M_{t-1}^{-1}f_t(y_t - f_t^T\alpha_{t-1})}{f_t^T\frac{1}{1-\lambda}M_{t-1}^{-1}f_t + \frac{1}{\lambda}}, \tag{15}$$

and (14) can be simplified as

$$\alpha_t = \alpha_{t-1} + \lambda M_t^{-1}f_t(y_t - f_t^T\alpha_{t-1}). \tag{16}$$

In (14), the new estimate α_t is calculated using the previous estimate α_{t-1}, the inversion of M_{t-1} and the new training data $\{f_t, y_t\}$. Also, in (16), the calculation is simplified using the newly computed M_t^{-1}. Thus, these equations are recursive solution for the optimal parameter vector α in (3).

Summary of RM-RLS Algorithm
Input: Training set $D = \{x_i, y_i\}, i = 1, 2, \ldots, N$
Output: Parameter vector α

1. Initialization: $M_0^{-1} = \frac{1}{b}I, t = 1, \alpha_0$ is random.
2. At time t, calculate f_t in (1) from $\{x_t, y_t\}$.
3. Update M_t^{-1} and α_t using (13) and (16).
4. Assign $t \leftarrow t + 1$. If $t > N$ then $\alpha \leftarrow \alpha_N$ and stop, otherwise repeat from step 2.

Remarks:

1. With M_0^{-1} being initiated deterministically, RM-RLS requires no matrix inversion like the original RM algorithm.
2. The storage size of RM-RLS consisting of the inversion of M_t ($K \times K$) and the current data ($K \times 1$) is smaller than the storage size of RM which is $N \times K$ in size where N is the number of training samples.

5   Feature Scaling-Space Learning

Let $x \in \mathcal{R}^l$ be a l-dimensional pattern feature. The feature scaling-space is defined as $\{x, \gamma_1 x, \gamma_2 x, \ldots\}$ where $\gamma_i \in \mathcal{R}, i = 1, 2, \ldots$ are the scaling factors for each derived feature $\gamma_i x$ [8]. In other words, for each data sample x, there corresponds additional scaled samples $\gamma_i x$ which can be used for training. In our learning framework, we adopt a symmetrical scaling and define γ_1, γ_2 as follows: $\gamma_1 = (1-\rho)$ and $\gamma_2 = (1+\rho)$ where $0 \leqslant \rho < 1$. The final feature scaling-space is thus the set of original and scaled samples containing $\{\gamma_1 x, x, \gamma_2 x\}$. The training target vector contains replicates of the original target vector without scaling, i.e. $\{\mathbf{y}, \mathbf{y}, \mathbf{y}\}$. Notice that $\rho = 0$ corresponds to two redundant sets of data added to the original data x. This approach can turn an under-determined system to an over-determined system where the number of training samples is larger than the number of parameters.[1]

An Illustrative Example. Let x be a scalar regressing feature input and $g(\alpha, x) = \alpha_0 + \alpha_1 x + \alpha_2 x^2$ be the regressor function to fit the data. For 20 data samples obtained from randomly generated $x \in [0, 1]$ and suppose we have a target class output given by

$$ y = \begin{cases} 0, x < 0.5 \\ 1, x \geqslant 0.5 \end{cases}. \tag{17} $$

Three cases of training are performed as:

Case (i): use the original x and y for training;
Case (ii): use the sets $\{(1-\rho)x, \ x, \ (1+\rho)x\}$ and $\{y, y, y\}$ for training; and
Case (iii): use the sets $\{(1-\rho_2)x, (1-\rho_1)x, \ x, \ (1+\rho_1)x, (1+\rho_2)x\}$ and $\{y, y, y, y, y\}$ for training.

For convenience, Case (i) is abbreviated as '*original*', Case (ii) with $\rho = 0$ is abbreviated as '*original*× 3', Case (ii) with $\rho = 0.2$ is abbreviated as '*original+up-down scaled once*', Case (iii) with $\rho_1, \rho_2 = 0$ is abbreviated as '*original*× 5', Case (iii) with $\rho_1 = 0.2$ and $\rho_2 = 0.4$ is abbreviated as '*original+up-down scaled twice*'.

As indicated by a plot (not shown here) of the error function $(y - g(\alpha, x))^2$ for the above cases, the addition of scalings allows additional variation to the steepness of error function and position of minimum point. The result of the shift of minimum point towards the origin (especially for coefficient of high power terms) would be like weight decay regularization keeping the estimates within small values.

Fig. 1 shows the decision outputs for different scaling-spaces ('original' and 'scaling once' with $\rho = 0, 0.1, 0.2$) using another polynomial (10th-order) fitting the similar data using 50 random samples. It is seen from this plot that training using the scaling-space tends to smoothen the decision output (decision landscape for multivariate case). However, certain amount of bias have been introduced into the approximation, and care must be taken to find suitable scaling-spaces for good learning.

---

[1] If x and $\gamma_i x$ are concatenated to form a large dimension feature (e.g. $[x^T, \gamma_1 x^T, \gamma_2 x^T, \cdots]$), under-determined system can arise for cases with small number of training samples.

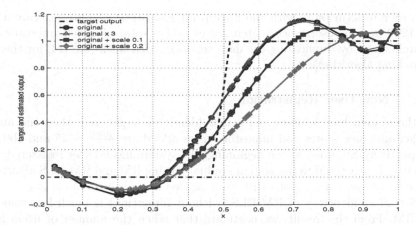

Fig. 1. Decision outputs for various scaling spaces (Legends: original×3 used the set $\{x,\ x,\ x\}$ for training; original + scale 0.1 used the set $\{(1-\rho)x,\ x,\ (1+\rho)x\}$ with $\rho = 0.1$ for training; original + scale 0.2 used the set $\{(1-\rho)x,\ x,\ (1+\rho)x\}$ with $\rho = 0.2$ for training)

6   Experiments

In the following experiments, we shall demonstrate the usefulness of RM-RLS for combining multiple biometric decisions using fingerprint and voice data. In the first experiment, users are registered one after another and the training times of RM and RM-RLS are recorded and compared. In the second experiment, we shall observe the performance of RM and RM-RLS when there is variation of sensor performance for the fingerprint data were collected over a period of 20 weeks and a static data set for voice was used. Our purpose is to observe possible decay in fingerprint sensor and to observe the tracking capability to time-varying noise.

6.1   Data Sets

Fingerpint: 12 fingerprint identities were collected over a period of 20 weeks using Veridicom sensor. For each fingerprint identity, in one week, we collected 10 samples. The total number of fingerprints is thus $12 \times 10 \times 20 = 2400$. All fingerprints collected from the second week and later are matched with the fingerprints collected in the first week to generate the genuine user match scores and impostor match scores (see [13] for the minutia matching algorithm). The resulted number of genuine scores generated in each week is $12 \times 10 \times 10 = 1200$. The number of impostor scores generated in each week is $12 \times 11 \times 10 \times 10 = 13200$.

   Voice: The voice data was obtained from six persons (3 males and 3 females) taken from TIDIGIT database. Each person was required to say two words. Thus, for text dependent case we had 12 voice identities in total. For each voice identity, we used 10 samples. The total number of voice samples is thus $12 \times 10 = 120$.

In order to form pairs with the fingerprint identities, we also generate a total of 1200 genuine-user voice match scores and a total of 13200 impostor voice match scores by duplicating the data sets over each week (see [14] for the voice matching algorithm).

6.2   New User Registration

If the system has N users and a new identity is registered, then the number of genuine user scores and impostor scores added are $\frac{10 \times 9}{2} = 45$ and $100 \times N$, respectively. Suppose, at the beginning, the system has no user registered. Each identity is registered to the system gradually using RM and RM-RLS algorithms. As can be seen in Fig. 2, the CPU time needed to find the final parameter vector α for all 12 identities of RM-RLS (without forgetting) is much less than that of RM. From this result, we postulate that when the number of users in the system is huge, the RM-RLS could save up considerable time for computation of learning parameters.

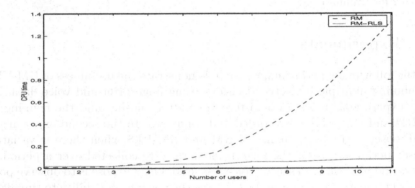

Fig. 2. CPU time (in sec.) required to find the parameter α of RM and RM-RLS algorithms

6.3   Tracking Accuracy Changes

Training Sets and Test Set: The data set (matching scores) obtained in each week is divided into 2 equal sets, one for training and the other for test. As we want to show the adaptive capability of the RM-RLS algorithm, we apply the following updating scheme which was used in [15]. The data from the first week was used to find the parameter α as a initial value. Then in each subsequent week, we use the current α to classify the training set. Only samples that are classified as genuine users are used to update the parameter vector α using either RM or RM-RLS (with forgetting factor). For RM-RLS, we chose the following values for the forgetting factor, $\lambda \in \{0.0005, 0.0007\}$ to see its effect on the training process. Finally, the test sets of all weeks were used to calculate the authentic acceptance rate (AAR), false rejection rate (FRR), false acceptance rate (FAR), equal error rate (EER) and the receiver operating characteristics (ROC). In a security system, the FAR is often kept at a small value (say, 10^{-4})) while the AAR (and $FRR = 1 - AAR$) which shows the probability that a genuine user is truly recognized is related to the user friendliness of the system. We shall observe the changes of these quantities over time for the test set.

Fig. 3 shows the weekly trend of FRR variation for both RM and RM-RLS algorithms at FAR = 0.0001. Also, as shown in the figure, in the first few weeks, the performance of RM and RM-RLS are similar. From week 12 onwards, RM-RLS with forgetting factor starts to perform better. This shows that there are some changes in the scores. RM-RLS can track these changes and therefore its performance is more steady and better than that of that of RM (the curve of RM-RLS is below that of RM after week 12).

Fig. 4 shows the weekly trend of EER variation of both RM and RM-RLS algorithms. Similar to the FRR study above, RM-RLS performs better than RM.

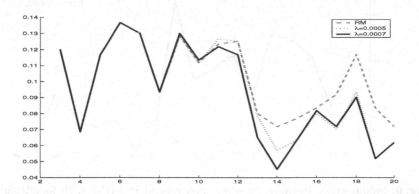

Fig. 3. False rejection rate of RM-RLS with different settings of forgetting factor λ at FAR = 0.0001

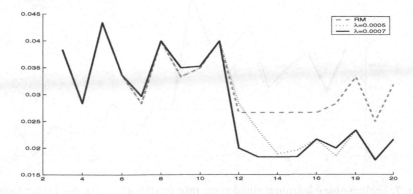

Fig. 4. Equal error rate of RM-RLS with different settings of forgetting factor λ

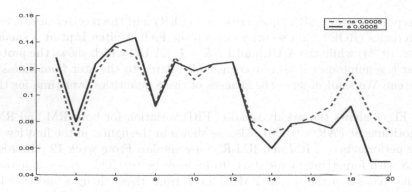

Fig. 5. Scaling-space learning: false rejection rate of RM-RLS with forgetting factor $\lambda = 0.0005$ at FAR = 0.0001

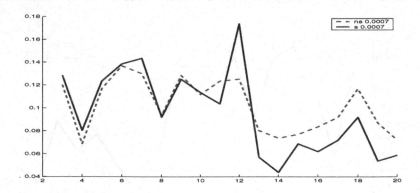

Fig. 6. Scaling-space learning: false rejection rate of RM-RLS with forgetting factor $\lambda = 0.0007$ at FAR = 0.0001

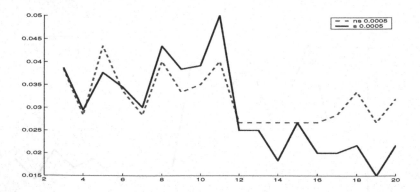

Fig. 7. Scaling-space learning: equal error rate of RM-RLS with forgetting factor $\lambda = 0.0005$

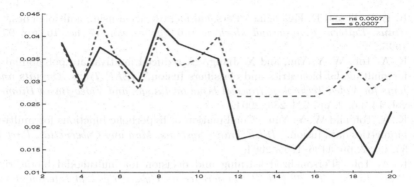

Fig. 8. Scaling-space learning: equal error rate of RM-RLS with forgetting factor $\lambda = 0.0007$

6.4 Tracking Accuracy Changes with Scaling-Space Learning

Fig. 5 and Fig. 6 show the learning FRR results at FAR $= 0.0001$ for two λ settings ($\lambda = 0.0005$ and 0.0007). Fig. 7 and Fig. 8 show the learning FRR results for similar λ settings. For both the FRR and EER plots, the dashed line indicates normal learning and the continuous line indicates learning using the feature scaling-space. These results show that the feature scaling-space learning provides possible room for learning stabilization.

7   Concluding Remarks

We addressed some issues pertaining to adaptive multimodal biometric authentication in this paper. These issues include the new user registration problem, the sensor decay problem and the small sample size problem. A recursive least squares formulation was introduced to track changes according to new user registration and sensor decay. The small sample size problem was stabilized using a feature scaling-space technique. Preliminary empirical experiments show some evidences for effective handling of these issues.

References

1. J. Schurmann, *Pattern Classification: A Unified View of Statistical and Neural Approaches.* New York: John Wiley & Sons, Inc, 1996.
2. L. Hong and A. Jain, "Integrating faces and fingerprints for person identification," *IEEE Trans. Pattern Analysis and Machine Intelligence*, vol. 20, no. 12, pp. 1295–1307, 1998.
3. S. Ben-Yacoub, Y. Abdeljaoued, and E. Mayoraz, "Fusion of face and speech data for person identity verification," *IEEE Trans. Neural Networks*, vol. 10, no. 5, pp. 1065–1074, 1999.
4. S. Prabhakar and A. K. Jain, "Decision-level fusion in fingerprint verification," *Pattern Recognition*, vol. 35, no. 4, pp. 861–874, 2002.

5. R. Brunelli and D. Falavigna, "Personal identification using multiple cues," *IEEE Trans. Pattern Analysis and Machine Intelligence*, vol. 17, no. 10, pp. 955–966, 1995.
6. K.-A. Toh, W.-Y. Yau, and X. Jiang, "A reduced multivariate polynomial model for multimodal biometrics and classifiers fusion," *IEEE Trans. Circuits and Systems for Video Technology (Special Issue on Image- and Video-Based Biometrics)*, vol. 14, no. 2, pp. 224–233, 2004.
7. K.-A. Toh and W.-Y. Yau, "Combination of hyperbolic functions for multi-modal biometrics data fusion," *IEEE Trans. Systems, Man and Cybernetics, Part-B*, vol. 34, no. 2, pp. 1196–1209, 2004.
8. K.-A. Toh, "Personalized learning and decision for multimodal biometrics," in *Proceedings of the 2004 IEEE Conference on Cybernetics and Intelligent Systems (CIS)*, (Singapore), 1-3 December 2004.
9. K.-A. Toh, "Fingerprint and speaker verification decisions fusion," in *International Conference on Image Analysis and Processing (ICIAP)*, (Mantova, Italy), pp. 626–631, September 2003.
10. K.-A. Toh, X. Jiang, and W.-Y. Yau, "Exploiting global and local decisions for multimodal biometrics verification," *IEEE Trans. Signal Processing*, vol. 52, no. 10, 2004.
11. K.-A. Toh, Q.-L. Tran, and D. Srinivasan, "Benchmarking a reduced multivariate polynomial pattern classifier," *IEEE Trans. Pattern Analysis and Machine Intelligence*, vol. 26, no. 6, pp. 740–755, 2004.
12. Q.-L. Tran, K.-A. Toh, and D. Srinivasan, "Adaptation to changes in multimodal biometric authentication," in *Proceedings of the 2004 IEEE Conference on Cybernetics and Intelligent Systems (CIS)*, (Singapore), 1-3 December 2004.
13. X. Jiang and W. Y. Yau, "Fingerprint minutiae matching based on the local and global structures," in *15th Internaional Conference on Pattern Recognition*, vol. 2, pp. 1042–1045, 2000.
14. C. Li and R. Venkateswarlu, "High accuracy connected digits recognition system with less computation," in *6th World Multiconference on Systemics, Cybernetics and Informatics (SCI 2002)*, (Orlando), July 2002.
15. X. Jiang and W. Ser, "Online fingerprint template improvement," *IEEE Transactions on Pattern Analysis and Machine Intelligence*, vol. 24, no. 8, pp. 1121–1126, 2002.

Protecting Biometric Data for Personal Identification

Muhammad Khurram Khan, Jiashu Zhang, and Lei Tian

Research Group for Biometrics (RGB), Sichuan Province Key Lab of Signal and Information
Processing, Southwest Jiaotong University, Chengdu, 610031, Sichuan, P.R. China.
Khurram.khan@scientist.com, itp@home.swjtu.edu.cn,
tyt619@163.com

Abstract. This paper presents a new chaotic watermarking and steganography
method to protect biometric data, which is sent over the networks for personal
identification. Unlike other methods, we utilized two keys, one for encrypting
the biometric template before embedding, which makes our method more
secure and another for watermark embedding that makes our method more
robust. The proposed method does not require original biometric image for the
extraction of watermarked data, and can provide high accuracy of extracted
watermarked data even under different noises and distortions. Experimental
results show that the performance of the proposed method is encouraging
comparable with other methods found in the current literature and can be used
in a practical system.

1 Introduction

Organizations search for more secure authentication methods for user access, e-
commerce, and other security applications; biometrics is getting an increasing
attention. Biometrics is an automated method for the personal recognition based on a
physiological or behavioral characteristic. Some kinds of biometrics are; face,
fingerprints, hand geometry, handwriting, iris, retina, vein, and voice [1], [2].

A biometric–based verification system works properly only if the verifier system
can guarantee that the biometric data came from the legitimate person at the time of
enrollment [3]. Furthermore, while biometric data provides uniqueness, they do not
provide secrecy. Only biometrics is not a panacea for the secrecy of data because it
has some risks of being hacked, modified and reused. So there is a need to protect
biometric data from different attacks.

In order to promote the wide spread utilization of biometric techniques; an
increased security of biometric data is necessary. Encryption, steganography and
watermarking are used to achieve this secrecy [3],[4].

Encryption is mostly used way of security. In Encryption, there are two basic
problems 1) Hackers have historically found ways to crack encryption, in effect,
obtaining the key without being a legitimate user; and 2) Once a single legitimate
copy of some content has been decrypted, a hacker is now free to make another copy
of the decrypted data.

Steganography is a technique of concealed data, where a secret message is hidden
within another unrelated message and then communicated to the other party. In
contrast to cryptography, the content of the sent message is a secret and only parties
involved in the communication know its presence.

S.Z. Li et al. (Eds.): Sinobiometrics 2004, LNCS 3338, pp. 629–638, 2004.

Watermarking can be considered as a special technique of steganography where one message is embedded in another and the two messages are related to each other in some way. The watermarking techniques prevent forgery and unauthorized replication of physical objects.

1.1 Related Work

There is only a little work done on the watermarking and steganography of biometrics data. In this area, only few papers are published during last years. Jain and Uludag [3] described two application scenarios based on amplitude modulation watermarking method for hiding biometric data. First application is based on steganography, while another is embedding the facial information in fingerprint images.

Gunsel et al. [4] proposed two spatial domain-watermarking methods. Their first method utilizes an image adaptive strength adjustment technique to make low visibility of watermark, while another method uses feature adaptive watermarking technique, thus applicable before feature extraction.

Sonia Jain [5] proposed a local average scheme where an executable compares the block-by-block local average of the transmitted image and the received image.

Pankanti and Yeung [6] investigated the effects of watermarking fingerprint images on the recognition and retrieval accuracy by using an invisible fragile watermarking technique for image verification. A spatial watermark image is embedded in the spatial domain by utilizing a verification key. According to our study this is the first attempt in the biometric based watermarking.

1.2 Outline

This paper is divided into four sections. Section I delineates the introduction and overview of biometrics, watermarking, steganography and encryption. Section II gives the detailed descriptions of our watermarking and steganography algorithm and method for embedding and extraction of iris template. Experiments and results are reported in Section III. At the end, Section IV concludes the findings and gives the consideration of future work.

2 Watermarking and Steganography Method

First step of our proposed system is to capture any biometric image from the sensor and perform image processing algorithms to extract the features for watermark generation as shown in Fig. 1. In this research iris template or iris code will be used as a watermark.

In this paper we utilized chaos to encrypt the iris template. The most attractive features of chaos in information hiding are its extreme sensitivity to initial conditions and the outspreading of orbits over the entire space. These special characteristics make chaotic maps excellent candidates for watermarking and encryption, based on the classic Shannon's requirement of confusion and diffusion [8]. In recent years, chaotic maps have been used for digital watermarking, to increase the security [7]. Here a chaotic sequence is applied on the iris code to encrypt and to make it more secure. The watermark embedding and extraction process is depicted in Fig. 2(a) and 2(b).

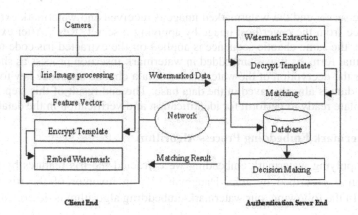

Client End   Authentication Sever End

Fig. 1. Proposed system depiction

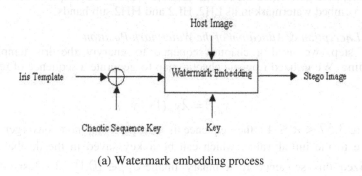

(a) Watermark embedding process

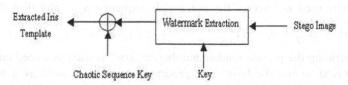

(b) Watermark extraction process

Fig. 2. Watermarking processes (a). Embedding process (b). Watermark Extraction

After encrypting the template, the watermark is embedded into the cover/host with a 'Key'; the end result of this step is a stego-watermarked image, which contains iris template hidden in the host image in the encrypted form. For this process we employed DWT based blind watermarking algorithm, which does not require the actual image to extract watermark from host/cover that contains watermarked data. The reason for using DWT is due to its superior robustness against various signal processing attacks and high data compression [9]. Watermarked data is sent to the authentication server over the network to identify a person's claimed identity as shown in Fig. 1.

At the server end the watermarked image is received and watermark extraction will take place from the cover/host image by applying a secret 'Key'. After extracting the template, the same chaotic sequence is applied on the extracted iris code to decrypt it in its actual form, as it was embedded in watermark insertion process as shown in Fig. 2(a). For the decryption of the watermarked data a chaotic sequence key together with relevant data is already saved in the data base. The end result of this step is extracted iris template ready to perform for identification and verification in the database.

A Watermark Embedding Process Algorithm

Before applying watermark embedding we extracted the iris features by the process and method described by John Daugman [2], an inventor of the iris recognition system. In the following, our watermark-embedding algorithm is described.

Step 1. Decomposition of the Original Image
In this step, we performed the second discrete wavelet decomposition of the original image to embed watermark in its LH2, HL2 and HH2 sub bands.

Step 2. Encryption & Allocation of the Watermark Position
In this step, we used a chaotic sequence to encrypt the iris template before embedding. We utilized Logistic chaotic map to generate a sequence of real numbers [7]:

$$y_{n+1} = \lambda y_n (1 - y_n) \tag{1}$$

Where $3.57 < \lambda \le 4$, the sequence is non-periodic, non-convergent, and very sensitive to the initial value, which can be a key saved in the database. Then we normalized this sequence to a binary image $c_{i,j} \in \{0,1\}$. Exclusive-OR (XOR) operation is used to encrypt the watermark sequence $s_{i,j}$, and then the encrypted watermark is $w_{i,j} = s_{i,j} \oplus c_{i,j}$.

In generating the pseudo random number, a "key" is used as a seed number, which is also saved in the database. The generated number is used as a watermarking position of LH2, HL2, and HH2 sub-band. To avoid overlapping of watermark allocation and modification of pixel value we select the watermarking position, separated with at least one pixel. The same pixel should not be selected as watermark embedding position in the selection procedure.

Step 3. Mean Value Computations
In this step, we computed neighboring symbol's mean value of selected pixel by using (2). If we denote the pixel value of the watermark embedding position as $x_{i,j}$, and the mean value of the neighboring value is $m_{i,j}$, then $m_{i,j}$ can be computed using the following formula:

$$m_{i,j} = mean(x_{i,j-1}, x_{i-1,j}, x_{i+1,j}, x_{i,j+1}) \tag{2}$$

Step 4. Watermark Embedding and Flag Generation
In Step 4, we decided whether to embed watermark into the selected pixel and generate flag ($f_{i,j}$) by the following criteria.

1) If the selected $x_{i,j}$ is bigger than the mean value $m_{i,j}$ and $w_{i,j} = 1$, change $x_{i,j}$ with $x'_{i,j}$ using (3) and create a flag $f_{i,j}$ with the value of 0. Where α denotes the watermark embedding strength

$$if\,(x_{i,j} > m_{i,j}\,and w_{i,j} = 1)then$$

$$x'_{i,j} = x_{i,j}(1 - \alpha w_{i,j}) \tag{3}$$

$$f_{i,j} = 0$$

2) If the selected $x_{i,j}$ is bigger than mean value $m_{i,j}$ and $w_{i,j} = 0$, change $x_{i,j}$ with $x'_{i,j}$ using (4) and create a flag $f_{i,j}$ with the value of 1. Where α denotes the watermark embedding strength

$$if\,(x_{i,j} > m_{i,j}\,and w_{i,j} = 0)then$$

$$x'_{i,j} = x_{i,j}(1 - \alpha) \tag{4}$$

$$f_{i,j} = 1$$

3) If the selected $x_{i,j}$ is smaller than the mean value $m_{i,j}$ and $w_{i,j} = 1$, change $x_{i,j}$ with $x'_{i,j}$ using (5) and create a flag $f_{i,j}$ with the value of 2. Where α denotes the watermark embedding strength.

$$if\,(x_{i,j} < m_{i,j}\,and w_{i,j} = 1)then$$

$$x'_{i,j} = x_{i,j}(1 + \alpha w_{i,j}) \tag{5}$$

$$f_{i,j} = 2$$

4) If the selected $x_{i,j}$ is smaller than the mean value $m_{i,j}$ and $w_{i,j} = 0$, change $x_{i,j}$ with $x'_{i,j}$ using (6) and create a flag $f_{i,j}$ with the value of 3. Where α denotes the watermark embedding strength.

$$if\,(x_{i,j} < m_{i,j}\,and w_{i,j} = 0)then$$

$$x'_{i,j} = x_{i,j}(1 + \alpha) \tag{6}$$

$$f_{i,j} = 3$$

These equations describe that the modified value $x'_{i,j}$ is proportional to the original value of the image $x_{i,j}$, which makes the watermark more robust. The generated flag

$f_{i,j}$ is stored in the database and is used in the watermark detection procedure. After the step 4, the image is inverse transformed by using inverse discrete wavelet transform (IDWT) to construct the watermarked image.

B Watermark Extraction Process Algorithm

In this process, we extracted the watermark from the host image and performed matching against the templates to assess the performance of the system. The algorithm is described in following steps.

Step 1. Decomposition of the Watermarked Image
In the watermark extraction process, we transformed the watermarked image by using second level discrete wavelet decomposition as it was decomposed in embedding process, to extract the watermark from LH2, HL2 and HH2 sub bands.

Step 2. Confirmation of Watermark Location
After transforming the image into wavelet domain, we found the watermark embedded location by using the same "key", which was used in watermark embedding procedure.

Step 3. Comparing Flags
In this step, we computed neighbor's mean value using the procedure described in Step3 of the watermark embedding and generated a flag $f'_{i,j}$, then generated $w'_{i,j}$ using the opposite procedure described in Step 4 of the watermark embedding process.

Step 4. Decryption and Matching
In decryption of the watermarked template, we utilized the formula $s'_{i,j} = w'_{i,j} \oplus c_{i,j}$ to decrypt the extracted data. Then we compared the extracted watermark $s'_{i,j}$ with the original template, which is stored in the database by using (7)

$$Match = \frac{NZ(xor(s_{i,j}, s'_{i,j}))}{N} \tag{7}$$

Where, NZ is total number of zeros by an Exclusive-OR (XOR) operation between an original template $s_{i,j}$ stored in the database, while $s'_{i,j}$ is an extracted and decrypted watermark sequence from the cover image. N is the size of the template.

3 Experiments and Results

In order to evaluate the performance of the proposed method portions of the research in this paper use the CASIA iris image database collected by Institute of Automation, Chinese Academy of Sciences. CASIA Iris Image Database (ver 1.0) contains 756 iris images from 108 eyes (hence 108 classes) [10].

The embedded watermark size is 512 bytes, which is normally a standard size of the iris template used in the industry. We performed many experiments on different images. These images are shown in Fig. 3. We use different images as host/cover e.g. Baboon, Lena, New York and Sailboat, and the extracted watermark data is exactly the same as it was encoded. The watermark data extraction performance in comparison with others is shown in Table I.

Furthermore, we applied cropping attack to watermarked images and evaluated the performance of our method against Gunsel et al. [4], as shown in Table II.

(a)   (b)   (c)   (d)

(e)   (f)   (g)   (h)

Fig. 3. Sample cover images (a-d) and watermarked stego images (e-h) (New York Image courtesy of Patrick Loo, University of Cambridge, others from USC-SIPI)

Table I. Comparison of the proposed methods (In %)

TImage	Method in [11]	Method in [4]	Our method
Lena	99.57	99.78	99.86
Baboon	91.79	100	99.84
Sailboat	73.87	99.78	99.81
New York	98.49	99.78	99.79

Table II. Comaprison of the proposed method after 50% cropping effect

Image	Method in [4]	Our method
Lena	93.52	97.29
Baboon	95.03	97.14
Sailboat	84.02	96.85
New York	93.74	94.13

Jain and Uludag [3] did not mention the effect of cropping in their method, so it is very difficult to judge the performance of their system against cropping and other noises.

There are two kinds of attacks on watermarking: one is through signal processing such as filtering, additive noise, and compression; the other is to use geometric transformations, which include cropping, scaling, rotating, and so on [8].

In most watermarking algorithms, the tolerance to the first type of attack is higher than that to the latter. Our scheme also aims at gaining high robustness against cropping attack as compare to Gunsel et al. [4] system. Even it tolerates against both kind of noises and distortions e.g. Wiener filtering, median filtering, resizing, JPEG compression, Gaussian noise, and cropping etc. The detailed experimental results on each image are shown in Table III.

If the watermarked image is significantly affected, the watermarked data can be a little distorted but is able to perform verification or identification of a person.

While on the other hand we don't need to apply any other encryption algorithms on the host image, which is a burden on the processing. Jain and Uludag [3] applied the secret key encryption, but the weak point of their system is that they send the key over the network before sending the watermarked image. If a hacker is already on the channel he will get the key and easily decrypt the data, but in our system there is no need of sending the key for the watermark decryption over a secure/non-secure channel. The watermark decryption key is already saved in the database on the server, because the probability of attacks over the network channel is higher than the data saved on the server. So to protect decryption key from threats we saved it in the database. It makes our system more robust, vigor and secure as compare to Jain and Uludag's system.

Table III. Detailed Experimental results on each image

(A) BABOON IMAGE

Attacks	PSNR (dB)	Accuracy (%)
Median Filtering (3x3)	20.42	87.19
Wiener Filtering (6x6)	23.40	88.66
Resize (50%)	19.48	87.08
Cropping (50%)	16.44	97.14
Gaussian Noise (0,0.001)	29.10	93.83
JPEG Compression (4:1)	23.73	94.84

(B) LENA IMAGE

Attacks	PSNR (dB)	Accuracy (%)
Median Filtering (3x3)	30.89	88.68
Wiener Filtering (6x6)	32.90	87.25
Resize (50%)	27.95	86.97
Cropping (50%)	17.20	97.29
Gaussian Noise (0,0.001)	29.61	87.27
JPEG Compression (4:1)	34.76	95.85

(C) SAILBOAT IMAGE

Attacks	PSNR (dB)	Accuracy (%)
Median Filtering (3x3)	26.33	88.14
Wiener Filtering (6x6)	28.91	88.11
Resize (50%)	24.12	86.76
Cropping (50%)	14.38	96.85
Gaussian Noise (0,0.001)	29.41	89.25
JPEG Compression (4:1)	30.41	94.84

(D) NEW YORK IMAGE

Attacks	PSNR (dB)	Accuracy (%)
Median Filtering (3x3)	20.48	92.26
Wiener Filtering (6x6)	23.02	90.47
Resize (50%)	18.35	89.59
Cropping (50%)	17.50	94.13
Gaussian Noise (0,0.001)	30.63	89.44
JPEG Compression (4:1)	22.99	88.03

Furthermore, Gunsel et al. [4] didn't apply any encryption on the template before or after the watermark embedding. So their method is also vulnerable if any hacker extracts the watermarked data. In addition, schemes proposed by Jain and Uludag [3] and Gunsel et al. [4] are vulnerable to the so-called copy attack [12], where any unauthorized person can copy hacked watermark from the host image and misuse it on purpose. So it makes their methods unreliable in authentication applications over the network. Sonia's [5] method does not provide the detailed results on the watermarked stego image and she did not give any signal or image processing effects on her method. Pankanti and Yeung [6] did not give the detail of effects on their method, but claimed that their method gives a significant performance. So it is difficult to compare performance of [5], [6] with our method.

4 Conclusion

In this work, we have proposed an innovative watermarking and steganography scheme for securing the biometric data with more emphasis on iris templates. Due to the excellent time-frequency features and the well matching to the human visual system (HVS) characteristic, we utilized DWT to implement our algorithm. We encrypted the iris templates by a chaotic sequence before embedding as a watermark and decrypted it after extraction from the host image to make it more secure and protected from copy attack.

Finally, we performed a series of experiments to evaluate the proposed algorithm. Moreover, we carried out extensive quantitative comparison among some existing methods and provided discussions on the overall experimental results. The novelty of our algorithm is that it can be applied for any biometric data for the security, which is sent over the networks e.g. fingerprint, face or palm print etc.

So our system is an open ended system for securing biometric templates. It is also experimented that our system is highly robust against different kinds of attacks and gives better performance than others. So the proposed scheme can be effectively used to ensure security and privacy in practical systems. Future research in this area can be to use both robust and fragile watermark simultaneously for hybrid watermark based identification.

Acknowledgements

This project is supported by 'Sichuan Youth Science and Technology Funds' under grant number: 03ZQ026-033. The system described in this paper is the subject of patent protection.

References

[1] Muhammad, K. K., and Zhang, J.: Optimizing WLAN Security by Biometrics. In: Ilyas, M. (ed.): Handbook of Wireless Local Area Networks: Applications, Technology, Security, and Standards: (In Press), CRC Press Boca Raton, Florida, USA (2004).

[2] Daugman, J.: High Confidence Visual Recognition of Persons by a Test of Statistical Independence. IEEE Transactions on PAMI. Vol 15(11) (1993) 1148-1161.

[3] Jain, A.K., and Uludag, U.: Hiding Biometric Data. IEEE Transaction on Pattern Analysis and Machine Intelligence. Vol 25(11) (2003) 1494-1498.

[4] Gunsel, B., Uludag, U., and Tekalp, A.M.: Robust Watermarking of Fingerprint Images. Pattern Recognition. Vol 35(12) (2002) 2739-2747.

[5] Sonia, J.: Digital Watermarking Techniques: A Case Study in Fingerprints and Faces. Proc. Indian Conference on Computer Vision, Graphics, and Image Processing, (2000) 139-144.

[6] Pankanti, S., and Yeung, M.M.: Verification Watermarks on Fingerprint Recognition and Retrieval. Proc. SPIE, Vol (3657) (1999) 66-78.

[7] Zhang, J., Tian, L., and Tai, H.M.: A New Watermarking Method Based on Chaotic Maps. Proc. IEEE ICME'04. (2004).

[8] Zhao, D., Chen, G., and Liu, W.: A Chaos-based Robust Wavelet-domain Watermarking Algorithm. Chaos, Solitons, and Fractals. Vol. 22(12) (2004) 47-54.

[9] Hong, I., Kim, I., and Han, S.S.: A Blind Watermarking Technique Using Wavelet Transform. Proc. ISIE Korea, Vol (3) (2001) 1946-1950.

[10] CASIA Iris Database Online: http://www.sinobiometrics.com (Sept. 2004).

[11] Uludag, U., Gunsel, B., and Tekalp, A.M.: Robust Watermarking of Busy Images. Proceedings of SPIE Electronic Imaging Conference, Security and Watermarking of Multimedia Contents. Vol (4314) (2001) 18–25.

[12] Deguillaume, F., Voloshynovskiy, S., and Pun, T.: Secure Hybrid Robust Watermarking Resistant Against Tampering and Copy Attack. Signal Processing, Elsevier Science Ltd. Vol (83) (2003) 2133-2170.

Digital Curvelet Transform for Palmprint Recognition

Kaifeng Dong, Guiyu Feng, and Dewen Hu*

Department of Automatic Control, College of Mechatronics and Automation,
National University of Defense Technology, Changsha, 410073, China
dwhu@nudt.edu.cn

Abstract. In this paper, we present a new feature extraction method for palmprint recognition. The digital curvelet transform is revised here and used to extract the palmprint features. In our algorithm, we use the discrete Meyer wavelet transform to replace the "à trous" transform, then apply the ridgelet transform to each block which is subbanded after the discrete Meyer wavelet transform from the palmprint image. Our work is carried on the PolyU Palmprint Database. Dealing with the palmprint image sized of 64×64, our new strategy acquires $4 \times 128 \times 128$ curvelet coefficients. Based on the system performance, the best coefficients threshold can be obtained. With this threshold the curvelet coefficients are filtered and less than 2% of coefficients are selected. With this compressed coefficients set, the correct recognition rate of our palmprint identification experiment is up to 95.25%.

1 Introduction

The personal identification and verification has existed since the beginning of our human beings. In some occasions (e.g. airport, bank, police station) and systems (e.g. ATM booths, computer system) which require reliable verification schemes, the users' identity is required considering the security factor. Traditionally, personal identification needs to take something (such as a key, an ID card) or remember something (such as password). However, what these approaches based on may be lost or forgotten.

Biometrics is a person's physiological or behavioral characteristics [1]. It is universal, but different between each other. Most of these characteristics are stable for many years even the whole life, and usually can't be taken away or copied from the one person to the other. Therefore, the researches of using biometrics to identify person are becoming more and more popular.

There may be problems or limitations for any biometrics identification system. For example, face identification needs face images captured under constrained lighting conditions and the face identification system can be cheated if someone mimics the authorized face. The iris identification system can provide a high accuracy, but it needs high performance camera to catch the exiguous veins of iris.

---

* Corresponding author.

S.Z. Li et al. (Eds.): Sinobiometrics 2004, LNCS 3338, pp. 639–645, 2004.
© Springer-Verlag Berlin Heidelberg 2004

Compared with other biometric characteristics, palmprint authentication is a relatively new branch of biometric technology. Palmprint authentication has several advantages [2]. The principal lines and wrinkles of palm are permanent, which can be easily obtained from a low-resolution image, and most users accept to offer their palmprint to identify their identity. Recently, many palmprint recognition methods have been proposed and achieved encouraging results. Lu et al. gave a method based on eigenspace technology [3]. Wai Kin Kong et al. used 2-D gabor filters to extract palmprint features [2]. Wu et al. proposed a novel method for palmprint recognition, called Fisherpalms [4]. Han et al. introduced a feature extraction method using soble and morphological operations [5].

The main purpose of this paper is to apply the digital curvelet transform to exact palmprint features. Candès and Donoho developed a new multi-scale transform which they called the curvelet transform [6] [7] [8]. The curvelet transform has been used for image processing, such as image denoising [6] and contrast enhancement [7]. The wavelet transform only has limited directional elements and scale concepts, so when the wavelet transform deals with the important edges in the image, it exhibits many wavelet coefficients even at fine scale. It is the limitation of the wavelet transform. In contrast, the basis elements of curvelet transform are high directional sensitive and highly anisotropic. With these properties, the curvelet transform can easily describe the edges with only a small number of curvelet coefficients, and the results are better than other traditional transforms, such as Fourier transform and wavelet transform. In this paper, we apply the curvelet transform to palmprint features extraction, and the experimental result is satisfactory.

The rest of this paper is organized as follows: section 2 gives a brief introduction to the feature extraction using digital curvelet transform, section 3 reports experimental results and some analysis. Section 4 presents our conclusions and future work.

2 Digital Curvelet Transform

The curvelet transform can be seen as the combination of two-dimension wavelet transform and the ridgelet transform. It was a reversible transformation. Fig. 1 shows the flowgraph of the digital curvelet transform. It contains two parts. First, we apply the two-dimension wavelet transform algorithm to the image, decompose the image into subbands, and partition each subband into blocks. Then, apply the digital ridgelet transform to each block, it is the most important step of the digital curvelet transform.

2.1 Two-Dimension Wavelet Transform (WT2D)

According to the definition of curvelet transform, we need a spatial bandpass filter to decompose the image into subbands. In Donoho's opinion, the "à trous" subband filtering algorithm can satisfy the needs of the digital curvelet transform. Dealing with an image sized of $n \times n$, the algorithm is defined as follows:

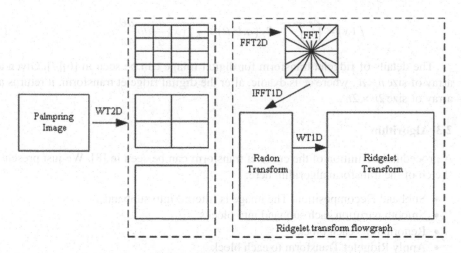

Fig. 1. Digital Curvelet Transform flowgraph

$$I(x, y) = c_J(x, y) + \sum_{j=1}^{J} w_j(x, y) \tag{1}$$

Where c_J is the corresponding smooth level version of the original image, w_j represents the details of the image at scale 2^{-j}. The algorithm outputs $(J+1)$ subband arrays of size $n \times n$.

2.2 Ridgelet Transform

The two-dimension (2-D) continuous ridgelet transform in R^2 is defined as follows:

$$\int |\hat{\psi}(\xi)|^2 / |\xi|^2 \, d\xi < \infty \tag{2}$$

Where ψ is a smooth univariate function and satisfies the condition of $\int \psi(t) dt = 0$.

Considering the special case, ψ is normalized so that $\int |\hat{\psi}(\xi)|^2 / |\xi|^2 \, d\xi = 1$.

The bivariate ridgelet $\psi_{a,b,\theta} : R^2 \to R^2$ is defined as follows:

$$\psi_{a,b,\theta} = a^{-1/2} \cdot \psi\left((x_1 \cos\theta + x_2 \sin\theta - b)/a\right) \tag{3}$$

Here, $a > 0$, $b \in R$, $\theta \in [0, 2\pi)$.

Given an integrable bivariate function $f(x)$, its ridgelet coefficients are defined as follows:

$$R_f(a, b, \theta) = \int \psi_{a,b,\theta}(x) f(x) dx \tag{4}$$

And the exact reconstruction formula

$$f(x) = \int_0^{2\pi} \int_{-\infty}^{\infty} \int_0^{\infty} R_f(a,b,\theta) \psi_{a,b,\theta}(x) \frac{da}{a^3} db \frac{d\theta}{4\pi} \qquad (5)$$

The details of ridgelet transform for digital image can be seen in [6][7]. Given an array of size $n \times n$, where n is dyadic, after the digital ridgelet transform, it returns an array of size $2n \times 2n$.

2.3 Algorithm

A procedural definition of the curvelet transform can be seen in [8]. We just present a sketch of the transform algorithm here:

- Subband Decomposition. The image is filtered into subbands.
- Smooth partition each subband into blocks.
- Renormalize each block.
- Apply Ridgelet Transform to each block.

3 Experimental Results

3.1 Palmprint Database

This work is carried on the PolyU Palmprint Database [10]. The database includes 100 different palms, and each of these palms has six samples. The samples for each palm were collected in two sessions, which means that the first three samples were captured in one session and the other three samples in another session. An example of one palm can be seen in Fig. 2a.

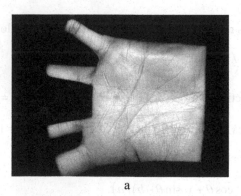

a   b

Fig. 2. A sample of one palm in the PolyU palmprint database (a), and the corresponding palmprint image (b)

From Fig.2a, we can see that the palmprint image contains background and the other part of the palm that we don't need. After palmprint image preprocessing [9], we get the region of interest (Fig. 2b), an image sized of 120×120.

3.2 Experimental Algorithm

In our experiment, we make a little revision on the digital curvelet transform. On the 2D wavelet transform step, we select 2D discrete stationary wavelet transform, and use discrete Meyer wavelet instead of à trous subband filtering algorithm. The image is filtered into 4 subbands. Because the size of the original image is small, we don't partition the subbands into block. Then we apply the digital ridgelet transform to each subband. For details see Fig. 3. The ridgelet transform toolbox can be available at http://www-stat.stanford.edu/~donoho/.

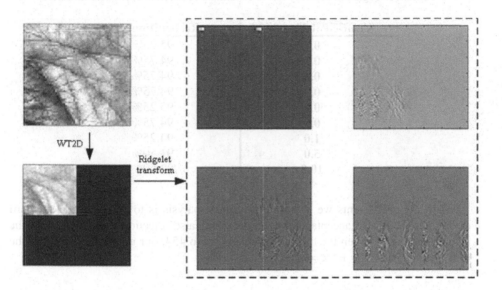

Fig. 3. The transform flowgraph of our method

3.3 Experimental Results and Analysis

We select two samples (the first and the fourth sample of each palm) as the training set, the other four samples as the test set. The images were resized to 64×64 .

By applying the digital curvelet transform to the palmprint image, we acquire a curvelet coefficients array of size $4 \times 128 \times 128$. The number of the coefficients is so large that we need to filter some data to reduce it. Observing the coefficients, most of them are less than 1. From Table 1, we can see that when the coefficient threshold is 0.4 the recognition result is the best (when the coefficient threshold is smaller than 0.4, the curvelet coefficients are still too much for calculation, and when the coefficient threshold is bigger than 10, the curvelet coefficients are not enough for recognition, so we just consider the conditions when the coefficient threshold is between 0.4 and 10), and when the coefficient threshold increases, the recognition rate decreases, therefore we use the following hard-thresholding rule to the coefficients:

$$Y = y, \text{if } |y| > 0.4 \tag{6}$$

$$Y = 0, \text{if } |y| \leq 0.4 \tag{7}$$

Where y is the original curvelet coefficients, and Y is the new coefficients; we only need to record the nonzero coefficients (less than 2% of the curvelet coefficients) and their positions. These data are the feature values of the palmprint we select. Finally, we use the Euclidian distance classifier to give the final decision.

Table 1. Recognition accuracy rate in conditions of different coefficient threshold

Coefficient Threshold	Recognition rate
0.4	95.25%
0.5	94.75%
0.6	94.75%
0.7	94.75%
0.8	95.25%
0.9	94.75%
1.0	94.25%
5.0	91.50%
10.0	83.50%

With the coefficients we acquired, a further analysis is to calculate the standard error rates, i.e., false acceptance rate (FAR) and false rejection rate (FRR). For the results, see Fig. 4.When the threshold value is set to 453, our method can achieve the best result with FRR = FAR =6.25%.

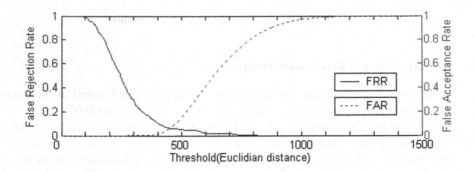

Fig. 4. Verification test results (the FRR and FAR of our algorithm)

From Table 1 and Fig. 4, although only using two samples of each palm as training set, it can be seen that our method for personal recognition can still achieves satisfactory results.

4   Conclusion and Future Work

In this paper, the digital curvelet transform is developed for palmprint recognition. Using our approach, the correct recognition rate of our experiments is up to 95.25% under the PolyU palmprint database. Compared with other feature extract methods (e.g. PCA and ICA showed in [11], by which the accuracy rates are 92.50% and 85.83% respectively), our experimental results are more encouraging.

Our future work would include making some revisions on the curvelet transform, and investigating other wavelet transform instead of the "à trous" algorithm. We are also interested in multi-modal biometrics, for example, fusion of palmprint with face, which is our another ongoing project [11].

Acknowledgement

This work is partially supported by the Distinguished Young Scholars Fund of China (60225015), Chinese National Hi-Tech R-D Program (2001AA114180), Natural Science Foundation of China (60171003), Ministry of Science and Technology of China (2001 CCA04100), Ministry of Education of China (TRAPOYT Project). Portions of the work tested on the PolyU Palmprint Database.

References

1. Jain, A.K., Bolle, R., Pankanti, S. (ed.): Biometrics: Personal Identification in Networked Society. Kluwer Academic, Dordrecht(1999)
2. Kong W.K., Zhang D., Li W.X.: Palmprint feature extraction using 2-D Gabor filters. Pattern Recognition 36 (2003) 2339–2347
3. Lu G.M., Zhang D., Wang K.Q.: Palmprint recognition using eigenpalms features. Pattern Recognition 24 (2003) 1463–1467
4. Wu X.Q., Zhang D., Wang K.Q.: Fisherpalms based palmprint recognition. Pattern Recognition Letters 24 (2003) 2829–2838
5. Han C.C., Cheng H.L., Fan K.C., Lin C.L.: Personal authentication using palmprint features. Pattern Recognition 36 (2003) 371–381
6. Starck J.L., Candès E.J., Dohono D.L.: The Curvelet Transform for Image Denoising. IEEE Trans. Image Processing. 11 (2002) 670–683
7. Starck J.L., Murtagh F., Candès E.J., Dohono D.L.: Gray and Color Image Contrast Enhancement by the Curvelet Transform. IEEE Trans. Image Processing. 12 (2003) 706–717
8. Dohono D.L., Duncan M.R.: Digital Curvelet Transform Strategy, Implementation and Experiments. Available at http://www-stat.stanford.edu/~beamlab/.
9. Zhang D., Kong W.K., You J., Wong M., Online palmprint identification. IEEE Trans. Pattern Anal. Mach. Intell. 25 (2003) 1041–1050
10. The PolyU Palmprint Database. Available at http://www.comp.polyu.edu.hk /~biometrics/
11. Feng G.Y., Dong K.F., Hu D.W., Zhang D.: When faces are combined with palmprints: a novel biometric fusion strategy. in Proc. of the 1ˢᵗ International Conference on Biometric Authentication, Hong Kong, China, LNCS 3072 (2004) 701–707

On-line Writer Verification Using Force Features of Basic Strokes

Ming Meng[1,2], ZhongCheng Wu[1], Ping Fang[1,2], YunJian Ge[1], and Yong Yu[1]

[1] Institute of Intelligent Machine, Chinese Academy of Sciences,
Hefei 230031 China
[2] Dept. of Automation, University of Science & Technology of China,
Hefei 230026 China
{mnming, pingfang}@ustc.edu,
{zcwu, yjge, yuyong}@iim.ac.cn

Abstract. Writing force is an important biometric attribute for on-line writer verification. But it is often neglected or introduced deficiently for the limitation of the existing input device. In this paper, a text-independent on-line writer verification algorithm based on force feature is presented. A novel digital tablet is used to collect data, which can capture all three-dimensional writing forces in addition to pen position. Four force features are extracted from the writing force information of significant basic strokes, which are segmented and determined by the normal force, length and direction of the strokes. The Euclidean distance of feature vectors is measured to verify the input characters with the template. A preliminary experiment shows that the writing force is an effective feature for the writer verification.

1 Introduction

As a biometric attribute, human handwriting reflects a great degree of individuality both in spatial and temporal domains. For this fact, writer or signature verification systems, which verify claimed identity, are used for person identification in financial transactions, access control, electronic signature, and so on. Reference [1] summarized a comprehensive survey of biometric applications based on handwriting.

Signature verification requires the writer to write fixed text, for example the name. In this sense, signature verification may be called text-dependent writer verification. In the contrary, text-independent writer verification can verify arbitrary characters or other hand written objects [2, 3]. Therefore, the text-independent writer verification can be available in wider range of applications [4] and reject forgery strategically [2].

Writer verification can be classified into two methods depending on the data acquisition approach: off-line method and on-line method. In the first method, handwriting is usually represented as a pixel matrix such as a scanned image. Generally, the off-line writer verification is implemented using different computer image processing and pattern recognition techniques. And various features are extracted to represent individual characteristics, such as texture analysis [4], integrated features of element, sting and histogram [5], shape features extracted from text-line [6].

S.Z. Li et al. (Eds.): Sinobiometrics 2004, LNCS 3338, pp. 646–653, 2004.

In contrast, in the on-line method, the variation of dynamic information in time, for example, pen motion, writing force and writing speed are recorded using special hardware. For the on-line writer verification, it is hard to imitate the handwriting, because the verification text can be changed at every test. However this characteristic makes it more difficult to detect the forged handwriting than the previous methods using only signatures. The main problem is how to extract reliable individual characteristics from different characters. So the writer verification is not well developed comparing to on-line signature verification. Previous work by [2] has deal with this problem by a category Hidden Markov Models based text-indicated method. In [3], the possibility of the stroke based writer verification, in which stroke direction and pen inclination of several handwritten objects are used.

This paper presents a text-independent writer verification system based on the writing force feature extracted from basic strokes. Data is collected using a novel digital tablet, which can capture all three-dimensional writing forces as well as pen position. The previous research [7, 8] reveals that the writing pressure is an effective feature that is used to discriminate authentic handwriting from forged one. To evaluate the contribution of writing force to the verification, we adopt four features extracted from the writing force information of segmented basic strokes. The Euclidean distance between the corresponding features of test set and template are calculated to determine acceptance or rejection. The result of a preliminary small-scale experiment shows that the writing force is an effective feature for the writer verification.

2 Data Acquisition and Preprocessing

In most on-line writer verification system, a special hardware is selected for dynamic data acquisition. A series of Wacom digital tablets are popularly used in various on-line writer or signature verification systems [3, 7]. The tablets can capture pen position, pen pressure (along pen direction) and pen inclination. A speedy and high sensitive electronic pen has developed to capture writing pressure precisely [8]. But it can't record other handwriting information, such as pen position. Furthermore, writing forces is a three-dimensional vector between the pen tip and writing panel actually as shown in Fig.1. This three-dimensional force can provide more individual characteristics. Several electronic pens using various sensors have developed to detect full writing forces [9, 10]. But they can't capture the pen position simultaneously, either.

To acquire the writing force as well as the trajectory of the pen tip, we have developed a novel digital tablet based on multi-axis sensor [11]. The tablet, which is connected with a personal computer through USB port, outputs five raw data, i.e., x-y position, $x(t)$ and $y(t)$, three-dimensional writing forces, $F_x(t)$, $F_y(t)$, and $F_z(t)$ at a sampling rate of 100 sample per second. Fig.2 shows an example of the shape of a Chinese character obtained by the tablet. And Fig.3 presents the three-dimensional writing force captured during the writing.

The raw data often include noise coming from the digital tablet and the hand jitters. So it is necessary to smooth the data with a low-pass filter. In the proposed system, a Gaussian filter is applied independently to each component of the sample sequence:

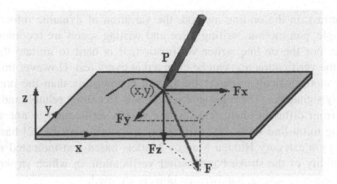

Fig. 1. Three-dimensional writing force vector

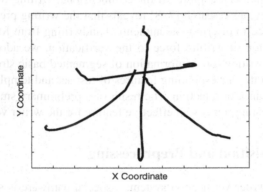

Fig. 2. Example of a Chinese character

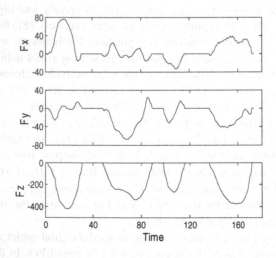

Fig. 3. Three-dimensional writing force versus time of the character

$$x'(t) = \sum_{i=-3\sigma}^{3\sigma} \omega_i x(t+i) \tag{1}$$

where

$$\omega_i = e^{-\frac{i^2}{2\sigma^2}} \bigg/ \sum_{j=-3\sigma}^{3\sigma} e^{-\frac{j^2}{2\sigma^2}} \tag{2}$$

This is defined similarly for other component of the data. The parameter σ in our experiment is 2.

3 Feature Extraction

3.1 Character Segmentation

Generally, a Chinese character is composed several simple strokes. According to the orientation and length of the stroke, these strokes are classified into seven types: dot, horizontal, vertical, slash, back slash, tick and hook [12]. A long stroke is more stable in variation of writing force than a short stroke. That is to say, more reliable individual characteristics can be extracted from long strokes. Consequently, we select four relatively long stroke types as basic strokes in our experiments. These strokes are horizontal (H), vertical (V), slash (S) and back slash (B).

We use the writing force as well as shape of character in segmentation. Firstly, strokes are extracted between pen-down and pen-up. But some of the obtained strokes may be cursive strokes, which are composed of several line segments in different direction. Those strokes can be separated using the significant points, which are selected depending on the angle change between the visited point and the neighbor [13]. For each basic type strokes of a character, one of them with maximum length is selected as significant basic stroke for the verification. Fig.4 shows segmentation and significant basic strokes of a typical character. The red square and blue square label start-point and endpoint of each stroke respectively. The solid lines represent the significant basic strokes and dash lines represent the ordinary strokes that will be discarded in verification.

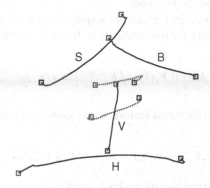

Fig. 4. Segmentation and significant basic strokes

3.2 Feature Extraction

The result of segmentation is one to four significant basic strokes for each character depending on its shape. Four kinds of feature are extracted from the writing force information of each stroke. The writing force of the sample point at time t includes three components: $F_x(t)$, $F_y(t)$, and $F_z(t)$.

Among them, $F_z(t)$ is the normal force needed for inking by pressing the pen tip on the paper. $F_x(t)$ and $F_y(t)$ are the tangential force need for combating surface friction. The ratio of tangential force to normal force is given by

$$r = \sqrt{(F_x^{mean})^2 + (F_y^{mean})^2}\Big/ F_z^{mean} \qquad (3)$$

where F_i^{mean}, $i=x, y, z$ is the average writing force in each direction.

The force sample sequence of each stroke can be represented as a curve along the writing time of the stroke. The centroid of the curve can be obtained as

$$C_i = \sum_{t=1}^{N} t \cdot F_i(t)\Big/ \sum_{t=1}^{N} F_i(t), i = x, y, z \qquad (4)$$

where N is the total number of the sample point. Then the normalized centroid is defined as the second feature. It is expressed as

$$c_i = C_i / N, i = x, y, z \qquad (5)$$

To describe the variation of writing force distribution along the time, a pseudo inertia radius of the curve is defined and normalized as

$$p_i = \sqrt{\sum_{t=1}^{N}(t-N/2)^2 \cdot F_i(t)\Big/ \sum_{t=1}^{N}F_z(t)}\Big/ N, i=x,y,z \qquad (6)$$

Generally speaking, the magnitude of the force in z-axis direction is obviously larger than it in other direction. Therefore, the features in all three directions are normalized by the variable in z-axis direction.

Maximum writing force in the sample sequence of each significant basic stroke also is an important feature for the verification. It can be normalized by average force in z-axis direction as

$$m_i = \operatorname*{Max}_{t=1,N}(|F_i(t)|)\Big/ F_z^{mean}, i = x, y, z \qquad (7)$$

At last, we get the stroke based feature vector consists of the following ten dimensional data

$$f_k = (r, c_i, p_i, m_i), i = x, y, z; k = 1,2,3,4 \qquad (8)$$

where k denote the four type significant basic stroke.

4 Verification

The verification is done by measuring the distance between the feature vector of the input characters and that of the template. In our experiments, we adopt the square root of the Euclidean distance

$$D_k = \sqrt{\sum_{i=1}^{10} (f_i^{input} - f_i^{template})^2}, k = 1,2,3,4 \tag{9}$$

Then the total distance is obtained by

$$D = \lambda_1 \cdot D_1 + \lambda_2 \cdot D_2 + \lambda_3 \cdot D_3 + \lambda_4 \cdot D_4, \tag{10}$$

where λ_k, k=1,2,3,4 are coefficients determined according to the writer and the number of each type of basic strokes extracted from the input characters.

The template of a writer has four feature vectors corresponding to four types of basic strokes, which are extracted from training character sets of this writer. Several feature values of all extracted strokes are calculated. Then the mean values f^{mean} and standard deviations σ of these features for each basic stroke are obtained using statistical method. The former are used to constitute the template of the writer and the later are references for the threshold. In the verification, if the total distance is less then the threshold, we accept input characters as genuine handwriting, otherwise, reject it as a forger.

5 Experiment Result

An experiment was performed to evaluate the verification system based on the force features using the algorithm described above. A total of 480 characters were collected from six individuals using the digital tablet mention above. They all are required to write eight specified characters ten times regularly at different time. Each same character set is divided into two groups. One including five characters is used as training sample for template generation and the others is used for writer verification. For each individual, twenty characters are randomly chosen from the characters written by other writers as the forgery set.

In the experiment, false rejection rate (FRR) and false acceptance rate (FAR) are measured to characterize the performance of the system. As we set the threshold to be the average 2σ of five reference characters. The verification gives a FRR of 37.6% and a FAR of 22.5%. Although the experimental result was not quite well in comparison to the successful verification system ever reported [2, 5, 13], it indicated that the writing force is an effective feature for the writer verification, especially for the text-independent writer verification. It also shows that the four extracted features have different contributions to compare the characters, so the features should be weighted differently for each stroke template.

6 Conclusion

A text-independent on-line writer verification algorithm was proposed based on force feature. Data is collected using a novel digital tablet, which can capture all three-dimensional writing forces as well as trajectory of pen position. Four force features are extracted from the writing force information of significant basic strokes, which are segmented and determined by the normal force, length and direction of the strokes. The Euclidean distance of feature vectors is measured to verify the input characters with the template. For the purpose of studying the effect of the writing force feature, only force features are used in the preliminary experiment. The experimental result shows that the algorithm using force feature of basic strokes is a promising method for the text-independent writer verification. In the future, the force features will be refined and combined with more features that are associated with shape and other dynamic features to improve the performance of the verification.

Acknowledgment

This research is supported by Center for Computational Science, Hefei Institutes of Physical Sciences under Grant No.0330405002. The authors express their thanks for the support.

References

1. F. Romann, C. vielhuer and R. Steinmetz, "Biometric Applications based on Handwriting," in Proc. Of the 2002 IEEE ICME'02, Vol.2, pp.573-576, Aug 2002.
2. Y. Yamazaki, T. Nagao and N. Komatu, "Text-indicated Writer Verification Using Hidden Markov Models," in Proc. Of the 7th ICDAR, Vol.1, pp.329-332, Aug 2003.
3. Y. Kato, T. Hamamoto and S. Hangai, "A Proposal of Writer Verification of Hand Written Objects," in Proc. Of the 2002 IEEE ICME'02, Vol.2, pp.585-588, Aug 2002.
4. H. E. S. Said, T. N. Tan and K. D. Baker, "Personal Identification Based on Handwriting," Pattern Recognition, vol.33, pp.149-160, 2000.
5. S. Cha and S. N. Srihari, "Multiple Feature Integration for Writer Verification," the Proceedings of the 7th IWFHR2000, pp.333-342, September 2000.
6. H. Bunke, Dr. U.-V. Marti, R. Messerli, "Writer Identification Using Text Line Based Features," in Proc. of the 6th ICDAR, pp.101-105, Sept 2001.
7. F. R. Rioja, M. N. Miyatake, M. H. Perez and M. K. Toscano, "Dynamics Features Extraction for Online Signature Verification," in Proc. of the 14th CONIELECOMP'04, pp.156-161, Feb 2004.
8. M. Kikuchi and N. Akamatsu, "Development of Speedy and High Sensitive Pen System for Writing Pressure and Writer Identification," in Proc. of the 6th ICDAR, pp.1040-1044, Sept 2001.
9. H. Shimizu, S. Kiyono, T. Motoki and W. Gao, "An Electrical Pen for Signature Verification Using a Two-dimensional Optical Angle Sensor," Sensors and Actuators A, vol.111, pp.216-221, 2004.

10. R. Martens and L. Claesen, "On-line Signature Verification by Dynamic Time-Warping," in Proc. of the 13th Int. Conf. on Pattern Recognition, vol.3, pp.38-42, Aug 1996.
11. P. Fang, Z. C. Wu, M. Meng, Y. J. Ge and Y. Yu, "A Novel Tablet for On-Line Handwriting Signal Capture," in Proc. of the 5th WCICA, pp.3714-3717, June 2004.
12. C. L. Liu, I. J. Kim and J. H. Kim, "Model-based Stroke Extraction and Matching for Handwritten Chinese Character Recognition," Pattern Recognition, vol.34, pp.2339-2352, 2001.
13. M. M. Shafiei and H. R. Rabiee, "A New Online Signature Verification Algorithm Using Variable Length Segmentation and Hidden Markov Models," in Proc. Of the 7th ICDAR, Vol.1, pp.443-446, Aug 2003.

A Novel Force Sensitive Tablet for Handwriting Information Acquisition

Zhongcheng Wu, Ping Fang, Ming Meng, and Fei Shen

Institute of Intelligent Machines, Chinese Academy of Science,
P.O. Box 1130, HeFei, 230031, China
Department of Automation, University of Science & Technology of China,
Hefei, 230026, China
zcwu@iim.ac.cn

Abstract. At present, many researches have been done on the handwriting using static or dynamic signals, but no tools could acquire all handwriting information including kinematics and kinetics of pen-point, including strokes of pen-up and pen-down, velocity and acceleration of pen-tip, three dimension forces of pen-plate contacting point and shape of character etc.. We have been designing a force sensitive tablet (F-Tablet), which is capable of capturing both the dynamic hand writing forces information and the static trajectory of the writing pen-tip. With the core part of the multi-dimension force/torque sensor, the F-Tablet can capture the two torques and three forces directly and simultaneously. With the specially designed structure, some other dynamic and static information, such as stroke, velocity, acceleration etc., can also be calculated from above data. Pen-like tools is used to write on the tablet, that means no ink is needed and no special designing is necessary. The tablet can also be used as an input device for computers or as a development tool for children to improve handwriting skills. As more information about the writers handwriting can be got by F-Tablet, it may be a choice of signature identification/verification input device for person recongnition.[1]

1 Introduction

Biometrics has become a hot subject in recent years because the need to prevent unauthorized access to all kinds of e-data during this information age. Data from physical biometrics such as fingerprints, hand geometry and iris scans, behavioral biometrics such as signature, voiceprint, gait and mannerisms, and chemical biometrics such as DNA and body odor have been acquired and analyzed for security applications[1].

During writing, a writer writes not only the context, but also his identity, which is implied in the dynamic writing process and the static handwriting. And because of the long history of signature and the convenience of the pen and papers, we are all accustomed to having a signature signed on file to be used as a basis of

---

[1] The work was funded by the Natural Science Foundation of China with grant No. 60375027.

comparison for verifying our signature [2]. Many researches have been done on signature. Rejean Plamondon has studied the models and the dynamic characters of writing; Sargur N. Srihari has done much work on the static handwriting information. The work of Sung-Hyuk Cha.K deals with the establishing handwriting individuality. The Name and Address Block Reader (NABR) developed at CEDAR was installed at most United States IRS processing centers, beginning in 1995. Cyber-SIGN provides products for signature verification by analyzing the shape, speed, stroke, pressure and timing information during the act of signing. Communication Intelligence Corporation has developed transaction and communication enabling technologies for electronic signatures, handwritten biometric signature verification, data security, and data compression. Softpro SignPlus, Valyd, WonderNet, LCI SMARTpen and some other companies have all provide solutions for signature identification/verification.

Generally, the signature can be studied using the dynamic handwriting signals, static handwriting signals or both the dynamic signals and the static signals at the same time. As the dynamic signals are apparently much harder to be imitated by others than the static signals, so a wide variety of devices have been devised for capturing the dynamic handwriting signals. An accelerometer pen is used to capture the two direction accelerations and pressure in the z-axis [3]. A dual axis accelerometer is used to get the signature's dynamics [4]. The SmartPen is used to capture forces on the pen-tip in three directions and angles of the pen-shaft in two dimensions (relative to the writing surface) [5]. A "digital pen" is used for detecting z-axis pressure [6].

Up to now, no tools can obtain all handwriting information acquisition, such as strokes of pen-up and pen-down, velocity and acceleration of pen-tip, three dimension forces of pen-plate contacting point and shape of character etc. As we can see that the existing devices designed for capture dynamic handwriting signals can only get the Z-force or can only get the forces with no other handwriting trajectory signals. In this paper, we introduces a novel multi-dimension force sensitive tablet (F-Tablet) for handwriting signal capture based on USB. The device is capable of capturing both the dynamic and static handwriting information, and a pen-like tool is used for the writing. First, the three perpendicular forces between the writing pen and the writing tablet directly are captured with a multi-dimension force/torque sensor. Then, the other handwriting signals such as trajectory, velocities and accel erations of the writing pen can also be calculated indirectly.

The work here is mainly based on the work of [6]. The problem of the tablet is analyzed and improvement is made to the structure to get better performance. The software is also modified to show the forces and trajectories of the writing. An USB interface and some filtering circuit are added to the conditioning circuit. In the next chapter, the structure and working principles of the force sensitive tablet for handwriting signal capture are described at first. Then the signal conditioning circuit is given in the chapter followed. The experimental results are presented and discussed in part 4. And conclusions about the device and some future work are given in the last part.

2 The F-Tablet Design

As handwriting is the process of human hand acting on contacting plate (such as paper) with pen, the writing information includes pen-tip trajectory, contacting force direction and amplitude. It is ideal to acquire all those information simultaneously.

In our design, the F-Tablet is capable of capturing three perpendicular forces of the pen-tip to the contacting plane and torques in two directions directly with a multi-dimension force/torque sensor. With the specially designed structure, the other dynamic signals and the static trajectory of the pen-tip can also be calculated indirectly.

Fig. 1 shows the frame diagram of the tablet. It consists of 4 parts. Part 1 is a cuboid box which wraps all the other parts, part 2 is the circuit, part 3 is a multi-dimension force/torque sensor, and part 4 is the input tablet of 60×60 mm^2 for writing, which is assembled together with the top of the sensor and there is a small clearance to the wrap box. The signal conditioning circuit (part 2) processes the signals from the multi-dimension force/torque sensor (part 3).

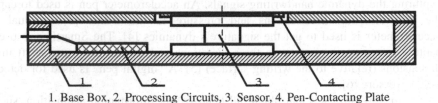

1. Base Box, 2. Processing Circuits, 3. Sensor, 4. Pen-Contacting Plate

Fig. 1. Frame Diagram of the Tablet

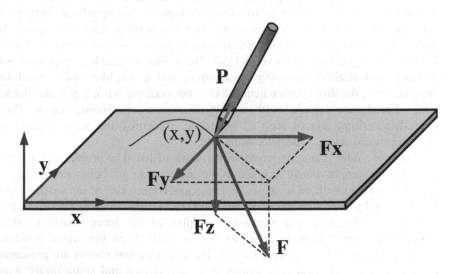

Fig. 2. Schematic Diagram of Force Action

The multi-dimension force/torque sensor, of which the bottom is assembled into the wrap box, is the core part of this tablet. It measures the forces and torques of the pen-tip. The details of the sensor's working principle can be found in [7].

The working principle can be learned from Fig.2. When a pen writes on the input tablet at point P, force F can be decomposed into forces in three perpendicular directions, $F_x(t_i)$, $F_y(t_i)$, $F_z(t_i)$. At the same time, $M_x(t_i)$ and $M_y(t_i)$ are exerted on the input tablet. These five force elements are all functions of time t_i and can be measured directly by the multi-dimension force/torque sensor. The coordinates of the point P can be calculated from the equilibrium of moments. They can be expressed as (1):

$$x_p(t_i) = \frac{M_y(t_i) - F_x(t_i) \cdot h}{F_z(t_i)}$$

$$y_p(t_i) = \frac{-M_x(t_i) - F_y(t_i) \cdot h}{F_z(t_i)}$$

(1)

where h denotes the distance between he input tablet and the origin of the coordinate of force sensor, that is z_p; $i = 0, 1, 2, \ldots$ The velocities and accelerations are the derivative of the two coordinates, which can be expressed as (2) and (3).

$$v_x(t_j) = \frac{x(t_j) - x(t_{j-1})}{\Delta t}$$

$$v_y(t_j) = \frac{y(t_j) - y(t_{j-1})}{\Delta t}$$

(2)

$$a_x(t_k) = \frac{v_x(t_k) - v_x(t_{k-1})}{\Delta t}$$

$$a_y(t_k) = \frac{v_y(t_k) - v_y(t_{k-1})}{\Delta t}$$

(3)

3   Conditioning Circuit Design

The upper limit of the frequency of handwriting is about 20Hz [3]. Results from our research shows that the maxim writing force is about 5N, the normal writing force is about 1~3N and the value is various to different person. So the F-Tablet is designed to measure forces between 0~10N, and the system resonance frequency is 140Hz, so the tablet is capable of capture the dynamic handwriting signal without distortion. The conditioning circuit as Fig.3 shows is designed to get the 5 channel output from the multi-dimension sensor. As the 5 channel have the same structure, only the 5th channel is presented in details.

First the 5 output signals from the Wheatstone bridge are amplified to big enough to be sampled. As the 5 channel have different measurement range, we adjust the operational amplifier suitably so that the maxim force or torque doesn't cause any saturation and the small signals can be observed at the same time. After that, a RC filtering circuit is used so that only signals with frequency between 0 and 20Hz can get across. A 12 bit AD is decided to do the conversion. And every channel will be sampled at the frequency of 100Hz.

Fz can be decomposed into three parts, the gravitation of the input tablet, the force exerted to the input tablet when writing and the fluctuation of the offset value with the time. The other forces and torques don't have the gravitation of the input tablet. During calibration, the effect of the input tablet will be eliminated. And the offset value can be viewed as a constant during writing and can be subtracted from the captured value at the beginning of writing with specially designed protocol. USB has many advantages such as self-identifying peripherals, automatic mapping of function to driver and configuration, dynamically attachable and reconfigurable peripherals. USB as a new interface standard with a long term perspective is preferred external connection to a host PC. And the calculation results show that the whole conditioning circuit can be driven by the power from the USB interface. USB interface is added to the conditioning circuit. MCU get power from USB and regulates it to power other devices. The USB is sure to give users more convenience.

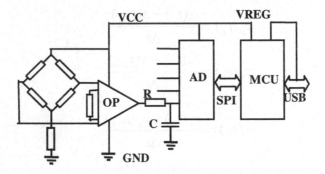

Fig. 3. Diagram of Conditioning Circuit

4 Experimental Results

This experiment is designed to verify whether the novel writing tablet is capable of capture both the dynamic and the static handwriting information. Because the forces and torques are measured by the tablet, so there is no requirement on the writing pen. An ordinary pen is used to write a Chinese character "中" on the input tablet. The conditioning circuit gets the 5 channel signals and transmits them to the host PC through USB interface. Test software is developed to display the trajectory using (1) and draw the three forces at the same time. The time-interval width of the stroke can obstained from the pressure between the pen-tip and the input tablet or Fz. And because the coordinates of the trajectory are calculated from Fx, Fy, Fz, Mx and My, so the shape of the displayed character implies all the forces and torques of the writing.

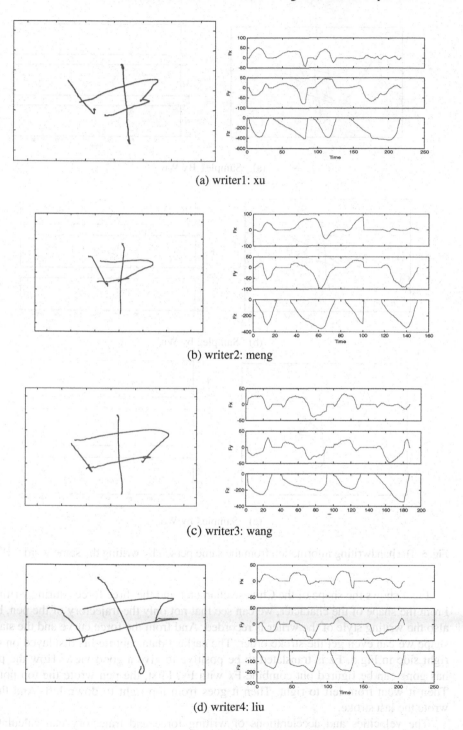

(a) writer1: xu

(b) writer2: meng

(c) writer3: wang

(d) writer4: liu

Fig. 4. The Chinese "中" by F-tablet and its forces

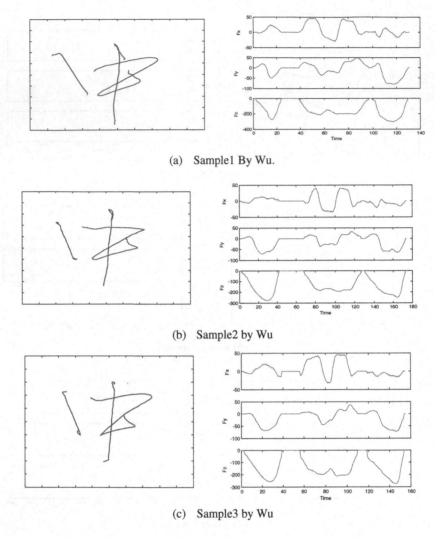

(a)   Sample1 By Wu.

(b)   Sample2 by Wu

(c)   Sample3 by Wu

Fig. 5. The handwriting information from the same person by writing the same word "中"

Fig.4 shows the shape of the Chinese character and the three forces during writing. From the shape of the character, we can see that not only the trajectory of the pen, but also the writing style of the writer is recorded. And from the force curve and the static shape we can even get the stroke order. The earliest data captured is displayed on the right side in Fig.4. Fz is translated to be positive to give a good view. How the pen has gone can be figured out combine Fx with Fy. First, the pen wrote the top point. Then it went from left to right. Then it goes from top right to down left. And then wrote the last stroke.

The velocities and accelerations of writing force and trajectory can calculated from the former information respectively. Other handwriting information such as the angle between the writing pen and the input tablet can also be calculated from the three perpendicular forces.

As a comparison, another experiment was done to acquire handwriting information from the same person by writing the same word "中", as Fig.5 was shown.

From the experiments results, we can find that the contacting force curves have some differences to the four persons. But from fig, 5, we could find that the force curves written by the author Wu have some consistency. From the figures, we can get all handwriting information, including strokes of pen-up and pen-down, velocity and acceleration of pen-tip, three dimension forces of pen-plate contacting point and shape of character.

5   Conclusion and Future Work

In this paper, a novel multi-dimension force sensitive tablet for handwriting signal capture based on USB is introduced. With a special multi-dimension force/torque sensor, we can get the three perpendicular forces of the pen-tip to the contacting plane and torques in two directions directly. All handwriting information, including strokes of pen-up and pen-down, velocity and acceleration of pen-tip, three dimension forces of pen-plate contacting point and shape of character etc can be obtained from the device directly or indirectly. And there is no special requirement for the writing pen. A pen-like tool is enough for handwriting input. As it can get pen-tip trajectory, F-Tablet could also be used as a new writing input tool for computers. With designed software, this tablet can even be used as a development tool for children to improve their writing skills.

A number of experiments have been conducted using the tablet. Experimental results show that the tablet is indeed capable of obtaining forces, trajectory, velocities and acceleration signals of the pen-tip. From the experiment results, we can find the different writing styles from the shape and curves of forces. So in this way, we could get more information about the writers handwriting and those information could be used for biometric recognition. The further work is to do some research work on writer identification/verification using one kind or several kinds of the signals captured with the force sensitive tablet.

References

1. http://www.cubs.buffalo.edu/about.shtml;
2. R. Plamondon, and S.N. Srihari, "On-line and off-line handwriting recognition: a comprehensive survey," IEEE Trans. on Pattern Analysis and Machine and Machine Intelligence, vol.22, pp. 63–85, 2000;
3. R. Baron and R Plamondon, "Acceleration Measurement with an Instrumented Pen for Signature Verification and Handwriting Analysis," IEEE Transactions on Instrumentation and Measurement, Vol. 38, pp. 1132–1138, 1989;

4. J. Martinez, J. de J. Lopez, and F. Luna Rosas, "A low-cost system for signature recognition," 42nd Midwest Symposium on Circuits and Systems, vol. 1, pp. 101-104, 1999;
5. R. Martens and L. Claesen, "Incorporating local consistency information into the online signature verification process," International Journal on Document Analysis and Recognition, vol. 1, pp. 110–115, 1998;
6. K. Tanabe, M. Yoshihara, H. Kameya and S. Mori, "Automatic Signature Verification Based on the Dynamic Feature of Pressure," Sixth International Conference on Document Analysis and Recognition, Proceedings, pp. 1045–1049, 2001;
7. Ping Fang, ZhongCheng Wu and Ming Meng, "A Novel Tablet for On-Line Handwriting Signal Capture", The 5th World Congress on Intelligent Control and Automation, June 20~25,2004, Hangzhou;
8. M. F. Bobbert and H. C. Schamhardt, "Accuracy of determining the point of force application with piezoelectric force plates," J. Biomechan., vol. 23, no. 7, pp. 705–710, 1990;
9. Heinz-Bodo Schmiedmayer and Josef Kastner, "Parameters influencing the accuracy of the point of force application determined with piezoelectric force plates", Journal of Biomechanics 32, pp1237–1242, 1999.

Shape and Structural Feature Based Ear Recognition[1]

Zhichun Mu, Li Yuan, Zhengguang Xu, Dechun Xi, and Shuai Qi

School of Information Engineering, Univ. of Science and Technology Beijing,
Beijing 100083
mu@ies.ustb.edu.cn

Abstract. Application and research of ear recognition technology is a new subject in the field of biometric recognition. The earlier research has shown that
human ear is one of the representative human biometrics with uniqueness and
stability. The paper discusses the edge-based ear recognition method including
ear edge detection, ear description and feature extraction, recognition method
and ear database construction. The feature vector is composed of the shape
feature vector of the outer ear and the structural feature vector of the inner ear.
The local feature vectors are proved to be invariant to ear image's parallel
move, scale and rotation.

1 Introduction

Earlier research has shown that human ear is one of the representative human biometrics with uniqueness and stability [1]. The special location of the ear makes it worthy
of our research. Ear recognition is also a non-intrusive recognition as the face recognition. Application and research of ear recognition technology is a new subject in the
field of biometrics recognition [2].

Generally, ear recognition uses a given static or dynamic image, and compares it
against the template data stored in a database to identify one or more persons or to
verify a claimed identity. At present, ear recognition methods fall into two categories:
the first one uses statistical approaches (such as PCA method [3]) to obtain a set of
eigenvectors. Then, any image can be represented using a weighted combination of
eigenvectors. The weights are obtained by projecting the image into eigenvector
components using an inner product operation. The identification of the image is done
by locating the image in the database whose weights are the closest to the weights of
the test image. The second category is based on the local features of the ear, such as
the geometry features composed of distance and curve relationship [4], or the force
field feature composed of potential wells and potential channels [5].

In this paper, we introduce a new local feature based recognition method. The ear
automatic identification system presented in this paper consists of the following parts:
image capture, ear detection, ear image preprocessing, ear edge detection, ear feature
extraction, ear classification and identification. The system structure is shown in figure 1.

---

[1] This work is supported by the National Natural Science Foundation of China under the Grant
No. 60375002.

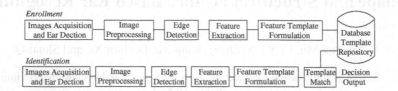

Fig. 1. Ear identification system structure

After ear image preprocessing and ear edge detection, we extract the shape feature vector of the outer ear and the structural feature vector of the inner ear to form the local feature vectors which are invariant to ear image's parallel move, scale and rotation.

The rest of the paper is organized as follows, section 2 discusses the edge extraction, section 3 describes feature extraction, section 4 presents results of the classification experiment and conclusion is provided in section 5.

2 Edge Detection of the Ear Image

2.1 Ear Image Preprocessing

First, we use the median filtering to remove the noise and remain the edge details of the ear. Then gray level stretch is employed to stretch certain gray level region, and improve the image quality. After the gray level adjustment, the contrast between the ear and the surrounding skin, the hair is much stronger.

2.2 Edge Detection of the Ear Image

We use the Sobel operator to extract the edges of the ear image. The edge information $N_1(x, y)$ (x and y denote the coordinates of a pixel) of the inner ear image is valid, but the outer contour is hard to be extracted because the ear color is similar to the skin color of the neck and face, and the low gradient change creates discontinuity in the outer ear contour as shown in figure 2(1). So we use appropriate threshold to get the binary image, and extract the valid outer ear contour $W_2(x, y)$. But the inner ear edge information $N_2(x, y)$ will be lost or invalid as shown in figure 2(2). Finally, we use the algebra operation to combine the valid edge information in figure 2(1) and 2(2). The image is segmented into outer ear region and inner ear region. The outer regions of figure 2(1) and 2(2) are added (equation 1) to connect the discontinuity of the edge; the inner regions of figure 2(1) and 2(2) are multiplied (equation 2) to keep the valid edge in figure 2 (1). $W(x, y)$ denotes the outer ear contour of the synthetical image, $N(x, y)$ denotes the inner ear information of the synthetical image.

$$W(x, y) = W_1(x, y) + W_2(x, y)$$
(1)

$$N(x, y) = N_1(x, y) * (255,255,255) + N_2(x, y) * (0,0,0)$$
(2)

2.3 Remove the Noise Lines

There are lots of noise lines spattering around the image because of the hair, the lighting or other reasons. So threshold method is used to remove these lines. With statistical measure, the average length of the noise lines in the edge image is less than 20 pixels, so the threshold length St is set to be 20. The noise lines shorter than St are set to be the background color, as shown in figure 2 (4).

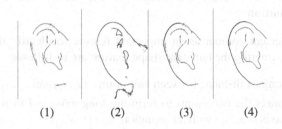

(1)   (2)   (3)   (4)

Fig. 2. Extract the outer contour and the inner ear edges. (1) edge detection with Sobel operator, (2) edge detection with threshold method, (3) composed image, (4) remove the noise lines

3 Feature Extraction

The most representative research of the feature extraction was done by Alfred Iannarelli. He created a 12-measurement "Iannarelli System" illustrated in figure 3 in 1949. The distance between each of the numbered areas is measured and assigned an integer distance value. The identification consists of the 12 measurements and the information about sex and race. It is believed that the method is not suitable for machine vision because of the difficulty of localizing the anatomical points [1]. If the first point is not defined accurately, none of the measurements are useful.

Burge and Burger [2] have researched automating ear biometrics with adjacency graph built from Voronoi diagram of its curve segments. The feature vectors are composed of the adjacency relationship of the curve segments. They introduce a graph matching based algorithm for authentication which takes into account the erroneous curve segments which can occur due to changes (e.g. lighting, shadowing and occlusion) in the ear images.

In this paper, we introduce a long axis based shape and structural feature extraction method (LABSSFE). The shape feature vector of the outer ear and the structural feature vector of the inner ear are extracted to form the local feature vectors.

Fig. 3. The locations of the anthropometric measurements used in the "Iannarelli System"

3.1   Shape Feature Vector Extraction of the Outer Ear Based on Curve Approximation

We take the outer ear contour as an important feature to identify the ear. The main procedures for extracting the outer ear shape feature are as follows:

1. Search the longest distance between two points (x_1, y_1) and (x_2, y_2) on the outer ear contour, connect the two points to form the long axis, and then get the midpoint on the long axis $O(x_0, y_0)$ with the equation $x_0 = (x_1 + x_2)/2$, $y_0 = (y_1 + y_2)/2$.

2. The upper curve and ear lobe of the ear edge image contain much information, so the outer ear curve is separated into two parts Line1 and Line2 at the midpoint $O(x_0, y_0)$ along axis X , each part is monotonous as shown in figure 4.

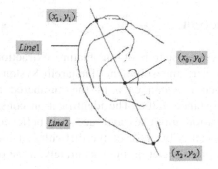

Fig. 4. Long axis segmentation of the outer ear contour

3. For each curve, get the pixel coordinates at equal intervals and apply the Least Square curve approximation. Then we get two curve approximation equations $L_1 = a_n x^n + a_{n-1} x^{n-1} + \cdots + a_0$ and $L_2 = b_n x^n + b_{n-1} x^{n-1} + \cdots + b_0$ .The coefficient vector $[a_n a_{n-1} \cdots a_0]$ of curve equation $L1$ is the shape feature of the curve $Line1$; the coefficient vector $[b_n b_{n-1} \cdots b_0]$ of curve equation $L2$ is the shape feature of the curve $Line2$. In case of edge deformity because of occlusion or other reasons, we can use one of the two vectors mentioned above.

3.2 Structural Feature Vector Extraction of the Inner Ear

The two main curves of the inner ear are used to extract feature vectors. The main procedure for extracting the inner ear structural feature is as follows:

1. Calculate the length of the long axis AB in figure 5. A and B are the intersection points between the long axis and the outer ear curve. $|AB|$ is the length of the long axis.

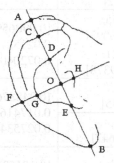

Fig. 5. Feature points of the inner ear

2. Get the perpendicular bisector of the long axis, which is the short axis FOH perpendicular to AOB and passing through midpoint O.
3. Get the intersection points C, D and E between the long axis and the inner ear curve. Get the intersection points F, G and H between the short axis and the inner ear curve. Record the coordinate of these points.
4. If we use the length between these points as feature vector, when the image scale is changed, the feature vector will change. The position of the long axis is relatively fixed in the edge image, so we use the ratio of the length between the points and the long axis to form the feature vector: $[OA/AB, OB/AB, OC/AB, OD/AB, OE/AB, OF/AB, OG/AB, OH/AB]$. This feature vector is invariant to ear image's scale and rotation.

In figure 6, there are five ear edge images, the corresponding outer ear feature vector and the inner ear feature vector are shown respectively in table 1.

Fig. 6. 5 ear edge images (ear1, ear2, ear3, ear4, ear5 respectively)

Table 1. Outer ear shape feature and inner ear structural feature vector

Edge Images	Outer Ear Shape Feature Vector	Inner Ear Structural Feature Vector
ear1	[-0.0006, 0.1386, -14.7975, 713.0572]	[0.094529, 0.250833, 0.036126, 0.135886, 0.036126, 0.027890, 0.011541, 0.250833]
	[0.0001, -0.0388, 5.4423, 43.6722]	
ear2	[-0.0006, 0.1455, -16.4672, 837.0093]	[0.090659, 0.249282, 0.167105, 0.021527, 0.024338, 0.009394, 0.072040, 0.250901]
	[0.0005, -0.1421, 16.5953, -375.9378]	
ear3	[-0.0005, 0.1163, -12.2659, 27.1885]	[0.248876, 0.083079, 0.128430, 0.017416, 0.035671, 0.010099, 0.027534, 0.251372]
	[0.0007, -0.1354, 13.2262, -212.1647]	
ear4	[-0.0006, 0.1405, -15.7944, 56.7026]	[0.151536, 0.250876, 0.067349, 0.131078, 0.040140, 0.027243, 0.026148, 0.250876]
	[0.0005, -0.1262, 14.1431, -291.7838]	
ear5	[-0.0012, 0.2032, -20.021, 932.2356]	[0.249407, 0.184991, 0.063847, 0.009704, 0.019741, 0.019741, 0.014154, 0.249407]
	[0.0012, -0.2108, 16.6412, -183.3683]	

4   Ear Recognition Experiment Result

This section describes how our database of ear images was defined as well as the experiment results.

4.1   Description of the Ear Database

Ear database is a very important part in an ear recognition system. At present, there is no standard ear image database. We have constructed an ear database composed of 77 subjects. The images of each subject are taken under two conditions: illumination variation and orientation variation (referred to the face image variation [7]) and individuals were invited to be seated 2m from the camera and change his/her face orientation. The 4 images are 300×400 pixels in size. The first image and the fourth image are the profile view of the head under different lighting condition. The second image and the third image are -30° and +30° rotation respectively as shown in figure 7.

4.2 Experiment Result

The LABSSFE method mentioned above is applied to the ear images of 77 subjects to extract the outer ear shape feature vector and the inner ear structural feature vector, and then combine the two vectors to form a unique feature vector for each ear image.

For the experiment, two sets of images were acquired. The first set is composed of the first image and the fourth image of subject No1 to No 60. The second set is composed of the first image of subject No 61 to No 60. The first set of images is organized into two subsets: the training set (first image of No1-60) and the test set (TS1, fourth image of No1-60). The second set is used for test (TS2).

In [3], a recognition rate of 72.7% is presented with the standard PCA approach. In this paper, using the BP network as classifier, we get an 85% of recognition accuracy over the TS1 set, and obtain a 98% of rejection over the TS2 set.

Fig. 7. 5 Ear image database (First one is taken under normal lighting condition, the second and the third one are taken -30° and +30° rotation respectively, the foruth one is taken under different lighting condition)

5 Conclusion

This paper proposes the long axis based shape and structural feature extraction method (LABSSFE) and a new feature based ear recognition technique. Future research will focus on feature sets construction composed of outer ear shape feature vector and the inner ear structural feature vector, and find the minimum feature sets to recognize images with bad quality or with occluding contours and shadow edges. Based on the previous research and its own features [6], we believe that ear biometric is ideal for passive identification because the features are robust and can be reliably extracted from a distance and ear recognition will be a promising technology in the field of access control, video surveillance or law enforcement applications etc.

References

1. Iannarelli Afred: Ear Identification. Forensic Identification Series. Paramount Publishing Company, Fremont, California (1989)
2. Rodrigo de L. G., Carlos A.L., Otman Aghzoutb, Juan R. A.: Biometric identification systems. Signal Processing, Vol. 83 (2003) 2539–2557
3. Chang, K., Bowyer. K.W., Sarkar, S., Victor, B: Comparison and Combination of Ear and Face Images in Appearance-Based Biometrics. IEEE Transactions on Pattern Analysis and Machine Intelligence. Vol. 25(9) (2003) 1160–1165
4. Hurley, D.J., Nixon, M. S., Carter, J.N: Force field energy functions for image feature extraction. Image and Vision Computing. Vol. 20 (2002) 311–317
5. Burge, M. and Burger, W: Ear Biometrics in Computer Vision. The 15th International Conference of Pattern Recognition, ICPR. (2000) 822–826
6. Yuan Li, Mu Zhichen, Xu Zhengguang, Liu Ke: Ear Recognition in Computer Vision. Pattern Recognition and Artificial Intelligence (Chinese), accepted.
7. P.Jonathan Philips, Hyeonjoon Moon, Syed A. Rizvi and Patrick J. Rauss.: The FERET Evaluation Methodology for Face-Recognition Algorithms. IEEE trans. on Pattern Analysis and Machine Intelligence. Vol. 22(10) (2000) 1090–1103

LLE Based Gait Analysis and Recognition

Honggui Li[1] and Xingguo Li[2]

[1] Electronic Department, Physics College, Yangzhou University, Yangzhou, China
Hgli@yzu.edu.cn
[2] Department of Electronic Engineering, Nanjing University of Science & Technology,
Nanjing, China
Xgli@njust.edu.cn

Abstract. This paper discusses LLE based nonlinear dimensionality reduction of gait images and its application in gait analysis and recognition. Firstly Gaussian derivative based gait segmentation method is given and it is better than classical background subtraction based method. Secondly self-similarity plot based gait alignment method is proposed. Then 1d LLE representation is used for gait analysis. Zero crossing, local maximum and minimum show gait cycle. The shape of 1d LLE representation shows dynamic feature of gait. 1d LLE representation is view independent. Finally the FFT module of 1d LLE representation is used for view independent gait recognition. Experiments results and its theory analysis show, LLE representation has the potential ability for view independent gait analysis and recognition.

1 Introduction

Gait recognition is one of the main technologies for identifying a person at a long distance. Other biometrics technologies, such as fingerprint recognition, iris recognition and face recognition, can't work effectively when person is far away.

Feature used for gait recognition includes static feature and dynamic feature [1]. The main static feature is the profile of person. An example of dynamic feature is the joint-angle trajectories of limbs. Static feature is unstable, because it can be easily influenced by cloth, visual angle, background, illumination and distance. Dynamic feature is expected to be invariant to cloth, visual angle, background, illumination and distance. Most of the gait recognition methods use static features, and only a few of the gait recognition methods use dynamic feature. Dynamic feature extraction methods can be divided into two kinds [2]. One is recovering the high-level dynamic information of gait, the other is directly modeling human motion. Tanawongsuwan recovers high-level dynamic information of gait: time-normalized joint-angle trajectories, and uses it for gait recognition [3]. BenAbdelkader directly models human motion, and believes the dynamic feature of gait is encoded in pairwise image similarities of gait images, and gives the definition of self-similarity plot (SSP) [2]. Liang Wang fuses static and dynamic feature for gait recognition [1]. This paper will use LLE for dynamic feature extraction. That is to say, LLE is used for directly modeling human motion.

S.Z. Li et al. (Eds.): Sinobiometrics 2004, LNCS 3338, pp. 671–679, 2004.

LLE (locally linear embedding) is one of the nonlinear dimensionality reduction (NDR) methods [4], and ISOMAP is another famous NDR method [5]. LLE is a fast NDR algorithm, which finds local geometry in high dimension space and generates a projection to lower dimension space that preserves original local geometry. LLE gives a low dimensional representation of gait images, and it shows the inherent relationship among gait images. Because dynamic feature of gait hides in gait sequences and LLE representation is based on image similarity, LLE is suitable to extraction dynamic feature from gait sequences. Following experiments results show, LLE representation can be viewed as a kind of dynamic feature.

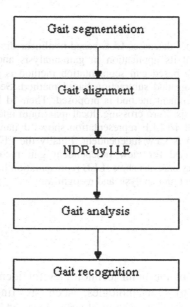

Fig. 1. The flow chart of this paper

The rest part of this paper is arranged as follows. The flow chart of this paper is in figure 1. LLE algorithm is introduced briefly in section 2. Gait segmentation will be discussed in section 3. Gait alignment is depicted in section 4. LLE based NDR of gait images is in section 5. View-independent gait cycle detection and dynamic feature extraction based on 1d LLE representation of gait images are given in section 6. In section 7, 1d LLE representation of gait is used for view independent gait recognition.

2 LLE Algorithm

The input is matrix $X = \{\vec{X}_1, \vec{X}_2, ..., \vec{X}_N\}$, where $\vec{X}_i \in R^D$. The output is matrix $Y = \{\vec{Y}_1, \vec{Y}_2, ..., \vec{Y}_N\}$, where $\vec{Y}_i \in R^d$ and $d << D$. For each vector $\vec{X}_i$, repeat following three steps:

(1) Find K nearest neighbors $\left\{ \vec{X}_{i1}, \vec{X}_{i2}, ..., \vec{X}_{iK} \right\}$;

(2) Find weight matrix $W = \left\{ W_{ij} \mid i = 1,2,...,N; \ j = 1,2,...,K \right\}$, which minimizes following cost function,

$$\varepsilon(W) = \sum_{i=1}^{N} \left| \vec{X}_i - \sum_{j=1}^{K} W_{ij} \vec{X}_{ij} \right|^2 \tag{1}$$

where W also satisfies conditions: $\sum_{j=1}^{K} W_{ij} = 1$ and $W_{ij} = 0$ if $\vec{X}_j$ is not a neighbor of $\vec{X}_i$;

(3) Find d dimension embedding vector $\vec{Y}_i$, which minimizes following cost function,

$$\Phi(Y) = \sum_{i=1}^{N} \left| \vec{Y}_i - \sum_{j=1}^{K} W_{ij} \vec{Y}_j \right|^2 \tag{2}$$

3 Gait Segmentation

Gait segmentation is the first step for gait analysis and recognition. We define gait segmentation as extracting human body from background in gait image. Usually the result of gait segmentation is a silhouette image. Classical gait segmentation method is background subtraction [6]. This method can't work well when pixel of foreground image has similar gray level value as that of pixel of background image in same position. Because there are new edges at human body contour in foreground image, human body counter can be found through comparing the edge information between foreground image and background image. We propose a new gait segmentation method, which is based on comparing filtering results between foreground image and background image using multi-scale and multi-direction Gaussian derivative filters [7]. The definition of Gaussian derivative filter is

$$gd(x, y) = -\frac{x}{\sigma^2} \frac{1}{2\pi\sigma^2} e^{-\frac{x^2+y^2}{2\sigma^2}}. \tag{3}$$

The difference of Gaussian derivative between foreground image and background image at position (x, y) is defined as

$$err(x, y) = \sum_{i=1}^{N} \left(gd_i * f_f(x, y) - gd_i * f_b(x, y) \right)^2. \tag{4}$$

where, N is the total number of multi-scale and multi-direction Gaussian derivative filters, f_f is foreground image, and f_b is background image.

Figure 2 shows results of gait segmentation. Figure 2(a) is foreground image, figure 2(b) is background image, figure 2(c) is the result of background subtraction method, and figure 2(d) is the result of Gaussian derivative based method. Figure 2 shows that, Gaussian derivative based method is better than background subtraction method.

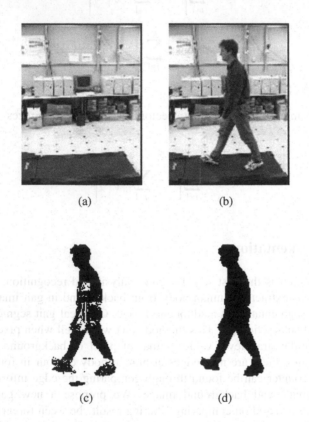

(a)   (b)

(c)   (d)

Fig. 2. Results of gait segmentation. (a) foreground image, (b) background image, (c) segmentation results of background subtraction, (d) segmentation result of Gaussian derivative based method

4 Gait Alignment

For linear and nonlinear dimensionality reduction methods, such as PCA, ICA, LLE and ISOMAP, it is very important to align image properly. As well known, face alignment is a very important step in face recognition, which is based on statistical learning and subspace analysis methods. The input of gait alignment is silhouette image from gait segmentation. We use SSP for gait alignment [2]. The definition of SSP is

$$\min_{|dx,dy|<r} \sum_{(x,y)\in B_{t_1}} \left| f_{t_1}(x+dx, y+dy) - f_{t_2}(x, y) \right| \tag{5}$$

where, t_1 and t_2 are numbers of silhouette images, B_{t_1} is the bounding box of silhouette image t_1, r is a small search radius, and f_{t_1} and f_{t_2} are silhouette images. When SSP is used for gait alignment, we let $t_2 = 1$ and f_{t_1} is aligned with dx and dy.

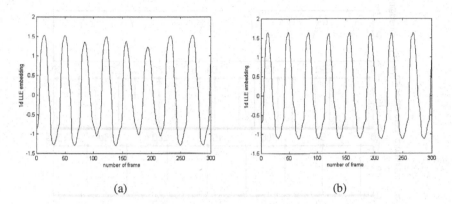

(a)   (b)

Fig. 3. 1d LLE representation of gait. (a) 1d LLE representation without alignment, (b) 1d LLE representation with alignment

5 NDR by LLE

Because simple gait can be viewed as simple motion in a plane, 1d LLE representation of gait images is sufficient for gait analysis and recognition. Further experiments results show, 2d LLE representation of gait images has almost the same information as that of 1d LLE representation. 3d or higher dimension LLE representation of gait images may have more information, which is useful for gait analysis and recognition. Figure 3(a) is 1d LLE representation of silhouette gait sequence without alignment, and figure 3(b) is 1d LLE representation of silhouette gait sequence with alignment. Figure 3 shows, gait alignment gives better result of LLE representation.

6 Gait Analysis

Zero crossing, local maximum and local minimum of 1d LLE representation show gait cycle respectively. Figure 4 shows zero crossing, local maximum and local minimum of 1d LLE representation is related to gait cycle. Further analysis shows, zero crossing of 1d LLE representation is related to maximum space extension of gait, and local maximum and local minimum of 1d LLE representation are related to minimum space extension of gait. Further experiments results show, zero crossing, local maximum and local minimum of 1d LLE representation are view independent. Classical gait cycle detection method is view dependent [2] [6].

The shape of 1d LLE representation shows dynamic feature of gait. Figure 4 shows, the shape of 1d LLE representation can be viewed as a kind of dynamic feature, which can be used for gait recognition.

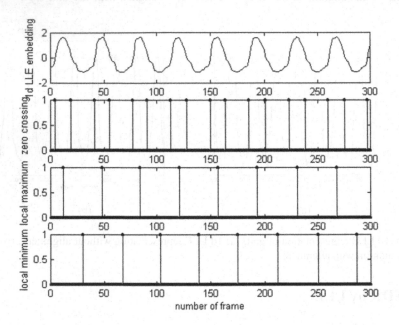

Fig. 4. Zero crossing, local maximum and local minimum of 1d LLE embedding

Further experiments results show, the shape of 1d LLE representation is view-independent.

Because maximum space extension of gait in one visual angle is also maximum space extension in another visual angle, maximum space extension is view independent. Because zero crossing of 1d LLE representation is corresponding to maximum space extension, zero crossing of 1d LLE representation is view independent. So minimum space extension of gait is also view independent, and local maximum and minimum of 1d LLE representation is view independent. Further 1d LLE representation is view independent.

7 Gait Recognition

Gait images come from CMU MOBO database. CMU MOBO database has 25 persons, 6 visual angles and 4 kinds of walk: slow walk, fast walk, slow incline walk and slow walk with a ball.

1d LLE representation is used for view-independent gait recognition. Slow walk of view 1 is used as training samples, and slow walk of view 2 is used as testing samples. Figure 5(a) is an example of view 1, and figure 5(b) is an example of view 2.

Because slow walk of view 1 has the same gait cycle as that of slow walk of view 2, the module of FFT (fast Fourier transform) for 1d LLE representation is used as feature vector. The module of FFT is shift invariant, so it is suitable as shift invariant feature vector. If the training samples and testing samples have different gait cycle, time-normalization is needed to make training samples and testing samples have same gait cycle, then the module of FFT for 1d LLE representation can be used as shift invariant feature vector.

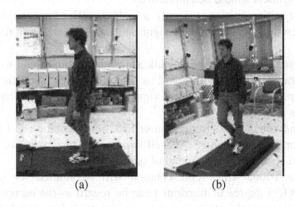

(a)   (b)

Fig. 5. Gait images of different visual angles. (a) view 1, (b) view 2

Experiments results show, it is not suitable to use 1d LLE representation as feature vector directly. It needs exact gait cycle detection and complex time-normalization.

Nearest neighbor classifier is used for classification. The similarity measurement between two feature vectors is Euclidean distance. Obviously, more sophisticated classifier may have higher recognition rate than that of nearest neighbor classifier.

Table 1 is the recognition rate. Because the recognition rate of rank 1 is very low, we don't calculate FAR (false acceptance rate), FRR (false rejection rate) and EER (equal error rate).

Table 1. Recognition rate

Rank	1	2	3	4	5
Recognition rate	68%	76%	88%	92%	92%

8 Conclusions

This paper studies LLE based nonlinear dimensionality reduction of gait images and its application in gait analysis and recognition. Firstly Gaussian derivative based gait segmentation method is given, which is better than classical background subtraction method. Secondly SSP based gait alignment method is proposed, and it is very important for linear or nonlinear dimensionality reduction methods. Then 1d LLE representation is used for view-independent gait cycle detection and dynamic feature extraction. Finally the module of FFT for 1d LLE representation is used for view-independent gait recognition.

In gait segmentation section, more robust segmentation method is needed and shade removing should be included.

In gait alignment section, more robust alignment method, such as ASM (active shape model), may be used. Because gait segmentation couldn't always give well silhouette image and LLE and ISOMAP are very sensitive to gait segmentation results, gait alignment should be emphasized.

In gait recognition section, we only use slow walk of view 1 and slow walk of view 2 for view-independent gait recognition, and the recognition rate of rank 1 is very low.

In future work, we will use slow walk as training samples and use fast walk, slow incline walk and slow walk with a ball as testing samples respectively. We will also use view1 as training samples and use view 2, view 3, view 4, view 5 and view 6 as testing samples respectively.

We will find robust classifier. Because LLE representation is time series, HMM will be used for gait recognition. As well known, HMM is very successful in speech recognition and speech signal is a kind of typical time series.

Higher dimensional LLE representation will be studied for gait analysis and recognition. DOF (degree of freedom) can be regard as the number of independent motion for a moving object. In order to extract true dynamic feature of gait, the dimensions of LLE representation should be not less than the DOF of gait. Liang Wang divides human body into 14 rigid components and uses 10 joint angles to represent dynamic features of gait [1]. If we regard gait as a motion in a plane, 10d LLE representation may be effective dynamic feature of gait.

LLE and ISOMAP can give good low dimensional representation for simple, nature and cyclic gait, but can't give good results for complex, pretend and random gait. Improved LLE and ISOMAP algorithm may be needed [8] [9].

Acknowledgement

I deeply thank education department biometrics advanced seminar at Beijing Jiaotong University in 2003, for the opportunity to learn new and advanced biometrics technologies, especially LLE and ISOMAP. I sincerely thank Sam T. Roweis and J. B. Tenebaum for free download of LLE and ISOMAP Matlab source codes from their web sites. I would like to thank Ralph Gross for warm-hearted help of CMU MOBO database download from their web site and excellent suggestions of gait recognition, especially view dependent and independent of gait cycle detection. I also want to thank Pattern Recognition Letters for the chance of reviewing paper "low cost fast stereo 3d reconstruction of the human face", because ideas in the reviewed paper and its references are the sources of the proposed gait segmentation method.

References

1. Liang Wang, Huazhong Ning, Tieniu Tan and Weiming Hu: Fusion of Static and Dynamic Body Biometrics for Gait Recognition. Proc. of the Ninth IEEE Int. Conf. On Computer Vision. (2003) 1449–1454
2. Chiraz BenAbdelkader, Ross Cutler and Larry Davis: Motion-based Recognition of People in EigenGait Space. Proc. of the Fifth IEEE Int. Conf. On Automatic Face and Gesture Recognition. (2002) 254–259
3. R. Tanawongsuwan and A. Bobic: Gait Recognition from Time-normalized Joint-angle Trajectories in the Walking Plane. Proc. of Int. Conf. On Computer Vision and Pattern Recognition. (2001) 726–731
4. Sam T. Roweis: Nonlinear Dimensionality Reduction by Locally Linear Embedding. Science Vol. 290. (2000) 2323–2326
5. J. B. Tenebaum: A Global Geometric Framework for Nonlinear Dimensionality Reduction. Science Vol. 290. (2000) 2319–2323
6. Robert T. Collins, Ralph Gross and Jianbo Shi: Silhouette-based Human Identification from Body Shape and Gait. Proc. of Int. Conf. On Automatic Face and Gesture Recognition. (2002) 366–371
7. Gui Yun Tian, Duke Gledhill and David Taylor: Comprehensive Interest Points Based Imaging Mosaic. Pattern Recognition Letters Vol. 24. (2003) 1171–1179
8. Ming-Hsuan Yang: Face Recognition Using Extended ISOMAP. Proc. of IEEE Int. Conf. On Image Processing. (2002) 117–120
9. Yiming Wu, Kapluk CHAN: An Extended Isomap Algorithm for Learning Multi-Class Manifold. Proc. of IEEE Int. Conf. On Machine Learning and Cybernetics. (2004) 3429–3434

Personal Identification Using Knuckleprint[1]

Qiang Li, Zhengding Qiu, Dongmei Sun, and Jie Wu

Institute of Information Science,
Beijing Jiaotong University, Beijing 100044, P.R. China
liqianglq@126.com

Abstract. A novel biometric defined as "knuckleprint" is presented in this paper. The Line feature of the knuckleprint with its distribution in the finger (which is defined as location feature) is extracted to identify a person. To enhance the performance of identification, hierarchical classification method is used to classify the location feature and line feature in different levels. Though this is the first attempt of knuckleprint identification, the accuracy rate reaches 96.88% on the database that contains 1,432 image samples, which testifies that knuckleprint is reliable as a biometric, and demonstrates the effectiveness and robustness of the features.

1 Introduction

Hand-based biometrics, such as hand geometry and fingerprint, are the oldest but most successful biometric technologies in the market, and they are also considered as the most reliable means to identify a person[1]. However, each biometric has its own shortcoming. As preponderant as it is, fingerprint recognition needs quite high quality samples (about 500dpi), and this brings about more than 4% of population fails to enroll[2]. Therefore, new kind of biometrics that based on low-resolution images should be developed. Knuckleprint, which would be a new member of hand-based biometrics, is one of these solutions.

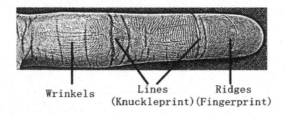

Wrinkels   Lines   Ridges
(Knuckleprint) (Fingerprint)

Fig. 1. Flexion shrinks, wrinkles and ridges in the middle finger

---

[1] This work was supported by grant 2003RC069 from Research Foundation of Beijing Jiaotong University.

While studying the inner cuticle in a finger(Fig.1), we find that there are much more lines, wrinkles and ridges in a finger than those in a fingerprint. And like fingerprint, these patterns are formed even before born and determined by gene[3], thus can be used in biometrics. The requirements of image quality for extracting these three patterns (lines, wrinkles and ridges) are different[8]. Ridges (which are the main feature of fingerprint) can only be derived from fine resolution images, but this is not expected. While wrinkles and lines can be extracted from low quality images, the patterns of them are much simpler than ridges. Thus, their features should be more robust. However, the wrinkles have relatively low contrast compared with lines, and some hands have few wrinkles or even lack for them. Besides, wrinkles are changeable according to one's physical condition[4]. As a result, we use the lines for identification, and because the lines are in the inner skin of knuckle, we name the lines knuckleprint.

Knuckleprint refers to the flexion shrinks in the inner skin of knuckles, especially the second knuckle for it contains more lines and more complex pattern than that of the first knuckle while more stable than the third knuckle. Consequently, image of the middle finger is gathered to obtain knuckleprint. According to our observation and prior knowledge[4], knuckleprint has mainly two intuitionistic features: the location of the lines (where the lines are) and the patterns of each line (what the lines look like). Our approach of identification is based on these two features. First, the location of the lines can be measured simply by projecting the image along the direction of lines. Second, line feature that can represent the knuckleprint exactly is extracted. Hierarchical scheme[6] is employed in the stage of classification. Location feature classifier gives four most likely results at first, and then line-matching classifier may find the final result in these candidates.

This paper is organized as follows: Section 2 illustrates the method of data acquisition and acquirement of the ROI (region of interest) of knuckleprint. Knuckleprint feature analysis is introduced in Section 3. Hierarchical matching strategy is discussed in Section 4. Section 5 presents the experiments and their results. Section 6 summarizes the paper.

2   Knuckleprint Acquisition

CCD digital camera is used to get the original image samples. We capture the whole hand image with it (Fig.2(a)). The resolution of the original image is 1792x1200 (after preprocessing, the resolution is less than 70dpi). A capture device is designed to fix the illumination and to place the hand.

The two features (location feature and line feature) should be extracted in different ROIs respectively. Whole finger is needed to extract the location feature of knuckleprint. As to line feature, there are three knuckles in the middle finger, and it is evident that the second one contains more meaningful information. Thus we extract lines around second knuckle, and name the line feature ROI as "knuckleprint ROI" because it can describe the knuckleprint more exactly. To find these two ROIs in the original image, three steps are needed and detailed below.

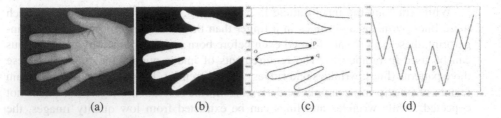

(a)   (b)   (c)   (d)

Fig. 2. Datum point determination: (a) Original image sample; (b) Binarized image; (c) Edge and datum points; (d) X coordinate of (c)

Datum Point Determination. Many papers had discussed this problem in the field of palmprint recognition[5][8]. While taking advantage of Han's method[5], we improve the algorithm and apply it to get knuckleprint.

As Fig.2(b) shows, we apply a threshold to the gray image (a). Since the illumination is well controlled and rather stable, the threshold value is fixed to 75 after studying several samples' histogram. After border tracing, we get a set of coordinates $(x_i, y_i), i = 1, 2, \ldots$, which make up of the edge of the hand. The curve in Fig.2(c) is a plot of the point set. Obviously, X coordinate of the curve Fig.2(d) contains enough information of the location of datum points o, p and q shown in Fig.2(c). These points should be located where curve (d)'s derivative is zero while its curvature is crossing zero.

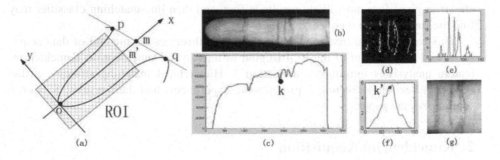

(a)   (c)   (f)   (g)

Fig. 3. Finger ROI and knuckleprint

Datum Coordinates and Finger ROI. Datum coordinates should be set up after we got the datum points. Given datum points p, q and o as illustrated in Fig.3(a), the point o is defined as origin of the coordinates. Point m, which is the middle point of p and q, defines the axis X along with point o (It is interesting to find that point m is more stable than point p and q.). Knuckleprint can be obtained after setting up this datum coordinates. The shadowed square in Fig.3(a) is defined to be the ROI. Though point m is steady enough to get ROI, we use another point m' to get rid of the nonlinear transformation caused by variation of hand poses. And point m' is 20 pixels closer to o than m. The ROI of finger is about 400x200 as shown in Fig.3 (b), whose size is related to the size of finger. Though the length and width of finger seem discriminable, we discard this information by unify the size of image to 300x100 (<70dpi). This is mainly because we need a scaling invariant feature.

Knuckleprint ROI Production. We take out the knuckleprint ROI around second knuckle from the finger ROI. The process of it is illustrated in Fig.3(c)-(g). Fig.3(c) is the radon projection of (b) down to the X-axis. Then the location of knuckleprint k is calculated by smoothing the curve. However, k is not stable enough because of the low contrast of knuckleprint. Consequently, the surrounding region is segmented for a more elaborate processing. Line detection is employed to find the precise datum point of knuckleprint, and the method is part of feature extraction as described in section 3. Fig.3(d) is the line feature around k, (e) is the radon projection of it, a low pass filter is used to get (f). And it is quite simple to find k' in (f). (As the accumulation of energy run up to 1/2 of the total energy along X-axis, the curve reaches k'.) Finally, a 64x64 knuckleprint ROI is generated based on point k' (the y coordinate of k' is the mean value of finger edge around k). Fig3.(g) is the result.

ROI of finger and knuckleprint is shifting, rotating, scaling invariant as described above, which ensures that the features would be stable.

3   Feature Analysis and Extraction

Location feature and line feature of knuckleprint are investigated in our experiment. The location feature lies on the length of each knuckle, which is different from person to person. And the lines in knuckleprint are determined by gene, influenced by the way of clenching, working condition, etc[4]. These two features are visible, thus the features can be described as "knowledge based" because we human can distinguish them by our eyes. To demonstrate the effectiveness of knuckleprint, we use several general methods to extract the features. It is evident that these two features are independent and are prone to be classified by a coarse to fine strategy.

3.1   Location Feature of Knuckleprint

Location feature of knuckleprint can be obtained by projecting $\mathbf{I}_{adj}$ onto its X-axis. Radon transform is employed to achieve this.

Fig.4(a),(b) show two different curves (which defined as location feature later) of knuckleprint after radon transform. It is evident that the patterns are discriminable. Without loss of generality, the location of second knuckle (point k as described in section 2) is studied first. Fig4.(c) shows different k points of 70 persons. Taking the location of each k as a variable, the standard deviation of it is 8.44, which is about 3% of the whole range. Hence the value of k is not sufficient as a feature to identify in a large group. So we use the whole radon curve

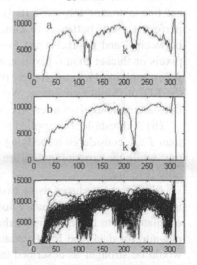

Fig. 4. Radon transformation

for identification instead of point k, and we define the curve as location feature. Experimental results suggest that it has a good ability of discrimination.

3.2 Line Feature of Knuckleprint

Lots of line extraction methods, such as edge detection[6], template operator[5][8] method have been proposed for extracting lines in palmprint. Though palmprint is similar to knuckleprint in many aspects, we shouldn't use these methods to extract lines in knuckleprint. The structures of these two biometrics are by no mean the same. The lines in knuckleprint are simpler than those in palmprint because all the lines are nearly vertical, and may not be influenced by fluctuant surface of hand; moreover, they should be treated subtler than those in palmprint because they are shorter and need more detailed description. Hence, we should find a better method specialized for knuckleprint.

Fig. 5. Line feature extraction

Following steps are our approach of line extraction for knuckleprint:

(i) A mask is designed to make the line clearer. The 1x7 mask **H** is defined as:

$$\mathbf{H} = [-1, -1, -1, 6, -1, -1, -1] \tag{1}$$

This is because most of the lines are nearly but not absolutely vertical, so a vertical line extractor may lose its function here. Nevertheless, a row vector as a mask performs much better as to knuckleprint. The width of lines we want to extract is between 3 and 6 pixels, and this determines the length of **H**. Lines thinner than 3 pixels or thicker than 6 pixels cannot generate a high value after convolving with **H**. After applying **H** to the image, the range of the data value is widened, which makes the ROI no longer an image. We regulate the data to the range [0,255](Fig.5(b)), the lines are more distinct after processing.

(ii) A threshold T is applied to the masked image. The points whose values greater than T are considered to be lying on a line, these data are hold still (for noise canceling) while the remaining data are set to 0 as background. T is fixed to 50 experimentally (Fig.5(c)).

(iii)Noise is reduced using two-dimensional adaptive wiener filter. Wiener method is based on statistics (mean value μ and variance value v^2 in the windowed image) estimated from a local neighborhood for each pixel[7]. When a local region has few meaningful data, the local variance is smaller, while the smoothing effect of filter would be stronger as described in (2) (v^2 is the variance of the whole image). So, the wiener filter is adaptive and it can preserve edges and high frequency parts better than linear filters. The window size of wiener filter is set to 5x5, which is determined by the width of lines that we need. The filtered image $\mathbf{I}_{out}$ is shown in Fig.5(d).

$$\mathbf{I}_{out}(x, y) = \mu + \frac{\sigma^2 - v^2}{\sigma^2}(\mathbf{I}_{in}(x, y) - \mu) \tag{2}$$

(iv) $\mathbf{I}_{out}$ mentioned above is still a grayscale image. Thresholding performs again to binarize the image and to extract the lines. The threshold T' is fixed to 150 here, and the value bigger than 150 is set to 0, while the others set to 1. Fig.5(e) is the binarized knuckleprint image.

(v) A set of morphological operations is performed to find the feature lines. Spur pixels removing, image skeleton extraction and isolated points cleaning are used in turn to obtain feature lines (Fig.5(f)).

(vi) Feature lines have been extracted successfully through five steps above. However, different knuckleprints have different amount of feature lines. To obtain more stable and unitary feature sets, we regular the lines by restricting the number of points in feature lines. After successive morphological shrink and clean operations, shorter lines are erased and longer lines are shortened. While preserving the most significant features of knuckleprint, the number of point is reduced. Fig.5(g) is obtained by limiting the point number to be less than 100, and this is the final result of line feature extraction.

4   Hierarchical Classification

Classification is based on two classifiers employed in different levels. The coarse level classifier emphasizes on location feature of knuckleprint, and the fine level one is dedicated to the line features.

4.1   Coarse Level Classification (for Location Feature of Knuckleprint)

To reveal the effectiveness of the feature, a general method, which is based on Euclidean distance, is used for classification. Suppose there are W classes knuckleprint $K_i(i=1,2,...,W)$ and each class contains P training samples. R_i which stands for the ith class's location feature, is defined as:

$$R_i = \frac{1}{P}\sum_{r=1}^{P} R_{ir}, \quad i \in [1, N] \tag{3}$$

where R_{ir} is the radon transform of rth sample of the ith class. Given two location feature vectors R_i and R_j, the distance in the feature space is defined as:

$$d_E(R_i, R_j) = \sum_{x=1}^{N}(R_i(x) - R_j(x))^2 \tag{4}$$

For a testing sample $\mathbf{I}$, the location feature R_I is worked out at first. Then the classification based on (4) would be performed to deicide which class the sample $\mathbf{I}$ belongs to. That is, if

$$d_E(R_I, R_{res}) = \min_j d_E(R_I, R_j), \qquad j = 1, 2, \cdots, W \tag{5}$$

then we could arrive at $\mathbf{I} \in K_{res}$.

Based on equation (4) and (5), we can rank the distances of one testing sample to all the classes. Several nearest results (that is, most likely result) are selected for the next step: fine level classification.

4.2 Fine Level Classification (for Line Feature of Knuckleprint)

Unlike location feature, each line feature is not a vector but a point set. The principle of classification is to measure the degree of similarity of two point sets. Here we use Hausdorff distance[6] which is a non-linear way for classification. Moreover, we improve the method and propose a novel scheme to enhance its power.

Given two point sets $L_1 = \{a_1, \ldots, a_m\}$ and $L_2 = \{b_1, \ldots, b_n\}$, the Hausdorff distance d_H between them is defined as:

$$d_H = \max(d_{L_1 L_2}, d_{L_2 L_1}) \tag{6}$$

where $d_{L_1 L_2} = \max_{a_i \in L_1}(d_{a_i L_2})$, $d_{a_i L_2} = \min_{b_j \in L_2}(d_{a_i b_j})$, and $d_{a_i b_j}$ is Euclidean distance between two points.

Actually, d_H is based on point matching. Each point in one set could find a nearest point in another set as its matching point, and distance of these two points is calculated. The maximum distance of these matched points is defined as Hausdorff distance. However, the method is sensitive to noise because the maximum distance is often generated by meaningless point in our experiment. So, we use mean value of the distances instead of the maximum value to reduce the effect of noise.

Furthermore, to lower the complexity, we only calculate $d_{L_1 L_2}$ without calculate $d_{L_2 L_1}$. But this would generate a wrong value when L_1 contains much more points than L_2. So we fix L_2 to be the "template point set", which is generated by training samples as shown in Fig.5(f) without point number limitation. In correspondence, L_1 is fixed to be the "test point set", and the point number is limited as described in section 3.2(Fig.5(g)). Then, the improved Hausdorff distance can be expressed as:

$$d_H' = d_{L_1 L_2} = \underset{a_i \in L_1}{mean}(d_{a_i L_2}) = \underset{a_i \in L_1}{mean}(\underset{b_j \in L_2}{\min}(d_{a_i b_j})) \tag{7}$$

And the smallest d_H' indicates the most likely result.

5 Experiments and Discussions

The original database is set up using the hand image capture device. 1423 sample images from 73 hands are gathered in the database. 5 samples of each person are taken out to form training set, while the remaining 1058 images are taken as testing set. The identification system is programmed using Matlab6.2 under Microsoft Windows XP environment, and the computer has PIV 2.66G CPU and 256M RAM.

5.1   Experiment on Two Features Separately

Before performing the two-layer scheme, location feature and line feature are studied separately, and the results are given in Fig.6.

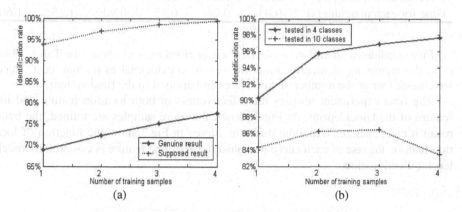

Fig. 6. The performance of location feature (a) and line feature (b) of knuckleprint

The test of knuckleprint's location feature(Fig.6(a)) is carried out on the entire database, that is, we use location feature to identify a person. The identification rate reaches 77.60% using four training samples. Though the rate is not so high, the result shows that location feature can describe a knuckleprint roughly. Moreover, after we analyze the samples that are classified incorrectly, we find that most of the right classes are ranking as second or third most likely result. So an experiment is conducted to test location feature classification as a coarse level operation. In the test, four most likely classes are picked out, and if these four classes contain the right one, the identification is considered to be right. The identification rate of the test reaches 99.30%(only 10 of 1058 samples are classified incorrectly). That is, the rate 99.30% may be reached if there is no mistake in the stage of fine level classification.

Line feature matching is a rather time-consuming operation, and we tested it in a limited scope from four to ten classes (each match would take up 3 second for a ten classes scope which can not be used in real time applications), and a part of the results are plotted in Fig.6(b). It illustrates that line feature matching can perform better in a smaller scope. The identification rate reaches 97.68% in the case of 4 classes.

5.2   Experiment on Hierarchical Classification

With the increasing of class number, the performance of line feature matching degrades dramatically. So choosing the number of candidates appropriately is important. An experiment is designed for this. The results are given in Tab.1, one training sample of each class is used for test.

Table 1. Choose the number of candidates for fine level classification

Number of candidate	1	2	3	4	5	6
Identification rate (%)	68.8	81.6	83.0	85.0	85.1	84.6
Time for each matching(s)	0.03	0.25	0.55	0.90	1.25.	1.60

Five candidates should give out the best performance as shown in Tab.1. However, the increasing of identification rate is not so evidential as its time cost. Hence we choose four as the number of candidates and apply it to the final system.

The final experiment testifies the effectiveness of both location feature and line feature of the knuckleprint. As Fig.7 shows, the more samples are trained, the better result it can generate. While the different curves in Fig.7 show the function of location feature, the rise of each curve demonstrates that line feature is essential to knuckleprint identification.

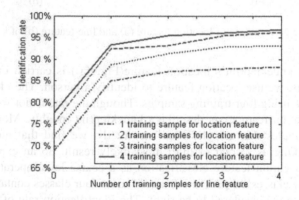

Fig. 7. Identification rate of different number of training samples

Up to 96.88% of the 1058 testing samples are classified correctly in the system by using four training samples in each class, which shows the effectiveness of knuckleprint as a biometric.

6 Summary

We have presented a preliminary study of knuckleprint as a biometric, and proposed two features: location feature and line feature to characterize a knuckleprint.

Knuckleprint has the advantage that the feature pattern of it is much simpler than many kinds of biometrics (such as fingerprint, palmprint and face), because the main feature of it is vertical wrinkles that are easier to extract. Moreover, knuckleprint can be obtained in low resolution and low contrast images, and thus we can set up a more robust system based on it. We proposed a method of knuckleprint identification, and build up a system based on it. The experimental results demonstrate the effectiveness of knuckleprint, and provide the basis for further development of a more effective, accurate and robust system.

References

1. Hand-based Biometrics. Biometric Technology Today. Vol.11(7) (2003) 9–11
2. Jain, A.K., Ross, A.: Multibiometric Systems. Communications of ACM, Special Issue on Multimodal Interfaces. Vol.47(1) (2004) 34–40
3. Rodriguez, P.A.R., et al.: Biometric Identification by Dermatoglyphics, Proc. Of ICIP (1996) 312–322
4. Wang, C.X.: Elementary Diagnosis by Palmprint. ZHISHI Press, China. (2003)
5. Han, C.-C., Cheng, H.-L., Lin, C.-L., Fan, K.C.: Personal Authentication using Palm-print Features. Pattern Recognition. Vol.36 (2003) 371–381
6. You, J., .Li, W.-X., Zhang, D.: Hierarchical palmprint identification via multiple feature extraction. Pattern Recognition. Vol.35 (2002) 847–859
7. Image Processing Toolbox for Use with Matlab, User's Guide. version 3 (2001). http://www.mathworks.com
8. Zhang, D., Shu, W.: Two Novel Characteristics in Palmprint Verification: Datum Point Invariance and Line Feature Matching. Pattern Recognition. Vol.32 (1999) 691–702

AAM Based Matching of Hand Appearance for User Verification

Xiaolong Teng, Ying Liu, and Chongqing Liu

Shanghai Jiaotong University, Institute of Image Processing and Pattern recognition,
Room 1607, Haoran Building, 1954 Huashan Road, Shanghai, China
txlhot@sjtu.edu.cn

Abstract. We present a method for personal authentication bsed on deformable matching of hand appearance. Authentication systems are already employed in komains that require some sort of user verification. In this work, active appearance models, which has good ability of fast locating deformable objects in images, have been proposed for recognizing hand appearance and the results are compared with existing methods.

1 Introduction

Automatic human identification has become an important issue in today's information and network-based society. The techniques for automatically identifying an individual based on his physical or behavioral characteristics are called biometrics, which will be more convenient and reliable for practice application.

Candidate methods can be selected using various criteria, taking into account the expected threats, potential loss and installation and operation costs. The acceptability to the users should also be considered. A broad variety of physical characteristics have been used for personal identification. Up to now, biometric properties like fingerprints, face, voice, iris and hand geometry was the subjects of many research efforts and used in different types of identification and verification systems. But the main reason of increased interest in this research area is that as the technology develops, these kinds of systems are more likely to run on the PDA devices.

In general, it is known that fingerprint and iris patterns can uniquely define each member of an extremely large population that makes them appropriate for large-scale recognition (establishing a subject's identity). Nevertheless, in many applications, because of some privacy or limited resources, we only need to authenticate a person (confirm or deny the person's claimed identity). In these conditions, hand recognition systems are very suitable for these purposes, because they do not cause anxiety for the users like fingerprint and iris systems do.

Hand geometry-based verification systems have been commercialized for almost 30 years. Still, their technical descriptions are scarce and the available information is based mostly on patents [1,2]. However, the problem of matching hand shapes is not only important for biometric systems, but also it is part of a more general, shape-based object learning and recognition topic [3,4].

S.Z. Li et al. (Eds.): Sinobiometrics 2004, LNCS 3338, pp. 690–695, 2004.

In this paper, we propose a new method for recognizing hand appearances by using AAM. Both shape features and texture cues are combined for features extraction. First of all, the model is constructed based on the training image set on which some feature points have been manually labeled. Then every user's feature vector is computed according to their own hand images in training stage. In recognition stage, the model is fitted to the test image by using fitting algorithm and the feature is extracted accordingly. At last, the Mahalanobis distance is involved for the classification purpose. The performance of the proposed method will be compared with existing methods. We do not use any pegs, which are needed in previous literatures.

2   Active Appearance Models

Above all, we should have a collection of training images for a certain object class in which the locations of L feature points have been determined manually or in a semiautomatic manner. The 2D coordinates of the feature points in each image define a 2L×1 shape vector, X, which is called the shape in the image frame. Each of these shape vectors is normalized to a common reference frame to obtain x, which is called the shape in the normalized frame. This normalization typically consists of a translation, rotation, and scaling. A shape model can now be obtained by applying Principal Component Analysis (PCA) to the x vectors, $x_s = \bar{x} + E_x c_x$, where xs is the synthesized shape in the normalized frame, $\bar{x}$ is the mean shape in the normalized frame, Ex is a matrix that has the shape eigenvectors as its columns, and cx is a $N_{c_x} \times 1$ vector of shape coefficients with N_{c_x} being the number of shape coefficients. Given a synthesized shape, xs, in the normalized frame, a synthesized shape, Xs, in the image frame can be obtained by applying a transformation to xs:

$$X_s = S_{g_s}(x_s)$$

(1)

where $S_{g_s}(.)$ is a transformation that involves scaling, rotation, and translation, and gs is a 4×1 vector that contains the transformation parameters for $S_{g_s}(.)$ After having obtained the shape model, all of the training images are warped to the mean shape and scanned into a vector to obtain

$$I_w = W_X(I),$$

(2)

where Iw is the image in the normalized frame, I is one of the training images, and $W_X(.)$ means the warping operation from the image frame to the normalized frame followed by the scanning of the warped image into a vector. The next step is to normalize Iw to obtain tn, which we call the normalized texture. This normalization means that each normalized texture has zero mean and unit variance. A texture model can now be obtained by applying PCA to the normalized textures:

$$t_s = \bar{t} + E_t c_t$$

(3)

where ts is the synthesized texture, $\bar{t}$ is the mean texture, Et is a matrix that contains the texture eigenvectors as its columns, and ct is a $N_{c_t} \times 1$ vector of texture coefficients with N_{c_t} being the number of texture coefficients.

With the obtained shape and texture models, a combined appearance model can be obtained by applying PCA to the shape and texture coefficients,

$$c_{xt} = [\begin{matrix} \Lambda c_x \\ c_t \end{matrix}] \tag{4}$$

where cxt is the combined vector of shape and texture coefficients, and Λ is a diagonal scaling matrix to adjust for the difference in the units of the shape and texture coefficients. A simple choice for the diagonal entries of Λ is the square root of the ratio of the total intensity variation to the total shape variation [5]. As a result of PCA, we now have an appearance model,

$$c_{xts} = E_a c_a \tag{5}$$

where cxts is the vector of synthesized shape and texture coefficients, Ea is a matrix that has appearance eigenvectors as its columns, and ca is a $N_{c_a} \times 1$ vector of appearance coefficients with N_{c_a} being the number of appearance coefficients. Here, we do not use a mean vector in this model because that the means of the shape and texture coefficients are close to zero. Because of linearity, the shape and texture vectors can be represented in terms of the appearance coefficients as

$$x_s = \bar{x} + Q_s c_a \tag{6}$$

$$t_s = \bar{t} + Q_t c_a \tag{7}$$

where Qs and Qt depend on Ex, Et, Λ, and Ea.

To use AAM, we need a way to fit the model automatically to a previously unseen image. In other words, we need an automatic way to find the vector po that optimally reconstructs a given target image I. In [7], Cootes et al. propose a fast and robust iterative scheme to find po. The method starts with an initial value for p, and converges to the optimal value by minimizing the difference between the target image and the image synthesized by the model. Note that the difference should be computed in the normalized frame. During an iteration, using the current synthesized shape, Xs, the target image is warped into the normalized frame to obtain the normalized texture,

$$t_n = T_{g_i}^{-1}(W_{X_s}(I)) \tag{8}$$

Then, the difference between this normalized texture and the current synthesized texture is:

$$r(P) = t_n - t_s \tag{9}$$

For the given current model parameter c0, the iteration process is shown as following:

(1) Compute the vector difference based on equation (9);

(2) Compute the relative error value, Error $= \|r0(P)\|2$;

(3) Compute δ ca, $\delta c_a = A \delta I$;

(4) Let k=1;

(5) Let $c_1 = c_0 - k \delta c_a$;

(6) For the new vector difference r0(p), if $\|r1(p)\|2 <$ Error, then accept the new model parameterc1 and the current shape and texture; otherwise, try k at 1.5, 0.5, 0.25, etc, repeat the step (5) and (6). If the all of them fail to improve the error, convergence is declared.

In order to obtain A, which is in step(3), the changes of the model parameters δ c and the relative changes δ I are needed, and then the multiple linear regression analysis is carried through. Moreover, the pose parameters of appearance can also be changed, which can be taken as the additional elements of δ c.

3   Hand Appearance Identification

In order to construct an AAM, there should be a training data, which includes N images with n manual labeled feature points. The feature points can be labeled on the contour of the hand appearance and some special lines, which is shown as Figure1.

Following the method described above, the AAM of the hand appearance has been constructed. There are totally 120 training images, which belong to 9 sets of images. the main features (Fig.1).

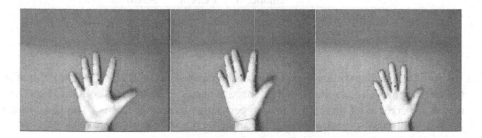

Fig. 1. Some training images with 45 manual labeled feature points

The AAM training stage can also be thought as the hand appearance features extraction process. The eigenvectors are the feature of the hand appearance.

Because the distance between hand and the scanner is fixed and the relative lighting condition is invariance, the influence caused by zoom can be ignored. Furthermore, applying the AAM can reduce the influence that is caused by ken-inside translation and small-angle rotation, and no pegs are needed.

In the above stage, model has been constructed and 9 average eigenvectors are obtained from the training data set, among which every eigenvector corresponding to a tester. Given a new example of a hand, the aim is to identify the hand in a way that is invariant to zoom, ken-inside translation and small-range rotation. If there exists a representative training set of hand appearance images, it is possible to do this using the Mahalonobis distance measure [8], which enhances the effect of inter-class variation (identity), meanwhile suppressing the effect of within class variation (lighting). This gives a scaled measure of the distance of an example from a particular class. The Mahalanobis distance di between the example and the class i, is shown as following:

$$d_i = (c - \bar{c}_i)C^{-1}(c - \bar{c}_i) \tag{10}$$

where c is the vector of extracted appearance parameters, $\bar{c}_i$ is the average vector for class i, and C is the common within-class covariance matrix for all the training examples.

4   Experiments

Throughout the experiments, Mahalanobis distance was used for classification purposes. Maximum interclass distance multiplied by 10 was used as a threshold for verification. This value was determined experimentally. Applying AAM is to combine shape features and texture cues in order to search for a better performance.

Table 1. Shows the results obtained using different methods

	Shape. %	PCA %	AAM %
Identification	88	93	95
Verification	97	98	98

Some of our experimental results are summarized in Table 1. The first column in the table shows the results of using shape features. The second column shows the results observed after the PCA has been performed to shape features. The last column in Table 1 illustrates results obtained by applying AAM.

As it is clearly seen, with shape features, we achieved a recognition rate of 88%, and a verification rate of 97%. Applying PCA to our shape features resulted in five dimensions projected feature space, retaining 99% of the original variance. Experiments show 93% performance in recognition and 98% in verification. While AAM is applied, both shape features and texture cues are involved. The proposed method increased the identification success above to 95%, the verification rate kept to 98% and the false acceptance rate decreased down to 1%.

The output over the whole test set is good since 97.04% were evaluated correctly. The average error rate is about 1.2% with roughly half the errors due to false rejections and half to false acceptances. This error rate needs to be reduced, but even so it could be acceptable for certain applications. And with other biometrics, the methods can be applied in secondary security field.

5   Conclusions

In this paper, Active Appearance Models have been proposed for extracting hand appearance and the results are compared with existing methods while researching the best features for identification-verification tasks. Not only shape, but also texture is involved.

The results show that the fusion of invariants from the shape and texture features improves the performance of identification and verification.

Future work may include using dynamic training data; and the observing the long run performance of the recognition system, which has the ability to update its training data during each use. Combining multiple classifiers could also increase system's reliability. A more successful hand recognition system will contribute to the other biometric methods' effectiveness and can wildly be used in applications that require low-medium security.

References

1. Ballard DH. "Generalizing the Hough transform to detect arbitrary shapes". Pattern Recognition 1981; 13:111–22.
2. Duda RO, Hart PE. Use of Hough transformation to detect lines in pictures. Commnu ACM 1972; 15(1): 11-5.
3. Shapiro SD. Feature space transforms for curve detection," Pattern Recognition 1978; 10: 129–43
4. Moenssens AA. "Fingerprint techniques". Radnor, PA: Clifton Book Company, 1971
5. X. Hou, S. Z. Li, H. Zhang, and Q. Cheng. "Direct Appearance Models". IEEE Conf. Computer Vision and Pattern Recognition, 1:828–33, 2001.
6. T. Ahmad, C. J. Taylor, A. Lanitis, T. F. Cootes. "Tracking and recognizing hand gestures, using statistical shape models". Image and Vision Computing, 1997, 15: 345~352
7. Cootes, T.F.; Edwards, G.J.; Taylor, C.J.: "Active appearance models" Lecture Notes in Computer Science, v 1407, 1998, p 484
8. Hand D. J. "Discrimination and Classification". New York: John Wiley & Sons, Inc.
9. Mikkel B. Stegmann: "The AAM-API: An Open Source Active Appearance Model Implementation". MICCAI (2) 2003: 951–952

Author Index

Lecture Notes in Computer Science

For information about Vols. 1–3236

please contact your bookseller or Springer

Vol. 3285: S. Manandhar, J. Austin, U.B. Desai, Y. Oyanagi, A. Talukder (Eds.), Applied Computing. XII, 334 pages. 2004.

Vol. 3284: A. Karmouch, L. Korba, E.R.M. Madeira (Eds.), Mobility Aware Technologies and Applications. XII, 382 pages. 2004.

Vol. 3283: F.A. Aagesen, C. Anutariya, V. Wuwongse (Eds.), Intelligence in Communication Systems. XIII, 327 pages. 2004.

Vol. 3282: V. Guruswami, List Decoding of Error-Correcting Codes. XIX, 350 pages. 2004.

Vol. 3281: T. Dingsøyr (Ed.), Software Process Improvement. X, 207 pages. 2004.

Vol. 3280: C. Aykanat, T. Dayar, İ. Körpeoğlu (Eds.), Computer and Information Sciences - ISCIS 2004. XVIII, 1009 pages. 2004.

Vol. 3278: A. Sahai, F. Wu (Eds.), Utility Computing. XI, 272 pages. 2004.

Vol. 3275: P. Perner (Ed.), Advances in Data Mining. VIII, 173 pages. 2004. (Subseries LNAI).

Vol. 3274: R. Guerraoui (Ed.), Distributed Computing. XIII, 465 pages. 2004.

Vol. 3273: T. Baar, A. Strohmeier, A. Moreira, S.J. Mellor (Eds.), <<UML>> 2004 - The Unified Modelling Language. XIII, 454 pages. 2004.

Vol. 3271: J. Vicente, D. Hutchison (Eds.), Management of Multimedia Networks and Services. XIII, 335 pages. 2004.

Vol. 3270: M. Jeckle, R. Kowalczyk, P. Braun (Eds.), Grid Services Engineering and Management. X, 165 pages. 2004.

Vol. 3269: J. Lopez, S. Qing, E. Okamoto (Eds.), Information and Communications Security. XI, 564 pages. 2004.

Vol. 3268: W. Lindner, M. Mesiti, C. Türker, Y. Tzitzikas, A. Vakali (Eds.), Current Trends in Database Technology - EDBT 2004 Workshops. XVIII, 608 pages. 2004.

Vol. 3266: J. Solé-Pareta, M. Smirnov, P.V. Mieghem, J. Domingo-Pascual, E. Monteiro, P. Reichl, B. Stiller, R.J. Gibbens (Eds.), Quality of Service in the Emerging Networking Panorama. XVI, 390 pages. 2004.

Vol. 3265: R.E. Frederking, K.B. Taylor (Eds.), Machine Translation: From Real Users to Research. XI, 392 pages. 2004. (Subseries LNAI).

Vol. 3264: G. Paliouras, Y. Sakakibara (Eds.), Grammatical Inference: Algorithms and Applications. XI, 291 pages. 2004. (Subseries LNAI).

Vol. 3263: M. Weske, P. Liggesmeyer (Eds.), Object-Oriented and Internet-Based Technologies. XII, 239 pages. 2004.

Vol. 3262: M.M. Freire, P. Chemouil, P. Lorenz, A. Gravey (Eds.), Universal Multiservice Networks. XIII, 556 pages. 2004.

Vol. 3261: T. Yakhno (Ed.), Advances in Information Systems. XIV, 617 pages. 2004.

Vol. 3260: I.G.M.M. Niemegeers, S.H. de Groot (Eds.), Personal Wireless Communications. XIV, 478 pages. 2004.

Vol. 3259: J. Dix, J. Leite (Eds.), Computational Logic in Multi-Agent Systems. XII, 251 pages. 2004. (Subseries LNAI).

Vol. 3258: M. Wallace (Ed.), Principles and Practice of Constraint Programming - CP 2004. XVII, 822 pages. 2004.

Vol. 3257: E. Motta, N.R. Shadbolt, A. Stutt, N. Gibbins (Eds.), Engineering Knowledge in the Age of the Semantic Web. XVII, 517 pages. 2004. (Subseries LNAI).

Vol. 3256: H. Ehrig, G. Engels, F. Parisi-Presicce, G. Rozenberg (Eds.), Graph Transformations. XII, 451 pages. 2004.

Vol. 3255: A. Benczúr, J. Demetrovics, G. Gottlob (Eds.), Advances in Databases and Information Systems. XI, 423 pages. 2004.

Vol. 3254: E. Macii, V. Paliouras, O. Koufopavlou (Eds.), Integrated Circuit and System Design. XVI, 910 pages. 2004.

Vol. 3253: Y. Lakhnech, S. Yovine (Eds.), Formal Techniques, Modelling and Analysis of Timed and Fault-Tolerant Systems. X, 397 pages. 2004.

Vol. 3252: H. Jin, Y. Pan, N. Xiao, J. Sun (Eds.), Grid and Cooperative Computing - GCC 2004 Workshops. XVIII, 785 pages. 2004.

Vol. 3251: H. Jin, Y. Pan, N. Xiao, J. Sun (Eds.), Grid and Cooperative Computing - GCC 2004. XXII, 1025 pages. 2004.

Vol. 3250: L.-J. (LJ) Zhang, M. Jeckle (Eds.), Web Services. X, 301 pages. 2004.

Vol. 3249: B. Buchberger, J.A. Campbell (Eds.), Artificial Intelligence and Symbolic Computation. X, 285 pages. 2004. (Subseries LNAI).

Vol. 3246: A. Apostolico, M. Melucci (Eds.), String Processing and Information Retrieval. XIV, 332 pages. 2004.

Vol. 3245: E. Suzuki, S. Arikawa (Eds.), Discovery Science. XIV, 430 pages. 2004. (Subseries LNAI).

Vol. 3244: S. Ben-David, J. Case, A. Maruoka (Eds.), Algorithmic Learning Theory. XIV, 505 pages. 2004. (Subseries LNAI).

Vol. 3243: S. Leonardi (Ed.), Algorithms and Models for the Web-Graph. VIII, 189 pages. 2004.

Vol. 3242: X. Yao, E. Burke, J.A. Lozano, J. Smith, J.J. Merelo-Guervós, J.A. Bullinaria, J. Rowe, P. Tiño, A. Kabán, H.-P. Schwefel (Eds.), Parallel Problem Solving from Nature - PPSN VIII. XX, 1185 pages. 2004.

Vol. 3241: D. Kranzlmüller, P. Kacsuk, J.J. Dongarra (Eds.), Recent Advances in Parallel Virtual Machine and Message Passing Interface. XIII, 452 pages. 2004.

Vol. 3240: I. Jonassen, J. Kim (Eds.), Algorithms in Bioinformatics. IX, 476 pages. 2004. (Subseries LNBI).

Vol. 3239: G. Nicosia, V. Cutello, P.J. Bentley, J. Timmis (Eds.), Artificial Immune Systems. XII, 444 pages. 2004.

Vol. 3238: S. Biundo, T. Frühwirth, G. Palm (Eds.), KI 2004: Advances in Artificial Intelligence. XI, 467 pages. 2004. (Subseries LNAI).

Vol. 3237: C. Peters, J. Gonzalo, M. Braschler, M. Kluck (Eds.), Comparative Evaluation of Multilingual Information Access Systems. XIV, 702 pages. 2004.